THE GREAT
WRITERS
L I B R A R Y

Comedies

This edition is the copyright © 1988 of Marshall Cavendish Ltd. Published in 1988 for
The Great Writers library by Marshall Cavendish Partworks Ltd., 58 Old Compton Street,
London W1V 5PA. Printed and bound in Spain by Printer Industria Gráfica, Barcelona.

D.L.B. 32482-1988
This is a facsimile reproduction of an edition first published in 1906 by J. M. Dent & Sons Ltd., London

ISBN 0-86307-709-9

"O, when mine eyes did see Olivia first,
Methought she purged the air of pestilence!
That instant was I turn'd into a hart;
And my desires, like fell and cruel hounds,
E'er since pursue me."

Orsino,
TWELFTH NIGHT I, i

Comedies

WILLIAM SHAKESPEARE

CONTENTS

Leon Palmarino fecit

THE TEMPEST

DRAMATIS PERSONÆ

ALONSO, *King of Naples.*
SEBASTIAN, *his brother.*
PROSPERO, *the right Duke of Milan.*
ANTONIO, *his brother, the usurping Duke of Milan.*
FERDINAND, *son to the King of Naples.*
GONZALO, *an honest old Counsellor.*
ADRIAN, } *Lords.*
FRANCISCO, }
CALIBAN, *a savage and deformed Slave.*
TRINCULO, *a Jester.*
STEPHANO, *a drunken Butler.*

Master of a Ship.
Boatswain.
Mariners.

MIRANDA, *daughter to Prospero.*

ARIEL, *an airy Spirit.*
IRIS,
CERES,
JUNO, } *presented by Spirits.*
Nymphs,
Reapers,
Other Spirits attending on Prospero.

ACT I—SCENE I

On a ship at sea : a tempestuous noise of thunder and lightning heard.

Enter a Ship-Master and a Boatswain.

Mast. Boatswain !

Boats. Here, master : what cheer ?

Mast. Good, speak to the mariners : fall to 't, yarely, or we run ourselves aground : bestir, bestir.   [*Exit.*

Enter Mariners.

Boats. Heigh, my hearts ! cheerly, cheerly, my hearts ! yare, yare ! Take in the topsail. Tend to the master's whistle. Blow, till thou burst thy wind, if room enough !

Enter Alonso, Sebastian, Antonio, Ferdinand, Gonzalo, and others.

Alon. Good boatswain, have care. Where's the master ? Play

Boats. I pray now, keep below.   [the men.

Ant. Where is the master, boatswain ?

Boats. Do you not hear him ? You mar our labour : keep your cabins : you do assist the storm.

Gon. Nay, good, be patient.

Boats. When the sea is. Hence ! What cares these roarers for the name of king ? To cabin : silence ! trouble us not.

Gon. Good, yet remember whom thou hast aboard.

Boats. None that I more love than myself. You are a counsellor ; if you can command these elements to silence, and work the peace of the present, we will not hand a rope more ; use your authority : if you cannot, give thanks you have lived so long, and make yourself ready in your cabin for the mischance of the hour, if it so hap. Cheerly, good hearts ! Out of our way, I say.   [*Exit.*

Gon. I have great comfort from this fellow : methinks he hath no drowning mark upon him ; his complexion is perfect gallows. Stand fast, good Fate, to his hanging : make the

1

rope of his destiny our cable, for our own doth little advantage. If he be not born to be hanged, our case is miserable. *[Exeunt.*

Re-enter Boatswain.

Boats. Down with the topmast! yare! lower, lower! Bring her to try with main-course. [*A cry within.*] A plague upon this howling! they are louder than the weather or our office.

Re-enter Sebastian, Antonio, and Gonzalo.

Yet again! what do you here? Shall we give o'er, and drown? Have you a mind to sink?

Seb. A pox o' your throat, you bawling, blasphemous, incharit-
Boats. Work you, then.   [able dog!
Ant. Hang, cur! hang, you whoreson, insolent noise-maker. We are less afraid to be drowned than thou art.
Gon. I'll warrant him for drowning; though the ship were no stronger than a nutshell, and as leaky as an unstanched wench.
Boats. Lay her a-hold, a-hold! set her two courses; off to sea again; lay her off.

Enter Mariners wet.

Mariners. All lost! to prayers, to prayers! all lost!
Boats. What, must our mouths be cold?
Gon. The king and prince at prayers! let's assist them,
For our case is as theirs.
Seb.   I'm out of patience.
Ant. We are merely cheated of our lives by drunkards:
This wide-chapp'd rascal,—would thou mightst lie drowning
The washing of ten tides!
Gon.   He'll be hang'd yet,
Though every drop of water swear against it,
And gape at widest to glut him.
[*A confused noise within:* 'Mercy on us!'—
'We split, we split!'—'Farewell my wife and children''—
'Farewell, brother!'—'We split, we split, we split!']
Ant. Let's all sink with the king.
Seb. Let's take leave of him.   [*Exeunt Ant. and Seb.*
Gon. Now would I give a thousand furlongs of sea for an acre of barren ground, long heath, brown furze, any thing. The wills above be done! but I would fain die a dry death. [*Exeunt.*

SCENE II

The island. Before Prospero's cell.
Enter Prospero and Miranda.

Mir. If by your art, my dearest father, you have
Put the wild waters in this roar, allay them.
The sky, it seems, would pour down stinking pitch,

2

But that the sea, mounting to the welkin's cheek,
Dashes the fire out.   O, I have suffer'd
With those that I saw suffer! a brave vessel,
Who had, no doubt, some noble creature in her,
Dash'd all to pieces.   O, the cry did knock
Against my very heart!   Poor souls, they perish'd!
Had I been any god of power, I would
Have sunk the sea within the earth, or ere
It should the good ship so have swallow'd and
The fraughting souls within her.

Pros.   Be collected:
No more amazement: tell your piteous heart
There's no harm done.

Mir.   O, woe the day!

Pros.   No harm.
I have done nothing but in care of thee,
Of thee, my dear one, thee, my daughter, who
Art ignorant of what thou art, nought knowing
Of whence I am, nor that I am more better
Than Prospero, master of a full poor cell,
And thy no greater father.

Mir.   More to know
Did never meddle with my thoughts.

Pros.   'Tis time
I should inform thee farther.   Lend thy hand,
And pluck my magic garment from me.—So:

                        [*Lays down his mantle.*
Lie there, my art.   Wipe thou thine eyes; have comfort.
The direful spectacle of the wreck, which touch'd
The very virtue of compassion in thee,
I have with such provision in mine art
So safely ordered, that there is no soul,
No, not so much perdition as an hair
Betid to any creature in the vessel
Which thou heard'st cry, which thou saw'st sink.   Sit down;
For thou must now know farther.

Mir.   You have often
Begun to tell me what I am; but stopp'd,
And left me to a bootless inquisition,
Concluding 'Stay: not yet.'

Pros.   The hour's now come;
The very minute bids thee ope thine ear;
Obey, and be attentive.   Canst thou remember
A time before we came unto this cell?
I do not think thou canst, for then thou wast not

3

    Out three years old.
Mir.   Certainly, sir, I can.
Pros. By what? by any other house or person?
    Of any thing the image tell me, that
    Hath kept with thy remembrance.
Mir.   'Tis far off,
    And rather like a dream than an assurance
    That my remembrance warrants. Had I not
    Four or five women once that tended me?
Pros Thou hadst, and more, Miranda. But how is it
    That this lives in thy mind? What seest thou else
    In the dark backward and abysm of time?
    If thou remember'st aught ere thou camest here,
    How thou camest here thou mayst.
Mir.   But that I do not.
Pros. Twelve year since, Miranda, twelve year since,
    Thy father was the Duke of Milan, and
    A prince of power.
Mir.   Sir, are not you my father?
Pros. Thy mother was a piece of virtue, and
    She said thou wast my daughter; and thy father
    Was Duke of Milan; and his only heir
    A princess, no worse issued.
Mir.   O the heavens!
    What foul play had we, that we came from thence?
    Or blessed was 't we did?
Pros.   Both, both, my girl:
    By foul play, as thou say'st, were we heaved thence;
    But blessedly holp thither.
Mir.   O, my heart bleeds
    To think o' the teen that I have turn'd you to,
    Which is from my remembrance! Please you, farther.
Pros. My brother, and thy uncle, call'd Antonio,—
    I pray thee, mark me,—that a brother should
    Be so perfidious!—he whom, next thyself,
    Of all the world I loved, and to him put
    The manage of my state; as at that time
    Through all the signories it was the first,
    And Prospero the prime duke, being so reputed
    In dignity, and for the liberal arts
    Without a parallel; those being all my study,
    The government I cast upon my brother,
    And to my state grew stranger, being transported
    And rapt in secret studies. Thy false uncle—
    Dost thou attend me?

4

Mir.   Sir, most heedfully.
Pros. Being once perfected how to grant suits,
   How to deny them, who to advance, and who
   To trash for over-topping, new created
   The creatures that were mine, I say, or changed 'em,
   Or else new form'd 'em; having both the key
   Of officer and office, set all hearts i' the state
   To what tune pleased his ear; that now he was
   The ivy which had hid my princely trunk,
   And suck'd my verdure out on 't.   Thou attend'st not.
Mir. O, good sir, I do.
Pros.   I pray thee, mark me.
   I, thus neglecting worldly ends, all dedicated
   To closeness and the bettering of my mind
   With that which, but by being so retired,
   O'er-prized all popular rate, in my false brother
   Awaked an evil nature; and my trust,
   Like a good parent, did beget of him
   A falsehood in its contrary, as great
   As my trust was; which had indeed no limit,
   A confidence sans bound.   He being thus lorded,
   Not only with what my revenue yielded,
   But what my power might else exact, like one
   Who having into truth, by telling of it,
   Made such a sinner of his memory,
   To credit his own lie, he did believe
   He was indeed the duke; out o' the substitution,
   And executing the outward face of royalty,
   With all prerogative:—hence his ambition growing,—
   Dost thou hear?
Mir.   Your tale, sir, would cure deafness.
Pros. To have no screen between this part he play'd
   And him he play'd it for, he needs will be
   Absolute Milan.   Me, poor man, my library
   Was dukedom large enough: of temporal royalties
   He thinks me now incapable; confederates,
   So dry he was for sway, wi' the King of Naples
   To give him annual tribute, do him homage,
   Subject his coronet to his crown, and bend
   The dukedom, yet unbow'd,—alas, poor Milan!—
   To most ignoble stooping.
Mir.   O the heavens!
Pros. Mark his condition, and the event; then tell me
   If this might be a brother.
Mir.   I should sin

5

To think but nobly of my grandmother:
Good wombs have borne bad sons.

Pros.   Now the condition.
This King of Naples, being an enemy
To me inveterate, hearkens my brother's suit;
Which was, that he, in lieu o' the premises,
Of homage and I know not how much tribute,
Should presently extirpate me and mine
Out of the dukedom, and confer fair Milan,
With all the honours, on my brother: whereon,
A treacherous army levied, one midnight
Fated to the purpose, did Antonio open
The gates of Milan; and, i' the dead of darkness,
The ministers for the purpose hurried thence
Me and thy crying self.

Mir.   Alack, for pity!
I, not remembering how I cried out then,
Will cry it o'er again: it is a hint
That wrings mine eyes to 't.

Pros.   Hear a little further,
And then I 'll bring thee to the present business
Which now 's upon 's; without the which, this story
Were most impertinent.

Mir.   Wherefore did they not
That hour destroy us?

Pros.   Well demanded, wench:
My tale provokes that question.   Dear, they durst not,
So dear the love my people bore me; nor set
A mark so bloody on the business; but
With colours fairer painted their foul ends.
In few, they hurried us aboard a bark,
Bore us some leagues to sea; where they prepared
A rotten carcass of a butt, not rigg'd,
Nor tackle, sail, nor mast; the very rats
Instinctively have quit it: there they hoist us,
To cry to the sea that roar'd to us; to sigh
To the winds, whose pity, sighing back again,
Did us but loving wrong.

Mir.   Alack, what trouble
Was I then to you!

Pros.   O, a cherubin
Thou wast that did preserve me.   Thou didst smile,
Infused with a fortitude from heaven,
When I have deck'd the sea with drops full salt,
Under my burthen groan'd; which raised in me

An undergoing stomach, to bear up
Against what should ensue.
Mir.   How came we ashore?
Pros. By Providence divine.
Some food we had, and some fresh water, that
A noble Neapolitan, Gonzalo,
Out of his charity, who being then appointed
Master of this design, did give us, with
Rich garments, linens, stuffs and necessaries,
Which since have steaded much; so, of his gentleness,
Knowing I loved my books, he furnish'd me
From mine own library with volumes that
I prize above my dukedom.
Mir.   Would I might
But ever see that man!
Pros.   Now I arise: [*Resumes his mantle.*
Sit still, and hear the last of our sea-sorrow.
Here in this island we arrived; and here
Have I, thy schoolmaster, made thee more profit
Than other princess' can, that have more time
For vainer hours, and tutors not so careful.
Mir. Heavens thank you for 't! And now, I pray you, sir,
For still 'tis beating in my mind, your reason
For raising this sea-storm?
Pros.   Know thus far forth.
By accident most strange, bountiful Fortune,
Now my dear lady, hath mine enemies
Brought to this shore; and by my prescience
I find my zenith doth depend upon
A most auspicious star, whose influence
If now I court not, but omit, my fortunes
Will ever after droop.   Here cease more questions:
Thou art inclined to sleep; 'tis a good dulness,
And give it way: I know thou canst not choose.
                                        [*Miranda sleeps.*
Come away, servant, come.   I am ready now.
Approach, my Ariel, come.
                    Enter Ariel.
Ari. All hail, great master! grave sir, hail! I come
To answer thy best pleasure; be 't to fly,
To swim, to dive into the fire, to ride
On the curl'd clouds, to thy strong bidding task
Ariel and all his quality.
Pros.   Hast thou, spirit,
Perform'd to point the tempest that I bade thee?

7

Ari. To every article.
  I boarded the king's ship; now on the beak,
  Now in the waist, the deck, in every cabin,
  I flamed amazement: sometime I 'ld divide,
  And burn in many places; on the topmast,
  The yards and bowsprit, would I flame distinctly,
  Then meet and join.   Jove's lightnings, the precursors
  O' the dreadful thunder-claps, more momentary
  And sight-outrunning were not: the fire and cracks
  Of sulphurous roaring the most mighty Neptune
  Seem to besiege, and make his bold waves tremble
  Yea, his dread trident shake.
Pros.   My brave spirit!
  Who was so firm, so constant, that this coil
  Would not infect his reason?
Ari.   Not a soul
  But felt a fever of the mad, and play'd
  Some tricks of desperation.   All but mariners
  Plunged in the foaming brine, and quit the vessel,
  Then all afire with me: the king's son, Ferdinand,
  With hair up-staring,—then like reeds, not hair,—
  Was the first man that leap'd; cried, 'Hell is empty,
  And all the devils are here.'
Pros.   Why, that's my spirit!
  But was not this nigh shore?
Ari.   Close by, my master.
Pros. But are they, Ariel, safe?
Ari.   Not a hair perish'd;
  On their sustaining garments not a blemish,
  But fresher than before: and, as thou badest me,
  In troops I have dispersed them 'bout the isle.
  The king's son have I landed by himself;
  Whom I left cooling of the air with sighs
  In an odd angle of the isle, and sitting,
  His arms in this sad knot.
Pros.   Of the king's ship
  The mariners, say how thou hast disposed,
  And all the rest o' the fleet.
Ari.   Safely in harbour
  Is the king's ship; in the deep nook, where once
  Thou call'dst me up at midnight to fetch dew
  From the still-vex'd Bermoothes, there she 's hid:
  The mariners all under hatches stow'd;
  Who, with a charm join'd to their suffer'd labour,
  I have left asleep: and for the rest o' the fleet,

Which I dispersed, they all have met again,
And are upon the Mediterranean flote,
Bound sadly home for Naples ;
Supposing that they saw the king's ship wreck'd,
And his great person perish.

Pros.   Ariel, thy charge
Exactly is perform'd : but there's more work.
What is the time o' the day ?

Ari.   Past the mid season.

Pros. At least two glasses.   The time 'twixt six and now
Must by us both be spent most preciously.

Ari. Is there more toil ?   Since thou dost give me pains,
Let me remember thee what thou hast promised,
Which is not yet perform'd me.

Pros.   How now ? moody ?
What is 't thou canst demand ?

Ari.   My liberty.

Pros. Before the time be out ? no more !

Ari.   I prithee,
Remember I have done thee worthy service ;
Told thee no lies, made thee no mistakings, served
Without or grudge or grumblings : thou didst promise
To bate me a full year.

Pros.   Dost thou forget
From what a torment I did free thee ?

Ari.   No.

Pros. Thou dost, and think'st it much to tread the ooze
Of the salt deep,
To run upon the sharp wind of the north,
To do me business in the veins o' the earth
When it is baked with frost.

Ari.   I do not, sir.

Pros. Thou liest, malignant thing !   Hast thou forgot
The foul witch Sycorax, who with age and envy
Was grown into a hoop ? hast thou forgot her ?

Ari. No, sir.

Pros.   Thou hast. Where was she born ? speak ; tell me.

Ari. Sir, in Argier.

Pros.   O, was she so ?   I must
Once in a month recount what thou hast been,
Which thou forget'st.   This damn'd witch Sycorax,
For mischiefs manifold, and sorceries terrible
To enter human hearing, from Argier,
Thou know'st, was banish'd : for one thing she did
They would not take her life.   Is not this true ?

9

Ari. Ay, sir.

Pros. This blue-eyed hag was hither brought with child,
  And here was left by the sailors.   Thou, my slave,
  As thou report'st thyself, wast then her servant ;
  And, for thou wast a spirit too delicate
  To act her earthy and abhorr'd commands,
  Refusing her grand hests, she did confine thee,
  By help of her more potent ministers,
  And in her most unmitigable rage,
  Into a cloven pine ; within which rift
  Imprison'd thou didst painfully remain
  A dozen years ; within which space she died,
  And left thee there ; where thou didst vent thy groans
  As fast as mill-wheels strike.   Then was this island—
  Save for the son that she did litter here,
  A freckled whelp hag-born—not honour'd with
  A human shape.

Ari.   Yes, Caliban her son.

Pros. Dull thing, I say so ; he, that Caliban,
  Whom now I keep in service.   Thou best know'st
  What torment I did find thee in ; thy groans
  Did make wolves howl, and penetrate the breasts
  Of ever-angry bears : it was a torment
  To lay upon the damn'd, which Sycorax
  Could not again undo : it was mine art,
  When I arrived and heard thee, that made gape
  The pine, and let thee out.

Ari.   I thank thee, master.

Pros. If thou more murmur'st, I will rend an oak,
  And peg thee in his knotty entrails, till
  Thou hast howl'd away twelve winters.

Ari.   Pardon, master :
  I will be correspondent to command,
  And do my spiriting gently.

Pros.   Do so ; and after two days
  I will discharge thee.

Ari.   That 's my noble master !
  What shall I do ? say what ; what shall I do ?

Pros. Go make thyself like a nymph o' the sea : be subject
  To no sight but thine and mine ; invisible
  To every eyeball else.   Go take this shape,
  And hither come in 't: go hence with diligence ! [*Exit Ariel.*
  Awake, dear heart, awake ! thou hast slept well ;
  Awake !

Mir.   The strangeness of your story put

10

Heaviness in me.

Pros.   Shake it off.   Come on ;
We'll visit Caliban my slave, who never
Yields us kind answer.

Mir.   'T is a villain, sir,
I do not love to look on.

Pros   But, as 't is,
We cannot miss him : he does make our fire,
Fetch in our wood, and serves in offices
That profit us.   What, ho ! slave ! Caliban !
Thou earth, thou ! speak.

Cal.   [*Within*] There 's wood enough within.

Pros. Come forth, I say ! there 's other business for thee :
Come, thou tortoise ! when ?

Re-enter Ariel like a water-nymph.

Fine apparition !   My quaint Ariel,
Hark in thine ear.

Ari.   My lord, it shall be done.   [*Exit.*

Pros. Thou poisonous slave, got by the devil himself
Upon thy wicked dam, come forth !

Enter Caliban.

Cal. As wicked dew as e'er my mother brush'd
With raven's feather from unwholesome fen
Drop on you both ! a south-west blow on ye
And blister you all o'er !

Pros. For this, be sure, to-night thou shalt have cramps,
Side-stitches that shall pen thy breath up ; urchins
Shall, for that vast of night that they may work,
All exercise on thee ; thou shalt be pinch'd
As thick as honeycomb, each pinch more stinging
Than bees that made 'em.

Cal.   I must eat my dinner.
This island's mine, by Sycorax my mother,
Which thou takest from me.   When thou camest first,
Thou strokedst me, and madest much of me ; wouldst give me
Water with berries in 't ; and teach me how
To name the bigger light, and how the less,
That burn by day and night : and then I loved thee,
And show'd thee all the qualities o' th' isle,
The fresh springs, brine-pits, barren place and fertile :
Cursed be I that did so !   All the charms
Of Sycorax, toads, beetles, bats, light on you !
For I am all the subjects that you have,
Which first was mine own king : and here you sty me
In this hard rock, whiles you do keep from me

The rest o' th' island.

Pros.   Thou most lying slave,
Whom stripes may move, not kindness! I have used thee,
Filth as thou art, with human care; and lodged thee
In mine own cell, till thou didst seek to violate
The honour of my child.

Cal. O ho, O ho! would 't had been done!
Thou didst prevent me; I had peopled else
This isle with Calibans.

Pros.   Abhorred slave,
Which any print of goodness wilt not take,
Being capable of all ill! I pitied thee,
Took pains to make thee speak, taught thee each hour
One thing or other: when thou didst not, savage,
Know thine own meaning, but wouldst gabble like
A thing most brutish, I endow'd thy purposes
With words that made them known. But thy vile race,
Though thou didst learn, had that in 't which good natures
Could not abide to be with; therefore wast thou
Deservedly confined into this rock,
Who hadst deserved more than a prison.

Cal. You taught me language; and my profit on 't
Is, I know how to curse. The red plague rid you
For learning me your language!

Pros.   Hag-seed, hence!
Fetch us in fuel; and be quick, thou'rt best,
To answer other business. Shrug'st thou, malice
If thou neglect'st, or dost unwillingly
What I command, I'll rack thee with old cramps,
Fill all thy bones with aches, make thee roar,
That beasts shall tremble at thy din.

Cal.   No, pray thee.
[*Aside*] I must obey: his art is of such power,
It would control my dam's god, Setebos,
And make a vassal of him.

Pros.   So, slave! hence! [*Exit Caliban.*
          Re-enter Ariel, invisible, playing and singing ,
                    Ferdinand following.
                    Ariel's song.
          Come unto these yellow sands,
                    And then take hands :
          Courtsied when you have and kiss'd
                    The wild waves whist :
          Foot it featly here and there ,
          And, sweet sprites, the burthen bear.

                         Hark, hark !
              Burthen [*dispersedly*]. Bow-wow.
        Ari. The watch dogs bark :
              Burthen [*dispersedly*]. Bow-wow.
        Ari. Hark, hark ! I hear
              The strain of strutting chanticleer
              Cry, Cock-a-diddle-dow.
Fer. Where should this music be ? i' th' air or th' earth ?
    It sounds no more : and, sure, it waits upon
    Some god o' th' island.   Sittting on a bank,
    Weeping again the king my father's wreck,
    This music crept by me upon the waters,
    Allaying both their fury and my passion
    With its sweet air : thence I have follow'd it,
    Or it hath drawn me rather.   But 'tis gone.
    No, it begins again.
                         Ariel sings.
              Full fathom five thy father lies ;
                  Of his bones are coral made ;
              Those are pearls that were his eyes :
                  Nothing of him that doth fade,
              But doth suffer a sea-change
              Into something rich and strange.
              Sea-nymphs hourly ring his knell :
                         Burthen : Ding-dong
Ari. Hark ! now I hear them,—Ding-dong, bell.
Fer. The ditty does remember my drown'd father.
    This is no mortal business, nor no sound
    That the earth owes :—I hear it now above me.
Pros. The fringed curtains of thine eye advance,
    And say what thou seest yond.
Mir.   What is 't ? a spirit ?
    Lord, how it looks about !   Believe me, sir,
    It carries a brave form.   But 'tis a spirit.
Pros. No, wench ; it eats and sleeps and hath such senses
    As we have, such.   This gallant which thou seest
    Was in the wreck ; and, but he's something stain'd
    With grief, that's beauty's canker, thou mightst call him
    A goodly person : he hath lost his fellows,
    And strays about to find 'em.
Mir.   I might call him
    A thing divine ; for nothing natural
    I ever saw so noble.
Pros.   [*Aside*] It goes on, I see,
    As my soul prompts it.   Spirit, fine spirit ! I'll free thee

                              13

Within two days for this.

Fer.   Most sure, the goddess
On whom these airs attend !   Vouchsafe my prayer
May know if you remain upon this island;
And that you will some good instruction give
How I may bear me here : my prime request,
Which I do last pronounce, is, O you wonder !
If you be maid or no?

Mir.   No wonder, sir ;
But certainly a maid.

Fer.   My language ! heavens !
I am the best of them that speak this speech,
Were I but where 'tis spoken.

Pros.   How ? the best?
What wert thou, if the King of Naples heard thee?

Fer. A single thing, as I am now, that wonders
To hear thee speak of Naples.   He does hear me ;
And that he does I weep : myself am Naples,
Who with mine eyes, never since at ebb, beheld
The king my father wreck'd.

Mir.   Alack, for mercy !

Fer. Yes, faith, and all his lords ; the Duke of Milan
And his brave son being twain.

Pros.   [*Aside*] The Duke of Milan
And his more braver daughter could control thee,
If now 'twere fit to do 't.   At the first sight
They have changed eyes.   Delicate Ariel,
I'll set thee free for this.   [*To Fer.*]   A word, good sir ;
I fear you have done yourself some wrong : a word.

Mir. Why speaks my father so ungently?   This
Is the third man that e'er I saw ; the first
That e'er I sigh'd for : pity move my father
To be inclined my way !

Fer.   O, if a virgin,
And your affection not gone forth, I'll make you
The queen of Naples.

Pros.   Soft, sir ! one word more.
[*Aside*] They are both in either's powers : but this swift business
I must uneasy make, lest too light winning
Make the prize light. [*To Fer.*] One word more ; I charge thee
That thou attend me : thou dost here usurp
The name thou owest not ; and hast put thyself
Upon this island as a spy, to win it
From me, the lord on 't.

Fer.   No, as I am a man.

14

Mir. There's nothing ill can dwell in such a temple :
  If the ill spirit have so fair a house,
  Good things will strive to dwell with 't.
Pros.   Follow me.
  Speak not you for him ; he 's a traitor.   Come ;
  I 'll manacle thy neck and feet together :
  Sea-water shalt thou drink ; thy food shall be
  The fresh-brook muscles, wither'd roots, and husks
  Wherein the acorn cradled.   Follow.
Fer.   No ;
  I will resist such entertainment till
  Mine enemy has more power.
              [Draws, and is charmed from moving.
Mir.   O dear father,
  Make not too rash a trial of him, for
  He 's gentle, and not fearful.
Pros.   What ! I say,
  My foot my tutor ?   Put thy sword up, traitor ;
  Who makest a show, but darest not strike, thy conscience
  Is so possess'd with guilt : come from thy ward ;
  For I can here disarm thee with this stick
  And make thy weapon drop.
Mir.   Beseech you, father.
Pros. Hence ! hang not on my garments.
Mir.   Sir, have pity ;
  I'll be his surety.
Pros.   Silence ! one word more
  Shall make me chide thee, if not hate thee.   What !
  An advocate for an impostor ! hush !
  Thou think'st there is no more such shapes as he,
  Having seen but him and Caliban : foolish wench !
  To the most of men this is a Caliban,
  And they to him are angels.
Mir.   My affections
  Are, then, most humble ; I have no ambition
  To see a goodlier man.
Pros.   Come on ; obey :
  Thy nerves are in their infancy again,
  And have no vigour in them.
Fer.   So they are :
  My spirits, as in a dream, are all bound up.
  My father's loss, the weakness which I feel,
  The wreck of all my friends, nor this man's threats,
  To whom I am subdued, are but light to me,
  Might I but through my prison once a day

Behold this maid : all corners else o' th' earth
Let liberty make use of ; space enough
Have I in such a prison.
Pros.   [*Aside*] It works. [*To Fer.*] Come on.
Thou hast done well, fine Ariel ! [*To Fer.*] Follow me.
[*To Ari.*] Hark what thou else shalt do me
Mir.   Be of comfort ;
My father 's of a better nature, sir,
Than he appears by speech : this is unwonted
Which now came from him.
Pros.   Thou shalt be as free
As mountain winds : but then exactly do
All points of my command.
Ari.   To the syllable.
Pros. Come, follow.   Speak not for him.   [*Exeunt.*

ACT II—Scene I

Another part of the island.
Enter Alonso, Sebastian, Antonio, Gonzalo,
Adrian, Francisco, and others.

Gon. Beseech you, sir, be merry ; you have cause,
So have we all, of joy ; for our escape
Is much beyond our loss.   Our hint of woe
Is common ; every day, some sailor's wife,
The masters of some merchant, and the merchant,
Have just our theme of woe ; but for the miracle,
I mean our preservation, few in millions
Can speak like us : then wisely, good sir, weigh
Our sorrow with our comfort.
Alon.   Prithee, peace.
Seb. He receives comfort like cold porridge.
Ant. The visitor will not give him o'er so.   [will strike.
Seb. Look, he 's winding up the watch of his wit ; by and by it
Gon. Sir,—
Seb. One : tell.   [entertainer—
Gon. When every grief is entertain'd that's offer'd, Comes to the
Seb. A dollar.   [you purposed.
Gon. Dolour comes to him, indeed : you have spoken truer than
Seb. You have taken it wiselier than I meant you should.
Gon. Therefore, my lord,—
Ant. Fie, what a spendthrift is he of his tongue !
Alon. I prithee, spare.
Gon. Well, I have done : but yet,—
Seb. He will be talking.

16

Ant. Which, of he or Adrian, for a good wager, first begins

Seb. The old cock.   [to crow?

Ant. The cockerel.

Seb. Done.   The wager?

Ant. A laughter.

Seb. A match!

Adr. Though this island seem to be desert,—

Seb. Ha, ha, ha!—So, you 're paid.

Adr. Uninhabitable, and almost inaccessible,—

Seb. Yet,—

Adr. Yet,—

Ant. He could not miss 't.

Adr. It must needs be of subtle, tender and delicate temper-

Ant. Temperance was a delicate wench.   [ance.

Seb. Ay, and a subtle ; as he most learnedly delivered.

Adr. The air breathes upon us here most sweetly.

Seb. As if it had lungs, and rotten ones.

Ant. Or as 'twere perfumed by a fen.

Gon. Here is everything advantageous to life.

Ant. True ; save means to live.

Seb. Of that there 's none, or little.

Gon. How lush and lusty the grass looks ! how green !

Ant. The ground, indeed, is tawny.

Seb. With an eye of green in 't.

Ant. He misses not much.

Seb. No ; he doth but mistake the truth totally.

Gon. But the rarity of it is,—which is indeed almost beyond

Seb. As many vouched rarities are.   [credit,—

Gon. That our garments, being, as they were, drenched in the
    sea, hold, notwithstanding, their freshness and glosses, being
    rather new-dyed than stained with salt water.

Ant. If but one of his pockets could speak, would it not say

Seb. Ay, or very falsely pocket up his report.   [he lies?

Gon. Methinks our garments are now as fresh as when we put
    them on first in Afric, at the marriage of the king's fair
    daughter Claribel to the King of Tunis.

Seb. 'Twas a sweet marriage, and we prosper well in our return.

Adr. Tunis was never graced before with such a paragon to

Gon. Not since widow Dido's time.   [their queen.

Ant. Widow ! a pox o' that ! How came that widow in?
    widow Dido !

Seb. What if he had said 'widower Æneas' too? Good Lord,
    how you take it !

Adr. 'Widow Dido' said you? you make me study of that:
    she was of Carthage, not of Tunis.

Gon. This Tunis, sir, was Carthage.

Adr. Carthage?

Gon. I assure you, Carthage.

Ant. His word is more than the miraculous harp.

Seb. He hath raised the wall, and houses too.

Ant. What impossible matter will he make easy next?

Seb. I think he will carry this island home in his pocket, and give it his son for an apple.

Ant. And, sowing the kernels of it in the sea, bring forth more

Gon. Ay.　　　　　　　　　　　　　　　　　　[islands.

Ant. Why, in good time.

Gon. Sir, we were talking that our garments seem now as fresh as when we were at Tunis at the marriage of your daughter,

Ant. And the rarest that e'er came there.　[who is now queen.

Seb. Bate, I beseech you, widow Dido.

Ant. O, widow Dido! ay, widow Dido.

Gon. Is not, sir, my doublet as fresh as the first day
　I wore it? I mean, in a sort.

Ant. That sort was well fished for.

Gon. When I wore it at your daughter's marriage?

Alon. You cram these words into mine ears against
　The stomach of my sense. Would I had never
　Married my daughter there! for, coming thence,
　My son is lost, and, in my rate, she too,
　Who is so far from Italy removed
　I ne'er again shall see her. O thou mine heir
　Of Naples and of Milan, what strange fish
　Hath made his meal on thee?

Fran. 　　　　　　　　　　Sir, he may live:
　I saw him beat the surges under him,
　And ride upon their backs; he trod the water,
　Whose enmity he flung aside, and breasted
　The surge most swoln that met him; his bold head
　'Bove the contentious waves he kept, and oar'd
　Himself with his good arms in lusty stroke
　To the shore, that o'er his wave-worn basis bow'd,
　As stooping to relieve him: I not doubt
　He came alive to land:

Alon. 　　　　　　No, no, he's gone.

Seb. Sir, you may thank yourself for this great loss,
　That would not bless our Europe with your daughter,
　But rather lose her to an African;
　Where she, at least, is banish'd from your eye,
　Who hath cause to wet the grief on 't.

Alon. 　　　　　　　　　Prithee, peace.

Seb. You were kneel'd to, and importuned otherwise,
  By all of us ; and the fair soul herself
  Weigh'd between loathness and obedience, at
  Which end o' the beam should bow. We have lost your son,
  I fear, for ever : Milan and Naples have
  Mo widows in them of this business' making
  Than we bring men to comfort them :
  The fault 's your own.
Alon.   So is the dear'st o' the loss.
Gon. My lord Sebastian,
  The truth you speak doth lack some gentleness,
  And time to speak it in : you rub the sore,
  When you should bring the plaster.
Seb.   Very well.
Ant. And most chirurgeonly.
Gon. It is foul weather in us all, good sir,
  When you are cloudy.
Seb.   Foul weather ?
Ant.   Very foul.
Gon. Had I plantation of this isle, my lord,—
Ant. He 'ld sow 't with nettle-seed.
Seb.   Or docks, or mallows.
Gon. And were the king on 't, what would I do?
Seb. 'Scape being drunk for want of wine.
Gon. I' the commonwealth I would by contraries
  Execute all things ; for no kind of traffic
  Would I admit ; no name of magistrate ;
  Letters should not be known ; riches, poverty,
  And use of service, none ; contract, succession,
  Bourn, bound of land, tilth, vineyard, none ;
  No use of metal, corn, or wine, or oil ;
  No occupation ; all men idle, all ;
  And women too, but innocent and pure ;
  No sovereignty ;—
Seb.   Yet he would be king on 't.
Ant. The latter end of his commonwealth forgets the beginning.
Gon. All things in common nature should produce
  Without sweat or endeavour : treason, felony,
  Sword, pike, knife, gun, or need of any engine,
  Would I not have ; but nature should bring forth,
  Of it own kind, all foison, all abundance,
  To feed my innocent people.
Seb. No marrying 'mong his subjects ?
Ant. None, man ; all idle ; whores and knaves.
Gon. I would with such perfection govern, sir,

To excel the golden age.

Seb.   'Save his majesty !

Ant. Long live Gonzalo !

Gon.   And,—do you mark me, sir?

Alon. Prithee, no more : thou dost talk nothing to me.

Gon. I do well believe your highness ; and did it to minister
   occasion to these gentlemen, who are of such sensible and
   nimble lungs that they always use to laugh at nothing.

Ant. 'Twas you we laughed at.

Gon. Who in this kind of merry fooling am nothing to you :
   so you may continue, and laugh at nothing still.

Ant. What a blow was there given !

Seb. An it had not fallen flat-long.

Gon. You are gentlemen of brave mettle ; you would lift the
   moon out of her sphere, if she would continue in it five
   weeks without changing.

             Enter Ariel (invisible) playing solemn music.

Seb. We would so, and then go a bat-fowling.

Ant. Nay, good my lord, be not angry.

Gon. No, I warrant you ; I will not adventure my discretion
   so weakly.   Will you laugh me asleep, for I am very heavy?

Ant. Go sleep, and hear us.

                       [*All sleep except Alon., Seb., and Ant.*

Alon. What, all so soon asleep ! I wish mine eyes
   Would, with themselves, shut up my thoughts : I find
   They are inclined to do so.

Seb.   Please you, sir,
   Do not omit the heavy offer of it :
   It seldom visits sorrow ; when it doth,
   It is a comforter.

Ant.   We two, my lord,
   Will guard your person while you take your rest,
   And watch your safety.

Alon.   Thank you.—Wondrous heavy.

                       [*Alonso sleeps.   Exit Ariel.*

Seb. What a strange drowsiness possesses them !

Ant. It is the quality o' the climate.

Seb.   Why
   Doth it not then our eyelids sink ? I find not
   Myself disposed to sleep.

Ant.   Nor I ; my spirits are nimble.
   They fell together all, as by consent ;
   They dropp'd, as by a thunder-stroke.   What might,
   Worthy Sebastian ?—O, what might ?—No more :—
   And yet methinks I see it in thy face,

What thou shouldst be : the occasion speaks thee ; and
My strong imagination sees a crown
Dropping upon thy head.

Seb.   What, art thou waking ?

Ant. Do you not hear me speak ?

Seb.   I do ; and surely
It is a sleepy language, and thou speak'st
Out of thy sleep.   What is it thou didst say ?
This is a strange repose, to be asleep
With eyes wide open ; standing, speaking, moving,
And yet so fast asleep.

Ant.   Noble Sebastian,
Thou let'st thy fortune sleep—die, rather ; wink'st
Whiles thou art waking.

Seb.   Thou dost snore distinctly ;
There's meaning in thy snores.

Ant. I am more serious than my custom : you
Must be so too, if heed me ; which to do
Trebles thee o'er.

Seb.   Well, I am standing water.

Ant. I'll teach you how to flow.

Seb.   Do so : to ebb
Hereditary sloth instructs me.

Ant.   O,
If you but knew how you the purpose cherish
Whiles thus you mock it ! how, in stripping it,
You more invest it !   Ebbing men, indeed,
Most often do so near the bottom run
By their own fear or sloth.

Seb.   Prithee, say on :
The setting of thine eye and cheek proclaim
A matter from thee ; and a birth, indeed,
Which throes thee much to yield.

Ant.   Thus, sir :
Although this lord of weak remembrance, this,
Who shall be of as little memory
When he is earth'd, hath here almost persuaded,—
For he 's a spirit of persuasion, only
Professes to persuade,—the king his son's alive,
'Tis as impossible that he's undrown'd
As he that sleeps here swims.

Seb.   I have no hope
That he 's undrown'd.

Ant.   O, out of that 'no hope'
What great hope have you ! no hope that way is

Another way so high a hope that even
Ambition cannot pierce a wink beyond,
But doubt discovery there.   Will you grant with me
That Ferdinand is drown'd?

Seb.   He's gone.

Ant.   Then, tell me,
Who's the next heir of Naples?

Seb.   Claribel.

Ant. She that is queen of Tunis; she that dwells
Ten leagues beyond man's life; she that from Naples
Can have no note, unless the sun were post,—
The man i' the moon's too slow,—till new-born chins
Be rough and razorable; she that from whom
We all were sea-swallow'd, though some cast again,
And by that destiny, to perform an act
Whereof what's past is prologue; what to come,
In yours and my discharge.

Seb.   What stuff is this! how say you:
'Tis true, my brother's daughter's queen of Tunis;
So is she heir of Naples; 'twixt which regions
There is some space.

Ant.   A space whose every cubit
Seems to cry out, 'How shall that Claribel
Measure us back to Naples?   Keep in Tunis,
And let Sebastian wake.'   Say, this were death
That now hath seized them; why, they were no worse
Than now they are.   There be that can rule Naples
As well as he that sleeps; lords that can prate
As amply and unnecessarily
As this Gonzalo; I myself could make
A chough of as deep chat.   O, that you bore
The mind that I do! what a sleep were this
For your advancement!   Do you understand me?

Seb. Methinks I do.

Ant.   And how does your content
Tender your own good fortune?

Seb.   I remember
You did supplant your brother Prospero.

Ant.   True:
And look how well my garments sit upon me;
Much feater than before: my brother's servants
Were then my fellows: now they are my men.

Seb. But, for your conscience.

Ant. Ay, sir; where lies that? if 'twere a kibe,
'Twould put me to my slipper: but I feel not

22

This deity in my bosom : twenty consciences,
That stand 'twixt me and Milan, candied be they,
And melt, ere they molest !   Here lies your brother,
No better than the earth he lies upon,
If he were that which now he's like, that's dead ;
Whom I, with this obedient steel, three inches of it,
Can lay to bed for ever ; whiles you, doing thus,
To the perpetual wink for aye might put
This ancient morsel, this Sir Prudence, who
Should not upbraid our course.   For all the rest,
They 'll take suggestion as a cat laps milk ;
They 'll tell the clock to any business that
We say befits the hour.

Seb.   Thy case, dear friend,
Shall be my precedent ; as thou got'st Milan,
I 'll come by Naples.   Draw thy sword : one stroke
Shall free thee from the tribute which thou payest ;
And I the king shall love thee.

Ant.   Draw together ;
And when I rear my hand, do you the like,
To fall it on Gonzalo.

Seb.   O, but one word.   [*They talk apart.*
                   Re-enter Ariel invisible.

Ari. My master through his art foresees the danger
That you, his friend, are in ; and sends me forth,—
For else his project dies,—to keep them living.
                              [*Sings in Gonzalo's ear.*
            While you here do snoring lie,
            Open-eyed conspiracy
                  His time doth take.
            If of life you keep a care,
            Shake off slumber, and beware :
                  Awake, awake !

Ant. Then let us both be sudden.

Gon.   Now, good angels
Preserve the king !   [*They wake.*

Alon. Why, how now ? ho, awake !—Why are you drawn ?
Wherefore this ghastly looking ?

Gon.   What's the matter ?

Seb. Whiles we stood here securing your repose,
Even now, we heard a hollow burst of bellowing
Like bulls, or rather lions : did 't not wake you ?
It struck mine ear most terribly.

Alon.   I heard nothing.

Ant. O, 'twas a din to fright a monster's ear,

23

To make an earthquake! sure, it was the roar
Of a whole herd of lions.
Alon.   Heard you this, Gonzalo?
Gon. Upon mine honour, sir, I heard a humming,
And that a strange one too, which did awake me:
I shaked you, sir, and cried: as mine eyes open'd,
I saw their weapons drawn:—there was a noise,
That's verily.   'Tis best we stand upon our guard,
Or that we quit this place: let's draw our weapons.
Alon. Lead off this ground; and let's make further search
For my poor son.
Gon.   Heavens keep him from these beasts!
For he is, sure, 'i th' island.
Alon.   Lead away.
Ari. Prospero my lord shall know what I have done:
So, king, go safely on to seek thy son.   [*Exeunt.*

Scene II

Another part of the island.
*Enter Caliban with a burden of wood.   A noise of
thunder heard.*

Cal. All the infections that the sun sucks up
From bogs, fens, flats, on Prosper fall, and make him
By inch-meal a disease! his spirits hear me,
And yet I needs must curse.   But they'll nor pinch,
Fright me with urchin-shows, pitch me i' the mire,
Nor lead me, like a firebrand, in the dark
Out of my way, unless he bid 'em: but
For every trifle are they set upon me;
Sometime like apes, that mow and chatter at me,
And after bite me; then like hedgehogs, which
Lie tumbling in my barefoot way, and mount
Their pricks at my footfall; sometime am I
All wound with adders, who with cloven tongues
Do hiss me into madness.

Enter Trinculo.
                              Lo, now, lo!
Here comes a spirit of his, and to torment me
For bringing wood in slowly.   I'll fall flat;
Perchance he will not mind me.

Trin. Here's neither bush nor shrub, to bear off any weather at
all, and another storm brewing; I hear it sing i' the wind:
yond same black cloud, yond huge one, looks like a foul
bombard that would shed his liquor.   If it should thunder
as it did before, I know not where to hide my head: yond

same cloud cannot choose but fall by pailfuls. What have we here? a man or a fish? dead or alive? A fish: he smells like a fish; a very ancient and fish-like smell; a kind of not of the newest Poor-John. A strange fish! Were I in England now, as once I was, and had but this fish painted, not a holiday fool there but would give a piece of silver: there would this monster make a man; any strange beast there makes a man: when they will not give a doit to relieve a lame beggar, they will lay out ten to see a dead Indian. Legged like a man! and his fins like arms! Warm o' my troth! I do now let loose my opinion; hold it no longer: this is no fish, but an islander, that hath lately suffered by a thunderbolt. [*Thunder.*] Alas, the storm is come again! my best way is to creep under his gaberdine; there is no other shelter hereabout: misery acquaints a man with strange bed-fellows. I will here shroud till the dregs of the storm be past.

Enter Stephano, singing: a bottle in his hand.

I shall no more to sea, to sea,
    Here shall I die a-shore,—

This is a very scurvy tune to sing at a man's funeral: well, here's my comfort.   [*Drinks.*
[*Sings.*

The master, the swabber, the boatswain, and I,
    The gunner, and his mate,
Loved Moll, Meg, and Marian, and Margery,
    But none of us cared for Kate;
    For she had a tongue with a tang,
    Would cry to a sailor, Go hang!
She loved not the savour of tar nor of pitch;
Yet a tailor might scratch her where'er she did itch.
    Then, to sea, boys, and let her go hang!

This is a scurvy tune too: but here's my comfort. [*Drinks.*
Cal. Do not torment me:—O!
Ste. What's the matter? Have we devils here? Do you put tricks upon's with salvages and men of Ind, ha? I have not scaped drowning, to be afeard now of your four legs; for it hath been said, As proper a man as ever went on four legs cannot make him give ground; and it shall be said so again, while Stephano breathes at nostrils.
Cal. The spirit torments me:—O!
Ste. This is some monster of the isle with four legs, who hath got, as I take it, an ague. Where the devil should he learn our language? I will give him some relief, if it be but for that. If I can recover him, and keep him tame, and get to

Naples with him, he 's a present for any emperor that ever trod on neat's-leather.

Cal. Do not torment me, prithee; I 'll bring my wood home faster.

Ste. He 's in his fit now, and does not talk after the wisest. He shall taste of my bottle: if he have never drunk wine afore, it will go near to remove his fit. If I can recover him, and keep him tame, I will not take too much for him; he shall pay for him that hath him, and that soundly.

Cal. Thou dost me yet but little hurt; thou wilt anon, I know it by thy trembling: now Prosper works upon thee.

Ste. Come on your ways; open your mouth; here is that which will give language to you, cat: open your mouth; this will shake your shaking, I can tell you, and that soundly: you cannot tell who 's your friend: open your chaps again.

Trin. I should know that voice: it should be—but he is drowned; and these are devils:—O defend me!

Ste. Four legs and two voices,—a most delicate monster! His forward voice, now, is to speak well of his friend; his backward voice is to utter foul speeches and to detract. If all the wine in my bottle will recover him, I will help his ague. Come:—Amen! I will pour some in thy other

Trin. Stephano!　　　　　　　　　　　　　　　　[mouth.

Ste. Doth thy other mouth call me? Mercy, mercy! This is a devil, and no monster: I will leave him; I have no long spoon.

Trin. Stephano! If thou beest Stephano, touch me, and speak to me; for I am Trinculo,—be not afeard,—thy good friend Trinculo.

Ste. If thou beest Trinculo, come forth: I 'll pull thee by the lesser legs: if any be Trinculo's legs, these are they. Thou art very Trinculo indeed! How camest thou to be the siege of this moon-calf? can he vent Trinculos?

Trin. I took him to be killed with a thunder-stroke. But art thou not drowned, Stephano? I hope, now, thou art not drowned. Is the storm overblown? I hid me under the dead moon-calf's gaberdine for fear of the storm. And art thou living, Stephano? O Stephano, two Neapolitans scaped!

Ste. Prithee, do not turn me about; my stomach is not constant.

Cal. [*Aside*] These be fine things, an if they be not sprites. That 's a brave god, and bears celestial liquor: I will kneel to him.

Ste. How didst thou scape? How camest thou hither? swear, by this bottle, how thou camest hither. I escaped upon a butt of sack, which the sailors heaved o'erboard, by this bottle! which I made of the bark of a tree with mine own hands, since I was cast ashore.

Cal. I 'll swear, upon that bottle, to be thy true subject; for the liquor is not earthly.

Ste. Here; swear, then, how thou escapedst. [I 'll be sworn.

Trin. Swum ashore, man, like a duck: I can swim like a duck,

Ste. Here, kiss the book. Though thou canst swim like a duck, thou art made like a goose.

Trin. O Stephano, hast any more of this?

Ste. The whole butt, man: my cellar is in a rock by the sea-side, where my wine is hid. How now, moon-calf! how

Cal. Hast thou not dropp'd from heaven? [does thine ague?

Ste. Out o' the moon, I do assure thee: I was the man i' the moon when time was.

Cal. I have seen thee in her, and I do adore thee: my mistress show'd me thee, and thy dog, and thy bush.

Ste. Come, swear to that; kiss the book: I will furnish it anon with new contents: swear.

Trin. By this good light, this is a very shallow monster! I afeard of him! A very weak monster! The man i' the moon! A most poor credulous monster! Well drawn, monster, in good sooth!

Cal. I 'll show thee every fertile inch o' th' island; and I will kiss thy foot: I prithee, be my god.

Trin. By this light, a most perfidious and drunken monster! when 's god 's asleep, he 'll rob his bottle.

Cal. I 'll kiss thy foot; I 'll swear myself thy subject.

Ste. Come on, then; down, and swear.

Trin. I shall laugh myself to death at this puppy-headed monster. A most scurvy monster! I could find in my

Ste. Come, kiss. [heart to beat him,—

Trin. But that the poor monster 's in drink. An abominable monster!

Cal. I 'll show thee the best springs; I 'll pluck thee berries;
  I 'll fish for thee, and get thee wood enough.
  A plague upon the tyrant that I serve!
  I 'll bear him no more sticks, but follow thee,
  Thou wondrous man. [drunkard!

Trin. A most ridiculous monster, to make a wonder of a poor

Cal. I prithee, let me bring thee where crabs grow;
  And I with my long nails will dig thee pig-nuts;
  Show thee a jay's nest, and instruct thee how
  To snare the nimble marmoset; I 'll bring thee
  To clustering filberts, and sometimes I 'll get thee
  Young scamels from the rock. Wilt thou go with me?

Ste. I prithee now, lead the way, without any more talking.
  Trinculo, the king and all our company else being drowned,
  we will inherit here : here ; bear my bottle : fellow Trinculo,
Cal. [*Sings drunkenly*]   [we 'll fill him by and by again.
            Farewell, master ; farewell, farewell !
Trin. A howling monster ; a drunken monster !
Cal.   No more dams I 'll make for fish ;
                    Nor fetch in firing
                    At requiring ;
            Nor scrape trencher, nor wash dish :
                    'Ban, 'Ban, Cacaliban
            Has a new master :—get a new man.
    Freedom, hey-day ! hey-day, freedom ! freedom, hey-day,
    freedom !
Ste. O brave monster ! Lead the way.   [*Exeunt*.

ACT III—Scene I
Before Prospero's cell.
Enter Ferdinand, bearing a log.

Fer. There be some sports are painful, and their labour
    Delight in them sets off : some kinds of baseness
    Are nobly undergone, and most poor matters
    Point to rich ends.   This my mean task
    Would be as heavy to me as odious, but
    The mistress which I serve quickens what 's dead,
    And makes my labours pleasures : O, she is
    Ten times more gentle than her father 's crabbed,
    And he 's composed of harshness.   I must remove
    Some thousands of these logs, and pile them up,
    Upon a sore injunction : my sweet mistress
    Weeps when she sees me work, and says, such baseness
    Had never like executor.   I forget :
    But these sweet thoughts do even refresh my labours,
    Most busy lest, when I do it.

Enter Miranda ; and Prospero at a distance, unseen.

Mir.   Alas, now, pray you,
    Work not so hard : I would the lightning had
    Burnt up those logs that you are enjoin'd to pile !
    Pray, set it down, and rest you : when this burns,
    'Twill weep for having wearied you.   My father
    Is hard at study ; pray, now, rest yourself ;
    He 's safe for these three hours.
Fer.   O most dear mistress,
    The sun will set before I shall discharge
    What I must strive to do.

Mir.   If you 'll sit down,
  I'll bear your logs the while : pray, give me that ;
  I'll carry it to the pile.
Fer.   No, precious creature ;
  I had rather crack my sinews, break my back,
  Than you should such dishonour undergo,
  While I sit lazy by.
Mir.   It would become me
  As well as it does you : and I should do it
  With much more ease ; for my good will is to it,
  And yours it is against.
Pros.   Poor worm, thou art infected
  This visitation shows it.
Mir.   You look wearily.
Fer. No, noble mistress ; 'tis fresh morning with me
  When you are by at night.   I do beseech you,—
  Chiefly that I might set it in my prayers,—
  What is your name ?
Mir.   Miranda.—O my father,
  I have broke your hest to say so !
Fer.   Admired Miranda !
  Indeed the top of admiration ! worth
  What 's dearest to the world !   Full many a lady
  I have eyed with best regard, and many a time
  The harmony of their tongues hath into bondage
  Brought my too diligent ear : for several virtues
  Have I liked several women ; never any
  With so full soul, but some defect in her
  Did quarrel with the noblest grace she owed,
  And put it to the foil : but you, O you,
  So perfect and so peerless, are created
  Of every creature's best !
Mir.   I do not know
  One of my sex ; no woman's face remember,
  Save, from my glass, mine own ; nor have I seen
  More that I may call men than you, good friend,
  And my dear father : how features are abroad,
  I am skilless of ; but, by my modesty,
  The jewel in my dower, I would not wish
  Any companion in the world but you ;
  Nor can imagination form a shape,
  Besides yourself, to like of.   But I prattle
  Something too wildly, and my father's precepts
  I therein do forget.
Fer.   I am, in my condition,

29

A prince, Miranda; I do think, a king;
I would, not so!—and would no more endure
This wooden slavery than to suffer
The flesh-fly blow my mouth.   Hear my soul speak:
The very instant that I saw you, did
My heart fly to your service; there resides,
To make me slave to it; and for your sake
Am I this patient log-man.

Mir.   Do you love me?

Fer. O heaven, O earth, bear witness to this sound,
And crown what I profess with kind event,
If I speak true! if hollowly, invert
What best is boded me to mischief!   I,
Beyond all limit of what else i' the world,
Do love, prize, honour you.

Mir.   I am a fool
To weep at what I am glad of.

Pros.   Fair encounter
Of two most rare affections!   Heavens rain grace
On that which breeds between 'em!

Fer.   Wherefore weep you?

Mir. At mine unworthiness, that dare not offer
What I desire to give; and much less take
What I shall die to want.   But this is trifling;
And all the more it seeks to hide itself,
The bigger bulk it shows.   Hence, bashful cunning!
And prompt me, plain and holy innocence!
I am your wife, if you will marry me;
If not, I'll die your maid: to be your fellow
You may deny me; but I'll be your servant,
Whether you will or no.

Fer.   My mistress, dearest;
And I thus humble ever.

Mir.   My husband, then?

Fer. Ay, with a heart as willing
As bondage e'er of freedom: here's my hand.

Mir. And mine, with my heart in't: and now farewell
Till half an hour hence.

Fer.   A thousand thousand!

                    [*Exeunt Fer. and Mir. severally.*

Pros. So glad of this as they I cannot be,
Who are surprised withal; but my rejoicing
At nothing can be more.   I'll to my book;
For yet, ere supper-time, must I perform
Much business appertaining.   [*Exit.*

SCENE II

Another part of the Island.
Enter Caliban, Stephano, and Trinculo.

Ste. Tell not me ;—when the butt is out, we will drink water ; not a drop before: therefore bear up, and board 'em. Servant-monster, drink to me.

Trin. Servant-monster! the folly of this island! They say there's but five upon this isle : we are three of them ; if th' other two be brained like us, the state totters.

Ste. Drink, servant-monster, when I bid thee: thy eyes are almost set in thy head.

Trin. Where should they be set else? he were a brave monster indeed, if they were set in his tail.

Ste. My man-monster hath drowned his tongue in sack : for my part, the sea cannot drown me; I swam, ere I could recover the shore, five-and-thirty leagues off and on. By this light, thou shalt be my lieutenant, monster, or my standard.

Trin. Your lieutenant, if you list; he's no standard.

Ste. We'll not run, Monsieur Monster.

Trin. Nor go neither; but you'll lie, like dogs, and yet say nothing neither.

Ste. Moon-calf, speak once in thy life, if thou beest a good moon-calf.

Cal. How does thy honour? Let me lick thy shoe. I'll not serve him, he is not valiant.

Trin. Thou liest, most ignorant monster : I am in case to justle a constable. Why, thou deboshed fish, thou, was there ever man a coward that hath drunk so much sack as I to-day? Wilt thou tell a monstrous lie, being but half a fish and half a monster?

Cal. Lo, how he mocks me! wilt thou let him, my lord?

Trin. 'Lord,' quoth he! That a monster should be such a natural!

Cal. Lo, lo, again! bite him to death, I prithee.

Ste. Trinculo, keep a good tongue in your head : if you prove a mutineer,—the next tree! The poor monster's my subject, and he shall not suffer indignity.

Cal. I thank my noble lord. Wilt thou be pleased to hearken once again to the suit I made to thee?

Ste. Marry, will I : kneel and repeat it; I will stand, and so shall Trinculo.

Enter Ariel, invisible.

Cal. As I told thee before, I am subject to a tyrant, a sorcerer, that by his cunning hath cheated me of the island.

31

Ari. Thou liest.

Cal. Thou liest, thou jesting monkey, thou:
  I would my valiant master would destroy thee!
  I do not lie.

Ste. Trinculo, if you trouble him any more in's tale, by this
  hand, I will supplant some of your teeth.

Trin. Why, I said nothing.

Ste. Mum, then, and no more.   Proceed.

Cal. I say, by sorcery he got this isle;
  From me he got it.   If thy greatness will
  Revenge it on him,—for I know thou darest,
  But this thing dare not,—

Ste. That's most certain.

Cal. Thou shalt be lord of it, and I'll serve thee.

Ste. How now shall this be compassed?   Canst thou bring
  me to the party?

Cal. Yea, yea, my lord: I'll yield him thee asleep,
  Where thou mayst knock a nail into his head.

Ari. Thou liest; thou canst not.

Cal. What a pied ninny's this!   Thou scurvy patch!
  I do beseech thy greatness, give him blows,
  And take his bottle from him: when that's gone,
  He shall drink nought but brine; for I'll not show him
  Where the quick freshes are.

Ste. Trinculo, run into no further danger: interrupt the monster
  one word further, and, by this hand, I'll turn my mercy out
  o' doors, and make a stock-fish of thee.

Trin. Why, what did I?   I did nothing.   I'll go farther off.

Ste. Didst thou not say he lied?

Ari. Thou liest.

Ste. Do I so? take thou that.   [*Beats him.*]
  As you like this, give me the lie another time

Trin. I did not give the lie.   Out o' your wits,
  and hearing too?   A pox o' your bottle! this can sack and
  drinking do.   A murrain on your monster, and the devil take
  your fingers!

Cal. Ha, ha, ha!

Ste. Now, forward with your tale.—Prithee, stand farther off.

Cal. Beat him enough: after a little time,
  I'll beat him too.

Ste.   Stand farther.—Come, proceed.

Cal. Why, as I told thee, 'tis a custom with him
  I' th' afternoon to sleep: there thou mayst brain him,
  Having first seized his books; or with a log
  Batter his skull, or paunch him with a stake,

32

Or cut his wezand with thy knife. Remember.
First to possess his books; for without them
He's but a sot, as I am, nor hath not
One spirit to command: they all do hate him
As rootedly as I. Burn but his books.
He has brave utensils,—for so he calls them,—
Which, when he has a house, he'll deck withal.
And that most deeply to consider is
The beauty of his daughter; he himself
Calls her a nonpareil: I never saw a woman,
But only Sycorax my dam and she;
But she as far surpasseth Sycorax
As great'st does least.

Ste.   Is it so brave a lass?

Cal. Ay, lord; she will become thy bed, I warrant,
And bring thee forth brave brood.

Ste. Monster, I will kill this man: his daughter and I will be
king and queen,—save our graces!—and Trinculo and thyself shall be viceroys. Dost thou like the plot, Trinculo?

Trin. Excellent.

Ste. Give me thy hand: I am sorry I beat thee; but, while thou
livest, keep a good tongue in thy head.

Cal. Within this half hour will he be asleep:
Wilt thou destroy him then?

Ste.   Ay, on mine honour.

Ari. This will I tell my master.

Cal. Thou makest me merry; I am full of pleasure:
Let us be jocund: will you troll the catch
You taught me but while-ere?

Ste. At thy request, monster, I will do reason, any reason.—
Come on, Trinculo, let us sing.   [*Sings.*

       Flout 'em and scout 'em
       And scout 'em and flout 'em;
           Thought is free.

Cal. That's not the tune.

       [*Ariel plays the tune on a tabor and pipe.*

Ste. What is this same?

Trin. This is the tune of our catch, played by the picture of
Nobody.

Ste. If thou beest a man, show thyself in thy likeness: if thou
beest a devil, take't as thou list.

Trin. O, forgive me my sins!

Ste. He that dies pays all debts: I defy thee. Mercy upon us!

Cal. Art thou afeard?

Ste. No, monster, not I.

Cal. Be not afeard; the isle is full of noises,
Sounds and sweet airs, that give delight, and hurt not.
Sometimes a thousand twangling instruments
Will hum about mine ears; and sometime voices,
That, if I then had waked after long sleep,
Will make me sleep again: and then, in dreaming,
The clouds methought would open, and show riches
Ready to drop upon me; that, when I waked,
I cried to dream again.

Ste. This will prove a brave kingdom to me, where
I shall have my music for nothing.

Cal. When Prospero is destroyed.

Ste. That shall be by and by: I remember the story.

Trin. The sound is going away; let's follow it, and after do our
work.

Ste. Lead, monster; we'll follow. I would I could see this taborer;
he lays it on.

Trin. Wilt come? I'll follow, Stephano.   [*Exeunt.*

SCENE III

Another part of the island.
Enter Alonso, Sebastian, Antonio, Gonzalo,
Adrian, Francisco, and others.

Gon. By'r lakin, I can go no further, sir;
My old bones ache: here's a maze trod, indeed,
Through forth-rights and meanders! By your patience,
I needs must rest me.

Alon.   Old lord, I cannot blame thee,
Who am myself attach'd with weariness,
To the dulling of my spirits: sit down, and rest.
Even here I will put off my hope, and keep it
No longer for my flatterer: he is drown'd
Whom thus we stray to find; and the sea mocks
Our frustrate search on land. Well, let him go.

Ant. [*Aside to Seb.*] I am right glad that he's so out of hope.
Do not, for one repulse, forego the purpose
That you resolved to effect.

Seb.   [*Aside to Ant.*]   The next advantage
Will we take thoroughly.

Ant.   [*Aside to Seb.*] Let it be to-night;
For, now they are oppress'd with travel, they
Will not, nor cannot, use such vigilance
As when they are fresh.

Seb.   [*Aside to Ant.*] I say, to-night: no more.

[*Solemn and strange music.*

The Tempest

Alon. What harmony is this?—My good friends, hark !

Gon. Marvellous sweet music !

> *Enter Prospero above, invisible. Enter several strange Shapes, bringing in a banquet: they dance about it with gentle actions of salutation ; and, inviting the King, &c. to eat, they depart.*

Alon. Give us kind keepers, heavens !—What were these?

Seb. A living drollery. Now I will believe
That there are unicorns; that in Arabia
There is one tree, the phœnix' throne ; one phœnix
At this hour reigning there.

Ant.   I 'll believe both ;
And what does else want credit, come to me,
And I 'll be sworn 'tis true : travellers ne'er did lie,
Though fools at home condemn 'em.

Gon.   If in Naples
I should report this now, would they believe me?
If I should say, I saw such islanders,—
For, certes, these are people of the island,—
Who, though they are of monstrous shape, yet, note,
Their manners are more gentle-kind than of
Our human generation you shall find
Many, nay, almost any.

Pros.   [*Aside*] Honest lord,
Thou hast said well; for some of you there present
Are worse than devils.

Alon.   I cannot too much muse
Such shapes, such gesture, and such sound, expressing—
Although they want the use of tongue—a kind
Of excellent dumb discourse.

Pros.   [*Aside*] Praise in departing.

Fran. They vanish'd strangely.

Seb.   No matter, since
They have left their viands behind ; for we have stomachs.—
Will 't please you taste of what is here ?

Alon.   Not I.

Gon. Faith, sir, you need not fear. When we were boys,
Who would believe that there were mountaineers
Dew-lapp'd like bulls, whose throats had hanging at 'em
Wallets of flesh ? or that there were such men
Whose heads stood in their breasts? which now we find
Each putter-out of five for one will bring us
Good warrant of.

Alon.   I will stand to, and feed,
Although my last : no matter, since I feel

The best is past.   Brother, my lord the duke,
Stand to, and do as we.

*Thunder and lightning.   Enter Ariel, like a harpy ; claps his
    wings upon the table ; and, with a quaint device, the
    banquet vanishes.*

Ari. You are three men of sin, whom Destiny,—
That hath to instrument this lower world
And what is in 't,—the never-surfeited sea
Hath caused to belch up you ; and on this island,
Where man doth not inhabit,—you 'mongst men
Being most unfit to live.   I have made you mad ;
And even with such-like valour men hang and drown
Their proper selves.

              [*Alon., Seb. etc. draw their swords.*
              You fools ! I and my fellows
Are ministers of Fate : the elements,
Of whom your swords are temper'd, may as well
Wound the loud winds, or with bemock'd-at stabs
Kill the still-closing waters, as diminish
One dowle that 's in my plume : my fellow-ministers
Are like invulnerable.   If you could hurt,
Your swords are now too massy for your strengths,
And will not be uplifted.   But remember,—
For that 's my business to you,—that you three
From Milan did supplant good Prospero ;
Exposed unto the sea, which hath requit it,
Him and his innocent child : for which foul deed
The powers, delaying, not forgetting, have
Incensed the seas and shores, yea, all the creatures,
Against your peace.   Thee of thy son, Alonso,
They have bereft ; and do pronounce by me :
Lingering perdition—worse than any death
Can be at once—shall step by step attend
You and your ways ; whose wraths to guard you from,—
Which here, in this most desolate isle, else falls
Upon your heads,—is nothing but heart-sorrow
And a clear life ensuing.

*He vanishes in thunder ; then, to soft music, enter the Shapes
    again, and dance, with mocks and mows, and carrying
    out the table.*

Pros. Bravely the figure of this harpy hast thou
Perform'd, my Ariel ; a grace it had, devouring :
Of my instruction hast thou nothing bated
In what thou hadst to say : so, with good life
And observation strange, my meaner ministers

Their several kinds have done.   My high charms work,
And these mine enemies are all knit up
In their distractions : they now are in my power ;
And in these fits I leave them, while I visit
Young Ferdinand,—whom they suppose is drown'd,—
And his and mine loved darling.   [*Exit above.*

Gon. I' the name of something holy, sir, why stand you
In this strange stare?

Alon.   O, it is monstrous, monstrous!
Methought the billows spoke, and told me of it ;
The winds did sing it to me ; and the thunder,
That deep and dreadful organ-pipe, pronounced
The name of Prosper : it did bass my trespass.
Therefore my son i' th' ooze is bedded ; and
I 'll seek him deeper than e'er plummet sounded,
And with him there lie mudded.   [*Exit.*

Seb.   But one fiend at a time,
I 'll fight their legions o'er.

Ant.   I 'll be thy second.
                    [*Exeunt Seb. and Ant.*

Gon. All three of them are desperate : their great guilt,
Like poison given to work a great time after,
Now 'gins to bite the spirits.   I do beseech you,
That are of suppler joints, follow them swiftly,
And hinder them from what this ecstasy
May now provoke them to.

Adr.   Follow, I pray you.   [*Exeunt.*

ACT IV—Scene I
Before Prospero's cell.
Enter Prospero, Ferdinand, and Miranda.

Pros. If I have too austerely punish'd you,
Your compensation makes amends ; for I
Have given you here a third of mine own life,
Or that for which I live ; who once again
I tender to thy hand : all thy vexations
Were but my trials of thy love, and thou
Hast strangely stood the test : here, afore Heaven,
I ratify this my rich gift.   O Ferdinand,
Do not smile at me that I boast her off,
For thou shalt find she will outstrip all praise,
And make it halt behind her.

Fer.   I do believe it
Against an oracle.

Pros. Then, as my gift and thine own acquisition

Worthily purchased, take my daughter : but
If thou dost break her virgin-knot before
All sanctimonious ceremonies may
With full and holy rite be minister'd,
No sweet aspersion shall the heavens let fall
To make this contract grow ; but barren hate,
Sour-eyed disdain and discord shall bestrew
The union of your bed with weeds so loathly
That you shall hate it both : therefore take heed,
As Hymen's lamps shall light you.

Fer.   As I hope
For quiet days, fair issue and long life,
With such love as 'tis now, the murkiest den,
The most opportune place, the strong'st suggestion
Our worser genius can, shall never melt
Mine honour into lust, to take away
The edge of that day's celebration
When I shall think, or Phœbus' steeds are founder'd,
Or Night kept chain'd below.

Pros.   Fairly spoke.
Sit, then, and talk with her ; she is thine own.
What, Ariel ! my industrious servant, Ariel !

Enter Ariel.

Ari. What would my potent master ? here I am.

Pros. Thou and thy meaner fellows your last service
Did worthily perform ; and I must use you
In such another trick.   Go bring the rabble,
O'er whom I give thee power, here to this place ı
Incite them to quick motion ; for I must
Bestow upon the eyes of this young couple
Some vanity of mine art : it is my promise,
And they expect it from me.

Ari.   Presently ?

Pros. Ay, with a twink.

Ari.   Before you can say, 'come,' and 'go,'
And breathe twice, and cry, 'so, so,'
Each one, tripping on his toe,
Will be here with mop and mow.
Do you love me, master ? no ?

Pros. Dearly, my delicate Ariel.   Do not approach
Till thou dost hear me call.

Ari.   Well, I conceive.   [*Exit.*

Pros. Look thou be true ; do not give dalliance
Too much the rein : the strongest oaths are straw
To the fire i' the blood : be more abstemious,

38

Or else, good night your vow!

Fer.   I warrant you, sir;
  The white cold virgin snow upon my heart
  Abates the ardour of my liver.

Pros.   Well.
  Now come, my Ariel! bring a corollary,
  Rather than want a spirit: appear, and pertly!
  No tongue! all eyes! be silent.   [*Soft music.*
                    Enter Iris.

Iris. Ceres, most bounteous lady, thy rich leas
  Of wheat, rye, barley, vetches, oats, and pease;
  Thy turfy mountains, where live nibbling sheep,
  And flat meads thatch'd with stover, them to keep;
  Thy banks with pioned and twilled brims,
  Which spongy April at thy hest betrims,
  To make cold nymphs chaste crowns; and thy broom-groves,
  Whose shadow the dismissed bachelor loves,
  Being lass-lorn; thy pole-clipt vineyard;
  And thy sea-marge, sterile and rocky-hard,
  Where thou thyself dost air;—the queen o' the sky,
  Whose watery arch and messenger am I,
  Bids thee leave these; and with her sovereign grace,
  Here, on this grass-plot, in this very place,
  To come and sport:—her peacocks fly amain:
  Approach, rich Ceres, her to entertain.
                    Enter Ceres.

Cer. Hail, many-colour'd messenger, that ne'er
  Dost disobey the wife of Jupiter;
  Who, with thy saffron wings, upon my flowers
  Diffusest honey-drops, refreshing showers;
  And with each end of thy blue bow dost crown
  My bosky acres and my unshrubb'd down,
  Rich scarf to my proud earth;—why hath thy queen
  Summon'd me hither, to this short-grass'd green?

Iris. A contract of true love to celebrate;
  And some donation freely to estate
  On the blest lovers.

Cer.   Tell me, heavenly bow,
  If Venus or her son, as thou dost know,
  Do now attend the queen? Since they did plot
  The means that dusky Dis my daughter got,
  Her and her blind boy's scandal'd company
  I have forsworn.

Iris.   Of her society
  Be not afraid: I met her deity

39

    Cutting the clouds towards Paphos, and her son
    Dove-drawn with her.   Here thought they to have done
    Some wanton charm upon this man and maid,
    Whose vows are, that no bed-right shall be paid
    Till Hymen's torch be lighted : but in vain ;
    Mars's hot minion is return'd again ;
    Her waspish-headed son has broke his arrows,
    Swears he will shoot no more, but play with sparrows,
    And be a boy right out.
Cer.   High'st queen of state,
    Great Juno, comes ; I know her by her gait.

                   Enter Juno.

Juno. How does my bounteous sister?   Go with me
    To bless this twain, that they may prosperous be,
    And honour'd in their issue.   *[They sing.*
Juno.   Honour, riches, marriage-blessing,
             Long continuance, and increasing,
             Hourly joys be still upon you !
             Juno sings her blessings on you.
Cer   Earth's increase, foison plenty,
             Barns and garners never empty ;
             Vines with clustering bunches growing
             Plants with goodly burthen bowing ;
             Spring come to you at the farthest
             In the very end of harvest !
             Scarcity and want shall shun you ;
             Ceres' blessing so is on you.
Fer. This is a most majestic vision, and
    Harmonious charmingly.   May I be bold
    To think these spirits?
Pros.   Spirits, which by mine art
    I have from their confines call'd to enact
    My present fancies.
Fer.   Let me live here ever ;
    So rare a wonder'd father and a wise
    Makes this place Paradise.
      [Juno and Ceres whisper, and send Iris on employment.
Pros.   Sweet, now, silence !
    Juno and Ceres whisper seriously ;
    There's something else to do : hush, and be mute,
    Or else our spell is marr'd.
Iris. You nymphs, call'd Naiads, of the wind'ring brooks,
    With your sedged crowns and ever-harmless looks,
    Leave your crisp channels, and on this green land
    Answer your summons ; Juno does command :

Come, temperate nymphs, and help to celebrate
A contract of true love; be not too late.

Enter certain Nymphs.

You sunburn'd sicklemen, of August weary,
Come hither from the furrow, and be merry:
Make holiday; your rye-straw hats put on,
And these fresh nymphs encounter every one
In country footing.

*Enter certain Reapers, properly habited: they join with the
Nymphs in a graceful dance; towards the end whereof Prospero
starts suddenly, and speaks; after which, to a strange, hollow,
and confused noise, they heavily vanish.*

Pros. [*Aside*] I had forgot that foul conspiracy
Of the beast Caliban and his confederates
Against my life: the minute of their plot
Is almost come [*To the Spirits.*] Well done! avoid; no more!

Fer. This is strange: your father's in some passion
That works him strongly.

Mir.   Never till this day
Saw I him touch'd with anger so distemper'd.

Pros. You do look, my son, in a moved sort,
As if you were dismay'd: be cheerful, sir.
Our revels now are ended.   These our actors,
As I foretold you, were all spirits, and
Are melted into air, into thin air:
And, like the baseless fabric of this vision,
The cloud-capp'd towers, the gorgeous palaces,
The solemn temples, the great globe itself,
Yea, all which it inherit, shall dissolve,
And, like this insubstantial pageant faded,
Leave not a rack behind.   We are such stuff
As dreams are made on; and our little life
Is rounded with a sleep.   Sir, I am vex'd;
Bear with my weakness; my old brain is troubled:
Be not disturb'd with my infirmity:
If you be pleased, retire into my cell,
And there repose: a turn or two I'll walk,
To still my beating mind

Fer. Mir.   We wish your peace.   [*Exeunt.*
Pros. Come with a thought.   I thank thee, Ariel: come.

Enter Ariel.

Ari. Thy thoughts I cleave to.   What's thy pleasure?
Pros.   Spirit,
We must prepare to meet with Caliban.

41

Ari. Ay, my commander : when I presented Ceres
  I thought to have told thee of it ; but I fear'd
  Lest I might anger thee.
Pros. Say again, where didst thou leave these varlets ?
Ari. I told you, sir, they were red-hot with drinking ;
  So full of valour that they smote the air
  For breathing in their faces ; beat the ground
  For kissing of their feet ; yet always bending
  Towards their project.   Then I beat my tabor ;
  At which, like unback'd colts, they prick'd their ears,
  Advanced their eyelids, lifted up their noses
  As they smelt music : so I charm'd their ears,
  That, calf-like, they my lowing followed through
  Tooth'd briers, sharp furzes, pricking goss, and thorns,
  Which enter'd their frail shins : at last I left them
  I' the filthy-mantled pool beyond your cell,
  There dancing up to the chins, that the foul lake
  O'erstunk their feet.
Pros.   This was well done, my bird.
  Thy shape invisible retain thou still :
  The trumpery in my house, go bring it hither,
  For stale to catch these thieves.
Ari.   I go, I go.   [*Exit.*
Pros. A devil, a born devil, on whose nature
  Nurture can never stick ; on whom my pains,
  Humanely taken, all, all lost, quite lost ;
  And as with age his body uglier grows,
  So his mind cankers.   I will plague them all,
  Even to roaring.

   Re-enter Ariel, loaden with glistering apparel, &c.
            Come, hang them on this line.

        Prospero and Ariel remain, invisible.
    Enter Caliban, Stephano, and Trinculo, all wet.

Cal. Pray you, tread softly, that the blind mole may not
  Hear a foot fall : we now are near his cell.
Ste. Monster, your fairy, which you say is a harmless fairy, has
  done little better than played the Jack with us.
Trin. Monster, I do smell all horse-piss ; at which my nose is
  in great indignation.
Ste. So is mine.   Do you hear, monster ?   If I should take a
  displeasure against you, look you,—
Trin. Thou wert but a lost monster.
Cal. Good my lord, give me thy favour still.
  Be patient, for the prize I 'll bring thee to

Shall hoodwink this mischance: therefore speak softly.
All's hush'd as midnight yet.
Trin. Ay, but to lose our bottles in the pool,—
Ste. There is not only disgrace and dishonour in that, monster,
but an infinite loss.   [*harmless fairy, monster.*
Trin. That's more to me than my wetting: yet this is your
Ste. I will fetch off my bottle, though I be o'er ears for my labour.
Cal. Prithee, my king, be quiet. See'st thou here,
This is the mouth o' the cell: no noise, and enter.
Do that good mischief which may make this island
Thine own for ever, and I, thy Caliban,
For aye thy foot-licker.
Ste. Give me thy hand. I do begin to have bloody thoughts.
Trin. O King Stephano! O peer! O worthy Stephano! look
what a wardrobe here is for thee!
Cal. Let it alone, thou fool; it is but trash.   [*King Stephano!*
Trin. O, ho, monster! we know what belongs to a frippery. O
Ste. Put off that gown, Trinculo; by this hand, I'll have that gown
Trin. Thy grace shall have it.
Cal. The dropsy drown this fool! what do you mean
To dote thus on such luggage? Let's alone,
And do the murder first: if he awake,
From toe to crown he'll fill our skins with pinches,
Make us strange stuff.
Ste. Be you quiet, monster. Mistress line, is not this my
jerkin? Now is the jerkin under the line: now, jerkin, you
are like to lose your hair, and prove a bald jerkin.
Trin. Do, do: we steal by line and level, an't like your grace.
Ste. I thank thee for that jest; here's a garment for't: wit shall
not go unrewarded while I am king of this country. 'Steal
by line and level' is an excellent pass of pate; there's another
garment for't.   [*away with the rest.*
Trin. Monster, come, put some lime upon your fingers, and
Cal. I will have none on't: we shall lose our time,
And all be turn'd to barnacles, or to apes
With foreheads villanous low.
Ste. Monster, lay-to your fingers: help to bear this away where
my hogshead of wine is, or I'll turn you out of my kingdom:
Trin. And this.   [*go to, carry this.*
Ste. Ay, and this.
*A noise of hunters heard. Enter divers Spirits, in shape of dogs
and hounds, hunting them about; Prospero and Ariel setting
them on.*
Pros. Hey, Mountain, hey!
Ari. Silver! there it goes, Silver!

Pros. Fury, Fury! there, Tyrant, there! hark, hark!

               [*Cal., Ste., and Trin. are driven out.*

  Go charge my goblins that they grind their joints

  With dry convulsions; shorten up their sinews

  With aged cramps; and more pinch-spotted make them

  Than pard or cat o' mountain.

Ari.   Hark, they roar!

Pros. Let them be hunted soundly.   At this hour

  Lie at my mercy all mine enemies:

  Shortly shall all my labours end, and thou

  Shalt have the air at freedom: for a little

  Follow, and do me service.   [*Exeunt.*

ACT V—Scene I

Before the cell of Prospero.

Enter Prospero in his magic robes, and Ariel.

Pros. Now does my project gather to a head:

  My charms crack not; my spirits obey; and time

  Goes upright with his carriage.   How's the day?

Ari. On the sixth hour; at which time, my lord,

  You said our work should cease.

Pros.   I did say so,

  When first I raised the tempest.   Say, my spirit,

  How fares the king and's followers?

Ari.   Confined together

  In the same fashion as you gave in charge,

  Just as you left them; all prisoners, sir,

  In the line-grove which weather-fends your cell;

  They cannot budge till your release.   The king,

  His brother, and yours, abide all three distracted,

  And the remainder mourning over them,

  Brimful of sorrow and dismay; but chiefly

  Him that you term'd, sir, 'The good old lord, Gonzalo';

  His tears run down his beard, like winter's drops

  From eaves of reeds.   Your charm so strongly works 'em,

  That if you now beheld them, your affections

  Would become tender.

Pros.   Dost thou think so, spirit?

Ari. Mine would, sir, were I human.

Pros.   And mine shall.

  Hast thou, which art but air, a touch, a feeling

  Of their afflictions, and shall not myself,

  One of their kind, that relish all as sharply,

  Passion as they, be kindlier moved than thou art?

  Though with their high wrongs I am struck to the quick,

Yet with my nobler reason 'gainst my fury
Do I take part : the rarer action is
In virtue than in vengeance : they being penitent,
The sole drift of my purpose doth extend
Not a frown further.   Go release them, Ariel :
My charms I 'll break, their senses I 'll restore,
And they shall be themselves.

Ari.   I 'll fetch them, sir.   [*Exit.*
Pros. Ye elves of hills, brooks, standing lakes, and groves ;
And ye that on the sands with printless foot
Do chase the ebbing Neptune, and do fly him
When he comes back ; you demi-puppets that
By moonshine do the green sour ringlets make,
Whereof the ewe not bites ; and you whose pastime
Is to make midnight mushrooms, that rejoice
To hear the solemn curfew ; by whose aid—
Weak masters though ye be—I have bedimm'd
The noontide sun, call'd forth the mutinous winds,
And 'twixt the green sea and the azured vault
Set roaring war : to the dread rattling thunder
Have I given fire, and rifted Jove's stout oak
With his own bolt ; the strong-based promontory
Have I made shake, and by the spurs pluck'd up
The pine and cedar : graves at my command
Have waked their sleepers, oped, and let 'em forth
By my so potent art.   But this rough magic
I here abjure ; and, when I have required
Some heavenly music,—which even now I do,—
To work mine end upon their senses, that
This airy charm is for, I 'll break my staff,
Bury it certain fathoms in the earth,
And deeper than did ever plummet sound
I 'll drown my book.   [*Solemn music.*

*Re-enter Ariel before: then Alonso, with a frantic gesture,
attended by Gonzalo ; Sebastian and Antonio in like manner,
attended by Adrian and Francisco: they all enter the circle
which Prospero had made, and there stand charmed ; which
Prospero observing, speaks:*

A solemn air, and the best comforter
To an unsettled fancy, cure thy brains,
Now useless, boil'd within thy skull ! There stand,
For you are spell-stopp'd.
Holy Gonzalo, honourable man,
Mine eyes, even sociable to the show of thine,

45

Fall fellowly drops.   The charm dissolves apace ;
And as the morning steals upon the night,
Melting the darkness, so their rising senses
Begin to chase the ignorant fumes that mantle
Their clearer reason.   O good Gonzalo,
My true preserver, and a loyal sir
To him thou follow'st !   I will pay thy graces
Home both in word and deed.   Most cruelly
Didst thou, Alonso, use me and my daughter :
Thy brother was a furtherer in the act.
Thou art pinch'd for 't now, Sebastian.   Flesh and blood,
You, brother mine, that entertain'd ambition,
Expell'd remorse and nature ; who, with Sebastian,—
Whose inward pinches therefore are most strong,—
Would here have kill'd your king ; I do forgive thee,
Unnatural though thou art.   Their understanding
Begins to swell ; and the approaching tide
Will shortly fill the reasonable shore,
That now lies foul and muddy.   Not one of them
That yet looks on me, or would know me : Ariel,
Fetch me the hat and rapier in my cell :
I will discase me, and myself present
As I was sometime Milan : quickly, spirit ;
Thou shalt ere long be free.

Ariel sings and helps to attire him.

Where the bee sucks, there suck I :
In a cowslip's bell I lie ;
There I couch when owls do cry.
On the bat's back I do fly
After summer merrily.
Merrily, merrily shall I live now
Under the blossom that hangs on the bough.

Pros. Why, that 's my dainty Ariel !   I shall miss thee ;
But yet thou shalt have freedom : so, so, so.
To the king's ship, invisible as thou art :
There shalt thou find the mariners asleep
Under the hatches ; the master and the boatswain
Being awake, enforce them to this place,
And presently, I prithee.

Ari. I drink the air before me, and return
Or ere your pulse twice beat.   [*Exit.*

Gon. All torment, trouble, wonder and amazement
Inhabits here : some heavenly power guide us
Out of this fearful country !

46

Pros.   Behold, sir king,
The wronged Duke of Milan, Prospero:
For more assurance that a living prince
Does now speak to thee, I embrace thy body;
And to thee and thy company I bid
A hearty welcome.

Alon.   Whether thou be'st he or no,
Or some enchanted trifle to abuse me,
As late I have been, I not know: thy pulse
Beats, as of flesh and blood; and, since I saw thee,
The affliction of my mind amends, with which,
I fear, a madness held me: this must crave—
An if this be at all—a most strange story.
Thy dukedom I resign, and do entreat
Thou pardon me my wrongs.—But how should Prospero
Be living and be here?

Pros.   First, noble friend,
Let me embrace thine age, whose honour cannot
Be measured or confined.

Gon.   Whether this be
Or be not, I'll not swear.

Pros.   You do yet taste
Some subtilties o' the isle, that will not let you
Believe things certain.   Welcome, my friends all!
[*Aside to Seb. and Ant.*] But you, my brace of lords, were I
   so minded,
I here could pluck his highness' frown upon you,
And justify you traitors: at this time
I will tell no tales.

Seb.   [*Aside*] The devil speaks in him.

Pros.   No.
For you, most wicked sir, whom to call brother
Would even infect my mouth, I do forgive
Thy rankest fault,—all of them; and require
My dukedom of thee, which perforce, I know,
Thou must restore.

Alon.   If thou be'st Prospero,
Give us particulars of thy preservation;
How thou hast met us here, who three hours since
Were wreck'd upon this shore; where I have lost—
How sharp the point of this remembrance is!—
My dear son Ferdinand.

Pros.   I am woe for't, sir.

Alon. Irreparable is the loss; and patience
Says it is past her cure.

47

Pros.   I rather think
You have not sought her help, of whose soft grace
For the like loss I have her sovereign aid,
And rest myself content.
Alon.   You the like loss!
Pros. As great to me as late; and, supportable
To make the dear loss, have I means much weaker
Than you may call to comfort you, for I
Have lost my daughter.
Alon.   A daughter?
O heavens, that they were living both in Naples,
The king and queen there! that they were, I wish
Myself were mudded in that oozy bed
Where my son lies.   When did you lose your daughter?
Pros. In this last tempest.   I perceive, these lords
At this encounter do so much admire,
That they devour their reason, and scarce think
Their eyes do offices of truth, their words
Are natural breath: but, howsoe'er you have
Been justled from your senses, know for certain
That I am Prospero, and that very duke
Which was thrust forth of Milan; who most strangely
Upon this shore, where you were wreck'd, was landed,
To be the lord on 't.   No more yet of this;
For 'tis a chronicle of day by day,
Not a relation for a breakfast, nor
Befitting this first meeting.   Welcome, sir;
This cell's my court: here have I few attendants,
And subjects none abroad: pray you, look in.
My dukedom since you have given me again,
I will requite you with as good a thing;
At least bring forth a wonder, to content ye
As much as me my dukedom.

*Here Prospero discovers Ferdinand and Miranda playing
at chess.*

Mir. Sweet lord, you play me false.
Fer.   No, my dear'st love,
I would not for the world.
Mir. Yes, for a score of kingdoms you should wrangle,
And I would call it fair play.
Alon.   If this prove
A vision of the island, one dear son
Shall I twice lose.
Seb.   A most high miracle!

48

Fer. Though the seas threaten, they are merciful ;
  I have cursed them without cause.   *[Kneels.*
Alon.   Now all the blessings
  Of a glad father compass thee about !
  Arise, and say how thou camest here.
Mir.   O, wonder !
  How many goodly creatures are there here !
  How beauteous mankind is ! O brave new world,
  That has such people in 't !
Pros.   'Tis new to thee.
Alon. What is this maid with whom thou wast at play ?
  Your eld'st acquaintance cannot be three hours :
  Is she the goddess that hath sever'd us,
  And brought us thus together ?
Fer.   Sir, she is mortal ;
  But by immortal Providence she 's mine :
  I chose her when I could not ask my father
  For his advice, nor thought I had one. She
  Is daughter to this famous Duke of Milan,
  Of whom so often I have heard renown,
  But never saw before ; of whom I have
  Received a second life ; and second father
  This lady makes him to me.
Alon.   I am hers :
  But, O, how oddly will it sound that I
  Must ask my child forgiveness !
Pros.   There, sir, stop :
  Let us not burthen our remembrances with
  A heaviness that 's gone.
Gon.   I have inly wept,
  Or should have spoke ere this. Look down, you gods,
  And on this couple drop a blessed crown !
  For it is you that have chalk'd forth the way
  Which brought us hither.
Alon.   I say, Amen, Gonzalo !
Gon. Was Milan thrust from Milan, that his issue
  Should become kings of Naples ? O, rejoice
  Beyond a common joy ! and set it down
  With gold on lasting pillars ; In one voyage
  Did Claribel her husband find at Tunis,
  And Ferdinand, her brother, found a wife
  Where he himself was lost, Prospero his dukedom
  In a poor isle, and all of us ourselves
  When no man was his own.
Alon.   *[To Fer. and Mir.]* Give me your hands :

Let grief and sorrow still embrace his heart
That doth not wish you joy!
Gon.   Be it so! Amen!

Re-enter Ariel, with the Master and Boatswain amazedly
following.

O, look, sir, look, sir! here is more of us:
I prophesied, if a gallows were on land,
This fellow could not drown.   Now, blasphemy,
That swear'st grace o'erboard, not an oath on shore?
Hast thou no mouth by land?   What is the news?
Boats. The best news is, that we have safely found
Our king and company; the next, our ship—
Which, but three glasses since, we gave out split—
Is tight and yare and bravely rigg'd, as when
We first put out to sea.
Ari.   [*Aside to Pros.*] Sir, all this service
Have I done since I went.
Pros.   [*Aside to Ari.*] My tricksy spirit!
Alon. These are not natural events; they strengthen
From strange to stranger.   Say, how came you hither?
Boats. If I did think, sir, I were well awake,
I 'ld strive to tell you.   We were dead of sleep,
And—how we know not—all clapp'd under hatches;
Where, but even now, with strange and several noises
Of roaring, shrieking, howling, jingling chains,
And mo diversity of sounds, all horrible,
We were awaked; straightway, at liberty;
Where we, in all her trim, freshly beheld
Our royal, good, and gallant ship; our master
Capering to eye her:—on a trice, so please you,
Even in a dream, were we divided from them,
And were brought moping hither.
Ari.   [*Aside to Pros.*] Was 't well done?
Pros. [*Aside to Ari.*] Bravely, my diligence.   Thou shalt be free.
Alon. This is as strange a maze as e'er men trod;
And there is in this business more than nature
Was ever conduct of: some oracle
Must rectify our knowledge.
Pros.   Sir, my liege,
Do not infest your mind with beating on
The strangeness of this business; at pick'd leisure
Which shall be shortly, single I 'll resolve you,
Which to you shall seem probable, of every
These happen'd accidents; till when, be cheerful,

And think of each thing well. [*Aside to Ari.*] Come hither,
Set Caliban and his companions free ;   [spirit :
Untie the spell. [*Exit Ariel.*] How fares my gracious sir ?
There are yet missing of your company
Some few odd lads that you remember not.

*Re-enter Ariel, driving in Caliban, Stephano, and Trinculo,
in their stolen apparel.*

Ste. Every man shift for all the rest, and let no man take care
for himself ; for all is but fortune.—Coragio, bully-monster,
coragio !
Trin. If these be true spies which I wear in my head, here's a
Cal. O Setebos, these be brave spirits indeed !   [goodly sight.
How fine my master is !   I am afraid
He will chastise me.
Seb.   Ha, ha !
What things are these, my lord Antonio ?
Will money buy 'em ?
Ant.   Very like ; one of them
Is a plain fish, and, no doubt, marketable.
Pros. Mark but the badges of these men, my lords,
Then say if they be true.   This mis-shapen knave,
His mother was a witch ; and one so strong
That could control the moon, make flows and ebbs,
And deal in her command, without her power.
These three have robb'd me ; and this demi-devil—
For he's a bastard one—had plotted with them
To take my life.   Two of these fellows you
Must know and own ; this thing of darkness I
Acknowledge mine.
Cal.   I shall be pinch'd to death.
Alon. Is not this Stephano, my drunken butler ?
Seb. He is drunk now : where had he wine ?
Alon. And Trinculo is reeling ripe : where should they
Find this grand liquor that hath gilded 'em ?—
How camest thou in this pickle ?
Trin. I have been in such a pickle, since I saw you last, that,
I fear me, will never out of my bones : I shall not fear fly-
Seb. Why, how now, Stephano !   [blowing.
Ste. O, touch me not ;—I am not Stephano, but a cramp.
Pros. You'ld be king o' the isle, sirrah ?
Ste. I should have been a sore one, then.
Alon. This is a strange thing as e'er I look'd on.
                                [*Pointing to Caliban.*
Pros. He is as disproportion'd in his manners

As in his shape.   Go, sirrah, to my cell;
Take with you your companions; as you look
To have my pardon, trim it handsomely.
Cal. Ay, that I will; and I'll be wise hereafter,
And seek for grace.   What a thrice-double ass
Was I, to take this drunkard for a god,
And worship this dull fool!
Pros.   Go to; away!
Alon. Hence, and bestow your luggage where you found it.
Seb. Or stole it, rather.
                          [*Exeunt Cal., Ste., and Trin.*
Pros. Sir, I invite your Highness and your train
To my poor cell, where you shall take your rest
For this one night; which, part of it, I'll waste
With such discourse as, I not doubt, shall make it
Go quick away: the story of my life,
And the particular accidents gone by
Since I came to this isle: and in the morn
I'll bring you to your ship, and so to Naples,
Where I have hope to see the nuptial
Of these our dear beloved solemnized;
And thence retire me to my Milan, where
Every third thought shall be my grave.
Alon.   I long
To hear the story of your life, which must
Take the ear strangely.
Pros.   I'll deliver all;
And promise you calm seas, auspicious gales,
And sail so expeditious, that shall catch
Your royal fleet far off   [*Aside to Ari.*] My Ariel, chick,
That is thy charge: then to the elements
Be free, and fare thou well! Please you, draw near. [*Exeunt.*

EPILOGUE.

Spoken by Prospero.

Now my charms are all o'erthrown,
And what strength I have 's mine own,
Which is most faint: now, 'tis true,
I must be here confined by you,
Or sent to Naples.   Let me not,
Since I have my dukedom got,
And pardon'd the deceiver, dwell
In this bare island by your spell;
But release me from my bands
With the help of your good hands:

Gentle breath of yours my sails
Must fill, or else my project fails,
Which was to please.   Now I want
Spirits to enforce, art to enchant ;
And my ending is despair,
Unless I be relieved by prayer,
Which pierces so, that it assaults
Mercy itself, and frees all faults.
As you from crimes would pardon'd be,
Let your indulgence set me free.

THE MERCHANT OF VENICE

DRAMATIS PERSONÆ

The DUKE OF VENICE.
The PRINCE OF MOROCCO, ⎫ *suitors to*
The PRINCE OF ARRAGON, ⎭ *Portia.*
ANTONIO, *a merchant of Venice.*
BASSANIO, *his friend, suitor likewise to Portia.*
SALANIO,
SALARINO, ⎫ *friends to Antonio and*
GRATIANO, ⎬ *Bassanio.*
SALERIO, ⎭
LORENZO, *in love with Jessica.*
SHYLOCK, *a rich Jew.*

TUBAL, *a Jew, his friend.*
LAUNCELOT GOBBO, *the clown, servant to Shylock.*
OLD GOBBO, *father to Launcelot.*
LEONARDO, *servant to Bassanio.*
BALTHASAR, ⎫ *servants to Portia.*
STEPHANO, ⎭

PORTIA, *a rich heiress.*
NERISSA, *her waiting-maid.*
JESSICA, *daughter to Shylock.*

Magnificoes of Venice, Officers of the Court of Justice, Gaoler, Servants to Portia, and other Attendants.

SCENE : *Partly at Venice, and partly at Belmont, the seat of Portia, on the Continent.*

ACT I—SCENE I

Venice. A street.
Enter Antonio, Salarino, and Salanio.

Ant. In sooth, I know not why I am so sad :
    It wearies me ; you say it wearies you ;
    But how I caught it, found it, or came by it,
    What stuff 'tis made of, whereof it is born,
    I am to learn ;
    And such a want-wit sadness makes of me,
    That I have much ado to know myself.
Salar. Your mind is tossing on the ocean ;
    There, where your argosies with portly sail,
    Like signiors and rich burghers on the flood,
    Or, as it were, the pageants of the sea,
    Do overpeer the petty traffickers,
    That curt'sy to them, do them reverence,
    As they fly by them with their woven wings.
Salan. Believe me, sir, had I such venture forth,
    The better part of my affections would
    Be with my hopes abroad.   I should be still
    Plucking the grass, to know where sits the wind ;
    Peering in maps for ports, and piers, and roads ;
    And every object, that might make me fear
    Misfortune to my ventures, out of doubt
    Would make me sad.
Salar.   My wind, cooling my broth,
    Would blow me to an ague, when I thought
    What harm a wind too great at sea might do.
    I should not see the sandy hour-glass run,
    But I should think of shallows and of flats,
    And see my wealthy Andrew dock'd in sand

Vailing her high top lower than her ribs
To kiss her burial.　Should I go to church
And see the holy edifice of stone,
And not bethink me straight of dangerous rocks,
Which touching but my gentle vessel's side
Would scatter all her spices on the stream,
Enrobe the roaring waters with my silks;
And, in a word, but even now worth this,
And now worth nothing?　Shall I have the thought
To think on this; and shall I lack the thought,
That such a thing bechanced would make me sad?
But tell not me; I know, Antonio
Is sad to think upon his merchandise.

Ant. Believe me, no: I thank my fortune for it,
My ventures are not in one bottom trusted,
Nor to one place; nor is my whole estate
Upon the fortune of this present year:
Therefore my merchandise makes me not sad.

Salar. Why, then you are in love.

Ant.　　　　　　　　　　　　Fie, fie!

Salar. Not in love neither?　Then let us say you are sad,
Because you are not merry: and 'twere as easy
For you to laugh, and leap, and say you are merry,
Because you are not sad.　Now, by two-headed Janus.
Nature hath framed strange fellows in her time:
Some that will evermore peep through their eyes,
And laugh like parrots at a bag-piper;
And other of such vinegar aspect,
That they'll not show their teeth in way of smile,
Though Nestor swear the jest be laughable.

　　　　　　Enter Bassanio, Lorenzo, and Gratiano.

Salan. Here comes Bassanio, your most noble kinsman,
Gratiano, and Lorenzo.　Fare ye well:
We leave you now with better company.

Salar. I would have stay'd till I had made you merry,
If worthier friends had not prevented me.

Ant. Your worth is very dear in my regard.
I take it, your own business calls on you,
And you embrace the occasion to depart.

Salar. Good morrow, my good lords.

Bass. Good signiors both, when shall we laugh? say, when?
You grow exceeding strange: must it be so?

Salar. We'll make our leisures to attend on yours.

　　　　　　　　　　　[Exeunt Salarino and Salanio.

Lor. My Lord Bassanio, since you have found Antonio,

We two will leave you : but, at dinner-time,
I pray you, have in mind where we must meet.
Bass. I will not fail you.
Gra. You look not well, Signior Antonio ;
You have too much respect upon the world :
They lose it that do buy it with much care :
Believe me, you are marvellously changed.
Ant. I hold the world but as the world, Gratiano ;
A stage, where every man must play a part,
And mine a sad one.
Gra.   Let me play the fool :
With mirth and laughter let old wrinkles come ;
And let my liver rather heat with wine
Than my heart cool with mortifying groans.
Why should a man, whose blood is warm within,
Sit like his grandsire cut in alabaster ?
Sleep when he wakes, and creep into the jaundice
By being peevish ?   I tell thee what, Antonio—
I love thee, and it is my love that speaks,—
There are a sort of men, whose visages
Do cream and mantle like a standing pond ;
And do a wilful stillness entertain,
With purpose to be dress'd in an opinion
Of wisdom, gravity, profound conceit ;
As who should say, ' I am Sir Oracle,
And, when I ope my lips, let no dog bark ! '
O my Antonio, I do know of these,
That therefore only are reputed wise
For saying nothing ; when, I am very sure,
If they should speak, would almost damn those ears,
Which, hearing them, would call their brothers fools.
I 'll tell thee more of this another time :
But fish not, with this melancholy bait,
For this fool gudgeon, this opinion.
Come, good Lorenzo.   Fare ye well awhile :
I 'll end my exhortation after dinner.
Lor. Well, we will leave you, then, till dinner-time :
I must be one of these same dumb wise men,
For Gratiano never lets me speak.
Gra. Well, keep me company but two years moe,
Thou shalt not know the sound of thine own tongue.
Ant. Farewell : I 'll grow a talker for this gear.
Gra. Thanks, i' faith ; for silence is only commendable
In a neat's tongue dried, and a maid not vendible.
                              [*Exeunt Gratiano and Lorenzo.*

Ant. Is that any thing now?

Bass. Gratiano speaks an infinite deal of nothing, more than
any man in all Venice. His reasons are as two grains of
wheat hid in two bushels of chaff : you shall seek all day ere
you find them : and when you have them, they are not worth
the search.

Ant. Well, tell me now, what lady is the same
To whom you swore a secret pilgrimage,
That you to-day promised to tell me of?

Bass. 'Tis not unknown to you, Antonio,
How much I have disabled mine estate,
By something showing a more swelling port
Than my faint means would grant continuance :
Nor do I now make moan to be abridged
From such a noble rate ; but my chief care
Is, to come fairly off from the great debts,
Wherein my time, something too prodigal,
Hath left me gaged. To you, Antonio,
I owe the most, in money and in love ;
And from your love I have a warranty
To unburthen all my plots and purposes
How to get clear of all the debts I owe.

Ant. I pray you, good Bassanio, let me know it ;
And if it stand, as you yourself still do,
Within the eye of honour, be assured,
My purse, my person, my extremest means,
Lie all unlock'd to your occasions.

Bass. In my school-days, when I had lost one shaft,
I shot his fellow of the self-same flight
The self-same way with more advised watch,
To find the other forth ; and by adventuring both,
I oft found both : I urge this childhood proof,
Because what follows is pure innocence.
I owe you much ; and, like a wilful youth,
That which I owe is lost : but if you please
To shoot another arrow that self way
Which you did shoot the first, I do not doubt,
As I will watch the aim, or to find both,
Or bring your latter hazard back again,
And thankfully rest debtor for the first.

Ant. You know me well ; and herein spend but time
To wind about my love with circumstance :
And out of doubt you do me now more wrong
In making question of my uttermost,
Than if you had made waste of all I have :

57

Then do but say to me what I should do,
That in your knowledge may by me be done,
And I am prest unto it: therefore, speak.
Bass. In Belmont is a lady richly left;
And she is fair, and, fairer than that word,
Of wondrous virtues: sometimes from her eyes
I did receive fair speechless messages:
Her name is Portia; nothing undervalued
To Cato's daughter, Brutus' Portia:
Nor is the wide world ignorant of her worth;
For the four winds blow in from every coast
Renowned suitors: and her sunny locks
Hang on her temples like a golden fleece;
Which makes her seat of Belmont Colchos' strond,
And many Jasons come in quest of her.
O my Antonio, had I but the means
To hold a rival place with one of them,
I have a mind presages me such thrift,
That I should questionless be fortunate!
Ant. Thou know'st that all my fortunes are at sea;
Neither have I money, nor commodity
To raise a present sum: therefore go forth;
Try what my credit can in Venice do:
That shall be rack'd, even to the uttermost,
To furnish thee to Belmont, to fair Portia.
Go, presently inquire, and so will I,
Where money is; and I no question make,
To have it of my trust, or for my sake.   [*Exeunt.*

SCENE II

Belmont.   A room in Portia's house.
Enter Portia and Nerissa.

Por. By my troth, Nerissa, my little body is aweary of this
great world.
Ner. You would be, sweet madam, if your miseries were in the
same abundance as your good fortunes are: and yet, for
aught I see, they are as sick that surfeit with too much, as
they that starve with nothing. It is no mean happiness,
therefore, to be seated in the mean: superfluity comes sooner
by white hairs; but competency lives longer.
Por. Good sentences, and well pronounced.
Ner. They would be better, if well followed.
Por. If to do were as easy as to know what were good to do,
chapels had been churches, and poor men's cottages princes'
palaces. It is a good divine that follows his own instructions:

I can easier teach twenty what were good to be done, than
be one of the twenty to follow mine own teaching.   The
brain may devise laws for the blood ; but a hot temper leaps
o'er a cold decree : such a hare is madness the youth, to
skip o'er the meshes of good counsel the cripple.   But this
reasoning is not in the fashion to choose me a husband.   O
me, the word 'choose'!   I may neither choose whom I
would, nor refuse whom I dislike ; so is the will of a living
daughter curbed by the will of a dead father.   Is it not hard,
Nerissa, that I cannot choose one, nor refuse none?

Ner. Your father was ever virtuous ; and holy men, at their
death, have good inspirations : therefore, the lottery, that he
hath devised in these three chests of gold, silver, and lead,—
whereof who chooses his meaning chooses you,—will, no
doubt, never be chosen by any rightly, but one who shall
rightly love.   But what warmth is there in your affection
towards any of these princely suitors that are already come?

Por. I pray thee, over-name them ; and as thou namest them,
I will describe them ; and, according to my description, level
at my affection.

Ner. First, there is the Neapolitan prince.

Por. Ay, that's a colt indeed, for he doth nothing but talk of
his horse ; and he makes it a great appropriation to his own
good parts, that he can shoe him himself.   I am much afeard
my lady his mother played false with a smith.

Ner. Then there is the County Palatine.

Por. He doth nothing but frown ; as who should say, 'if you
will not have me, choose :' he hears merry tales, and smiles
not : I fear he will prove the weeping philosopher when he
grows old, being so full of unmannerly sadness in his youth.
I had rather be married to a death's-head with a bone in his
mouth than to either of these.   God defend me from these
two !

Ner. How say you by the French lord, Monsieur Le Bon?

Por. God made him, and therefore let him pass for a man.
In truth, I know it is a sin to be a mocker : but, he !—why,
he hath a horse better than the Neapolitan's ; a better bad
habit of frowning than the Count Palatine : he is every man
in no man ; if a throstle sing, he falls straight a capering :
he will fence with his own shadow : if I should marry him, I
should marry twenty husbands.   If he would despise me, I
would forgive him ; for if he love me to madness, I shall
never requite him.   [England?

Ner. What say you, then, to Falconbridge, the young baron of

Por. You know I say nothing to him ; for he understands not

me, nor I him : he hath neither Latin, French, nor Italian ;
and you will come into the court and swear that I have a
poor pennyworth in the English. He is a proper man's
picture ; but, alas, who can converse with a dumb-show ?
How oddly he is suited ! I think he bought his doublet in
Italy, his round hose in France, his bonnet in Germany, and
his behaviour every where.

Ner. What think you of the Scottish lord, his neighbour?

Por. That he hath a neighbourly charity in him ; for he
borrowed a box of the ear of the Englishman, and swore
he would pay him again when he was able : I think the
Frenchman became his surety, and sealed under for another.

Ner. How like you the young German, the Duke of Saxony's
nephew ?

Por. Very vilely in the morning, when he is sober ; and most
vilely in the afternoon, when he is drunk : when he is best,
he is a little worse than a man ; and when he is worst, he is
little better than a beast : an the worst fall that ever fell, I
hope I shall make shift to go without him.

Ner. If he should offer to choose, and choose the right casket,
you should refuse to perform your father's will, if you should
refuse to accept him.

Por. Therefore, for fear of the worst, I pray thee, set a deep
glass of Rhenish wine on the contrary casket ; for, if the devil
be within and that temptation without, I know he will choose
it. I will do any thing, Nerissa, ere I 'll be married to a
sponge.

Ner. You need not fear, lady, the having any of these lords :
they have acquainted me with their determinations ; which
is, indeed, to return to their home, and to trouble you with
no more suit, unless you may be won by some other sort
than your father's imposition, depending on the caskets.

Por. If I live to be as old as Sibylla, I will die as chaste as
Diana, unless I be obtained by the manner of my father's
will. I am glad this parcel of wooers are so reasonable ; for
there is not one among them but I dote on his very
absence ; and I pray God grant them a fair departure.

Ner. Do you not remember, lady, in your father's time, a
Venetian, a scholar, and a soldier, that came hither in
company of the Marquis of Montferrat?

Por. Yes, yes, it was Bassanio ; as I think he was so called.

Ner. True, madam : he, of all the men that ever my foolish
eyes looked upon, was the best deserving a fair lady.

Por. I remember him well ; and I remember him worthy of
thy praise.

Enter a Serving-man.

How now! what news?

Serv. The four strangers seek for you, madam, to take their leave : and there is a forerunner come from a fifth, the Prince of Morocco ; who brings word, the prince his master will be here to-night.

Por. If I could bid the fifth welcome with so good a heart as I can bid the other four farewell, I should be glad of his approach : if he have the condition of a saint and the complexion of a devil, I had rather he should shrive me than wive me.

Come, Nerissa. Sirrah, go before.

Whiles we shut the gates upon one wooer, another knocks at the door.   [*Exeunt.*

SCENE III

Venice. A public place.
Enter Bassanio and Shylock.

Shy. Three thousand ducats ; well.

Bass. Ay, sir, for three months.

Shy. For three months ; well.

Bass. For the which, as I told you, Antonio shall be bound.

Shy. Antonio shall become bound ; well.

Bass. May you stead me? will you pleasure me? shall I know your answer?

Shy. Three thousand ducats for three months, and Antonio

Bass. Your answer to that.   [bound.

Shy. Antonio is a good man.

Bass. Have you heard any imputation to the contrary?

Shy. Ho, no, no, no, no : my meaning, in saying he is a good man, is to have you understand me, that he is sufficient. Yet his means are in supposition : he hath an argosy bound to Tripolis, another to the Indies ; I understand, moreover, upon the Rialto, he hath a third at Mexico, a fourth for England, and other ventures he hath, squandered abroad. But ships are but boards, sailors but men : there be land-rats and water-rats, water-thieves and land-thieves, I mean pirates ; and then there is the peril of waters, winds, and rocks. The man is, notwithstanding, sufficient. Three thousand ducats ; I think I may take his bond.

Bass. Be assured you may.

Shy. I will be assured I may ; and, that I may be assured, I will bethink me. May I speak with Antonio?

Bass. If it please you to dine with us.

Shy. Yés, to smell pork ; to eat of the habitation which your

prophet the Nazarite conjured the devil into. I will buy
with you, sell with you, talk with you, walk with you, and so
following ; but I will not eat with you, drink with you, nor
pray with you.   What news on the Rialto ?   Who is he
comes here ?

Enter Antonio.

Bass. This is Signior Antonio.

Shy. [*Aside*] How like a fawning publican he looks !
  I hate him for he is a Christian ;
  But more for that in low simplicity
  He lends out money gratis and brings down
  The rate of usance here with us in Venice.
  If I can catch him once upon the hip,
  I will feed fat the ancient grudge I bear him.
  He hates our sacred nation ; and he rails,
  Even there where merchants most do congregate,
  On me, my bargains, and my well-won thrift,
  Which he calls interest.   Cursed be my tribe,
  If I forgive him !

Bass.   Shylock, do you hear ?

Shy. I am debating of my present store ;
  And, by the near guess of my memory,
  I cannot instantly raise up the gross
  Of full three thousand ducats.   What of that ?
  Tubal, a wealthy Hebrew of my tribe,
  Will furnish me.   But soft ! how many months
  Do you desire ?   [*To Ant.*]   Rest you fair, good signior ;
  Your worship was the last man in our mouths.

Ant. Shylock, although I neither lend nor borrow,
  By taking nor by giving of excess,
  Yet, to supply the ripe wants of my friend,
  I 'll break a custom.   Is he yet possess'd
  How much ye would ?

Shy.   Ay, ay, three thousand ducats.

Ant. And for three months.

Shy. I had forgot ; three months, you told me so.
  Well then, your bond ; and let me see ; but hear you ;
  Methought you said you neither lend nor borrow
  Upon advantage.

Ant.   I do never use it.

Shy. When Jacob grazed his uncle Laban's sheep,—
  This Jacob from our holy Abram was,
  As his wise mother wrought in his behalf,
  The third possessor ; ay, he was the third,—

Ant. And what of him ? did he take interest ?

Shy. No, not take interest; not, as you would say,
  Directly interest: mark what Jacob did.
  When Laban and himself were compromised
  That all the eanlings which were streak'd and pied
  Should fall as Jacob's hire, the ewes, being rank,
  In the end of Autumn turned to the rams;
  And when the work of generation was
  Between these woolly breeders in the act,
  The skilful shepherd peel'd me certain wands,
  And, in the doing of the deed of kind,
  He stuck them up before the fulsome ewes,
  Who, then conceiving, did in eaning time
  Fall parti-colour'd lambs, and those were Jacob's.
  This was a way to thrive, and he was blest:
  And thrift is blessing, if men steal it not.

Ant. This was a venture, sir, that Jacob served for;
  A thing not in his power to bring to pass,
  But sway'd and fashion'd by the hand of heaven.
  Was this inserted to make interest good?
  Or is your gold and silver ewes and rams?

Shy. I cannot tell; I make it breed as fast:
  But note me, signior.

Ant.   Mark you this, Bassanio,
  The devil can cite Scripture for his purpose.
  An evil soul, producing holy witness,
  Is like a villain with a smiling cheek;
  A goodly apple rotten at the heart:
  O, what a goodly outside falsehood hath!

Shy. Three thousand ducats; 'tis a good round sum.
  Three months from twelve; then, let me see; the rate—

Ant. Well, Shylock, shall we be beholding to you?

Shy. Signior Antonio, many a time and oft
  In the Rialto you have rated me
  About my moneys and my usances:
  Still have I borne it with a patient shrug;
  For sufferance is the badge of all our tribe.
  You call me misbeliever, cut-throat dog,
  And spit upon my Jewish gaberdine,
  And all for use of that which is mine own.
  Well then, it now appears you need my help:
  Go to, then; you come to me, and you say
  'Shylock, we would have moneys:' you say so;
  You, that did void your rheum upon my beard,
  And foot me as you spurn a stranger cur
  Over your threshold: moneys is your suit.

63

What should I say to you?   Should I not say
' Hath a dog money? is it possible
A cur can lend three thousand ducats?' or
Shall I bend low and in a bondman's key,
With bated breath and whispering humbleness,
Say this,—
' Fair sir, you spit on me on Wednesday last;
You spurn'd me such a day; another time
You call'd me dog; and for these courtesies
I 'll lend you thus much moneys'?

Ant. I am as like to call thee so again,
To spit on thee again, to spurn thee too.
If thou wilt lend this money, lend it not
As to thy friends; for when did friendship take
A breed for barren metal of his friend?
But lend it rather to thine enemy;
Who if he break, thou mayest with better face
Exact the penalty.

Shy.   Why, look you, how you storm!
I would be friends with you, and have your love,
Forget the shames that you have stain'd me with,
Supply your present wants, and take no doit
Of usance for my moneys, and you 'll not hear me:
This is kind I offer.

Bass. This were kindness.

Shy.   This kindness will I show.
Go with me to a notary, seal me there
Your single bond; and, in a merry sport,
If you repay me not on such a day,
In such a place, such sum or sums as are
Express'd in the condition, let the forfeit
Be nominated for an equal pound
Of your fair flesh, to be cut off and taken
In what part of your body pleaseth me.

Ant. Content, i' faith: I 'll seal to such a bond,
And say there is much kindness in the Jew.

Bass. You shall not seal to such a bond for me:
I 'll rather dwell in my necessity.

Ant. Why, fear not, man; I will not forfeit it:
Within these two months, that 's a month before
This bond expires, I do expect return
Of thrice three times the value of this bond.

Shy. O father Abram, what these Christians are,
Whose own hard dealings teaches them suspect
The thoughts of others!   Pray you, tell me this;

64

If he should break his day, what should I gain
By the exaction of the forfeiture?
A pound of man's flesh taken from a man
Is not so estimable, profitable neither,
As flesh of muttons, beefs, or goats. I say,
To buy his favour, I extend this friendship:
If he will take it, so; if not, adieu;
And, for my love, I pray you wrong me not.

Ant. Yes, Shylock, I will seal unto this bond.

Shy. Then meet me forthwith at the notary's;
Give him direction for this merry bond;
And I will go and purse the ducats straight;
See to my house, left in the fearful guard
Of an unthrifty knave; and presently
I will be with you.

Ant.   Hie thee, gentle Jew.   [*Exit Shylock.*
The Hebrew will turn Christian: he grows kind.

Bass. I like not fair terms and a villain's mind.

Ant. Come on: in this there can be no dismay;
My ships come home a month before the day.   [*Exeunt.*

ACT II—SCENE I

Belmont. A room in Portia's house.

*Flourish of cornets. Enter the Prince of Morocco and his
train; Portia, Nerissa, and others attending.*

Mor. Mislike me not for my complexion,
The shadow'd livery of the burnish'd sun,
To whom I am a neighbour and near bred.
Bring me the fairest creature northward born,
Where Phœbus' fire scarce thaws the icicles,
And let us make incision for your love,
To prove whose blood is reddest, his or mine.
I tell thee, lady, this aspect of mine
Hath fear'd the valiant: by my love, I swear
The best-regarded virgins of our clime
Hath loved it too: I would not change this hue,
Except to steal your thoughts, my gentle queen.

Por. In terms of choice I am not solely led
By nice direction of a maiden's eyes;
Besides, the lottery of my destiny
Bars me the right of voluntary choosing:
But if my father had not scanted me
And hedged me by his wit, to yield myself
His wife who wins me by that means I told you,

Yourself, renowned prince, then stood as fair
As any comer I have look'd on yet
For my affection.

Mor.   Even for that I thank you:
Therefore, I pray you, lead me to the caskets,
To try my fortune.   By this scimitar
That slew the Sophy and a Persian prince
That won three fields of Sultan Solyman,
I would outstare the sternest eyes that look,
Outbrave the heart most daring on the earth,
Pluck the young sucking cubs from the she-bear,
Yea, mock the lion when he roars for prey,
To win thee, lady.   But, alas the while !
If Hercules and Lichas play at dice
Which is the better man, the greater throw
May turn by fortune from the weaker hand :
So is Alcides beaten by his page ;
And so may I, blind fortune leading me,
Miss that which one unworthier may attain,
And die with grieving.

Por.   You must take your chance
And either not attempt to choose at all,
Or swear before you choose, if you choose wrong,
Never to speak to lady afterward.
In way of marriage : therefore be advised.

Mor. Nor will not.   Come, bring me unto my chance.

Por. First, forward to the temple : after dinner
Your hazard shall be made.

Mor.   Good fortune then !
To make me blest or cursed'st among men.

                              [*Cornets, and exeunt.*

Scene II

Venice.   A street.

Enter Launcelot.

Laun. Certainly my conscience will serve me to run from this
Jew my master.   The fiend is at mine elbow, and tempts me,
saying to me, 'Gobbo, Launcelot Gobbo, good Launcelot,'
or 'good Gobbo,' or 'good Launcelot Gobbo, use your legs,
take the start, run away.'   My conscience says, 'No ; take
heed, honest Launcelot ; take heed, honest Gobbo,' or, as
aforesaid, 'honest Launcelot Gobbo ; do not run ; scorn
running   with   thy   heels.'   Well,   the   most   courageous
fiend bids me pack : 'Via !' says the fiend ; 'away !'
says the fiend ; 'for the heavens, rouse up a brave mind,'

says the fiend, 'and run.' Well, my conscience, hanging
about the neck of my heart, says very wisely to me,
'My honest friend Launcelot, being an honest man's son,'—
or rather an honest woman's son ;—for, indeed, my father
did something smack, something grow to, he had a kind of
taste ;—well, my conscience says, 'Launcelot, budge not.'
'Budge,' says the fiend.   'Budge not,' says my conscience.
'Conscience,' say I, 'you counsel well ;' 'Fiend,' say I, 'you
counsel well :' to be ruled by my conscience, I should stay
with the Jew my master, who, God bless the mark, is a kind
of devil ; and, to run away from the Jew, I should be ruled
by the fiend, who, saving your reverence, is the devil himself.
Certainly the Jew is the very devil incarnal ; and, in my
conscience, my conscience is but a kind of hard conscience,
to offer to counsel me to stay with the Jew. The fiend
gives the more friendly counsel : I will run, fiend ; my heels
are at your command ; I will run.

Enter Old Gobbo, with a basket.

Gob. Master young man, you, I pray you, which is the way to
master Jew's ?

Laun. [*Aside*] O heavens, this is my true-begotten father !
who, being more than sand-blind, high-gravel blind, knows
me not : I will try confusions with him.

Gob. Master young gentleman, I pray you, which is the way to
master Jew's ?

Laun. Turn up on your right hand at the next turning, but,
at the next turning of all, on your left ; marry, at the very next
turning, turn of no hand, but turn down indirectly to the
Jew's house.

Gob. By God's sonties, 'twill be a hard way to hit. Can you
tell me whether one Launcelot, that dwells with him, dwell
with him or no ?

Laun. Talk you of young Master Launcelot ? [*Aside*] Mark me
now ; now will I raise the waters. Talk you of young
Master Launcelot ?

Gob. No master, sir, but a poor man's son : his father, though
I say it, is an honest exceeding poor man, and, God be
thanked, well to live.

Laun. Well, let his father be what a' will, we talk of young
Master Launcelot.

Gob. Your worship's friend, and Launcelot, sir.

Laun. But I pray you, ergo, old man, ergo, I beseech you, talk
you of young Master Launcelot ?

Gob. Of Launcelot, an 't please your mastership.

Laun. Ergo, Master Launcelot. Talk not of Master Launcelot,

father ; for the young gentleman, according to Fates and
Destinies and such odd sayings, the Sisters Three and such
branches of learning, is indeed deceased ; or, as you would
say in plain terms, gone to heaven.

Gob. Marry, God forbid ! the boy was the very staff of my
age, my very prop.

Laun. Do I look like a cudgel or a hovel-post, a staff or a
prop ? Do you know me, father ?

Gob. Alack the day, I know you not, young gentleman : but,
I pray you, tell me, is my boy, God rest his soul, alive or

Laun. Do you not know me, father ?   [dead ?

Gob. Alack, sir, I am sand-blind ; I know you not.

Laun. Nay, indeed, if you had your eyes, you might fail
of the knowing me : it is a wise father that knows his own
child.   Well, old man, I will tell you news of your son : give
me your blessing : truth will come to light ; murder cannot
be hid long ; a man's son may ; but, at the length, truth
will out.   [my boy.

Gob. Pray you, sir, stand up : I am sure you are not Launcelot,

Laun. Pray you, let 's have no more fooling about it, but
give me your blessing : I am Launcelot, your boy that was
your son that is, your child that shall be.

Gob. I cannot think you are my son.

Laun. I know not what I shall think of that : but I am
Launcelot, the Jew's man ; and I am sure Margery your wife
is my mother.

Gob. Her name is Margery, indeed : I 'll be sworn, if thou be
Launcelot, thou art mine own flesh and blood. Lord
worshipped might he be ! what a beard hast thou got ! thou
hast got more hair on thy chin than Dobbin my fill-horse
has on his tail.

Laun. It should seem, then, that Dobbin's tail grows backward :
I am sure he had more hair of his tail than I have of my
face when I last saw him.

Gob. Lord, how art thou changed !   How dost thou and thy
master agree ? I have brought him a present. How 'gree
you now ?

Laun. Well, well : but, for mine own part, as I have set up
my rest to run away, so I will not rest till I have run some
ground.   My master 's a very Jew : give him a present ! give
him a halter : I am famished in his service ; you may tell
every finger I have with my ribs. Father, I am glad you
are come : give me your present to one Master Bassanio,
who, indeed, gives rare new liveries : if I serve not him, I
will run as far as God has any ground. O rare fortune ! here

comes the man: to him, father; for I am a Jew, if I serve the Jew any longer.

Enter Bassanio, with Leonardo and other followers.

Bass. You may do so; but let it be so hasted, that supper be ready at the farthest by five of the clock. See these letters delivered; put the liveries to making; and desire Gratiano to come anon to my lodging.   *[Exit a Servant.*

Laun. To him, father.

Gob. God bless your worship!

Bass. Gramercy! wouldst thou aught with me?

Gob. Here's my son, sir, a poor boy,—

Laun. Not a poor boy, sir, but the rich Jew's man; that would, sir,—as my father shall specify,—

Gob. He hath a great infection, sir, as one would say, to serve—

Laun. Indeed, the short and the long is, I serve the Jew, and have a desire,—as my father shall specify,—

Gob. His master and he, saving your worship's reverence, are scarce cater-cousins,—

Laun. To be brief, the very truth is that the Jew, having done me wrong, doth cause me,—as my father, being, I hope, an old man, shall frutify unto you,—

Gob. I have here a dish of doves that I would bestow upon your worship, and my suit is,—

Laun. In very brief, the suit is impertinent to myself, as your worship shall know by this honest old man; and, though I say it, though old man, yet poor man, my father.

Bass. One speak for both. What would you?

Laun. Serve you, sir.

Gob. That is the very defect of the matter, sir.

Bass. I know thee well; thou hast obtain'd thy suit:
Shylock thy master spoke with me this day,
And hath preferr'd thee, if it be preferment
To leave a rich Jew's service, to become
The follower of so poor a gentleman.

Laun. The old proverb is very well parted between my master Shylock and you, sir: you have the grace of God, sir, and he hath enough.

Bass. Thou speak'st it well. Go, father, with thy son.
Take leave of thy old master and inquire
My lodging out. Give him a livery
More guarded than his fellows': see it done.

Laun. Father, in. I cannot get a service, no; I have ne'er a tongue in my head. Well, if any man in Italy have a fairer table which doth offer to swear upon a book, I shall

have good fortune.　Go to, here's a simple line of life:
here's a small trifle of wives: alas, fifteen wives is nothing!
a'leven widows and nine maids is a simple coming-in for
one man: and then to 'scape drowning thrice, and to be in
peril of my life with the edge of a feather-bed; here are
simple scapes.　Well, if Fortune be a woman, she's a good
wench for this gear.　Father, come; I'll take my leave of
the Jew in the twinkling of an eye.

[Exeunt Launcelot and Old Gobbo.

Bass.　I pray thee, good Leonardo, think on this:
These things being bought and orderly bestow'd,
Return in haste, for I do feast to-night
My best-esteem'd acquaintance: hie thee, go.

Leon.　My best endeavours shall be done herein.

Enter Gratiano.

Gra.　Where is your master?
Leon.　　　　　　　　Yonder, sir, he walks.　　　*[Exit.*
Gra.　Signior Bassanio,—
Bass.　Gratiano!
Gra.　I have a suit to you.
Bass.　　　　　　　You have obtain'd it.
Gra.　You must not deny me: I must go with you to Belmont.
Bass.　Why, then you must.　But hear thee, Gratiano:
Thou art too wild, too rude, and bold of voice;
Parts that become thee happily enough,
And in such eyes as ours appear not faults;
But where thou art not known, why there they show
Something too liberal.　Pray thee, take pain
To allay with some cold drops of modesty
Thy skipping spirit; lest, through thy wild behaviour,
I be misconstrued in the place I go to,
And lose my hopes.
Gra.　　　　　　　Signior Bassanio, hear me:
If I do not put on a sober habit,
Talk with respect, and swear but now and then,
Wear prayer-books in my pocket, look demurely;
Nay more, while grace is saying, hood mine eyes
Thus with my hat, and sigh, and say 'amen;'
Use all the observance of civility,
Like one well studied in a sad ostent
To please his grandam, never trust me more.
Bass.　Well, we shall see your bearing.
Gra.　Nay, but I bar to-night: you shall not gauge me
By what we do to-night.
Bass.　　　　　　　No, that were pity:

I would entreat you rather to put on
Your boldest suit of mirth, for we have friends
That purpose merriment. But fare you well:
I have some business.

Gra. And I must to Lorenzo and the rest:
But we will visit you at supper-time.   [*Exeunt.*

SCENE III

The same. A room in Shylock's house.
Enter Jessica and Launcelot.

Jes. I am sorry thou wilt leave my father so:
Our house is hell; and thou, a merry devil,
Didst rob it of some taste of tediousness.
But fare thee well; there is a ducat for thee:
And, Launcelot, soon at supper shalt thou see
Lorenzo, who is thy new master's guest:
Give him this letter; do it secretly;
And so farewell: I would not have my father
See me in talk with thee.

Laun. Adieu! tears exhibit my tongue. Most beautiful pagan,
most sweet Jew! if a Christian did not play the knave,
and get thee, I am much deceived. But, adieu: these
foolish drops do something drown my manly spirit: adieu.

Jes. Farewell, good Launcelot.   [*Exit Launcelot.*
Alack, what heinous sin is it in me
To be ashamed to be my father's child!
But though I am a daughter to his blood,
I am not to his manners. O Lorenzo,
If thou keep promise, I shall end this strife,
Become a Christian, and thy loving wife.   [*Exit.*

SCENE IV

The same. A street.
Enter Gratiano, Lorenzo, Salarino, and Salanio.

Lor. Nay, we will slink away in supper-time,
Disguise us at my lodging, and return
All in an hour.

Gra. We have not made good preparation.

Salar. We have not spoke us yet of torch-bearers.

Salan. 'Tis vile, unless it may be quaintly order'd,
And better in my mind not undertook.

Lor. 'Tis now but four o'clock: we have two hours
To furnish us.

Enter Launcelot, with a letter.

                Friend Launcelot, what's the news?

Laun. An it shall please you to break up this, it shall seem to

Lor. I know the hand: in faith, 'tis a fair hand;   [*signify.*

   And whiter than the paper it writ on

   Is the fair hand that writ.

Gra.   Love-news, in faith.

Laun. By your leave, sir.

Lor. Whither goest thou?

Laun. Marry, sir, to bid my old master the Jew to sup to-night

   with my new master the Christian.

Lor. Hold here, take this: tell gentle Jessica

   I will not fail her; speak it privately.

   Go, gentlemen,   [*Exit Launcelot.*

   Will you prepare you for this masque to-night?

   I am provided of a torch-bearer.

Salar. Ay, marry, I'll begone about it straight.

Salan. And so will I.

Lor.   Meet me and Gratiano

   At Gratiano's lodging some hour hence.

Salar. 'Tis good we do so.   [*Exeunt Salar. and Salan.*

Gra. Was not that letter from fair Jessica?

Lor. I must needs tell thee all.   She hath directed

   How I shall take her from her father's house;

   What gold and jewels she is furnish'd with;

   What page's suit she hath in readiness.

   If e'er the Jew her father come to heaven,

   It will be for his gentle daughter's sake:

   And never dare misfortune cross her foot,

   Unless she do it under this excuse,

   That she is issue to a faithless Jew.

   Come, go with me; peruse this as thou goest:

   Fair Jessica shall be my torch-bearer.   [*Exeunt.*

Scene V

The same.   Before Shylock's house.

Enter Shylock and Launcelot.

Shy. Well, thou shalt see, thy eyes shall be thy judge,

   The difference of old Shylock and Bassanio:—

   What, Jessica!—thou shalt not gormandise,

   As thou hast done with me:—What, Jessica!—

   And sleep and snore, and rend apparel out;—

   Why, Jessica, I say!

Laun.   Why, Jessica!

Shy. Who bids thee call? I do not bid thee call.

Laun. Your worship was wont to tell me that I could do
nothing without bidding.

Enter Jessica.

Jes. Call you? what is your will?

Shy. I am bid forth to supper, Jessica :
There are my keys. But wherefore should I go?
I am not bid for love; they flatter me :
But yet I'll go in hate, to feed upon
The prodigal Christian. Jessica, my girl,
Look to my house. I am right loath to go :
There is some ill a-brewing towards my rest,
For I did dream of money-bags to-night.

Laun. I beseech you, sir, go : my young master doth expect

Shy. So do I his.   [your reproach.

Laun. And they have conspired together, I will not say you
shall see a masque ; but if you do, then it was not for
nothing that my nose fell a-bleeding on Black-Monday last
at six o'clock i' the morning, falling out that year on Ash-
Wednesday was four year, in the afternoon.

Shy. What, are there masques? Hear you me, Jessica :
Lock up my doors ; and when you hear the drum,
And the vile squealing of the wry-neck'd fife,
Clamber not you up to the casements then,
Nor thrust your head into the public street
To gaze on Christian fools with varnish'd faces ;
But stop my house's ears, I mean my casements.
Let not the sound of shallow foppery enter
My sober house. By Jacob's staff, I swear
I have no mind of feasting forth to-night :
But I will go. Go you before me, sirrah ;
Say I will come.

Laun. I will go before, sir. Mistress, look out at window, for
all this ;
> There will come a Christian by,
> Will be worth a Jewess' eye.   [*Exit.*

Shy. What says that fool of Hagar's offspring, ha?

Jes. His words were, 'Farewell, mistress ;' nothing else.

Shy. The patch is kind enough, but a huge feeder ;
Snail-slow in profit, and he sleeps by day
More than the wild-cat : drones hive not with me :
Therefore I part with him ; and part with him
To one that I would have him help to waste
His borrow'd purse. Well, Jessica, go in :
Perhaps I will return immediately.

Do as I bid you ; shut doors after you :
Fast bind, fast find,
A proverb never stale in thrifty mind.   [*Exit.*
Jes. Farewell ; and if my fortune be not crost,
I have a father, you a daughter, lost.   [*Exit.*

SCENE VI

The same.

Enter Gratiano and Salarino, masqued.

Gra. This is the pent-house under which Lorenzo
Desired us to make stand.
Salar.   His hour is almost past.
Gra. And it is marvel he out-dwells his hour,
For lovers ever run before the clock.
Salar. O, ten times faster Venus' pigeons fly
To seal love's bonds new-made, than they are wont
To keep obliged faith unforfeited !
Gra. That ever holds : who riseth from a feast
With that keen appetite that he sits down ?
Where is the horse that doth untread again
His tedious measures with the unbated fire
That he did pace them first ?   All things that are,
Are with more spirit chased than enjoy'd.
How like a younker or a prodigal
The scarfed bark puts from her native bay,
Hugg'd and embraced by the strumpet wind !
How like the prodigal doth she return,
With over-weather'd ribs and ragged sails,
Lean, rent, and beggar'd by the strumpet wind !
Salar. Here comes Lorenzo : more of this hereafter.

Enter Lorenzo.

Lor. Sweet friends, your patience for my long abode ;
Not I, but my affairs, have made you wait :
When you shall please to play the thieves for wives,
I 'll watch as long for you then.   Approach ;
Here dwells my father Jew.   Ho ! who 's within ?

Enter Jessica, above, in boy's clothes.

Jes. Who are you ?   Tell me, for more certainty,
Albeit I 'll swear that I do know your tongue.
Lor. Lorenzo, and thy love.
Jes. Lorenzo, certain ; and my love, indeed,
For who love I so much ?   And now who knows
But you, Lorenzo, whether I am yours ?
Lor. Heaven and thy thoughts are witness that thou art.
Jes. Here, catch this casket ; it is worth the pains.

74

I am glad 'tis night, you do not look on me,
For I am much ashamed of my exchange:
But love is blind, and lovers cannot see
The pretty follies that themselves commit;
For if they could, Cupid himself would blush
To see me thus transformed to a boy!

Lor. Descend, for you must be my torch-bearer.

Jes. What, must I hold a candle to my shames?
They in themselves, good sooth, are too too light.
Why, 'tis an office of discovery, love;
And I should be obscured.

Lor.   So are you, sweet,
Even in the lovely garnish of a boy.
But come at once;
For the close night doth play the runaway,
And we are stay'd for at Bassanio's feast.

Jes. I will make fast the doors, and gild myself
With some mo ducats, and be with you straight. [*Exit above.*

Gra. Now, by my hood, a Gentile, and no Jew.

Lor. Beshrew me but I love her heartily;
For she is wise, if I can judge of her;
And fair she is, if that mine eyes be true;
And true she is, as she hath proved herself;
And therefore, like herself, wise, fair, and true,
Shall she be placed in my constant soul.

Enter Jessica, below.

What, art thou come? On, gentlemen; away!
Our masquing mates by this time for us stay.

[*Exit with Jessica and Salarino.*
Enter Antonio.

Ant. Who's there?

Gra. Signior Antonio!

Ant. Fie, fie, Gratiano; where are all the rest?
'Tis nine o'clock: our friends all stay for you.
No masque to-night: the wind is come about;
Bassanio presently will go aboard:
I have sent twenty out to seek for you.

Gra. I am glad on't: I desire no more delight
Than to be under sail and gone to-night.   [*Exeunt.*

SCENE VII

Belmont.   A room in Portia's house.
*Flourish of cornets.   Enter Portia, with the Prince of
Morocco, and their trains.*

Por. Go draw aside the curtains, and discover

    The several caskets to this noble prince.
    Now make your choice.
Mor. The first, of gold, who this inscription bears,
  'Who chooseth me shall gain what many men desire;'
  The second, silver, which this promise carries,
  'Who chooseth me shall get as much as he deserves;
  This third, dull lead, with warning all as blunt,
  'Who chooseth me must give and hazard all he hath.'
  How shall I know if I do choose the right?
Por. The one of them contains my picture, prince,
  If you choose that, then I am yours withal.
Mor. Some god direct my judgement! Let me see;
  I will survey the inscriptions back again.
  What says this leaden casket?
  'Who chooseth me must give and hazard all he hath.'
  Must give,—for what? for lead? hazard for lead?
  This casket threatens. Men that hazard all
  Do it in hope of fair advantages:
  A golden mind stoops not to shows of dross;
  I'll then nor give nor hazard aught for lead.
  What says the silver with her virgin hue?
  'Who chooseth me shall get as much as he deserves.'
  As much as he deserves! Pause there, Morocco,
  And weigh thy value with an even hand:
  If thou be'st rated by thy estimation,
  Thou dost deserve enough; and yet enough
  May not extend so far as to the lady:
  And yet to be afeared of my deserving
  Were but a weak disabling of myself.
  As much as I deserve! Why, that's the lady:
  I do in birth deserve her, and in fortunes,
  In graces and in qualities of breeding;
  But more than these, in love I do deserve.
  What if I stray'd no further, but chose here?
  Let's see once more this saying graved in gold;
  'Who chooseth me shall gain what many men desire.'
  Why, that's the lady; all the world desires her;
  From the four corners of the earth they come,
  To kiss this shrine, this mortal-breathing saint:
  The Hyrcanian deserts and the vasty wilds
  Of wide Arabia are as throughfares now
  For princes to come view fair Portia:
  The watery kingdom, whose ambitious head
  Spits in the face of heaven, is no bar
  To stop the foreign spirits; but they come,

As o'er a brook, to see fair Portia.
One of these three contains her heavenly picture.
Is 't like that lead contains her? 'Twere damnation
To think so base a thought : it were too gross
To rib her cerecloth in the obscure grave.
Or shall I think in silver she 's immured,
Being ten times undervalued to tried gold?
O sinful thought ! Never so rich a gem
Was set in worse than gold. They have in England
A coin that bears the figure of an angel
Stamped in gold, but that 's insculp'd upon ;
But here an angel in a golden bed
Lies all within. Deliver me the key :
Here do I choose, and thrive I as I may !
Por. There, take it, prince ; and if my form lie there,
   Then I am yours.   [*He unlocks the golden casket.*
Mor.   O hell ! what have we here?
A carrion Death, within whose empty eye
There is a written scroll ! I 'll read the writing.
   [*Reads*] All that glisters is not gold ;
           Often have you heard that told :
           Many a man his life hath sold
           But my outside to behold :
           Gilded tombs do worms infold.
           Had you been as wise as bold,
           Young in limbs, in judgement old,
           Your answer had not been inscroll'd :
           Fare you well ; your suit is cold.
Cold, indeed ; and labour lost :
Then, farewell, heat, and welcome, frost !
Portia, adieu. I have too grieved a heart
To take a tedious leave : thus losers part.
               [*Exit with his train. Flourish of cornets.*
Por. A gentle riddance. Draw the curtains, go.
Let all of his complexion choose me so.   [*Exeunt.*

Scene VIII
Venice. A street.
Enter Salarino and Salanio.

Salar. Why, man, I saw Bassanio under sail :
   With him is Gratiano gone along ;
   And in their ship I am sure Lorenzo is not.
Salan. The villain Jew with outcries raised the Duke,
   Who went with him to search Bassanio's ship.

Salar. He came too late, the ship was under sail:
  But there the Duke was given to understand
  That in a gondola were seen together
  Lorenzo and his amorous Jessica:
  Besides, Antonio certified the Duke
  They were not with Bassanio in his ship.
Salan. I never heard a passion so confused,
  So strange, outrageous, and so variable,
  As the dog Jew did utter in the streets:
  'My daughter! O my ducats! O my daughter!
  Fled with a Christian! O my Christian ducats!
  Justice! the law! my ducats, and my daughter!
  A sealed bag, two sealed bags of ducats,
  Of double ducats, stolen from me by my daughter!
  And jewels, two stones, two rich and precious stones,
  Stolen by my daughter! Justice! find the girl!
  She hath the stones upon her, and the ducats!'
Salar. Why, all the boys in Venice follow him,
  Crying, his stones, his daughter, and his ducats.
Salan. Let good Antonio look he keep his day,
  Or he shall pay for this.
Salar.   Marry, well remember'd.
  I reason'd with a Frenchman yesterday,
  Who told me, in the narrow seas that part
  The French and English, there miscarried
  A vessel of our country richly fraught:
  I thought upon Antonio when he told me;
  And wish'd in silence that it were not his.
Salan. You were best to tell Antonio what you hear;
  Yet do not suddenly, for it may grieve him.
Salar. A kinder gentleman treads not the earth.
  I saw Bassanio and Antonio part:
  Bassanio told him he would make some speed
  Of his return: he answer'd, 'Do not so;
  Slubber not business for my sake, Bassanio,
  But stay the very riping of the time;
  And for the Jew's bond which he hath of me,
  Let it not enter in your mind of love:
  Be merry; and employ your chiefest thoughts
  To courtship, and such fair ostents of love
  As shall conveniently become you there:'
  And even there, his eye being big with tears,
  Turning his face, he put his hand behind him,
  And with affection wondrous sensible
  He wrung Bassanio's hand; and so they parted.

Salan. I think he only loves the world for him.
   I pray thee, let us go and find him out,
   And quicken his embraced heaviness
   With some delight or other.
Salar.   Do we so.   [*Exeunt.*

SCENE IX

Belmont.   A room in Portia's house.
Enter Nerissa and a Servitor.

Ner. Quick, quick, I pray thee : draw the curtain straight :
   The Prince of Arragon hath ta'en his oath,
   And comes to his election presently.
Flourish of cornets.   Enter the Prince of Arragon, Portia, and
their trains.

Por. Behold, there stand the caskets, noble prince :
   If you choose that wherein I am contain'd,
   Straight shall our nuptial rites be solemnized :
   But if you fail, without more speech, my lord,
   You must be gone from hence immediately.
Ar. I am enjoin'd by oath to observe three things :
   First, never to unfold to any one
   Which casket 'twas I chose ; next, if I fail
   Of the right casket, never in my life
   To woo a maid in way of marriage :
   Lastly,
   If I do fail in fortune of my choice,
   Immediately to leave you and be gone.
Por. To these injunctions every one doth swear
   That comes to hazard for my worthless self.
Ar. And so have I address'd me.   Fortune now
   To my heart's hope !   Gold ; silver ; and base lead.
   'Who chooseth me must give and hazard all he hath.'
   You shall look fairer, ere I give or hazard.
   What says the golden chest ? ha ! let me see :
   'Who chooseth me shall gain what many men desire.'
   What many men desire ! that 'many' may be meant
   By the fool multitude, that choose by show,
   Not learning more than the fond eye doth teach ;
   Which pries not to the interior, but, like the martlet,
   Builds in the weather on the outward wall,
   Even in the force and road of casualty.
   I will not choose what many men desire,
   Because I will not jump with common spirits,
   And rank me with the barbarous multitudes.

79

Why, then to thee, thou silver treasure-house ;
Tell me once more what title thou dost bear :
'Who chooseth me shall get as much as he deserves:'
And well said too ; for who shall go about
To cozen fortune, and be honourable
Without the stamp of merit?   Let none presume
To wear an undeserved dignity.
O, that estates, degrees and offices
Were not derived corruptly, and that clear honour
Were purchased by the merit of the wearer !
How many then should cover that stand bare !
How many be commanded that command !
How much low peasantry would then be glean'd
From the true seed of honour ! and how much honour
Pick'd from the chaff and ruin of the times,
To be new-varnish'd !   Well, but to my choice :
'Who chooseth me shall get as much as he deserves.'
I will assume desert.   Give me a key for this,
And instantly unlock my fortunes here.

        [He opens the silver casket.

Por. [*Aside*] Too long a pause for that which you find there.
Ar. What's here? the portrait of a blinking idiot,
 Presenting me a schedule !   I will read it.
 How much unlike art thou to Portia !
 How much unlike my hopes and my deservings !
 'Who chooseth me shall have as much as he deserves.'
 Did I deserve no more than a fool's head?
 Is that my prize? are my deserts no better?
Por. To offend, and judge, are distinct offices,
 And of opposed natures.
Ar.   What is here?

 [*Reads*] The fire seven times tried this :
     Seven times tried that judgement is,
     That did never choose amiss.
     Some there be that shadows kiss ;
     Such have but a shadow's bliss :
     There be fools alive, I wis,
     Silver'd o'er ; and so was this.
     Take what wife you will to bed,
     I will ever be your head :
     So be gone : you are sped.
     Still more fool I shall appear
     By the time I linger here :
     With one fool's head I came to woo,
     But I go away with two.

Sweet, adieu. I 'll keep my oath,
Patiently to bear my wroth.

[Exeunt Arragon and train.

Por. Thus hath the candle singed the moth.
O, these deliberate fools ! when they do choose,
They have the wisdom by their wit to lose.

Ner. The ancient saying is no heresy,
Hanging and wiving goes by destiny.

Por. Come, draw the curtain, Nerissa.

Enter a Servant.

Serv. Where is my lady ?

Por.   Here : what would my lord?

Serv. Madam, there is alighted at your gate
A young Venetian, one that comes before
To signify the approaching of his lord ;
From whom he bringeth sensible regreets,
To wit, besides commends and courteous breath,
Gifts of rich value. Yet I have not seen
So likely an ambassador of love :
A day in April never came so sweet,
To show how costly summer was at hand,
As this fore-spurrer comes before his lord.

Por. No more, I pray thee : I am half afeard
Thou wilt say anon he is some kin to thee,
Thou spend'st such high-day wit in praising him.
Come, come, Nerissa ; for I long to see
Quick Cupid's post that comes so mannerly.

Ner. Bassanio, lord Love, if thy will it be !   *[Exeunt.*

ACT III—Scene I

Venice. A street.

Enter Salanio and Salarino.

Salan. Now, what news on the Rialto ?

Salar. Why, yet it lives there unchecked, that Antonio hath a
ship of rich lading wrecked on the narrow seas ; the Goodwins,
I think they call the place ; a very dangerous flat and fatal,
where the carcases of many a tall ship lie buried, as they
say, if my gossip Report be an honest woman of her word.

Salan. I would she were as lying a gossip in that as ever
knapped ginger, or made her neighbours believe she wept
for the death of a third husband. But it is true, without
any slips of prolixity, or crossing the plain highway of talk,
that the good Antonio, the honest Antonio,—O that I had a
title good enough to keep his name company !—

Salar. Come, the full stop.

Salan. Ha! what sayest thou? Why, the end is, he hath lost

Salar. I would it might prove the end of his losses.   [a ship.

Salan. Let me say 'amen' betimes, lest the devil cross my
prayer, for here he comes in the likeness of a Jew.

Enter Shylock.

How now, Shylock! what news among the merchants?

Shy. You knew, none so well, none so well as you, of my
daughter's flight.

Salar. That's certain: I, for my part, knew the tailor that
made the wings she flew withal.

Salan. And Shylock, for his own part, knew the bird was
fledged; and then it is the complexion of them all to leave

Shy. She is damned for it.   [the dam.

Salar. That's certain, if the devil may be her judge.

Shy. My own flesh and blood to rebel!

Salan. Out upon it, old carrion! rebels it at these years?

Shy. I say, my daughter is my flesh and blood.

Salar. There is more difference between thy flesh and hers
than between jet and ivory; more between your bloods than
there is between red wine and rhenish. But tell us, do you
hear whether Antonio have had any loss at sea or no?

Shy. There I have another bad match: a bankrupt, a prodigal,
who dare scarce show his head on the Rialto; a beggar, that
was used to come so smug upon the mart; let him look to
his bond: he was wont to call me usurer; let him look to
his bond: he was wont to lend money for a Christian
courtesy; let him look to his bond.

Salar. Why, I am sure, if he forfeit, thou wilt not take his
flesh: what's that good for?

Shy. To bait fish withal: if it will feed nothing else, it will
feed my revenge. He hath disgraced me, and hindered me
half a million; laughed at my losses, mocked at my gains,
scorned my nation, thwarted my bargains, cooled my friends,
heated mine enemies; and what's his reason? I am a Jew.
Hath not a Jew eyes? hath not a Jew hands, organs,
dimensions, senses, affections, passions? fed with the same
food, hurt with the same weapons, subject to the same
diseases, healed by the same means, warmed and cooled by
the same winter and summer, as a Christian is? If you
prick us, do we not bleed? if you tickle us, do we not laugh?
if you poison us, do we not die? and if you wrong us, shall
we not revenge? if we are like you in the rest, we will
resemble you in that. If a Jew wrong a Christian, what is
his humility? Revenge. If a Christian wrong a Jew, what

should his sufferance be by Christian example? Why, revenge. The villany you teach me, I will execute; and it shall go hard but I will better the instruction.

Enter a Servant.

Serv. Gentlemen, my master Antonio is at his house, and desires to speak with you both.

Salar. We have been up and down to seek him.

Enter Tubal.

Salan. Here comes another of the tribe: a third cannot be matched, unless the devil himself turn Jew.

[*Exeunt Salan. Salar. and Servant.*

Shy. How now, Tubal! what news from Genoa? hast thou found my daughter?

Tub. I often came where I did hear of her, but cannot find her.

Shy. Why, there, there, there, there! a diamond gone, cost me two thousand ducats in Frankfort! The curse never fell upon our nation till now; I never felt it till now: two thousand ducats in that; and other precious, precious jewels. I would my daughter were dead at my foot, and the jewels in her ear! would she were hearsed at my foot, and the ducats in her coffin! No news of them? Why, so:—and I know not what's spent in the search: why, thou loss upon loss! the thief gone with so much, and so much to find the thief; and no satisfaction, no revenge: nor no ill luck stirring but what lights on my shoulders; no sighs but of my breathing; no tears but of my shedding.

Tub. Yes, other men have ill luck too: Antonio, as I heard in

Shy. What, what, what? ill luck, ill luck?   [Genoa,—

Tub. Hath an argosy cast away, coming from Tripolis.

Shy. I thank God, I thank God! Is't true, is't true?

Tub. I spoke with some of the sailors that escaped the wreck.

Shy. I thank thee, good Tubal: good news, good news! ha, ha! where? in Genoa?   [fourscore ducats.

Tub. Your daughter spent in Genoa, as I heard, in one night

Shy. Thou stick'st a dagger in me: I shall never see my gold again: fourscore ducats at a sitting! fourscore ducats!

Tub. There came divers of Antonio's creditors in my company to Venice, that swear he cannot choose but break.

Shy. I am very glad of it: I'll plague him; I'll torture him: I am glad of it.

Tub. One of them showed me a ring that he had of your daughter for a monkey.

Shy. Out upon her! Thou torturest me, Tubal: it was my turquoise; I had it of Leah when I was a bachelor: I would not have given it for a wilderness of monkeys.

83

Tub. But Antonio is certainly undone.

Shy. Nay, that's true, that's very true.   Go, Tubal, fee me an
officer; bespeak him a fortnight before.   I will have the
heart of him, if he forfeit; for, were he out of Venice, I can
make what merchandise I will.   Go, go, Tubal, and meet
me at our synagogue; go, good Tubal; at our synagogue,
Tubal.   [*Exeunt.*

SCENE II

Belmont.   A room in Portia's house.

Enter Bassanio, Portia, Gratiano, Nerissa, and Attendants.

Por. I pray you, tarry: pause a day or two
Before you hazard; for, in choosing wrong,
I lose your company: therefore forbear awhile.
There's something tells me, but it is not love,
I would not lose you; and you know yourself,
Hate counsels not in such a quality.
But lest you should not understand me well,—
And yet a maiden hath no tongue but thought,—
I would detain you here some month or two
Before you venture for me.   I could teach you
How to choose right, but I am then forsworn;
So will I never be: so may you miss me;
But if you do, you'll make me wish a sin,
That I had been forsworn.   Beshrew your eyes,
They have o'er-look'd me, and divided me;
One half of me is yours, the other half yours,
Mine own, I would say; but if mine, then yours,
And so all yours!   O, these naughty times
Put bars between the owners and their rights!
And so, though yours, not yours.   Prove it so,
Let fortune go to hell for it, not I.
I speak too long; but 'tis to peize the time,
To eke it and to draw it out in length,
To stay you from election.

Bass.   Let me choose;
For as I am, I live upon the rack.

Por. Upon the rack, Bassanio! then confess
What treason there is mingled with your love.

Bass. None but that ugly treason of mistrust,
Which makes me fear the enjoying of my love:
There may as well be amity and life
'Tween snow and fire, as treason and my love.

Por. Ay, but I fear you speak upon the rack,
Where men enforced do speak any thing.

Bass. Promise me life, and I'll confess the truth.

Por. Well then, confess and live.

Bass.   'Confess,' and 'love,'
    Had been the very sum of my confession:
    O happy torment, when my torturer
    Doth teach me answers for deliverance!
    But let me to my fortune and the caskets.

Por. Away, then! I am lock'd in one of them:
    If you do love me, you will find me out.
    Nerissa and the rest, stand all aloof.
    Let music sound while he doth make his choice;
    Then, if he lose, he makes a swan-like end,
    Fading in music: that the comparison
    May stand more proper, my eye shall be the stream,
    And watery death-bed for him. He may win;
    And what is music then? Then music is
    Even as the flourish when true subjects bow
    To a new-crowned monarch: such it is
    As are those dulcet sounds in break of day
    That creep into the dreaming bridegroom's ear,
    And summon him to marriage. Now he goes,
    With no less presence, but with much more love,
    Than young Alcides, when he did redeem
    The virgin tribute paid by howling Troy
    To the sea-monster: I stand for sacrifice;
    The rest aloof are the Dardanian wives,
    With bleared visages, came forth to view
    The issue of the exploit. Go, Hercules!
    Live thou, I live: with much much more dismay
    I view the fight than thou that makest the fray.

Music, whilst Bassanio comments on the caskets to himself.

SONG.

       Tell me where is fancy bred,
       Or in the heart or in the head?
       How begot, how nourished?
          Reply, reply.
       It is engender'd in the eyes,
       With gazing fed; and fancy dies
       In the cradle where it lies.
          Let us all ring fancy's knell;
          I 'll begin it,—Ding, dong, bell.

All.   Ding, dong, bell.

Bass. So may the outward shows be least themselves:

The world is still deceived with ornament.
In law, what plea so tainted and corrupt,
But, being season'd with a gracious voice,
Obscures the show of evil?   In religion,
What damned error, but some sober brow
Will bless it, and approve it with a text,
Hiding the grossness with fair ornament?
There is no vice so simple, but assumes
Some mark of virtue on his outward parts:
How many cowards, whose hearts are all as false
As stairs of sand, wear yet upon their chins
The beards of Hercules and frowning Mars;
Who, inward search'd, have livers white as milk;
And these assume but valour's excrement
To render them redoubted!   Look on beauty,
And you shall see 'tis purchased by the weight;
Which therein works a miracle in nature,
Making them lightest that wear most of it:
So are those crisped snaky golden locks
Which make such wanton gambols with the wind,
Upon supposed fairness, often known
To be the dowry of a second head,
The skull that bred them in the sepulchre.
Thus ornament is but the guiled shore
To a most dangerous sea; the beauteous scarf
Veiling an Indian beauty; in a word,
The seeming truth which cunning times put on
To entrap the wisest.   Therefore, thou gaudy gold,
Hard food for Midas, I will none of thee;
Nor none of thee, thou pale and common drudge
'Tween man and man; but thou, thou meagre lead,
Which rather threatenest than dost promise aught,
Thy paleness moves me more than eloquence;
And here choose I: joy be the consequence!

Por. [*Aside*] How all the other passions fleet to air,
As doubtful thoughts, and rash-embraced despair,
And shuddering fear, and green-eyed jealousy!
O love, be moderate; allay thy ecstasy;
In measure rain thy joy; scant this excess!
I feel too much thy blessing: make it less,
For fear I surfeit!

Bass.   What find I here?

[*Opening the leaden casket.*

Fair Portia's counterfeit!   What demi-god
Hath come so near creation?   Move these eyes?

86

Or whether, riding on the balls of mine,
Seem they in motion? Here are sever'd lips,
Parted with sugar breath : so sweet a bar
Should sunder such sweet friends. Here in her hairs
The painter plays the spider, and hath woven
A golden mesh to entrap the hearts of men,
Faster than gnats in cobwebs : but her eyes,—
How could he see to do them? having made one,
Methinks it should have power to steal both his
And leave itself unfurnish'd. Yet look, how far
The substance of my praise doth wrong this shadow
In underprizing it, so far this shadow
Doth limp behind the substance. Here 's the scroll,
The continent and summary of my fortune.
   [*Reads*] You that choose not by the view,
          Chance as fair, and choose as true !
          Since this fortune falls to you,
          Be content and seek no new.
          If you be well pleased with this,
          And hold your fortune for your bliss,
          Turn you where your lady is,
          And claim her with a loving kiss.
A gentle scroll. Fair lady, by your leave ;
I come by note, to give and to receive.
Like one of two contending in a prize,
That thinks he hath done well in people's eyes,
Hearing applause and universal shout,
Giddy in spirit, still gazing in a doubt
Whether those peals of praise be his or no ;
So, thrice-fair lady, stand I, even so ;
As doubtful whether what I see be true,
Until confirm'd, sign'd, ratified by you.
Por. You see me, Lord Bassanio, where I stand,
Such as I am : though for myself alone
I would not be ambitious in my wish,
To wish myself much better ; yet, for you
I would be trebled twenty times myself ;
A thousand times more fair, ten thousand times
More rich ;
That only to stand high in your account,
I might in virtues, beauties, livings, friends,
Exceed account ; but the full sum of me
Is sum of something, which, to term in gross,
Is an unlesson'd girl, unschool'd, unpractised ;
Happy in this, she is not yet so old

But she may learn ; happier than this,
She is not bred so dull but she can learn ;
Happiest of all is that her gentle spirit
Commits itself to yours to be directed,
As from her lord, her governor, her king.
Myself and what is mine to you and yours
Is now converted : but now I was the lord
Of this fair mansion, master of my servants,
Queen o'er myself ; and even now, but now,
This house, these servants, and this same myself,
Are yours, my lord : I give them with this ring ;
Which when you part from, lose, or give away,
Let it presage the ruin of your love,
And be my vantage to exclaim on you.

Bass. Madam, you have bereft me of all words,
Only my blood speaks to you in my veins ;
And there is such confusion in my powers,
As, after some oration fairly spoke
By a beloved prince, there doth appear
Among the buzzing pleased multitude ;
Where every something, being blent together,
Turns to a wild of nothing, save of joy,
Express'd and not express'd. But when this ring
Parts from this finger, then parts life from hence :
O, then be bold to say Bassanio's dead !

Ner. My lord and lady, it is now our time,
That have stood by and seen our wishes prosper,
To cry, good joy : good joy, my lord and lady !

Gra. My lord Bassanio and my gentle lady,
I wish you all the joy that you can wish ;
For I am sure you can wish none from me :
And when your honours mean to solemnize
The bargain of your faith, I do beseech you,
Even at that time I may be married too.

Bass. With all my heart, so thou canst get a wife.

Gra. I thank your lordship, you have got me one.
My eyes, my lord, can look as swift as yours :
You saw the mistress, I beheld the maid ;
You loved, I loved for intermission.
No more pertains to me, my lord, than you.
Your fortune stood upon the casket there,
And so did mine too, as the matter falls ;
For wooing here until I sweat again,
And swearing till my very roof was dry
With oaths of love, at last, if promise last,

88

I got a promise of this fair one here
To have her love, provided that your fortune
Achieved her mistress.
Por.   Is this true, Nerissa?
Ner. Madam, it is, so you stand pleased withal.
Bass. And do you, Gratiano, mean good faith?
Gra. Yes, faith, my lord.
Bass. Our feast shall be much honoured in your marriage.
Gra. We'll play with them the first boy for a thousand ducats.
Ner. What, and stake down?
Gra. No; we shall ne'er win at that sport, and stake down.
But who comes here? Lorenzo and his infidel?
What, and my old Venetian friend Salerio?

*Enter Lorenzo, Jessica, and Salerio, a Messenger from
Venice.*

Bass. Lorenzo and Salerio, welcome hither;
If that the youth of my new interest here
Have power to bid you welcome. By your leave,
I bid my very friends and countrymen,
Sweet Portia, welcome.
Por.   So do I, my lord:
They are entirely welcome.
Lor. I thank your honour. For my part, my lord,
My purpose was not to have seen you here;
But meeting with Salerio by the way,
He did entreat me, past all saying nay,
To come with him along.
Saler.   I did, my lord;
And I have reason for it. Signior Antonio
Commends him to you.   [*Gives Bassanio a letter.*
Bass.   Ere I ope his letter,
I pray you, tell me how my good friend doth.
Saler. Not sick, my lord, unless it be in mind;
Nor well, unless in mind: his letter there
Will show you his estate.
Gra. Nerissa, cheer yon stranger; bid her welcome.
Your hand, Salerio: what's the news from Venice?
How doth that royal merchant, good Antonio?
I know he will be glad of our success;
We are the Jasons, we have won the fleece.
Saler. I would you had won the fleece that he hath lost.
Por. There are some shrewd contents in yon same paper,
That steals the colour from Bassanio's cheek:
Some dear friend dead; else nothing in the world
Could turn so much the constitution

Of any constant man.　What, worse and worse!
With leave, Bassanio; I am half yourself,
And I must freely have the half of anything
That this same paper brings you.
Bass.　　　　　　　　　　　O sweet Portia,
Here are a few of the unpleasant'st words
That ever blotted paper!　Gentle lady,
When I did first impart my love to you,
I freely told you, all the wealth I had
Ran in my veins, I was a gentleman;
And then I told you true: and yet, dear lady.
Rating myself at nothing, you shall see
How much I was a braggart.　When I told you
My state was nothing, I should then have told you
That I was worse than nothing; for, indeed,
I have engaged myself to a dear friend,
Engaged my friend to his mere enemy,
To feed my means.　Here is a letter, lady;
The paper as the body of my friend,
And every word in it a gaping wound,
Issuing life-blood.　But is it true, Salerio?
Have all his ventures fail'd?　What, not one hit?
From Tripolis, from Mexico, and England,
From Lisbon, Barbary, and India?
And not one vessel scape the dreadful touch
Of merchant-marring rocks?
Saler.　　　　　　　　　　Not one, my lord.
Besides, it should appear, that if he had
The present money to discharge the Jew,
He would not take it.　Never did I know
A creature, that did bear the shape of man,
So keen and greedy to confound a man:
He plies the Duke at morning and at night;
And doth impeach the freedom of the state,
If they deny him justice: twenty merchants,
The Duke himself, and the magnificoes
Of greatest port, have all persuaded with him;
But none can drive him from the envious plea
Of forfeiture, of justice, and his bond.
Jes. When I was with him I have heard him swear
To Tubal and to Chus, his countrymen,
That he would rather have Antonio's flesh
Than twenty times the value of the sum
That he did owe him: and I know, my lord,
If law, authority and power deny not,

It will go hard with poor Antonio.

Por. Is it your dear friend that is thus in trouble ?

Bass. The dearest friend to me, the kindest man,
  The best-condition'd and unwearied spirit
  In doing courtesies ; and one in whom
  The ancient Roman honour more appears
  That any that draws breath in Italy.

Por. What sum owes he the Jew ?

Bass. For me three thousand ducats.

Por.   What, no more?
  Pay him six thousand, and deface the bond ;
  Double six thousand, and then treble that,
  Before a friend of this description
  Shall lose a hair through Bassanio's fault.
  First go with me to church and call me wife,
  And then away to Venice to your friend ;
  For never shall you lie by Portia's side
  With an unquiet soul. You shall have gold
  To pay the petty debt twenty times over :
  When it is paid, bring your true friend along.
  My maid Nerissa and myself meantime
  Will live as maids and widows. Come, away !
  For you shall hence upon your wedding-day :
  Bid your friends welcome, show a merry cheer :
  Since you are dear bought, I will love you dear.
  But let me hear the letter of your friend.

Bass. [*reads*] Sweet Bassanio, my ships have all miscarried,
my creditors grow cruel, my estate is very low, my bond to
the Jew is forfeit ; and since in paying it, it is impossible I
should live, all debts are cleared between you and I, if I
might but see you at my death. Notwithstanding, use your
pleasure : if your love do not persuade you to come, let not
my letter.

Por. O love, dispatch all business, and be gone !

Bass. Since I have your good leave to go away,
    I will make haste : but, till I come again,
    No bed shall e'er be guilty of my stay,
    No rest be interposer 'twixt us twain.   [*Exeunt.*

SCENE III

Venice. A street.
Enter Shylock, Salarino, Antonio, and Gaoler.

Shy. Gaoler, look to him : tell not me of mercy ;
  This is the fool that lent out money gratis :
  Gaoler, look to him.

91

Ant.　　　　　　　　　　Hear me yet, good Shylock.

Shy. I 'll have my bond; speak not against my bond :
　I have sworn an oath that I will have my bond.
　Thou call'dst me dog before thou hadst a cause ;
　But, since I am a dog, beware my fangs :
　The Duke shall grant me justice.　I do wonder,
　Thou naughty gaoler, that thou art so fond
　To come abroad with him at his request.

Ant. I pray thee, hear me speak.

Shy. I 'll have my bond ; I will not hear thee speak :
　I 'll have my bond ; and therefore speak no more.
　I 'll not be made a soft and dull-eyed fool,
　To shake the head, relent, and sigh, and yield
　To Christian intercessors.　Follow not ;
　I 'll have no speaking : I will have my bond.　　　　[*Exit.*

Salar. It is the most impenetrable cur
　That ever kept with men.

Ant.　　　　　　　　　　Let him alone :
　I 'll follow him no more with bootless prayers.
　He seeks my life ; this reason well I know :
　I oft deliver'd from his forfeitures
　Many that have at times made moan to me ;
　Therefore he hates me.

Salar.　　　　　　　　　I am sure the Duke
　Will never grant this forfeiture to hold.

Ant. The Duke cannot deny the course of law :
　For the commodity that strangers have
　With us in Venice, if it be denied,
　Will much impeach the justice of his state ;
　Since that the trade and profit of the city
　Consisteth of all nations.　Therefore, go :
　These griefs and losses have so bated me,
　That I shall hardly spare a pound of flesh
　To-morrow to my bloody creditor.
　Well, gaoler, on.　Pray God, Bassanio come
　To see me pay his debt, and then I care not !　　　　[*Exeunt.*

Scene IV

Belmont.　A room in Portia's house.
Enter Portia, Nerissa, Lorenzo, Jessica, and Balthasar.

Lor. Madam, although I speak it in your presence,
　You have a noble and a true conceit
　Of god-like amity ; which appears most strongly
　In bearing thus the absence of your lord.
　But if you knew to whom you show this honour,

How true a gentleman you send relief,
How dear a lover of my lord your husband,
I know you would be prouder of the work
Than customary bounty can enforce you.

Por. I never did repent for doing good,
Nor shall not now: for in companions
That do converse and waste the time together,
Whose souls do bear an equal yoke of love,
There must be needs a like proportion
Of lineaments, of manners and of spirit;
Which makes me think that this Antonio,
Being the bosom lover of my lord,
Must needs be like my lord. If it be so,
How little is the cost I have bestow'd
In purchasing the semblance of my soul
From out the state of hellish misery!
This comes too near the praising of myself;
Therefore no more of it: hear other things.
Lorenzo, I commit into your hands
The husbandry and manage of my house
Until my lord's return: for mine own part,
I have toward heaven breathed a secret vow
To live in prayer and contemplation,
Only attended by Nerissa here,
Until her husband and my lord's return:
There is a monastery two miles off;
And there will we abide. I do desire you
Not to deny this imposition;
The which my love and some necessity
Now lays upon you.

Lor.   Madam, with all my heart;
I shall obey you in all fair commands.

Por. My people do already know my mind,
And will acknowledge you and Jessica
In place of Lord Bassanio and myself.
And so farewell, till we shall meet again.

Lor. Fair thoughts and happy hours attend on you!

Jes. I wish your ladyship all heart's content.

Por. I thank you for your wish, and am well pleased
To wish it back on you: fare you well, Jessica.

                       [*Exeunt Jessica and Lorenzo.*

Now, Balthasar,
As I have ever found thee honest-true,
So let me find thee still. Take this same letter,
And use thou all the endeavour of a man

In speed to Padua: see thou render this
Into my cousin's hand, Doctor Bellario;
And, look, what notes and garments he doth give thee,
Bring them, I pray thee, with imagined speed
Unto the tranect, to the common ferry
Which trades to Venice.   Waste no time in words,
But get thee gone: I shall be there before thee.

Balth. Madam, I go with all convenient speed.   [*Exit.*

Por. Come on, Nerissa; I have work in hand
That you yet know not of; we'll see our husbands
Before they think of us.

Ner.   Shall they see us?

Por. They shall, Nerissa; but in such a habit,
That they shall think we are accomplished
With that we lack.   I'll hold thee any wager,
When we are both accoutred like young men,
I'll prove the prettier fellow of the two,
And wear my dagger with a braver grace,
And speak between the change of man and boy
With a reed voice, and turn two mincing steps
Into a manly stride, and speak of frays
Like a fine bragging youth; and tell quaint lies,
How honourable ladies sought my love,
Which I denying, they fell sick and died;
I could not do withal: then I'll repent,
And wish, for all that, that I had not kill'd them;
And twenty of these puny lies I'll tell,
That men shall swear I have discontinued school
Above a twelvemonth.   I have within my mind
A thousand raw tricks of these bragging Jacks,
Which I will practise.

Ner.   Why, shall we turn to men?

Por. Fie, what a question's that,
If thou wert near a lewd interpreter!
But come, I'll tell thee all my whole device
When I am in my coach, which stays for us
At the park-gate; and therefore haste away,
For we must measure twenty miles to-day.   [*Exeunt.*

SCENE V

The same. A garden.
Enter Launcelot and Jessica.

Laun. Yes, truly; for, look you, the sins of the father are to
be laid upon the children: therefore, I promise ye, I fear
you.   I was always plain with you, and so now I speak my

agitation of the matter : therefore be of good cheer ; for, truly, I think you are damned.   There is but one hope in it that can do you any good : and that is but a kind of bastard hope neither.

Jes. And what hope is that, I pray thee?

Laun. Marry, you may partly hope that your father got you not, that you are not the Jew's daughter.

Jes. That were a kind of bastard hope, indeed : so the sins of my mother should be visited upon me.

Laun. Truly then I fear you are damned both by father and mother : thus when I shun Scylla, your father, I fall into Charybdis, your mother : well, you are gone both ways.

Jes. I shall be saved by my husband ; he hath made me a Christian.

Laun. Truly, the more to blame he : we were Christians enow before ; e'en as many as could well live, one by another. This making of Christians will raise the price of hogs : if we grow all to be pork-eaters, we shall not shortly have a rasher on the coals for money.

Enter Lorenzo.

Jes. I'll tell my husband, Launcelot, what you say : here he comes.

Lor. I shall grow jealous of you shortly, Launcelot, if you thus get my wife into corners.

Jes. Nay, you need not fear us, Lorenzo : Launcelot and I are out.   He tells me flatly, there is no mercy for me in heaven, because I am a Jew's daughter : and he says, you are no good member of the commonwealth ; for, in converting Jews to Christians, you raise the price of pork.

Lor. I shall answer that better to the commonwealth than you can the getting up of the negro's belly : the Moor is with child by you, Launcelot.

Laun. It is much that the Moor should be more than reason : but if she be less than an honest woman, she is indeed more than I took her for.

Lor. How every fool can play upon the word!   I think the best grace of wit will shortly turn into silence ; and discourse grow commendable in none only but parrots.   Go in, sirrah ; bid them prepare for dinner.

Laun. That is done, sir ; they have all stomachs.

Lor. Goodly Lord, what a wit-snapper are you !   then bid them prepare dinner.

Laun. That is done too, sir ; only 'cover' is the word.

Lor. Will you cover, then, sir?

Laun. Not so, sir, neither ; I know my duty.

Lor. Yet more quarrelling with occasion! Wilt thou show the whole wealth of thy wit in an instant? I pray thee, understand a plain man in his plain meaning: go to thy fellows; bid them cover the table, serve in the meat, and we will come in to dinner.

Laun. For the table, sir, it shall be served in; for the meat, sir, it shall be covered; for your coming in to dinner, sir, why, let it be as humours and conceits shall govern.   [*Exit.*

Lor. O dear discretion, how his words are suited!
The fool hath planted in his memory
An army of good words; and I do know
A many fools, that stand in better place,
Garnish'd like him, that for a tricksy word
Defy the matter. How cheer'st thou, Jessica?
And now, good sweet, say thy opinion,
How dost thou like the Lord Bassanio's wife?

Jes. Past all expressing. It is very meet
The Lord Bassanio live an upright life;
For, having such a blessing in his lady,
He finds the joys of heaven here on earth;
And if on earth he do not mean it, then
In reason he should never come to heaven.
Why, if two gods should play some heavenly match
And on the wager lay two earthly women,
And Portia one, there must be something else
Pawn'd with the other; for the poor rude world
Hath not her fellow.

Lor.   Even such a husband
Hast thou of me as she is for a wife.

Jes. Nay, but ask my opinion too of that.

Lor. I will anon: first, let us go to dinner.

Jes. Nay, let me praise you while I have a stomach.

Lor. No, pray thee, let it serve for table-talk;
Then, howsoe'er thou speak'st, 'mong other things
I shall digest it.

Jes. Well, I'll set you forth.   [*Exeunt.*

ACT IV—Scene I

Venice. A court of justice.

Enter the Duke, the Magnificoes, Antonio, Bassanio,
Gratiano, Salerio, and others.

Duke. What, is Antonio here?

Ant. Ready, so please your Grace.

Duke. I am sorry for thee: thou art come to answer

A stony adversary, an inhuman wretch
Uncapable of pity, void and empty
From any dram of mercy.

Ant..   I have heard
Your Grace hath ta'en great pains to qualify
His rigorous course; but since he stands obdurate,
And that no lawful means can carry me
Out of his envy's reach, I do oppose
My patience to his fury; and am arm'd
To suffer, with a quietness of spirit,
The very tyranny and rage of his.

Duke. Go one, and call the Jew into the court.

Saler. He is ready at the door: he comes, my lord.

Enter Shylock.

Duke. Make room, and let him stand before our face.
Shylock, the world thinks, and I think so too,
That thou but lead'st this fashion of thy malice
To the last hour of act; and then 'tis thought
Thou 'lt show thy mercy and remorse more strange
Than is thy strange apparent cruelty;
And where thou now exact'st the penalty,
Which is a pound of this poor merchant's flesh,
Thou wilt not only loose the forfeiture,
But, touch'd with human gentleness and love,
Forgive a moiety of the principal;
Glancing an eye of pity on his losses,
That have of late so huddled on his back,
Enow to press a royal merchant down,
And pluck commiseration of his state
From brassy bosoms and rough hearts of flint,
From stubborn Turks and Tartars, never train'd
To offices of tender courtesy.
We all expect a gentle answer, Jew.

Shy. I have possess'd your Grace of what I purpose;
And by our holy Sabbath have I sworn
To have the due and forfeit of my bond:
If you deny it, let the danger light
Upon your charter and your city's freedom.
You 'll ask me, why I rather choose to have
A weight of carrion-flesh than to receive
Three thousand ducats: I 'll not answer that:
But, say, it is my humour: is it answer'd?
What if my house be troubled with a rat,
And I be pleased to give ten thousand ducats
To have it baned?   What, are you answer'd yet?

Some men there are love not a gaping pig;
Some, that are mad if they behold a cat;
And others, when the bagpipe sings i' the nose,
Cannot contain their urine: for affection,
Mistress of passion, sways it to the mood
Of what it likes or loathes.   Now, for your answer,
As there is no firm reason to be render'd,
Why he cannot abide a gaping pig;
Why he, a harmless necessary cat;
Why he, a woollen bag-pipe; but of force
Must yield to such inevitable shame
As to offend, himself being offended;
So can I give no reason, nor I will not,
More than a lodged hate and a certain loathing
I bear Antonio, that I follow thus
A losing suit against him.   Are you answer'd?

Bass. This is no answer, thou unfeeling man,
To excuse the current of thy cruelty.

Shy. I am not bound to please thee with my answer.

Bass. Do all men kill the things they do not love?

Shy. Hates any man the thing he would not kill?

Bass. Every offence is not a hate at first.

Shy. What, wouldst thou have a serpent sting thee twice?

Ant. I pray you, think you question with the Jew.
You may as well go stand upon the beach,
And bid the main flood bate his usual height;
You may as well use question with the wolf,
Why he hath made the ewe bleat for the lamb;
You may as well forbid the mountain pines
To wag their high tops, and to make no noise,
When they are fretten with the gusts of heaven;
You may as well do any thing most hard,
As seek to soften that—than which what's harder?—
His Jewish heart: therefore, I do beseech you,
Make no more offers, use no farther means,
But with all brief and plain conveniency
Let me have judgement and the Jew his will.

Bass. For thy three thousand ducats here is six.

Shy. If every ducat in six thousand ducats
Were in six parts and every part a ducat,
I would not draw them; I would have my bond.

Duke. How shalt thou hope for mercy, rendering none?

Shy. What judgement shall I dread, doing no wrong?
You have among you many a purchased slave,
Which, like your asses and your dogs and mules,

You use in abject and in slavish parts,
Because you bought them: shall I say to you,
Let them be free, marry them to your heirs?
Why sweat they under burthens? let their beds
Be made as soft as yours, and let their palates
Be season'd with such viands? You will answer
'The slaves are ours:' so do I answer you:
The pound of flesh, which I demand of him,
Is dearly bought; 'tis mine and I will have it.
If you deny me, fie upon your law!
There is no force in the decrees of Venice.
I stand for judgement: answer; shall I have it?
Duke. Upon my power I may dismiss this court,
Unless Bellario, a learned doctor,
Whom I have sent for to determine this,
Come here to-day.
Saler.   My lord, here stays without
A messenger with letters from the doctor,
New come from Padua.
Duke. Bring us the letters; call the messenger.
Bass. Good cheer, Antonio! What, man, courage yet!
The Jew shall have my flesh, blood, bones, and all,
Ere thou shalt lose for me one drop of blood.
Ant. I am a tainted wether of the flock,
Meetest for death: the weakest kind of fruit
Drops earliest to the ground; and so let me:
You cannot better be employ'd, Bassanio,
Than to live still, and write mine epitaph.
          Enter Nerissa, dressed like a lawyer's clerk.
Duke. Came you from Padua, from Bellario?
Ner. From both, my lord. Bellario greets your Grace.
                              [*Presenting a letter.*
Bass. Why dost thou whet thy knife so earnestly?
Shy. To cut the forfeiture from that bankrupt there.
Gra. Not on thy sole, but on thy soul, harsh Jew,
  Thou makest thy knife keen; but no metal can,
  No, not the hangman's axe, bear half the keenness
  Of thy sharp envy. Can no prayers pierce thee?
Shy. No, none that thou hast wit enough to make.
Gra. O, be thou damn'd, inexecrable dog!
  And for thy life let justice be accused.
  Thou almost makest me waver in my faith,
  To hold opinion with Pythagoras,
  That souls of animals infuse themselves
  Into the trunks of men: thy currish spirit

99

Govern'd a wolf, who hang'd for human slaughter,
Even from the gallows did his fell soul fleet,
And, whilst thou lay'st in thy unhallow'd dam,
Infused itself in thee ; for thy desires
Are wolvish, bloody, starved and ravenous.

Shy. Till thou canst rail the seal from off my bond,
Thou but offend'st thy lungs to speak so loud :
Repair thy wit, good youth, or it will fall
To cureless ruin.　I stand here for law.

Duke. This letter from Bellario doth commend
A young and learned doctor to our court.
Where is he ?

Ner.　　　　He attendeth here hard by,
To know your answer, whether you 'll admit him.

Duke. With all my heart.　Some three or four of you
Go give him courteous conduct to this place.
Meantime the court shall hear Bellario's letter.

Clerk. [*reads*] Your Grace shall understand that at the receipt
of your letter I am very sick : but in the instant that your
messenger came, in loving visitation was with me a young
doctor of Rome ; his name is Balthasar.　I acquainted him
with the cause in controversy between the Jew and Antonio
the merchant : we turned o'er many books together : he is
furnished with my opinion ; which, bettered with his own
learning,—the greatness whereof I cannot enough commend,
—comes with him, at my importunity, to fill up your Grace's
request in my stead.　I beseech you, let his lack of years
be no impediment to let him lack a reverend estimation ; for
I never knew so young a body with so old a head.　I leave
him to your gracious acceptance, whose trial shall better
publish his commendation.

Duke. You hear the learn'd Bellario, what he writes :
And here, I take it, is the doctor come.

Enter Portia for Balthasar.

Give me your hand.　Come you from old Bellario ?

Por. I did, my lord.

Duke.　　　　You are welcome : take your place.
Are you acquainted with the difference
That holds this present question in the court ?

Por. I am informed throughly of the cause.
Which is the merchant here, and which the Jew ?

Duke. Antonio and old Shylock, both stand forth.

Por. Is your name Shylock ?

Shy.　　　　　Shylock is my name.

Por. Of a strange nature is the suit you follow ;

Yet in such rule that the Venetian law
Cannot impugn you as you do proceed.
You stand within his danger, do you not?
Ant. Ay, so he says.
Por.   Do you confess the bond?
Ant. I do.
Por.   Then must the Jew be merciful:
Shy. On what compulsion must I? tell me that
Por. The quality of mercy is not strain'd,
    It droppeth as the gentle rain from heaven
    Upon the place beneath: it is twice blest;
    It blesseth him that gives, and him that takes:
    'Tis mightiest in the mightiest: it becomes
    The throned monarch better than his crown;
    His sceptre shows the force of temporal power,
    The attribute to awe and majesty,
    Wherein doth sit the dread and fear of kings;
    But mercy is above this sceptred sway;
    It is enthroned in the hearts of kings,
    It is an attribute to God himself;
    And earthly power doth then show likest God's
    When mercy seasons justice.   Therefore, Jew,
    Though justice be thy plea, consider this,
    That, in the course of justice, none of us
    Should see salvation: we do pray for mercy;
    And that same prayer doth teach us all to render
    The deeds of mercy.   I have spoke thus much
    To mitigate the justice of thy plea;
    Which if thou follow, this strict court of Venice
    Must needs give sentence 'gainst the merchant there.
Shy. My deeds upon my head! I crave the law,
    The penalty and forfeit of my bond.
Por. Is he not able to discharge the money?
Bass. Yes, here I tender it for him in the court;
    Yea, twice the sum: if that will not suffice,
    I will be bound to pay it ten times o'er,
    On forfeit of my hands, my head, my heart:
    If this will not suffice, it must appear
    That malice bears down truth.   And I beseech **you**,
    Wrest once the law to your authority:
    To do a great right, do a little wrong,
    And curb this cruel devil of his will.
Por. It must not be; there is no power in Venice
    Can alter a decree established:
    'Twill be recorded for a precedent,

And many an error, by the same example,
Will rush into the state : it cannot be.

Shy. A Daniel come to judgement! yea, a Daniel!
O wise young judge, how I do honour thee!

Por. I pray you, let me look upon the bond.

Shy. Here 'tis, most reverend doctor, here it is.

Por. Shylock, there 's thrice thy money offer'd thee.

Shy. An oath, an oath, I have an oath in heaven:
Shall I lay perjury upon my soul?
No, not for Venice.

Por. 　　　　　　　　Why, this bond is forfeit;
And lawfully by this the Jew may claim
A pound of flesh, to be by him cut off
Nearest the merchant's heart.　Be merciful:
Take thrice thy money; bid me tear the bond.

Shy. When it is paid according to the tenour.
It doth appear you are a worthy judge;
You know the law, your exposition
Hath been most sound: I charge you by the law,
Whereof you are a well-deserving pillar,
Proceed to judgement: by my soul I swear
There is no power in the tongue of man
To alter me: I stay here on my bond.

Ant. Most heartily I do beseech the court
To give the judgement.

Por. 　　　　　　　　Why then, thus it is:
You must prepare your bosom for his knife.

Shy. O noble judge! O excellent young man!

Por. For the intent and purpose of the law
Hath full relation to the penalty,
Which here appeareth due upon the bond.

Shy. 'Tis very true: O wise and upright judge!
How much more elder art thou than thy looks!

Por. Therefore lay bare your bosom.

Shy. 　　　　　　　　　　Ay, his breast:
So says the bond:—doth it not, noble judge?—
'Nearest his heart:' those are the very words.

Por. It is so.　Are there balance here to weigh
The flesh?

Shy. 　　　I have them ready.

Por. Have by some surgeon, Shylock, on your charge,
To stop his wounds, lest he do bleed to death.

Shy. Is it so nominated in the bond?

Por. It is not so express'd: but what of that?
'Twere good you do so much for charity.

Shy. I cannot find it; 'tis not in the bond.
Por. You, merchant, have you any thing to say?
Ant. But little: I am arm'd and well prepared.
  Give me your hand, Bassanio: fare you well!
  Grieve not that I am fallen to this for you;
  For herein Fortune shows herself more kind
  Than is her custom: it is still her use
  To let the wretched man outlive his wealth,
  To view with hollow eye and wrinkled brow
  An age of poverty; from which lingering penance
  Of such misery doth she cut me off.
  Commend me to your honourable wife:
  Tell her the process of Antonio's end;
  Say how I loved you, speak me fair in death;
  And, when the tale is told, bid her be judge
  Whether Bassanio had not once a love.
  Repent but you that you shall lose your friend,
  And he repents not that he pays your debt;
  For if the Jew do cut but deep enough,
  I 'll pay it presently with all my heart.
Bass. Antonio, I am married to a wife
  Which is as dear to me as life itself;
  But life itself, my wife, and all the world,
  Are not with me esteem'd above thy life:
  I would lose all, ay, sacrifice them all
  Here to this devil, to deliver you.
Por. Your wife would give you little thanks for that,
  If she were by, to hear you make the offer.
Gra. I have a wife, whom, I protest, I love:
  I would she were in heaven, so she could
  Entreat some power to change this currish Jew.
Ner. 'Tis well you offer it behind her back;
  The wish would make else an unquiet house.
Shy. These be the Christian husbands.   I have a daughter;
  Would any of the stock of Barrabas
  Had been her husband rather than a Christian!   [*Aside.*
  We trifle time: I pray thee, pursue sentence.
Por. A pound of that same merchant's flesh is thine:
  The court awards it, and the law doth give it.
Shy. Most rightful judge!
Por. And you must cut this flesh from off his breast:
  The law allows it, and the court awards it.
Shy. Most learned judge!   A sentence!   Come, prepare!
Por. Tarry a little; there is something else.
  This bond doth give thee here no jot of blood;

The words expressly are 'a pound of flesh:'
Take then thy bond, take thou thy pound of flesh;
But, in the cutting it, if thou dost shed
One drop of Christian blood, thy lands and goods
Are, by the laws of Venice, confiscate
Unto the state of Venice.

Gra. O upright judge! Mark, Jew: O learned judge!
Shy. Is that the law?
Por. Thyself shalt see the act:
For, as thou urgest justice, be assured
Thou shalt have justice, more than thou desirest.

Gra. O learned judge! Mark, Jew: a learned judge!
Shy. I take this offer, then; pay the bond thrice,
And let the Christian go.
Bass. Here is the money.

Por. Soft!
The Jew shall have all justice; soft! no haste:
He shall have nothing but the penalty.

Gra. O Jew! an upright judge, a learned judge!
Por. Therefore prepare thee to cut off the flesh.
Shed thou no blood; nor cut thou less nor more
But just a pound of flesh: if thou cut'st more
Or less than a just pound, be it but so much
As makes it light or heavy in the substance,
Or the division of the twentieth part
Of one poor scruple, nay, if the scale do turn
But in the estimation of a hair,
Thou diest and all thy goods are confiscate.

Gra. A second Daniel, a Daniel, Jew!
Now, infidel, I have you on the hip.
Por. Why doth the Jew pause? take thy forfeiture.
Shy. Give me my principal, and let me go.
Bass. I have it ready for thee; here it is.
Por. He hath refused it in the open court:
He shall have merely justice and his bond.

Gra. A Daniel, still say I, a second Daniel!
I thank thee, Jew, for teaching me that word.
Shy. Shall I not have barely my principal?
Por. Thou shalt have nothing but the forfeiture,
To be so taken at thy peril, Jew.
Shy. Why, then the devil give him good of it!
I'll stay no longer question.
Por. Tarry, Jew:
The law hath yet another hold on you.
It is enacted in the laws of Venice,

If it be proved against an alien
That by direct or indirect attempts
He seek the life of any citizen,
The party 'gainst the which he doth contrive
Shall seize one half his goods; the other half
Comes to the privy coffer of the state;
And the offender's life lies in the mercy
Of the Duke only, 'gainst all other voice.
In which predicament, I say, thou stand'st:
For it appears, by manifest proceeding,
That indirectly, and directly too,
Thou hast contrived against the very life
Of the defendant; and thou hast incurr'd
The danger formerly by me rehearsed.
Down, therefore, and beg mercy of the Duke.

Gra. Beg that thou mayst have leave to hang thyself:
And yet, thy wealth being forfeit to the state,
Thou hast not left the value of a cord;
Therefore thou must be hang'd at the state's charge.

Duke. That thou shalt see the difference of our spirits,
I pardon thee thy life before thou ask it:
For half thy wealth, it is Antonio's;
The other half comes to the general state,
Which humbleness may drive unto a fine.

Por. Ay, for the state, not for Antonio.

Shy. Nay, take my life and all; pardon not that:
You take my house, when you do take the prop
That doth sustain my house; you take my life,
When you do take the means whereby I live.

Por. What mercy can you render him, Antonio?

Gra. A halter gratis; nothing else, for God's sake.

Ant. So please my lord the Duke and all the court
To quit the fine for one half of his goods,
I am content; so he will let me have
The other half in use, to render it,
Upon his death, unto the gentleman
That lately stole his daughter:
Two things provided more, that, for this favour,
He presently become a Christian;
The other, that he do record a gift,
Here in the court, of all he dies possess'd,
Unto his son Lorenzo and his daughter.

Duke. He shall do this, or else I do recant
The pardon that I late pronounced here.

Por. Art thou contented, Jew? what dost thou say?

Shy. I am content.
Por.   Clerk, draw a deed of gift.
Shy. I pray you, give me leave to go from hence ;
  I am not well : send the deed after me,
  And I will sign it.
Duke.   Get thee gone, but do it.
Gra. In christening shalt thou have two godfathers :
  Had I been judge, thou shouldst have had ten more,
  To bring thee to the gallows, not the font.   [*Exit Shylock.*
Duke. Sir, I entreat you home with me to dinner.
Por. I humbly do desire your Grace of pardon :
  I must away this night toward Padua,
  And it is meet I presently set forth.
Duke. I am sorry that your leisure serves you not.
  Antonio, gratify this gentleman,
  For, in my mind, you are much bound to him.
               [*Exeunt Duke and his train.*
Bass. Most worthy gentleman, I and my friend
  Have by your wisdom been this day acquitted
  Of grievous penalties ; in lieu whereof,
  Three thousand ducats, due unto the Jew,
  We freely cope your courteous pains withal.
Ant. And stand indebted, over and above,
  In love and service to you evermore.
Por. He is well paid that is well satisfied ;
  And I, delivering you, am satisfied,
  And therein do account myself well paid :
  My mind was never yet more mercenary.
  I pray you, know me when we meet again :
  I wish you well, and so I take my leave.
Bass. Dear sir, of force I must attempt you further :
  Take some remembrance of us, as a tribute,
  Not as a fee : grant me two things, I pray you,
  Not to deny me, and to pardon me.
Por. You press me far, and therefore I will yield.
  Give me your gloves, I 'll wear them for your sake ;   [*To Ant.*
  And, for your love, I 'll take this ring from you :   [*To Bass.*
  Do not draw back your hand ; I 'll take no more ;
  And you in love shall not deny me this.
Bass. This ring, good sir, alas, it is a trifle !
  I will not shame myself to give you this.
Por. I will have nothing else but only this ;
  And now methinks I have a mind to it.
Bass. There 's more depends on this than on the value.
  The dearest ring in Venice will I give you,

And find it out by proclamation :
Only for this, I pray you, pardon me.
Por. I see, sir, you are liberal in offers :
You taught me first to beg ; and now methinks
You teach me how a beggar should be answer'd.
Bass. Good sir, this ring was given me by my wife ;
And when she put it on, she made me vow
That I should neither sell nor give nor lose it.
Por. That 'scuse serves many men to save their gifts.
An if your wife be not a mad-woman,
And know how well I have deserved the ring,
She would not hold out enemy for ever,
For giving it to me.   Well, peace be with you !
                              [*Exeunt Portia and Nerissa.*
Ant. My Lord Bassanio, let him have the ring :
Let his deservings and my love withal
Be valued 'gainst your wife's commandment.
Bass. Go, Gratiano, run and overtake him ;
Give him the ring ; and bring him, if thou canst,
Unto Antonio's house : away ! make haste.   [*Exit Gratiano.*
Come, you and I will thither presently ;
And in the morning early will we both
Fly toward Belmont : come, Antonio.   [*Exeunt.*

SCENE II
The same.   A street.
Enter Portia and Nerissa.

Por. Inquire the Jew's house out, give him this deed
And let him sign it : we 'll away to-night
And be a day before our husbands home :
This deed will be well welcome to Lorenzo.

Enter Gratiano.

Gra. Fair sir, you are well o'erta'en :
My Lord Bassanio upon more advice
Hath sent you here this ring, and doth entreat
Your company at dinner.
Por.   That cannot be :
His ring I do accept most thankfully :
And so, I pray you, tell him : furthermore,
I pray you, show my youth old Shylock's house.
Gra. That will I do.
Ner.   Sir, I would speak with you.
I 'll see if I can get my husband's ring,   [*Aside to Portia.*
Which I did make him swear to keep for ever.

Por. [*Aside to Ner.*] Thou mayst, I warrant. We shall have old
   That they did give the rings away to men ;   [swearing
   But we 'll outface them, and outswear them too.
   [*Aloud*] Away ! make haste : thou know'st where I will tarry.
Ner. Come, good sir, will you show me to this house ?

                                [*Exeunt.*

ACT V—SCENE I
Belmont.   Avenue to Portia's house.
Enter Lorenzo and Jessica.

Lor. The moon shines bright : in such a night as this,
   When the sweet wind did gently kiss the trees
   And they did make no noise, in such a night
   Troilus methinks mounted the Troyan walls,
   And sigh'd his soul toward the Grecian tents,
   Where Cressid lay that night.
Jes.   In such a night
   Did Thisbe fearfully o'ertrip the dew,
   And saw the lion's shadow ere himself,
   And ran dismay'd away.
Lor.   In such a night
   Stood Dido with a willow in her hand
   Upon the wild sea banks, and waft her love
   To come again to Carthage.
Jes.   In such a night
   Medea gather'd the enchanted herbs
   That did renew old Æson.
Lor.   In such a night
   Did Jessica steal from the wealthy Jew,
   And with an unthrift love did run from Venice
   As far as Belmont.
Jes.   In such a night
   Did young Lorenzo swear he loved her well,
   Stealing her soul with many vows of faith
   And ne'er a true one.
Lor.   In such a night
   Did pretty Jessica, like a little shrew,
   Slander her love, and he forgave it her.
Jes. I would out-night you, did no body come :
   But, hark, I hear the footing of a man.

               Enter Stephano.

Lor. Who comes so fast in silence of the night ?
Steph. A friend.
Lor. A friend ! what friend ? your name, I pray you, friend ?
Steph. Stephano is my name ; and I bring word

My mistress will before the break of day
Be here at Belmont: she doth stray about
By holy crosses, where she kneels and prays
For happy wedlock hours.

Lor.   Who comes with her?

Steph. None but a holy hermit and her maid.
I pray you, is my master yet return'd?

Lor. He is not, nor we have not heard from him.
But go we in, I pray thee, Jessica,
And ceremoniously let us prepare
Some welcome for the mistress of the house.

Enter Launcelot.

Laun. Sola, sola! wo ha, ho! sola, sola!

Lor. Who calls?

Laun. Sola! did you see Master Lorenzo? Master Lorenzo,

Lor. Leave hollaing, man: here.   [sola, sola!

Laun. Sola! where? where?

Lor. Here.

Laun. Tell him there's a post come from my master, with his
horn full of good news: my master will be here ere morning.
                                                    [*Exit.*

Lor. Sweet soul, let's in, and there expect their coming.
And yet no matter: why should we go in?
My friend Stephano, signify, I pray you,
Within the house, your mistress is at hand;
And bring your music forth into the air.   [*Exit Stephano.*
How sweet the moonlight sleeps upon this bank!
Here will we sit, and let the sounds of music
Creep in our ears: soft stillness and the night
Become the touches of sweet harmony.
Sit, Jessica. Look how the floor of heaven
Is thick inlaid with patines of bright gold:
There's not the smallest orb which thou behold'st
But in his motion like an angel sings,
Still quiring to the young-eyed cherubins;
Such harmony is in immortal souls;
But whilst this muddy vesture of decay
Doth grossly close it in, we cannot hear it.

Enter Musicians.

Come, ho, and wake Diana with a hymn!
With sweetest touches pierce your mistress' ear,
And draw her home with music.   [*Music.*

Jes. I am never merry when I hear sweet music.

Lor. The reason is, your spirits are attentive:
For do but note a wild and wanton herd,

Or race of youthful and unhandled colts,
Fetching mad bounds, bellowing and neighing loud,
Which is the hot condition of their blood;
If they but hear perchance a trumpet sound,
Or any air of music touch their ears,
You shall perceive them make a mutual stand,
Their savage eyes turn'd to a modest gaze
By the sweet power of music: therefore the poet
Did feign that Orpheus drew trees, stones and floods;
Since nought so stockish, hard and full of rage,
But music for the time doth change his nature.
The man that hath no music in himself,
Nor is not moved with concord of sweet sounds,
Is fit for treasons, stratagems and spoils;
The motions of his spirit are dull as night,
And his affections dark as Erebus:
Let no such man be trusted.   Mark the music.

Enter Portia and Nerissa.

Por. That light we see is burning in my hall.
How far that little candle throws his beams!
So shines a good deed in a naughty world.
Ner. When the moon shone, we did not see the candle.
Por. So doth the greater glory dim the less:
A substitute shines brightly as a king,
Until a king be by; and then his state
Empties itself, as doth an inland brook
Into the main of waters.   Music! hark!
Ner. It is your music, madam, of the house.
Por. Nothing is good, I see, without respect:
Methinks it sounds much sweeter than by day.
Ner. Silence bestows that virtue on it, madam.
Por. The crow doth sing as sweetly as the lark,
When neither is attended; and I think
The nightingale, if she should sing by day,
When every goose is cackling, would be thought
No better a musician than the wren.
How many things by season season'd are
To their right praise and true perfection!
Peace, ho! the moon sleeps with Endymion,
And would not be awaked.   [*Music ceases.*
Lor.   That is the voice,
Or I am much deceived, of Portia.
Por. He knows me as the blind man knows the cuckoo,
By the bad voice.
Lor.   Dear lady, welcome home.

Por. We have been praying for our husbands' healths,
Which speed, we hope, the better for our words.
Are they return'd?

Lor.   Madam, they are not yet;
But there is come a messenger before,
To signify their coming.

Por.   Go in, Nerissa;
Give order to my servants that they take
No note at all of our being absent hence;
Nor you, Lorenzo; Jessica, nor you.   [*A tucket sounds.*

Lor. Your husband is at hand; I hear his trumpet:
We are no tell-tales, madam; fear you not.

Por. This night methinks is but the daylight sick;
It looks a little paler: 'tis a day,
Such as the day is when the sun is hid.

   Enter Bassanio, Antonio, Gratiano, and their followers.

Bass. We should hold day with the Antipodes,
If you would walk in absence of the sun.

Por. Let me give light, but let me not be light;
For a light wife doth make a heavy husband,
And never be Bassanio so for me:
But God sort all! You are welcome home, my lord.

Bass. I thank you, madam. Give welcome to my friend.
This is the man, this is Antonio,
To whom I am so infinitely bound.

Por. You should in all sense be much bound to him,
For, as I hear, he was much bound for you.

Ant. No more than I am well acquitted of.

Por. Sir, you are very welcome to our house:
It must appear in other ways than words,
Therefore I scant this breathing courtesy.

Gra. [*To Nerissa*] By yonder moon I swear you do me wrong;
In faith, I gave it to the judge's clerk:
Would he were gelt that had it, for my part,
Since you do take it, love, so much at heart.

Por. A quarrel, ho, already! what's the matter?

Gra. About a hoop of gold, a paltry ring
That she did give me, whose posy was
For all the world like cutler's poetry
Upon a knife, 'Love me, and leave me not.'

Ner. What talk you of the posy or the value?
You swore to me, when I did give it you,
That you would wear it till your hour of death,
And that it should lie with you in your grave:
Though not for me, yet for your vehement oaths,

You should have been respective, and have kept it.
Gave it a judge's clerk ! no, God 's my judge,
The clerk will ne'er wear hair on 's face that had it.
Gra. He will, an if he live to be a man.
Ner. Ay, if a woman live to be a man.
Gra. Now, by this hand, I gave it to a youth,
A kind of boy, a little scrubbed boy,
No higher than thyself, the judge's clerk,
A prating boy, that begg'd it as a fee :
I could not for my heart deny it him.
Por. You were to blame, I must be plain with you,
To part so slightly with your wife's first gift ;
A thing stuck on with oaths upon your finger
And so riveted with faith unto your flesh.
I gave my love a ring, and made him swear
Never to part with it ; and here he stands ;
I dare be sworn for him he would not leave it
Nor pluck it from his finger, for the wealth
That the world masters.   Now, in faith, Gratiano,
You give your wife too unkind a cause of grief :
An 'twere to me, I should be mad at it.
Bass. [*Aside*] Why, I were best to cut my left hand off,
And swear I lost the ring defending it.
Gra. My Lord Bassanio gave his ring away
Unto the judge that begg'd it, and indeed
Deserved it too ; and then the boy, his clerk,
That took some pains in writing, he begg'd mine ;
And neither man nor master would take aught
But the two rings.
Por.   What ring gave you, my lord?
Not that, I hope, which you received of me.
Bass. If I could add a lie unto a fault,
I would deny it ; but you see my finger
Hath not the ring upon it, it is gone.
Por. Even so void is your false heart of truth.
By heaven, I will ne'er come in your bed
Until I see the ring.
Ner.   Nor I in yours
Till I again see mine.
Bass.   Sweet Portia,
If you did know to whom I gave the ring,
If you did know for whom I gave the ring,
And would conceive for what I gave the ring,
And how unwillingly I left the ring,
When nought would be accepted but the ring,

You would abate the strength of your displeasure.

Por. If you had known the virtue of the ring,
Or half her worthiness that gave the ring,
Or your own honour to contain the ring,
You would not then have parted with the ring.
What man is there so much unreasonable,
If you had pleased to have defended it
With any terms of zeal, wanted the modesty
To urge the thing held as a ceremony?
Nerissa teaches me what to believe:
I 'll die for 't but some woman had the ring.

Bass. No, by my honour, madam, by my soul,
No woman had it, but a civil doctor,
Which did refuse three thousand ducats of me,
And begg'd the ring; the which I did deny him,
And suffer'd him to go displeased away;
Even he that did uphold the very life
Of my dear friend. What should I say, sweet lady?
I was enforced to send it after him;
I was beset with shame and courtesy;
My honour would not let ingratitude
So much besmear it. Pardon me, good lady;
For, by these blessed candles of the night,
Had you been there, I think you would have begg'd
The ring of me to give the worthy doctor.

Por. Let not that doctor e'er come near my house:
Since he hath got the jewel that I loved,
And that which you did swear to keep for me,
I will become as liberal as you;
I 'll not deny him any thing I have,
No, not my body nor my husband's bed:
Know him I shall, I am well sure of it:
Lie not a night from home; watch me like Argus:
If you do not, if I be left alone,
Now, by mine honour, which is yet mine own,
I 'll have that doctor for my bedfellow.

Ner. And I his clerk; therefore be well advised
How you do leave me to mine own protection.

Gra. Well, do you so: let not me take him, then;
For if I do, I 'll mar the young clerk's pen.

Ant. I am the unhappy subject of these quarrels.

Por. Sir, grieve not you; you are welcome notwith**standing**.

Bass. Portia, forgive me this enforced wrong;
And, in the hearing of these many friends,
I swear to thee, even by thine own fair eyes,

Wherein I see myself,—

Por.   Mark you but that !
In both my eyes he doubly sees himself ;
In each eye, one : swear by your double self,
And there 's an oath of credit.

Bass.   Nay, but hear me :
Pardon this fault, and by my soul I swear
I never more will break an oath with thee.

Ant. I once did lend my body for his wealth ;
Which, but for him that had your husband's ring,
Had quite miscarried : I dare be bound again,
My soul upon the forfeit, that your lord
Will never more break faith advisedly.

Por. Then you shall be his surety.   Give him this,
And bid him keep it better than the other.

Ant. Here, Lord Bassanio ; swear to keep this ring.

Bass. By heaven, it is the same I gave the doctor !

Por. I had it of him : pardon me, Bassanio ;
For, by this ring, the doctor lay with me.

Ner. And pardon me, my gentle Gratiano ;
For that same scrubbed boy, the doctor's clerk,
In lieu of this last night did lie with me.

Gra. Why, this is like the mending of highways
In summer, where the ways are fair enough :
What, are we cuckolds ere we have deserved it ?

Por. Speak not so grossly.   You are all amazed :
Here is a letter ; read it at your leisure ;
It comes from Padua, from Bellario :
There you shall find that Portia was the doctor,
Nerissa there her clerk : Lorenzo here
Shall witness I set forth as soon as you,
And even but now return'd ; I have not yet
Enter'd my house.   Antonio, you are welcome ;
And I have better news in store for you
Than you expect : unseal this letter soon ;
There you shall find three of your argosies
Are richly come to harbour suddenly :
You shall not know by what strange accident
I chanced on this letter.

Ant.   I am dumb.

Bass. Were you the doctor and I knew you not ?

Gra. Were you the clerk that is to make me cuckold ?

Ner. Ay, but the clerk that never means to do it,
Unless he live until he be a man.

Bass. Sweet doctor, you shall be my bedfellow :

The Merchant of Venice [Act V, Sc. 1

When I am absent, then lie with my wife.

Ant. Sweet lady, you have given me life and living;
For here I read for certain that my ships
Are safely come to road.

Por.　　　　　　　How now, Lorenzo!
My clerk hath some good comforts too for you.

Ner. Ay, and I'll give them him without a fee.
There do I give to you and Jessica,
From the rich Jew, a special deed of gift,
After his death, of all he dies possess'd of.

Lor. Fair ladies, you drop manna in the way
Of starved people.

Por.　　　　　　It is almost morning,
And yet I am sure you are not satisfied
Of these events at full. Let us go in;
And charge us there upon inter'gatories,
And we will answer all things faithfully.

Gra. Let it be so: the first inter'gatory
That my Nerissa shall be sworn on is,
Whether till the next night she had rather stay,
Or go to bed now, being two hours to day:
But were the day come, I should wish it dark,
That I were couching with the doctor's clerk.
Well, while I live I'll fear no other thing
So sore as keeping safe Nerissa's ring.　　　[*Exeunt.*

115

AS YOU LIKE IT

DRAMATIS PERSONÆ

DUKE, *living in banishment.*
FREDERICK, *his brother, and usurper of his dominions.*
AMIENS, } *lords attending on the banished*
JAQUES, } *Duke.*
LE BEAU, *a courtier attending upon Frederick.*
CHARLES, *wrestler to Frederick.*
OLIVER,
JAQUES, } *sons of Sir Rowland de Boys.*
ORLANDO,
ADAM, } *servants to Oliver.*
DENNIS,

TOUCHSTONE, *a clown.*
SIR OLIVER MARTEXT, *a vicar.*
CORIN, } *shepherds.*
SYLVIUS, }
WILLIAM, *a country fellow, in love with Audrey.*
A person representing Hymen.

ROSALIND, *daughter to the banished Duke.*
CELIA, *daughter to Frederick.*
PHEBE, *a shepherdess.*
AUDREY, *a country wench.*

Lords, pages, and attendants, &c.
SCENE: *Oliver's house; Duke Frederick's court; and the Forest of Arden.*

ACT I—SCENE I

Orchard of Oliver's house.
Enter Orlando and Adam.

Orl. As I remember, Adam, it was upon this fashion, bequeathed me by will but poor a thousand crowns, and, as thou sayest, charged my brother, on his blessing, to breed me well: and there begins my sadness. My brother Jaques he keeps at school, and report speaks goldenly of his profit: for my part, he keeps me rustically at home, or, to speak more properly, stays me here at home unkept; for call you that keeping for a gentleman of my birth, that differs not from the stalling of an ox? His horses are bred better; for, besides that they are fair with their feeding, they are taught their manage, and to that end riders dearly hired: but I, his brother, gain nothing under him but growth; for the which his animals on his dunghills are as much bound to him as I. Besides this nothing that he so plentifully gives me, the something that nature gave me his countenance seems to take from me: he lets me feed with his hinds, bars me the place of a brother, and, as much as in him lies, mines my gentility with my education. This is it, Adam, that grieves me; and the spirit of my father, which I think is within me, begins to mutiny against this servitude: I will no longer endure it, though yet I know no wise remedy how to avoid it.

Adam. Yonder comes my master, your brother.   [me up.

Orl. Go apart, Adam, and thou shalt hear how he will shake

Enter Oliver.

Oli. Now, sir! what make you here?

Orl. Nothing: I am not taught to make any thing.

Oli. What mar you then, sir?

Orl. Marry, sir, I am helping you to mar that which God made, a poor unworthy brother of yours, with idleness.

Oli. Marry, sir, be better employed, and be naught awhile.

Orl. Shall I keep your hogs and eat husks with them? What prodigal portion have I spent, that I should come to such

Oli. Know you where you are, sir?   [penury?

Orl. O, sir, very well; here in your orchard.

Oli. Know you before whom, sir?

Orl. Ay, better than him I am before knows me. I know you are my eldest brother; and, in the gentle condition of blood, you should so know me. The courtesy of nations allows you my better, in that you are the first-born; but the same tradition takes not away my blood, were there twenty brothers betwixt us: I have as much of my father in me as you; albeit, I confess, your coming before me is nearer to

Oli. What, boy!   [his reverence.

Orl. Come, come, elder brother, you are too young in this.

Oli. Wilt thou lay hands on me, villain?

Orl. I am no villain; I am the youngest son of Sir Rowland de Boys; he was my father, and he is thrice a villain that says such a father begot villains. Wert thou not my brother, I would not take this hand from thy throat till this other had pulled out thy tongue for saying so: thou hast railed on thyself.

Adam. Sweet masters, be patient: for your father's remembrance, be at accord.

Oli. Let me go, I say.

Orl. I will not, till I please: you shall hear me. My father charged you in his will to give me good education: you have trained me like a peasant, obscuring and hiding from me all gentlemanlike qualities. The spirit of my father grows strong in me, and I will no longer endure it: therefore allow me such exercises as may become a gentleman, or give me the poor allottery my father left me by testament; with that I will go buy my fortunes.

Oli. And what wilt thou do? beg, when that is spent? Well, sir, get you in: I will not long be troubled with you; you shall have some part of your will: I pray you, leave me.

Orl. I will no further offend you than becomes me for my

Oli. Get you with him, you old dog.   [good.

Adam. Is 'old dog' my reward? Most true, I have lost my teeth in your service. God be with my old master! he would not have spoken such a word.

                                    [*Exeunt Orlando and Adam.*

Oli. Is it even so? begin you to grow upon me? I will physic your rankness, and yet give no thousand crowns neither. Holla, Dennis !

Enter Dennis.

Den. Calls your worship?   [me ?
Oli. Was not Charles, the Duke's wrestler, here to speak with
Den. So please you, he is here at the door and importunes access to you.
Oli. Call him in. [*Exit Dennis.*] 'Twill be a good way ; and to-morrow the wrestling is.

Enter Charles.

Cha. Good morrow to your worship.   [court ?
Oli. Good Monsieur Charles, what 's the new news at the new
Cha. There 's no news at the court, sir, but the old news : that is, the old Duke is banished by his younger brother the new Duke ; and three or four loving lords have put themselves into voluntary exile with him, whose lands and revenues enrich the new Duke ; therefore he gives them good leave to wander.
Oli. Can you tell if Rosalind, the Duke's daughter, be banished with her father?
Cha. O, no ; for the Duke's daughter, her cousin, so loves her, being ever from their cradles bred together, that she would have followed her exile, or have died to stay behind her. She is at the court, and no less beloved of her uncle than his own daughter ; and never two ladies loved as they do.
Oli. Where will the old Duke live?
Cha. They say he is already in the forest of Arden, and a many merry men with him ; and there they live like the old Robin Hood of England : they say many young gentlemen flock to him every day, and fleet the time carelessly, as they did in the golden world.
Oli. What, you wrestle to-morrow before the new Duke?
Cha. Marry, do I, sir ; and I came to acquaint you with a matter.   I am given, sir, secretly to understand that your younger brother, Orlando, hath a disposition to come in disguised against me to try a fall.   To-morrow, sir, I wrestle for my credit ; and he that escapes me without some broken limb shall acquit him well.   Your brother is but young and tender ; and, for your love, I would be loath to foil him, as I must, for my own honour, if he come in : therefore, out of my love to you, I came hither to acquaint you withal ; that either you might stay him from his intendment, or brook such disgrace well as he shall run into ; in that it is a thing of his own search, and altogether against my will.

Oli. Charles, I thank thee for thy love to me, which thou shalt
  find I will most kindly requite. I had myself notice of my
  brother's purpose herein, and have by underhand means
  laboured to dissuade him from it, but he is resolute. I 'll
  tell thee, Charles :—it is the stubbornest young fellow of
  France ; full of ambition, an envious emulator of every man's
  good parts, a secret and villanous contriver against me his
  natural brother : therefore use thy discretion ; I had as lief
  thou didst break his neck as his finger. And thou wert best
  look to 't ; for if thou dost him any slight disgrace, or if he
  do not mightily grace himself on thee, he will practise against
  thee by poison, entrap thee by some treacherous device, and
  never leave thee till he hath ta'en thy life by some indirect
  means or other ; for, I assure thee, and almost with tears
  I speak it, there is not one so young and so villanous this
  day living. I speak but brotherly of him ; but should I
  anatomize him to thee as he is, I must blush and weep,
  and thou must look pale and wonder.

Cha. I am heartily glad I came hither to you. If he come to-
  morrow, I 'll give him his payment : if ever he go alone again,
  I 'll never wrestle for prize more : and so, God keep your
  worship !

Oli. Farewell, good Charles. [*Exit Charles.*] Now will I stir
  this gamester : I hope I shall see an end of him ; for my soul,
  yet I know not why, hates nothing more than he. Yet he 's
  gentle ; never schooled, and yet learned ; full of noble
  device ; of all sorts enchantingly beloved ; and indeed so
  much in the heart of the world, and especially of my own
  people, who best know him, that I am altogether misprised :
  but it shall not be so long ; this wrestler shall clear all :
  nothing remains but that I kindle the boy thither ; which
  now I 'll go about.   [*Exit.*

SCENE II

Lawn before the Duke's palace.
Enter Rosalind and Celia.

Cel. I pray thee, Rosalind, sweet my coz, be merry.

Ros. Dear Celia, I show more mirth than I am mistress of ;
  and would you yet I were merrier ? Unless you could teach
  me to forget a banished father, you must not learn me how
  to remember any extraordinary pleasure.

Cel. Herein I see thou lovest me not with the full weight that
  I love thee. If my uncle, thy banished father, had banished
  thy uncle, the Duke my father, so thou hadst been still with
  me, I could have taught my love to take thy father for mine :

so wouldst thou, if the truth of thy love to me were so
righteously tempered as mine is to thee.   [yours.

Ros. Well, I will forget the condition of my estate, to rejoice in

Cel. You know my father hath no child but I, nor none is
like to have : and, truly, when he dies, thou shalt be his
heir ; for what he hath taken away from thy father perforce,
I will render thee again in affection ; by mine honour, I
will ; and when I break that oath, let me turn monster :
therefore, my sweet Rose, my dear Rose, be merry.

Ros. From henceforth I will, coz, and devise sports. Let me
see ; what think you of falling in love ?

Cel. Marry, I prithee, do, to make sport withal : but love no
man in good earnest ; nor no further in sport neither, than
with safety of a pure blush thou mayst in honour come off

Ros. What shall be our sport, then ?   [again.

Cel. Let us sit and mock the good housewife Fortune from her
wheel, that her gifts may henceforth be bestowed equally.

Ros. I would we could do so ; for her benefits are mightily
misplaced ; and the bountiful blind woman doth most
mistake in her gifts to women.

Cel. 'Tis true ; for those that she makes fair she scarce makes
honest ; and those that she makes honest she makes very
ill-favouredly.

Ros. Nay, now thou goest from Fortune's office to Nature's :
Fortune reigns in gifts of the world, not in the lineaments of
Nature.

Enter Touchstone.

Cel. No ? when Nature hath made a fair creature, may she not
by Fortune fall into the fire?   Though Nature hath given us
wit to flout at Fortune, hath not Fortune sent in this fool to
cut off the argument?

Ros. Indeed, there is Fortune too hard for Nature, when
Fortune makes Nature's natural the cutter-off of Nature's
wit.

Cel. Peradventure this is not Fortune's work neither, but
Nature's ; who perceiveth our natural wits too dull to reason
of such goddesses, and hath sent this natural for our whetstone ; for always the dulness of the fool is the whetstone of
the wits.   How now, wit ! whither wander you ?

Touch. Mistress, you must come away to your father.

Cel. Were you made the messenger ?

Touch. No, by mine honour, but I was bid to come for you.

Ros. Where learned you that oath, fool ?

Touch. Of a certain knight that swore by his honour they were
good pancakes, and swore by his honour the mustard was

naught ; now I 'll stand to it, the pancakes were naught and the mustard was good, and yet was not the knight forsworn.

Cel. How prove you that, in the great heap of your knowledge?

Ros. Ay, marry, now unmuzzle your wisdom.

Touch. Stand you both forth now : stroke your chins, and swear by your beards that I am a knave.

Cel. By our beards, if we had them, thou art.

Touch. By my knavery, if I had it, then I were ; but if you swear by that that is not, you are not forsworn : no more was this knight, swearing by his honour, for he never had any ; or if he had, he had sworn it away before ever he saw those pancakes or that mustard.

Cel. Prithee, who is 't that thou meanest?

Touch. One that old Frederick, your father, loves.

Cel. My father's love is enough to honour him : enough ! speak no more of him ; you 'll be whipped for taxation one of these days.

Touch. The more pity, that fools may not speak wisely what wise men do foolishly.

Cel. By my troth, thou sayest true ; for since the little wit that fools have was silenced, the little foolery that wise men have makes a great show. Here comes Monsieur Le Beau.

Ros. With his mouth full of news.

Cel. Which he will put on us, as pigeons feed their young.

Ros. Then shall we be news-crammed

Cel. All the better ; we shall be the more marketable.

Enter Le Beau.

Bon jour, Monsieur Le Beau ; what 's the news?

Le Beau. Fair princess, you have lost much good sport.

Cel. Sport ! of what colour?

Le Beau. What colour, madam ! how shall I answer you?

Ros. As wit and fortune will.

Touch. Or as the Destinies decree.

Cel. Well said : that was laid on with a trowel.

Touch. Nay, if I keep not my rank,—

Ros. Thou losest thy old smell.

Le Beau. You amaze me, ladies : I would have told you of good wrestling, which you have lost the sight of.

Ros. Yet tell us the manner of the wrestling.

Le Beau. I will tell you the beginning ; and, if it please your ladyships, you may see the end ; for the best is yet to do ; and here, where you are, they are coming to perform it.

Cel. Well, the beginning, that is dead and buried.

Le Beau. There comes an old man and his three sons,—

Cel. I could match this beginning with an old tale.

Le Beau. Three proper young men, of excellent growth and presence.

Ros. With bills on their necks, 'Be it known unto all men by these presents.'

Le Beau. The eldest of the three wrestled with Charles, the Duke's wrestler; which Charles in a moment threw him, and broke three of his ribs, that there is little hope of life in him : so he served the second, and so the third. Yonder they lie; the poor old man, their father, making such pitiful dole over them that all the beholders take his part with weeping.

Ros. Alas !

Touch. But what is the sport, monsieur, that the ladies have lost?

Le Beau. Why, this that I speak of.

Touch. Thus men may grow wiser every day : it is the first time that ever I heard breaking of ribs was sport for ladies.

Cel. Or I, I promise thee.

Ros. But is there any else longs to see this broken music in his sides? is there yet another dotes upon rib-breaking? Shall we see this wrestling, cousin?

Le Beau. You must, if you stay here; for here is the place appointed for the wrestling, and they are ready to perform it.

Cel. Yonder, sure, they are coming : let us now stay and see it.

Flourish. Enter Duke Frederick, Lords, Orlando, Charles, and Attendants.

Duke F. Come on : since the youth will not be entreated, his own peril on his forwardness.

Ros. Is yonder the man?

Le Beau. Even he, madam.

Cel. Alas, he is too young ! yet he looks successfully.

Duke F. How now, daughter and cousin ! are you crept hither to see the wrestling?

Ros. Ay, my liege, so please you give us leave.

Duke F. You will take little delight in it, I can tell you, there is such odds in the man. In pity of the challenger's youth I would fain dissuade him, but he will not be entreated. Speak to him, ladies ; see if you can move him.

Cel. Call him hither, good Monsieur Le Beau.

Duke F. Do so : I 'll not be by.

Le Beau. Monsieur the challenger, the princess calls for you.

Orl. I attend them with all respect and duty.

Ros. Young man, have you challenged Charles the wrestler?

Orl. No, fair princess ; he is the general challenger : I come but in, as others do, to try with him the strength of my youth.

Cel. Young gentleman, your spirits are too bold for your years. You have seen cruel proof of this man's strength : if you saw yourself with your eyes, or knew yourself with your judgement, the fear of your adventure would counsel you to a more equal enterprise. We pray you, for your own sake, to embrace your own safety, and give over this attempt.

Ros. Do, young sir; your reputation shall not therefore be misprised: we will make it our suit to the Duke that the wrestling might not go forward.

Orl. I beseech you, punish me not with your hard thoughts; wherein I confess me much guilty, to deny so fair and excellent ladies any thing. But let your fair eyes and gentle wishes go with me to my trial: wherein if I be foiled, there is but one shamed that was never gracious; if killed, but one dead that is willing to be so: I shall do my friends no wrong, for I have none to lament me; the world no injury, for in it I have nothing: only in the world I fill up a place, which may be better supplied when I have made it empty.

Ros. The little strength that I have, I would it were with you.

Cel. And mine, to eke out hers.

Ros. Fare you well: pray heaven I be deceived in you!

Cel. Your heart's desires be with you!

Cha. Come, where is this young gallant that is so desirous to lie with his mother earth?

Orl. Ready, sir; but his will hath in it a more modest working.

Duke F. You shall try but one fall.

Cha. No, I warrant your Grace, you shall not entreat him to a second, that have so mightily persuaded him from a first.

Orl. You mean to mock me after; you should not have mocked me before: but come your ways.

Ros. Now Hercules be thy speed, young man!

Cel. I would I were invisible, to catch the strong fellow by the leg. [*They wrestle.*

Ros. O excellent young man!

Cel. If I had a thunderbolt in mine eye, I can tell who should down. [*Shout. Charles is thrown.*

Duke F. No more, no more.

Orl. Yes, I beseech your Grace: I am not yet well breathed.

Duke F. How dost thou, Charles?

Le Beau. He cannot speak, my lord.

Duke F. Bear him away. What is thy name, young man?

Orl. Orlando, my liege; the youngest son of Sir Rowland de Boys.

Duke F. I would thou hadst been son to some man else:
The world esteem'd thy father honourable,
But I did find him still mine enemy:
Thou shouldst have better pleased me with this deed,
Hadst thou descended from another house.

But fare thee well; thou art a gallant youth:
I would thou hadst told me of another father.

[Exeunt Duke Fred., train, and Le Beau.

Cel. Were I my father, coz, would I do this?

Orl. I am more proud to be Sir Rowland's son,
His youngest son; and would not change that calling,
To be adopted heir to Frederick.

Ros. My father loved Sir Rowland as his soul,
And all the world was of my father's mind:
Had I before known this young man his son,
I should have given him tears unto entreaties,
Ere he should thus have ventured.

Cel.   Gentle cousin,
Let us go thank him and encourage him:
My father's rough and envious disposition
Sticks me at heart. Sir, you have well deserved:
If you do keep your promises in love
But justly, as you have exceeded all promise,
Your mistress shall be happy.

Ros.   Gentleman,

[Giving him a chain from her neck.

Wear this for me, one out of suits with fortune,
That could give more, but that her hand lacks means.
Shall we go, coz?

Cel.   Ay.   Fare you well, fair gentleman.

Orl. Can I not say, I thank you?   My better parts
Are all thrown down, and that which here stands up
Is but a quintain, a mere lifeless block.

Ros. He calls us back: my pride fell with my fortunes;
I 'll ask him what he would.   Did you call, sir?
Sir, you have wrestled well and overthrown
More than your enemies.

Cel.   Will you go, coz?

Ros. Have with you.   Fare you well.

[Exeunt Rosalind and Celia.

Orl. What passion hangs these weights upon my tongue?
I cannot speak to her, yet she urged conference.
O poor Orlando, thou art overthrown!
Or Charles or something weaker masters thee.

Re-enter Le Beau.

Le Beau. Good sir, I do in friendship counsel you
To leave this place.   Albeit you have deserved
High commendation, true applause, and love,
Yet such is now the Duke's condition,
That he misconstrues all that you have done.

The Duke is humorous : what he is, indeed,
More suits you to conceive than I to speak of.

Orl. I thank you, sir : and, pray you, tell me this ;
Which of the two was daughter of the Duke,
That here was at the wrestling ?

Le Beau. Neither his daughter, if we judge by manners ;
But yet, indeed, the taller is his daughter :
The other is daughter to the banish'd Duke,
And here detain'd by her usurping uncle,
To keep his daughter company ; whose loves
Are dearer than the natural bond of sisters.
But I can tell you that of late this Duke
Hath ta'en displeasure 'gainst his gentle niece,
Grounded upon no other argument
But that the people praise her for her virtues,
And pity her for her good father's sake ;
And, on my life, his malice 'gainst the lady
Will suddenly break forth.   Sir, fare you well :
Hereafter, in a better world than this,
I shall desire more love and knowledge of you.

Orl. I rest much bounden to you : fare you well.

[*Exit Le Beau.*

Thus must I from the smoke into the smother ;
From tyrant Duke unto a tyrant brother :
But heavenly Rosalind !   [*Exit.*

Scene III

A room in the palace.
Enter Celia and Rosalind.

Cel. Why, cousin ! why, Rosalind !   Cupid have mercy ! not a

Ros. Not one to throw at a dog.   [word ?

Cel. No, thy words are too precious to be cast away upon curs ;
throw some of them at me ; come, lame me with reasons.

Ros. Then there were two cousins laid up ; when the one
should be lamed with reasons and the other mad without

Cel. But is all this for your father?   [any.

Ros. No, some of it is for my child's father.   O, how full of
briers is this working-day world !

Cel. They are but burs, cousin, thrown upon thee in holiday
foolery : if we walk not in the trodden paths, our very
petticoats will catch them.

Ros. I could shake them off my coat : these burs are in my

Cel. Hem them away.   [heart.

Ros. I would try, if I could cry hem and have him.

Cel. Come, come, wrestle with thy affections.

Ros. O, they take the part of a better wrestler than myself!

Cel. O, a good wish upon you! you will try in time, in despite
of a fall. But, turning these jests out of service, let us talk
in good earnest: is it possible, on such a sudden, you should
fall into so strong a liking with old Sir Rowland's youngest

Ros. The Duke my father loved his father dearly.   [son?

Cel. Doth it therefore ensue that you should love his son
dearly? By this kind of chase, I should hate him, for my
father hated his father dearly; yet I hate not Orlando.

Ros. No, faith, hate him not, for my sake.

Cel. Why should I not? doth he not deserve well?

Ros. Let me love him for that, and do you love him because I
do. Look, here comes the Duke.

Cel. With his eyes full of anger.

Enter Duke Frederick, with Lords.

Duke F. Mistress, dispatch you with your safest haste
And get you from our court.

Ros.   Me, uncle?

Duke F.   You, cousin:
Within these ten days if that thou be'st found
So near our public court as twenty miles,
Thou diest for it.

Ros.   I do beseech your Grace,
Let me the knowledge of my fault bear with me
If with myself I hold intelligence,
Or have acquaintance with mine own desires;
If that I do not dream, or be not frantic,—
As I do trust I am not,—then, dear uncle,
Never so much as in a thought unborn
Did I offend your Highness.

Duke F.   Thus do all traitors:
If their purgation did consist in words,
They are as innocent as grace itself:
Let it suffice thee that I trust thee not.

Ros. Yet your mistrust cannot make me a traitor:
Tell me whereon the likelihood depends.

Duke F. Thou art thy father's daughter; there's enough.

Ros. So was I when your Highness took his dukedom;
So was I when your Highness banish'd him:
Treason is not inherited, my lord;
Or, if we did derive it from our friends,
What's that to me? my father was no traitor:
Then, good my liege, mistake me not so much
To think my poverty is treacherous.

Cel. Dear sovereign, hear me speak.

Duke F. Ay, Celia; we stay'd her for your sake,
   Else had she with her father ranged along.
Cel. I did not then entreat to have her stay;
   It was your pleasure and your own remorse:
   I was too young that time to value her;
   But now I know her: if she be a traitor,
   Why so am I; we still have slept together,
   Rose at an instant, learn'd, play'd, eat together,
   And wheresoe'er we went, like Juno's swans,
   Still we went coupled and inseparable.
Duke F. She is too subtle for thee; and her smoothness,
   Her very silence and her patience
   Speak to the people, and they pity her.
   Thou art a fool: she robs thee of thy name;
   And thou wilt show more bright and seem more virtuous
   When she is gone. Then open not thy lips:
   Firm and irrevocable is my doom
   Which I have pass'd upon her; she is banish'd.
Cel. Pronouce that sentence then on me, my liege:
   I cannot live out of her company.
Duke F. You are a fool. You, niece, provide yourself:
   If you outstay the time, upon mine honour,
   And in the greatness of my word, you die.
                    [*Exeunt Duke Frederick and Lords.*
Cel. O my poor Rosalind, whither wilt thou go?
   Wilt thou change fathers? I will give thee mine.
   I charge thee, be not thou more grieved than I am.
Ros. I have more cause.
Cel.   Thou hast not, cousin;
   Prithee, be cheerful: know'st thou not, the Duke
   Hath banish'd me, his daughter?
Ros.   That he hath not.
Cel. No, hath not? Rosalind lacks then the love
   Which teacheth thee that thou and I am one:
   Shall we be sunder'd? shall we part, sweet girl?
   No: let my father seek another heir.
   Therefore devise with me how we may fly,
   Whither to go and what to bear with us;
   And do not seek to take your charge upon you
   To bear your griefs yourself and leave me out;
   For, by this heaven, now at our sorrows pale,
   Say what thou canst, I'll go along with thee.
Ros. Why, whither shall we go?
Cel. To seek my uncle in the forest of Arden.
Ros. Alas, what danger will it be to us,

Maids as we are, to travel forth so far !
Beauty provoketh thieves sooner than gold.

Cel. I 'll put myself in poor and mean attire
And with a kind of umber smirch my face ;
The like do you : so shall we pass along
And never stir assailants.

Ros.   Were it not better,
Because that I am more than common tall,
That I did suit me all points like a man ?
A gallant curtle-axe upon my thigh,
A boar-spear in my hand ; and—in my heart
Lie there what hidden woman's fear there will—
We 'll have a swashing and a martial outside,
As many other mannish cowards have
That do outface it with their semblances.

Cel. What shall I call thee when thou art a man?

Ros. I 'll have no worse a name than Jove's own page ;
And therefore look you call me Ganymede.
But what will you be call'd?

Cel. Something that hath a reference to my state :
No longer Celia, but Aliena.

Ros. But, cousin, what if we assay'd to steal
The clownish fool out of your father's court?
Would he not be a comfort to our travel?

Cel. He 'll go along o'er the wide world with me ;
Leave me alone to woo him.   Let 's away,
And get our jewels and our wealth together ;
Devise the fittest time and safest way
To hide us from pursuit that will be made
After my flight.   Now go we in content
To liberty and not to banishment.   [*Exeunt.*

ACT II—Scene I

The Forest of Arden.
Enter Duke senior, Amiens, and two or three Lords, like foresters.

Duke S. Now, my co-mates and brothers in exile,
Hath not old custom made this life more sweet
Than that of painted pomp ?   Are not these woods
More free from peril than the envious court?
Here feel we but the penalty of Adam,
The seasons' difference ; as the icy fang
And churlish chiding of the winter's wind,
Which, when it bites and blows upon my boay,

Even till I shrink with cold, I smile and say
' This is no flattery : these are counsellors
That feelingly persuade me what I am.'
Sweet are the uses of adversity ;
Which, like the toad, ugly and venomous,
Wears yet a precious jewel in his head :
And this our life exempt from public haunt
Finds tongues in trees, books in the running brooks,
Sermons in stones and good in every thing.
I would not change it.

Ami.   Happy is your Grace,
That can translate the stubbornness of fortune
Into so quiet and so sweet a style.

Duke S. Come, shall we go and kill us venison ?
And yet it irks me the poor dappled fools,
Being native burghers of this desert city,
Should in their own confines with forked heads
Have their round haunches gored.

First Lord.   Indeed, my lord,
The melancholy Jaques grieves at that,
And, in that kind, swears you do more usurp
Than doth your brother that hath banish'd you.
To-day my Lord of Amiens and myself
Did steal behind him as he lay along
Under an oak whose antique root peeps out
Upon the brook that brawls along this wood :
To the which place a poor sequester'd stag,
That from the hunter's aim had ta'en a hurt,
Did come to languish, and indeed, my lord,
The wretched animal heaved forth such groans,
That their discharge did stretch his leathern coat
Almost to bursting, and the big round tears
Coursed one another down his innocent nose
In piteous chase ; and thus the hairy fool,
Much marked of the melancholy Jaques,
Stood on the extremest verge of the swift brook,
Augmenting it with tears.

Duke S.   But what said Jaques ?
Did he not moralise this spectacle ?

First Lord. O, yes, into a thousand similes.
First, for his weeping into the needless stream ;
' Poor deer,' quoth he, ' thou makest a testament
As worldlings do, giving thy sum of more
To that which had too much : ' then, being there alone,
Left and abandon'd of his velvet friends ;

' 'Tis right,' quoth he ; ' thus misery doth part
The flux of company : ' anon a careless herd,
Full of the pasture, jumps along by him
And never stays to greet him ; ' Ay,' quoth Jaques,
' Sweep on, you fat and greasy citizens ;
'Tis just the fashion : wherefore do you look
Upon that poor and broken bankrupt there ? '
Thus most invectively he pierceth through
The body of the country, city, court,
Yea, and of this our life ; swearing that we
Are mere usurpers, tyrants and what 's worse,
To fright the animals and to kill them up
In their assign'd and native dwelling-place.
Duke S. And did you leave him in this contemplation ?
Sec. Lord. We did, my lord, weeping and commenting
Upon the sobbing deer.
Duke S.   Show me the place :
I love to cope him in these sullen fits,
For then he 's full of matter.
First Lord. I 'll bring you to him straight.   [*Exeunt.*

SCENE II

A room in the palace.
Enter Duke Frederick, with Lords.

Duke F. Can it be possible that no man saw them ?
It cannot be : some villains of my court
Are of consent and sufferance in this.
First Lord. I cannot hear of any that did see her.
The ladies, her attendants of her chamber,
Saw her a-bed, and in the morning early
They found the bed untreasured of their mistress.
Sec. Lord. My lord, the roynish clown, at whom so oft
Your Grace was wont to laugh, is also missing.
Hisperia, the princess' gentlewoman,
Confesses that she secretly o'erheard
Your daughter and her cousin much commend
The parts and graces of the wrestler
That did but lately foil the sinewy Charles ;
And she believes, wherever they are gone,
That youth is surely in their company.
Duke F. Send to his brother ; fetch that gallant hither ;
If he be absent, bring his brother to me ;
I 'll make him find him : do this suddenly,
And let not search and inquisition quail
To bring again these foolish runaways.   [*Exeunt.*

SCENE III
Before Oliver's house.
Enter Orlando and Adam, meeting.

Orl. Who's there?

Adam. What, my young master? O my gentle master!
  O my sweet master! O you memory
  Of old Sir Rowland! why, what make you here?
  Why are you virtuous? why do people love you?
  And wherefore are you gentle, strong and valiant?
  Why would you be so fond to overcome
  The bonny priser of the humorous Duke?
  Your praise is come too swiftly home before you.
  Know you not, master, to some kind of men
  Their graces serve them but as enemies?
  No more do yours: your virtues, gentle master,
  Are sanctified and holy traitors to you.
  O, what a world is this, when what is comely
  Envenoms him that bears it!

Orl. Why, what's the matter?

Adam.   O unhappy youth!
  Come not within these doors; within this roof
  The enemy of all your graces lives:
  Your brother—no, no brother; yet the son—
  Yet not the son, I will not call him son,
  Of him I was about to call his father,—
  Hath heard your praises, and this night he means
  To burn the lodging where you use to lie
  And you within it: if he fail of that,
  He will have other means to cut you off.
  I overheard him and his practices.
  This is no place; this house is but a butchery:
  Abhor it, fear it, do not enter it.

Orl. Why, whither, Adam, wouldst thou have me go?

Adam. No matter whither, so you come not here.

Orl. What, wouldst thou have me go and beg my food?
  Or with a base and boisterous sword enforce
  A thievish living on the common road?
  This I must do, or know not what to do:
  Yet this I will not do, do how I can;
  I rather will subject me to the malice
  Of a diverted blood and bloody brother.

Adam. But do not so. I have five hundred crowns,
  The thrifty hire I saved under your father,
  Which I did store to be my foster-nurse

When service should in my old limbs lie lame,
And unregarded age in corners thrown :
Take that, and He that doth the ravens feed,
Yea, providently caters for the sparrow,
Be comfort to my age !   Here is the gold ;
All this I give you.   Let me be your servant :
Though I look old, yet I am strong and lusty ;
For in my youth I never did apply
Hot and rebellious liquors in my blood,
Nor did not with unbashful forehead woo
The means of weakness and debility ;
Therefore my age is as a lusty winter,
Frosty, but kindly : let me go with you :
I 'll do the service of a younger man
In all your business and necessities.

Orl. O good old man, how well in thee appears
The constant service of the antique world,
When service sweat for duty, not for meed !
Thou art not for the fashion of these times,
Where none will sweat but for promotion,
And having that do choke their service up
Even with the having : it is not so with thee.
But, poor old man, thou prunest a rotten tree,
That cannot so much as a blossom yield
In lieu of all thy pains and husbandry.
But come thy ways ; we 'll go along together,
And ere we have thy youthful wages spent,
We 'll light upon some settled low content.

Adam. Master, go on, and I will follow thee,
To the last gasp, with truth and loyalty.
From seventeen years till now almost fourscore
Here lived I, but now live here no more.
At seventeen years many their fortunes seek ;
But at fourscore it is too late a week :
Yet fortune cannot recompense me better
Than to die well and not my master's debtor.   [*Exeunt.*

SCENE IV

The Forest of Arden.
*Enter Rosalind for Ganymede, Celia for Aliena, and
Touchstone.*

Ros. O Jupiter, how weary are my spirits !
Touch. I care not for my spirits, if my legs were not weary.
Ros. I could find in my heart to disgrace my man's apparel
and to cry like a woman ; but I must comfort the weaker

vessel, as doublet and hose ought to show itself courageous to petticoat : therefore, courage, good Aliena.

Cel. I pray you, bear with me ; I cannot go no further.

Touch. For my part, I had rather bear with you than bear you : yet I should bear no cross, if I did bear you ; for I think you have no money in your purse.

Ros. Well, this is the forest of Arden.

Touch. Ay, now am I in Arden ; the more fool I ; when I was at home, I was in a better place : but travellers must be

Ros. Ay, be so, good Touchstone.   [content.

Enter Corin and Silvius.

Look you, who comes here ; a young man and an old in solemn talk.

Cor. That is the way to make her scorn you still.

Sil. O Corin, that thou knew'st how I do love her !

Cor. I partly guess ; for I have loved ere now.

Sil. No, Corin, being old, thou canst not guess,
Though in thy youth thou wast as true a lover
As ever sigh'd upon a midnight pillow :
But if thy love were ever like to mine,—
As sure I think did never man love so,—
How many actions most ridiculous
Hast thou been drawn to by thy fantasy ?

Cor. Into a thousand that I have forgotten.

Sil. O, thou didst then ne'er love so heartily !
If thou remember'st not the slightest folly
That ever love did make thee run into,
Thou hast not loved :
Or if thou hast not sat as I do now,
Wearing thy hearer in thy mistress' praise,
Thou hast not loved :
Or if thou hast not broke from company
Abruptly, as my passion now makes me,
Thou hast not loved.
O Phebe, Phebe, Phebe !   [*Exit.*

Ros. Alas, poor shepherd ! searching of thy wound,
I have by hard adventure found mine own.

Touch. And I mine. I remember, when I was in love I broke my sword upon a stone and bid him take that for coming a-night to Jane Smile : and I remember the kissing of her batlet and the cow's dugs that her pretty chopt hands had milked : and I remember the wooing of a peascod instead of her ; from whom I took two cods and, giving her them again, said with weeping tears 'Wear these for my sake.' We that

are true lovers run into strange capers ; but as all is mortal
in nature, so is all nature in love mortal in folly.

Ros. Thou speakest wiser than thou art ware of.

Touch. Nay, I shall ne'er be ware of mine own wit till I break
my shins against it.

Ros. Jove, Jove ! this shepherd's passion
  Is much upon my fashion.

Touch. And mine ; but it grows something stale with me.

Cel. I pray you, one of you question yond man
  If he for gold will give us any food :
  I faint almost to death.

Touch.   Holla, you clown !

Ros. Peace, fool : he 's not thy kinsman.

Cor.   Who calls ?

Touch. Your betters, sir.

Cor.   Else are they very wretched.

Ros. Peace, I say.   Good even to you, friend.

Cor. And to you, gentle sir, and to you all.

Ros. I prithee, shepherd, if that love or gold
  Can in this desert place buy entertainment,
  Bring us where we may rest ourselves and feed :
  Here 's a young maid with travel much oppress'd
  And faints for succour.

Cor.   Fair sir, I pity her
  And wish, for her sake more than for mine own,
  My fortunes were more able to relieve her ;
  But I am shepherd to another man
  And do not shear the fleeces that I graze :
  My master is of churlish disposition
  And little recks to find the way to heaven
  By doing deeds of hospitality :
  Besides, his cote, his flocks and bounds of feed
  Are now on sale, and at our sheepcote now,
  By reason of his absence, there is nothing
  That you will feed on ; but what is, come see,
  And in my voice most welcome shall you be.

Ros. What is he that shall buy his flock and pasture ?

Cor. That young swain that you saw here but erewhile,
  That little cares for buying any thing.

Ros. I pray thee, if it stand with honesty,
  Buy thou the cottage, pasture and the flock,
  And thou shalt have to pay for it of us.

Cel. And we will mend thy wages.   I like this place,
  And willingly could waste my time in it.

Cor. Assuredly the thing is to be sold :

Go with me : if you like upon report
The soil, the profit and this kind of life,
I will your very faithful feeder be
And buy it with your gold right suddenly.   [*Exeunt.*

SCENE V

The forest.
Enter Amiens, Jaques, and others.

SONG.

Ami.   Under the greenwood tree
              Who loves to lie with me,
              And turn his merry note
              Unto the sweet bird's throat,
        Come hither, come hither, come hither :
                Here shall he see
                No enemy
        But winter and rough weather.

Jaq. More, more, I prithee, more.
Ami. It will make you melancholy, Monsieur Jaques.
Jaq. I thank it. More, I prithee, more. I can suck
  melancholy out of a song, as a weasel sucks eggs. More,
  I prithee, more.
Ami. My voice is ragged : I know I cannot please you.
Jaq. I do not desire you to please me ; I do desire you to sing.
  Come, more ; another stanzo : call you 'em stanzos ?
Ami. What you will, Monsieur Jaques.
Jaq. Nay, I care not for their names ; they owe me nothing.
  Will you sing ?
Ami. More at your request than to please myself.
Jaq. Well then, if ever I thank any man, I 'll thank you ; but
  that they call compliment is like the encounter of two dog-
  apes, and when a man thanks me heartily, methinks I have
  given him a penny and he renders me the beggarly thanks.
  Come, sing ; and you that will not, hold your tongues.
Ami. Well, I 'll end the song. Sirs, cover the while ; the Duke
  will drink under this tree. He hath been all this day to look
  you.
Jaq. And I have been all this day to avoid him. He is too
  disputable for my company : I think of as many matters as
  he ; but I give heaven thanks, and make no boast of them.
  Come, warble, come.

SONG.

Who doth ambition shun,   [*All together here.*
And loves to live i' the sun,
Seeking the food he eats,
And pleased with what he gets,
Come hither, come hither, come hither :
Here shall he see
No enemy
But winter and rough weather.

Jaq. I 'll give you a verse to this note, that I made yesterday
in despite of my invention.
Ami. And I 'll sing it.
Jaq. Thus it goes :—

If it do come to pass
That any man turn ass,
Leaving his wealth and ease
A stubborn will to please,
Ducdame, ducdame, ducdame :
Here shall he see
Gross fools as he,
And if he will come to me

Ami. What 's that 'ducdame'?
Jaq. 'Tis a Greek invocation, to call fools into a circle.   I 'll
go sleep, if I can ; if I cannot, I 'll rail against all the first-
born of Egypt.
Ami. And I 'll go seek the Duke : his banquet is prepared.
                                          [*Exeunt severally.*

SCENE VI
The forest.
Enter Orlando and Adam.

Adam. Dear master, I can go no further ; O, I die for food !
Here lie I down, and measure out my grave. Farewell, kind
master.
Orl. Why, how now, Adam ! no greater heart in thee?   Live
a little ; comfort a little ; cheer thyself a little.   If this uncouth forest yield any thing savage, I will either be food for
it or bring it for food to thee.   Thy conceit is nearer death
than thy powers.   For my sake be comfortable ; hold death
awhile at the arm's end : I will here be with thee presently ;
and if I bring thee not something to eat, I will give thee
leave to die : but if thou diest before I come, thou art a

136

mocker of my labour.   Well said! thou lookest cheerly, and
I 'll be with thee quickly.   Yet thou liest in the bleak air:
come, I will bear thee to some shelter; and thou shalt not
die for lack of a dinner, if there live any thing in this desert.
Cheerly, good Adam!   [*Exeunt.*

SCENE VII
The forest.
A table set out.   Enter Duke senior, Amiens, and Lords
like outlaws.

Duke S. I think he be transform'd into a beast;
For I can no where find him like a man.

First Lord. My lord, he is but even now gone hence:
Here was he merry, hearing of a song.

Duke S. If he, compact of jars, grow musical,
We shall have shortly discord in the spheres.
Go, seek him: tell him I would speak with him.

Enter Jaques.

First Lord. He saves my labour by his own approach.

Duke S. Why, how now, monsieur! what a life is this,
That your poor friends must woo your company?
What, you look merrily!

Jaq. A fool, a fool!   I met a fool i' the forest,
A motley fool; a miserable world!
As I do live by food, I met a fool;
Who laid him down and bask'd him in the sun,
And rail'd on Lady Fortune in good terms,
In good set terms, and yet a motley fool.
'Good morrow, fool,' quoth I.   'No, sir,' quoth he,
'Call me not fool till heaven hath sent me fortune:'
And then he drew a dial from his poke,
And, looking on it with lack-lustre eye,
Says very wisely, 'It is ten o'clock:
Thus we may see,' quoth he, 'how the world wags:
'Tis but an hour ago since it was nine;
And after one hour more 'twill be eleven;
And so, from hour to hour, we ripe and ripe,
And then, from hour to hour, we rot and rot;
And thereby hangs a tale.'   When I did hear
The motley fool thus moral on the time,
My lungs began to crow like chanticleer,
That fools should be so deep-contemplative;
And I did laugh sans intermission
An hour by his dial.   O noble fool!
A worthy fool!   Motley's the only wear.

Duke S. What fool is this?

Jaq. O worthy fool! One that hath been a courtier,
　And says, if ladies be but young and fair,
　They have the gift to know it: and in his brain,
　Which is as dry as the remainder biscuit
　After a voyage, he hath strange places cramm'd
　With observation, the which he vents
　In mangled forms. O that I were a fool!
　I am ambitious for a motley coat.

Duke S. Thou shalt have one.

Jaq.　　　　　　　　　　It is my only suit;
　Provided that you weed your better judgements
　Of all opinion that grows rank in them
　That I am wise. I must have liberty
　Withal, as large a charter as the wind,
　To blow on whom I please; for so fools have;
　And they that are most galled with my folly,
　They most must laugh. And why, sir, must they so?
　The ' why ' is plain as way to parish church:
　He that a fool doth very wisely hit
　Doth very foolishly, although he smart,
　Not to seem senseless of the bob: if not,
　The wise man's folly is anatomized
　Even by the squandering glances of the fool.
　Invest me in my motley; give me leave
　To speak my mind, and I will through and through
　Cleanse the foul body of the infected world,
　If they will patiently receive my medicine.

Duke S. Fie on thee! I can tell what thou wouldst do.

Jaq. What, for a counter, would I do but good?

Duke S. Most mischievous foul sin, in chiding sin:
　For thou thyself hast been a libertine,
　As sensual as the brutish sting itself;
　And all the embossed sores and headed evils,
　That thou with license of free foot has caught,
　Wouldst thou disgorge into the general world.

Jaq. Why, who cries out on pride,
　That can therein tax any private party?
　Doth it not flow as hugely as the sea,
　Till that the weary very means do ebb?
　What woman in the city do I name,
　When that I say the city-woman bears
　The cost of princes on unworthy shoulders?
　Who can come in and say that I mean her,
　When such a one as she such is her neighbour?

Or what is he of basest function,
That says his bravery is not on my cost,
Thinking that I mean him, but therein suits
His folly to the mettle of my speech?
There then; how then? what then?   Let me see wherein
My tongue hath wrong'd him: if it do him right,
Then he hath wrong'd himself; if he be free,
Why then my taxing like a wild-goose flies,
Unclaim'd of any man.   But who comes here?

Enter Orlando, with his sword drawn.

Orl. Forbear, and eat no more.
Jaq.   Why, I have eat none yet.
Orl. Nor shalt not, till necessity be served.
Jaq. Of what kind should this cock come of?
Duke S. Art thou thus bolden'd, man, by thy distress?
   Or else a rude despiser of good manners,
   That in civility thou seem'st so empty?
Orl. You touch'd my vein at first: the thorny point
   Of bare distress hath ta'en from me the show
   Of smooth civility: yet am I inland bred
   And know some nurture.   But forbear, I say:
   He dies that touches any of this fruit
   Till I and my affairs are answered.
Jaq. An you will not be answered with reason, I must die.
Duke S. What would you have?   Your gentleness shall force,
   More than your force move us to gentleness.
Orl. I almost die for food; and let me have it.
Duke S. Sit down and feed, and welcome to our table.
Orl. Speak you so gently?   Pardon me, I pray you:
   I thought that all things had been savage here;
   And therefore put I on the countenance
   Of stern commandment.   But whate'er you are
   That in this desert inaccessible,
   Under the shade of melancholy boughs,
   Lose and neglect the creeping hours of time;
   If ever you have look'd on better days,
   If ever been where bells have knoll'd to church,
   If ever sat at any good man's feast,
   If ever from your eyelids wiped a tear
   And know what 'tis to pity and be pitied,
   Let gentleness my strong enforcement be:
   In the which hope I blush, and hide my sword.
Duke S. True is it that we have seen better days,
   And have with holy bell been knoll'd to church,

And sat at good men's feasts, and wiped our eyes
Of drops that sacred pity hath engender'd:
And therefore sit you down in gentleness
And take upon command what help we have
That to your wanting may be minister'd.

Orl. Then but forbear your food a little while,
Whiles, like a doe, I go to find my fawn
And give it food. There is an old poor man,
Who after me hath many a weary step
Limp'd in pure love: till he be first sufficed,
Oppress'd with two weak evils, age and hunger,
I will not touch a bit.

Duke S.   Go find him out,
And we will nothing waste till you return.

Orl. I thank ye; and be blest for your good comfort! [*Exit.*

Duke S. Thou seest we are not all alone unhappy:
This wide and universal theatre
Presents more woeful pageants than the scene
Wherein we play in.

Jaq.   All the world's a stage,
And all the men and women merely players:
They have their exits and their entrances;
And one man in his time plays many parts,
His acts being seven ages. At first the infant,
Mewling and puking in the nurse's arms.
Then the whining school-boy, with his satchel
And shining morning face, creeping like snail
Unwillingly to school. And then the lover,
Sighing like furnace, with a woeful ballad
Made to his mistress' eyebrow. Then a soldier,
Full of strange oaths, and bearded like the pard,
Jealous in honour, sudden and quick in quarrel,
Seeking the bubble reputation
Even in the cannon's mouth. And then the justice,
In fair round belly with good capon lined,
With eyes severe and beard of formal cut,
Full of wise saws and modern instances;
And so he plays his part. The sixth age shifts
Into the lean and slipper'd pantaloon,
With spectacles on nose and pouch on side,
His youthful hose, well saved, a world too wide
For his shrunk shank; and his big manly voice,
Turning again toward childish treble, pipes
And whistles in his sound. Last scene of all,
That ends this strange eventful history,

Is second childishness and mere oblivion,
Sans teeth, sans eyes, sans taste, sans every thing.

Re-enter Orlando, with Adam.

Duke S. Welcome. Set down your venerable burthen,
  And let him feed.
Orl. I thank you most for him.
Adam.   So had you need:
  I scarce can speak to thank you for myself.
Duke S. Welcome; fall to: I will not trouble you
  As yet, to question you about your fortunes.
  Give us some music; and, good cousin, sing.

SONG.

Ami.   Blow, blow, thou winter wind,
             Thou art not so unkind
                 As man's ingratitude;
             Thy tooth is not so keen,
             Because thou art not seen,
                 Although thy breath be rude.
    Heigh-ho! sing, heigh-ho! unto the green holly:
    Most friendship is feigning, most loving mere folly:
             Then, heigh-ho, the holly!
                 This life is most jolly.

             Freeze, freeze, thou bitter sky,
             That dost not bite so nigh
                 As benefits forgot:
             Though thou the waters warp,
             Thy sting is not so sharp
                 As friend remember'd not.
    Heigh-ho! sing, &c.

Duke S. If that you were the good Sir Rowland's son,
  As you have whisper'd faithfully you were,
  And as mine eye doth his effigies witness
  Most truly limn'd and living in your face,
  Be truly welcome hither: I am the Duke
  That loved your father: the residue of your fortune,
  Go to my cave and tell me. Good old man,
  Thou art right welcome as thy master is.
  Support him by the arm. Give me your hand,
  And let me all your fortunes understand.   [*Exeunt.*

ACT III—Scene I

A room in the palace.
Enter Duke Frederick, Lords, and Oliver.

Duke F. Not see him since? Sir, sir, that cannot be:
But were I not the better part made mercy,
I should not seek an absent argument
Of my revenge, thou present. But look to it:
Find out thy brother, wheresoe'er he is;
Seek him with candle; bring him dead or living
Within this twelvemonth, or turn thou no more
To seek a living in our territory.
Thy lands and all things that thou dost call thine
Worth seizure do we seize into our hands,
Till thou canst quit thee by thy brother's mouth
Of what we think against thee.
Oli. O that your Highness knew my heart in this!
I never loved my brother in my life.
Duke F. More villain thou. Well, push him out of doors;
And let my officers of such a nature
Make an extent upon his house and lands:
Do this expediently and turn him going.   [*Exeunt.*

Scene II

The forest.
Enter Orlando, with a paper.

Orl.   Hang there, my verse, in witness of my love:
            And thou, thrice-crowned queen of night, survey
          With thy chaste eye, from thy pale sphere above,
            Thy huntress' name that my full life doth sway.
          O Rosalind! these trees shall be my books
            And in their barks my thoughts I 'll character;
          That every eye which in this forest looks
            Shall see thy virtue witness'd every where.
          Run, run, Orlando; carve on every tree
          The fair, the chaste and unexpressive she.   [*Exit.*
Enter Corin and Touchstone.

Cor. And how like you this shepherd's life, Master Touchstone?
Touch. Truly, shepherd, in respect of itself, it is a good life;
but in respect that it is a shepherd's life, it is naught. In
respect that it is solitary, I like it very well; but in respect
that it is private, it is a very vile life. Now, in respect it is
in the fields, it pleaseth me well; but in respect it is not in
the court, it is tedious. As it is a spare life, look you, it fits
my humour well; but as there is no more plenty in it, it

goes much against my stomach. Hast any philosophy in thee, shepherd?

Cor. No more but that I know the more one sickens the worse at ease he is; and that he that wants money, means and content is without three good friends; that the property of rain is to wet and fire to burn; that good pasture makes fat sheep, and that a great cause of the night is lack of the sun; that he that hath learned no wit by nature nor art may complain of good breeding or comes of very dull kindred.

Touch. Such a one is a natural philosopher. Wast ever in court, shepherd?

Cor. No, truly.

Touch. Then thou art damned.

Cor. Nay, I hope.

Touch. Truly, thou art damned, like an ill-roasted egg all on

Cor. For not being at court? Your reason.   [one side.

Touch. Why, if thou never wast at court, thou never sawest good manners; if thou never sawest good manners, then thy manners must be wicked; and wickedness is sin, and sin is damnation. Thou art in a parlous state, shepherd.

Cor. Not a wit, Touchstone: those that are good manners at the court are as ridiculous in the country as the behaviour of the country is most mockable at the court. You told me you salute not at the court, but you kiss your hands: that courtesy would be uncleanly, if courtiers were shepherds.

Touch. Instance, briefly; come, instance.

Cor. Why, we are still handling our ewes, and their fells, you know, are greasy.

Touch. Why, do not your courtier's hands sweat? and is not the grease of a mutton as wholesome as the sweat of a man? Shallow, shallow. A better instance, I say; come.

Cor. Besides, our hands are hard.

Touch. Your lips will feel them the sooner. Shallow again. A more sounder instance, come.

Cor. And they are often tarred over with the surgery of our sheep; and would you have us kiss tar? The courtier's hands are perfumed with civet.

Touch. Most shallow man! thou worm's-meat, in respect of a good piece of flesh indeed! Learn of the wise, and perpend: civet is of a baser birth than tar, the very uncleanly flux of a cat. Mend the instance, shepherd.

Cor. You have too courtly a wit for me: I'll rest.

Touch. Wilt thou rest damned? God help thee, shallow man! God make incision in thee! thou art raw.

Cor. Sir, I am a true labourer: I earn that I eat, get that I

wear, owe no man hate, envy no man's happiness, glad of
other men's good, content with my harm, and the greatest
of my pride is to see my ewes graze and my lambs suck.

Touch. That is another simple sin in you, to bring the ewes
and the rams together and to offer to get your living by the
copulation of cattle; to be bawd to a bell-wether, and to
betray a she-lamb of a twelvemonth to a crooked-pated, old,
cuckoldly ram, out of all reasonable match. If thou beest
not damned for this, the devil himself will have no shepherds; I cannot see else how thou shouldst 'scape.

Cor. Here comes young Master Ganymede, my new mistress's
brother.

> *Enter Rosalind, with a paper, reading.*

Ros.   From the east to western Ind,
>   No jewel is like Rosalind.
>   Her worth, being mounted on the wind,
>   Through all the world bears Rosalind.
>   All the pictures fairest lined
>   Are but black to Rosalind.
>   Let no face be kept in mind
>   But the fair of Rosalind.

Touch. I 'll rhyme you so eight years together, dinners and
suppers and sleeping-hours excepted: it is the right butter-
women's rank to market.

Ros. Out, fool!

Touch. For a taste:

>   If a hart do lack a hind,
>   Let him seek out Rosalind.
>   If the cat will after kind,
>   So be sure will Rosalind.
>   Winter garments must be lined,
>   So must slender Rosalind.
>   They that reap must sheaf and bind;
>   Then to cart with Rosalind.
>   Sweetest nut hath sourest rind,
>   Such a nut is Rosalind.
>   He that sweetest rose will find,
>   Must find love's prick and Rosalind.

This is the very false gallop of verses: why do you infect
yourself with them?

Ros. Peace, you dull fool! I found them on a tree.

Touch. Truly, the tree yields bad fruit.

Ros. I'll graff it with you, and then I shall graff it with a
  medlar : then it will be the earliest fruit i' the country ; for
  you'll be rotten ere you be half ripe, and that's the right
  virtue of the medlar.

Touch. You have said ; but whether wisely or no, let the forest
  judge.

          Enter Celia, with a writing.

Ros. Peace !
  Here comes my sister, reading : stand aside.

Cel. [*reads*] Why should this a desert be ?
        For it is unpeopled ? No ;
     Tongues I'll hang on every tree,
        That shall civil sayings show :
     Some, how brief the life of man
        Runs his erring pilgrimage,
     That the stretching of a span
        Buckles in his sum of age ;
     Some, of violated vows
        'Twixt the souls of friend and friend :
     But upon the fairest boughs,
        Or at every sentence end,
     Will I Rosalinda write,
        Teaching all that read to know
     The quintessence of every sprite
        Heaven would in little show.
     Therefore Heaven Nature charged
        That one body should be fill'd
     With all graces wide-enlarged :
        Nature presently distill'd
     Helen's cheek, but not her heart,
        Cleopatra's majesty,
     Atalanta's better part,
        Sad Lucretia's modesty.
     Thus Rosalind of many parts
        By heavenly synod was devised ;
     Of many faces, eyes and hearts,
        To have the touches dearest prized.
    Heaven would that she these gifts should have,
    And I to live and die her slave.

Ros. O most gentle pulpiter ! what tedious homily of love have
  you wearied your parishioners withal, and never cried 'Have
  patience, good people' !

Cel. How now ! back, friends ! Shepherd, go off a little. Go
  with him, sirrah.

Touch. Come, shepherd, let us make an honourable retreat ;

though not with bag and baggage, yet with scrip and
scrippage.   [*Exeunt Corin and Touchstone.*

Cel. Didst thou hear these verses?

Ros. O, yes, I heard them all, and more too; for some of them
had in them more feet than the verses would bear.

Cel. That's no matter: the feet might bear the verses.

Ros. Ay, but the feet were lame and could not bear themselves
without the verse and therefore stood lamely in the verse.

Cel. But didst thou hear without wondering how thy name
should be hanged and carved upon these trees?

Ros. I was seven of the nine days out of the wonder before
you came; for look here what I found on a palm tree. I
was never so be-rhymed since Pythagoras' time, that I was
an Irish rat, which I can hardly remember.

Cel. Trow you who hath done this?

Ros. Is it a man?

Cel. And a chain, that you once wore, about his neck. Change

Ros. I prithee, who?   [you colour?

Cel. O Lord, Lord! it is a hard matter for friends to meet;
but mountains may be removed with earthquakes and so
encounter.

Ros. Nay, but who is it?

Cel. Is it possible?

Ros. Nay, I prithee now with most petitionary vehemence, tell
me who it is.

Cel. O wonderful, wonderful, and most wonderful wonderful!
and yet again wonderful, and after that, out of all hooping!

Ros. Good my complexion! dost thou think, though I am
caparisoned like a man, I have a doublet and hose in my
disposition? One inch of delay more is a South-sea of
discovery; I prithee, tell me who is it quickly, and speak
apace. I would thou couldst stammer, that thou might'st
pour this concealed man out of thy mouth, as wine comes
out of a narrow-mouthed bottle, either too much at once, or
none at all. I prithee, take the cork out of thy mouth that
I may drink thy tidings.

Cel. So you may put a man in your belly.

Ros. Is he of God's making? What manner of man? Is his
head worth a hat? Or his chin worth a beard?

Cel. Nay, he hath but a little beard.

Ros. Why, God will send more, if the man will be thankful:
let me stay the growth of his beard, if thou delay me not
the knowledge of his chin.

Cel. It is young Orlando, that tripped up the wrestler's heels
and your heart both in an instant.

Ros. Nay, but the devil take mocking: speak sad brow and
Cel. I' faith, coz, 'tis he.   [true maid.
Ros. Orlando?
Cel. Orlando.
Ros. Alas the day! what shall I do with my doublet and hose?
    What did he when thou sawest him? What said he? How
    looked he? Wherein went he? What makes he here? Did
    he ask for me? Where remains he? How parted he with
    thee? and when shalt thou see him again? Answer me in
    one word.
Cel. You must borrow me Gargantua's mouth first: 'tis a word
    too great for any mouth of this age's size. To say ay and no
    to these particulars is more than to answer in a catechism.
Ros. But doth he know that I am in this forest and in man's
    apparel? Looks he as freshly as he did the day he wrestled?
Cel. It is as easy to count atomies as to resolve the propositions
    of a lover; but take a taste of my finding him, and relish it
    with good observance. I found him under a tree, like a
    dropped acorn.
Ros. It may well be called Jove's tree, when it drops forth such
Cel. Give me audience, good madam.   [fruit.
Ros. Proceed.
Cel. There lay he, stretched along, like a wounded knight.
Ros. Though it be pity to see such a sight, it well becomes the
    ground.
Cel. Cry 'holla' to thy tongue, I prithee; it curvets unseason-
    ably. He was furnished like a hunter.
Ros. O, ominous! he comes to kill my heart.
Cel. I would sing my song without a burden: thou bringest
    me out of tune.
Ros. Do you not know I am a woman? when I think, I must
    speak. Sweet, say on.
Cel. You bring me out. Soft! comes he not here?
              Enter Orlando and Jaques.
Ros. 'Tis he: slink by, and note him.
Jaq. I thank you for your company; but, good faith, I had as
    lief have been myself alone.
Orl. And so had I; but yet, for fashion sake,
    I thank you too for your society.
Jaq. God buy you: let's meet as little as we can.
Orl. I do desire we may be better strangers.   [their barks.
Jaq. I pray you, mar no more trees with writing love-songs in
Orl. I pray you, mar no moe of my verses with reading them
Jaq. Rosalind is your love's name?   [ill-favouredly
Orl. Yes, just.

Jaq. I do not like her name.

Orl. There was no thought of pleasing you when she was

Jaq. What stature is she of?   [christened.

Orl. Just as high as my heart.

Jaq. You are full of pretty answers. Have you not been acquainted with goldsmiths' wives, and conned them out of rings?

Orl. Not so; but I answer you right painted cloth, from whence
you have studied your questions.

Jaq. You have a nimble wit: I think 'twas made of Atalanta's
heels. Will you sit down with me? and we two will rail
against our mistress the world, and all our misery.

Orl. I will chide no breather in the world but myself, against
whom I know most faults.

Jaq. The worst fault you have is to be in love.

Orl. 'Tis a fault I will not change for your best virtue. I am
weary of you.

Jaq. By my troth, I was seeking for a fool when I found you.

Orl. He is drowned in the brook: look but in, and you shall
see him.

Jaq. There I shall see mine own figure.

Orl. Which I take to be either a fool or a cipher.

Jaq. I'll tarry no longer with you: farewell, good Signior Love.

Orl. I am glad of your departure: adieu, good Monsieur
Melancholy.   [*Exit Jaques.*

Ros. [*Aside to Celia*] I will speak to him like a saucy lackey,
and under that habit play the knave with him. Do you hear,

Orl. Very well: what would you?   [forester?

Ros. I pray you, what is 't o' clock?

Orl. You should ask me what time o' day: there's no clock in
the forest.

Ros. Then there is no true lover in the forest; else sighing
every minute and groaning every hour would detect the lazy
foot of Time as well as a clock.   [proper?

Orl. And why not the swift foot of Time? had not that been as

Ros. By no means, sir: Time travels in divers paces with divers
persons. I'll tell you who Time ambles withal, who Time
trots withal, who Time gallops withal and who he stands still

Orl. I prithee, who doth he trot withal?   [withal.

Ros. Marry, he trots hard with a young maid between the
contract of her marriage and the day it is solemnized: if the
interim be but a se'nnight, Time's pace is so hard that it
seems the length of seven year.

Orl. Who ambles Time withal?

Ros. With a priest that lacks Latin, and a rich man that hath
not the gout; for the one sleeps easily because he cannot

study, and the other lives merrily because he feels no pain ;
the one lacking the burden of lean and wasteful learning, the
other knowing no burden of heavy tedious penury : these
Time ambles withal.

Orl. Who doth he gallop withal?

Ros. With a thief to the gallows ; for though he go as softly as
foot can fall, he thinks himself too soon there.

Orl. Who stays it still withal?

Ros. With lawyers in the vacation ; for they sleep between
term and term and then they perceive not how Time moves.

Orl. Where dwell you, pretty youth?

Ros. With this shepherdess, my sister : here in the skirts of the
forest, like fringe upon a petticoat.

Orl. Are you native of this place?

Ros. As the cony that you see dwell where she is kindled.

Orl. Your accent is something finer than you could purchase
in so removed a dwelling.

Ros. I have been told so of many : but indeed an old religious
uncle of mine taught me to speak, who was in his youth an
inland man ; one that knew courtship too well, for there he
fell in love. I have heard him read many lectures against it,
and I thank God I am not a woman, to be touched with so
many giddy offences as he hath generally taxed their whole
sex withal.

Orl. Can you remember any of the principal evils that he laid
to the charge of women?

Ros. There were none principal ; they were all like one another
as half-pence are, every one fault seeming monstrous till his
fellow-fault came to match it.

Orl. I prithee, recount some of them.

Ros. No, I will not cast away my physic but on those that are
sick. There is a man haunts the forest, that abuses our
young plants with carving Rosalind on their barks ; hangs
odes upon hawthorns and elegies on brambles ; all, forsooth,
deifying the name of Rosalind : if I could meet that fancy-
monger, I would give him some good counsel, for he seems
to have the quotidian of love upon him.   [remedy.

Orl. I am he that is so love-shaked : I pray you, tell me your

Ros. There is none of my uncle's marks upon you : he taught
me how to know a man in love ; in which cage of rushes I
am sure you are not prisoner.

Orl. What were his marks?

Ros. A lean cheek, which you have not ; a blue eye and sunken,
which you have not ; an unquestionable spirit, which you
have not ; a beard neglected, which you have not ; but I

pardon you for that, for simply your having in beard is a younger brother's revenue: then your hose should be ungartered, your bonnet unbanded, your sleeve unbuttoned, your shoe untied and every thing about you demonstrating a careless desolation; but you are no such man; you are rather point-device in your accoutrements, as loving yourself than seeming the lover of any other.

Orl. Fair youth, I would I could make thee believe I love.

Ros. Me believe it! you may as soon make her that you love believe it; which, I warrant, she is apter to do than to confess she does: that is one of the points in the which women still give the lie to their consciences. But, in good sooth, are you he that hangs the verses on the trees, wherein Rosalind is so admired?

Orl. I swear to thee, youth, by the white hand of Rosalind, I am that he, that unfortunate he.

Ros. But are you so much in love as your rhymes speak?

Orl. Neither rhyme nor reason can express how much.

Ros. Love is merely a madness; and, I tell you, deserves as well a dark house and a whip as madmen do: and the reason why they are not so punished and cured is, that the lunacy is so ordinary that the whippers are in love too. Yet I profess curing it by counsel.

Orl. Did you ever cure any so?

Ros. Yes, one, and in this manner. He was to imagine me his love, his mistress; and I set him every day to woo me: at which time would I, being but a moonish youth, grieve, be effeminate, changeable, longing and liking; proud, fantastical, apish, shallow, inconstant, full of tears, full of smiles; for every passion something and for no passion truly any thing, as boys and women are for the most part cattle of this colour: would now like him, now loathe him; then entertain him, then forswear him; now weep for him, then spit at him; that I drave my suitor from his mad humour of love to a living humour of madness; which was, to forswear the full stream of the world and to live in a nook merely monastic. And thus I cured him; and this way will I take upon me to wash your liver as clean as a sound sheep's heart, that there shall not be one spot of love in 't.

Orl. I would not be cured, youth.

Ros. I would cure you, if you would but call me Rosalind and come every day to my cote and woo me.

Orl. Now, by the faith of my love, I will: tell me where it is.

Ros. Go with me to it and I 'll show it you: and by the way you shall tell me where in the forest you live. Will you go?

Orl. With all my heart, good youth.

Ros. Nay, you must call me Rosalind.   Come, sister, will you
go?   [*Exeunt.*

SCENE III

The forest.

Enter Touchstone and Audrey; Jaques behind.

Touch. Come apace, good Audrey: I will fetch up your goats,
Audrey.   And how, Audrey? am I the man yet? doth my
simple feature content you?

Aud. Your features! Lord warrant us! what features?

Touch. I am here with thee and thy goats, as the most capricious poet, honest Ovid, was among the Goths.

Jaq. [*Aside*] O knowledge ill-inhabited, worse than Jove in a
thatched house!

Touch. When a man's verses cannot be understood, nor a man's
good wit seconded with the forward child, understanding, it
strikes a man more dead than a great reckoning in a little
room.   Truly, I would the gods had made thee poetical.

Aud. I do not know what 'poetical' is: is it honest in deed and
word? is it a true thing?

Touch. No, truly; for the truest poetry is the most feigning; and
lovers are given to poetry, and what they swear in poetry may
be said as lovers they do feign.

Aud. Do you wish then that the gods had made me poetical?

Touch. I do, truly; for thou swearest to me thou art honest:
now, if thou wert a poet, I might have some hope thou didst

Aud. Would you not have me honest?   [feign.

Touch. No, truly, unless thou wert hard-favoured; for honesty
coupled to beauty is to have honey a sauce to sugar.

Jaq. [*Aside*] A material fool!

Aud. Well, I am not fair; and therefore I pray the gods make
me honest.

Touch. Truly, and to cast away honesty upon a foul slut were
to put good meat into an unclean dish.

Aud. I am not a slut, though I thank the gods I am foul.

Touch. Well, praised be the gods for thy foulness! sluttishness
may come hereafter.   But be it as it may be, I will marry
thee, and to that end I have been with Sir Oliver Martext
the vicar of the next village, who hath promised to meet me
in this place of the forest and to couple us.

Jaq. [*Aside*] I would fain see this meeting.

Aud. Well, the gods give us joy!

Touch. Amen.   A man may, if he were of a fearful heart, stagger
in this attempt; for here we have no temple but the wood, no

151

assembly but horn-beasts. But what though? Courage! As horns are odious, they are necessary. It is said, 'many a man knows no end of his goods:' right; many a man has good horns, and knows no end of them. Well, that is the dowry of his wife; 'tis none of his own getting. Horns?— even so:—poor men alone? No, no; the noblest deer hath them as huge as the rascal. Is the single man therefore blessed? No: as a walled town is more worthier than a village, so is the forehead of a married man more honourable than the bare brow of a bachelor; and by how much defence is better than no skill, by so much is a horn more precious than to want. Here comes Sir Oliver.

Enter Sir Oliver Martext.

Sir Oliver Martext, you are well met: will you dispatch us here under this tree, or shall we go with you to your chapel?

Sir Oli. Is there none here to give the woman?

Touch. I will not take her on gift of any man.

Sir Oli. Truly, she must be given, or the marriage is not lawful.

Jaq. Proceed, proceed: I'll give her.

Touch. Good even, good Master What-ye-call't: how do you, sir? You are very well met: God 'ild you for your last company: I am very glad to see you: even a toy in hand here, sir: nay, pray be covered.

Jaq. Will you be married, motley?

Touch. As the ox hath his bow, sir, the horse his curb and the falcon her bells, so man hath his desires; and as pigeons bill, so wedlock would be nibbling.

Jaq. And will you, being a man of your breeding, be married under a bush like a beggar? Get you to church, and have a good priest that can tell you what marriage is: this fellow will but join you together as they join wainscot; then one of you will prove a shrunk panel, and like green timber warp, warp.

Touch. [*Aside*] I am not in the mind but I were better to be married of him than of another: for he is not like to marry me well; and not being well married, it will be a good excuse for me hereafter to leave my wife.

Jaq. Go thou with me, and let me counsel thee.

Touch. Come, sweet Audrey:
We must be married, or we must live in bawdry.
Farewell, good Master Oliver: not,—
                    O sweet Oliver,
                    O brave Oliver,
            Leave me not behind thee:
but,—

Wind away,
Begone, I say,
I will not to wedding with thee.

[Exeunt Jaques, Touchstone, and Audrey.

Sir Oli. 'Tis no matter : ne'er a fantastical knave of them all shall flout me out of my calling. *[Exit.*

SCENE IV

The forest.
Enter Rosalind and Celia.

Ros. Never talk to me ; I will weep.

Cel. Do, I prithee ; but yet have the grace to consider that tears do not become a man.

Ros. But have I not cause to weep ?

Cel. As good cause as one would desire ; therefore weep.

Ros. His very hair is of the dissembling colour.

Cel. Something browner than Judas's : marry, his kisses are Judas's own children.

Ros. I' faith, his hair is of a good colour. [our.

Cel. An excellent colour : your chestnut was ever the only col-

Ros. And his kissing is as full of sanctity as the touch of holy bread.

Cel. He hath bought a pair of cast lips of Diana : a nun of winter's sisterhood kisses not more religiously ; the very ice of chastity is in them.

Ros. But why did he swear he would come this morning, and comes not ?

Cel. Nay, certainly, there is no truth in him.

Ros. Do you think so ?

Cel. Yes ; I think he is not a pick-purse nor a horse-stealer ; but for his verity in love, I do think him as concave as a covered goblet or a worm-eaten nut.

Ros. Not true in love ?

Cel. Yes, when he is in ; but I think he is not in.

Ros. You have heard him swear downright he was.

Cel. 'Was' is not 'is' : besides, the oath of a lover is no stronger than the word of a tapster ; they are both the confirmer of false reckonings. He attends here in the forest on the Duke your father.

Ros. I met the Duke yesterday and had much question with him : he asked me of what parentage I was ; I told him, of as good as he ; so he laughed and let me go. But what talk we of fathers, when there is such a man as Orlando ?

Cel. O, that's a brave man ! he writes brave verses, speaks brave words, swears brave oaths and breaks them bravely,

quite traverse, athwart the heart of his lover; as a puisny
tilter, that spurs his horse but on one side, breaks his staff
like a noble goose: but all's brave that youth mounts and
folly guides.   Who comes here?

Enter Corin.

Cor. Mistress and master, you have oft inquired
After the shepherd that complain'd of love,
Who you saw sitting by me on the turf,
Praising the proud disdainful shepherdess
That was his mistress.

Cel.   Well, and what of him?

Cor. If you will see a pageant truly play'd,
Between the pale complexion of true love
And the red glow of scorn and proud disdain,
Go hence a little and I shall conduct you,
If you will mark it.

Ros.   O, come, let us remove:
The sight of lovers feedeth those in love.
Bring us to this sight, and you shall say
I'll prove a busy actor in their play.   [*Exeunt.*

SCENE V

Another part of the forest.
Enter Silvius and Phebe.

Sil. Sweet Phebe, do not scorn me; do not, Phebe;
Say that you love me not, but say not so
In bitterness.   The common executioner,
Whose heart the accustom'd sight of death makes hard,
Falls not the axe upon the humbled neck
But first begs pardon: will you sterner be
Than he that dies and lives by bloody drops?

Enter Rosalind, Celia, Corin, behind.

Phe. I would not be thy executioner:
I fly thee, for I would not injure thee.
Thou tell'st me there is murder in mine eye:
'Tis pretty, sure, and very probable,
That eyes, that are the frail'st and softest things,
Who shut their coward gates on atomies,
Should be call'd tyrants, butchers, murderers!
Now I do frown on thee with all my heart;
And if mine eyes can wound, now let them kill thee:
Now counterfeit to swoon; why now fall down;
Or if thou canst not, O, for shame, for shame,
Lie not, to say mine eyes are murderers!
Now show the wound mine eye hath made in thee:

154

Scratch thee but with a pin, and there remains
Some scar of it; lean but upon a rush,
The cicatrice and capable impressure
Thy palm some moment keeps; but now mine eyes,
Which I have darted at thee, hurt thee not,
Nor, I am sure, there is no force in eyes
That can do hurt.

Sil.   O dear Phebe,
If ever,—as that ever may be near,—
Yoo meet in some fresh cheek the power of fancy,
Then shall you know the wounds invisible
That love's keen arrows make.

Phe.   But till that time
Come not thou near me: and when that time comes,
Afflict me with thy mocks, pity me not;
As till that time I shall not pity thee.

Ros. And why, I pray you? Who might be your mother,
That you insult, exult, and all at once,
Over the wretched? What though you have no beauty,—
As, by my faith, I see no more in you
Than without candle may go dark to bed,—
Must you be therefore proud and pitiless?
Why, what means this? Why do you look on me?
I see no more in you than in the ordinary
Of nature's sale-work. 'Od's my little life,
I think she means to tangle my eyes too!
No, faith, proud mistress, hope not after it:
'Tis not your inky brows, your black silk hair,
Your bugle eyeballs, nor your cheek of cream,
That can entame my spirits to your worship.
You foolish shepherd, wherefore do you follow her,
Like foggy south, puffing with wind and rain?
You are a thousand times a properer man
Than she a woman: 'tis such fools as you
That makes the world full of ill-favour'd children:
'Tis not her glass, but you, that flatters her;
And out of you she sees herself more proper
Than any of her lineaments can show her.
But, mistress, know yourself: down on your knees,
And thank heaven, fasting, for a good man's love:
For I must tell you friendly in your ear,
Sell when you can: you are not for all markets:
Cry the man mercy; love him; take his offer:
Foul is most foul, being foul to be a scoffer.
So take her to thee, shepherd: fare you well.

Phe. Sweet youth, I pray you, chide a year together:
   I had rather hear you chide than this man woo.
Ros. He 's fallen in love with your foulness and she 'll fall in
   love with my anger.   If it be so, as fast as she answers thee
   with frowning looks, I 'll sauce her with bitter words.   Why
   look you so upon me?
Phe. For no ill will I bear you.
Ros. I pray you, do not fall in love with me,
   For I am falser than vows made in wine:
   Besides, I like you not.   If you will know my house,
   'Tis at the tuft of olives here hard by.
   Will you go, sister?   Shepherd, ply her hard.
   Come, sister.   Shepherdess, look on him better,
   And be not proud: though all the world could see,
   None could be so abused in sight as he.
   Come, to our flock.   [*Exeunt Rosalind, Celia and Corin.*
Phe. Dead shepherd, now I find thy saw of might,
   ' Who ever loved that loved not at first sight?'
Sil. Sweet Phebe,—
Phe.   Ha, what say'st thou, Silvius?
Sil. Sweet Phebe, pity me.
Phe. Why, I am sorry for thee, gentle Silvius.
Sil. Wherever sorrow is, relief would be:
   If you do sorrow at my grief in love,
   By giving love your sorrow and my grief
   Were both extermined.
Phe. Thou hast my love: is not that neighbourly.
Sil. I would have you.
Phe.   Why, that were covetousness.
   Silvius, the time was that I hated thee,
   And yet it is not that I bear thee love;
   But since that thou canst talk of love so well,
   Thy company, which erst was irksome to me,
   I will endure, and I 'll employ thee too:
   But do not look for further recompense
   Than thine own gladness that thou art employ'd.
Sil. So holy and so perfect is my love,
   And I in such a poverty of grace,
   That I shall think it a most plenteous crop
   To glean the broken ears after the man
   That the main harvest reaps: loose now and then
   A scatter'd smile, and that I 'll live upon.
Phe. Know'st thou the youth that spoke to me erewhile?
Sil. Not very well, but I have met him oft;
   And he hath bought the cottage and the bounds

That the old carlot once was master of
Phe. Think not I love him, though I ask for him ;
  'Tis but a peevish boy ; yet he talks well ;
  But what care I for words ? yet words do well
  When he that speaks them pleases those that hear.
  It is a pretty youth : not very pretty :
  But, sure, he 's proud, and yet his pride becomes him :
  He 'll make a proper man : the best thing in him
  Is his complexion ; and faster than his tongue
  Did make offence his eye did heal it up.
  He is not very tall ; yet for his years he 's tall :
  His leg is but so so ; and yet 'tis well :
  There was a pretty redness in his lip,
  A little riper and more lusty red
  Than that mix'd in his cheek ; 'twas just the difference
  Betwixt the constant red and mingled damask.
  There be some women, Silvius, had they mark'd him
  In parcels as I did, would have gone near
  To fall in love with him : but, for my part,
  I love him not nor hate him not ; and yet
  I have more cause to hate him than to love him :
  For what had he to do to chide at me ?
  He said mine eyes were black and my hair black
  And, now I am remember'd, scorn'd at me :
  I marvel why I answer'd not again :
  But that 's all one ; omittance is no quittance.
  I 'll write to him a very taunting letter,
  And thou shalt bear it : wilt thou, Silvius ?
Sil. Phebe, with all my heart.
Phe.   I 'll write it straight
  The matter 's in my head and in my heart :
  I will be bitter with him and passing short.
  Go with me, Silvius.   *[Exeunt.*

ACT IV—Scene I
The forest.
Enter Rosalind, Celia, and Jaques.

Jaq. I prithee, pretty youth, let me be better acquainted with
Ros. They say you are a melancholy fellow.   [thee.
Jaq. I am so ; I do love it better than laughing.
Ros. Those that are in extremity of either are abominable
fellows, and betray themselves to every modern censure
worse than drunkards.
Jaq. Why, 'tis good to be sad and say nothing.

Ros. Why then, 'tis good to be a post.

Jaq. I have neither the scholar's melancholy, which is emula-
tion ; nor the musician's, which is fantastical ; nor the
courtier's, which is proud ; nor the soldier's, which is
ambitious ; nor the lawyer's, which is politic ; nor the lady's,
which is nice ; nor the lover's, which is all these : but it is a
melancholy of mine own, compounded of many simples,
extracted from many objects ; and indeed the sundry
contemplation of my travels, in which my often rumination
wraps me in a most humorous sadness.

Ros. A traveller ! By my faith, you have great reason to be
sad : I fear you have sold your own lands to see other men's ;
then, to have seen much, and to have nothing, is to have rich
eyes and poor hands.

Jaq. Yes, I have gained my experience.

Ros. And your experience makes you sad : I had rather have a
fool to make me merry than experience to make me sad ;
and to travel for it too !

Enter Orlando.

Orl. Good-day and happiness, dear Rosalind !

Jaq. Nay, then, God buy you, an you talk in blank verse. [*Exit.*

Ros. Farewell, Monsieur Traveller : look you lisp and wear
strange suits ; disable all the benefits of your own country ;
be out of love with your nativity and almost chide God for
making you that countenance you are ; or I will scarce think
you have swam in a gondola. Why, how now, Orlando !
where have you been all this while ? You a lover ! An you
serve me such another trick, never come in my sight more.

Orl. My fair Rosalind, I come within an hour of my promise.

Ros. Break an hour's promise in love ! He that will divide a
minute into a thousand parts, and break but a part of the
thousandth part of a minute in the affairs of love, it may be
said of him that Cupid hath clapped him o' the shoulder, but
I 'll warrant him heart-whole.

Orl. Pardon me, dear Rosalind.

Ros. Nay, an you be so tardy, come no more in my sight : I
had as lief be wooed of a snail.

Orl. Of a snail ?

Ros. Ay, of a snail ; for though he comes slowly, he carries his
house on his head ; a better jointure, I think, than you make
a woman : besides, he brings his destiny with him.

Orl. What 's that ?

Ros. Why, horns, which such as you are fain to be beholding
to your wives for : but he comes armed in his fortune and
prevents the slander of his wife.

Orl. Virtue is no horn-maker ; and my Rosalind is virtuous.

Ros. And I am your Rosalind.

Cel. It pleases him to call you so ; but he hath a Rosalind of a better leer than you.

Ros. Come, woo me, woo me ; for now I am in a holiday humour and like enough to consent. What would you say to me now, an I were your very very Rosalind ?

Orl. I would kiss before I spoke.

Ros. Nay, you were better speak first ; and when you were gravelled for lack of matter, you might take occasion to kiss. Very good orators, when they are out, they will spit ; and for lovers lacking—God warn us !—matter, the cleanliest shift is

Orl. How if the kiss be denied ?   [to kiss.

Ros. Then she puts you to entreaty and there begins new matter.

Orl. Who could be out, being before his beloved mistress ?

Ros. Marry, that should you, if I were your mistress, or I should think my honesty ranker than my wit.

Orl. What, of my suit ?

Ros. Not out of your apparel, and yet out of your suit. Am not I your Rosalind ?

Orl. I take some joy to say you are, because I would be talking of her.

Ros. Well, in her person, I say I will not have you.

Orl. Then in mine own person I die.

Ros. No, faith, die by attorney.   The poor world is almost six thousand years old, and in all this time there was not any man died in his own person, videlicet, in a love-cause. Troilus had his brains dashed out with a Grecian club ; yet he did what he could to die before, and he is one of the patterns of love.   Leander, he would have lived many a fair year, though Hero had turned nun, if it had not been for a hot midsummer night ; for, good youth, he went but forth to wash him in the Hellespont and being taken with the cramp was drowned : and the foolish chroniclers of that age found it was 'Hero of Sestos.'   But these are all lies : men have died from time to time and worms have eaten them, but not for love.

Orl. I would not have my right Rosalind of this mind ; for, I protest, her frown might kill me.

Ros. By this hand, it will not kill a fly.   But come, now I will be your Rosalind in a more coming-on disposition, and ask me what you will, I will grant it.

Orl. Then love me, Rosalind.

Ros. Yes, faith, will I, Fridays and Saturdays and all.

Orl. And wilt thou have me ?

Ros. Ay, and twenty such.

Orl. What sayest thou?

Ros. Are you not good?

Orl. I hope so.

Ros. Why then, can one desire too much of a good thing? Come, sister, you shall be the priest and marry us. Give me your hand, Orlando. What do you say, sister?

Orl. Pray thee, marry us.

Cel. I cannot say the words.

Ros. You must begin, 'Will you, Orlando—'

Cel. Go to. Will you, Orlando, have to wife this Rosalind?

Orl. I will.

Ros. Ay, but when?

Orl. Why now; as fast as she can marry us.

Ros. Then you must say 'I take thee, Rosalind, for wife.

Orl. I take thee, Rosalind, for wife.

Ros. I might ask you for your commission; but I do take thee, Orlando, for my husband: there's a girl goes before the priest; and certainly a woman's thought runs before her

Orl. So do all thoughts; they are winged.   [actions.

Ros. Now tell me how long you would have her after you have possessed her.

Orl. For ever and a day.

Ros. Say 'a day,' without the 'ever'. No, no, Orlando; men are April when they woo, December when they wed: maids are May when they are maids, but the sky changes when they are wives. I will be more jealous of thee than a Barbary cock-pigeon over his hen, more clamorous than a parrot against rain, more new-fangled than an ape, more giddy in my desires than a monkey: I will weep for nothing, like Diana in the fountain, and I will do that when you are disposed to be merry; I will laugh like a hyen, and that when thou art inclined to sleep.

Orl. But will my Rosalind do so?

Ros. By my life, she will do as I do.

Orl. O, but she is wise.

Ros. Or else she could not have the wit to do this: the wiser, the waywarder: make the doors upon a woman's wit and it will out at the casement; shut that and 'twill out at the keyhole; stop that, 'twill fly with the smoke out at the chimney.

Orl. A man that had a wife with such a wit, he might say, 'Wit, whither wilt?'

Ros. Nay, you might keep that check for it till you met your wife's wit going to your neighbour's bed.

Orl. And what wit could wit have to excuse that?

Ros. Marry, to say she came to seek you there. You shall never take her without her answer, unless you take her without her tongue. O, that woman that cannot make her fault her husband's occasion, let her never nurse her child herself, for she will breed it like a fool!

Orl. For these two hours, Rosalind, I will leave thee.

Ros. Alas, dear love, I cannot lack thee two hours!

Orl. I must attend the Duke at dinner: by two o'clock I will be with thee again.

Ros. Ay, go your ways, go your ways; I knew what you would prove: my friends told me as much, and I thought no less: that flattering tongue of yours won me: 'tis but one cast away, and so, come, death! Two o'clock is your hour?

Orl. Ay, sweet Rosalind.

Ros. By my troth, and in good earnest, and so God mend me, and by all pretty oaths that are not dangerous, if you break one jot of your promise or come one minute behind your hour, I will think you the most pathetical break-promise, and the most hollow lover, and the most unworthy of her you call Rosalind, that may be chosen out of the gross band of the unfaithful: therefore beware my censure and keep your promise.

Orl. With no less religion than if thou wert indeed my Rosalind: so adieu.

Ros. Well, Time is the old justice that examines all such offenders, and let Time try: adieu.   [*Exit Orlando.*

Cel. You have simply misused our sex in your love-prate: we must have your doublet and hose plucked over your head, and show the world what the bird hath done to her own nest.

Ros. O coz, coz, coz, my preety little coz, that thou didst know how many fathom deep I am in love! But it cannot be sounded: my affection hath an unknown bottom, like the bay of Portugal.

Cel. Or rather, bottomless; that as fast as you pour affection in, it runs out.

Ros. No, that same wicked bastard of Venus that was begot of thought, conceived of spleen, and born of madness, that blind rascally boy that abuses every one's eyes because his own are out, let him be judge how deep I am in love. I'll tell thee, Aliena, I cannot be out of the sight of Orlando: I'll go find a shadow and sigh till he come.

Cel. And I'll sleep.   [*Exeunt.*

Scene II

The forest.
Enter Jaques, Lords, and Foresters.

Jaq. Which is he that killed the deer?

A Lord. Sir, it was I.

Jaq. Let's present him to the Duke, like a Roman conqueror;
and it would do well to set the deer's horns upon his head,
for a branch of victory.   Have you no song, forester, for this
purpose?

For. Yes, sir.

Jaq. Sing it: 'tis no matter how it be in tune, so it make noise
enough.

Song.

For.   What shall he have that kill'd the deer?
His leather skin and horns to wear.
      Then sing him home:
         [The rest shall bear this burden.
Take thou no scorn to wear the horn;
It was a crest ere thou wast born:
      Thy father's father wore it,
      And thy father bore it:
The horn, the horn, the lusty horn
Is not a thing to laugh to scorn.   *[Exeunt.*

Scene III

The forest.
Enter Rosalind and Celia.

Ros. How say you now?   Is it not past two o'clock; and here
much Orlando!

Cel. I warrant you, with pure love and troubled brain, he hath
ta'en his bow and arrows and is gone forth to sleep.   Look,
who comes here.

Enter Silvius.

Sil. My errand is to you, fair youth;
My gentle Phebe bid me give you this.
I know not the contents; but, as I guess
By the stern brow and waspish action
Which she did use as she was writing of it,
It bears an angry tenour: pardon me;
I am but as a guiltless messenger.

Ros. Patience herself would startle at this letter
And play the swaggerer; bear this, bear all:
She says I am not fair, that I lack manners;
She calls me proud, and that she could not love me,

162

Were man as rare as phœnix. 'Od's my will!
Her love is not the hare that I do hunt:
Why writes she so to me? Well, shepherd, well,
This is a letter of your own device.

Sil. No, I protest, I know not the contents:
Phebe did write it.

Ros.   Come, come, you are a fool,
And turn'd into the extremity of love.
I saw her hand: she has a leathern hand,
A freestone-colour'd hand; I verily did think
That her old gloves were on, but 'twas her hands:
She has a huswife's hand; but that's no matter:
I say she never did invent this letter;
This is a man's invention and his hand.

Sil. Sure, it is hers.

Ros. Why, 'tis a boisterous and a cruel style,
A style for challengers; why, she defies me,
Like Turk to Christian: women's gentle brain
Could not drop forth such giant-rude invention,
Such Ethiope words, blacker in their effect
Than in their countenance. Will you hear the letter?

Sil. So please you, for I never heard it yet;
Yet heard too much of Phebe's cruelty.

Ros. She Phebes me: mark how the tyrant writes.
    [*Reads*]   Art thou god to shepherd turn'd,
            That a maiden's heart hath burn'd?
    Can a woman rail thus?

Sil. Call you this railing?

Ros. [*reads*]
            Why, thy godhead laid apart,
            Warr'st thou with a woman's heart?
    Did you ever hear such railing?
            Whiles the eye of man did woo me,
            That could do no vengeance to me.
    Meaning me a beast.
            If the scorn of your bright eyne
            Have power to raise such love in mine.
            Alack, in me what strange effect
            Would they work in mild aspect!
            Whiles you chide me, I did love;
            How then might your prayers move
            He that brings this love to thee
            Little knows this love in me:
            And by him seal up thy mind;
            Whether that thy youth and kind

163

Will the faithful offer take
Of me and all that I can make;
Or else by him my love deny,
And then I'll study how to die.

Sil. Call you this chiding?

Cel. Alas, poor shepherd!

Ros. Do you pity him? no, he deserves no pity. Wilt thou
love such a woman? What, to make thee an instrument
and play false strains upon thee! not to be endured!
Well, go your way to her, for I see love hath made thee a
tame snake, and say this to her: that if she love me, I
charge her to love thee; if she will not, I will never have
her unless thou entreat for her. If you be a true lover,
hence, and not a word; for here comes more company.

[*Exit Silvius.*

Enter Oliver.

Oli. Good morrow, fair ones: pray you, if you know,
Where in the purlieus of this forest stands
A sheep-cote fenced about with olive-trees?

Cel. West of this place, down in the neighbour bottom:
The rank of osiers by the murmuring stream
Left on your right hand brings you to the place.
But at this hour the house doth keep itself;
There's none within.

Oli. If that an eye may profit by a tongue,
Then should I know you by description;
Such garments and such years: 'The boy is fair,
Of female favour, and bestows himself
Like a ripe sister: the woman low,
And browner than her brother.' Are not you
The owner of the house I did enquire for?

Cel. It is no boast, being ask'd, to say we are.

Oli. Orlando doth commend him to you both,
And to that youth he calls his Rosalind
He sends this bloody napkin. Are you he?

Ros. I am: what must we understand by this?

Oli. Some of my shame; if you will know of me
What man I am, and how, and why, and where
This handkercher was stain'd.

Cel.   I pray you, tell it.

Oli. When last the young Orlando parted from you
He left a promise to return again
Within an hour, and pacing through the forest,
Chewing the food of sweet and bitter fancy,
Lo, what befel! he threw his eye aside,

And mark what object did present itself:
Under an oak, whose boughs were moss'd with age
And high top bald with dry antiquity,
A wretched ragged man, o'ergrown with hair,
Lay sleeping on his back: about his neck
A green and gilded snake had wreathed itself,
Who with her head nimble in threats approach'd
The opening of his mouth; but suddenly,
Seeing Orlando, it unlink'd itself,
And with indented glides did slip away
Into a bush: under which bush's shade
A lioness, with udders all drawn dry,
Lay couching, head on ground, with catlike watch,
When that the sleeping man should stir; for 'tis
The royal disposition of that beast
To prey on nothing that doth seem as dead:
This seen, Orlando did approach the man
And found it was his brother, his elder brother.

Cel. O, I have heard him speak of that same brother:
And he did render him the most unnatural
That lived amongst men.

Oli.   And well he might so do,
For well I know he was unnatural.

Ros. But, to Orlando: did he leave him there,
Food to the suck'd and hungry lioness?

Oli. Twice did he turn his back and purposed so;
But kindness, nobler ever than revenge,
And nature, stronger than his just occasion,
Made him give battle to the lioness,
Who quickly fell before him: in which hurtling
From miserable slumber I awaked.

Cel. Are you his brother?

Ros.   Was 't you he rescued?

Cel. Was 't you that did so oft contrive to kill him?

Oli. 'Twas I; but 'tis not I: I do not shame
To tell you what I was, since my conversion
So sweetly tastes, being the thing I am.

Ros. But, for the bloody napkin?

Oli.   By and by.
When from the first to last betwixt us two
Tears our recountments had most kindly bathed,
As how I came into that desert place;·
In brief, he led me to the gentle Duke,
Who gave me fresh array and entertainment,
Committing me unto my brother's love;

Who led me instantly unto his cave,
There stripp'd himself, and here upon his arm
The lioness had torn some flesh away,
Which all this while had bled; and now he fainted
And cried, in fainting, upon Rosalind.
Brief, I recover'd him, bound up his wound;
And, after some small space, being strong at heart,
He sent me hither, stranger as I am,
To tell this story, that you might excuse
His broken promise, and to give this napkin,
Dyed in his blood, unto the shepherd youth
That he in sport doth call his Rosalind.   [*Rosalind swoons.*

Cel. Why, how now, Ganymede! sweet Ganymede!

Oli. Many will swoon when they do look on blood.

Cel. There is more in it.   Cousin Ganymede!

Oli. Look, he recovers.

Ros. I would I were at home.

Cel.   We 'll lead you thither.
I pray you, will you take him by the arm?   [heart.

Oli. Be of good cheer, youth: you a man! you lack a man's

Ros. I do so, I confess it.   Ah, sirrah, a body would think this was well counterfeited!   I pray you, tell your brother how well I counterfeited.   Heigh-ho!

Oli. This was not counterfeit: there is too great testimony in your complexion that it was a passion of earnest.

Ros. Counterfeit, I assure you.

Oli. Well then, take a good heart and counterfeit to be a man.

Ros. So I do: but, i' faith, I should have been a woman by right.

Cel. Come, you look paler and paler: pray you, draw homewards. Good sir, go with us.

Oli. That will I, for I must bear answer back
How you excuse my brother, Rosalind.

Ros. I shall devise something: but, I pray you, commend my counterfeiting to him.   Will you go?   [*Exeunt.*

ACT V—Scene I

The forest.
Enter Touchstone and Audrey.

Touch. We shall find a time, Audrey; patience, gentle Audrey.

Aud. Faith, the priest was good enough, for all the old gentleman's saying.

Touch. A most wicked Sir Oliver, Audrey, a most vile Martext.

But, Audrey, there is a youth here in the forest lays claim to
you.

Aud. Ay, I know who 'tis : he hath no interest in me in the
world : here comes the man you mean.

Touch. It is meat and drink to me to see a clown : by my troth,
we that have good wits have much to answer for ; we shall
be flouting ; we cannot hold.

Enter William.

Will. Good even, Audrey.

Aud. God ye good even, William.

Will. And good even to you, sir.

Touch. Good even, gentle friend.   Cover thy head, cover thy
head ; nay, prithee, be covered.   How old are you, friend ?

Will. Five and twenty, sir.

Touch. A ripe age.   Is thy name William ?

Will. William, sir.

Touch. A fair name.   Wast born i' the forest here ?

Will. Ay, sir, I thank God.

Touch. 'Thank God ;' a good answer.   Art rich ?

Will. Faith, sir, so so.

Touch. 'So so' is good, very good, very excellent good ; and yet
it is not ; it is but so so.   Art thou wise ?

Will. Ay, sir, I have a pretty wit.

Touch. Why, thou sayest well.   I do now remember a saying,
'The fool doth think he is wise, but the wise man knows
himself to be a fool.'   The heathen philosopher, when he
had a desire to eat a grape, would open his lips when he put
it into his mouth ; meaning thereby that grapes were made to
eat and lips to open.   You do love this maid ?

Will. I do, sir.

Touch. Give me your hand.   Art thou learned ?

Will. No, sir.

Touch. Then learn this of me : to have, is to have ; for it is a
figure in rhetoric that drink, being poured out of a cup into
a glass, by filling the one doth empty the other ; for all your
writers do consent that ipse is he : now you are not ipse, for
I am he.

Will. Which he, sir ?

Touch. He, sir, that must marry this woman.   Therefore, you
clown, abandon,—which is in the vulgar leave,—the society,
—which in the boorish is company,—of this female,—which
in the common is woman ; which together is, abandon the
society of this female, or, clown, thou perishest ; or, to thy
better understanding, diest ; or, to wit, I kill thee, make thee
away, translate thy life into death, thy liberty into bondage: I

will deal in poison with thee, or in bastinado, or in steel ; I
will bandy with thee in faction ; I will o'er-run thee with
policy ; I will kill thee a hundred and fifty ways : therefore
tremble, and depart.

Aud. Do, good William.

Will. God rest you merry, sir.   [*Exit.*

Enter Corin.

Cor. Our master and mistress seeks you ; come, away, away !

Touch. Trip, Audrey ! trip, Audrey !   I attend, I attend.

[*Exeunt.*

SCENE II

The forest.
Enter Orlando and Oliver.

Orl. Is 't possible that on so little acquaintance you should like
her ? that but seeing you should like her ? and loving woo ?
and, wooing, she should grant ? and will you persever to
enjoy her ?

Oli. Neither call the giddiness of it in question, the poverty of
her, the small acquaintance, my sudden wooing, nor her
sudden consenting ; but say with me, I love Aliena ; say
with her that she loves me ; consent with both that we may
enjoy each other : it shall be to your good ; for my father's
house and all the revenue that was old Sir Rowland's will I
estate upon you, and here live and die a shepherd.

Orl. You have my consent.   Let your wedding be to-morrow :
thither will I invite the Duke and all 's contented followers.
Go you and prepare Aliena ; for look you, here comes my
Rosalind.

Enter Rosalind.

Ros. God save you, brother.

Oli. And you, fair sister.   [*Exit.*

Ros. O, my dear Orlando, how it grieves me to see thee wear
thy heart in a scarf !

Orl. It is my arm.

Ros. I thought thy heart had been wounded with the claws of

Orl. Wounded it is, but with the eyes of a lady.   [a lion.

Ros. Did your brother tell you how I counterfeited to swoon
when he showed me your handkercher ?

Orl. Ay, and greater wonders than that.

Ros. O, I know where you are : nay, 'tis true : there was never
any thing so sudden but the fight of two rams, and Cæsar's
thrasonical brag of ' I came, saw, and overcame :' for your
brother and my sister no sooner met but they looked ; no
sooner looked but they loved ; no sooner loved but they

sighed; no sooner sighed but they asked one another the reason; no sooner knew the reason but they sought the remedy: and in these degrees have they made a pair of stairs to marriage which they will climb incontinent, or else be incontinent before marriage: they are in the very wrath of love and they will together; clubs cannot part them.

Orl. They shall be married to-morrow, and I will bid the Duke to the nuptial. But, O, how bitter a thing it is to look into happiness, through another man's eyes! By so much the more shall I to-morrow be at the height of heart-heaviness, by how much I shall think my brother happy in having what he wishes for.

Ros. Why, then, to-morrow I cannot serve your turn for

Orl. I can live no longer by thinking.   [Rosalind?

Ros. I will weary you then no longer with idle talking. Know of me then, for now I speak to some purpose, that I know you are a gentleman of good conceit: I speak not this that you should bear a good opinion of my knowledge, insomuch I say I know you are; neither do I labour for a greater esteem than may in some little measure draw a belief from you, to do yourself good and not to grace me. Believe then, if you please, that I can do strange things: I have, since I was three year old, conversed with a magician, most profound in his art and yet not damnable. If you do love Rosalind so near the heart as your gesture cries it out, when your brother marries Aliena, shall you marry her: I know into what straits of fortune she is driven; and it is not impossible to me, if it appear not inconvenient to you, to set her before your eyes to-morrow human as she is and without any

Orl. Speakest thou in sober meanings?   [danger.

Ros. By my life, I do; which I tender dearly, though I say I am a magician. Therefore, put you in your best array; bid your friends; for if you will be married to-morrow, you shall; and to Rosalind, if you will.

Enter Silvius and Phebe.

Look, here comes a lover of mine and a lover of hers.

Phe. Youth, you have done me much ungentleness,
To show the letter that I writ to you.

Ros. I care not if I have: it is my study
To seem despiteful and ungentle to you:
You are there followed by a faithful shepherd;
Look upon him, love him; he worships you.

Phe. Good shepherd, tell this youth what 'tis to love.

Sil. It is to be all made of sighs and tears;
And so am I for Phebe.

Phe. And I for Ganymede.

Orl. And I for Rosalind.

Ros. And I for no woman.

Sil. It is to be all made of faith and service;
  And so am I for Phebe.

Phe. And I for Ganymede.

Orl. And I for Rosalind.

Ros. And I for no woman.

Sil. It is to be all made of fantasy,
  All made of passion, and all made of wishes;
  All adoration, duty, and observance,
  All humbleness, all patience, and impatience,
  All purity, all trial, all observance;
  And so am I for Phebe.

Phe. And so am I for Ganymede.

Orl. And so am I for Rosalind.

Ros. And so am I for no woman.

Phe. If this be so, why blame you me to love you?

Sil. If this be so, why blame you me to love you?

Orl. If this be so, why blame you me to love you?

Ros. Who do you speak to, 'Why blame you me to love you?'

Orl. To her that is not here, nor doth not hear.

Ros. Pray you, no more of this; 'tis like the howling of Irish
  wolves against the moon. [*To Sil.*] I will help you, if I
  can: [*To Phe.*] I would love you, if I could.   To-morrow
  meet me all together. [*To Phe.*] I will marry you, if ever I
  marry woman, and I'll be married to-morrow: [*To Orl.*] I
  will satisfy you, if ever I satisfied man, and you shall be
  married to-morrow: [*To Sil.*] I will content you, if what
  pleases you contents you, and you shall be married to-
  morrow. [*To Orl.*] As you love Rosalind, meet: [*To Sil.*]
  as you love Phebe, meet: and as I love no woman, I'll
  meet.   So, fare you well: I have left you commands.

Sil. I'll not fail, if I live.

Phe. Nor I.

Orl. Nor I.   [*Exeunt.*

SCENE III

The forest.

Enter Touchstone and Audrey.

Touch. To-morrow is the joyful day, Audrey; to-morrow will
  we be married.

Aud. I do desire it with all my heart; and I hope it is no dishonest desire to desire to be a woman of the world.   Here
  come two of the banished Duke's pages.

Enter two Pages.

First Page. Well met, honest gentleman.

Touch. By my troth, well met. Come, sit, sit, and a song.

Sec. Page. We are for you: sit i' the middle.

First Page. Shall we clap into 't roundly, without hawking or spitting or saying we are hoarse, which are the only prologues to a bad voice? [on a horse.

Sec. Page. I' faith, i' faith; and both in a tune, like two gipsies

SONG.

It was a lover and his lass,
    With a hey, and a ho, and a hey nonino,
That o'er the green corn-field did pass
    In the spring time, the only pretty ring time,
When birds do sing, hey ding a ding, ding:
    Sweet lovers love the spring.

Between the acres of the rye,
    With a hey, and a ho, and a hey nonino,
These pretty country folks would lie,
    In spring time, &c.

This carol they began that hour,
    With a hey, and a ho, and a hey nonino,
How that a life was but a flower
    In spring time, &c.

And therefore take the present time,
    With a hey, and a ho, and a hey nonino;
For love is crowned with the prime
    In spring time, &c.

Touch. Truly, young gentlemen, though there was no great matter in the ditty, yet the note was very untuneable.

First Page. You are deceived, sir: we kept time, we lost not our time.

Touch. By my troth, yes; I count it but time lost to hear such a foolish song. God be wi' you: and God mend your voices! Come, Audrey. [*Exeunt.*

SCENE IV
The forest.
Enter Duke senior, Amiens, Jaques, Orlando, Oliver, and Celia.

Duke S. Dost thou believe, Orlando, that the boy
Can do all this that he hath promised?

Orl. I sometimes do believe, and sometimes do not;
    As those that fear they hope, and know they fear.

Enter Rosalind, Silvius, and Phebe.

Ros. Patience once more, whiles our compact is urged:
    You say, if I bring in your Rosalind,
    You will bestow her on Orlando here?
Duke S. That would I, had I kingdoms to give with her.
Ros. And you say, you will have her, when I bring her.
Orl. That would I, were I of all kingdoms king.
Ros. You say, you'll marry me, if I be willing?
Phe. That will I, should I die the hour after.
Ros. But if you do refuse to marry me,
    You'll give yourself to this most faithful shepherd?
Phe. So is the bargain.
Ros. You say, that you'll have Phebe, if she will?
Sil. Though to have her and death were both one thing.
Ros. I have promised to make all this matter even.
    Keep you your word, O Duke, to give your daughter;
    You yours, Orlando, to receive his daughter:
    Keep your word, Phebe, that you'll marry me,
    Or else refusing me, to wed this shepherd:
    Keep your word, Silvius, that you'll marry her,
    If she refuse me: and from hence I go,
    To make these doubts all even.

[*Exeunt Rosalind and Celia.*

Duke S. I do remember in this shepherd boy
    Some lively touches of my daughter's favour.
Orl. My lord, the first time that I ever saw him
    Methought he was a brother to your daughter:
    But, my good lord, this boy is forest-born,
    And hath been tutor'd in the rudiments
    Of many desperate studies by his uncle,
    Whom he reports to be a great magician,
    Obscured in the circle of this forest.

Enter Touchstone and Audrey.

Jaq. There is, sure, another flood toward, and these couples are
    coming to the ark. Here comes a pair of very strange beasts,
    which in all tongues are called fools.
Touch. Salutation and greeting to you all!
Jaq. Good my lord, bid him welcome: this is the motley-
    minded gentleman that I have so often met in the forest:
    he hath been a courtier, he swears.
Touch. If any man doubt that, let him put me to my purgation.
    I have trod a measure; I have flattered a lady; I have been
    politic with my friend, smooth with mine enemy; I have un-

done three tailors; I have had four quarrels, and like to have
Jaq. And how was that ta'en up?   [fought one.
Touch. Faith, we met, and found the quarrel was upon the
seventh cause.
Jaq. How seventh cause? Good my lord, like this fellow.
Duke S. I like him very well.
Touch. God 'ild you, sir; I desire you of the like. I press in
here, sir, amongst the rest of the country copulatives, to
swear and to forswear; according as marriage binds and
blood breaks: a poor virgin, sir, an ill-favoured thing, sir,
but mine own; a poor humour of mine, sir, to take that that
no man else will: rich honesty dwells like a miser, sir, in a
poor house; as your pearl in your foul oyster.
Duke S. By my faith, he is very swift and sententious.
Touch. According to the fool's bolt, sir, and such dulcet diseases.
Jaq. But, for the seventh cause; how did you find the quarrel
on the seventh cause?
Touch. Upon a lie seven times removed:—bear your body
more seeming, Audrey:—as thus, sir. I did dislike the
cut of a certain courtier's beard: he sent me word, if I said
his beard was not cut well, he was in the mind it was: this
is called the Retort Courteous. If I sent him word again
'it was not well cut,' he would send me word, he cut it to
please himself: this is called the Quip Modest. If again 'it
was not well cut,' he disabled my judgement: this is called
the Reply Churlish. If again 'it was not well cut,' he would
answer, I spake not true: this is called the Reproof Valiant.
If again 'it was not well cut,' he would say, I lie: this is
called the Countercheck Quarrelsome: and so to the Lie
Circumstantial and the Lie Direct.
Jaq. And how oft did you say his beard was not well cut?
Touch. I durst go no further than the Lie Circumstantial, nor
he durst not give me the Lie Direct; and so we measured
swords and parted.
Jaq. Can you nominate in order now the degrees of the lie?
Touch. O sir, we quarrel in print, by the book; as you have
books for good manners: I will name you the degrees. The
first, the Retort Courteous; the second, the Quip Modest;
the third, the Reply Churlish; the fourth, the Reproof
Valiant; the fifth, the Countercheck Quarrelsome; the sixth,
the Lie with Circumstance; the seventh, the Lie Direct. All
these you may avoid but the Lie Direct; and you may avoid
that too, with an If. I knew when seven justices could not
take up a quarrel, but when the parties were met themselves,
one of them thought but of an If, as, 'If you said so, then I

said so;' and they shook hands and swore brothers.   Your
   If is the only peace-maker; much virtue in If.
Jaq. Is not this a rare fellow, my lord? he's as good at any
   thing and yet a fool.
Duke S. He uses his folly like a stalking-horse and under the
   presentation of that he shoots his wit.

> *Enter Hymen, Rosalind, and Celia.*
> *Still Music.*

Hym.   Then is there mirth in heaven,
                  When earthly things made even
                       Atone together.
                  Good Duke, receive thy daughter:
                  Hymen from heaven brought her,
                       Yea, brought her hither,
                  That thou mightst join her hand with his
                  Whose heart within his bosom is.

Ros. To you I give myself, for I am yours.
   To you I give myself, for I am yours.
Duke S. If there be truth in sight, you are my daughter.
Orl. If there be truth in sight, you are my Rosalind.
Phe.   If sight and shape be true,
                  Why then, my love adieu!

Ros. I'll have no father, if you be not he:
   I'll have no husband, if you be not he:
   Nor ne'er wed woman, if you be not she.
Hym.   Peace, ho! I bar confusion:
                  'Tis I must make conclusion
                       Of these most strange events:
                  Here's eight that must take hands
                  To join in Hymen's bands,
                       If truth holds true contents.
                  You and you no cross shall part:
                  You and you are heart in heart:
                  You to his love must accord,
                  Or have a woman to your lord:
                  You and you are sure together,
                  As the winter to foul weather.
                  Whiles a wedlock-hymn we sing,
                  Feed yourselves with questioning;
                  That reason wonder may diminish,
                  How thus we met, and these things finish.

SONG.

Wedding is great Juno's crown:
   O blessed bond of board and bed!

> 'Tis Hymen peoples every town ;
> High wedlock then be honoured :
> Honour, high honour and renown,
> To Hymen, god of every town !

Duke S. O my dear niece, welcome thou art to me !
Even daughter, welcome, in no less degree.
Phe. I will not eat my word, now thou art mine ;
Thy faith my fancy to thee doth combine.

Enter Jaques de Boys.

Jaq. de B. Let me have audience for a word or two :
I am the second son of old Sir Rowland,
That bring these tidings to this fair assembly.
Duke Frederick, hearing how that every day
Men of great worth resorted to this forest,
Address'd a mighty power ; which were on foot,
In his own conduct, purposely to take
His brother here and put him to the sword :
And to the skirts of this wild wood he came ;
Where meeting with an old religious man,
After some question with him, was converted
Both from his enterprise and from the world ;
His crown bequeathing to his banish'd brother,
And all their lands restored to them again
That were with him exiled.   This to be true,
I do engage my life.
Duke S.   Welcome, young man ;
Thou offer'st fairly to thy brothers' wedding :
To one his lands withheld ; and to the other
A land itself at large, a potent dukedom.
First, in this forest let us do those ends
That here were well begun and well begot :
And after, every of this happy number,
That have endured shrewd days and nights with us,
Shall share the good of our returned fortune,
According to the measure of their states.
Meantime, forget this new-fallen dignity,
And fall into our rustic revelry.
Play, music !   And you, brides and bridegrooms all,
With measure heap'd in joy, to the measures fall.
Jaq. Sir, by your patience.   If I heard you rightly,
The Duke hath put on a religious life
And thrown into neglect the pompous court ?
Jaq. de B. He hath.

Jaq. To him will I : out of these convertites
　There is much matter to be heard and learn'd.
[*To Duke S.*] You to your former honour I bequeath ;
　Your patience and your virtue well deserves it :
[*To Orl.*] You to a love, that your true faith doth merit :
[*To Oli.*] You to your land, and love, and great allies :
[*To Sil.*] You to a long and well-deserved bed :
[*To Touch.*] And you to wrangling ; for thy loving voyage
　Is but for two months victuall'd.　So, to your pleasures :
　I am for other than for dancing measures.
Duke S. Stay, Jaques, stay.
Jaq. To see no pastime I : what you would have
　I 'll stay to know at your abandon'd cave.　　　　　[*Exit.*
Duke S. Proceed, proceed : we will begin these rites,
　As we do trust they 'll end, in true delights.　　　[*A dance.*

EPILOGUE

Ros. It is not the fashion to see the lady the epilogue ; but it
is no more unhandsome than to see the lord the prologue.
If it be true that good wine needs no bush, 'tis true that a
good play needs no epilogue : yet to good wine they do use
good bushes ; and good plays prove the better by the help
of good epilogues.　What a case am I in then, that am
neither a good epilogue, nor cannot insinuate with you in the
behalf of a good play !　I am not furnished like a beggar,
therefore to beg will not become me : my way is to conjure
you ; and I 'll begin with the women.　I charge you, O
women, for the love you bear to men, to like as much of this
play as please you : and I charge you, O men, for the love
you bear to women,—as I perceive by your simpering, none
of you hates them,—that between you and the women the
play may please.　If I were a woman I would kiss as many
of you as had beards that pleased me, complexions that
liked me and breaths that I defied not : and, I am sure, as
many as have good beards or good faces or sweet breaths
will, for my kind offer, when I make curtsy, bid me farewell.
　　　　　　　　　　　　　　　　　　　　　　　[*Exeunt.*

THE TAMING OF THE SHREW

DRAMATIS PERSONÆ

A Lord.
CHRISTOPHER SLY, *a tinker.* } *Persons in the*
Hostess, Page, Players, *Induction.*
   Huntsmen and Servants.

GREMIO, } *suitors to Bianca.*
HORTENSIO,
TRANIO, } *servants to Lucentio.*
BIONDELLO,
GRUMIO, } *servants to Petruchio.*
CURTIS,
A Pedant.

BAPTISTA, *a rich gentleman of Padua.*
VINCENTIO, *an old gentleman of Pisa.*
LUCENTIO, *son to Vincentio, in love with*
   Bianca.
PETRUCHIO, *a gentleman of Verona, a*
   suitor to Katharina.

KATHARINA, *the shrew,* } *daughters to*
BIANCA, } *Baptista*
Widow.

Tailor, Haberdasher, and Servants attending on Baptista and Petruchio.
SCENE: *Padua, and Petruchio's country house.*

INDUCTION—SCENE I

Before an alehouse on a heath.
Enter Hostess and Sly.

Sly. I 'll pheeze you, in faith.

Host. A pair of stocks, you rogue!

Sly. Y' are a baggage: the Slys are no rogues; look in the
chronicles; we came in with Richard Conqueror. Therefore paucas pallabris; let the world slide: sessa!

Host. You will not pay for the glasses you have burst?

Sly. No, not a denier. Go by, Jeronimy: go to thy cold bed,
and warm thee.

Host. I know my remedy; I must go fetch the thirdborough.
                                         [Exit.

Sly. Third, or fourth, or fifth borough, I 'll answer him by law:
I 'll not budge an inch, boy: let him come, and kindly.
                                         [Falls asleep.

Horns winded. Enter a Lord from hunting, with his train.

Lord. Huntsman, I charge thee, tender well my hounds:
Brach Merriman, the poor cur is emboss'd;
And couple Clowder with the deep-mouth'd brach.
Saw'st thou not, boy, how Silver made it good
At the hedge-corner, in the coldest fault?
I would not lose the dog for twenty pound.

First Hun. Why, Belman is as good as he, my lord;
He cried upon it at the merest loss,
And twice to-day picked out the dullest scent:
Trust me, I take him for the better dog.

Lord. Thou art a fool: if Echo were as fleet,
I would esteem him worth a dozen such.
But sup them well and look unto them all:
To-morrow I intend to hunt again.

First Hun. I will, my lord.

Lord. What's here? one dead, or drunk? See, doth he
    breathe?
Sec. Hun. He breathes, my lord. Were he not warm'd with ale,
    This were a bed but cold to sleep so soundly.
Lord. O monstrous beast! how like a swine he lies!
    Grim death, how foul and loathsome is thine image!
    Sirs, I will practise on this drunken man.
    What think you, if he were convey'd to bed,
    Wrapp'd in sweet clothes, rings put upon his fingers,
    A most delicious banquet by his bed,
    And brave attendants near him when he wakes,
    Would not the beggar then forget himself?
First Hun. Believe me, lord, I think he cannot choose.
Sec. Hun. It would seem strange unto him when he waked.
Lord. Even as a flattering dream or worthless fancy.
    Then take him up and manage well the jest:
    Carry him gently to my fairest chamber
    And hang it round with all my wanton pictures:
    Balm his foul head in warm distilled waters
    And burn sweet wood to make the lodging sweet:
    Procure me music ready when he wakes,
    To make a dulcet and a heavenly sound;
    And if he chance to speak, be ready straight
    And with a low submissive reverence
    Say 'What is it your honour will command?'
    Let one attend him with a silver basin
    Full of rose-water and bestrew'd with flowers;
    Another bear the ewer, the third a diaper,
    And say 'Will 't please your lordship cool your hands?'
    Some one be ready with a costly suit,
    And ask him what apparel he will wear;
    Another tell him of his hounds and horse,
    And that his lady mourns at his disease:
    Persuade him that he hath been lunatic;
    And when he says he is, say that he dreams,
    For he is nothing but a mighty lord.
    This do and do it kindly, gentle sirs:
    It will be pastime passing excellent,
    If it be husbanded with modesty.
First Hun. My lord, I warrant you we will play our part,
    As he shall think by our true diligence
    He is no less than what we say he is.
Lord. Take him up gently and to bed with him;
    And each one to his office when he wakes.
                    [*Some bear out Sly.   A trumpet sounds.*

Sirrah, go see what trumpet 'tis that sounds :
[Exit Servingman.

Belike, some noble gentleman that means,
Travelling some journey, to repose him here.
Re-enter Servingman.

How now ! who is it?
Serv. An't please your honour, players
That offer service to your lordship.
Lord. Bid them come near.
Enter Players.

Now, fellows, you are welcome.
Players. We thank your honour.
Lord. Do you intend to stay with me to-night ?
A Player. So please your lordship to accept our duty.
Lord. With all my heart. This fellow I remember,
Since once he play'd a farmer's eldest son :
'Twas where you woo'd the gentlewoman so well :
I have forgot your name ; but, sure, that part
Was aptly fitted and naturally perform'd.
A Player. I think 'twas Soto that your honour means
Lord. 'Tis very true : thou didst it excellent.
Well, you are come to me in happy time ;
The rather for I have some sport in hand
Wherein your cunning can assist me much.
There is a lord will hear you play to-night :
But I am doubtful of your modesties ;
Lest over-eyeing of his odd behaviour,—
For yet his honour never heard a play,—
You break into some merry passion
And so offend him ; for I tell you, sirs,
If you should smile he grows impatient.
A Player. Fear not, my lord : we can contain ourselves,
Were he the veriest antic in the world.
Lord. Go, sirrah, take them to the buttery,
And give them friendly welcome every one :
Let them want nothing that my house affords.
[Exit one with the Players.

Sirrah, go you to Barthol'mew my page,
And see him dress'd in all suits like a lady :
That done, conduct him to the drunkard's chamber ;
And call him ' madam,' do him obeisance.
Tell him from me, as he will win my love,
He bear himself with honourable action,
Such as he hath observed in noble ladies
Unto their lords, by them accomplished :

179

Such duty to the drunkard let him do
With soft low tongue and lowly courtesy,
And say, 'What is 't your honour will command,
Wherein your lady and your humble wife
May show her duty and make known her love ? '
And then with kind embracements, tempting kisses,
And with declining head into his bosom,
Bid him shed tears, as being overjoy'd
To see her noble lord restored to health,
Who for this seven years hath esteemed him
No better than a poor and loathsome beggar :
And if the boy have not a woman's gift
To rain a shower of commanded tears,
An onion will do well for such a shift,
Which in a napkin being close convey'd
Shall in despite enforce a watery eye.
See this dispatch'd with all the haste thou canst :
Anon I 'll give thee more instructions.　[*Exit a Servingman.*
I know the boy will well usurp the grace,
Voice, gait and action of a gentlewoman :
I long to hear him call the drunkard husband,
And how my men will stay themselves from laughter
When they do homage to this simple peasant.
I 'll in to counsel them ; haply my presence
May well abate the over-merry speen
Which otherwise would grow into extremes.　　　[*Exeunt.*

SCENE II

A bedchamber in the Lord's house.

*Enter aloft Sly, with Attendant; some with apparel, others
with basin and ewer and other appurtenances, and Lord.*

Sly. For God's sake, a pot of small ale.
First Serv. Will 't please your lordship drink a cup of sack ?
Sec. Serv. Will 't please your honour taste of these conserves ?
Third Serv. What raiment will your honour wear to-day ?
Sly. I am Christophero Sly ; call not me 'honour' nor 'lord-
ship :' I ne'er drank sack in my life ; and if you give me
any conserves, give me conserves of beef : ne'er ask me
what raiment I 'll wear ; for I have no more doublets than
backs, no more stockings than legs, nor no more shoes
than feet ; nay, sometime more feet than shoes, or such
shoes as my toes look through the overleather.
Lord. Heaven cease this idle humour in your honour !
O, that a mighty man of such descent,
Of such possessions and so high esteem,

Should be infused with so foul a spirit !

Sly. What, would you make me mad? Am not I Christopher
Sly, old Sly's son of Burton-heath, by birth a pedlar, by
education a card-maker, by transmutation a bear-herd, and
now by present profession a tinker? Ask Marian Hacket,
the fat ale-wife of Wincot, if she know me not : if she say
I am not fourteen pence on the score for sheer ale, score
me up for the lyingest knave in Christendom. What! I
am not bestraught : here 's—

Third Serv. O, this it is that makes your lady mourn !

Sec. Serv. O, this it is that makes your servants droop !

Lord. Hence comes it that your kindred shuns your house,
As beaten hence by your strange lunacy.
O noble lord, bethink thee of thy birth,
Call home thy ancient thoughts from banishment,
And banish hence these abject lowly dreams.
Look how thy servants do attend on thee,
Each in his office ready at thy beck.
Wilt thou have music? hark ! Apollo plays,   [*Music.*
And twenty caged nightingales do sing :
Or wilt thou sleep? we 'll have thee to a couch
Softer and sweeter than the lustful bed
On purpose trimm'd up for Semiramis.
Say thou wilt walk ; we will bestrew the ground :
Or wilt thou ride? thy horses shall be trapp'd,
Their harness studded all with gold and pearl.
Dost thou love hawking? thou hast hawks will soar
Above the morning lark : or wilt thou hunt?
Thy hounds shall make the welkin answer them,
And fetch shrill echoes from the hollow earth.

First Serv. Say thou wilt course ; thy greyhounds are as swift
As breathed stags, ay, fleeter than the roe.

Sec. Serv. Dost thou love pictures? we will fetch thee straight
Adonis painted by a running brook,
And Cytherea all in sedges hid,
Which seem to move and wanton with her breath,
Even as the waving sedges play with wind.

Lord. We 'll show thee Io as she was a maid ;
And how she was beguiled and surprised,
As lively painted as the deed was done.

Third Serv. Or Daphne roaming through a thorny wood,
Scratching her legs that one shall swear she bleeds,
And at that sight shall sad Apollo weep,
So workmanly the blood and tears are drawn.

Lord. Thou art a lord and nothing but a lord :

Thou hast a lady far more beautiful
Than any woman in this waning age.

First Serv. And till the tears that she hath shed for thee
Like envious floods o'er-run her lovely face,
She was the fairest creature in the world ;
And yet she is inferior to none.

Sly. Am I a lord? and have I such a lady?
Or do I dream? or have I dream'd till now?
I do not sleep : I see, I hear, I speak ;
I smell sweet savours and I feel soft things :
Upon my life, I am a lord indeed,
And not a tinker nor Christophero Sly.
Well, bring our lady hither to our sight ;
And once again, a pot o' the smallest ale.

Sec. Serv. Will 't please your mightiness to wash your hands?
O, how we joy to see your wit restored !
O, that once more you knew but what you are !
These fifteen years you have been in a dream ;
Or when you waked, so waked as if you slept.

Sly. These fifteen years ! by my fay, a goodly nap.
But did I never speak of all that time?

First Serv. O, yes, my lord, but very idle words :
For though you lay here in this goodly chamber,
Yet would you say ye were beaten out of door ;
And rail upon the hostess of the house ;
And say you would present her at the leet,
Because she brought stone jugs and no seal'd quarts :
Sometimes you would call out for Cicely Hacket.

Sly. Ay, the woman's maid of the house.

Third Serv. Why, sir, you know no house nor no such maid,
Nor no such men as you have reckon'd up,
As Stephen Sly and old John Naps of Greece
And Peter Turph and Henry Pimpernell
And twenty more such names and men as these
Which never were nor no man ever saw.

Sly. Now Lord be thanked for my good amends !

All. Amen.

Sly. I thank thee : thou shalt not lose by it.

　　　　　Enter the Page as a lady, attended.

Page. How fares my noble lord?

Sly. Marry, I fare well ; for here is cheer enough.
Where is my wife?

Page Here, noble lord : what is thy will with her?

Sly. Are you my wife and will not call me husband?
My men should call me ' lord : ' I am your goodman.

Page. My husband and my lord, my lord and husband;
    I am your wife in all obedience.
Sly. I know it well. What must I call her?
Lord. Madam.
Sly. Al'ce madam, or Joan madam?
Lord. 'Madam' and nothing else: so lords call ladies.
Sly. Madam wife, they say that I have dream'd
    And slept above some fifteen year or more.
Page. Ay, and the time seems thirty unto me,
    Being all this time abandon'd from your bed.
Sly. 'Tis much. Servants, leave me and her alone.
    Madam, undress you and come now to bed.
Page. Thrice-noble lord, let me entreat of you
    To pardon me yet for a night or two;
    Or, if not so, until the sun be set:
    For your physicians have expressly charged,
    In peril to incur your former malady,
    That I should yet absent me from your bed:
    I hope this reason stands for my excuse.
Sly. Ay, it stands so that I may hardly tarry so long. But I
    would be loath to fall into my dreams again: I will therefore
    tarry in despite of the flesh and the blood.
                Enter a Messenger.
Mess. Your honour's players, hearing your amendment,
    Are come to play a pleasant comedy;
    For so your doctors hold it very meet,
    Seeing too much sadness hath congeal'd your blood,
    And melancholy is the nurse of frenzy:
    Therefore they thought it good you hear a play
    And frame your mind to mirth and merriment,
    Which bars a thousand harms and lengthens life.
Sly. Marry, I will, let them play it. Is not a comonty a Christ-
    mas gambold or a tumbling-trick?
Page. No, my good lord; it is more pleasing stuff.
Sly. What, household stuff?
Page. It is a kind of history.
Sly. Well, we'll see't. Come, madam wife, sit by my side and
    let the world slip: we shall ne'er be younger.
                Flourish.

ACT I—Scene I
Padua. A public place.
Enter Lucentio and his man Tranio.

Luc. Tranio, since for the great desire I had
    To see fair Padua, nursery of arts,

I am arrived for fruitful Lombardy,
The pleasant garden of great Italy;
And by my father's love and leave am arm'd
With his good will and thy good company,
My trusty servant, well approved in all,
Here let us breathe and haply institute
A course of learning and ingenious studies.
Pisa renowned for grave citizens
Gave me my being and my father first,
A merchant of great traffic through the world,
Vincentio, come of the Bentivolii.
Vincentio's son brought up in Florence
It shall become to serve all hopes conceived,
To deck his fortune with his virtuous deeds:
And therefore, Tranio, for the time I study,
Virtue and that part of philosophy
Will I apply that treats of happiness
By virtue specially to be achieved.
Tell me thy mind; for I have Pisa left
And am to Padua come, as he that leaves
A shallow plash to plunge him in the deep,
And with satiety seeks to quench his thirst.

Tra. *Mi perdonato*, gentle master mine,
I am in all affected as yourself;
Glad that you thus continue your resolve
To suck the sweets of sweet philosophy.
Only, good master, while we do admire
This virtue and this moral discipline,
Let's be no stoics nor no stocks, I pray;
Or so devote to Aristotle's checks
As Ovid be an outcast quite abjured:
Balk logic with acquaintance that you have,
And practise rhetoric in your common talk;
Music and poesy use to quicken you;
The mathematics and the metaphysics,
Fall to them as you find your stomach serves you;
No profit grows where is no pleasure ta'en:
In brief, sir, study what you most affect.

Luc. Gramercies, Tranio, well dost thou advise.
If, Biondello, thou wert come ashore,
We could at once put us in readiness,
And take a lodging fit to entertain
Such friends as time in Padua shall beget.
But stay a while: what company is this?

Tra. Master, some show to welcome us to town.

The Taming of the Shrew [Act I, Sc. i

Enter Baptista, Katharina, Bianca, Gremio, and Hortensio.
Lucentio and Tranio stand by.

Bap. Gentlemen, importune me no farther,
  For how I firmly am resolved you know;
  That is, not to bestow my youngest daughter
  Before I have a husband for the elder:
  If either of you both love Katharina,
  Because I know you well and love you well,
  Leave shall you have to court her at your pleasure.

Gre. [*Aside*] To cart her rather: she's too rough for me.
  There, there, Hortensio, will you any wife?

Kath. I pray you, sir, is it your will
  To make a stale of me amongst these mates?

Hor. Mates, maid! how mean you that? no mates for you,
  Unless you were of gentler, milder mould.

Kath. I' faith, sir, you shall never need to fear:
  I wis it is not half way to her heart;
  But if it were, doubt not her care should be
  To comb your noddle with a three-legg'd stool
  And paint your face and use you like a fool.

Hor. From all such devils, good Lord deliver us!

Gre. And me too, good Lord!

Tra. Husht, master! here's some good pastime toward:
  That wench is stark mad or wonderful froward.

Luc. But in the other's silence do I see
  Maid's mild behaviour and sobriety.
  Peace, Tranio!

Tra. Well said, master; mum! and gaze your fill.

Bap. Gentlemen, that I may soon make good
  What I have said, Bianca, get you in:
  And let it not displease thee, good Bianca,
  For I will love thee ne'er the less, my girl.

Kath. A pretty peat! it is best
  Put finger in the eye, an she knew why.

Bian. Sister, content you in my discontent.
  Sir, to your pleasure humbly I subscribe:
  My books and instruments shall be my company,
  On them to look and practise by myself.

Luc. Hark, Tranio! thou may'st hear Minerva speak.

Hor. Signior Baptista, will you be so strange?
  Sorry am I that our good will effects
  Bianca's grief.

Gre.   Why will you mew her up,
  Signior Baptista, for this fiend of hell,
  And make her bear the penance of her tongue?

Bap. Gentlemen, content ye; I am resolved:
Go in, Bianca: [*Exit Bianca.*
And for I know she taketh most delight
In music, instruments and poetry,
Schoolmasters will I keep within my house,
Fit to instruct her youth.   If you, Hortensio,
Or Signior Gremio, you, know any such,
Prefer them hither; for to cunning men
I will be very kind, and liberal
To mine own children in good bringing-up:
And so, farewell.   Katharina, you may stay;
For I have more to commune with Bianca.   [*Exit.*

Kath. Why, and I trust I may go too, may I not? What,
shall I be appointed hours; as though, belike, I knew not
what to take, and what to leave, ha?   [*Exit.*

Gre. You may go to the devil's dam: your gifts are so good,
here's none will hold you.   Their love is not so great,
Hortensio, but we may blow our nails together, and fast it
fairly out: our cake's dough on both sides.   Farewell: yet,
for the love I bear my sweet Bianca, if I can by any means
light on a fit man to teach her that wherein she delights,
I will wish him to her father.

Hor. So will I, Signior Gremio: but a word, I pray.   Though
the nature of our quarrel yet never brooked parle, know now,
upon advice, it toucheth us both, that we may yet again have
access to our fair mistress, and be happy rivals in Bianca's
love, to labour and effect one thing specially.

Gre. What's that, I pray?

Hor. Marry, sir, to get a husband for her sister.

Gre. A husband! a devil.

Hor. I say, a husband.

Gre. I say, a devil.   Thinkest thou, Hortensio, though her
father be very rich, any man is so very a fool to be married
to hell?

Hor. Tush, Gremio! though it pass your patience and mine to
endure her loud alarums, why, man, there be good fellows in
the world, an a man could light on them, would take her
with all faults, and money enough.

Gre. I cannot tell; but I had as lief take her dowry with this
condition, to be whipped at the high-cross every morning.

Hor. Faith, as you say, there's small choice in rotten apples.
But come; since this bar in law makes us friends, it shall be
so far forth friendly maintained till by helping Baptista's
eldest daughter to a husband we set his youngest free for a
husband, and then have to 't afresh.   Sweet Bianca!   Happy

186

man be his dole ! He that runs fastest gets the ring. How
say you, Signior Gremio ?

Gre. I am agreed ; and would I had given him the best horse
in Padua to begin his wooing that would thoroughly woo her,
wed her and bed her and rid the house of her ! Come on.

[*Exeunt Gremio and Hortensio.*

Tra. I pray, sir, tell me, is it possible
That love should of a sudden take such hold !

Luc. O Tranio, till I found it to be true,
I never thought it possible or likely ;
But see, while idly I stood looking on,
I found the effect of love in idleness :
And now in plainness do confess to thee,
That art to me as secret and as dear
As Anna to the Queen of Carthage was,
Tranio, I burn, I pine, I perish, Tranio,
If I achieve not this young modest girl.
Counsel me, Tranio, for I know thou canst ;
Assist me, Tranio, for I know thou wilt.

Tra. Master, it is no time to chide you now ;
Affection is not rated from the heart :
If love have touch'd you, nought remains but so,
' Redime te captum quam queas minimo.'

Luc. Gramercies, lad, go forward ; this contents :
The rest will comfort, for thy counsel's sound.

Tra. Master, you look'd so longly on the maid,
Perhaps you mark'd not what's the pith of all.

Luc. O yes, I saw sweet beauty in her face,
Such as the daughter of Agenor had,
That made great Jove to humble him to her hand,
When with his knees he kiss'd the Cretan strond.

Tra. Saw you no more ? mark'd you not how her sister
Began to scold and raise up such a storm
That mortal ears might hardly endure the din ?

Luc. Tranio, I saw her coral lips to move
And with her breath she did perfume the air :
Sacred and sweet was all I saw in her.

Tra. Nay, then, 'tis time to stir him from his trance.
I pray, awake, sir : if you love the maid,
Bend thoughts and wits to achieve her. Thus it stands :
Her elder sister is so curst and shrewd
That till the father rid his hands of her,
Master, your love must live a maid at home ;
And therefore has he closely mew'd her up,
Because she will not be annoy'd with suitors.

Luc. Ah, Tranio, what a cruel father 's he!
   But art thou not advised, he took some care
   To get her cunning schoolmasters to instruct her?
Tra. Ay, marry, am I, sir; and now 'tis plotted.
Luc. I have it, Tranio.
Tra.   Master, for my hand,
   Both our inventions meet and jump in one.
Luc. Tell me thine first.
Tra.   You will be schoolmaster
   And undertake the teaching of the maid:
   That 's your device.
Luc.   It is: may it be done?
Tra. Not possible; for who shall bear your part,
   And be in Padua here Vincentio's son;
   Keep house and ply his book, welcome his friends,
   Visit his countrymen and banquet them?
Luc. Basta; content thee, for I have it full.
   We have not yet been seen in any house,
   Nor can we be distinguish'd by our faces
   For man or master; then it follows thus;
   Thou shalt be master, Tranio, in my stead,
   Keep house and port and servants, as I should:
   I will some other be; some Florentine,
   Some Neapolitan, or meaner man of Pisa.
   'Tis hatch'd and shall be so: Tranio, at once
   Uncase thee; take my colour'd hat and cloak:
   When Biondello comes, he waits on thee;
   But I will charm him first to keep his tongue.
Tra. So had you need.
   In brief, sir, sith it your pleasure is,
   And I am tied to be obedient,
   For so your father charged me at our parting;
   ' Be serviceable to my son,' quoth he,
   Although I think 'twas in another sense;
   I am content to be Lucentio,
   Because so well I love Lucentio.
Luc. Tranio, be so, because Lucentio loves:
   And let me be a slave, to achieve that maid
   Whose sudden sight hath thrall'd my wounded eye.
   Here comes the rogue.

Enter Biondello.

                Sirrah, where have you been?
Bion. Where have I been! Nay, how now! where are you?
   Master, has my fellow Tranio stolen your clothes? Or you
   stolen his? or both? pray, what 's the news?

Luc. Sirrah, come hither : 'tis no time to jest,
    And therefore frame your manners to the time.
    Your fellow Tranio here, to save my life,
    Puts my apparel and my countenance on,
    And I for my escape have put on his ;
    For in a quarrel since I came ashore
    I kill'd a man and fear I was descried :
    Wait you on him, I charge you, as becomes,
    While I make way from hence to save my life :
    You understand me ?
Bion.   I, sir ! ne'er a whit.
Luc. And not a jot of Tranio in your mouth :
    Tranio is changed into Lucentio.
Bion. The better for him. Would I were so too !
Tra. So could I, faith, boy, to have the next wish after,
    That Lucentio indeed had Baptista's youngest daughter.
    But, sirrah, not for my sake, but your master's I advise
    You use your manners discreetly in all kind of companies :
    When I am alone, why, then I am Tranio ;
    But in all places else your master Lucentio.
Luc. Tranio, let 's go : one thing more rests, that thyself execute,
    to make one among these wooers : if thou ask me why,
    sufficeth, my reasons are both good and weighty. [*Exeunt.*
             The presenters above speak.
First Serv. My lord, you nod ; you do not mind the play.
Sly. Yes, by Saint Anne, do I. A good matter, surely : comes
    there any more of it ?
Page. My lord, 'tis but begun.
Sly. 'Tis a very excellent piece of work, madam lady : would
    'twere done !   [*They sit and mark.*

SCENE II
Padua.   Before Hortensio's house.
Enter Petruchio and his man Grumio.

Pet. Verona, for a while I take my leave,
    To see my friends in Padua, but of all
    My best beloved and approved friend,
    Hortensio ; and I trow this is his house.
    Here, sirrah Grumio ; knock, I say.
Gru. Knock, sir ! whom should I knock ? is there any man
    has rebused your worship ?
Pet. Villain, I say, knock me here soundly.
Gru. Knock you here, sir ! why, sir, what am I, sir, that I
    should knock you here, sir ?
Pet. Villain, I say, knock me at this gate

 And rap me well, or I 'll knock your knave's pate.

Gru. My master is grown quarrelsome. I should knock you
 And then I know after who comes by the worst.   [first,

Pet. Will it not be?

 Faith, sirrah, an you 'll not knock, I 'll wring it ;
 I 'll try how you can *sol, fa,* and sing it.

          [*He wrings him by the ears.*

Gru. Help, masters, help ! my master is mad.

Pet. Now, knock when I bid you, sirrah villain !

       Enter Hortensio.

Hor. How now ! what 's the matter? My old friend Grumio !
 and my good friend Petruchio ! How do you all at Verona?

Pet. Signior Hortensio, come you to part the fray?
 'Con tutto il core ben trovato,' may I say.   [Petrucio.'

Hor. 'Alla nostra casa ben venuto, molto honorato signor mio
 Rise, Grumio, rise : we will compound this quarrel.

Gru. Nay, 'tis no matter, sir, what he 'leges in Latin. If
 this be not a lawful cause for me to leave his service, look
 you, sir, he bid me knock him and rap him soundly, sir :
 well, was it fit for a servant to use his master so, being
 perhaps, for aught I see, two-and-thirty, a pip out?
 Whom would to God I had well knock'd at first,
 Then had not Grumio come by the worst.

Pet. A senseless villain ! Good Hortensio,
 I bade the rascal knock upon your gate
 And could not get him for my heart to do it.

Gru. Knock at the gate ! O heavens ! Spake you not these
 words plain, 'Sirrah, knock me here, rap me here, knock me
 well, and knock me soundly' ? And. come you now with,
 'knocking at the gate' ?

Pet. Sirrah, be gone, or talk not, I advise you.

Hor. Petruchio, patience ; I am Grumio's pledge :
 Why, this 's a heavy chance 'twixt him and you,
 Your ancient, trusty, pleasant servant Grumio.
 And tell me now, sweet friend, what happy gale
 Blows you to Padua here from old Verona?

Pet. Such wind as scatters young men through the world,
 To seek their fortunes farther than at home,
 Where small experience grows. But in a few,
 Signior Hortensio, thus it stands with me :
 Antonio, my father, is deceased ;
 And I have thrust myself into this maze,
 Haply to wive and thrive as best I may :
 Crowns in my purse I have and goods at home,
 And so am come abroad to see the world.

Hor. Petruchio, shall I then come roundly to thee,
And wish thee to a shrewd ill-favour'd wife?
Thou 'ldst thank me but a little for my counsel:
And yet I 'll promise thee she shall be rich,
And very rich: but thou 'rt too much my friend,
And I 'll not wish thee to her.

Pet. Signior Hortensio, 'twixt such friends as we
Few words suffice; and therefore, if thou know
One rich enough to be Petruchio's wife,
As wealth is burden of my wooing dance,
Be she as foul as was Florentius' love,
As old as Sibyl, and as curst and shrewd
As Socrates' Xanthippe, or a worse,
She moves me not, or not removes, at least,
Affection's edge in me, were she as rough
As are the swelling Adriatic seas:
I come to wife it wealthily in Padua;
If wealthily, then happily in Padua.

Gru. Nay, look you, sir, he tells you flatly what his mind is:
why, give him gold enough and marry him to a puppet or an
aglet-baby; or an old trot with ne'er a tooth in her head
though she have as many diseases as two and fifty horses:
why, nothing comes amiss, so money comes withal.

Hor. Petruchio, since we are stepp'd thus far in,
I will continue that I broach'd in jest.
I can, Petruchio, help thee to a wife
With wealth enough and young and beauteous,
Brought up as best becomes a gentlewoman:
Her only fault, and that is faults enough,
Is that she is intolerable curst
And shrewd and froward, so beyond all measure,
That, were my state far worser than it is,
I would not wed her for a mine of gold.

Pet. Hortensio, peace! thou know'st not gold's effect:
Tell me her father's name and 'tis enough;
For I will board her, though she chide as loud
As thunder when the clouds in autumn crack.

Hor. Her father is Baptista Minola,
An affable and courteous gentleman:
Her name is Katharina Minola,
Renown'd in Padua for her scolding tongue.

Pet. I know her father, though I know not her;
And he knew my deceased father well.
I will not sleep, Hortensio, till I see her;
And therefore let me be thus bold with you

To give you over at this first encounter,
Unless you will accompany me thither.

Gru. I pray you, sir, let him go while the humour lasts.   O' my word, an she knew him as well as I do, she would think scolding would do little good upon him : she may perhaps call him half a score knaves or so : why, that 's nothing ; an he begin at once, he 'll rail in his rope-tricks.   I 'll tell you what, sir, an she stand him but a little, he will throw a figure in her face and so disfigure her with it that she shall have no more eyes to see withal than a cat.   You know him not, sir.

Hor. Tarry, Petruchio, I must go with thee ;
For in Baptista's keep my treasure is :
He hath the jewel of my life in hold,
His youngest daughter, beautiful Bianca ;
And her withholds from me and other more,
Suitors to her and rivals in my love ;
Supposing it a thing impossible,
For those defects I have before rehearsed,
That ever Katharina will be woo'd ;
Therefore this order hath Baptista ta'en,
That none shall have access unto Bianca
Till Katharine the curst have got a husband.

Gru. Katharine the curst !
A title for a maid of all titles the worst.

Hor. Now shall my friend Petruchio do me grace ;
And offer me disguised in sober robes
To old Baptista as a schoolmaster
Well seen in music, to instruct Bianca ;
That so I may, by this device, at least
Have leave and leisure to make love to her,
And unsuspected court her by herself.

Gru. Here 's no knavery !   See, to beguile the old folks, how the young folks lay their heads together !
                    Enter Gremio and Lucentio disguised.
Master, master, look about you : who goes there, ha ?

Hor. Peace, Grumio ! it is the rival of my love.
Petruchio, stand by a while.

Gru. A proper stripling and an amorous !

Gre. O, very well ; I have perused the note.
Hark you, sir ; I 'll have them very fairly bound :
All books of love, see that at any hand ;
And see you read no other lectures to her :
You understand me : over and beside
Signior Baptista's liberality,
I 'll mend it with a largess.   Take your paper too,

And let me have them very well perfumed :
For she is sweeter than perfume itself
To whom they go to. What will you read to her ?

Luc. Whate'er I read to her, I 'll plead for you
As for my patron, stand you so assured,
As firmly as yourself were still in place :
Yea, and perhaps with more successful words
Than you, unless you were a scholar, sir.

Gre. O this learning, what a thing it is !

Gru. O this woodcock, what an ass it is !

Pet. Peace, sirrah !

Hor. Grumio, mum ! God save you, Signior Gremio.

Gre. And you are well met, Signior Hortensio.
Trow you whither I am going ? To Baptista Minola.
I promised to inquire carefully
About a schoolmaster for the fair Bianca :
And by good fortune I have lighted well
On this young man, for learning and behaviour
Fit for her turn, well read in poetry
And other books, good ones, I warrant ye.

Hor. 'Tis well ; and I have met a gentleman
Hath promised me to help me to another,
A fine musician to instruct our mistress ;
So shall I no whit be behind in duty
To fair Bianca, so beloved of me.

Gre. Beloved of me ; and that my deeds shall prove.

Gru. And that his bags shall prove.

Hor. Gremio, 'tis now no time to vent our love :
Listen to me, and if you speak me fair,
I 'll tell you news indifferent good for either
Here is a gentleman whom by chance I met,
Upon agreement from us to his liking,
Will undertake to woo curst Katharine,
Yea, and to marry her, if her dowry please.

Gre. So said, so done, is well.
Hortensio, have you told him all her faults ?

Pet. I know she is an irksome brawling scold :
If that be all, masters, I hear no harm.

Gre. No, say'st me so, friend ? What countryman ?

Pet. Born in Verona, old Antonio's son :
My father dead, my fortune lives for me ;
And I do hope good days and long to see.

Gre. O sir, such a life, with such a wife, were strange !
But if you have a stomach, to 't i' God's name :
You shall have me assisting you in all.

But will you woo this wild-cat?
Pet.   Will I live?
Gru. Will he woo her? ay, or I'll hang her.
Pet. Why came I hither but to that intent?
　Think you a little din can daunt my ears?
　Have I not in my time heard lions roar?
　Have I not heard the sea puff'd up with winds
　Rage like an angry boar chafed with sweat?
　Have I not heard great ordnance in the field,
　And heaven's artillery thunder in the skies?
　Have I not in a pitched battle heard
　Loud 'larums, neighing steeds, and trumpets' clang?
　And do you tell me of a woman's tongue,
　That gives not half so great a blow to hear
　As will a chestnut in a farmer's fire?
　Tush, tush! fear boys with bugs.
Gru.   For he fears none.
Gre. Hortensio, hark:
　This gentleman is happily arrived,
　My mind presumes, for his own good and ours.
Hor. I promised we would be contributors
　And bear his charge of wooing, whatsoe'er.
Gre. And so we will, provided that he win her.
Gru. I would I were as sure of a good dinner.

Enter Tranio brave, and Biondello.

Tra. Gentlemen, God save you.   If I may be bold,
　Tell me, I beseech you, which is the readiest way
　To the house of Signior Baptista Minola?
Bion. He that has the two fair daughters: is 't he you mean?
Tra. Even he, Biondello.
Gre. Hark you, sir; you mean not her to—
Tra. Perhaps, him and her, sir: what have you to do?
Pet. Not her that chides, sir, at any hand, I pray.
Tra. I love no chiders, sir.   Biondello, let's away.
Luc. Well begun, Tranio.
Hor.   Sir, a word ere you go;
　Are you a suitor to the maid you talk of, yea or no?
Tra. And if I be, sir, is it any offence?
Gre. No; if without more words you will get you hence.
Tra. Why, sir, I pray, are not the streets as free
　For me as for you?
Gre.   But so is not she.
Tra. For what reason, I beseech you?
Gre.   For this reason, if you'll know,

That she 's the choice love of Signior Gremio.
Hor. That she 's the chosen love of Signior Hortensio.
Tra. Softly, my masters ! if you be gentlemen,
 Do me this right ; hear me with patience.
 Baptista is a noble gentleman,
 To whom my father is not all unknown ;
 And were his daughter fairer than she is,
 She may more suitors have and me for one.
 Fair Leda's daughter had a thousand wooers ;
 Then well one more may fair Bianca have :
 And so she shall ; Lucentio shall make one,
 Though Paris came in hope to speed alone.
Gre. What, this gentleman will out-talk us all !
Luc. Sir, give him head : I know he 'll prove a jade.
Pet. Hortensio, to what end are all these words ?
Hor. Sir, let me be so bold as ask you,
 Did you yet ever see Baptista's daughter ?
Tra. No, sir ; but hear I do that he hath two,
 The one as famous for a scolding tongue
 As is the other for beauteous modesty.
Pet. Sir, sir, the first 's for me ; let her go by.
Gre. Yea, leave that labour to great Hercules ;
 And let it be more than Alcides' twelve.
Pet. Sir, understand you this of me in sooth :
 The youngest daughter whom you hearken for
 Her father keeps from all access of suitors ;
 And will not promise her to any man
 Until the elder sister first be wed :
 The younger then is free and not before.
Tra. If it be so, sir, that you are the man
 Must stead us all and me amongst the rest ;
 And if you break the ice and do this feat,
 Achieve the elder, set the younger free
 For our access, whose hap shall be to have her
 Will not so graceless be to be ingrate.
Hor. Sir, you say well and well you do conceive ;
 And since you do profess to be a suitor,
 You must, as we do, gratify this gentleman,
 To whom we all rest generally beholding.
Tra. Sir, I shall not be slack : in sign whereof,
 Please ye we may contrive this afternoon,
 And quaff carouses to our mistress' health,
 And do as adversaries do in law,
 Strive mightily, but eat and drink as friends.
Gru. Bion. O excellent motion ! Fellows, let 's be gone.

Hor. The motion's good indeed and be it so ;
    Petruchio, I shall be your ben venuto.   *[Exeunt.*

ACT II—Scene I

Padua.   A room in Baptista's house.
Enter Katharina and Bianca.

Bian. Good sister, wrong me not, nor wrong yourself,
    To make a bondmaid and a slave of me ;
    That I disdain : but for these other gawds,
    Unbind my hands, I 'll pull them off myself,
    Yea, all my raiment, to my petticoat ;
    Or what you will command me will I do,
    So well I know my duty to my elders.
Kath. Of all thy suitors, here I charge thee, tell
    Whom thou lovest best : see thou dissemble not,
Bian. Believe me, sister, of all the men alive
    I never yet beheld that special face
    Which I could fancy more than any other.
Kath. Minion, thou liest. Is 't not Hortensio ?
Bian. If you affect him, sister, here I swear
    I 'll plead for you myself, but you shall have him.
Kath. O then, belike, you fancy riches more :
    You will have Gremio to keep you fair.
Bian. Is it for him you do envy me so ?
    Nay, then you jest, and now I well perceive
    You have but jested with me all this while :
    I prithee, sister Kate, untie my hands.
Kath. If that be jest, then all the rest was so.   *[Strikes her.*
          Enter Baptista.
Bap. Why, how now, dame ! whence grows this insolence ?
    Bianca, stand aside. Poor girl ! she weeps.
    Go ply thy needle ; meddle not with her.
    For shame, thou hilding of a devilish spirit,
    Why dost thou wrong her that did ne'er wrong thee ?
    When did she cross thee with a bitter word ?
Kath. Her silence flouts me, and I 'll be revenged.
                  [Flies after Bianca.
Bap. What, in my sight ? Bianca, get thee in. *[Exit Bianca.*
Kath. What, will you not suffer me ? Nay, now I see
    She is your treasure, she must have a husband ;
    I must dance bare-foot on her wedding day
    And for your love to her lead apes in hell.
    Talk not to me : I will go sit and weep
    Till I can find occasion of revenge.   *[Exit.*

Bap. Was ever gentleman thus grieved as I?
  But who comes here?

Enter Gremio, Lucentio in the habit of a mean man; Petruchio, with Hortensio as a musician; and Tranio, with Biondello bearing a lute and books.

Gre. Good morrow, neighbour Baptista.

Bap. Good morrow, neighbour Gremio. God save you, gentlemen!

Pet. And you, good sir! Pray, have you not a daughter
  Call'd Katharina, fair and virtuous?

Bap. I have a daughter, sir, called Katharina.

Gre. You are too blunt: go to it orderly.

Pet. You wrong me, Signior Gremio: give me leave.
  I am a gentleman of Verona, sir,
  That, hearing of her beauty and her wit,
  Her affability and bashful modesty,
  Her wondrous qualities and mild behaviour,
  Am bold to show myself a forward guest
  Within your house, to make mine eye the witness
  Of that report which I so oft have heard.
  And, for an entrance to my entertainment,
  I do present you with a man of mine, [*Presenting Hortensio.*
  Cunning in music and the mathematics,
  To instruct her fully in those sciences,
  Whereof I know she is not ignorant:
  Accept of him, or else you do me wrong:
  His name is Licio, born in Mantua.

Bap. You're welcome, sir; and he, for your good sake.
  But for my daughter Katharine, this I know,
  She is not for your turn, the more my grief.

Pet. I see you do not mean to part with her,
  Or else you like not of my company.

Bap. Mistake me not; I speak but as I find.
  Whence are you, sir? what may I call your name?

Pet. Petruchio is my name; Antonio's son,
  A man well known throughout all Italy.

Bap. I know him well; you are welcome for his sake.

Gre. Saving your tale, Petruchio, I pray,
  Let us, that are poor petitioners, speak too:
  Baccare! you are marvellous forward.

Pet. O, pardon me, Signior Gremio; I would fain be doing.

Gre. I doubt it not, sir; but you will curse your wooing
  Neighbour, this is a gift very grateful, I am sure of it. To
  express the like kindness, myself, that have been more kindly
  beholden to you than any, I freely give unto you this young

scholar [*presenting Lucentio*], that hath been long studying at
Rheims ; as cunning in Greek, Latin, and other languages,
as the other in music and mathematics : his name is Cambio ;
pray, accept his service.

Bap. A thousand thanks, Signior Gremio. Welcome, good
Cambio. But, gentle sir [*to Tranio*], methinks you walk like a
stranger : may I be so bold to know the cause of your coming ?

Tra. Pardon me, sir, the boldness is mine own ;
That, being a stranger in this city here,
Do make myself a suitor to your daughter,
Unto Bianca, fair and virtuous.
Nor is your firm resolve unknown to me,
In the preferment of the eldest sister.
This liberty is all that I request,
That, upon knowledge of my parentage,
I may have welcome 'mongst the rest that woo,
And free access and favour as the rest :
And, toward the education of your daughters,
I here bestow a simple instrument,
And this small packet of Greek and Latin books :
If you accept them, then their worth is great.

Bap. Lucentio is your name ; of whence, I pray ?

Tra. Of Pisa, sir ; son to Vincentio.

Bap. A mighty man of Pisa ; by report
I know him well : you are very welcome, sir.
Take you the lute, and you the set of books ;
You shall go see your pupils presently.
Holla, within !

                Enter a Servant.
          Sirrah, lead these gentlemen
To my daughters ; and tell them both,
These are their tutors : bid them use them well.
       [*Exit Servant, with Luc. and Hor., Bio. following.*
We will go walk a little in the orchard,
And then to dinner. You are passing welcome,
And so I pray you all to think yourselves.

Pet. Signior Baptista, my business asketh haste,
And every day I cannot come to woo.
You knew my father well, and in him me,
Left solely heir to all his lands and goods,
Which I have better'd rather than decreased :
Then tell me, if I get your daughter's love,
What dowry shall I have with her to wife ?

Bap. After my death the one half of my lands,
And in possession twenty thousand crowns.

Pet. And, for that dowry, I 'll assure her of
   Her widowhood, be it that she survive me,
   In all my lands and leases whatsoever :
   Let specialties be therefore drawn between us,
   That covenants may be kept on either hand.
Bap. Ay, when the special thing is well obtain'd,
   That is, her love ; for that is all in all.
Pet. Why, that is nothing ; for I tell you, father,
   I am as peremptory as she proud-minded ;
   And where two raging fires meet together
   They do consume the thing that feeds their fury :
   Though little fire grows great with little wind,
   Yet extreme gusts will blow out fire and all :
   So I to her and so she yields to me ;
   For I am rough and woo not like a babe.
Bap. Well mayst thou woo, and happy be thy speed !
   But be thou arm'd for some unhappy words.
Pet. Ay, to the proof ; as mountains are for winds,
   That shake not, though they blow perpetually.

Re-enter Hortensio, with his head broke.

Bap. How now, my friend ! why dost thou look so pale?
Hor. For fear, I promise you, if I look pale.
Bap. What, will my daughter prove a good musician?
Hor. I think she 'll sooner prove a soldier :
   Iron may hold with her, but never lutes.
Bap. Why, then thou canst not break her to the lute?
Hor. Why, no ; for she hath broke the lute to me.
   I did but tell her she mistook her frets,
   And bow'd her hand to teach her fingering ;
   When, with a most impatient devilish spirit,
   ' Frets, call you these?' quoth she ; ' I 'll fume with them :'
   And, with that word, she struck me on the head,
   And through the instrument my pate made way ;
   And there I stood amazed for a while,
   As on a pillory, looking through the lute ;
   While she did call me rascal fiddler
   And twangling Jack ; with twenty such vile terms,
   As had she studied to misuse me so.
Pet. Now, by the world, it is a lusty wench ;
   I love her ten times more than e'er I did :
   O, how I long to have some chat with her !
Bap. Well, go with me and be not so discomfited :
   Proceed in practice with my younger daughter ;
   She 's apt to learn and thankful for good turns.

Signior Petruchio, will you go with us,
Or shall I send my daughter Kate to you?
Pet. I pray you do ; I will attend her here,
      [*Exeunt Baptista, Gremio, Tranio, and Hortensio.*
And woo her with some spirit when she comes.
Say that she rail ; why then I 'll tell her plain
She sings as sweetly as a nightingale :
Say that she frown ; I 'll say she looks as clear
As morning roses newly wash'd with dew :
Say she be mute and will not speak a word ;
Then I 'll commend her volubility,
And say she uttereth piercing eloquence :
If she do bid me pack, I 'll give her thanks,
As though she bid me stay by her a week :
If she deny to wed, I 'll crave the day
When I shall ask the banns, and when be married.
But here she comes ; and now, Petruchio, speak.

Enter Katharina.

Good morrow, Kate ; for that 's your name, I hear.
Kath. Well have you heard, but something hard of hearing :
      They call me Katharine that do talk of me.
Pet. You lie, in faith ; for you are call'd plain Kate,
      And bonny Kate, and sometimes Kate the curst ;
      But Kate, the prettiest Kate in Christendom,
      Kate of Kate-Hall, my super-dainty Kate,
      For dainties are all Kates, and therefore, Kate,
      Take this of me, Kate of my consolation ;
      Hearing thy mildness praised in every town,
      Thy virtues spoke of, and thy beauty sounded,
      Yet not so deeply as to thee belongs,
      Myself am moved to woo thee for my wife.
Kath. Moved ! in good time : let him that moved you hither
      Remove you hence : I knew you at the first
      You were a moveable.
Pet.   Why, what's a moveable ?
Kath. A join'd-stool.
Pet.   Thou hast hit it : come, sit on me.
Kath. Asses are made to bear, and so are you.
Pet. Women are made to bear, and so are you.
Kath. No such jade as you, if me you mean.
Pet. Alas, good Kate, I will not burden thee !
      For, knowing thee to be but young and light,—
Kath. Too light for such a swain as you to catch ;
      And yet as heavy as my weight should be.
200

Pet. Should be! should—buzz!

Kath.   Well ta'en, and like a buzzard.

Pet. O slow-wing'd turtle! shall a buzzard take thee?

Kath. Ay, for a turtle, as he takes a buzzard.

Pet. Come, come, you wasp; i' faith, you are too angry.

Kath. If I be waspish, best beware my sting.

Pet. My remedy is then, to pluck it out.

Kath. Ay, if the fool could find it where it lies.

Pet. Who knows not where a wasp does wear his sting? In

Kath. In his tongue.   [his tail.

Pet.   Whose tongue?

Kath. Yours, if you talk of tails: and so farewell.

Pet. What, with my tongue in your tail? nay, come again,
   Good Kate; I am a gentleman.

Kath.   That I 'll try. [*She strikes him.*

Pet. I swear I 'll cuff you, if you strike again.

Kath. So may you lose your arms:
   If you strike me, you are no gentleman;
   And if no gentleman, why then no arms.

Pet. A herald, Kate? O, put me in thy books!

Kath. What is your crest? a coxcomb?

Pet. A combless cock, so Kate will be my hen.

Kath. No cock of mine; you crow too like a craven.

Pet. Nay, come, Kate, come; you must not look so sour.

Kath. It is my fashion, when I see a crab.

Pet. Why, here 's no crab; and therefore look not sour.

Kath. There is, there is.

Pet. Then show it me.

Kath.   Had I a glass, I would.

Pet. What, you mean my face?

Kath.   Well aim'd of such a young one.

Pet. Now, by Saint George, I am too young for you.

Kath. Yet you are wither'd.

Pet.   'Tis with cares.

Kath.   I care not.

Pet. Nay, hear you, Kate: in sooth, you 'scape not so.

Kath. I chafe you, if I tarry; let me go.

Pet. No, not a whit: I find you passing gentle.
   'Twas told me you were rough and coy and sullen,
   And now I find report a very liar;
   For thou art pleasant, gamesome, passing courteous,
   But slow in speech, yet sweet as spring-time flowers:
   Thou canst not frown, thou canst not look askance,
   Nor bite the lip, as angry wenches will,
   Nor hast thou pleasure to be cross in talk,

But thou with mildness entertain'st thy wooers,
With gentle conference, soft and affable.
Why does the world report that Kate doth limp?
O slanderous world! Kate, like the hazel-twig,
Is straight and slender, and as brown in hue
As hazel-nuts and sweeter than the kernels.
O, let me see thee walk: thou dost not halt.

Kath. Go, fool, and whom thou keep'st command.

Pet. Did ever Dian so become a grove
As Kate this chamber with her princely gait?
O, be thou Dian, and let her be Kate;
And then let Kate be chaste and Dian sportful!

Kath. Where did you study all this goodly speech?

Pet. It is extempore, from my mother-wit.

Kath. A witty mother! witless else her son.

Pet. Am I not wise?

Kath.   Yes; keep you warm.

Pet. Marry, so I mean, sweet Katharine, in thy bed:
And therefore, setting all this chat aside,
Thus in plain terms: Your father hath consented
That you shall be my wife; your dowry 'greed on;
And, will you, nill you, I will marry you.
Now, Kate, I am a husband for your turn;
For, by this light, whereby I see thy beauty,
Thy beauty, that doth make me like thee well,
Thou must be married to no man but me;
For I am he am born to tame you, Kate,
And bring you from a wild Kate to a Kate
Conformable as other household Kates.
Here comes your father: never make denial;
I must and will have Katharine to my wife.

Re-enter Baptista, Gremio, and Tranio.

Bap. Now, Signior Petruchio, how speed you with my daughter?

Pet. How but well, sir? how but well?
It were impossible I should speed amiss.

Bap. Why, how now, daughter Katharine! in your dumps?

Kath. Call you me daughter? now, I promise you
You have show'd a tender fatherly regard,
To wish me wed to one half lunatic;
A mad-cap ruffian and a swearing Jack,
That thinks with oaths to face the matter out.

Pet. Father, 'tis thus: yourself and all the world,
That talk'd of her, have talk'd amiss of her:
If she be curst, it is for policy,
For she's not froward, but modest as the dove;

She is not hot, but temperate as the morn ;
For patience she will prove a second Grissel,
And Roman Lucrece for her chastity :
And to conclude, we have 'greed so well together,
That upon Sunday is the wedding-day.

Kath. I'll see thee hang'd on Sunday first.

Gre. Hark, Petruchio ! she says she 'll see thee hang'd first.

Tra. Is this your speeding ? nay, then, good night our part !

Pet. Be patient, gentlemen ; I choose her for myself :
If she and I be pleased, what 's that to you ?
'Tis bargain'd 'twixt us twain, being alone,
That she shall still be curst in company.
I tell you, 'tis incredible to believe
How much she loves me : O, the kindest Kate !
She hung about my neck ; and kiss on kiss
She vied so fast, protesting oath on oath,
That in a twink she won me to her love.
O, you are novices ! 'tis a world to see,
How tame, when men and women are alone,
A meacock wretch can make the curstest shrew.
Give me thy hand, Kate : I will unto Venice,
To buy apparel 'gainst the wedding-day.
Provide the feast, father, and bid the guests ;
I will be sure my Katharine shall be fine.

Bap. I know not what to say : but give me your hands ;
God send you joy, Petruchio ! 'tis a match.

Gre. Tra. Amen, say we : we will be witnesses.

Pet. Father, and wife, and gentlemen, adieu ;
I will to Venice ; Sunday comes apace :
We will have rings, and things, and fine array ;
And kiss me, Kate, we will be married o' Sunday.

[*Exeunt Petruchio and Katharina severally.*

Gre. Was ever match clapp'd up so suddenly ?

Bap. Faith, gentlemen, now I play a merchant's part,
And venture madly on a desperate mart.

Tra. 'Twas a commodity lay fretting by you :
'Twill bring you gain, or perish on the seas.

Bap. The gain I seek is, quiet in the match.

Gre. No doubt but he hath got a quiet catch.
But now, Baptista, to your younger daughter :
Now is the day we long have looked for :
I am your neighbour, and was suitor first.

Tra. And I am one that love Bianca more
Than words can witness, or your thoughts can guess.

Gre. Youngling, thou canst not love so dear as I.

Tra. Greybeard, thy love doth freeze.
Gre.   But thine doth fry.
   Skipper, stand back : 'tis age that nourisheth.
Tra. But youth in ladies' eyes that flourisheth.
Bap. Content you, gentlemen : I will compound this strife :
   'Tis deeds must win the prize ; and he, of both,
   That can assure my daughter greatest dower
   Shall have my Bianca's love.
   Say, Signior Gremio, what can you assure her ?
Gre. First, as you know, my house within the city
   Is richly furnished with plate and gold ;
   Basins and ewers to lave her dainty hands ;
   My hangings all of Tyrian tapestry ;
   In ivory coffers I have stuff'd my crowns ;
   In cypress chests my arras, counterpoints,
   Costly apparel, tents, and canopies,
   Fine linen, Turkey cushions boss'd with pearl,
   Valance of Venice gold in needlework,
   Pewter and brass, and all things that belong
   To house or housekeeping : then, at my farm
   I have a hundred milch-kine to the pail,
   Sixscore fat oxen standing in my stalls,
   And all things answerable to this portion.
   Myself am struck in years, I must confess ;
   And if I die to-morrow, this is hers,
   If whilst I live she will be only mine.
Tra. That ' only ' came well in.   Sir, list to me :
   I am my father's heir and only son :
   If I may have your daughter to my wife,
   I 'll leave her houses three or four as good,
   Within rich Pisa walls, as any one
   Old Signior Gremio has in Padua ;
   Besides two thousand ducats by the year
   Of fruitful land, all which shall be her jointure.
   What ! have I pinch'd you, Signior Gremio ?
Gre. Two thousand ducats by the year of land !
   My land amounts not to so much in all :
   That she shall have ; besides an argosy
   That now is lying in Marseilles' road.
   What ! have I choked you with an argosy ?
Tra. Gremio, 'tis known my father had no less
   Than three great argosies ; besides two galliasses,
   And twelve tight galleys : these I will assure her,
   And twice as much, whate'er thou offer'st next.
Gre. Nay, I have offer'd all, I have no more ;

And she can have no more than all I have :
If you like me, she shall have me and mine.
Tra. Why, then the maid is mine from all the world,
By your firm promise : Gremio is out-vied.
Bap. I must confess your offer is the best ;
And, let your father make her the assurance,
She is your own ; else, you must pardon me,
If you should die before him, where 's her dower ?
Tra. That 's but a cavil : he is old, I young.
Gre. And may not young men die, as well as old ?
Bap. Well, gentlemen,
I am thus resolved : on Sunday next you know
My daughter Katharine is to be married :
Now, on the Sunday following, shall Bianca
Be bride to you, if you make this assurance ;
If not, to Signior Gremio :
And so, I take my leave, and thank you both.
Gre. Adieu, good neighbour.   [*Exit Baptista.*
                    Now I fear thee not :
Sirrah young gamester, your father were a fool
To give thee all, and in his waning age
Set foot under thy table : tut, a toy !
An old Italian fox is not so kind, my boy.   [*Exit.*
Tra. A vengeance on your crafty wither'd hide !
Yet I have faced it with a card of ten.
'Tis in my head to do my master good :
I see no reason but supposed Lucentio
Must get a father, call'd—supposed Vincentio ;
And that 's a wonder : fathers commonly
Do get their children ; but in this case of wooing,
A child shall get a sire, if I fail not of my cunning.   [*Exit.*

ACT III—Scene I
Padua.   Baptista's house.
Enter Lucentio, Hortensio, and Bianca.

Luc. Fiddler, forbear ; you grow too forward, sir :
Have you so soon forgot the entertainment
Her sister Katharine welcomed you withal ?
Hor. But, wrangling pedant, this is
The patroness of heavenly harmony :
Then give me leave to have prerogative ;
And when in music we have spent an hour,
Your lecture shall have leisure for as much.
Luc. Preposterous ass, that never read so far

To know the cause why music was ordain'd!
Was it not to refresh the mind of man
After his studies or his usual pain?
Then give me leave to read philosophy,
And while I pause, serve in your harmony.

Hor. Sirrah, I will not bear these braves of thine.

Bian. Why, gentlemen, you do me double wrong,
To strive for that which resteth in my choice:
I am no breeching scholar in the schools;
I'll not be tied to hours nor 'pointed times,
But learn my lessons as I please myself.
And, to cut off all strife, here sit we down:
Take you your instrument, play you the whiles;
His lecture will be done ere you have tuned.

Hor. You'll leave his lecture when I am in tune?

Luc. That will be never: tune your instrument.

Bian. Where left we last?

Luc. Here, madam:
        'Hic ibat Simois; hic est Sigeia tellus;
         Hic steterat Priami regia celsa senis.'

Bian. Construe them.

Luc. 'Hic ibat,' as I told you before,—'Simois,' I am Lucentio,—'hic est,' son unto Vincentio of Pisa,—'Sigeia
tellus,' disguised thus to get your love;—'Hic steterat,' and
that Lucentio that comes a-wooing,—'Priami,' is my man
Tranio,—'regia,' bearing my port,—'celsa senis,' that we
might beguile the old pantaloon.

Hor. Madam, my instrument's in tune.

Bian. Let's hear. O fie! the treble jars.

Luc. Spit in the hole, man, and tune again.

Bian. Now let me see if I can construe it:
'Hic ibat Simois,' I know you not,—'hic est Sigeia tellus,' I
trust you not,—'Hic steterat Priami,' take heed he hear us
not,—'regia,' presume not,—'celsa senis,' despair not.

Hor. Madam, 'tis now in tune.

Luc.   All but the base.

Hor. The base is right; 'tis the base knave that jars.
[*Aside*] How fiery and forward our pedant is!
Now, for my life, the knave doth court my love:
Pedascule, I'll watch you better yet.

Bian. In time I may believe, yet I mistrust.

Luc. Mistrust it not; for, sure, Æacides
Was Ajax, call'd so from his grandfather.

Bian. I must believe my master; else, I promise you,
I should be arguing still upon that doubt:

But let it rest. Now, Licio, to you :
Good masters, take it not unkindly, pray,
That I have been thus pleasant with you both.
Hor. You may go walk, and give me leave a while :
My lessons make no music in three parts.
Luc. Are you so formal, sir ? well, I must wait,
[*Aside*] And watch withal ; for, but I be deceived,
Our fine musician groweth amorous.
Hor. Madam, before you touch the instrument,
To learn the order of my fingering,
I must begin with rudiments of art ;
To teach you gamut in a briefer sort,
More pleasant, pithy, and effectual,
Than hath been taught by any of my trade :
And there it is in writing, fairly drawn.
Bian. Why, I am past my gamut long ago.
Hor. Yet read the gamut of Hortensio.
Bian. [*reads*] "'Gamut' I am, the ground of all accord,
　'A re,' to plead Hortensio's passion ;
'B mi,' Bianca, take him for thy lord,
　'C fa ut,' that loves with all affection :
'D sol re,' one clef, two notes have I :
'E la mi,' show pity, or I die."
Call you this gamut ? tut, I like it not :
Old fashions please me best ; I am not so nice,
To change true rules for old inventions.
Enter a Servant.
Serv. Mistress, your father prays you leave your books,
And help to dress your sister's chamber up :
You know to-morrow is the wedding-day.
Bian. Farewell, sweet masters both ; I must be gone.
[*Exeunt Bianca and Servant.*
Luc. Faith, mistress, then I have no cause to stay. [*Exit.*
Hor. But I have cause to pry into this pedant :
Methinks he looks as though he were in love :
Yet if thy thoughts, Bianca, be so humble,
To cast thy wandering eyes on every stale,
Seize thee that list : if once I find thee ranging,
Hortensio will be quit with thee by changing. [*Exit.*

SCENE II
Padua. Before Baptista's house.
Enter Baptista, Gremio, Tranio, Katharina, Bianca,
Lucentio, and others, attendants.
Bap. Signior Lucentio [*To Tranio*], this is the 'pointed day
207

That Katharine and Petruchio should be married,
And yet we hear not of our son-in-law.
What will be said? what mockery will it be,
To want the bridegroom when the priest attends
To speak the ceremonial rites of marriage!
What says Lucentio to this shame of ours?

Kath. No shame but mine: I must, forsooth, be forced
To give my hand, opposed against my heart,
Unto a mad-brain rudesby, full of spleen;
Who woo'd in haste, and means to wed at leisure.
I told you, I, he was a frantic fool,
Hiding his bitter jests in blunt behaviour:
And, to be noted for a merry man,
He'll woo a thousand, 'point the day of marriage,
Make friends, invite, and proclaim the banns;
Yet never means to wed where he hath woo'd.
Now must the world point at poor Katharine,
And say, 'Lo, there is mad Petruchio's wife,
If it would please him come and marry her!'

Tra. Patience, good Katharine, and Baptista too.
Upon my life, Petruchio means but well,
Whatever fortune stays him from his word:
Though he be blunt, I know him passing wise;
Though he be merry, yet withal he's honest.

Kath. Would Katharine had never seen him though!
                    [*Exit weeping, followed by Bianca and others.*

Bap. Go, girl; I cannot blame thee now to weep;
For such an injury would vex a very saint,
Much more a shrew of thy impatient humour.
                    Enter Biondello.

Bion. Master, master! news, old news, and such news as you
    never heard of!

Bap. Is it new and old too? how may that be?

Bion. Why, is it not news, to hear of Petruchio's coming?

Bap. Is he come?

Bion. Why, no, sir.

Bap. What then?

Bion. He is coming.

Bap. When will he be here?

Bion. When he stands where I am and sees you there.

Tra. But say, what to thine old news?

Bion. Why, Petruchio is coming in a new hat and an old
    jerkin, a pair of old breeches thrice turned, a pair of boots
    that have been candle-cases, one buckled, another laced, an
    old rusty sword ta'en out of the town-armoury, with a broken

hilt, and chapeless; with two broken points: his horse
hipped with an old mothy saddle and stirrups of no kindred;
besides, possessed with the glanders and like to mose in the
chine; troubled with the lampass, infected with the fashions,
full of windgalls, sped with spavins, rayed with the yellows,
past cure of the fives, stark spoiled with the staggers, be-
gnawn with the bots, swayed in the back and shoulder-
shotten; near-legged before and with a half-cheeked bit and
a head-stall of sheep's leather which, being restrained to
keep him from stumbling, hath been often burst and now
repaired with knots; one girth six times pieced and a
woman's crupper of velure, which hath two letters for her
name fairly set down in studs, and here and there pieced
with pack-thread.

Bap. Who comes with him?

Bion. O, sir, his lackey, for all the world caparisoned like the
horse; with a linen stock on one leg, and a kersey boot-
hose on the other, gartered with a red and blue list; an old
hat, and 'the humour of forty fancies' pricked in't for a
feather: a monster, a very monster in apparel, and not like a
Christian footboy or a gentleman's lackey.

Tra. 'Tis some odd humour pricks him to this fashion;
Yet oftentimes he goes but mean-apparell'd.

Bap. I am glad he's come, howsoe'er he comes.

Bion. Why, sir, he comes not.

Bap. Didst thou not say he comes?

Bion. Who? that Petruchio came?

Bap. Ay, that Petruchio came.

Bion. No, sir; I say his horse comes, with him on his back.

Bap. Why, that's all one.

Bion. Nay, by Saint Jamy,
      I hold you a penny,
      A horse and a man
      Is more than one,
      And yet not many.

Enter Petruchio and Grumio.

Pet. Come, where be these gallants? who's at home?

Bap. You are welcome, sir.

Pet.   And yet I come not well.

Bap. And yet you halt not.

Tra.   Not so well apparell'd
      As I wish you were.

Pet. Were it better, I should rush in thus.
      But where is Kate? where is my lovely bride?
      How does my father? Gentles, methinks you frown:

209

And wherefore gaze this goodly company,
As if they saw some wondrous monument,
Some comet or unusual prodigy?
Bap. Why, sir, you know this is your wedding-day:
First were we sad, fearing you would not come;
Now sadder, that you come so unprovided.
Fie, doff this habit, shame to your estate,
An eye-sore to our solemn festival!
Tra. And tell us, what occasion of import
Hath all so long detain'd you from your wife,
And sent you hither so unlike yourself?
Pet. Tedious it were to tell, and harsh to hear:
Sufficeth, I am come to keep my word,
Though in some part enforced to digress;
Which, at more leisure, I will so excuse
As you shall well be satisfied withal.
But where is Kate? I stay too long from her:
The morning wears, 'tis time we were at church.
Tra. See not your bride in these unreverent robes:
Go to my chamber; put on clothes of mine.
Pet. Not I, believe me: thus I'll visit her.
Bap. But thus, I trust, you will not marry her.
Pet. Good sooth, even thus; therefore ha' done with words.
To me she's married, not unto my clothes:
Could I repair what she will wear in me,
As I can change these poor accoutrements,
'Twere well for Kate and better for myself.
But what a fool am I to chat with you,
When I should bid good morrow to my bride,
And seal the title with a lovely kiss!
                    [*Exeunt Petruchio and Grumio.*
Tra. He hath some meaning in his mad attire:
We will persuade him, be it possible,
To put on better ere he go to church.
Bap. I'll after him, and see the event of this.
                [*Exeunt Baptista, Gremio, and attendants.*
Tra. But to her love concerneth us to add
Her father's liking: which to bring to pass,
As I before imparted to your worship,
I am to get a man,—whate'er he be,
It skills not much, we'll fit him to our turn,—
And he shall be Vincentio of Pisa;
And make assurance here in Padua
Of greater sums than I have promised.
So shall you quietly enjoy your hope,

And marry sweet Bianca with consent.
Luc. Were it not that my fellow-schoolmaster
   Doth watch Bianca's steps so narrowly,
   'Twere good, methinks, to steal our marriage;
   Which once perform'd, let all the world say no,
   I'll keep mine own, despite of all the world.
Tra. That by degrees we mean to look into,
   And watch our vantage in this business:
   We'll over-reach the greybeard, Gremio,
   The narrow-prying father, Minola,
   The quaint musician, amorous Licio;
   All for my master's sake, Lucentio.

                    Re-enter Gremio.

   Signior Gremio, came you from the church?
Gre. As willingly as e'er I came from school.
Tra. And is the bride and bridegroom coming home?
Gre. A bridegroom say you? 'tis a groom indeed,
   A grumbling groom, and that the girl shall find.
Tra. Curster than she? why, 'tis impossible.
Gre. Why, he's a devil, a devil, a very fiend.
Tra. Why, she's a devil, a devil, the devil's dam.
Gre. Tut, she's a lamb, a dove, a fool to him!
   I'll tell you, Sir Lucentio: when the priest
   Should ask, if Katharine should be his wife,
   'Ay, by gogs-wouns,' quoth he; and swore so loud,
   That, all amazed, the priest let fall the book;
   And, as he stoop'd again to take it up,
   This mad-brain'd bridegroom took him such a cuff,
   That down fell priest and book, and book and priest:
   'Now take them up,' quoth he, 'if any list.'
Tra. What said the wench when he rose again?
Gre. Trembled and shook; for why he stamp'd and swore,
   As if the vicar meant to cozen him.
   But after many ceremonies done,
   He calls for wine: 'A health!' quoth he; as if
   He had been aboard, carousing to his mates
   After a storm: quaff'd off the muscadel,
   And threw the sops all in the sexton's face;
   Having no other reason
   But that his beard grew thin and hungerly
   And seem'd to ask him sops as he was drinking.
   This done, he took the bride about the neck
   And kiss'd her lips with such a clamorous smack
   That at the parting all the church did echo:
   And I seeing this came thence for very shame;

And after me, I know, the rout is coming.
Such a mad marriage never was before :
Hark, hark !   I hear the minstrels play.   [*Music.*
Re-enter Petruchio, Katharina, Bianca, Baptista, Hortensio,
       Grumio, and Train.

Pet. Gentlemen and friends, I thank you for your pains :
I know you think to dine with me to-day,
And have prepared great store of wedding cheer ?
But so it is, my haste doth call me hence,
And therefore here I mean to take my leave.

Bap. Is 't possible you will away to-night ?

Pet. I must away to-day, before night come :
Make it no wonder; if you knew my business,
You would entreat me rather go than stay.
And, honest company, I thank you all,
That have beheld me give away myself
To this most patient, sweet, and virtuous wife .
Dine with my father, drink a health to me ;
For I must hence ; and farewell to you all.

Tra. Let us entreat you stay till after dinner.

Pet. It may not be.

Gre.   Let me entreat you.

Pet. It cannot be.

Kath.   Let me entreat you.

Pet. I am content.

Kath.   Are you content to stay ?

Pet. I am content you shall entreat me stay ;
But yet not stay, entreat me how you can.

Kath. Now, if you love me, stay.

Pet.   Grumio, my horse.

Gru. Ay, sir, they be ready : the oats have eaten the horses.

Kath. Nay, then,
Do what thou canst, I will not go to-day ;
No, nor to-morrow, not till I please myself.
The door is open, sir ; there lies your way ;
You may be jogging whiles your boots are green ;
For me, I 'll not be gone till I please myself :
'Tis like you 'll prove a jolly surly groom,
That take it on you at the first so roundly.

Pet. O Kate, content thee ; prithee, be not angry.

Kath. I will be angry : what hast thou to do ?
Father, be quiet : he shall stay my leisure.

Gre. Ay, marry, sir, now it begins to work.

Kath. Gentlemen, forward to the bridal dinner :
I see a woman may be made a fool,

212

If she had not a spirit to resist.

Pet. They shall go forward, Kate, at thy command.
Obey the bride, you that attend on her ;
Go to the feast, revel and domineer,
Carouse full measure to her maidenhead.
Be mad and merry, or go hang yourselves :
But for my bonny Kate, she must with me.
Nay, look not big, nor stamp, nor stare, nor fret ;
I will be master of what is mine own :
She is my goods, my chattels ; she is my house,
My household stuff, my field, my barn,
My horse, my ox, my ass, my any thing ;
And here she stands, touch her whoever dare ;
I 'll bring mine action on the proudest he
That stops my way in Padua. Grumio,
Draw forth thy weapon, we are beset with thieves ;
Rescue thy mistress, if thou be a man.
Fear not, sweet wench, they shall not touch thee, Kate :
I 'll buckler thee against a million.
                  [*Exeunt Petruchio, Katharina, and Grumio.*

Bap. Nay, let them go, a couple of quiet ones.
Gre. Went they not quickly, I should die with laughing.
Tra. Of all mad matches never was the like.
Luc. Mistress, what 's your opinion of your sister ?
Bian. That, being mad herself, she 's madly mated.
Gre. I warrant him, Petruchio is Kated.
Bap. Neighbours and friends, though bride and bridegroom
For to supply the places at the table,   [wants
You know there wants no junkets at the feast.
Lucentio, you shall supply the bridegroom's place ;
And let Bianca take her sister's room.
Tra. Shall sweet Bianca practise how to bride it ?
Bap. She shall, Lucentio. Come, gentlemen, let 's go.
                                         [*Exeunt.*

ACT IV—SCENE I
Petruchio's country house.
Enter Grumio.

Gru. Fie, fie on all tired jades, on all mad masters, and all
foul ways ! Was ever man so beaten? was ever man so
rayed? was ever man so weary ? I am sent before to make
a fire, and they are coming after to warm them. Now, were
not I a little pot, and soon hot, my very lips might freeze to
my teeth, my tongue to the roof of my mouth, my heart in
my belly ere I should come by a fire to thaw me : but I,

with blowing the fire, shall warm myself; for, considering the weather, a taller man than I will take cold. Holla, ho! Curtis.

Enter Curtis.

Curt. Who is that calls so coldly?

Gru. A piece of ice: if thou doubt it, thou mayst slide from my shoulder to my heel with no greater a run but my head and my neck. A fire, good Curtis.

Curt. Is my master and his wife coming, Grumio?

Gru. O, ay, Curtis, ay: and therefore fire, fire; cast on no

Curt. Is she so hot a shrew as she's reported?   [water.

Gru. She was, good Curtis, before this frost: but, thou knowest, winter tames man, woman, and beast; for it hath tamed my old master, and my new mistress, and myself, fellow Curtis.

Curt. Away, you three-inch fool! I am no beast.

Gru. Am I but three inches? why, thy horn is a foot; and so long am I at the least. But wilt thou make a fire, or shall I complain on thee to our mistress, whose hand, she being now at hand, thou shalt soon feel, to thy cold comfort, for being slow in thy hot office?

Curt. I prithee, good Grumio, tell me, how goes the world?

Gru. A cold world, Curtis, in every office but thine; and therefore fire: do thy duty, and have thy duty; for my master and mistress are almost frozen to death.   [news.

Curt. There's fire ready; and therefore, good Grumio, the

Gru. Why, 'Jack, boy! ho! boy!' and as much news as thou

Curt. Come, you are so full of cony-catching!   [wilt.

Gru. Why, therefore fire; for I have caught extreme cold. Where's the cook? is supper ready, the house trimmed, rushes strewed, cobwebs swept; the serving-men in their new fustian, their white stockings, and every officer his wedding-garment on? Be the jacks fair within, the jills fair without, the carpets laid, and everything in order?

Curt. All ready; and therefore, I pray thee, news.

Gru. First, know, my horse is tired; my master and mistress fallen out.

Curt. How?

Gru. Out of their saddles into the dirt: and thereby hangs a

Curt. Let's ha't, good Grumio.   [tale.

Gru. Lend thine ear.

Curt. Here.

Gru. There.   [*Strikes him.*

Curt. This is to feel a tale, nor to hear a tale.

Gru. And therefore 'tis called a sensible tale: and this cuff was but to knock at your ear, and beseech listening. Now I

begin : *Imprimis*, we came down a foul hill, my master riding
behind my mistress,—

Curt. Both of one horse?

Gru. What's that to thee?

Curt. Why, a horse.

Gru. Tell thou the tale ; but hadst thou not crossed me, thou
shouldst have heard how her horse fell and she under her
horse ; thou shouldst have heard in how miry a place, how
she was bemoiled, how he left her with the horse upon her,
how he beat me because her horse stumbled, how she waded
through the dirt to pluck him off me, how he swore, how
she prayed, that never prayed before, how I cried, how the
horses ran away, how her bridle was burst, how I lost my
crupper, with many things of worthy memory, which now shall
die in oblivion and thou return unexperienced to thy grave.

Curt. By this reckoning he is more shrew than she.

Gru. Ay ; and that thou and the proudest of you all shall find
when he comes home. But what talk I of this ? Call forth
Nathaniel, Joseph, Nicholas, Philip, Walter, Sugarsop and
the rest : let their heads be sleekly combed, their blue coats
brushed, and their garters of an indifferent knit : let them
curtsy with their left legs, and not presume to touch a hair
of my master's horse-tail till they kiss their hands. Are they
all ready ?

Curt. They are.

Gru Call them forth.

Curt. Do you hear, ho ? you must meet my master to counten
ance my mistress !

Gru. Why, she hath a face of her own.

Curt. Who knows not that ?

Gru. Thou, it seems, that calls for company to countenance her.

Curt. I call them forth to credit her.

Gru. Why, she comes to borrow nothing of them.

Enter four or five serving-men.

Nath. Welcome home, Grumio !

Phil. How now, Grumio !

Jos. What, Grumio !

Nich. Fellow Grumio !

Nath. How now, old lad ?

Gru. Welcome, you ;—how now, you ;—what, you ;—fellow,
you ;—and thus much for greeting. Now, my spruce companions, is all ready, and all things neat ?

Nath. All things is ready. How near is our master ?

Gru. E'en at hand, alighted by this ; and therefore be not—
Cock's passion, silence ! I hear my master.

Enter Petruchio and Katharina.

Pet. Where be these knaves? What, no man at door
   To hold my stirrup nor to take my horse!
   Where is Nathaniel, Gregory, Philip?
All Serv. Here, here, sir; here, sir.
Pet. Here, sir! here, sir! here, sir! here, sir!
   You logger-headed and unpolish'd grooms!
   What, no attendance? no regard? no duty?
   Where is the foolish knave I sent before?
Gru. Here, sir; as foolish as I was before.
Pet. You peasant swain! you whoreson malt-horse drudge!
   Did I not bid thee meet me in the park,
   And bring along these rascal knaves with thee?
Gru. Nathaniel's coat, sir, was not fully made,
   And Gabriel's pumps were all unpink'd i' the heel;
   There was no link to colour Peter's hat,
   And Walter's dagger was not come from sheathing:
   There were none fine but Adam, Ralph, and Gregory;
   The rest were ragged, old, and beggarly;
   Yet, as they are, here are they come to meet you.
Pet. Go, rascals, go, and fetch my supper in. [*Exeunt Servants.*

[*Singing*]   Where is the life that late I led—

   Where are those—Sit down, Kate, and welcome.—
   Soud, soud, soud, soud!

Re-enter Servants with supper.

   Why, when, I say? Nay, good sweet Kate, be merry.
   Off with my boots, you rogues! you villains, when?

[*Sings*]   It was the friar of orders grey,
            As he forth walked on his way:—

   Out, you rogue! you pluck my foot awry:
   Take that, and mend the plucking off the other. [*Strikes him.*
   Be merry, Kate. Some water, here; what, ho!
   Where's my spaniel Troilus? Sirrah, get you hence,
   And bid my cousin Ferdinand come hither:
   One, Kate, that you must kiss, and be acquainted with.
   Where are my slippers? Shall I have some water?

Enter one with water.

   Come, Kate, and wash, and welcome heartily.
   You whoreson villain! will you let it fall! [*Strikes him.*
Kath. Patience, I pray you; 'twas a fault unwilling.
Pet. A whoreson beetle-headed, flap-ear'd knave!

216

Come, Kate, sit down ; I know you have a stomach.
Will you give thanks, sweet Kate ; or else shall I ?
What 's this ? mutton ?
First Serv.   Ay.
Pet.   Who brought it ?
Peter.   I.
Pet. 'Tis burnt ; and so is all the meat.
    What dogs are these ! where is the rascal cook ?
    How durst you, villains, bring it from the dresser,
    And serve it thus to me that love it not ?
    There, take it to you, trenches, cups, and all :
        [*Throws the meat, &c. about the stage.*
    You heedless joltheads and unmanner'd slaves !
    What, do you grumble ?   I 'll be with you straight.
Kath. I pray you, husband, be not so disquiet :
    The meat was well, if you were so contented.
Pet. I tell thee, Kate, 'twas burnt and dried away ;
    And I expressly am forbid to touch it,
    For it engenders choler, planteth anger ;
    And better 'twere that both of us did fast,
    Since, of ourselves, ourselves are choleric,
    Than feed it with such over-roasted flesh.
    Be patient ; to-morrow 't shall be mended,
    And, for this night, we 'll fast for company :
    Come, I will bring thee to thy bridal chamber.   [*Exeunt.*
        Re-enter Servants severally.
Nath. Peter, didst ever see the like ?
Peter. He kills her in her own humour.
          Re-enter Curtis.
Gru. Where is he ?
Curt. In her chamber, making a sermon of continency to her ;
    And rails, and swears, and rates, that she, poor soul,
    Knows not which way to stand, to look, to speak,
    And sits as one new-risen from a dream.
    Away, away ! for he is coming hither.   [*Exeunt.*
        Re-enter Petruchio.
Pet. Thus have I politicly begun my reign,
    And 'tis my hope to end successfully.
    My falcon now is sharp and passing empty ;
    And till she stoop she must not be full-gorged,
    For then she never looks upon her lure.
    Another way I have to man my haggard,
    To make her come and know her keeper's call,
    That is, to watch her, as we watch these kites
    That bate and beat and will not be obedient.

She eat no meat to-day, nor none shall eat ;
Last night she slept not, nor to-night she shall not ;
As with the meat, some undeserved fault
I 'll find about the making of the bed ;
And here I 'll fling the pillow, there the bolster,
This way the coverlet, another way the sheets :
Ay, and amid this hurly I intend
That all is done in reverend care of her ;
And in conclusion she shall watch all night :
And if she chance to nod, I 'll rail and brawl,
And with the clamour keep her still awake.
This is a way to kill a wife with kindness ;
And thus I 'll curb her mad and headstrong humour.
He that knows better how to tame a shrew,
Now let him speak : 'tis charity to show.   [*Exit.*

Scene II

Padua.   Before Baptista's house.
Enter Tranio and Hortensio.

Tra. Is 't possible, friend Licio, that Mistress Bianca
    Doth fancy any other but Lucentio ?
    I tell you, sir, she bears me fair in hand.
Hor. Sir, to satisfy you in what I have said,
    Stand by and mark the manner of his teaching.
            Enter Bianca and Lucentio.
Luc. Now, mistress, profit you in what you read ?
Bian. What, master, read you ? first resolve me that.
Luc. I read that I profess, the Art to Love.
Bian. And may you prove, sir, master of your art !
Luc. While you, sweet dear, prove mistress of my heart !
Hor. Quick proceeders, marry !   Now, tell me, I pray,
    You that durst swear that your mistress Bianca
    Loved none in the world so well as Lucentio.
Tra. O despiteful love ! unconstant womankind !
    I tell thee, Licio, this is wonderful.
Hor. Mistake no more : I am not Licio,
    Nor a musician, as I seem to be ;
    But one that scorn to live in this disguise,
    For such a one as leaves a gentleman,
    And makes a god of such a cullion :
    Know, sir, that I am call'd Hortensio.
Tra. Signior Hortensio, I have often heard
    Of your entire affection to Bianca ;
    And since mine eyes are witness of her lightness,

Forswear Bianca and her love for ever.

Hor. See, how they kiss and court! Signior Lucentio,
Here is my hand, and here I firmly vow
Never to woo her more, but do forswear her,
As one unworthy all the former favours
That I have fondly flatter'd her withal.

Tra. And here I take the like unfeigned oath,
Never to marry with her though she would entreat:
Fie on her! see, how beastly she doth court him!

Hor. Would all the world but he had quite forsworn!
For me, that I may surely keep mine oath,
I will be married to a wealthy widow,
Ere three days pass, which hath as long loved me
As I have loved this proud disdainful haggard.
And so farewell, Signior Lucentio.
Kindness in women, not their beauteous looks,
Shall win my love: and so I take my leave,
In resolution as I swore before.   [*Exit.*

Tra. Mistress Bianca, bless you with such grace
As 'longeth to a lover's blessed case?
Nay, I have ta'en you napping, gentle love,
And have forsworn you with Hortensio.

Bian. Tranio, you jest: but have you both forsworn me?

Tra. Mistress, we have.

Luc.   Then we are rid of Licio.

Tra. I' faith, he'll have a lusty widow now,
That shall be woo'd and wedded in a day.

Bian. God give him joy.

Tra. Ay, and he'll tame her.

Bian.   He says so, Tranio.

Tra. Faith, he is gone unto the taming-school.

Bian. The taming-school! what, is there such a place?

Tra. Ay, mistress, and Petruchio is the master;
That teacheth tricks eleven and twenty long,
To tame a shrew and charm her chattering tongue.

Enter Biondello.

Bion. O master, master, I have watch'd so long
That I am dog-weary! but at last I spied
An ancient angel coming down the hill,
Will serve the turn.

Tra.   What is he, Biondello?

Bion. Master, a mercatante, or a pedant,
I know not what; but formal in apparel,
In gait and countenance surely like a father.

219

Luc. And what of him, Tranio?

Tra. If he be credulous and trust my tale,
    I 'll make him glad to seem Vincentio,
    And give assurance to Baptista Minola,
    As if he were the right Vincentio.
    Take in your love, and then let me alone.

[Exeunt Lucentio and Bianca.
Enter a Pedant.

Ped. God save you, sir!

Tra.   And you, sir! you are welcome.
    Travel you far on, or are you at the farthest?

Ped. Sir, at the farthest for a week or two:
    But then up farther, and as far as Rome;
    And so to Tripoli, if God lend me life.

Tra. What countryman, I pray?

Ped.   Of Mantua.

Tra. Of Mantua, sir? marry, God forbid!
    And come to Padua, careless of your life?

Ped. My life, sir! how, I pray? for that goes hard.

Tra. 'Tis death for any one in Mantua
    To come to Padua.   Know you not the cause?
    Your ships are stay'd at Venice; and the Duke,
    For private quarrel 'twixt your duke and him,
    Hath publish'd and proclaim'd it openly:
    'Tis marvel, but that you are but newly come,
    You might have heard it else proclaim'd about.

Ped. Alas, sir, it is worse for me than so!
    For I have bills for money by exchange
    From Florence, and must here deliver them.

Tra. Well, sir, to do you courtesy,
    This will I do, and this I will advise you:
    First, tell me, have you ever been at Pisa?

Ped. Ay, sir, in Pisa have I often been;
    Pisa renowned for grave citizens.

Tra. Among them know you one Vincentio?

Ped. I know him not, but I have heard of him;
    A merchant of incomparable wealth.

Tra. He is my father, sir; and, sooth to say,
    In countenance somewhat doth resemble you.

Bion. As much as an apple doth an oyster, and all one. [*Aside.*

Tra. To save your life in this extremity,
    This favour will I do you for his sake;
    And think it not the worst of all your fortunes
    That you are like to Sir Vincentio.
    His name and credit shall you undertake,

220

And in my house you shall be friendly lodged :
Look that you take upon you as you should ;
You understand me, sir : so shall you stay
Till you have done your business in the city :
If this be courtesy, sir, accept of it.

Ped. O sir, I do ; and will repute you ever
  The patron of my life and liberty.

Tra. Then go with me to make the matter good.
  This, by the way, I let you understand ;
  My father is here look'd for every day,
  To pass assurance of a dower in marriage
  'Twixt me and one Baptista's daughter here :
  In all these circumstances I 'll instruct you :
  Go with me to clothe you as becomes you.   [*Exeunt.*

Scene III

A room in Petruchio's house.
Enter Katharina and Grumio.

Gru. No, no, forsooth ; I dare not for my life.

Kath. The more my wrong, the more his spite appears :
  What, did he marry me to famish me ?
  Beggars, that come unto my father's door,
  Upon entreaty have a present alms ;
  If not, elsewhere they meet with charity :
  But I, who never knew how to entreat,
  Nor never needed that I should entreat,
  Am starved for meat, giddy for lack of sleep ;
  With oaths kept waking, and with brawling fed :
  And that which spites me more than all these wants,
  He does it under name of perfect love ;
  As who should say, if I should sleep or eat,
  'Twere deadly sickness or else present death.
  I prithee go and get me some repast ;
  I care not what, so it be wholesome food.

Gru. What say you to a neat's foot ?

Kath. 'Tis passing good : I prithee let me have it.

Gru. I fear it is too choleric a meat.
  How say you to a fat tripe finely broil'd ?

Kath. I like it well : good Grumio, fetch it me.

Gru. I cannot tell ; I fear 'tis choleric.
  What say you to a piece of beef and mustard ?

Kath. I dish that I do love to feed upon.

Gru. Ay, but the mustard is too hot a little.

Kath. Why then, the beef, and let the mustard rest.

Gru. Nay then, I will not : you shall have the mustard,

Or else you get no beef of Grumio.

Kath. Then both, or one, or anything thou wilt.

Gru. Why then, the mustard without the beef.

Kath. Go, get thee gone, thou false deluding slave, [*Beats him.*
That feed'st me with the very name of meat:
Sorrow on thee and all the pack of you
That triumph thus upon my misery!
Go, get thee gone, I say.

        Enter Petruchio and Hortensio with meat.

Pet. How fares my Kate? What, sweeting, all amort?

Hor. Mistress, what cheer?

Kath.   Faith, as cold as can be.

Pet. Pluck up thy spirits; look cheerfully upon me.
Here, love; thou see'st how diligent I am
To dress thy meat myself and bring it thee:
I am sure, sweet Kate, this kindness merits thanks.
What, not a word? Nay, then thou lovest it not;
And all my pains is sorted to no proof.
Here, take away this dish.

Kath.   I pray you, let it stand.

Pet. The poorest service is repaid with thanks;
And so shall mine, before you touch the meat.

Kath. I thank you, sir.

Hor. Signior Petruchio, fie! you are to blame.
Come, Mistress Kate, I'll bear you company.

Pet. Eat it all up, Hortensio, if thou lovest me.   [*Aside.*
Much good do it unto thy gentle heart!
Kate, eat apace: and now, my honey love,
Will we return unto thy father's house,
And revel it as bravely as the best,
With silken coats and caps and golden rings,
With ruffs and cuffs and fardingales and things;
With scarfs and fans and double change of bravery,
With amber bracelets, beads and all this knavery.
What, hast thou dined? The tailor stays thy leisure,
To deck thy body with his ruffling treasure.

                Enter Tailor.

Come, tailor, let us see these ornaments;
Lay forth the gown.

             Enter Haberdasher.

            What news with you, sir?

Hab. Here is the cap your worship did bespeak.

Pet. Why, this was moulded on a porringer;
A velvet dish: fie, fie! 'tis lewd and filthy:
Why, 'tis a cockle or a walnut shell,

A knack, a toy, a trick, a baby's cap:
Away with it! come, let me have a bigger.
Kath. I 'll have no bigger: this doth fit the time,
And gentlewomen wear such caps as these.
Pet. When you are gentle, you shall have one too,
And not till then.
Hor.   That will not be in haste.   [*Aside.*
Kath. Why, sir, I trust I may have leave to speak;
And speak I will; I am no child, no babe:
Your betters have endured me say my mind,
And if you cannot, best you stop your ears.
My tongue will tell the anger of my heart,
Or else my heart concealing it will break;
And rather than it shall, I will be free
Even to the uttermost, as I please, in words.
Pet. Why, thou say'st true; it is a paltry cap,
A custard-coffin, a bauble, a silken pie:
I love thee well, in that thou likest it not.
Kath. Love me or love me not, I like the cap;
And it I will have, or I will have none. [*Exit Haberdasher.*
Pet. Thy gown? why, ay: come, tailor, let us see 't.
O mercy, God! what masquing stuff is here?
What 's this? a sleeve? 'tis like a demi-cannon:
What, up and down, carved like an apple-tart?
Here 's snip and nip and cut and slish and slash,
Like to a censer in a barber's shop:
Why, what, i' devil's name, tailor, call'st thou this?
Hor. I see she 's like to have neither cap nor gown.   [*Aside.*
Tai. You bid me make it orderly and well,
According to the fashion and the time.
Pet. Marry, and did; but if you be remember'd,
I did not bid you mar it to the time.
Go, hop me over every kennel home,
For you shall hop without my custom, sir:
I 'll none of it: hence! make your best of it.
Kath. I never saw a better-fashion'd gown,
More quaint, more pleasing, nor more commendable:
Belike you mean to make a puppet of me.
Pet. Why, true; he means to make a puppet of thee.
Tai. She says your worship means to make a puppet of her.
Pet. O monstrous arrogance! Thou liest, thou thread, thou
Thou yard, three-quarters, half-yard, quarter, nail! [thimble,
Thou flea, thou nit, thou winter-cricket thou!
Braved in mine own house with a skein of thread?
Away, thou rag, thou quantity, thou remnant;

Or I shall so be-mete thee with thy yard,
As thou shalt think on prating whilst thou livest!
I tell thee, I, that thou hast marr'd her gown.

Tai. Your worship is deceived; the gown is made
Just as my master had direction:
Grumio gave order how it should be done.

Gru. I gave him no order; I gave him the stuff.

Tai. But how did you desire it should be made?

Gru. Marry, sir, with needle and thread.

Tai. But did you not request to have it cut?

Gru. Thou hast faced many things.

Tai. I have.

Gru. Face not me: thou hast braved many men; brave not
me; I will neither be faced nor braved. I say unto thee,
I bid thy master cut out the gown, but I did not bid him cut
it to pieces: ergo, thou liest.

Tai. Why, here is the note of the fashion to testify.

Pet. Read it.

Gru. The note lies in 's throat if he say I said so.

Tai. [*reads*] 'Imprimis, a loose-bodied gown:'

Gru. Master, if ever I said loose-bodied gown, sew me in the
skirts of it, and beat me to death with a bottom of brown
thread: I said a gown.

Pet. Proceed.

Tai. [*reads*] 'With a small compassed cape:'

Gru. I confess the cape.

Tai. [*reads*] 'With a trunk sleeve:'

Gru. I confess two sleeves.

Tai. [*reads*] 'The sleeves curiously cut.'

Pet. Ay, there's the villany.

Gru. Error i' the bill, sir; error i' the bill. I commanded the
sleeves should be cut out, and sewed up again; and that
I'll prove upon thee, though thy little finger be armed in a
thimble.

Tai. This is true that I say: an I had thee in place where, thou
shouldst know it.

Gru. I am for thee straight: take thou the bill, give me thy
mete-yard, and spare not me.

Hor. God-a-mercy, Grumio! then he shall have no odds.

Pet. Well, sir, in brief, the gown is not for me.

Gru. You are i' the right, sir: 'tis for my mistress.

Pet. Go, take it up unto thy master's use.

Gru. Villain, not for thy life: take up my mistress' gown for
thy master's use!

Pet. Why, sir, what's your conceit in that?

Gru. O, sir, the conceit is deeper than you think for:
  Take up my mistress' gown to his master's use!
  O, fie, fie, fie!
Pet. Hortensio, say thou wilt see the tailor paid.   [*Aside.*
  Go take it hence; be gone, and say no more.
Hor. Tailor, I 'll pay thee for thy gown to-morrow:
  Take no unkindness of his hasty words:
  Away! I say; commend me to thy master.   [*Exit Tailor.*
Pet. Well, come, my Kate; we will unto your father's
  Even in these honest mean habiliments:
  Our purses shall be proud, our garments poor;
  For 'tis the mind that makes the body rich;
  And as the sun breaks through the darkest clouds,
  So honour peereth in the meanest habit.
  What, is the jay more precious than the lark,
  Because his feathers are more beautiful?
  Or is the adder better than the eel,
  Because his painted skin contents the eye?
  O, no, good Kate; neither art thou the worse
  For this poor furniture and mean array.
  If thou account'st it shame, lay it on me;
  And therefore frolic: we will hence forthwith,
  To feast and sport us at thy father's house.
  Go, call my men, and let us straight to him;
  And bring our horses unto Long-lane end;
  There will we mount, and thither walk on foot.
  Let 's see; I think 'tis now some seven o'clock,
  And well we may come there by dinner-time.
Kath. I dare assure you, sir, 'tis almost two;
  And 'twill be supper-time ere you come there.
Pet. It shall be seven ere I go to horse:
  Look, what I speak, or do, or think to do,
  You are still crossing it. Sirs, let 't alone:
  I will not go to-day; and ere I do,
  It shall be what o'clock I say it is.
Hor. Why, so this gallant will command the sun.   [*Exeunt.*

SCENE IV

Padua. Before Baptista's house.
Enter Tranio, and the Pedant dressed like Vincentio.

Tra. Sir, this is the house: please it you that I call?
Ped. Ay, what else? and but I be deceived
  Signior Baptista may remember me,
  Near twenty years ago, in Genoa,
  Where we were lodgers at the Pegasus.

Tra. 'Tis well; and hold your own, in any case,
  With such austerity as 'longeth to a father.
Ped. I warrant you.

Enter Biondello.

                    But, sir, here comes your boy;
  'Twere good he were school'd.
Tra. Fear you not him.   Sirrah Biondello,
  Now do your duty throughly, I advise you:
  Imagine 'twere the right Vincentio.
Bion. Tut, fear not me.
Tra. But hast thou done thy errand to Baptista?
Bion. I told him that your father was at Venice;
  And that you look'd for him this day in Padua.
Tra. Thou 'rt a tall fellow: hold thee that to drink.
  Here comes Baptista: set your countenance, sir.

Enter Baptista and Lucentio.

  Signior Baptista, you are happily met.
  [*To the Pedant*] Sir, this is the gentleman I told you of:
  I pray you, stand good father to me now,
  Give me Bianca for my patrimony.
Ped. Soft, son!
  Sir, by your leave: having come to Padua
  To gather in some debts, my son Lucentio
  Made me acquainted with a weighty cause
  Of love between your daughter and himself:
  And, for the good report I hear of you,
  And for the love he beareth to your daughter,
  And she to him, to stay him not too long,
  I am content, in a good father's care,
  To have him match'd; and, if you please to like
  No worse than I, upon some agreement
  Me shall you find ready and willing
  With one consent to have her so bestow'd;
  For curious I cannot be with you,
  Signior Baptista, of whom I hear so well.
Bap. Sir, pardon me in what I have to say:
  Your plainness and your shortness please me well.
  Right true it is, your son Lucentio here
  Doth love my daughter, and she loveth him,
  Or both dissemble deeply their affections:
  And therefore, if you say no more than this,
  That like a father you will deal with him,
  And pass my daughter a sufficient dower,
  The match is made, and all is done:
  Your son shall have my daughter with consent.

226

Tra. I thank you, sir.   Where then do you know best
  We be affied and such assurance ta'en
  As shall with either part's agreement stand?
Bap. Not in my house, Lucentio; for, you know,
  Pitchers have ears, and I have many servants:
  Besides, old Gremio is hearkening still;
  And happily we might be interrupted.
Tra. Then at my lodging, an it like you:
  There doth my father lie; and there, this night,
  We'll pass the business privately and well.
  Send for your daughter by your servant here;
  My boy shall fetch the scrivener presently.
  The worst is this, that, at so slender warning,
  You are like to have a thin and slender pittance.
Bap. It likes me well.   Cambio, hie you home,
  And bid Bianca make her ready straight;
  And, if you will, tell what hath happened,
  Lucentio's father is arrived in Padua,
  And how she's like to be Lucentio's wife.
Bion. I pray the gods she may with all my heart!
Tra. Dally not with the gods, but get thee gone.   [*Exit Bion.*
  Signior Baptista, shall I lead the way?
  Welcome! one mess is like to be your cheer:
  Come, sir; we will better it in Pisa.
Bap. I follow you.   [*Exeunt Tranio, Pedant, and Baptista.*
                   Re-enter Biondello.
Bion. Cambio.
Luc. What sayest thou, Biondello?
Bion. You saw my master wink and laugh upon you?
Luc. Biondello, what of that?
Bion. Faith, nothing; but has left me here behind, to expound
  the meaning or moral of his signs and tokens.
Luc. I pray thee, moralize them.
Bion. Then thus.   Baptista is safe, talking with the deceiving
  father of a deceitful son.
Luc. And what of him?
Bion. His daughter is to be brought by you to the supper.
Luc. And then?
Bion. The old priest at Saint Luke's church is at your com-
  mand at all hours.
Luc. And what of all this?
Bion. I cannot tell; expect they are busied about a counterfeit
  assurance: take your assurance of her, 'cum privilegio ad
  imprimendum solum:' to the church; take the priest, clerk,
  and some sufficient honest witnesses:

227

If this be not that you look for, I have no more to say,
But bid Bianca farewell for ever and a day.

Luc. Hearest thou, Biondello?

Bion. I cannot tarry: I knew a wench married in an afternoon
as she went to the garden for parsley to stuff a rabbit; and
so may you, sir: and so, adieu, sir. My master hath appointed
me to go to Saint Luke's, to bid the priest be ready to come
against you come with your appendix.   [*Exit.*

Luc. I may, and will, if she be so contented:
She will be pleased; then wherefore should I doubt?
Hap what hap may, I'll roundly go about her:
It shall go hard if Cambio go without her.   [*Exit.*

Scene V

A public road.

Enter Petruchio, Katharina, Hortensio, and Servants.

Pet. Come on, i' God's name; once more toward our father's.
Good Lord, how bright and goodly shines the moon!

Kath. The moon! the sun: it is not moonlight now.

Pet. I say it is the moon that shines so bright.

Kath. I know it is the sun that shines so bright.

Pet. Now, by my mother's son, and that's myself,
It shall be moon, or star, or what I list,
Or ere I journey to your father's house.
Go on, and fetch our horses back again.
Evermore cross'd and cross'd; nothing but cross'd!

Hor. Say as he says, or we shall never go.

Kath. Forward, I pray, since we have come so far,
And be it moon, or sun, or what you please:
An if you please to call it a rush-candle,
Henceforth I vow it shall be so for me.

Pet. I say it is the moon.

Kath.   I know it is the moon.

Pet. Nay, then you lie: it is the blessed sun.

Kath. Then, God be bless'd, it is the blessed sun:
But sun it is not, when you say it is not;
And the moon changes even as your mind.
What you will have it named, even that it is;
And so it shall be so for Katharine.

Hor. Petruchio, go thy ways; the field is won.

Pet. Well, forward, forward! thus the bowl should run,
And not unluckily against the bias.
But, soft! company is coming here.

Enter Vincentio.

[*To Vincentio*] Good morrow, gentle mistress: where away?

Tell me, sweet Kate, and tell me truly too,
Hast thou beheld a fresher gentlewoman?
Such war of white and red within her cheeks!
What stars do spangle heaven with such beauty,
As those two eyes become that heavenly face?
Fair lovely maid, once more good day to thee.
Sweet Kate, embrace her for her beauty's sake.

Hor. A' will make the man mad, to make a woman of him.

Kath. Young budding virgin, fair and fresh and sweet,
Whither away, or where is thy abode?
Happy the parents of so fair a child;
Happier the man, whom favourable stars
Allot thee for his lovely bed-fellow!

Pet. Why, how now, Kate! I hope thou art not mad:
This is a man, old, wrinkled, faded, wither'd;
And not a maiden, as thou say'st he is.

Kath. Pardon, old father, my mistaking eyes,
That have been so bedazzled with the sun,
That every thing I look on seemeth green:
Now I perceive thou art a reverend father;
Pardon, I pray thee, for my mad mistaking.

Pet. Do, good old grandsire; and withal make known
Which way thou travellest: if along with us,
We shall be joyful of thy company.

Vin. Fair sir, and you my merry mistress,
That with your strange encounter much amazed me,
My name is call'd Vincentio; my dwelling Pisa;
And bound I am to Padua; there to visit
A son of mine, which long I have not seen.

Pet. What is his name?

Vin. Lucentio, gentle sir.

Pet. Happily met; the happier for thy son.
And now by law, as well as reverend age,
I may entitle thee my loving father:
The sister to my wife, this gentlewoman,
Thy son by this hath married. Wonder not,
Nor be not grieved: she is of good esteem,
Her dowry wealthy, and of worthy birth;
Beside, so qualified as may beseem
The spouse of any noble gentleman.
Let me embrace with old Vincentio,
And wander we to see thy honest son,
Who will of thy arrival be full joyous.

Vin. But is this true? or is it else your pleasure,
Like pleasant travellers, to break a jest

Upon the company you overtake?

Hor. I do assure thee, father, so it is.

Pet. Come, go along, and see the truth hereof;

For our first merriment hath made thee jealous.

> *[Exeunt all but Hortensio.*

Hor. Well, Petruchio, this has put me in heart.

Have to my widow! and if she be froward,

Then hast thou taught Hortensio to be untoward.   *[Exit.*

ACT V—Scene I

Padua.   Before Lucentio's house.

*Gremio discovered.   Enter behind Biondello, Lucentio, and
Bianca.*

Bion. Softly and swiftly, sir; for the priest is ready.

Luc. I fly, Biondello: but they may chance to need thee at
home; therefore leave us.

Bion. Nay, faith, I'll see the church o' your back; and then
come back to my master's as soon as I can.

> *[Exeunt Lucentio, Bianca, and Biondello.*

Gre. I marvel Cambio comes not all this while.

*Enter Petruchio, Katharina, Vincentio, Grumio, with
Attendants.*

Pet. Sir, here's the door, this is Lucentio's house:

My father's bears more toward the market-place;

Thither must I, and here I leave you, sir.

Vin. You shall not choose but drink before you go:

I think I shall command your welcome here,

And, by all likelihood, some cheer is toward.   *[Knocks.*

Gre. They're busy within; you were best knock louder.

Pedant looks out of the window.

Ped. What's he that knocks as he would beat down the gate?

Vin. Is Signior Lucentio within, sir?

Ped. He's within, sir, but not to be spoken withal.

Vin. What if a man bring him a hundred pound or two, to
make merry withal?

Ped. Keep your hundred pounds to yourself: he shall need
none, so long as I live.

Pet. Nay, I told you your son was well beloved in Padua.   Do
you hear, sir?—to leave frivolous circumstances,—I pray
you, tell Signior Lucentio, that his father is come from Pisa,
and is here at the door to speak with him.

Ped. Thou liest: his father has come from Padua and here
looking out at the window.

Vin. Art thou his father?

The Taming of the Shrew [Act V, Sc. i

Ped. Ay, sir; so his mother says, if I may believe her.
Pet. [*To Vincentio*] Why, how now, gentleman! why, this is flat
    knavery, to take upon you another man's name.
Ped. Lay hands on the villain: I believe a' means to cozen
    somebody in this city under my countenance.

Re-enter Biondello.

Bion. I have seen them in the church together: God send 'em
    good shipping! But who is here? mine old master Vin-
    centio! now we are undone, and brought to nothing.
Vin. [*Seeing Biondello*] Come hither, crack-hemp.
Bion. I hope I may choose, sir.
Vin. Come hither, you rogue. What, have you forgot me?
Bion. Forgot you! no, sir: I could not forget you, for I never
    saw you before in all my life.
Vin. What, you notorious villain, didst thou never see thy
    master's father, Vincentio?
Bion. What, my old worshipful old master? yes, marry, sir:
    see where he looks out of the window.
Vin. Is't so, indeed? [*Beats Biondello.*
Bion. Help, help, help! here's a madman will murder me.
    [*Exit.*
Ped. Help, son! help, Signior Baptista! [*Exit from above.*
Pet. Prithee, Kate, let's stand aside, and see the end of this
    controversy. [*They retire.*

Re-enter Pedant below; Tranio, Baptista, and Servants.

Tra. Sir, what are you, that offer to beat my servant?
Vin. What am I, sir! nay, what are you, sir? O immortal
    gods! O fine villain! A silken doublet! a velvet hose! a
    scarlet cloak! and a copatain hat! O, I am undone! I am
    undone! while I play the good husband at home, my son
    and my servant spend all at the university.
Tra. How now! what's the matter?
Bap. What, is the man lunatic?
Tra. Sir, you seem a sober ancient gentleman by your habit,
    but your words show you a madman. Why, sir, what 'cerns
    it you if I wear pearl and gold? I thank my good father, I
    am able to maintain it.
Vin. Thy father! O villain! he is a sail-maker in Bergamo.
Bap. You mistake, sir, you mistake, sir. Pray, what do you
    think is his name?
Vin. His name! as if I knew not his name: I have brought
    him up ever since he was three years old, and his name is
    Tranio.

Ped. Away, away, mad ass! his name is Lucentio; and he is
mine only son, and heir to the lands of me, Signior
Vincentio.

Vin. Lucentio! O, he hath murdered his master! Lay hold
on him, I charge you, in the Duke's name. O, my son, my
son! Tell me, thou villain, where is my son Lucentio?

Tra. Call forth an officer.

Enter one with an Officer.

Carry this mad knave to the gaol. Father Baptista, I charge
you see that he be forthcoming.

Vin. Carry me to the gaol!

Gre. Stay, officer: he shall not go to prison.

Bap. Talk not, Signior Gremio: I say he shall go to prison.

Gre. Take heed, Signior Baptista, lest you be cony-catched in
this business: I dare swear this is the right Vincentio.

Ped. Swear, if thou darest.

Gre. Nay, I dare not swear it.

Tra. Then thou wert best say that I am not Lucentio.

Gre. Yes, I know thee to be Signior Lucentio.

Bap. Away with the dotard! to the gaol with him!

Vin. Thus strangers may be haled and abused:
O monstrous villain!

Re-enter Biondello, with Lucentio and Bianca.

Bian. O, we are spoiled! and—yonder he is: deny him, forswear him, or else we are all undone.

Luc. Pardon, sweet father.   [*Kneeling.*

Vin.   Lives my sweet son?

[Exeunt Biondello, Tranio, and Pedant, as fast as may be.

Bian. Pardon, dear father.

Bap.   How hast thou offended?
Where is Lucentio?

Luc.   Here's Lucentio.
Right son to the right Vincentio;
That have by marriage made thy daughter mine,
While counterfeit supposes blear'd thine eyne.

Gre. Here's packing, with a witness, to deceive us all!

Vin. Where is that damned villain Tranio,
That faced and braved me in this matter so?

Bap. Why, tell me, is not this my Cambio?

Bian. Cambio is changed into Lucentio.

Luc. Love wrought these miracles. Bianca's love
Made me exchange my state with Tranio,
While he did bear my countenance in the town;
And happily I have arrived at the last
Unto the wished haven of my bliss.

232

The Taming of the Shrew [Act V, Sc. ii

What Tranio did, myself enforced him to;
Then pardon him, sweet father, for my sake.   [gaol.
Vin. I 'll slit the villain's nose, that would have sent me to the
Bap. But do you hear, sir? have you married my daughter
    without asking my good will?
Vin. Fear not, Baptista; we will content you, go to: but I will
    in, to be revenged for this villany.   [*Exit.*
Bap. And I, to sound the depth of this knavery.   [*Exit.*
Luc. Look not pale, Bianca; thy father will not frown.
                  [*Exeunt Lucentio and Bianca.*
Gre. My cake is dough: but I 'll in among the rest;
    Out of hope of all, but my share of the feast.   [*Exit.*
Kath. Husband, let 's follow, to see the end of this ado.
Pet. First kiss me, Kate, and we will.
Kath. What, in the midst of the street?
Pet. What, art thou ashamed of me?
Kath. No, sir, God forbid; but ashamed to kiss.
Pet. Why, then let 's home again.   Come, sirrah, let 's away.
Kath. Nay, I will give thee a kiss: now pray thee, love, stay.
Pet. Is not this well?   Come, my sweet Kate:
    Better once than never, for never too late.   [*Exeunt.*

SCENE II

Padua.   Lucentio's house.

*Enter Baptista, Vincentio, Gremio, the Pedant, Lucentio, Bianca,
Petruchio, Katharina, Hortensio, and Widow, Tranio, Biondello, and Grumio: the Serving-men with Tranio bringing in
a banquet.*

Luc. At last, though long, our jarring notes agree:
    And time it is, when raging war is done,
    To smile at scapes and perils overblown.
    My fair Bianca, bid my father welcome,
    While I with self-same kindness welcome thine.
    Brother Petruchio, sister Katharina,
    And thou, Hortensio, with thy loving widow,
    Feast with the best, and welcome to my house:
    My banquet is to close our stomachs up,
    After our great good cheer.   Pray you, sit down;
    For now we sit to chat, as well as eat.
Pet. Nothing but sit and sit, and eat and eat!
Bap. Padua affords this kindness, son Petruchio.
Pet. Padua affords nothing but what is kind.
Hor. For both our sakes, I would that word were true
Pet. Now, for my life, Hortensio fears his widow.
Wid. Then never trust me, if I be afeard.

233

Pet. You are very sensible, and yet you miss my sense:
　I mean, Hortensio is afeard of you.
Wid. He that is giddy thinks the world turns round.
Pet. Roundly replied.
Kath.　　　　　　　　　Mistress, how mean you that?
Wid. Thus I conceive by him.
Pet. Conceives by me! How likes Hortensio that?
Hor. My widow says, thus she conceives her tale.
Pet. Very well mended. Kiss him for that, good widow.
Kath. 'He that is giddy thinks the world turns round:'
　I pray you, tell me what you meant by that.
Wid. Your husband, being troubled with a shrew,
　Measures my husband's sorrow by his woe:
　And now you know my meaning.
Kath. A very mean meaning.
Wid.　　　　　　　　　Right, I mean you.
Kath. And I am mean, indeed, respecting you.
Pet. To her, Kate!
Hor. To her, widow!
Pet. A hundred marks, my Kate does put her down.
Hor. That's my office.
Pet. Spoke like an officer: ha' to thee, lad.
　　　　　　　　　　　　　　　[*Drinks to Hortensio.*
Bap. How likes Gremio these quick-witted folks?
Gre. Believe me, sir, they butt together well.
Bian. Head, and butt! an hasty-witted body
　Would say your head and butt were head and horn.
Vin. Ay, mistress bride, hath that awaken'd you?
Bian. Ay, but not frighted me; therefore I'll sleep again.
Pet. Nay, that you shall not: since you have begun,
　Have at you for a bitter jest or two!
Bian. Am I your bird? I mean to shift my bush;
　And then pursue me as you draw your bow.
　You are welcome all.
　　　　　　　　　[*Exeunt Bianca, Katharina, and Widow.*
Pet. She hath prevented me. Here, Signior Tranio,
　This bird you aim'd at, though you hit her not;
　Therefore a health to all that shot and miss'd.
Tra. O, sir, Lucentio slipp'd me like his greyhound,
　Which runs himself, and catches for his master.
Pet. A good swift simile, but something currish.
Tra. 'Tis well, sir, that you hunted for yourself:
　'Tis thought your deer does hold you at bay.
Bap. O ho, Petruchio! Tranio hits you now.
Luc. I thank thee for that gird, good Tranio.

Hor. Confess, confess, hath he not hit you here?
Pet. A' has a little gall'd me, I confess;
   And, as the jest did glance away from me,
   'Tis ten to one it maim'd you two outright.
Bap. Now, in good sadness, son Petruchio,
   I think thou hast the veriest shrew of all.
Pet. Well, I say no: and therefore for assurance
   Let's each one send unto his wife;
   And he whose wife is most obedient,
   To come at first when he doth send for her,
   Shall win the wager which we will propose.
Hor. Content.   What is the wager?
Luc.   Twenty crowns.
Pet. Twenty crowns!
   I'll venture so much of my hawk or hound,
   But twenty times so much upon my wife.
Luc. A hundred then.
Hor.   Content.
Pet.   A match! 'tis done.
Hor. Who shall begin?
Luc.   That will I.
   Go, Biondello, bid your mistress come to me.
Bion. I go.   [*Exit.*
Bap. Son, I'll be your half, Bianca comes.
Luc. I'll have no halves; I'll bear it all myself.

               Re-enter Biondello.

   How now! what news?
Bion.   Sir, my mistress sends you word
   That she is busy, and she cannot come.
Pet. How! she is busy, and she cannot come!
   Is that an answer?
Gre.   Ay, and a kind one too:
   Pray God, sir, your wife send you not a worse.
Pet. I hope, better.
Hor. Sirrah Biondello, go and entreat my wife
   To come to me forthwith.   [*Exit Biondello.*
Pet.   O, ho! entreat her!
   Nay, then she must needs come.
Hor.   I am afraid, sir,
   Do what you can, yours will not be entreated.

               Re-enter Biondello.

   Now, where's my wife?
Bion. She says you have some goodly jest in hand:
   She will not come; she bids you come to her.
Pet. Worse and worse; she will not come!   O vile,

    Intolerable, not to be endured !

    Sirrah Grumio, go to your mistress ;

    Say, I command her come to me.   *[Exit Grumio.*

Hor. I know her answer.

Pet.   What ?

Hor.   She will not.

Pet. The fouler fortune mine, and there an end.

Bap. Now, by my holidame, here comes Katharina !

              Re-enter Katharina.

Kath. What is your will, sir, that you send for me ?

Pet. Where is your sister, and Hortensio's wife?

Kath. They sit conferring by the parlour fire.

Pet. Go, fetch them hither : if they deny to come,

    Swinge me them soundly forth unto their husbands :

    Away, I say, and bring them hither straight.

                    [Exit Katharina.

Luc. Here is a wonder, if you talk of a wonder.

Hor. And so it is : I wonder what it bodes.

Pet. Marry, peace it bodes, and love, and quiet life,

    An awful rule, and right supremacy ;

    And, to be short, what not, that 's sweet and happy ?

Bap. Now, fair befal thee, good Petruchio !

    The wager thou hast won ; and I will add

    Unto their losses twenty thousand crowns ;

    Another dowry to another daughter,

    For she is changed, as she had never. been.

Pet. Nay, I will win my wager better yet,

    And show more sign of her obedience,

    Her new-built virtue and obedience.

    See where she comes and brings your froward wives

    As prisoners to her womanly persuasion.

      Re-enter Katharina, with Bianca and Widow.

    Katharine, that cap of yours becomes you not :

    Off with that bauble, throw it under-foot.

Wid. Lord, let me never have a cause to sigh,

    Till I be brought to such a silly pass !

Bian. Fie, what a foolish duty call you this?

Luc. I would your duty were as foolish too :

    The wisdom of your duty, fair Bianca,

    Hath cost me an hundred crowns since supper-time.

Bian. The more fool you, for laying on my duty.

Pet. Katharine, I charge thee, tell these headstrong **women**

    What duty they do owe their lords and husbands.

Wid. Come, come, you 're mocking : we will have no **telling.**

Pet. Come on, I say ; and first begin with her.

Wid. She shall not.

Pet. I say she shall: and first begin with her.

Kath. Fie, fie! unknit that threatening unkind brow;
  And dart not scornful glances from those eyes,
  To wound thy lord, thy king, thy governor:
  It blots thy beauty as frosts do bite the meads,
  Confounds thy fame as whirlwinds shake fair buds,
  And in no sense is meet or amiable.
  A woman moved is like a fountain troubled,
  Muddy, ill-seeming, thick, bereft of beauty;
  And while it is so, none so dry or thirsty
  Will deign to sip or touch one drop of it.
  Thy husband is thy lord, thy life, thy keeper,
  Thy head, thy sovereign; one that cares for thee,
  And for thy maintenance commits his body
  To painful labour both by sea and land,
  To watch the night in storms, the day in cold,
  Whilst thou liest warm at home, secure and safe;
  And craves no other tribute at thy hands
  But love, fair looks and true obedience;
  Too little payment for so great a debt.
  Such duty as the subject owes the prince
  Even such a woman oweth to her husband;
  And when she is froward, peevish, sullen, sour,
  And not obedient to his honest will,
  What is she but a foul contending rebel,
  And graceless traitor to her loving lord?
  I am ashamed that women are so simple
  To offer war where they should kneel for peace;
  Or seek for rule, supremacy and sway,
  When they are bound to serve, love and obey.
  Why are our bodies soft and weak and smooth,
  Unapt to toil and trouble in the world,
  But that our soft conditions and our hearts
  Should well agree with our external parts?
  Come, come, you froward and unable worms!
  My mind hath been as big as one of yours,
  My heart as great, my reason haply more,
  To bandy word for word and frown for frown;
  But now I see our lances are but straws,
  Our strength as weak, our weakness past compare,
  That seeming to be most which we indeed least are.
  Then vail your stomachs, for it is no boot,
  And place your hands below your husband's foot:
  In token of which duty, if he please,

My hand is ready, may it do him ease.

Pet. Why, there 's a wench ! Come on, and kiss me, Kate.

Luc. Well, go thy ways, old lad ; for thou shalt ha 't.

Vin. 'Tis a good hearing, when children are toward.

Luc. But a harsh hearing, when women are froward.

Pet. Come, Kate, we 'll to bed.

We three are married, but you two are sped.

'Twas I won the wager, though you hit the white ;

[To Lucentio.

And, being a winner, God give you good night !

[Exeunt Petruchio and Katharina.

Hor. Now, go thy ways ; thou hast tamed a curst shrew.

Luc. 'Tis a wonder, by your leave, she will be tamed so.

[Exeunt.

MEASURE FOR MEASURE

DRAMATIS PERSONÆ

VINCENTIO, *the Duke.*
ANGELO, *Deputy.*
ESCALUS, *an ancient Lord.*
CLAUDIO, *a young gentleman.*
LUCIO, *a fantastic.*
Two other gentlemen.
PROVOST.
THOMAS, } *two friars.*
PETER,
A Justice.
VARRIUS.

ELBOW, *a simple constable.*
FROTH, *a foolish gentleman.*
POMPEY, *servant to Mistress Overdone.*
ABHORSON, *an executioner.*
BARNARDINE, *a dissolute prisoner.*

ISABELLA, *sister to Claudio.*
MARIANA, *betrothed to Angelo.*
JULIET, *beloved of Claudio.*
FRANCISCA, *a nun.*
MISTRESS OVERDONE, *a bawd.*

Lords, Officers, Citizens, Boy, and Attendants.
SCENE: *Vienna.*

ACT I—SCENE I

An apartment in the Duke's palace.
Enter Duke, Escalus, Lords and Attendants.

Duke. Escalus.
Escal. My lord.
Duke. Of government the properties to unfold,
 Would seem in me to affect speech and discourse;
 Since I am put to know that your own science
 Exceeds, in that, the lists of all advice
 My strength can give you: then no more remains,
 But that to your sufficiency . . . .
 . . . . as your worth is able,
 And let them work. The nature of our people,
 Our city's institutions, and the terms
 For common justice, you 're as pregnant in
 As art and practice hath enriched any
 That we remember. There is our commission,
 From which we would not have you warp. Call hither,
 I say, bid come before us Angelo. [*Exit an Attendant.*
 What figure of us think you he will bear?
 For you must know, we have with special soul
 Elected him our absence to supply;
 Lent him our terror, dress'd him with our love,
 And given his deputation all the organs
 Of our own power: what think you of it?
Escal. If any in Vienna be of worth
 To undergo such ample grace and honour,
 It is Lord Angelo.
Duke.   Look where he comes.

Enter Angelo.

Ang. Always obedient to your Grace's will,
 I come to know your pleasure.

239

Duke.   Angelo,
   There is a kind of character in thy life,
   That to th' observer doth thy history
   Fully unfold.   Thyself and thy belongings
   Are not thine own so proper, as to waste
   Thyself upon thy virtues, they on thee.
   Heaven doth with us as we with torches do,
   Not light them for themselves; for if our virtues
   Did not go forth of us, 'twere all alike
   As if we had them not.   Spirits are not finely touch'd
   But to fine issues; nor Nature never lends
   The smallest scruple of her excellence,
   But, like a thrifty goddess, she determines
   Herself the glory of a creditor,
   Both thanks and use.   But I do bend my speech
   To one that can my part in him advertise;
   Hold therefore, Angelo :—
   In our remove be thou at full ourself;
   Mortality and mercy in Vienna
   Live in thy tongue and heart: old Escalus,
   Though first in question, is thy secondary.
   Take thy commission.
Ang.   Now, good my lord,
   Let there be some more test made of my metal,
   Before so noble and so great a figure
   Be stamped upon it.
Duke.   No more evasion :
   We have with a leaven'd and prepared choice
   Proceeded to you; therefore take your honours.
   Our haste from hence is of so quick condition,
   That it prefers itself, and leaves unquestion'd
   Matters of needful value.   We shall write to you,
   As time and our concernings shall importune
   How it goes with us; and do look to know
   What doth befall you here.   So, fare you well:
   To the hopeful execution do I leave you
   Of your commissions.
Ang.   Yet, give leave, my lord,
   That we may bring you something on the way.
Duke. My haste may not admit it;
   Nor need you, on mine honour, have to do
   With any scruple; your scope is as mine own,
   So to enforce or qualify the laws
   As to your soul seems good.   Give me your hand:
   I'll privily away.   I love the people,

But do not like to stage me to their eyes:
Though it do well, I do not relish well
Their loud applause and Aves vehement;
Nor do I think the man of safe discretion
That does affect it.   Once more, fare you well.
Ang. The heavens give safety to your purposes!
Escal. Lead forth and bring you back in happiness!
Duke. I thank you.   Fare you well.   [*Exit.*
Escal. I shall desire you, sir, to give me leave
 To have free speech with you; and it concerns me
 To look into the bottom of my place:
 A power I have, but of what strength and nature
 I am not yet instructed.
Ang. 'Tis so with me.   Let us withdraw together,
 And we may soon our satisfaction have
 Touching that point.
Escal.   I 'll wait upon your honour.
                              [*Exeunt.*

SCENE II

A street.
Enter Lucio and two Gentlemen.

Lucio. If the Duke, with the other dukes, come not to com-
 position with the King of Hungary, why then all the dukes
 fall upon the king.
First Gent. Heaven grant us its peace, but not the King of
Sec. Gent. Amen.   [Hungary's!
Lucio. Thou concludest like the sanctimonious pirate, that
 went to sea with the Ten Commandments, but scraped one
 out of the table.
Sec. Gent. 'Thou shalt not steal'?
Lucio. Ay, that he razed.
First Gent. Why, 'twas a commandment to command the cap-
 tain and all the rest from their functions: they put forth to
 steal.   There's not a soldier of us all, that, in the thanks-
 giving before meat, do relish the petition well that prays for
Sec. Gent. I never heard any soldier dislike it.   [peace.
Lucio. I believe thee; for I think thou never wast where grace
Sec. Gent. No? a dozen times at least.   [was said
First Gent. What, in metre?
Lucio. In any proportion or in any language.
First Gent. I think, or in any religion.
Lucio. Ay, why not?   Grace is grace, despite of all con-
 troversy: as, for example, thou thyself art a wicked villain,
 despite of all grace.

241

First Gent. Well, there went but a pair of shears between us.

Lucio. I grant; as there may between the lists and the velvet. Thou art the list.

First Gent. And thou the velvet: thou art good velvet; thou 'rt a three-piled piece, I warrant thee: I had as lief be a list of an English kersey, as be piled, as thou art piled, for a French velvet. Do I speak feelingly now?

Lucio. I think thou dost; and, indeed, with most painful feeling of thy speech: I will, out of thine own confession, learn to begin thy health; but, whilst I live, forget to drink after thee.

First Gent. I think I have done myself wrong, have I not?

Sec. Gent. Yes, that thou hast, whether thou art tainted or free.

Lucio. Behold, behold, where Madam Mitigation comes! I have purchased as many diseases under her roof as come to—

Sec. Gent. To what, I pray?

Lucio. Judge.

Sec. Gent. To three thousand dolours a year.

First Gent. Ay, and more.

Lucio. A French crown more.

First Gent. Thou art always figuring diseases in me; but thou art full of error; I am sound.

Lucio. Nay, not as one would say, healthy; but so sound as things that are hollow: thy bones are hollow: impiety has made a feast of thee.

Enter Mistress Overdone.

First Gent. How now! which of your hips has the most profound sciatica?

Mrs Ov. Well, well; there 's one yonder arrested and carried to prison was worth five thousand of you all.

Sec. Gent. Who 's that, I pray thee?

Mrs Ov. Marry, sir, that 's Claudio, Signior Claudio.

First Gent. Claudio to prison? 'tis not so.

Mrs Ov. Nay, but I know 'tis so: I saw him arrested; saw him carried away; and, which is more, within these three days his head 's to be chopped off.

Lucio. But after all this fooling, I would not have it so. Art thou sure of this?

Mrs Ov. I am too sure of it: and it is for getting Madam Julietta with child.

Lucio. Believe me, this may be: he promised to meet me two hours since, and he was ever precise in promise-keeping.

Sec. Gent. Besides, you know, it draws something near to the speech we had to such a purpose.

First Gent. But, most of all, agreeing with the proclamation.

Lucio. **Away!** let's go learn the truth of it.

         [*Exeunt Lucio and Gentlemen.*

Mrs Ov. Thus, what with the war, what with the sweat, what with the gallows, and what with poverty, I am custom-shrunk.

        Enter Pompey.

How now! what's the news with you?

Pom. Yonder man is carried to prison.

Mrs Ov. Well; what has he done?

Pom. A woman.

Mrs Ov. But what's his offence?

Pom. Groping for trouts in a peculiar river.

Mrs Ov. What, is there a maid with child by him?

Pom. No, but there's a woman with maid by him. You have not heard of the proclamation, have you?

Mrs Ov. What proclamation, man?

Pom. All houses in the suburbs of Vienna must be plucked

Mrs Ov. And what shall become of those in the city? [down.

Pom. They shall stand for seed: they had gone down too, but that a wise burgher put in for them.

Mrs Ov. But shall all our houses of resort in the suburbs be pulled down?

Pom. To the ground, mistress.

Mrs Ov. Why, here's a change indeed in the commonwealth! What shall become of me?

Pom. Come; fear not you: good counsellors lack no clients: though you change your place, you need not change your trade; I'll be your tapster still. Courage! there will be pity taken on you: you that have worn your eyes almost out in the service, you will be considered.

Mrs Ov. What's to do here, Thomas tapster? let's withdraw.

Pom. Here comes Signior Claudio, led by the provost to prison; and there's Madam Juliet.   [*Exeunt.*

   Enter Provost, Claudio, Juliet, and Officers.

Claud. Fellow, why dost thou show me thus to the world?
Bear me to prison, where I am committed.

Prov. I do it not in evil disposition,
But from Lord Angelo by special charge.

Claud. Thus can the demigod Authority
Make us pay down for our offence by weight
The words of heaven;—on whom it will, it will;
On whom it will not, so; yet still 'tis just.

   Re-enter Lucio and two Gentlemen.

Lucio. Why, how now, Claudio! whence comes this restraint?

Claud. From too much liberty, my Lucio, liberty:
As surfeit is the father of much fast,

So every scope by the immoderate use
Turns to restraint.   Our natures do pursue,
Like rats that ravin down their proper bane,
A thirsty evil; and when we drink we die.

Lucio. If I could speak so wisely under an arrest, I would send
for certain of my creditors : and yet, to say the truth, I had
as lief have the foppery of freedom as the morality of
imprisonment.   What's thy offence, Claudio?

Claud. What but to speak of would offend again.

Lucio. What, is't murder ?

Claud. No.

Lucio. Lechery?

Claud. Call it so.

Prov. Away, sir! you must go.

Claud. One word, good friend.   Lucio, a word with you.

Lucio. A hundred, if they'll do you any good.
    Is lechery so look'd after?

Claud. Thus stands it with me : upon a true contract
I got possession of Julietta's bed :
You know the lady; she is fast my wife,
Save that we do the denunciation lack
Of outward order : this we came not to,
Only for propagation of a dower
Remaining in the coffer of her friends ;
From whom we thought it meet to hide our love
Till time had made them for us.   But it chances
The stealth of our most mutual entertainment
With character too gross is writ on Juliet.

Lucio. With·child, perhaps ?

Claud.   Unhappily, even so.
And the new Deputy now for the Duke,—
Whether it be the fault and glimpse of newness,
Or whether that the body public be
A horse whereon the governor doth ride,
Who, newly in the seat, that it may know
He can command, lets it straight feel the spur ;
Whether the tyranny be in his place,
Or in his eminence that fills it up,
I stagger in :—but this new governor
Awakes me all the enrolled penalties
Which have, like unscour'd armour, hung by the wall
So long, that nineteen zodiacs have gone round,
And none of them been worn ; and, for a name,
Now puts the drowsy and neglected act
Freshly on me : 'tis surely for a name.

Lucio. I warrant it is: and thy head stands so tickle on thy
   shoulders, that a milkmaid, if she be in love, may sigh it off.
   Send after the Duke, and appeal to him.

Claud. I have done so, but he's not to be found.
   I prithee, Lucio, do me this kind service:
   This day my sister should the cloister enter
   And there receive her approbation:
   Acquaint her with the danger of my state;
   Implore her, in my voice, that she make friends
   To the strict deputy; bid herself assay him:
   I have great hope in that; for in her youth
   There is a prone and speechless dialect,
   Such as move men; beside, she hath prosperous art
   When she will play with reason and discourse,
   And well she can persuade.

Lucio. I pray she may; as well for the encouragement of the
   like, which else would stand under grievous imposition, as
   for the enjoying of thy life, who I would be sorry should be
   thus foolishly lost at a game of tick-tack. I'll to her.

Claud. I thank you, good friend Lucio.

Lucio. Within two hours.

Claud.   Come, officer, away!   [*Exeunt.*

SCENE III

A monastery.
Enter Duke and Friar Thomas.

Duke. No, holy father; throw away that thought;
   Believe not that the dribbling dart of love
   Can pierce a complete bosom. Why I desire thee
   To give me secret harbour, hath a purpose
   More grave and wrinkled than the aims and ends
   Of burning youth.

Fri. T.   May your Grace speak of it?

Duke. My holy sir, none better knows than you
   How I have ever loved the life removed,
   And held in idle price to haunt assemblies
   Where youth, and cost, and witless bravery keeps.
   I have deliver'd to Lord Angelo,
   A man of stricture and firm abstinence,
   My absolute power and place here in Vienna,
   And he supposes me travell'd to Poland;
   For so I have strew'd it in the common ear,
   And so it is received. Now, pious sir,
   You will demand of me why I do this?

Fri. T. Gladly, my lord.

Duke. We have strict statutes and most biting laws,
    The needful bits and curbs to headstrong weeds,
    Which for this fourteen years we have let slip ;
    Even like an o'ergrown lion in a cave,
    That goes not out to prey.   Now, as fond fathers,
    Having bound up the threatening twigs of birch,
    Only to stick it in their children's sight
    For terror, not to use, in time the rod
    Becomes more mock'd than fear'd ; so our decrees,
    Dead to infliction, to themselves are dead ;
    And liberty plucks justice by the nose ;
    The baby beats the nurse, and quite athwart
    Goes all decorum.
Fri. T.   It rested in your Grace
    To unloose this tied-up justice when you pleased :
    And it in you more dreadful would have seem'd
    Than in Lord Angelo.
Duke.   I do fear, too dreadful :
    Sith 'twas my fault to give the people scope,
    'Twould be my tyranny to strike and gall them
    For what I bid them do : for we bid this be done,
    When evil deeds have their permissive pass,
    And not the punishment.   Therefore, indeed, my father,
    I have on Angelo imposed the office ;
    Who may, in the ambush of my name, strike home,
    And yet my nature never in the fight
    To do in slander.   And to behold his sway,
    I will, as 'twere a brother of your order,
    Visit both prince and people : therefore, I prithee,
    Supply me with the habit, and instruct me
    How I may formally in person bear me
    Like a true friar.   Moe reasons for this action
    At our more leisure shall I render you ;
    Only, this one : Lord Angelo is precise ;
    Stands at a guard with envy ; scarce confesses
    That his blood flows, or that his appetite
    Is more to bread than stone : hence shall we see,
    If power change purpose, what our seemers be.

                                        [*Exeunt.*

SCENE IV

A nunnery.

Enter Isabella and Francisca.

Isab. And have you nuns no farther privileges ?
Fran. Are not these large enough ?

Isab. Yes, truly: I speak not as desiring more;
   But rather wishing a more strict restraint
   Upon the sisterhood, the votarists of Saint Clare.
Lucio [*within*]. Ho! Peace be in this place!
Isab.   Who's that which calls?
Fran. It is a man's voice.   Gentle Isabella,
   Turn you the key, and know his business of him;
   You may, I may not; you are yet unsworn.
   When you have vow'd, you must not speak with men
   But in the presence of the prioress:
   Then, if you speak, you must not show your face;
   Or, if you show your face, you must not speak.
   He calls again; I pray you, answer him.   [*Exit*.
Isab. Peace and prosperity!   Who is't that calls?

Enter Lucio.

Lucio. Hail, virgin, if you be, as those cheek-roses
   Proclaim you are no less!   Can you so stead me
   As bring me to the sight of Isabella,
   A novice of this place, and the fair sister
   To her unhappy brother Claudio?
Isab. Why, 'her unhappy brother'? let me ask
   The rather, for I now must make you know
   I am that Isabella and his sister.
Lucio. Gentle and fair, your brother kindly greets you:
   Not to be weary with you, he's in prison.
Isab. Woe me! for what?
Lucio. For that which, if myself might be his judge,
   He should receive his punishment in thanks:
   He hath got his friend with child.
Isab. Sir, make me not your story.
Lucio.   It is true.
   I would not—though 'tis my familiar sin
   With maids to seem the lapwing, and to jest,
   Tongue far from heart—play with all virgins so:
   I hold you as a thing ensky'd and sainted;
   By your renouncement, an immortal spirit;
   And to be talk'd with in sincerity,
   As with a saint.
Isab. You do blaspheme the good in mocking me.
Lucio. Do not believe it.   Fewness and truth, 'tis thus :—
   Your brother and his lover have embraced:
   As those that feed grow full,—as blossoming time,
   That from the seedness the bare fallow brings
   To teeming foison,—even so her plenteous womb
   Expresseth his full tilth and husbandry.

247

Isab. Some one with child by him?—My cousin Juliet?
Lucio. Is she your cousin?
Isab. Adoptedly; as school-maids change their names
   By vain, though apt, affection.
Lucio.   She it is.
Isab. O, let him marry her.
Lucio.   This is the point.
   The duke is very strangely gone from hence;
   Bore many gentlemen, myself being one,
   In hand, and hope of action: but we do learn
   By those that know the very nerves of state,
   His givings-out were of an infinite distance
   From his true-meant design.   Upon his place,
   And with full line of his authority,
   Governs Lord Angelo; a man whose blood
   Is very snow-broth; one who never feels
   The wanton stings and motions of the sense,
   But doth rebate and blunt his natural edge
   With profits of the mind, study and fast.
   He—to give fear to use and liberty,
   Which have for long run by the hideous law,
   As mice by lions—hath picked out an act,
   Under whose heavy sense your brother's life
   Falls into forfeit: he arrests him on it;
   And follows close the rigour of the statute,
   To make him an example.   All hope is gone,
   Unless you have the grace by your fair prayer
   To soften Angelo: and that's my pith of business
   'Twixt you and your poor brother.
Isab. Doth he so seek his life?
Lucio.   Has censured him
   Already; and, as I hear, the provost hath
   A warrant for his execution.
Isab. Alas! what poor ability 's in me
   To do him good?
Lucio.   Assay the power you have.
Isab. My power?   Alas, I doubt,—
Lucio.   Our doubts are traitors,
   And make us lose the good we oft might win
   By fearing to attempt.   Go to Lord Angelo,
   And let him learn to know, when maidens sue,
   Men give like gods; but when they weep and kneel,
   All their petitions are as freely theirs
   As they themselves would owe them.
Isab. I'll see what I can do.

Lucio.   But speedily.

Isab. I will about it straight;
  No longer staying but to give the Mother
  Notice of my affair. I humbly thank you:
  Commend me to my brother: soon at night
  I 'll send him certain word of my success.

Lucio. I take my leave of you.

Isab.   Good sir, adieu.   [*Exeunt.*

ACT II—SCENE I
A hall in Angelo's house.
*Enter Angelo, Escalus, and a Justice, Provost, Officers, and
other Attendants, behind.*

Ang. We must not make a scarecrow of the law,
  Setting it up to fear the birds of prey,
  And let it keep one shape, till custom make it
  Their perch, and not their terror.

Escal.   Ay, but yet
  Let us be keen, and rather cut a little,
  Than fall, and bruise to death. Alas, this gentleman,
  Whom I would save, had a most noble father!
  Let but your honour know,
  Whom I believe to be most strait in virtue,
  That, in the working of your own affections,
  Had time cohered with place or place with wishing,
  Or that the resolute acting of your blood
  Could have attain'd the effect of your own purpose,
  Whether you had not sometime in your life
  Err'd in this point which now you censure him,
  And pull'd the law upon you.

Ang. 'Tis one thing to be tempted, Escalus,
  Another thing to fall. I not deny,
  The jury, passing on the prisoners's life,
  May in the sworn twelve have a thief or two
  Guiltier than him they try. What 's open made to justice,
  That justice seizes: what know the laws
  That thieves do pass on thieves? 'Tis very pregnant,
  The jewel that we find, we stoop and take 't,
  Because we see it; but what we do not see
  We tread upon, and never think of it.
  You may not so extenuate his offence
  For I have had such faults; but rather tell me,
  When I that censure him, do so offend,
  Let mine own judgement pattern out my death,
  And nothing come in partial. Sir, he must die.

Escal. Be it as your wisdom will.

Ang.   Where is the provost?

Prov. Here, if it like your honour.

Ang.   See that Claudio
  Be executed by nine to-morrow morning:
  Bring him his confessor, let him be prepared;
  For that 's the utmost of his pilgrimage.   *[Exit Provost.*

Escal. [*Aside*] Well, heaven forgive him! and forgive us all!
  Some rise by sin, and some by virtue fall:
  Some run from brakes of ice, and answer none;
  And some condemned for a fault alone.

    Enter Elbow, and Officers with Froth and Pompey.

Elb. Come, bring them away: if these be good people in a
  commonweal that do nothing but use their abuses in common houses, I know no law: bring them away.

Ang. How now, sir! What 's your name? and what 's the
  matter?

Elb. If it please your honour, I am the poor Duke's constable, and my name is Elbow: I do lean upon justice, sir,
  and do bring in here before your good honour two notorious
  benefactors.

Ang. Benefactors? Well; what benefactors are they? are they
  not malefactors?

Elb. If it please your honour, I know not well what they are:
  but precise villains they are, that I am sure of; and void
  of all profanation in the world that good Christians ought
  to have.

Escal. This comes off well; here 's a wise officer.

Ang. Go to: what quality are they of? Elbow is your name?
  why dost thou not speak, Elbow?

Pom. He cannot, sir; he 's out at elbow.

Ang. What are you, sir?

Elb. He, sir! a tapster, sir; parcel-bawd; one that serves a
  bad woman; whose house, sir, was, as they say, plucked
  down in the suburbs; and now she professes a hot-house,
  which, I think, is a very ill house too.

Escal. How know you that?

Elb. My wife, sir, whom I detest before heaven and your

Escal. How? thy wife?   [honour,—

Elb. Ay, sir;—whom, I thank heaven, is an honest woman,—

Escal. Dost thou detest her therefore?

Elb. I say, sir, I will detest myself also, as well as she, that
  this house, if it be not a bawd's house, it is pity of her life,
  for it is a naughty house.

Escal. How dost thou know that, constable?

Elb. Marry, sir, by my wife; who, if she had been a woman cardinally given, might have been accused in fornication, adultery, and all uncleanliness there.

Escal. By the woman's means?

Elb. Ay, sir, by Mistress Overdone's means: but as she spit in his face, so she defied him.

Pom. Sir, if it please your honour, this is not so.

Elb. Prove it before these varlets here, thou honourable man;

Escal. Do you hear how he misplaces? [*prove it.*

Pom. Sir, she came in great with child; and longing, saving your honour's reverence, for stewed prunes; sir, we had but two in the house, which at that very distant time stood, as it were, in a fruit-dish, a dish of some three-pence; your honours have seen such dishes; they are not China dishes, but very good dishes,—

Escal. Go to, go to: no matter for the dish, sir.

Pom. No, indeed, sir, not of a pin; you are therein in the right: but to the point. As I say, this Mistress Elbow, being, as I say, with child, and being great-bellied, and longing, as I said, for prunes; and having but two in the dish, as I said, Master Froth here, this very man, having eaten the rest, as I said, and, as I say, paying for them very honestly; for, as you know, Master Froth, I could not give you

Froth. No, indeed. [*three-pence again.*

Pom. Very well;—you being then, if you be remembered, cracking the stones of the foresaid prunes,—

Froth. Ay, so I did indeed.

Pom. Why, very well; I telling you then, if you be remembered, that such a one and such a one were past cure of the thing you wot of, unless they kept very good diet, as I

Froth. All this is true. [*told you,—*

Pom. Why, very well, then,—

Escal. Come, you are a tedious fool: to the purpose. What was done to Elbow's wife, that he hath cause to complain of? Come me to what was done to her.

Pom. Sir, your honour cannot come to that yet.

Escal. No, sir, nor I mean it not.

Pom. Sir, but you shall come to it, by your honour's leave. And, I beseech you, look into Master Froth here, sir; a man of fourscore pound a year; whose father died at Hallowmas: —was 't not at Hallowmas, Master Froth?—

Froth. All-hallond eve.

Pom. Why, very well; I hope here be truths. He, sir, sitting, as I say, in a lower chair, sir; 'twas in the Bunch of Grapes, where, indeed, you have a delight to sit, have you not?

Froth. I have so; because it is an open room, and good for
Pom. Why, very well, then; I hope here be truths.   [winter.
Ang. This will last out a night in Russia,
    When nights are longest there : I 'll take my leave,
    And leave you to the hearing of the cause ;
    Hoping you 'll find good cause to whip them all.
Escal. I think no less.   Good morrow to your lordship.
                                                [*Exit Angelo.*
    Now, sir, come on : what was done to Elbow's wife, once
Pom. Once, sir ? there was nothing done to her once. [more ?
Elb. I beseech you, sir, ask him what this man did to my wife.
Pom. I beseech your honour, ask me.
Escal. Well, sir ; what did this gentleman to her ?
Pom. I beseech you, sir, look in this gentleman's face.   Good
    Master Froth, look upon his honour ; 'tis for a good purpose.
    Doth your honour mark his face ?
Escal. Ay, sir, very well.
Pom. Nay, I beseech you, mark it well.
Escal. Well, I do so.
Pom. Doth your honour see any harm in his face ?
Escal. Why, no.
Pom. I 'll be supposed upon a book, his face is the worst thing
    about him.   Good, then ; if his face be the worst thing about
    him, how could Master Froth do the constable's wife any
    harm ?   I would know that of your honour.
Escal. He 's in the right.   Constable, what say you to it ?
Elb. First, an it like you, the house is a respected house ; next,
    this is a respected fellow ; and his mistress is a respected
    woman.   [than any of us all.
Pom. By this hand, sir, his wife is a more respected person
Elb. Varlet, thou liest ; thou liest, wicked varlet ! the time is
    yet to come that she was ever respected with man, woman,
    or child.
Pom. Sir, she was respected with him before he married with her
Escal. Which is the wiser here ? Justice or Iniquity ?   Is this
    true ?
Elb. O thou caitiff ! O thou varlet ! O thou wicked Hannibal !
    I respected with her before I was married to her !   If ever I
    was respected with her, or she with me, let not your worship
    think me the poor Duke's officer.   Prove this, thou wicked
    Hannibal, or I 'll have mine action of battery on thee.
Escal. If he took you a box o' th' ear, you might have your
    action of slander too.
Elb. Marry, I thank your good worship for it.   What is 't your
    worship's pleasure I shall do with this wicked caitiff ?

Escal. Truly, officer, because he hath some offences in him that thou wouldst discover if thou couldst, let him continue in his courses till thou knowest what they are.

Elb. Marry, I thank your worship for it. Thou seest, thou wicked varlet, now, what's come upon thee : thou art to continue now, thou varlet; thou art to continue.

Escal. Where were you born, friend?

Froth. Here in Vienna, sir.

Escal. Are you of fourscore pounds a year?

Froth. Yes, an't please you, sir.

Escal. So. What trade are you of, sir?

Pom. A tapster; a poor widow's tapster.

Escal. Your mistress' name?

Pom. Mistress Overdone.

Escal. Hath she had any more than one husband?

Pom. Nine, sir; Overdone by the last.

Escal. Nine! Come hither to me, Master Froth. Master Froth, I would not have you acquainted with tapsters : they will draw you, Master Froth, and you will hang them. Get you gone, and let me hear no more of you.

Froth. I thank your worship. For mine own part, I never come into any room in a taphouse, but I am drawn in.

Escal. Well, no more of it, Master Froth : farewell. [*Exit Froth.*] Come you hither to me, Master tapster. What's your name, Master tapster?

Pom. Pompey.

Escal. What else?

Pom. Bum, sir.

Escal. Troth, and your bum is the greatest thing about you; so that, in the beastliest sense, you are Pompey the Great. Pompey, you are partly a bawd, Pompey, howsoever you colour it in being a tapster, are you not? come, tell me true : it shall be the better for you.

Pom. Truly, sir, I am a poor fellow that would live.

Escal. How would you live, Pompey? by being a bawd? What do you think of the trade, Pompey? is it a lawful

Pom. If the law would allow it, sir.   [trade?

Escal. But the law will not allow it, Pompey; nor it shall not be allowed in Vienna.

Pom. Does your worship mean to geld and splay all the youth of the city?

Escal. No, Pompey.

Pom. Truly, sir, in my poor opinion, they will to't, then. If your worship will take order for the drabs and the knaves, you need not to fear the bawds.

Escal. There are pretty orders beginning, I can tell you: it
is but heading and hanging.

Pom. If you head and hang all that offend that way but for
ten year together, you 'll be glad to give out a commission
for more heads: if this law hold in Vienna ten year, I 'll
rent the fairest house in it after three-pence a bay: if you
live to see this come to pass, say Pompey told you so.

Escal. Thank you, good Pompey; and, in requital of your
prophecy, hark you: I advise you, let me not find you
before me again upon any complaint whatsoever; no, not
for dwelling where you do: if I do, Pompey, I shall beat
you to your tent, and prove a shrewd Cæsar to you; in
plain dealing, Pompey, I shall have you whipt: so, for this
time, Pompey, fare you well.

Pom. I thank your worship for your good counsel: [*Aside*]
but I shall follow it as the flesh and fortune shall better
determine.

  Whip me? No, no; let carman whip his jade:
  The valiant heart 's not whipt out of his trade. [*Exit.*

Escal. Come hither to me, Master Elbow; come hither,
Master constable. How long have you been in this place
of constable?

Elb. Seven year and a half, sir.

Escal. I thought, by your readiness in the office, you had
continued in it some time. You say, seven years together?

Elb. And a half, sir.

Escal. Alas, it hath been great pains to you. They do you
wrong to put you so oft upon 't: are there not men in
your ward sufficient to serve it?

Elb. Faith, sir, few of any wit in such matters: as they are
chosen, they are glad to choose me for them; I do it for
some piece of money, and go through with all.

Escal. Look you bring me in the names of some six or seven,
the most sufficient of your parish.

Elb. To your worship's house, sir?

Escal. To my house. Fare you well.   [*Exit Elbow.*
  What 's o'clock, think you?

Just. Eleven, sir.

Escal. I pray you home to dinner with me.

Just. I humbly thank you.

Escal. It grieves me for the death of Claudio;
  But there 's no remedy.

Just. Lord Angelo is severe.

Escal.   It is but needful ›
  Mercy is not itself, that oft looks so;

254

Pardon is still the nurse of second woe :
But yet,—poor Claudio !   There is no remedy.
Come, sir.   [*Exeunt.*

Scene II
Another room in the same.
Enter Provost and a Servant.

Serv. He 's hearing of a cause ; he will come straight :
  I 'll tell him of you.
Prov.   Pray you, do.   [*Exit Servant.*
  I 'll know
His pleasure ; may be he will relent.   Alas,
He hath but as offended in a dream !
All sects, all ages smack of this vice ; and he
To die for 't !

                    Enter Angelo.

Ang. Now, what 's the matter, provost ?
Prov. Is it your will Claudio shall die to-morrow ?
Ang. Did not I tell thee yea ? hadst thou not order ?
  Why dost thou ask again ?
Prov.   Lest I might be too rash :
  Under your good correction, I have seen,
  When, after execution, Judgement hath
  Repented o 'er his doom.
Ang.   Go to ; let that be mine :
  Do you your office, or give up your place,
  And you shall well be spared.
Prov.   I crave your honour's pardon.
  What shall be done, sir, with the groaning Juliet ?
  She 's very near her hour.
Ang.   Dispose of her
  To some more fitter place, and that with speed.

                    Re-enter Servant.

Serv. Here is the sister of the man condemn'd
  Desires access to you.
Ang.   Hath he a sister ?
Prov. Ay, my good lord ; a very virtuous maid,
  And to be shortly of a sisterhood,
  If not already.
Ang.   Well, let her be admitted.   [*Exit Servant.*
  See you the fornicatress be removed :
  Let her have needful, but not lavish, means ;
  There shall be order for 't.

                    Enter Isabella and Lucio.

Prov.   God save your honour !

Ang. Stay a little while. [*To Isab.*] You're welcome: what's
    your will?

Isab. I am a woeful suitor to your honour.
    Please but your honour hear me.

Ang.   Well; what's your suit?

Isab. There is a vice that most I do abhor,
    And most desire should meet the blow of justice;
    For which I would not plead, but that I must;
    For which I must not plead, but that I am
    At war 'twixt will and will not.

Ang.   Well; the matter?

Isab. I have a brother is condemn'd to die:
    I do beseech you, let it be his fault,
    And not my brother.

Prov.   [*Aside*] Heaven give thee moving graces!

Ang. Condemn the fault, and not the actor of it?
    Why, every fault's condemn'd ere it be done:
    Mine were the very cipher of a function,
    To fine the faults whose fine stands in record,
    And let go by the actor.

Isab.   O just but severe law!
    I had a brother, then.—Heaven keep your honour!

Lucio. [*Aside to Isab.*] Give 't not o'er so: to him again, entreat
    Kneel down before him, hang upon his gown: [him ;
    You are too cold; if you should need a pin,
    You could not with more tame a tongue desire it:
    To him, I say!

Isab. Must he needs die?

Ang.   Maiden, no remedy.

Isab. Yes; I do think that you might pardon him,
    And neither heaven nor man grieve at the mercy.

Ang. I will not do 't.

Isab.   But can you, if you would?

Ang. Look, what I will not, that I cannot do.

Isab. But might you do 't, and do the world no wrong,
    If so your heart were touch'd with that remorse
    As mine is to him?

Ang.   He's sentenced; 'tis too late.

Lucio. [*Aside to Isab.*] You are too cold.

Isab. Too late? why, no; I, that do speak a word,
    May call it back again. Well, believe this,
    No ceremony that to great ones 'longs,
    Not the king's crown, nor the deputed sword,
    The marshal's truncheon, nor the judge's robe,
    Become them with one half so good a grace

As mercy does.
If he had been as you, and you as he,
You would have slipt like him; but he, like you,
Would not have been so stern.

Ang.   Pray you, be gone.

Isab. I would to heaven I had your potency,
And you were Isabel! should it then be thus?
No; I would tell what 'twere to be a judge,
And what a prisoner.

Lucio. [*Aside to Isab.*] Ay, touch him; there 's the vein.

Ang. Your brother is a forfeit of the law,
And you but waste your words.

Isab.   Alas, alas!
Why, all the souls that were were forfeit once;
And He that might the vantage best have took
Found out the remedy.   How would you be,
If He, which is the top of judgement, should
But judge you as you are?   O, think on that;
And mercy then will breathe within your lips,
Like man new made.

Ang.   Be you content, fair maid;
It is the law, not I condemn your brother:
Were he my kinsman, brother, or my son,
It should be thus with him: he must die to-morrow.

Isab. To-morrow! O, that 's sudden! Spare him, spare him!
He 's not prepared for death.   Even for our kitchens
We kill the fowl of season: shall we serve heaven
With less respect than we do minister
To our gross selves?   Good, good my lord, bethink you;
Who is it that hath died for this offence!
There 's many have committed it.

Lucio.   [*Aside to Isab.*] Ay, well said.

Aug. The law hath not been dead, though it hath slept:
Those many had not dared to do that evil,
If the first that did the edict infringe
Had answer'd for his deed: now 'tis awake,
Takes note of what is done; and, like a prophet,
Looks in a glass, that shows what future evils,
Either now, or by remissness new-conceived,
And so in progress to be hatch'd and born,
Are now to have no successive degrees,
But, ere they live, to end.

Isab.   Yet show some pity.

Ang. I show it most of all when I show justice;
For then I pity those I do not know,

257

    Which a dismiss'd offence would after gall;
    And do him right that, answering one foul wrong,
    Lives not to act another.   Be satisfied;
    Your brother dies to-morrow; be content.
Isab. So you must be the first that gives this sentence,
    And he, that suffers.   O, it is excellent
    To have a giant's strength; but it is tyrannous
    To use it like a giant.
Lucio. [*Aside to Isab.*]   That's well said.
Isab. Could great men thunder
    As Jove himself does, Jove would ne'er be quiet,
    For every pelting, petty officer
    Would use his heaven for thunder.
    Nothing but thunder!   Merciful Heaven,
    Thou rather with thy sharp and sulphurous bolt
    Split'st the unwedgeable and gnarled oak
    Than the soft myrtle: but man, proud man,
    Drest in a little brief authority,
    Most ignorant of what he's most assured,
    His glassy essence, like an angry ape,
    Plays such fantastic tricks before high heaven
    As make the angels weep; who, with our spleens,
    Would all themselves laugh mortal.
Lucio. [*Aside to Isab.*] O, to him, to him, wench! he will relent;
    He's coming; I perceive 't.
Prov.   [*Aside*] Pray heaven she win him!
Isab. We cannot weigh our brother with ourself:
    Great men may jest with saints; 'tis wit in them,
    But in the less foul profanation.
Lucio. Thou 'rt i' the right, girl; more o' that.
Isab. That in the captain's but a choleric word,
    Which in the soldier is flat blasphemy.
Lucio. [*Aside to Isab.*] Art avised o' that? more on 't.
Ang. Why do you put these sayings upon me?
Isab. Because authority, though it err like others,
    Hath yet a kind of medicine in itself,
    That skins the vice o' the top.   Go to your bosom;
    Knock there, and ask your heart what it doth know
    That 's like my brother's fault: if it confess
    A natural guiltiness such as is his,
    Let it not sound a thought upon your tongue
    Against my brother's life.
Ang.   [*Aside*] She speaks, and 'tis
    Such sense, that my sense breeds with it.   Fare you well.
Isab. Gentle my lord, turn back.

Ang. I will bethink me : come again to-morrow.
Isab. Hark how I 'll bribe you : good my lord, turn back.
Ang. How ? bribe me ?
Isab. Ay, with such gifts that heaven shall share with you.
Lucio. [*Aside to Isab.*] You had marr'd all else.
Isab. Not with fond sicles of the tested gold,
    Or stones whose rates are either rich or poor
    As fancy values them ; but with true prayers
    That shall be up at heaven and enter there
    Ere sun-rise, prayers from preserved souls,
    From fasting maids whose minds are dedicate
    To nothing temporal.
Ang.   Well ; come to me to-morrow.
Lucio. [*Aside to Isab.*] Go to ; 'tis well ; away !
Isab. Heaven keep your honour safe !
Ang.   [*Aside*] Amen :
    For I am that way going to temptation,
    Where prayers cross.
Isab.   At what hour to-morrow
    Shall I attend your worship ?
Ang.   At any time 'fore noon.
Isab. 'Save your honour ! [*Exeunt Isabella, Lucio, and Provost.*
Ang.   From thee,—even from thy virtue !
    What 's this, what 's this ? Is this her fault or mine ?
    The tempter or the tempted, who sins most ?
    Ha !
    Not she ; nor doth she tempt : but it is I
    That, lying by the violet in the sun,
    Do as the carrion does, not as the flower,
    Corrupt with virtuous season.   Can it be
    That modesty may more betray our sense
    Than woman's lightness ?   Having waste ground enough,
    Shall we desire to raze the sanctuary,
    And pitch our evils there ?   O, fie, fie, fie !
    What dost thou, or what art thou, Angelo ?
    Dost thou desire her foully for those things,
    That make her good ?   O, let her brother live :
    Thieves for their robbery have authority
    When judges steal themselves.   What, do I love her,
    That I desire to hear her speak again,
    And feast upon her eyes ?   What is 't I dream on ?
    O cunning enemy, that, to catch a saint,
    With saints dost bait thy hook !   Most dangerous
    Is that temptation that doth goad us on
    To sin in loving virtue : never could the strumpet,

With all her double vigour, art and nature,
Once stir my temper ; but this virtuous maid
Subdues me quite.   Ever till now,
When men were fond, I smiled, and wonder'd how.

                                           [Exit.

SCENE III

A room in a prison.
Enter, severally, Duke disguised as a friar, and Provost.

Duke. Hail to you, provost ! so I think you are.
Prov. I am the provost.   What 's your will, good friar ?
Duke. Bound by my charity and my blest order,
  I come to visit the afflicted spirits
  Here in the prison.   Do me the common right
  To let me see them, and to make me know
  The nature of their crimes, that I may minister
  To them accordingly.
Prov. I would do more than that, if more were needful.

Enter Juliet.

  Look, here comes one : a gentlewoman of mine,
  Who, falling in the flaws of her own youth,
  Hath blister'd her report : she is with child ;
  And he that got it, sentenced ; a young man
  More fit to do another such offence
  Than die for this.
Duke. When must he die ?
Prov.   As I do think, to-morrow.
  I have provided for you : stay awhile,   *[To Juliet.*
  And you shall be conducted.
Duke. Repent you, fair one, of the sin you carry ?
Jul. I do ; and bear the shame most patiently.
Duke. I 'll teach you how you shall arraign your conscience,
  And try your penitence, if it be sound,
  Or hollowly put on.
Jul.   I 'll gladly learn.
Duke. Love you the man that wronged you ?
Jul. Yes, as I love the woman that wrong'd him.
Duke. So, then, it seems your most offenceful act
  Was mutually committed ?
Jul.   Mutually.
Duke.   Then was your sin of heavier kind than his.
Jul. I do confess it, and repent it, father.
Duke. 'Tis meet so, daughter : but lest you do repent,
  As that the sin hath brought you to this shame,
  Which sorrow is always toward ourselves, not heaven,

Showing we would not spare heaven as we love it,
But as we stand in fear,—

Jul. I do repent me, as it is an evil,
And take the shame with joy.

Duke.   There rest.
Your partner, as I hear, must die to-morrow,
And I am going with instruction to him.
Grace go with you, *Benedicite !*   *[Exit.*

Jul. Must die to-morrow ! O injurious love,
That respites me a life, whose very comfort
Is still a dying horror !

Prov.   'Tis pity of him.   *[Exeunt.*

SCENE IV

A room in Angelo's house.
Enter Angelo.

Ang. When I would pray and think, I think and pray
To several subjects. Heaven hath my empty words ;
Whilst my invention, hearing not my tongue,
Anchors on Isabel : Heaven in my mouth,
As if I did but only chew his name ;
And in my heart the strong and swelling evil
Of my conception. The state, whereon I studied,
Is like a good thing, being often read,
Grown fear'd and tedious ; yea, my gravity,
Wherein—let no man hear me—I take pride,
Could I with boot change for an idle plume,
Which the air beats for vain. O place, O form
How often dost thou with thy case, thy habit,
Wrench awe from fools, and tie the wiser souls
To thy false seeming ! Blood, thou art blood :
Let 's write good angel on the devil's horn ;
'Tis not the devil's crest.

Enter a Servant.
                How now ! who 's there ?

Serv. One Isabel, a sister, desires access to you.

Ang. Teach her the way. O heavens !
Why does my blood thus muster to my heart,
Making both it unable for itself,
And dispossessing all my other parts
Of necessary fitness ?
So play the foolish throngs with one that swoons ;
Come all to help him, and so stop the air
By which he should revive : and even so
The general subject to a well-wish'd king

Quit their own part, and in obsequious fondness
Crowd to his presence, where their untaught love
Must needs appear offence.

Enter Isabella.

　　　　　　　　　　How now, fair maid?

Isab. I am come to know your pleasure.

Ang. That you might know it, would much better please me
　　Than to demand what 'tis.　Your brother cannot live.

Isab. Even so.—Heaven keep your honour!

Ang. Yet may he live awhile; and, it may be,
　　As long as you or I: yet he must die.

Isab. Under your sentence?

Ang. Yea.

Isab. When, I beseech you? that in his reprieve,
　　Longer or shorter, he may be so fitted
　　That his soul sicken not.

Ang. Ha! fie, these filthy vices!　It were as good
　　To pardon him that hath from nature stolen
　　A man already made, as to remit
　　Their saucy sweetness that do coin heaven's image
　　In stamps that are forbid: 'tis all as easy
　　Falsely to take away a life true made,
　　As to put metal in restrained means
　　To make a false one.

Isab. 'Tis set down so in heaven, but not in earth.

Ang. Say you so? then I shall pose you quickly.
　　Which had you rather,—that the most just law
　　Now took your brother's life; or, to redeem him,
　　Give up your body to such sweet uncleanness
　　As she that he hath stain'd!

Isab. 　　　　　　　　　　Sir, believe this,
　　I had rather give my body than my soul.

Ang. I talk not of your soul: our compell'd sins
　　Stand more for number than for accompt.

Isab. 　　　　　　　　　　How say you?

Ang. Nay, I'll not warrant that; for I can speak
　　Against the thing I say.　Answer to this:—
　　I, now the voice of the recorded law,
　　Pronounce a sentence on your brother's life:
　　Might there not be a charity in sin
　　To save this brother's life?

Isab. 　　　　　　　　　　Please you to do't,
　　I'll take it as a peril to my soul,
　　It is no sin at all, but charity.

Ang. Pleased you to do't at peril of your soul,

262

Were equal poise of sin and charity.

Isab. That I do beg his life, if it be sin,
Heaven let me bear it ! you granting of my suit,
If that be sin, I 'll make it my morn prayer
To have it added to the faults of mine,
And nothing of your answer.

Ang.   Nay, but hear me.
Your sense pursues not mine : either you are ignorant,
Or seem so, craftily ; and that 's not good.

Isab. Let me be ignorant, and in nothing good,
But graciously to know I am no better.

Ang. Thus wisdom wishes to appear most bright
When it doth tax itself; as these black masks
Proclaim an enshield beauty ten times louder
Than beauty could, display'd.   But mark me ;
To be received plain, I 'll speak more gross :
Your brother is to die.

Isab. So.

Ang. And his offence is so, as it appears,
Accountant to the law upon that pain.

Isab. True.

Ang. Admit no other way to save his life,—
As I subscribe not that, nor any other,
But in the loss of question,—that you, his sister,
Finding yourself desired of such a person,
Whose credit with the judge, or own great place,
Could fetch your brother from the manacles
Of the all-building law ; and that there were
No earthly mean to save him, but that either
You must lay down the treasures of your body
To this supposed, or else to let him suffer ;
What would you do ?

Isab. As much for my poor brother as myself :
That is, were I under the terms of death,
The impression of keen whips I 'ld wear as rubies,
And strip myself to death, as to a bed
That longing have been sick for, ere I 'ld yield
My body up to shame.

Ang.   Then must your brother die.

Isab. And 'twere the cheaper way :
Better it were a brother died at once,
Than that a sister, by redeeming him,
Should die for ever.

Ang. Were not you, then, as cruel as the sentence
That you have slander'd so?

263

Isab. Ignomy in ransom and free pardon
    Are of two houses: lawful mercy
    Is nothing kin to foul redemption.
Ang. You seem'd of late to make the law a tyrant;
    And rather proved the sliding of your brother
    A merriment than a vice.
Isab. O, pardon me, my lord; it oft falls out,
    To have what we would have, we speak not what we mean:
    I something do excuse the thing I hate,
    For his advantage that I dearly love.
Ang. We are all frail.
Isab.   Else let my brother die,
    If not a feodary, but only he
    Owe and succeed thy weakness.
Ang. Nay, women are frail too.
Isab. Ay, as the glasses where they view themselves;
    Which are as easy broke as they make forms.
    Women!—Help Heaven! men their creation mar
    In profiting by them.   Nay, call us ten times frail;
    For we are soft as our complexions are,
    And credulous to false prints.
Ang.   I think it well:
    And from this testimony of your own sex,—
    Since, I suppose, we are made to be no stronger
    Than faults may shake our frames,—let me be bold;—
    I do arrest your words.   Be that you are,
    That is, a woman; if you be more, you 're none;
    If you be one,—as you are well express'd
    By all external warrants,—show it now,
    By putting on the destined livery.
Isab. I have no tongue but one: gentle my lord,
    Let me entreat you speak the former language.
Ang. Plainly conceive, I love you.
Isab. My brother did love Juliet,
    And you tell me that he shall die for it.
Ang. He shall not, Isabel, if you give me love.
Isab. I know your virtue hath a license in 't,
    Which seems a little fouler than it is,
    To pluck on others.
Ang.   Believe me, on mine honour,
    My words express my purpose.
Isab. Ha! little honour to be much believed,
    And most pernicious purpose!—Seeming, seeming!—
    I will proclaim thee, Angelo; look for 't:
    Sign me a present pardon for my brother,

Or with an outstretch'd throat I 'll tell the world aloud
What man thou art.

Ang.   Who will believe thee, Isabel ?
My unsoil'd name, the austereness of my life,
My vouch against you, and my place i' the state,
Will so your accusation overweigh,
That you shall stifle in your own report,
And smell of calumny.   I have begun ;
And now I give my sensual race the rein :
Fit thy consent to my sharp appetite ;
Lay by all nicety and prolixious blushes,
That banish what they sue for ; redeem thy brother
By yielding up thy body to my will ;
Or else he must not only die the death,
But thy unkindness shall his death draw out
To lingering sufferance.   Answer me to-morrow,
Or, by the affection that now guides me most,
I 'll prove a tyrant to him.   As for you,
Say what you can, my false o'erweighs your true.   [*Exit.*

Isab. To whom should I complain ?   Did I tell this,
Who would believe me ?   O perilous mouths,
That bear in them one and the self-same tongue,
Either of condemnation or approof ;
Bidding the law make court'sy to their will ;
Hooking both right and wrong to the appetite,
To follow as it draws !   I 'll to my brother :
Though he hath fall'n by prompture of the blood,
Yet hath he in him such a mind of honour,
That, had he twenty heads to tender down
On twenty bloody blocks, he 'ld yield them up,
Before his sister should her body stoop
To such abhorr'd pollution.
Then, Isabel, live chaste, and, brother, die ;
More than our brother is our chastity.
I 'll tell him yet of Angelo's request,
And fit his mind to death, for his soul's rest.   [*Exit.*

ACT III—Scene I

A room in the prison.

Enter Duke disguised as before, Claudio, and Provost.

Duke. So, then, you hope of pardon from Lord Angelo ?
Claud. The miserable have no other medicine
But only hope :
I 've hope to live, and am prepared to die.

Duke. Be absolute for death ; either death or life
 Shall thereby be the sweeter. Reason thus with life :
 If I do lose thee, I do lose a thing
 That none but fools would keep : a breath thou art,
 Servile to all the skyey influences,
 That dost this habitation, where thou keep'st,
 Hourly afflict : merely, thou art death's fool ;
 For him thou labour'st by thy flight to shun,
 And yet runn'st toward him still. Thou art not noble ;
 For all the accommodations that thou bear'st
 Are nursed by baseness. Thou 'rt by no means valiant ;
 For thou dost fear the soft and tender fork
 Of a poor worm. Thy best of rest is sleep,
 And that thou oft provokest ; yet grossly fear'st
 Thy death, which is no more. Thou art not thyself ;
 For thou exist'st on many a thousand grains
 That issue out of dust. Happy thou art not ;
 For what thou hast not, still thou strivest to get,
 And what thou hast, forget'st. Thou art not certain ;
 For thy complexion shifts to strange effects,
 After the moon. If thou art rich, thou 'rt poor ;
 For, like an ass whose back with ingots bows,
 Thou bear'st thy heavy riches but a journey,
 And death unloads thee. Friend hast thou none ;
 For thine own bowels, which do call thee sire,
 The mere effusion of thy proper loins,
 Do curse the gout, serpigo, and the rheum,
 For ending thee no sooner. Thou hast nor youth nor age,
 But, as it were, an after-dinner's sleep,
 Dreaming on both ; for all thy blessed youth
 Becomes as aged, and doth beg the alms
 Of palsied eld ; and when thou art old and rich,
 Thou hast neither heat, affection, limb, nor beauty,
 To make thy riches pleasant. What 's yet in this
 That bears the name of life ? Yet in this life
 Lie hid moe thousand deaths : yet death we fear,
 That makes these odds all even.
Claud.   I humbly thank you.
 To sue to live, I find I seek to die ;
 And, seeking death, find life : let it come on.
Isab. [*within*] What, ho ! Peace here ; grace and good
 company !
Prov. Who 's there ? come in : the wish deserves a welcome.
Duke. Dear sir, ere long I 'll visit you again.
Claud. Most holy sir, I thank you.

Enter Isabella.

Isab. My business is a word or two with Claudio.

Prov. And very welcome.   Look, signior, here's your sister.

Duke. Provost, a word with you.

Prov. As many as you please.

Duke. Bring me to hear them speak, where I may be concealed.

                                  [Exeunt Duke and Provost.

Claud. Now, sister, what's the comfort?

Isab. Why,

  As all comforts are ; most good, most good indeed.
  Lord Angelo, having affairs to heaven,
  Intends you for his swift ambassador,
  Where you shall be an everlasting leiger :
  Therefore your best appointment make with speed ;
  To-morrow you set on.

Claud.   Is there no remedy?

Isab. None, but such remedy as, to save a head,
  To cleave a heart in twain.

Claud.   But is there any?

Isab. Yes, brother, you may live :
  There is a devilish mercy in the judge,
  If you'll implore it, that will free your life,
  But fetter you till death.

Claud.   Perpetual durance?

Isab. Ay, just; perpetual durance, a restraint,
  Though all the world's vastidity you had,
  To a determined scope.

Claud.   But in what nature?

Isab. In such a one as, you consenting to 't,
  Would bark your honour from that trunk you bear
  And leave you naked.

Claud.   Let me know the point.

Isab. O, I do fear thee, Claudio ; and I quake,
  Lest thou a feverous life shouldst entertain,
  And six or seven winters more respect
  Than a perpetual honour.   Darest thou die?
  The sense of death is most in apprehension ;
  And the poor beetle, that we tread upon,
  In corporal sufferance finds a pang as great
  As when a giant dies.

Claud.   Why give you me this shame?
  Think you I can a resolution fetch
  From flowery tenderness?   If I must die,
  I will encounter darkness as a bride,
  And hug it in mine arms.

Isab. There spake my brother; there my father's grave
　　Did utter forth a voice.　Yes, thou must die:
　　Thou art too noble to conserve a life
　　In base appliances.　This outward-sainted deputy,
　　Whose settled visage and deliberate word
　　Nips youth i' the head, and follies doth emmew
　　As falcon doth the fowl, is yet a devil;
　　His filth within being cast, he would appear
　　A pond as deep as hell.
Claud.　　　　　　　　　The prenzie Angelo!
Isab. O, 'tis the cunning livery of hell
　　The damned'st body to invest and cover
　　In prenzie guards!　Dost thou think, Claudio?—
　　If I would yield him my virginity,
　　Thou mightst be freed.
Claud.　　　　　　　　O heavens! it cannot be.
Isab. Yes, he would give't thee, from this rank offence,
　　So to offend him still.　This night's the time
　　That I should do what I abhor to name,
　　Or else thou diest to-morrow.
Claud.　　　　　　　　　Thou shalt not do't.
Isab. O, were it but my life,
　　I'ld throw it down for your deliverance
　　As frankly as a pin.
Claud.　　　　　　Thanks, dear Isabel.
Isab. Be ready, Claudio, for your death to-morrow.
Claud. Yes.　Has he affections in him,
　　That thus can make him bite the law by the nose,
　　When he would force it?　Sure, it is no sin;
　　Or of the deadly seven it is the least.
Isab. Which is the least?
Claud. If it were damnable, he being so wise,
　　Why would he for the momentary trick
　　Be perdurably fined?—O Isabel!
Isab. What says my brother?
Claud.　　　　　　　Death is a fearful thing.
Isab. And shamed life a hateful.
Claud. Ay, but to die, and go we know not where;
　　To lie in cold obstruction and to rot;
　　This sensible warm motion to become
　　A kneaded clod; and the delighted spirit
　　To bathe in fiery floods, or to reside
　　In thrilling region of thick-ribbed ice;
　　To be imprison'd in the viewless winds,
　　And blown with restless violence round about

The pendent world; or to be worse than worst
Of those that lawless and incertain thought
Imagine howling:—'tis too horrible!
The weariest and most loathed worldly life
That age, ache, penury, and imprisonment
Can lay on nature is a paradise
To what we fear of death.

Isab. Alas, alas!

Claud.   Sweet sister, let me live:
What sin you do to save a brother's life,
Nature dispenses with the deed so far
That it becomes a virtue.

Isab.   O you beast!
O faithless coward!   O dishonest wretch!
Wilt thou be made a man out of my vice?
Is 't not a kind of incest, to take life
From thine own sister's shame?   What should I think?
Heaven shield my mother play'd my father fair!
For such a warped slip of wilderness
Ne'er issued from his blood.   Take my defiance!
Die, perish!   Might but my bending down
Reprieve thee from thy fate, it should proceed:
I 'll pray a thousand prayers for thy death,
No word to save thee.

Claud. Nay, hear me, Isabel.

Isab.   O, fie, fie, fie!
Thy sin 's not accidental, but a trade.
Mercy to thee would prove itself a bawd:
'Tis best that thou diest quickly.

Claud.   O, hear me, Isabella!

Re-enter Duke.

Duke. Vouchsafe a word, young sister, but one word.

Isab. What is your will?

Duke. Might you dispense with your leisure, I would by and
by have some speech with you: the satisfaction I would
require is likewise your own benefit.

Isab. I have no superfluous leisure; my stay must be stolen
out of other affairs! but I will attend you awhile.

[*Walks apart.*

Duke. Son, I have overheard what hath passed between you
and your sister.   Angelo had never the purpose to corrupt
her; only he hath made an assay of her virtue to practise his
judgement with the disposition of natures: she, having the
truth of honour in her, hath made him that gracious denial
which he is most glad to receive.   I am confessor to Angelo,

and I know this to be true; therefore prepare yourself to
death: do not satisfy your resolution with hopes that are
fallible: to-morrow you must die; go to your knees, and
make ready.

Claud. Let me ask my sister pardon.   I am so out of love with
life, that I will sue to be rid of it.

Duke. Hold you there: farewell.   [*Exit Claudio.*
Provost, a word with you!

Re-enter Provost.

Prov. What's your will, father?

Duke. That now you are come, you will be gone.   Leave me
awhile with the maid: my mind promises with my habit no
loss shall touch her by my company.

Prov. In good time.   [*Exit Provost.   Isabella comes forward.*

Duke. The hand that hath made you fair hath made you
good: the goodness that is cheap in beauty makes beauty
brief in goodness; but grace, being the soul of your complexion, shall keep the body of it ever fair.   The assault that
Angelo hath made to you, fortune hath conveyed to my
understanding: and, but that frailty hath examples for his
falling, I should wonder at Angelo.   How will you do to
content this substitute, and to save your brother?

Isab. I am now going to resolve him: I had rather my brother
die by the law than my son should be unlawfully born.   But,
O, how much is the good Duke deceived in Angelo!   If
ever he return and I can speak to him, I will open my lips
in vain, or discover his government.

Duke. That shall not be much amiss: yet, as the matter now
stands, he will avoid your accusation; he made trial of you
only.   Therefore fasten your ear on my advisings: to the
love I have in doing good a remedy presents itself.   I do
make myself believe that you may most uprighteously do a
poor wronged lady a merited benefit; redeem your brother
from the angry law; do no stain to your own gracious person;
and much please the absent Duke, if peradventure he shall
ever return to have hearing of this business.

Isab. Let me hear you speak farther.   I have spirit to do any
thing that appears not foul in the truth of my spirit.

Duke. Virtue is bold, and goodness never fearful.   Have you
not heard speak of Mariana, the sister of Frederick the great
soldier who miscarried at sea?

Isab. I have heard of the lady, and good words went with her
name.

Duke. She should this Angelo have married; was affianced to
her by oath, and the nuptial appointed: between which

time of the contract and limit of the solemnity, her brother
Frederick was wrecked at sea, having in that perished vessel
the dowry of his sister.   But mark how heavily this befell to
the poor gentlewoman : there she lost a noble and renowned
brother, in his love toward her ever most kind and natural ;
with him, the portion and sinew of her fortune, her marriage-
dowry ; with both, her combinate husband, this well-seeming
Angelo.

Isab. Can this be so ? did Angelo so leave her ?

Duke. Left her in her tears, and dried not one of them with
his comfort ; swallowed his vows whole, pretending in her
discoveries of dishonour : in few, bestowed her on her own
lamentation, which she yet wears for his sake ; and he, a
marble to her tears, is washed with them, but relents not.

Isab. What a merit were it in death to take this poor maid from
the world !   What corruption in this life, that it will let this
man live !   But how out of this can she avail ?

Duke. It is a rupture that you may easily heal : and the cure of
it not only saves your brother, but keeps you from dishonour
in doing it.

Isab. Show me how, good father.

Duke. This forenamed maid hath yet in her the continuance of
her first affection : his unjust unkindness, that in all reason
should have quenched her love, hath, like an impediment in
the current, made it more violent and unruly.   Go you to
Angelo ; answer his requiring with a plausible obedience ;
agree with his demands to the point ; only refer yourself to
this advantage, first, that your stay with him may not be
long ; that the time may have all shadow and silence in it ;
and the place answer to convenience.   This being granted in
course,—and now follows all,—we shall advise this wronged
maid to stead up your appointment, go in your place ; if the
encounter acknowledge itself hereafter, it may compel him to
her recompence : and here, by this, is your brother saved,
your honour untainted, the poor Mariana advantaged, and
the corrupt Deputy scaled.   The maid will I frame and make
fit for his attempt.   If you think well to carry this as you
may, the doubleness of the benefit defends the deceit from
reproof.   What think you of it ?

Isab. The image of it gives me content already ; and I trust it
will grow to a most prosperous perfection.

Duke. It lies much in your holding up.   Haste you speedily to
Angelo : if for this night he entreat you to his bed, give him
promise of satisfaction.   I will presently to Saint Luke's :
there, at the moated grange, resides this dejected Mariana.

At that place call upon me ; and dispatch with Angelo, that
it may be quickly.

Isab. I thank you for this comfort. Fare you well, good
father.   [*Exeunt severally.*

SCENE II

The street before the prison.

*Enter, on one side, Duke disguised as before ; on the other, Elbow,
and Officers with Pompey.*

Elb. Nay, if there be no remedy for it, but that you will needs
buy and sell men and women like beasts, we shall have all
the world drink brown and white bastard.

Duke. O heavens ! what stuff is here ?

Pom. 'Twas never merry world since, of two usuries, the merriest
was put down, and the worser allowed by order of law a
furred gown to keep him warm ; and furred with fox and
lamb-skins too, to signify, that craft, being richer than
innocency, stands for the facing.

Elb. Come your way, sir. 'Bless you, good father friar.

Duke. And you, good brother father. What offence hath this
man made you, sir ?

Elb. Marry, sir, he hath offended the law : and, sir, we take
him to be a thief too, sir, for we have found upon him,
sir, a strange picklock, which we have sent to the Deputy.

Duke. Fie, sirrah ! a bawd, a wicked bawd !
The evil that thou causest to be done,
That is thy means to live. Do thou but think
What 'tis to cram a maw or clothe a back
From such a filthy vice : say to thyself,
From their abominable and beastly touches
I drink, I eat, array myself, and live.
Canst thou believe thy living is a life,
So stinkingly depending ? Go mend, go mend.

Pom. Indeed, it does stink in some sort, sir ; but yet, sir, I
would prove—

Duke. Nay, if the devil have given thee proofs for sin,
Thou wilt prove his. Take him to prison, officer :
Correction and instruction must both work
Ere this rude beast will profit.

Elb. He must before the Deputy, sir ; he has given him warning : the Deputy cannot abide a whoremaster : if he be a
whoremonger, and comes before him, he were as good go
a mile on his errand.

Duke. That we were all, as some would seem to be,
From our faults, as faults from seeming, free !

Measure for Measure   [Act III, Sc. ii

Elb. His neck will come to your waist,—a cord, sir.

Pom. I spy comfort; I cry bail. Here's a gentleman and a friend of mine.

Enter Lucio.

Lucio. How now, noble Pompey! What, at the wheels of Cæsar? art thou led in triumph? What, is there none of Pygmalion's images, newly made woman, to be had now, for putting the hand in the pocket and extracting it clutched? What reply, ha? What sayest thou to this tune, matter and method? Is't not drown'd i' the last rain, ha? What sayest thou, Trot? Is the world as it was, man? Which is the way? Is it sad, and few words? or how? The trick of it?

Duke. Still thus, and thus; still worse!   [she still, ha?

Lucio. How doth my dear morsel, thy mistress? Procures

Pom. Troth, sir, she hath eaten up all her beef, and she is herself in the tub.

Lucio. Why, 'tis good; it is the right of it; it must be so: ever your fresh whore and your powdered bawd: an unshunned consequence; it must be so. Art going to prison, Pompey?

Pom. Yes, faith, sir.

Lucio. Why, 'tis not amiss, Pompey. Farewell: go say I sent thee thither. For debt, Pompey? or how?

Elb. For being a bawd, for being a bawd.

Lucio. Well, then, imprison him: if imprisonment be the due of a bawd, why, 'tis his right: bawd is he doubtless, and of antiquity too; bawd-born. Farewell, good Pompey. Commend me to the prison, Pompey: you will turn good husband now, Pompey; you will keep the house.

Pom. I hope, sir, your good worship will be my bail.

Lucio. No, indeed, will I not, Pompey; it is not the wear. I will pray, Pompey, to increase your bondage: if you take it not patiently, why, your mettle is the more. Adieu, trusty Pompey. 'Bless you, friar.

Duke. And you.

Lucio. Does Bridget paint still, Pompey, ha?

Elb. Come your ways, sir; come.

Pom. You will not bail me, then, sir?   [what news?

Lucio. Then, Pompey, nor now. What news abroad, friar?

Elb. Come your ways, sir; come.

Lucio. Go to kennel, Pompey; go. [*Exeunt Elbow, Pompey and Officers.*] What news, friar, of the Duke?

Duke. I know none. Can you tell me of any?

Lucio. Some say he is with the Emperor of Russia; other some, he is in Rome: but where is he, think you?

273

Duke. I know not where; but wheresoever, I wish him well.

Lucio. It was a mad fantastical trick of him to steal from the
    state, and usurp the beggary he was never born to. Lord
    Angelo dukes it well in his absence; he put transgression to 't.

Duke. He does well in 't.

Lucio. A little more lenity to lechery would do no harm in
    him : something too crabbed that way, friar.

Duke. It is too general a vice, and severity must cure it.

Lucio. Yes, in good sooth, the vice is of a great kindred; it
    is well allied : but it is impossible to extirp it quite, friar,
    till eating and drinking be put down. They say this Angelo
    was not made by man and woman after this downright way
    of creation : is it true, think you ?

Duke. How should he be made, then ?

Lucio. Some report a sea-maid spawned him; some, that he
    was begot between two stock-fishes. But it is certain that
    when he makes water, his urine is congealed ice; that I know
    to be true : and he is a motion generative; that 's infallible.

Duke. You are pleasant, sir, and speak apace.

Lucio. Why, what a ruthless king is this in him, for the rebellion
    of a codpiece to take away the life of a man ! Would the
    Duke that is absent have done this? Ere he would
    have hanged a man for the getting a hundred bastards,
    he would have paid for the nursing a thousand : he had
    some feeling of the sport; he knew the service, and that
    instructed him to mercy.

Duke. I never heard the absent Duke much detected for
    women; he was not inclined that way.

Lucio. O, sir, you are deceived.

Duke. 'Tis not possible.

Lucio. Who, not the Duke? yes, your beggar of fifty; and his
    use was to put a ducat in her clackdish : the Duke had
    crotchets in him. He would be drunk too; that let me

Duke. You do him wrong, surely.   [inform you.

Lucio. Sir, I was an inward of his. A shy fellow was the
    Duke : and I believe I know the cause of his withdrawing.

Duke. What, I prithee, might be the cause ?

Lucio. No, pardon; 'tis a secret must be locked within the
    teeth and the lips : but this I can let you understand, the
    greater file of the subject held the Duke to be wise.

Duke. Wise ! why, no question but he was.

Lucio. A very superficial, ignorant, unweighing fellow.

Duke. Either this is envy in you, folly, or mistaking : the very
    stream of his life and the business he hath helmed must,
    upon a warranted need, give him a better proclamation. Let

him be but testimonied in his own bringings-forth, and he
shall appear to the envious a scholar, a statesman and a
soldier.   Therefore you speak unskilfully; or if your knowledge be more, it is much darkened in your malice.

Lucio. Sir, I know him, and I love him.

Duke. Love talks with better knowledge, and knowledge with
dearer love.

Lucio. Come, sir, I know what I know.

Duke. I can hardly believe that, since you know not what you
speak.   But, if ever the Duke return, as our prayers are he
may, let me desire you to make your answer before him.   If
it be honest you have spoke, you have courage to maintain
it: I am bound to call upon you; and, I pray you, your name?

Lucio. Sir, my name is Lucio; well known to the Duke.

Duke. He shall know you better, sir, if I may live to report

Lucio. I fear you not.   [you.

Duke. O, you hope the Duke will return no more; or you
imagine me too unhurtful an opposite.   But, indeed, I can
do you little harm; you'll forswear this again.

Lucio. I'll be hanged first: thou art deceived in me, friar.
But no more of this.   Canst thou tell if Claudio die to-
morrow or no?

Duke. Why should he die, sir?

Lucio. Why? For filling a bottle with a tun-dish.   I would
the Duke we talk of were returned again: this ungenitured
agent will unpeople the province with continency; sparrows
must not build in his house-eaves, because they are lecher-
ous.   The Duke yet would have dark deeds darkly answered;
he would never bring them to light: would he were returned!
Marry, this Claudio is condemned for untrussing.   Farewell,
good friar: I prithee, pray for me.   The Duke, I say to
thee again, would eat mutton on Fridays.   He's not past it
yet, and I say to thee, he would mouth with a beggar,
though she smelt brown bread and garlic: say that I said
so.   Farewell.   [*Exit.*

Duke. No might nor greatness in mortality
    Can censure 'scape; back-wounding calumny
    The whitest virtue strikes.   What king so strong
    Can tie the gall up in the slanderous tongue?
    But who comes here?

Enter Escalus, Provost, and Officers with Mistress Overdone.

Escal. Go; away with her to prison!

Mrs Ov. Good my lord, be good to me; your honour is
    accounted a merciful man; good my lord.

Escal. Double and treble admonition, and still forfeit in the same kind! This would make mercy swear and play the tyrant.

Prov. A bawd of eleven years' continuance, may it please your honour.

Mrs Ov. My lord, this is one Lucio's information against me. Mistress Kate Keepdown was with child by him in the Duke's time; he promised her marriage: his child is a year and a quarter old, come Philip and Jacob: I have kept it myself; and see how he goes about to abuse me!

Escal. That fellow is a fellow of much license: let him be called before us. Away with her to prison! Go to; no more words. [*Exeunt Officers with Mistress Ov.*] Provost, my brother Angelo will not be altered; Claudio must die to-morrow: let him be furnished with divines, and have all charitable preparation. If my brother wrought by my pity, it should not be so with him.

Prov. So please you, this friar hath been with him, and advised him for the entertainment of death.

Escal. Good even, good father.

Duke. Bliss and goodness on you!

Escal. Of whence are you?

Duke. Not of this country, though my chance is now
To use it for my time: I am a brother
Of gracious order, late come from the See
In special business from his Holiness.

Escal. What news abroad i' the world?

Duke. None, but that there is so great a fever on goodness, that the dissolution of it must cure it: novelty is only in request; and it is as dangerous to be aged in any kind of course, as it is virtuous to be constant in any undertaking. There is scarce truth enough alive to make societies secure; but security enough to make fellowships accurst:—much upon this riddle runs the wisdom of the world. This news is old enough, yet it is every day's news. I pray you, sir, of what disposition was the Duke?

Escal. One that, above all other strifes, contended especially to

Duke. What pleasure was he given to?　　　　[know himself.

Escal. Rather rejoicing to see another merry, than merry at any thing which professed to make him rejoice: a gentleman of all temperance. But leave we him to his events, with a prayer they may prove prosperous; and let me desire to know how you find Claudio prepared. I am made to understand that you have lent him visitation.

Duke. He professes to have received no sinister measure from

his judge, but most willingly humbles himself to the deter-
mination of justice : yet had he framed to himself, by the
instruction of his frailty, many deceiving promises of life;
which I, by my good leisure, have discredited to him, and
now is he resolved to die.

Escal. You have paid the heavens your function, and the
prisoner the very debt of your calling. I have laboured for
the poor gentleman to the extremest shore of my modesty :
but my brother justice have I found so severe, that he hath
forced me to tell him he is indeed Justice.

Duke. If his own life answer the straitness of his proceeding,
it shall become him well ; wherein if he chance to fail, he
hath sentenced himself.

Escal. I am going to visit the prisoner. Fare you well.

Duke.   Peace be with you ! [*Exeunt Escalus and Provost.*
    He who the sword of heaven will bear
    Should be as holy as severe ;
    Pattern in himself to know,
    Grace to stand, and virtue go ;
    More or less to others paying
    Than by self-offences weighing.
    Shame to him whose cruel striking
    Kills for faults of his own liking !
    Twice treble shame on Angelo,
    To weed my vice and let his grow !
    O, what may man within him hide,
    Though angel on the outward side !
    How many likeness made in crimes,
    Making practice on the times,
    To draw with idle spiders' strings
    Most ponderous and substantial things !
    Craft against vice I must apply :
    With Angelo to-night shall lie
    His old betrothed but despised ;
    So disguise shall, by the disguised,
    Pay with falsehood false exacting,
    And perform an old contracting.   [*Exit.*

ACT IV—Scene I

The moated grange at St. Luke's.
Enter Mariana and a Boy.
Boy sings.

Take, O, take thy lips away,
 That so sweetly were forsworn;

And those eyes, the break of day,
    Lights that do mislead the morn :
But my kisses bring again, bring again ;
    Seals of love, but seal'd in vain, seal'd in vain.

Mari. Break off thy song, and haste thee quick away :
  Here comes a man of comfort, whose advice
  Hath often still'd my brawling discontent.   [*Exit Boy.*
        Enter Duke disguised as before.
  I cry you mercy, sir ; and well could wish
  You had not found me here so musical :
  Let me excuse me, and believe me so,
  My mirth it much displeased, but pleased my woe.

Duke. 'Tis good ; though music oft hath such a charm
    To make bad good, and good provoke to harm.
  I pray you, tell me, hath anybody inquired for me here
  to-day ? much upon this time have I promised here to
  meet.

Mari. You have not been inquired after : I have sat here all
            Enter Isabella.   [day.

Duke. I do constantly believe you. The time is come even
  now. I shall crave your forbearance a little : may be I will
  call upon you anon, for some advantage to yourself.

Mari. I am always bound to you.   [*Exit.*

Duke. Very well met, and well come.
  What is the news from this good Deputy ?

Isab. He hath a garden circummured with brick,
  Whose western side is with a vineyard back'd ;
  And to that vineyard is a planched gate,
  That makes his opening with this bigger key :
  This other doth command a little door
  Which from the vineyard to the garden leads ;
  There have I made my promise
  Upon the heavy middle of the night
  To call upon him.

Duke. But shall you on your knowledge find this way ?

Isab. I have ta'en a due and wary note upon 't :
  With whispering and most guilty diligence,
  In action all of precept, he did show me
  The way twice o'er.

Duke.   Are there no other tokens
  Between you 'greed concerning her observance ?

Isab. No, none, but only a repair i' the dark ;
  And that I have possess'd him my most stay
  Can be but brief ; for I have made him know
  I have a servant comes with me along,

That stays upon me, whose persuasion is
I come about my brother.
Duke.   'Tis well borne up.
I have not yet made known to Mariana
A word of this.   What, ho! within! come forth!
                    Re-enter Mariana.
I pray you, be acquainted with this maid;
She comes to do you good.
Isab.   I do desire the like.
Duke. Do you persuade yourself that I respect you?
Mari. Good friar, I know you do, and have found it.
Duke. Take, then, this your companion by the hand,
Who hath a story ready for your ear.
I shall attend your leisure: but make haste;
The vaporous night approaches.
Mari. Will 't please you walk aside?
                            [*Exeunt Mariana and Isabella.*
Duke. O place and greatness, millions of false eyes
Are stuck upon thee! volumes of report
Run with these false and most contrarious quests
Upon thy doings! thousand escapes of wit
Make thee the father of their idle dreams,
And rack thee in their fancies!
                Re-enter Mariana and Isabella.
                            Welcome, how agreed?
Isab. She 'll take the enterprise upon her, father,
If you advise it.
Duke.   It is not my consent,
But my entreaty too.
Isab.   Little have you to say
When you depart from him, but, soft and low,
' Remember now my brother.'
Mari.   Fear me not.
Duke. Nor, gentle daughter, fear you not at all.
He is your husband on a pre-contract:
To bring you thus together, 'tis no sin,
Sith that the justice of your title to him
Doth flourish the deceit.   Come, let us go:
Our corn 's to reap, for yet our tithe 's to sow.   [*Exeunt.*

                        SCENE II

                  A room in the prison.
                Enter Provost and Pompey.

Prov. Come hither, sirrah.   Can you cut off a man's head?
Pom. If the man be a bachelor, sir, I can; but if he be a

married man, he's his wife's head, and I can never cut off a
woman's head.

Prov. Come, sir, leave me your snatches, and yield me a
direct answer. To-morrow morning are to die Claudio and
Barnardine. Here is in our prison a common executioner
who in his office lacks a helper: if you will take it on you
to assist him, it shall redeem you from your gyves; if not,
you shall have your full time of imprisonment, and your
deliverance with an unpitied whipping, for you have been a
notorious bawd.

Pom. Sir, I have been an unlawful bawd time out of mind;
but yet I will be content to be a lawful hangman. I would
be glad to receive some instruction from my fellow partner.

Prov. What, ho! Abhorson! Where's Abhorson, there?

Enter Abhorson.

Abhor. Do you call, sir?

Prov. Sirrah, here's a fellow will help you to-morrow in your
execution. If you think it meet, compound with him by
the year, and let him abide here with you; if not, use him
for the present, and dismiss him. He cannot plead his
estimation with you; he hath been a bawd.   [mystery.

Abhor. A bawd, sir? fie upon him! he will discredit our

Prov. Go to, sir; you weigh equally; a feather will turn the
scale.   [*Exit.*

Pom. Pray, sir, by your good favour,—for surely, sir, a good
favour you have, but that you have a hanging look,—do you
call, sir, your occupation a mystery?

Abhor. Ay, sir; a mystery.

Pom. Painting, sir, I have heard say, is a mystery; and your
whores, sir, being members of my occupation, using painting,
do prove my occupation a mystery: but what mystery there
should be in hanging, if I should be hanged, I cannot

Abhor. Sir, it is a mystery.   [imagine.

Pom. Proof?

Abhor. Every true man's apparel fits your thief: if it be too
little for your thief, your true man thinks it big enough; if
it be too big for your thief, your thief thinks it little enough:
so every true man's apparel fits your thief.

Re-enter Provost.

Prov. Are you agreed?

Pom. Sir, I will serve him; for I do find your hangman is a
more penitent trade than your bawd; he doth oftener ask
forgiveness.   [four o'clock.

Prov. You, sirrah, provide your block and your axe to-morrow

Abhor. Come on, bawd; I will instruct thee in my trade; follow.

Pom. I do desire to learn, sir: and I hope, if you have
occasion to use me for your own turn, you shall find me
yare; for, truly, sir, for your kindness I owe you a good turn.

Prov. Call hither Barnardine and Claudio:

[Exeunt Pompey and Abhorson.

The one has my pity; not a jot the other,
Being a murderer, though he were my brother.

Enter Claudio.

Look, here's the warrant, Claudio, for thy death:
'Tis now dead midnight, and by eight to-morrow
Thou must be made immortal. Where's Barnardine?

Claud. As fast lock'd up in sleep as guiltless labour
When it lies starkly in the traveller's bones:
He will not wake.

Prov.   Who can do good on him?
Well, go, prepare yourself. *[Knocking within.]* But, hark,
    what noise?—
Heaven give your spirits comfort! *[Exit Claudio.]* By and
I hope it is some pardon or reprieve   [by.—
For the most gentle Claudio.

Enter Duke disguised as before.

                              Welcome, father.

Duke. The best and wholesomest spirits of the night
Envelop you, good Provost! Who call'd here of late?

Prov. None, since the curfew rung.

Duke. Not Isabel?

Prov.   No.

Duke.   They will then, ere't be long.

Prov. What comfort is for Claudio?

Duke. There's some in hope.

Prov. It is a bitter deputy.

Duke. Not so, not so; his life is parallel'd
Even with the stroke and line of his great justice
He doth with holy abstinence subdue
That in himself which he spurs on his power
To qualify in others; were he mealed with that
Which he corrects, then were he tyrannous;
But this being so, he's just.   *[Knocking within.*
                    Now are they come.

                                        [Exit Provost.

This is a gentle provost: seldom when
The steeled gaoler is the friend of men.   *[Knocking within.*
How now! what noise? That spirit's possessed with haste
That wounds the unsisting postern with these strokes.

281

Re-enter Provost.

Prov. There he must stay until the officer
  Arise to let him in : he is call'd up.

Duke. Have you no countermand for Claudio yet,
  But he must die to-morrow ?

Prov.   None, sir, none.

Duke. As near the dawning, provost, as it is,
  You shall hear more ere morning.

Prov.   Happily
  You something know ; yet I believe there comes
  No countermand ; no such example have we :
  Besides, upon the very siege of justice
  Lord Angelo hath to the public ear
  Profess'd the contrary.

Enter a Messenger.
              This is his lordship's man.

Duke. And here comes Claudio's pardon.

Mes. [*Giving a paper*] My lord hath sent you this note ; and
by me this further charge, that you swerve not from the
smallest article of it, neither in time, matter, or other circumstance. Good morrow : for, as I take it, it is almost day.

Prov. I shall obey him.   [*Exit Messenger.*

Duke. [*Aside*] This is his pardon, purchased by such sin
  For which the pardoner himself is in.
  Hence hath offence his quick celerity,
  When it is borne in high authority :
  When vice makes mercy, mercy's so extended,
  That for the fault's love is the offender friended.
  Now, sir, what news ?

Prov. I told you. Lord Angelo, belike thinking me remiss in
mine office, awakens me with this unwonted putting-on ;
methinks strangely, for he hath not used it before.

Duke. Pray you, let's hear.

Prov. [*Reads*]
  Whatsoever you may hear to the contrary, let Claudio be executed by four of the clock ; and in the afternoon Barnardine ;
  for my better satisfaction, let me have Claudio's head sent
  me by five. Let this be duly performed ; with a thought
  that more depends on it than we must yet deliver. Thus
  fail not to do your office, as you will answer it at your peril.
  What say you to this, sir ?

Duke. What is that Barnardine who is to be executed in the
afternoon ?

Prov. A Bohemian born, but here nursed up and bred ; one
that is a prisoner nine years old.

Duke. How came it that the absent Duke had not either
delivered him to his liberty or executed him? I have heard
it was ever his manner to do so.

Prov. His friends still wrought reprieves for him : and, indeed,
his fact, till now in the government of Lord Angelo, came
not to an undoubtful proof.

Duke. It is now apparent?

Prov. Most manifest, and not denied by himself.

Duke. Hath he borne himself penitently in prison ? how seems
he to be touched?

Prov. A man that apprehends death no more dreadfully but
as a drunken sleep ; careless, reckless, and fearless of what's
past, present, or to come ; insensible of mortality, and

Duke. He wants advice.   [desperately mortal.

Prov. He will hear none ; he hath evermore had the liberty of
the prison ; give him leave to escape hence, he would not :
drunk many times a day, if not many days entirely drunk.
We have very oft awaked him, as if to carry him to execution,
and showed him a seeming warrant for it : it hath not moved
him at all.

Duke. More of him anon. There is written in your brow,
provost, honesty and constancy : if I read it not truly, my
ancient skill beguiles me ; but, in the boldness of my cunning,
I will lay my self in hazard. Claudio, whom here you have
warrant to execute, is no greater forfeit to the law than
Angelo who hath sentenced him. To make you understand
this in a manifested effect, I crave but four days' respite ; for
the which you are to do me both a present and a dangerous

Prov. Pray, sir, in what?   [courtesy.

Duke. In the delaying death.

Prov. Alack, how may I do it, having the hour limited, and an
express command, under penalty, to deliver his head in the
view of Angelo? I may make my case as Claudio's, to cross
this in the smallest.

Duke. By the vow of mine order I warrant you, if my instructions may be your guide. Let this Barnardine be this morning executed, and his head borne to Angelo.

Prov. Angelo hath seen them both, and will discover the favour.

Duke. O, death's a great disguiser ; and you may add to it.
Shave the head, and tie the beard ; and say it was the desire
of the penitent to be so bared before his death : you know
the course is common. If any thing fall to you upon this,
more than thanks and good fortune, by the Saint whom I
profess, I will plead against it with my life.

Prov. Pardon me, good father ; it is against my oath.

Duke. Were you sworn to the Duke, or to the Deputy?

Prov. To him, and to his substitutes.

Duke. You will think you have made no offence, if the Duke avouch the justice of your dealing?

Prov. But what likelihood is in that?

Duke. Not a resemblance, but a certainty. Yet since I see you fearful, that neither my coat, integrity, nor persuasion can with ease attempt you, I will go further than I meant, to pluck all fears out of you. Look you, sir, here is the hand and seal of the Duke: you know the character, I doubt not; and the signet is not strange to you.

Prov. I know them both.

Duke. The contents of this is the return of the Duke: you shall anon over-read it at your pleasure; where you shall find, within these two days he will be here. This is a thing that Angelo knows not; for he this very day receives letters of strange tenour; perchance of the Duke's death; perchance entering into some monastery; but, by chance, nothing of what is writ. Look, the unfolding star calls up the shepherd. Put not yourself into amazement how these things should be: all difficulties are but easy when they are known. Call your executioner, and off with Barnardine's head: I will give him a present shrift and advise him for a better place. Yet you are amazed; but this shall absolutely resolve you. Come away; it is almost clear dawn.   [*Exeunt.*

Scene III

Another room in the same.

Enter Pompey.

Pom. I am as well acquainted here as I was in our house of profession: one would think it were Mistress Overdone's own house, for here be many of her old customers. First, here's young Master Rash; he's in for a commodity of brown paper and old ginger, nine-score and seventeen pounds; of which he made five marks, ready money: marry, then ginger was not much in request, for the old women were all dead. Then is there here one Master Caper, at the suit of Master Three-pile the mercer, for some four suits of peach-coloured satin, which now peaches him a beggar. Then have we here young Dizy, and young Master Deep-vow, and Master Copper-spur, and Master Starve-lackey the rapier and dagger man, and young Drop-heir that killed lusty Pudding, and Master Forthlight the tilter, and brave Master Shooty the great traveller, and wild Half-can that stabbed Pots, and,

I think, forty more; all great doers in our trade, and are
now 'for the Lord's sake.'

Enter Abhorson.

Abhor. Sirrah, bring Barnardine hither.

Pom. Master Barnardine! you must rise and be hanged, Master

Abhor. What ho, Barnardine!   [Barnardine!

Bar. [*Within*] A pox o' your throats! Who makes that noise
there? What are you?

Pom. Your friends, sir; the hangman. You must be so good,
sir, to rise and be put to death.

Bar. [*Within*] Away, you rogue, away! I am sleepy.

Abhor. Tell him he must awake, and that quickly too.

Pom. Pray, Master Barnardine, awake till you are executed, and

Abhor. Go in to him, and fetch him out.   [sleep afterwards.

Pom. He is coming, sir, he is coming; I hear his straw rustle.

Abhor. Is the axe upon the block, sirrah?

Pom. Very ready, sir.

Enter Barnardine.

Bar. How now, Abhorson? what's the news with you?

Abhor. Truly, sir, I would desire you to clap into your prayers;
for, look you, the warrant's come.   [fitted for 't.

Bar. You rogue, I have been drinking all night; I am not

Pom. O, the better, sir; for he that drinks all night, and is
hanged betimes in the morning, may sleep the sounder all
the next day.   [jest now, think you?

Abhor. Look you, sir; here comes your ghostly father: do we

Enter Duke disguised as before.

Duke. Sir, induced by my charity, and hearing how hastily you
are to depart, I am come to advise you, comfort you and
pray with you.

Bar. Friar, not I: I have been drinking hard all night, and I will
have more time to prepare me, or they shall beat out my brains
with billets: I will not consent to die this day, that's certain.

Duke. O, sir, you must: and therefore I beseech you
Look forward on the journey you shall go.

Bar. I swear I will not die to-day for any man's persuasion.

Duke. But hear you.

Bar. Not a word: if you have any thing to say to me, come to
my ward; for thence will not I to-day.   [*Exit.*

Duke. Unfit to live or die: O gravel heart!
After him, fellows; bring him to the block.

                              [*Exeunt Abhorson and Pompey.*

Enter Provost.

Prov. Now, sir, how do you find the prisoner?

Duke. A creature unprepared, unmeet for death;

285

And to transport him in the mind he is
Were damnable.
Prov.   Here in the prison, father,
There died this morning of a cruel fever
One Ragozine, a most notorious pirate,
A man of Claudio's years; his beard and head
Just of his colour.   What if we do omit
This reprobate till he were well inclined;
And satisfy the Deputy with the visage
Of Ragozine, more like to Claudio?
Duke. O, 'tis an accident that heaven provides!
Dispatch it presently; the hour draws on
Prefix'd by Angelo: see this be done,
And sent according to command; whiles I
Persuade this rude wretch willingly to die.
Prov. This shall be done, good father, presently.
But Barnardine must die this afternoon:
And how shall we continue Claudio,
To save me from the danger that might come
If he were known alive?
Duke.   Let this be done.
Put them in secret holds, both Barnardine and Claudio:
Ere twice the sun hath made his journal greeting
To the under generation, you shall find
Your safety manifested.
Prov. I am your free dependant.
Duke. Quick, dispatch, and send the head to Angelo.

                                        [*Exit Provost.*

Now will I write letters to Angelo,—
The provost, he shall bear them,—whose contents
Shall witness to him I am near at home,
And that, by great injunctions, I am bound
To enter publicly: him I'll desire
To meet me at the consecrated fount,
A league below the city; and from thence,
By cold gradation and well-balanced form,
We shall proceed with Angelo.

                    Re-enter Provost.

Prov. Here is the head; I'll carry it myself.
Duke. Convenient is it.   Make a swift return;
For I would commune with you of such things
That want no ear but yours.
Prov.   I'll make all speed.   [*Exit.*
Isab. [*Within*] Peace, ho, be here!
Duke. The tongue of Isabel.   She's come to know

                          286

If yet her brother's pardon be come hither
But I will keep her ignorant of her good,
To make her heavenly comforts of despair,
When it is least expected.

Enter Isabella.

Isab.   Ho, by your leave!
Duke. Good morning to you, fair and gracious daughter.
Isab. The better, given me by so holy a man.
      Hath yet the Deputy sent my brother's pardon?
Duke. He hath released him, Isabel, from the world:
      His head is off, and sent to Angelo.
Isab. Nay, but it is not so.
Duke. It is no other: show your wisdom, daughter,
      In your close patience.
Isab. O, I will to him and pluck out his eyes!
Duke. You shall not be admitted to his sight.
Isab. Unhappy Claudio! wretched Isabel!
      Injurious world! most damned Angelo!
Duke. This nor hurts him nor profits you a jot;
      Forbear it therefore; give your cause to heaven.
      Mark what I say, which you shall find
      By every syllable a faithful verity:
      The Duke comes home to-morrow;—nay, dry your eyes;
      One of our convent, and his confessor,
      Gives me this instance: already he hath carried
      Notice to Escalus and Angelo;
      Who do prepare to meet him at the gates,
      There to give up their power. If you can, pace your wisdom
      In that good path that I would wish it go;
      And you shall have your bosom on this wretch,
      Grace of the Duke, revenges to your heart,
      And general honour.
Isab.   I am directed by you.
Duke. This letter, then, to Friar Peter give;
      'Tis that he sent me of the Duke's return:
      Say, by this token, I desire his company
      At Mariana's house to-night. Her cause and yours
      I'll perfect him withal; and he shall bring you
      Before the Duke; and to the head of Angelo
      Accuse him home and home. For my poor self,
      I am combined by a sacred vow,
      And shall be absent. Wend you with this letter:
      Command these fretting waters from your eyes
      With a light heart; trust not my holy order,
      If I pervert your course.—Who's here?

Enter Lucio.

Lucio. Good even.   Friar, where 's the provost ?

Duke. Not within, sir.

Lucio. O pretty Isabella, I am pale at mine heart to see thine
eyes so red : thou must be patient.   I am fain to dine and sup
with water and bran ; I dare not for my head fill my belly ;
one fruitful meal would set me to 't.   But they say the Duke
will be here to-morrow.   By my troth, Isabel, I loved thy
brother : if the old fantastical Duke of dark corners had been
at home, he had lived.   [*Exit Isabella.*

Duke. Sir, the Duke is marvellous little beholding to your
reports ; but the best is, he lives not in them.

Lucio. Friar, thou knowest not the Duke so well as I do : he 's
a better woodman than thou takest him for.

Duke. Well, you 'll answer this one day.   Fare ye well.

Lucio. Nay, tarry ; I 'll go along with thee : I can tell thee
pretty tales of the Duke.

Duke. You have told me too many of him already, sir, if they
be true ; if not true, none were enough.

Lucio. I was once before him for getting a wench with child.

Duke. Did you such a thing ?

Lucio. Yes, marry, did I : but I was fain to forswear it ; they
would else have married me to the rotten medlar.

Duke. Sir, your company is fairer than honest.   Rest you well.

Lucio. By my troth, I 'll go with thee to the lane's end : if
bawdy talk offend you, we 'll have very little of it.   Nay,
friar, I am a kind of burr ; I shall stick.   [*Exeunt.*

SCENE IV

A room in Angelo's house.
Enter Angelo and Escalus.

Escal. Every letter he hath writ hath disvouched other.

Ang. In most uneven and distracted manner.   His actions
show much like to madness : pray heaven his wisdom be not
tainted !   And why meet him at the gates, and redeliver our
authorities there ?

Escal. I guess not.

Ang. And why should we proclaim it in an hour before his
entering, that if any crave redress of injustice, they should
exhibit their petitions in the street ?

Escal. He shows his reason for that : to have a dispatch of
complaints, and to deliver us from devices hereafter, which
shall then have no power to stand against us.

Ang. Well, I beseech you, let it be proclaimed betimes i' the

morn; I 'll call you at your house: give notice to such men
of sort and suit as are to meet him.

Escal. I shall, sir.   Fare you well.

Ang. Good night.   [*Exit Escalus.*
  This deed unshapes me quite, makes me unpregnant,
And dull to all proceedings.   A deflower'd maid!
And by an eminent body that enforced
The law against it!   But that her tender shame
Will not proclaim against her maiden loss,
How might she tongue me!   Yet reason dares her no;
For my authority bears of a credent bulk,
That no particular scandal once can touch
But it confounds the breather.   He should have lived,
Save that his riotous youth, with dangerous sense,
Might in the times to come have ta'en revenge,
By so receiving a dishonour'd life
With ransom of such shame.   Would yet he had lived!
Alack, when once our grace we have forgot,
Nothing goes right: we would, and we would not.   [*Exit.*

SCENE V
Fields without the town.
Enter Duke in his own habit, and Friar Peter.

Duke. These letters at fit time deliver me: [*Giving letters.*
  The provost knows our purpose and our plot.
The matter being afoot, keep your instruction,
And hold you ever to our special drift;
Though sometimes you do blench from this to that,
As cause doth minister.   Go call at Flavius' house,
And tell him where I stay: give the like notice
To Valentius, Rowland, and to Crassus,
And bid them bring the trumpets to the gate;
But send me Flavius first.

Fri P.   It shall be speeded well.   [*Exit.*

Enter Varrius.

Duke. I thank thee, Varrius; thou hast made good haste:
  Come, we will walk.   There 's other of our friends
Will greet us here anon, my gentle Varrius.   [*Exeunt.*

SCENE VI
Street near the city-gate.
Enter Isabella and Mariana.

Isab. To speak so indirectly I am loath:
  I would say the truth; but to accuse him so,

289

That is your part : yet I am advised to do it ;
He says, to veil full purpose.
Mari.   Be ruled by him.
Isab. Besides, he tells me that, if peradventure
He speak against me on the adverse side,
I should not think it strange ; for 'tis a physic
That 's bitter to sweet end.
Mari. I would Friar Peter—
Isab.   O, peace ! the friar is come.

Enter Friar Peter.

Fri. P. Come, I have found you out a stand most fit,
Where you may have such vantage on the Duke,
He shall not pass you.   Twice have the trumpets sounded ;
The generous and gravest citizens
Have hent the gates, and very near upon
The Duke is entering : therefore, hence, away !   [*Exeunt.*

ACT V—SCENE I

The city-gate.

*Mariana veiled, Isabella, and Friar Peter, at their stand.
Enter Duke, Varrius, Lords, Angelo, Escalus, Lucio, Provost,
Officers, and Citizens, at several doors.*

Duke. My very worthy cousin, fairly met !
Our old and faithful friend, we are glad to see you.
Ang.
Escal. } Happy return be to your royal Grace !
Duke. Many and hearty thankings to you both.
We have made inquiry of you ; and we hear
Such goodness of your justice, that our soul
Cannot but yield you forth to public thanks,
Forerunning more requital.
Ang.   You make my bonds still greater.
Duke. O, your desert speaks loud ; and I should wrong it,
To lock it in the wards of covert bosom,
When it deserves, with characters of brass,
A forted residence 'gainst the tooth of time
And razure of oblivion.   Give me your hand,
And let the subject see, to make them know
That outward courtesies would fain proclaim
Favours that keep within.   Come, Escalus ;
You must walk by us on our other hand :
And good supporters are you.

Friar Peter and Isabella come forward.

Fri. P. Now is your time : speak loud, and kneel before him.

Isab. Justice, O royal Duke! Vail your regard
    Upon a wrong'd, I would fain have said, a maid!
    O worthy prince, dishonour not your eye
    By throwing it on any other object
    Till you have heard me in my true complaint,
    And given me justice, justice, justice, justice!
Duke. Relate your wrongs; in what? by whom? be brief.
    Here is Lord Angelo shall give you justice:
    Reveal yourself to him.
Isab.   O worthy Duke,
    You bid me seek redemption of the devil:
    Hear me yourself; for that which I must speak
    Must either punish me, not being believed,
    Or wring redress from you. Hear me, O hear me, here!
Ang. My lord, her wits, I fear me, are not firm:
    She hath been a suitor to me for her brother
    Cut off by course of justice,—
Isab.   By course of justice!
Ang. And she will speak most bitterly and strange.
Isab. Most strange, but yet most truly, will I speak:
    That Angelo's forsworn; is it not strange?
    That Angelo's a murderer; is 't not strange?
    That Angelo is an adulterous thief,
    An hypocrite, a virgin-violator;
    Is it not strange and strange?
Duke.   Nay, it is ten times strange.
Isab. It is not truer he is Angelo
    Than this is all as true as it is strange:
    Nay, it is ten times true; for truth is truth
    To the end of reckoning.
Duke.   Away with her!—Poor soul,
    She speaks this in the infirmity of sense.
Isab. O prince, I conjure thee, as thou believest
    There is another comfort than this world,
    That thou neglect me not, with that opinion
    That I am touch'd with madness! Make not impossible
    That which but seems unlike: 'tis not impossible
    But one, the wicked'st caitiff on the ground,
    May seem as shy, as grave, as just, as absolute
    As Angelo; even so may Angelo,
    In all his dressings, characts, titles, forms,
    Be an arch-villain; believe it, royal prince:
    If he be less, he's nothing; but he's more,
    Had I more name for badness.
Duke.   By mine honesty,

If she be mad,—as I believe no other,—
Her madness hath the oddest frame of sense,
Such a dependency of thing on thing,
As e'er I heard in madness.

Isab.   O gracious Duke,
Harp not on that; nor do not banish reason
For inequality: but let your reason serve
To make the truth appear where it seems hid,
And hide the false seems true.

Duke.   Many that are not mad
Have, sure, more lack of reason.   What would you say?

Isab. I am the sister of one Claudio,
Condemn'd upon the act of fornication
To lose his head; condemn'd by Angelo:
I, in probation of a sisterhood,
Was sent to by my brother; one Lucio
As then the messenger,—

Lucio.   That's I, an't like your Grace:
I came to her from Claudio, and desired her
To try her gracious fortune with Lord Angelo
For her poor brother's pardon.

Isab.   That's he indeed.

Duke. You were not bid to speak.

Lucio.   No, my good lord;
Nor wish'd to hold my peace.

Duke.   I wish you now, then;
Pray you, take note of it: and when you have
A business for yourself, pray heaven you then
Be perfect.

Lucio.   I warrant your honour.

Duke. The warrant's for yourself; take heed to 't.

Isab. This gentleman told somewhat of my tale,—

Lucio. Right.

Duke. It may be right; but you are i' the wrong
To speak before your time.   Proceed.

Isab.   I went
To this pernicious caitiff Deputy,—

Duke. That's somewhat madly spoken.

Isab.   Pardon it;
The phrase is to the matter.

Duke. Mended again.   The matter;—proceed.

Isab. In brief,—to set the needless process by,
How I persuaded, how I pray'd, and kneel'd,
How he refell'd me, and how I replied,—
For this was of much length,—the vile conclusion

I now begin with grief and shame to utter :
He would not, but by gift of my chaste body
To his concupiscible intemperate lust,
Release my brother ; and, after much debatement,
My sisterly remorse confutes mine honour,
And I did yield to him : but the next morn betimes,
His purpose surfeiting, he sends a warrant
For my poor brother's head.

Duke.   This is most likely !
Isab. O, that it were as like as it is true !
Duke. By heaven, fond wretch, thou know'st not what thou
  Or else thou art suborn'd against his honour   [speak'st,
  In hateful practice.   First, his integrity
  Stands without blemish.   Next, it imports no reason
  That with such vehemency he should pursue
  Faults proper to himself : if he had so offended,
  He would have weigh'd thy brother by himself,
  And not have cut him off.   Some one hath set you on :
  Confess the truth, and say by whose advice
  Thou camest here to complain.
Isab.   And is this all ?
  Then, O you blessed ministers above,
  Keep me in patience, and with ripen'd time
  Unfold the evil which is here wrapt up
  Incountenance !—Heaven shield your Grace from woe,
  As I, thus wrong'd, hence unbelieved go !
Duke. I know you 'ld fain be gone.—An officer !
  To prison with her !—Shall we thus permit
  A blasting and a scandalous breath to fall
  On him so near us ?   This needs must be a practice.
  Who knew of your intent and coming hither ?
Isab. One that I would were here, Friar Lodowick.
Duke. A ghostly father, belike.   Who knows that Lodowick ?
Lucio. My lord, I know him ; 'tis a meddling friar ;
  I do not like the man : had he been lay, my lord,
  For certain words he spake against your Grace
  In your retirement, I had swinged him soundly.
Duke. Words against me ! this 's a good friar belike !
  And to set on this wretched woman here
  Against our substitute !   Let this friar be found.
Lucio. But yesternight, my lord, she and that friar,
  I saw them at the prison : a saucy friar,
  A very scurvy fellow.
Fri. P. Blessed be your royal Grace !
  I have stood by, my lord, and I have heard

Your royal ear abused.   First, hath this woman
Most wrongfully accused your substitute,
Who is as free from touch or soil with her
As she from one ungot.

Duke.   We did believe no less.
Know you that Friar Lodowick that she speaks of?

Fri. P. I know him for a man divine and holy;
Not scurvy, nor a temporary meddler,
As he 's reported by this gentleman;
And, on my trust, a man that never yet
Did, as he vouches, misreport your Grace.

Lucio. My lord, most villanously; believe it.

Fri. P. Well, he in time may come to clear himself;
But at this instant he is sick, my lord,
Of a strange fever.   Upon his mere request,—
Being come to knowledge that there was complaint
Intended 'gainst Lord Angelo,—came I hither,
To speak, as from his mouth, what he doth know
Is true and false; and what he with his oath
And all probation will make up full clear,
Whensoever he 's convented.   First, for this woman,
To justify this worthy nobleman,
So vulgarly and personally accused,
Her shall you hear disproved to her eyes,
Till she herself confess it.

Duke.   Good friar, let 's hear it.
      [*Isabella is carried off guarded; and Mariana comes forward.*
Do you not smile at this, Lord Angelo?—
O heaven, the vanity of wretched fools!—
Give us some seats.   Come, cousin Angelo;
In this I 'll be impartial; be you judge
Of your own cause.   Is this the witness, friar?
First, let her show her face, and after speak.

Mari. Pardon, my lord; I will not show my face
Until my husband bid me.

Duke. What, are you married?

Mari. No, my lord.

Duke. Are you a maid?

Mari. No, my lord.

Duke. A widow, then?

Mari. Neither, my lord.

Duke. Why, you are nothing, then:—neither maid, widow, nor
wife?

Lucio. My lord, she may be a punk; for many of them **are**
neither maid, widow, nor wife.

Duke. Silence that fellow: I would he had some cause to
    prattle for himself.

Lucio. Well, my lord.

Mari. My lord, I do confess I ne'er was married:
    And I confess, besides, I am no maid:
    I have known my husband; yet my husband
    Knows not that ever he knew me.

Lucio. He was drunk, then, my lord: it can be no better.

Duke. For the benefit of silence, would thou wert so too !

Lucio. Well, my lord.

Duke. This is no witness for Lord Angelo.

Mari. Now I come to 't, my lord:
    She that accuses him of fornication,
    In self-same manner doth accuse my husband;
    And charges him, my lord, with such a time
    When I 'll depose I had him in mine arms
    With all the effect of love.

Ang. Charges she moe than me ?

Mari.   Not that I know.

Duke. No ? you say your husband.

Mari. Why, just, my lord, and that is Angelo,
    Who thinks he knows that he ne'er knew my body,
    But knows he thinks that he knows Isabel's.

Ang. This is a strange abuse. Let 's see thy face.

Mari. My husband bids me; now I will unmask. [*Unveiling.*
    This is that face, thou cruel Angelo,
    Which once thou sworest was worth the looking on;
    This is the hand which, with a vow'd contract,
    Was fast belock'd in thine; this is the body
    That took away the match from Isabel,
    And did supply thee at thy garden-house
    In her imagined person.

Duke.   Know you this woman ?

Lucio. Carnally, she says.

Duke.   Sirrah, no more !

Lucio. Enough, my lord.

Ang. My lord, I must confess I know this woman:
    And five years since there was some speech of marriage
    Betwixt myself and her; which was broke off,
    Partly for that her promised proportions
    Came short of composition; but in chief,
    For that her reputation was disvalued
    In levity: since which time of five years
    I never spake with her, saw her, nor heard from her,
    Upon my faith and honour.

Mari.   Noble prince,
As there comes light from heaven and words from breath,
As there is sense in truth and truth in virtue,
I am affianced this man's wife as strongly
As words could make up vows: and, my good lord,
But Tuesday night last gone in 's garden-house
He knew me as a wife.   As this is true,
Let me in safety raise me from my knees;
Or else for ever be confixed here,
A marble monument!
Ang.   I did but smile till now:
Now, good my lord, give me the scope of justice;
My patience here is touch'd.   I do perceive
These poor informal women are no more
But instruments of some more mightier member
That sets them on: let me have way, my lord,
To find this practice out.
Duke.   Ay, with my heart;
And punish them to your height of pleasure.
Thou foolish friar; and thou pernicious woman,
Compact with her that 's gone, think'st thou thy oaths,
Though they would swear down each particular saint,
Were testimonies against his worth and credit,
That 's seal'd in approbation? You, Lord Escalus,
Sit with my cousin; lend him your kind pains
To find out this abuse, whence 'tis derived.
There is another friar that set them on;
Let him be sent for.
Fri. P. Would he were here, my lord! for he, indeed,
Hath set the women on to this complaint:
Your provost knows the place where he abides,
And he may fetch him.
Duke.   Go, do it instantly.   [*Exit Provost.*
And you, my noble and well-warranted cousin,
Whom it concerns to hear this matter forth,
Do with your injuries as seems you best,
In any chastisement: I for a while will leave you;
But stir not you till you have well determined
Upon these slanderers.
Escal. My lord, we 'll do it thoroughly.   [*Exit Duke.*] Signor
Lucio, did not you say you knew that Friar Lodowick to be
a dishonest person?
Lucio. 'Cucullus non facit monachum:' honest in nothing but
in his clothes; and one that hath spoke most villanous
speeches of the Duke.

Escal. We shall entreat you to abide here till he come, and
enforce them against him : we shall find this friar a notable
Lucio. As any in Vienna, on my word.   [fellow.
Escal. Call that same Isabel here once again : I would speak
with her. [*Exit an Attendant.*] Pray you, my lord, give
me leave to question ; you shall see how I 'll handle her.
Lucio. Not better than he, by her own report.
Escal. Say you ?
Lucio. Marry, sir, I think, if you handled her privately, she
would sooner confess : perchance, publicly, she 'll be
Escal. I will go darkly to work with her.   [ashamed.
Lucio. That 's the way ; for women are light at midnight.
*Re-enter Officers with Isabella ; and Provost with the Duke
in his friar's habit.*
Escal. Come on, mistress : here 's a gentlewoman denies all that
you have said.   [provost.
Lucio. My lord, here comes the rascal I spoke of ; here with the
Escal. In very good time : speak not you to him till we call
Lucio. Mum.   [upon you.
Escal. Come, sir : did you set these women on to slander Lord
Angelo ? they have confessed you did.
Duke. 'Tis false.
Escal. How ! know you where you are ?
Duke. Respect to your great place ! and let the devil
Be sometime honour'd for his burning throne !
Where is the Duke ? 'tis he should hear me speak.
Escal. The Duke 's in us ; and we will hear you speak :
Look you speak justly.
Duke. Boldly ; at least. But, O, poor souls,
Come you to seek the lamb here of the fox ?
Good night to your redress ! Is the Duke gone ?
Then is your cause gone too. The Duke 's unjust,
Thus to retort your manifest appeal,
And put your trial in the villain's mouth
Which here you come to accuse.
Lucio. This is the rascal ; this is he I spoke of.
Escal. Why, thou unreverend and unhallow'd friar,
Is 't not enough thou hast suborn'd these women
To accuse this worthy man, but, in foul mouth,
And in the witness of his proper ear,
To call him villain ? and then to glance from him
To the Duke himself, to tax him with injustice ?
Take him hence ; to the rack with him ! We 'll touse you
Joint by joint, but we will know his purpose.
What, 'unjust' !

Duke.   Be not so hot; the Duke
    Dare no more stretch this finger of mine than he
    Dare rack his own: his subject am I not,
    Nor here provincial.   My business in this state
    Made me a looker-on here in Vienna,
    Where I have seen corruption boil and bubble
    Till it o'er-run the stew; laws for all faults,
    But faults so countenanced, that the strong statutes
    Stand like the forfeits in a barber's shop,
    As much in mock as mark.

Escal. Slander to the state!   Away with him to prison!

Ang. What can you vouch against him, Signor Lucio?   Is this
    the man that you did tell us of?   [you know me?

Lucio. 'Tis he, my lord.   Come hither, goodman baldpate: do

Duke. I remember you, sir, by the sound of your voice: I met
    you at the prison, in the absence of the Duke.

Lucio. O, did you so?   And do you remember what you said of

Duke. Most notedly, sir.   [the Duke?

Lucio. Do you so, sir?   And was the Duke a fleshmonger, a
    fool, and a coward, as you then reported him to be?

Duke. You must, sir, change persons with me, ere you make
    that my report: you, indeed, spoke so of him; and much
    more, much worse.

Lucio. O thou damnable fellow! Did not I pluck thee by the
    nose for thy speeches?

Duke. I protest I love the Duke as I love myself.

Ang. Hark, how the villain would close now, after his
    treasonable abuses!

Escal. Such a fellow is not to be talked withal.   Away with him
    to prison!   Where is the provost? Away with him to prison!
    lay bolts enough upon him: let him speak no more.   Away
    with those giglets too, and with the other confederate com-

Duke. [*To the Provost*] Stay, sir; stay awhile.   [panion!

Ang. What, resists he?   Help him, Lucio.

Lucio. Come, sir; come, sir; come, sir; foh, sir! Why, you
    bald-pated, lying rascal, you must be hooded, must you?
    Show your knave's visage, with a pox to you! show your
    sheep-biting face, and be hanged an hour! Will 't not off?
                    [*Pulls off the friar's hood, and discovers the Duke.*

Duke. Thou art the first knave that e'er madest a Duke.
    First, provost, let me bail these gentle three.
    [*To Lucio.*] Sneak not away, sir; for the friar and you
    Must have a word anon.   Lay hold on him.

Lucio. This may prove worse than hanging.   [down.

Duke. [*To Escalus*] What you have spoke I pardon: sit you

We 'll borrow place of him. [*To Angelo*] Sir, by your leave.
Hast thou or word, or wit, or impudence,
That yet can do thee office? If thou hast,
Rely upon it till my tale be heard,
And hold no longer out.

Ang.   O my dread lord,
I should be guiltier than my guiltiness,
To think I can be undiscernible,
When I perceive your Grace, like power divine,
Hath look'd upon my passes. Then, good prince,
No longer session hold upon my shame,
But let my trial be mine own confession:
Immediate sentence then, and sequent death,
Is all the grace I beg.

Duke.   Come hither, Mariana.
Say, wast thou e'er contracted to this woman?

Ang. I was, my lord.

Duke. Go, take her hence, and marry her instantly.
Do you the office, friar; which consummate,
Return him here again. Go with him, provost.

                [*Exeunt Angelo, Mariana, Friar Peter and Provost.*

Escal. My lord, I am more amazed at his dishonour
Than at the strangeness of it.

Duke.   Come hither, Isabel.
Your friar is now your prince: as I was then
Advertising and holy to your business,
Not changing heart with habit, I am still
Attorney'd at your service.

Isab.   O, give me pardon,
That I, your vassal, have employ'd and pain'd
Your unknown sovereignty!

Duke.   You are pardon'd, Isabel:
And now, dear maid, be you as free to us.
Your brother's death, I know, sits at your heart;
And you may marvel why I obscured myself,
Labouring to save his life, and would not rather
Make rash remonstrance of my hidden power
Than let him so be lost. O most kind maid,
It was the swift celerity of his death,
Which I did think with slower foot came on,
That brain'd my purpose. But, peace be with him!
That life is better life, past fearing death,
Than that which lives to fear: make it your comfort,
So happy is your brother.

Isab.   I do, my lord.

299

Re-enter Angelo, Mariana, Friar Peter, and Provost.

Duke. For this new-married man, approaching here,
　Whose salt imagination yet hath wrong'd
　Your well-defended honour, you must pardon
　For Mariana's sake : but as he adjudged your brother,—
　Being criminal, in double violation
　Of sacred chastity, and of promise-breach
　Thereon dependent, for your brother's life,—
　The very mercy of the law cries out
　Most audible, even from his proper tongue,
　'An Angelo for Claudio, death for death!'
　Haste still pays haste, and leisure answers leisure ;
　Like doth quit like, and MEASURE still FOR MEASURE.
　Then, Angelo, thy fault's thus manifested ;
　Which, though thou wouldst deny, denies thee vantage.
　We do condemn thee to the very block
　Where Claudio stoop'd to death, and with like haste.
　Away with him!
Mari.　　　　　　O my most gracious lord,
　I hope you will not mock me with a husband.
Duke. It is your husband mock'd you with a husband.
　Consenting to the safeguard of your honour,
　I thought your marriage fit ; else imputation,
　For that he knew you, might reproach your life,
　And choke your good to come : for his possessions,
　Although by confiscation they are ours,
　We do instate and widow you withal,
　To buy you a better husband.
Mari.　　　　　　　　O my dear lord,
　I crave no other, nor no better man.
Duke. Never crave him ; we are definitive.
Mari. Gentle my liege,—　　　　　　　　[*Kneeling*
Duke.　　　　　　You do but lose your labour.
　Away with him to death ! [*To Lucio*] Now, sir, to you.
Mari. O my good lord ! Sweet Isabel, take my part ;
　Lend me your knees, and all my life to come
　I 'll lend you all my life to do you service.
Duke. Against all sense you do importune her :
　Should she kneel down in mercy of this fact,
　Her brother's ghost his paved bed would break,
　And take her hence in horror.
Mari.　　　　　　　　　Isabel,
　Sweet Isabel, do yet but kneel by me ;
　Hold up your hands, say nothing, I 'll speak all.

They say, best men are moulded out of faults;
And, for the most, become much more the better
For being a little bad: so may my husband.
O Isabel, will you not lend a knee?

Duke. He dies for Claudio's death.

Isab.   Most bounteous sir, [*Kneeling.*
Look, if it please you, on this man condemn'd,
As if my brother lived: I partly think
A due sincerity govern'd his deeds,
Till he did look on me: since it is so,
Let him not die. My brother had but justice,
In that he did the thing for which he died:
For Angelo,
His act did not o'ertake his bad intent;
And must be buried but as an intent
That perish'd by the way: thoughts are no subjects;
Intents, but merely thoughts.

Mari.   Merely, my lord.

Duke. Your suit's unprofitable; stand up, I say.
I have bethought me of another fault.
Provost, how came it Claudio was beheaded
At an unusual hour?

Prov.   It was commanded so.

Duke. Had you a special warrant for the deed?

Prov. No, my good lord; it was by private message.

Duke. For which I do discharge you of your office:
Give up your keys.

Prov.   Pardon me, noble lord:
I thought it was a fault, but knew it not;
Yet did repent me, after more advice:
For testimony whereof, one in the prison,
That should by private order else have died,
I have reserved alive.

Duke.   What's he?

Prov.   His name is Barnardine.

Duke. I would thou hadst done so by Claudio.
Go fetch him hither; let me look upon him. [*Exit Provost.*

Escal. I am sorry, one so learned and so wise
As you, Lord Angelo, have still appear'd,
Should slip so grossly, both in the heat of blood,
And lack of temper'd judgement afterward.

Ang. I am sorry that such sorrow I procure:
And so deep sticks it in my penitent heart,
That I crave death more willingly than mercy;
'Tis my deserving, and I do entreat it.

Re-enter Provost, with Barnardine, Claudio muffled, and Juliet.

Duke. Which is that Barnardine?

Prov.   This, my lord.

Duke. There was a friar told me of this man.
    Sirrah, thou art said to have a stubborn soul,
    That apprehends no further than this world,
    And squarest thy life according.   Thou 'rt condemn'd :
    But, for those earthly faults, I quit them all ;
    And pray thee take this mercy to provide
    For better times to come.   Friar, advise him ;
    I leave him to your hand.   What muffled fellow's that ?

Prov. This is another prisoner that I saved,
    Who should have died when Claudio lost his head ;
    As like almost to Claudio as himself.   [*Unmuffles Claudio.*

Duke. [*To Isabella*] If he be like your brother, for his sake
    Is he pardon'd ; and, for your lovely sake,
    Give me your hand, and say you will be mine,
    He is my brother too : but fitter time for that.
    By this Lord Angelo perceives he 's safe ;
    Methinks I see a quickening in his eye.
    Well, Angelo, your evil quits you well :
    Look that you love your wife ; her worth worth yours.
    I find an apt remission in myself ;
    And yet here 's one in place I cannot pardon.
    [*To Lucio*] You, sirrah, that knew me for a fool, a coward,
    One all of luxury, an ass, a madman ;
    Wherein have I so deserved of you,
    That you extol me thus?

Lucio. 'Faith, my lord, I spoke it but according to the trick.
    If you will hang me for it, you may ; but I had rather it
    would please you I might be whipt.

Duke. Whipt first, sir, and hang'd after.
    Proclaim it, provost, round about the city,
    If any woman wrong'd by this lewd fellow,—
    As I have heard him swear himself there 's one
    Whom he begot with child, let her appear,
    And he shall marry her : the nuptial finish'd,
    Let him be whipt and hang'd.

Lucio. I beseech your highness, do not marry me to a whore.
    Your highness said even now, I made you a Duke : good
    my lord, do not recompense me in making me a cuckold.

Duke. Upon mine honour, thou shalt marry her.
    Thy slanders I forgive ; and therewithal
    Remit thy other forfeits.—Take him to prison ;
    And see our pleasure herein executed.

Lucio. Marrying a punk, my lord, is pressing to death, whipping, and hanging.

Duke. Slandering a prince deserves it.

> *[Exeunt Officers with Lucio.*

She, Claudio, that you wrong'd, look you restore.
Joy to you, Mariana ! Love her, Angelo :
I have confess'd her, and I know her virtue.
Thanks, good friend Escalus, for thy much goodness :
There 's more behind that is more gratulate.
Thanks, provost, for thy care and secrecy :
We shall employ thee in a worthier place.
Forgive him, Angelo, that brought you home
The head of Ragozine for Claudio's :
The offence pardons itself.   Dear Isabel,
I have a motion much imports your good ;
Whereto if you 'll a willing ear incline,
What 's mine is yours, and what is yours is mine.
So, bring us to our palace ! where we 'll show
What 's yet behind, that 's meet you all should know.

> *[Exeunt.*

MUCH ADO ABOUT NOTHING

DRAMATIS PERSONÆ

DON PEDRO, *prince of Arragon.*
DON JOHN, *his bastard brother.*
CLAUDIO, *a young lord of Florence.*
BENEDICK, *a young lord of Padua.*
LEONATO, *governor of Messina.*
ANTONIO, *his brother.*
BALTHASAR, *attendant on Don Pedro.*
CONRADE, } *followers of Don John.*
BORACHIO, }
FRIAR FRANCIS.

DOGBERRY, *a constable.*
VERGES, *a headborough.*
A SEXTON.
A BOY.

HERO, *daughter to Leonato.*
BEATRICE, *niece to Leonato.*
MARGARET, } *gentlewomen attending on*
URSULA, } *Hero.*
Messengers, Watch, Attendants, &c.

SCENE, *Messina.*

ACT I—SCENE I

Before Leonato's house.

Enter Leonato, Hero, and Beatrice, with a Messenger.

Leon. I learn in this letter that Don Pedro of Arragon comes
this night to Messina. [I left him.

Mess. He is very near by this : he was not three leagues off when

Leon. How many gentlemen have you lost in this action ?

Mess. But few of any sort, and none of name.

Leon. A victory is twice itself when the achiever brings home
full numbers. I find here that Don Pedro hath bestowed
much honour on a young Florentine called Claudio.

Mess. Much deserved on his part, and equally remembered by
Don Pedro : he hath borne himself beyond the promise of his
age ; doing, in the figure of a lamb, the feats of a lion : he
hath indeed better bettered expectation than you must expect
of me to tell you how. [of it.

Leon. He hath an uncle here in Messina will be very much glad

Mess. I have already delivered him letters, and there appears
much joy in him ; even so much, that joy could not show
itself modest enough without a badge of bitterness.

Leon. Did he break out into tears ?

Mess. In great measure.

Leon. A kind overflow of kindness : there are no faces truer
than those that are so washed. How much better is it to
weep at joy than to joy at weeping ! [or no ?

Beat. I pray you, is Signior Mountanto returned from the wars

Mess. I know none of that name, lady : there was none such
in the army of any sort.

Leon. What is he that you ask for, niece ?

Hero. My cousin means Signior Benedick of Padua.

Mess. O, he 's returned ; and as pleasant as ever was.

Beat. He set up his bills here in Messina and challenged Cupid at the flight; and my uncle's fool, reading the challenge, subscribed for Cupid, and challenged him at the bird-bolt. I pray you, how many hath he killed and eaten in these wars? But how many hath he killed? for, indeed, I promised to eat all of his killing.

Leon. Faith, niece, you tax Signior Benedick too much; but he'll be meet with you, I doubt it not.

Mess. He hath done good service, lady, in these wars.

Beat. You had musty victual, and he hath holp to eat it: he is a very valiant trencher-man; he hath an excellent stomach.

Mess. And a good soldier too, lady.

Beat. And a good soldier to a lady; but what is he to a lord?

Mess. A lord to a lord, a man to a man; stuffed with all honourable virtues.

Beat. It is so, indeed; he is no less than a stuffed man: but for the stuffing,—well, we are all mortal.

Leon. You must not, sir, mistake my niece. There is a kind of merry war betwixt Signior Benedick and her: they never meet but there's a skirmish of wit between them.

Beat. Alas! he gets nothing by that. In our last conflict four of his five wits went halting off, and now is the whole man governed with one: so that if he have wit enough to keep himself warm, let him bear it for a difference between himself and his horse; for it is all the wealth that he hath left, to be known a reasonable creature. Who is his companion now? He hath every month a new sworn brother.

Mess. Is't possible?

Beat. Very easily possible: he wears his faith but as the fashion of his hat; it ever changes with the next block.

Mess. I see, lady, the gentleman is not in your books.

Beat. No; an he were, I would burn my study. But, I pray you, who is his companion? Is there no young squarer now that will make a voyage with him to the devil?

Mess. He is most in the company of the right noble Claudio.

Beat. O Lord, he will hang upon him like a disease: he is sooner caught than the pestilence, and the taker runs presently mad. God help the noble Claudio! if he have caught the Benedick, it will cost him a thousand pound ere

Mess. I will hold friends with you, lady.   [a' be cured.

Beat. Do, good friend.

Leon. You will never run mad, niece.

Beat. No, not till a hot January.

Mess. Don Pedro is approached.

Enter Don Pedro, Don John, Claudio, Benedick and Balthasar.

D. Pedro. Good Signior Leonato, you are come to meet your

trouble: the fashion of the world is to avoid cost, and you encounter it.

Leon. Never came trouble to my house in the likeness of your Grace: for trouble being gone, comfort should remain; but when you depart from me, sorrow abides, and happiness takes his leave. [this is your daughter.

D. Pedro. You embrace your charge too willingly. I think

Leon. Her mother hath many times told me so.

Bene. Were you in doubt, sir, that you asked her?

Leon. Signior Benedick, no; for then were you a child.

D. Pedro. You have it full, Benedick: we may guess by this what you are, being a man. Truly, the lady fathers herself. Be happy, lady; for you are like an honourable father.

Bene. If Signior Leonato be her father, she would not have his head on her shoulders for all Messina, as like him as she is.

Beat. I wonder that you will still be talking, Signior Benedick: nobody marks you.

Bene. What, my dear Lady Disdain! are you yet living?

Beat. Is it possible disdain should die while she hath such meet food to feed it, as Signior Benedick? Courtesy itself must convert to disdain, if you come in her presence.

Bene. Then is courtesy a turncoat. But it is certain I am loved of all ladies, only you excepted: and I would I could find in my heart that I had not a hard heart; for, truly, I love none.

Beat. A dear happiness to women: they would else have been troubled with a pernicious suitor. I thank God and my cold blood, I am of your humour for that: I had rather hear my dog bark at a crow than a man swear he loves me.

Bene. God keep your ladyship still in that mind! so some gentleman or other shall 'scape a predestinate scratched face.

Beat. Scratching could not make it worse, an 'twere such a face as yours were.

Bene. Well, you are a rare parrot-teacher.

Beat. A bird of my tongue is better than a beast of yours.

Bene. I would my horse had the speed of your tongue, and so good a continuer. But keep your way, i' God's name; I have done.

Beat. You always end with a jade's trick: I know you of old.

D. Pedro. That is the sum of all, Leonato. Signior Claudio and Signior Benedick, my dear friend Leonato hath invited you all. I tell him we shall stay here at the least a month; and he heartily prays some occasion may detain us longer. I dare swear he is no hypocrite, but prays from his heart.

Leon. If you swear, my lord, you shall not be forsworn. [*To*

Don John] Let me bid you welcome, my lord : being recon-
  ciled to the prince your brother, I owe you all duty.
D. John. I thank you : I am not of many words, but I thank
Leon. Please it your Grace lead on ?   [you.
D. Pedro. Your hand, Leonato ; we will go together.
                    [*Exeunt all except Benedick and Claudio.*
Claud. Benedick, didst thou note the daughter of Signior
Bene. I noted her not ; but I looked on her.   [Leonato ?
Claud. Is she not a modest young lady ?
Bene. Do you question me, as an honest man should do, for
  my simple true judgement ? or would you have me speak
  after my custom, as being a professed tyrant to their sex ?
Claud. No : I pray thee speak in sober judgement.
Bene. Why, i' faith, methinks she 's too low for a high praise,
  too brown for a fair praise, and too little for a great praise :
  only this commendation I can afford her, that were she other
  than she is, she were unhandsome ; and being no other but
  as she is, I do not like her.
Claud. Thou thinkest I am in sport : I pray thee tell me truly
  how thou likest her.
Bene. Would you buy her, that you inquire after her ?
Claud. Can the world buy such a jewel ?
Bene. Yea, and a case to put it into.   But speak you this with
  a sad brow ? or do you play the flouting Jack, to tell us
  Cupid is a good hare-finder, and Vulcan a rare carpenter ?
  Come, in what key shall a man take you, to go in the song ?
Claud. In mine eye she is the sweetest lady that ever I
  looked on.
Bene. I can see yet without spectacles, and I see no such
  matter : there 's her cousin, an she were not possessed with a
  fury, exceeds her as much in beauty as the first of May doth
  the last of December.   But I hope you have no intent to
  turn husband, have you ?
Claud. I would scarce trust myself, though I had sworn the
  contrary, if Hero would be my wife.
Bene. Is 't come to this ?   In faith, hath not the world one
  man but he will wear his cap with suspicion ?   Shall I never
  see a bachelor of threescore again ?   Go to, i' faith ; an thou
  wilt needs thrust thy neck into a yoke, wear the print of it,
  and sigh away Sundays.   Look ; Don Pedro is returned to
  seek you.
                    Re-enter Don Pedro.
D. Pedro. What secret hath held you here, that you followed
  not to Leonato's ?
Bene. I would your Grace would constrain me to tell.

D. Pedro. I charge thee on thy allegiance.

Bene. You hear, Count Claudio : I can be secret as a dumb
man ; I would have you think so ; but, on my allegiance,
mark you this, on my allegiance. He is in love. With who ?
now that is your Grace's part. Mark how short his answer
is ;—With Hero, Leonato's short daughter.

Claud. If this were so, so were it uttered.

Bene. Like the old tale, my lord : ' it is not so, nor 'twas not
so, but, indeed, God forbid it should be so.'

Claud. If my passion change not shortly, God forbid it should
be otherwise.

D. Pedro. Amen, if you love her ; for the lady is very well

Claud. You speak this to fetch me in, my lord.   [worthy.

D. Pedro. By my troth, I speak my thought.

Claud. And, in faith, my lord, I spoke mine.

Bene. And, by my two faiths and troths, my lord, I spoke

Claud. That I love her, I feel.   [mine.

D. Pedro. That she is worthy, I know.

Bene. That I neither feel how she should be loved, nor know
how she should be worthy, is the opinion that fire cannot
melt out of me : I will die in it at the stake.

D. Pedro. Thou wast ever an obstinate heretic in the despite
of beauty.   [his will.

Claud. And never could maintain his part but in the force of

Bene. That a woman conceived me, I thank her ; that she
brought me up, I likewise give her most humble thanks :
but that I will have a recheat winded in my forehead, or
hang my bugle in an invisible baldrick, all women shall
pardon me. Because I will not do them the wrong to
mistrust any, I will do myself the right to trust none ;
and the fine is, for which I may go the finer, I will live a
bachelor.

D. Pedro. I shall see thee, ere I die, look pale with love.

Bene. With anger, with sickness, or with hunger, my lord ; not
with love : prove that ever I lose more blood with love than
I will get again with drinking, pick out mine eyes with a
ballad-maker's pen, and hang me up at the door of a brothel-
house for the sign of blind Cupid.

D. Pedro. Well, if ever thou dost fall from this faith, thou
wilt prove a notable argument.

Bene. If I do, hang me in a bottle like a cat, and shoot at me ;
and he that hits me, let him be clapped on the shoulder
and called Adam.

D. Pedro. Well, as time shall try :
' In time the savage bull doth bear the yoke.'

Bene. The savage bull may; but if ever the sensible Benedick
   bear it, pluck off the bull's horns, and set them in my forehead: and let me be vilely painted; and in such great letters
   as they write 'Here is good horse to hire,' let them signify
   under my sign 'Here you may see Benedick the married
   man.'

Claud. If this should ever happen, thou wouldst be horn-mad.

D. Pedro. Nay, if Cupid have not spent all his quiver in
   Venice, thou wilt quake for this shortly.

Bene. I look for an earthquake too, then.

D. Pedro. Well, you will temporize with the hours. In the
   meantime, good Signior Benedick, repair to Leonato's:
   commend me to him, and tell him I will not fail him
   at supper; for indeed he hath made great preparation.

Bene. I have almost matter enough in me for such an
   embassage; and so I commit you—

Claud. To the tuition of God: From my house, if I had it,—

D. Pedro. The sixth of July: Your loving friend, Benedick.

Bene. Nay, mock not, mock not. The body of your discourse
   is sometime guarded with fragments, and the guards are
   but slightly basted on neither: ere you flout old ends any
   further, examine your conscience: and so I leave you. [*Exit.*

Claud. My liege, your highness now may do me good.

D. Pedro. My love is thine to teach: teach it but how,
   And thou shalt see how apt it is to learn
   Any hard lesson that may do thee good.

Claud. Hath Leonato any son, my lord?

D. Pedro. No child but Hero; she's his only heir.
   Dost thou affect her, Claudio?

Claud.   O, my lord,
   When you went onward on this ended action,
   I look'd upon her with a soldier's eye,
   That liked, but had a rougher task in hand
   Than to drive liking to the name of love:
   But now I am return'd and that war-thoughts
   Have left their places vacant, in their rooms
   Come thronging soft and delicate desires,
   All prompting me how fair young Hero is,
   Saying, I liked her ere I went to wars.

D. Pedro. Thou wilt be like a lover presently,
   And tire the hearer with a book of words.
   If thou dost love fair Hero, cherish it;
   And I will break with her and with her father,
   And thou shalt have her. Was 't not to this end
   That thou began'st to twist so fine a story?

Claud. How sweetly you do minister to love,
   That know love's grief by his complexion!
   But lest my liking might too sudden seem,
   I would have salved it with a longer treatise.
D. Pedro. What need the bridge much broader than the flood?
   The fairest grant is the necessity.
   Look, what will serve is fit: 'tis once, thou lovest,
   And I will fit thee with the remedy.
   I know we shall have revelling to-night:
   I will assume thy part in some disguise,
   And tell fair Hero I am Claudio;
   And in her bosom I 'll unclasp my heart,
   And take her hearing prisoner with the force
   And strong encounter of my amorous tale:
   Then after to her father will I break;
   And the conclusion is, she shall be thine.
   In practice let us put it presently.   [*Exeunt.*

SCENE II

A room in Leonato's house.
Enter Leonato and Antonio, meeting.

Leon. How now, brother! Where is my cousin, your son?
   hath he provided this music?
Ant. He is very busy about it. But, brother, I can tell you
   strange news, that you yet dreamt not of.
Leon. Are they good?
Ant. As the event stamps them: but they have a good cover;
   they show well outward. The prince and Count Claudio,
   walking in a thick-pleached alley in mine orchard, were thus
   much overheard by a man of mine: the prince discovered
   to Claudio that he loved my niece your daughter, and
   meant to acknowledge it this night in a dance; and if he
   found her accordant, he meant to take the present time by
   the top, and instantly break with you of it.
Leon. Hath the fellow any wit that told you this?
Ant. A good sharp fellow: I will send for him; and question
   him yourself.
Leon. No, no; we will hold it as a dream till it appear itself:
   but I will acquaint my daughter withal, that she may be the
   better prepared for an answer, if peradventure this be true.
   Go you and tell her of it. [*Enter attendants.*] Cousins, you
   know what you have to do. O, I cry you mercy, friend; go
   you with me, and I will use your skill. Good cousin, have
   a care this busy time.   [*Exeunt.*

SCENE III
The same.

Enter Don John and Conrade.

Con. What the good-year, my lord! why are you thus out of measure sad?

D. John. There is no measure in the occasion that breeds; therefore the sadness is without limit.

Con. You should hear reason.

D. John. And when I have heard it, what blessing brings it?

Con. If not a present remedy, at least a patient sufferance.

D. John. I wonder that thou, being (as thou sayest thou art) born under Saturn, goest about to apply a moral medicine to a mortifying mischief. I cannot hide what I am: I must be sad when I have cause, and smile at no man's jests; eat when I have stomach, and wait for no man's leisure; sleep when I am drowsy, and tend on no man's business; laugh when I am merry, and claw no man in his humour.

Con. Yea, but you must not make the full show of this till you may do it without controlment. You have of late stood out against your brother, and he hath ta'en you newly into his grace; where it is impossible you should take true root but by the fair weather that you make yourself: it is needful that you frame the season for your own harvest.

D. John. I had rather be a canker in a hedge than a rose in his grace; and it better fits my blood to be disdained of all than to fashion a carriage to rob love from any: in this, though I cannot be said to be a flattering honest man, it must not be denied but I am a plain-dealing villain. I am trusted with a muzzle, and enfranchised with a clog; therefore I have decreed not to sing in my cage. If I had my mouth, I would bite; if I had my liberty, I would do my liking: in the meantime let me be that I am, and seek not to alter me.

Con. Can you make no use of your discontent?

D. John. I make all use of it, for I use it only.
Who comes here?

Enter Borachio.

What news, Borachio?

Bora. I came yonder from a great supper: the prince your brother is royally entertained by Leonato; and I can give you intelligence of an intended marriage.

D. John. Will it serve for any model to build mischief on? What is he for a fool that betroths himself to unquietness?

Bora. Marry, it is your brother's right hand.

D. John. Who? the most exquisite Claudio?

Bora. Even he.

D. John. A proper squire! And who, and who? which way looks he?

Bora. Marry, on Hero, the daughter and heir of Leonato.

D. John. A very forward March-chick! How came you to this?

Bora. Being entertained for a perfumer, as I was smoking a musty room, comes me the prince and Claudio, hand in hand, in sad conference: I whipt me behind the arras; and there heard it agreed upon, that the prince should woo Hero for himself, and having obtained her, give her to Count Claudio.

D. John. Come, come, let us thither: this may prove food to my displeasure. That young start-up hath all the glory of my overthrow: if I can cross him any way, I bless myself every way. You are both sure, and will assist me?

Con. To the death, my lord.

D. John. Let us to the great supper: their cheer is the greater that I am subdued. Would the cook were of my mind! Shall we go prove what's to be done?

Bora. We'll wait upon your lordship.   [*Exeunt.*

ACT II—Scene I

A hall in Leonato's house.

Enter Leonato, Antonio, Hero, Beatrice, and others.

Leon. Was not Count John here at supper?

Ant. I saw him not.

Beat. How tartly that gentleman looks! I never can see him but I am heart-burned an hour after.

Hero. He is of a very melancholy disposition.

Beat. He were an excellent man that were made just in the midway between him and Benedick: the one is too like an image and says nothing, and the other too like my lady's eldest son, evermore tattling.

Leon. Then half Signior Benedick's tongue in Count John's mouth, and half Count John's melancholy in Signior Benedick's face,—

Beat. With a good leg and a good foot, uncle, and money enough in his purse, such a man would win any woman in the world, if a' could get her good-will.

Leon. By my troth, niece, thou wilt never get thee a husband, if thou be so shrewd of thy tongue.

Ant. In faith, she's too curst.

Beat. Too curst is more than curst : I shall lessen God's send-
ing that way ; for it is said, ' God sends a curst cow short
horns ;' but to a cow too curst he sends none.

Leon. So, by being too curst, God will send you no horns.

Beat. Just, if he send me no husband ; for the which blessing
I am at him upon my knees every morning and evening.
Lord, I could not endure a husband with a beard on his
face : I had rather lie in the woollen.

Leon. You may light on a husband that hath no beard.

Beat. What should I do with him ? dress him in my apparel,
and make him my waiting-gentlewoman ? He that hath a
beard is more than a youth ; and he that hath no beard is
less than a man : and he that is more than a youth is not
for me ; and he that is less than a man, I am not for him :
therefore I will even take sixpence in earnest of the bear-
ward, and lead his apes into hell.

Leon. Well, then, go you into hell ?

Beat. No, but to the gate ; and there will the devil meet me,
like an old cuckold, with horns on his head, and say ' Get
you to heaven, Beatrice, get you to heaven ; here's no place
for you maids :' so deliver I up my apes, and away to Saint
Peter for the heavens ; he shows me where the bachelors
sit, and there live we as merry as the day is long.

Ant. [*To Hero*] Well, niece, I trust you will be ruled by your
father.

Beat. Yes, faith ; it is my cousin's duty to make courtesy, and
say, ' Father, as it please you.' But yet for all that, cousin,
let him be a handsome fellow, or else make another courtesy,
and say, ' Father, as it please me.'   [husband.

Leon. Well, niece, I hope to see you one day fitted with a

Beat. Not till God make men of some other metal than earth.
Would it not grieve a woman to be overmastered with a
piece of valiant dust ? to make an account of her life to a
clod of wayward marl ? No, uncle, I 'll none : Adam's sons
are my brethren ; and, truly, I hold it a sin to match in my
kindred.

Leon. Daughter, remember what I told you : if the prince do
solicit you in that kind, you know your answer.

Beat. The fault will be in the music, cousin, if you be not
wooed in good time : if the prince be too important, tell
him there is measure in every thing, and so dance out the
answer. For, hear me, Hero : wooing, wedding, and
repenting, is as a Scotch jig, a measure, and a cinque
pace : the first suit is hot and hasty, like a Scotch jig, and
full as fantastical ; the wedding, mannerly-modest, as a

measure, full of state and ancientry; and then comes
repentance, and, with his bad legs, falls into the cinque
pace faster and faster, till he sink into his grave.

Leon. Cousin, you apprehend passing shrewdly.

Beat. I have a good eye, uncle; I can see a church by
daylight.

Leon. The revellers are entering, brother: make good room.
　　　　　　　　　　　　　　　[All put on their masks.

*Enter Don Pedro, Claudio, Benedick, Balthasar, Don John,
Borachio, Margaret, Ursula, and others, masked.*

D. Pedro. Lady, will you walk about with your friend?

Hero. So you walk softly, and look sweetly, and say nothing, I
am yours for the walk; and especially when I walk away.

D. Pedro. With me in your company?

Hero. I may say so, when I please.

D. Pedro. And when please you to say so?

Hero. When I like your favour; for God defend the lute should
be like the case!

D. Pedro. My visor is Philemon's roof; within the house is

Hero. Why, then, your visor should be thatched.　　　*[Jove.*

D. Pedro. Speak low, if you speak love.　*[Drawing her aside.*

Balth. Well, I would you did like me.

Marg. So would not I, for your own sake; for I have many

Balth. Which is one?　　　　　　　　　　　　　　*[ill qualities.*

Marg. I say my prayers aloud.

Balth. I love you the better: the hearers may cry, Amen.

Marg. God match me with a good dancer!

Balth. Amen.

Marg. And God keep him out of my sight when the dance is
done! Answer, clerk.

Balth. No more words: the clerk is answered.

Urs. I know you well enough; you are Signior Antonio.

Ant. At a word, I am not.

Urs. I know you by the waggling of your head.

Ant. To tell you true, I counterfeit him.

Urs. You could never do him so ill-well, unless you were the
very man. Here's his dry hand up and down: you are he,
you are he.

Ant. At a word, I am not.

Urs. Come, come, do you think I do not know you by your
excellent wit? can virtue hide itself? Go to, mum, you are
he: graces will appear, and there's an end.

Beat. Will you not tell me who told you so?

Bene. No, you shall pardon me.

Beat. Nor will you not tell me who you are?

Bene. Not now.

Beat. That I was disdainful, and that I had my good wit out
of the 'Hundred Merry Tales':—well, this was Signior
Benedick that said so.

Bene. What's he?

Beat. I am sure you know him well enough.

Bene. Not I, believe me.

Beat. Did he never make you laugh?

Bene. I pray you, what is he?

Beat. Why, he is the prince's jester: a very dull fool; only his
gift is in devising impossible slanders: none but libertines
delight in him; and the commendation is not in his wit, but
in his villany; for he both pleases men and angers them, and
then they laugh at him and beat him. I am sure he is in
the fleet: I would he had boarded me.

Bene. When I know the gentleman, I'll tell him what you say.

Beat. Do, do: he'll but break a comparison or two on me;
which, peradventure not marked or not laughed at, strikes
him into melancholy; and then there's a partridge wing
saved, for the fool will eat no supper that night. [*Music.*]
We must follow the leaders.

Bene. In every good thing.   [*turning.*

Beat. Nay, if they lead to any ill, I will leave them at the next
                    [*Dance.   Then exeunt all except Don John,*
                                    Borachio, and Claudio.

D. John. Sure my brother is amorous on Hero, and hath with-
drawn her father to break with him about it. The ladies
follow her, and but one visor remains.

Bora. And that is Claudio: I know him by his bearing.

D. John. Are not you Signior Benedick?

Claud. You know me well; I am he.

D. John. Signior, you are very near my brother in his love;
he is enamoured on Hero; I pray you, dissuade him from
her: she is no equal for his birth: you may do the part of
an honest man in it.

Claud. How know you he loves her?

D. John. I heard him swear his affection.

Bora. So did I too; and he swore he would marry her to-night.

D. John. Come, let us to the banquet.
                        [*Exeunt Don John and Borachio.*

Claud. Thus answer I in name of Benedick,
    But hear these ill news with the ears of Claudio.
    'Tis certain so; the prince wooes for himself.
    Friendship is constant in all other things
    Save in the office and affairs of love:

Therefore all hearts in love use their own tongues;
Let every eye negotiate for itself,
And trust no agent; for beauty is a witch,
Against whose charms faith melteth into blood.
This is an accident of hourly proof,
Which I mistrusted not.   Farewell, therefore, Hero!

Re-enter Benedick.

Bene. Count Claudio?
Claud. Yea, the same.
Bene. Come, will you go with me?
Claud. Whither?
Bene. Even to the next willow, about your own business,
county.   What fashion will you wear the garland of? about
your neck, like an usurer's chain? or under your arm, like a
lieutenant's scarf?   You must wear it one way, for the
prince hath got your Hero.
Claud. I wish him joy of her.
Bene. Why, that's spoken like an honest drovier; so they sell
bullocks.   But did you think the prince would have served
Claud. I pray you, leave me.   [you thus?
Bene. Ho! now you strike like the blind man; 'twas the boy
that stole your meat, and you'll beat the post.
Claud. If it will not be, I'll leave you.   [*Exit.*
Bene. Alas, poor hurt fowl! now will he creep into sedges.
But, that my lady Beatrice should know me, and not
know me!   The prince's fool!   Ha?   It may be I go under
that title because I am merry.   Yea, but so I am apt
to do myself wrong; I am not so reputed: it is the base,
though bitter, disposition of Beatrice that puts the world
into her person, and so gives me out.   Well, I'll be revenged
as I may.

Re-enter Don Pedro.

D. Pedro. Now, signior, where's the count? did you see him?
Bene. Troth, my lord, I have played the part of Lady Fame.
I found him here as melancholy as a lodge in a warren: I
told him, and I think I told him true, that your grace had
got the good will of this young lady; and I offered him my
company to a willow-tree, either to make him a garland, as
being forsaken, or to bind him up a rod, as being worthy to
D. Pedro. To be whipped!   What's his fault? [be whipped.
Bene. The flat transgression of a school-boy, who, being over-
joyed with finding a birds' nest, shows it his companion, and
he steals it.
D. Pedro. Wilt thou make a trust a transgression?   The transgression is in the stealer.

Bene. Yet it had not been amiss the rod had been made, and the garland too; for the garland he might have worn himself, and the rod he might have bestowed on you, who, as I take it, have stolen his birds' nest.

D. Pedro. I will but teach them to sing, and restore them to the owner.   [honestly.

Bene. If their singing answer your saying, by my faith, you say

D. Pedro. The Lady Beatrice hath a quarrel to you : the gentleman that danced with her told her she is much wronged by you.

Bene. O, she misused me past the endurance of a block ! an oak but with one green leaf on it would have answered her; my very visor began to assume life and scold with her. She told me, not thinking I had been myself, that I was the prince's jester, that I was duller than a great thaw; huddling jest upon jest, with such impossible conveyance, upon me, that I stood like a man at a mark, with a whole army shooting at me. She speaks poniards, and every word stabs : if her breath were as terrible as her terminations, there were no living near her; she would infect to the north star. I would not marry her, though she were endowed with all that Adam had left him before he transgressed : she would have made Hercules have turned spit, yea, and have cleft his club to make the fire too. Come, talk not of her : you shall find her the infernal Ate in good apparel. I would to God some scholar would conjure her; for certainly, while she is here, a man may live as quiet in hell as in a sanctuary; and people sin upon purpose, because they would go thither; so, indeed, all disquiet, horror, and perturbation follows her.

D. Pedro. Look, here she comes.

      Re-enter Claudio, Beatrice, Hero, and Leonato.

Bene. Will your grace command me any service to the world's end? I will go on the slightest errand now to the Antipodes that you can devise to send me on; I will fetch you a toothpicker now from the furthest inch of Asia; bring you the length of Prester John's foot; fetch you a hair off the great Cham's beard; do you any embassage to the Pigmies; rather than hold three words' conference with this harpy. You have no employment for me?

D. Pedro. None, but to desire your good company.

Bene. O God, sir, here's a dish I love not : I cannot endure my Lady Tongue.   [*Exit.*

D. Pedro. Come, lady, come; you have lost the heart of Signior Benedick.

Beat. Indeed, my lord, he lent it me awhile; and I gave him

use for it, a double heart for his single one: marry, once
before he won it of me with false dice, therefore your Grace
may well say I have lost it.   [down.

D. Pedro. You have put him down, lady, you have put him

Beat. So I would not he should do me, my lord, lest I should
prove the mother of fools. I have brought Count Claudio,
whom you sent me to seek.

D. Pedro. Why, how now, count! wherefore are you sad?

Claud. Not sad, my lord.

D. Pedro. How then? sick?

Claud. Neither, my lord.

Beat. The count is neither sad, nor sick, nor merry, nor well;
but civil count, civil as an orange, and something of that
jealous complexion.

D. Pedro. I' faith, lady, I think your blazon to be true; though,
I'll be sworn, if he be so, his conceit is false. Here,
Claudio, I have wooed in thy name, and fair Hero is won:
I have broke with her father, and his good will obtained:
name the day of marriage, and God give thee joy!

Leon. Count, take of me my daughter, and with her my fortunes:
his Grace hath made the match, and all grace say Amen to it.

Beat. Speak, count, 'tis your cue.

Claud. Silence is the perfectest herald of joy: I were but
little happy, if I could say how much. Lady, as you are
mine, I am yours: I give away myself for you, and dote
upon the exchange.

Beat. Speak, cousin; or, if you cannot, stop his mouth with a
kiss, and let not him speak neither.

D. Pedro. In faith, lady, you have a merry heart.

Beat. Yea, my lord; I thank it, poor fool, it keeps on the
windy side of care. My cousin tells him in his ear that he
is in her heart.

Claud. And so she doth, cousin.

Beat. Good Lord, for alliance! Thus goes every one to the
world but I, and I am sun-burnt; I may sit in a corner, and
cry heigh-ho for a husband!

D. Pedro. Lady Beatrice, I will get you one.

Beat. I would rather have one of your father's getting. Hath
your Grace ne'er a brother like you? Your father got
excellent husbands, if a maid could come by them.

D. Pedro. Will you have me, lady?

Beat. No, my lord, unless I might have another for working-
days: your Grace is too costly to wear every day. But, I
beseech your Grace, pardon me: I was born to speak all
mirth and no matter.

D. Pedro. Your silence most offends me, and to be merry best
becomes you ; for, out of question, you were born in a
merry hour.

Beat. No, sure, my lord, my mother cried ; but then there was
a star danced, and under that was I born.   Cousins, God
give you joy !

Leon. Niece, will you look to those things I told you of ?

Beat. I cry you mercy, uncle.   By your Grace's pardon. [*Exit.*

D. Pedro. By my troth, a pleasant-spirited lady.

Leon. There's little of the melancholy element in her, my lord :
she is never sad but when she sleeps ; and not ever sad then ;
for I have heard my daughter say, she hath often dreamed
of unhappiness, and waked herself with laughing.

D. Pedro. She cannot endure to hear tell of a husband.

Lean. O, by no means : she mocks all her wooers out of suit.

D. Pedro. She were an excellent wife for Benedick.

Leon. O Lord, my lord, if they were but a week married, they
would talk themselves mad.

D. Pedro. County Claudio, when mean you to go to church ?

Claud. To-morrow, my lord : time goes on crutches till love
have all his rites.

Leon. Not till Monday, my dear son, which is hence a just
seven-night ; and a time too brief, too, to have all things
answer my mind.

D. Pedro. Come, you shake the head at so long a breathing :
but, I warrant thee, Claudio, the time shall not go dully by
us.   I will, in the interim, undertake one of Hercules'
labours ; which is, to bring Signior Benedick and the Lady
Beatrice into a mountain of affection the one with the other.
I would fain have it a match ; and I doubt not but to fashion
it, if you three will but minister such assistance as I shall
give you direction.

Leon. My lord, I am for you, though it cost me ten nights'
Claud. And I, my lord.   [watchings.

D. Pedro. And you too, gentle Hero?

Hero. I will do any modest office, my lord, to help my cousin
to a good husband.

D. Pedro. And Benedick is not the unhopefullest husband that
I know.   Thus far can I praise him ; he is of a noble strain,
of approved valour, and confirmed honesty.   I will teach
you how to humour your cousin, that she shall fall in love
with Benedick ; and I, with your two helps, will so practi
on Benedick, that, in despite of his quick wit and his queasy
stomach, he shall fall in love with Beatrice.   If we can do
this, Cupid is no longer an archer : his glory shall be ours

for we are the only love-gods.   Go in with me, and I will
tell you my drift.   [*Exeunt.*

SCENE II

The same.

Enter Don John and Borachio.

D. John. It is so ; the Count Claudio shall marry the daughter
Bora. Yea, my lord ; but I can cross it.   [of Leonato.
D. John. Any bar, any cross, any impediment will be medicin-
able to me : I am sick in displeasure to him ; and whatso-
ever comes athwart his affection ranges evenly with mine.
How canst thou cross this marriage ?
Bora. Not honestly, my lord ; but so covertly that no dis-
honesty shall appear in me.
D. John. Show me briefly how.
Bora. I think I told your lordship, a year since, how much I
am in the favour of Margaret, the waiting gentlewoman to
Hero.
D. John. I remember.
Bora. I can, at any unseasonable instant of the night, appoint
her to look out at her lady's chamber window.
D. John. What life is in that, to be the death of this marriage ?
Bora. The poison of that lies in you to temper.   Go you to
the prince your brother ; spare not to tell him that he hath
wronged his honour in marrying the renowned Claudio—
whose estimation do you mightily hold up—to a con-
taminated stale, such a one as Hero.
D. John. What proof shall I make of that ?
Bora. Proof enough to misuse the prince, to vex Claudio, to
undo Hero, and kill Leonato.   Look you for any other issue ?
D. John. Only to despite them I will endeavour any thing.
Bora. Go, then ; find me a meet hour to draw Don Pedro and
the Count Claudio alone : tell them that you know that
Hero loves me ; intend a kind of zeal both to the prince and
Claudio, as,—in love of your brother's honour, who hath
made this match, and his friend's reputation, who is thus
like to be cozened with the semblance of a maid,—that you
have discovered thus.   They will scarcely believe this without
trial : offer them instances ; which shall bear no less likelihood than to see me at her chamber-window ; hear me call
Margaret, Hero ; hear Margaret term me Claudio ; and bring
them to see this the very night before the intended wedding,—for in the meantime I will so fashion the matter that
Hero shall be absent,—and there shall appear such seeming

truth of Hero's disloyalty, that jealousy shall be called assurance and all the preparation overthrown.

D. John. Grow this to what adverse issue it can, I will put it in practice. Be cunning in the working this, and thy fee is a thousand ducats.

Bora. Be you constant in the accusation, and my cunning shall not shame me.

D. John. I will presently go learn their day of marriage.

[Exeunt.

SCENE III

Leonato's orchard.

Enter Benedick.

Bene. Boy!

Enter Boy.

Boy. Signior?

Bene. In my chamber-window lies a book: bring it hither to
Boy. I am here already, sir.   [me in the orchard.
Bene. I know that; but I would have thee hence, and here again. [*Exit Boy.*] I do much wonder that one man, seeing how much another man is a fool when he dedicates his behaviours to love, will, after he hath laughed at such shallow follies in others, become the argument of his own scorn by falling in love: and such a man is Claudio. I have known when there was no music with him but the drum and the fife; and now had he rather hear the tabor and the pipe: I have known when he would have walked ten mile a-foot to see a good armour; and now will he lie ten nights awake, carving the fashion of a new doublet. He was wont to speak plain and to the purpose, like an honest man and a soldier; and now is he turned orthography; his words are a very fantastical banquet,—just so many strange dishes. May I be so converted, and see with these eyes? I cannot tell; I think not: I will not be sworn but love may transform me to an oyster; but I'll take my oath on it, till he have made an oyster of me, he shall never make me such a fool. One woman is fair, yet I am well; another is wise, yet I am well; another virtuous, yet I am well: but till all graces be in one woman, one woman shall not come in my grace. Rich she shall be, that's certain; wise, or I'll none; virtuous, or I'll never cheapen her; fair, or I'll never look on her; mild, or come not near me; noble, or not I for an angel; of good discourse, an excellent musician, and her hair shall be of what colour it please God. Ha! the prince and Monsieur Love! I will hide me in the arbour. [*Withdraws.*

321

Enter Don Pedro, Claudio, and Leonato.

D. Pedro. Come, shall we hear this music?

Claud. Yea, my good lord.　How still the evening is,
　　As hush'd on purpose to grace harmony!

D. Pedro. See you where Benedick hath hid himself?

Claud. O, very well, my lord: the music ended,
　　We'll fit the kid-fox with a pennyworth.

Enter Balthasar with Music.

D. Pedro. Come, Balthasar, we'll hear that song again.

Balth. O, good my lord, tax not so bad a voice
　　To slander music any more than once.

D. Pedro. It is the witness still of excellency
　　To put a strange face on his own perfection.
　　I pray thee, sing, and let me woo no more.

Balth. Because you talk of wooing, I will sing;
　　Since many a wooer doth commence his suit
　　To her he thinks not worthy, yet he wooes,
　　Yet will he swear he loves.

D. Pedro.　　　　　　　　Nay, pray thee, come;
　　Or, if thou wilt hold longer argument,
　　Do it in notes.

Balth.　　　　　Note this before my notes;
　　There's not a note of mine that's worth the noting.

D. Pedro. Why, these are very crotchets that he speaks;
　　Note, notes, forsooth, and nothing.　　　　　　*[Air.*

Bene. Now, divine air! now is his soul ravished! Is it not
　strange that sheeps' guts should hale souls out of men's
　bodies? Well, a horn for my money, when all's done.

The Song.

Balth.　　　　Sigh no more, ladies, sigh no more,
　　　　　　　Men were deceivers ever,
　　　　　One foot in sea and one on shore,
　　　　　　　To one thing constant never:
　　　　　Then sigh not so, but let them go,
　　　　　　　And be you blithe and bonny,
　　　　　Converting all your sounds of woe
　　　　　　　Into Hey nonny, nonny.

　　　　　Sing no more ditties, sing no moe,
　　　　　　　Of dumps so dull and heavy;
　　　　　The fraud of men was ever so,
　　　　　　　Since summer first was leavy:
　　　　　　　Then sigh not so, &c.

322

D. Pedro. By my troth, a good song.

Balth. And an ill singer, my lord.   [shift.

D. Pedro. Ha, no, no, faith; thou singest well enough for a

Bene. An he had been a dog that should have howled thus, they would have hanged him: and I pray God his bad voice bode no mischief. I had as lief have heard the night-raven, come what plague could have come after it.

D. Pedro. Yea, marry, dost thou hear, Balthasar? I pray thee, get us some excellent music; for to-morrow night we would have it at the Lady Hero's chamber-window.

Balth. The best I can, my lord.

D. Pedro. Do so: farewell. [*Exit Balthasar.*] Come hither, Leonato. What was it you told me of to-day, that your niece Beatrice was in love with Signior Benedick?

Claud. O, ay: stalk on, stalk on; the fowl sits. I did never think that lady would have loved any man.

Leon. No, nor I neither; but most wonderful that she should so dote on Signior Benedick, whom she hath in all outward behaviours seemed ever to abhor.

Bene. Is 't possible? Sits the wind in that corner?

Leon. By my troth, my lord, I cannot tell what to think of it, but that she loves him with an enraged affection; it is past the infinite of thought.

D. Pedro. May be she doth but counterfeit.

Claud. Faith, like enough.

Leon. O God, counterfeit! There was never counterfeit of passion came so near the life of passion as she discovers it.

D. Pedro. Why, what effects of passion shows she?

Claud. Bait the hook well; this fish will bite.

Leon. What effects, my lord? She will sit you, you heard my daughter tell you how.

Claud. She did, indeed.

D. Pedro. How, how, I pray you? You amaze me: I would have thought her spirit had been invincible against all assaults of affection.   [Benedick.

Leon. I would have sworn it had, my lord; especially against

Bene. I should think this a gull, but that the white-bearded fellow speaks it: knavery cannot, sure, hide himself in such reverence.

Claud. He hath ta'en the infection: hold it up.

D. Pedro. Hath she made her affection known to Benedick?

Leon. No; and swears she never will: that 's her torment.

Claud. 'Tis true, indeed; so your daughter says: 'Shall I,' says she, 'that have so oft encountered him with scorn, write to him that I love him?'

323

Leon. This says she now when she is beginning to write to him ; for she 'll be up twenty times a night ; and there will she sit in her smock till she have writ a sheet of paper : my daughter tells us all.

Claud. Now you talk of a sheet of paper, I remember a pretty jest your daughter told us of.

Leon. O, when she had writ it, and was reading it over, she found Benedick and Beatrice between the sheet ?

Claud. That.

Leon. O, she tore the letter into a thousand halfpence ; railed at herself, that she should be so immodest to write to one that she knew would flout her ; ' I measure him,' says she, ' by my own spirit ; for I should flout him, if he writ to me ; yea, though I love him, I should.'

Claud. Then down upon her knees she falls, weeps, sobs, beats her heart, tears her hair, prays, curses ; ' O sweet Benedick ! God give me patience ! '

Leon. She doth indeed ; my daughter says so : and the ecstasy hath so much overborne her, that my daughter is sometime afeard she will do a desperate outrage to herself : it is very true.

D. Pedro. It were good that Benedick knew of it by some other, if she will not discover it.

Claud. To what end ?   He would make but a sport of it, and torment the poor lady worse.

D. Pedro. An he should, it were an alms to hang him.   She's an excellent sweet lady ; and, out of all suspicion, she is

Claud. And she is exceeding wise.   [virtuous.

D. Pedro. In every thing but in loving Benedick.

Leon. O, my lord, wisdom and blood combating in so tender a body, we have ten proofs to one that blood hath the victory. I am sorry for her, as I have just cause, being her uncle and her guardian.

D. Pedro. I would she had bestowed this dotage on me : I would have daffed all other respects, and made her half myself.   I pray you, tell Benedick of it, and hear what a' will

Leon. Were it good, think you ?   [say.

Claud. Hero thinks surely she will die ; for she says she will die, if he love her not ; and she will die, ere she makes her love known ; and she will die, if he woo her, rather than she will bate one breath of her accustomed crossness.

D. Pedro. She doth well : if she should make tender of her love, 'tis very possible he 'll scorn it ; for the man, as you know all, hath a contemptible spirit.

Claud. He is a very proper man.

D. Pedro. He hath indeed a good outward happiness.

Claud. Before God ! and in my mind, very wise.

D. Pedro. He doth indeed show some sparks that are like wit.

Claud. And I take him to be valiant.

D. Pedro. As Hector, I assure you : and in the managing of
quarrels you may say he is wise ; for either he avoids them
with great discretion, or undertakes them with a most
Christian-like fear.

Leon. If he do fear God, a' must necessarily keep peace : if he
break the peace, he ought to enter into a quarrel with fear
and trembling.

D. Pedro. And so will he do ; for the man doth fear God,
howsoever it seems not in him by some large jests he will
make.   Well, I am sorry for your niece.   Shall we go seek
Benedick, and tell him of her love ?   [counsel.

Claud. Never tell him, my lord : let her wear it out with good

Leon. Nay, that's impossible : she may wear her heart out first.

D. Pedro. Well, we will hear further of it by your daughter :
let it cool the while.   I love Benedick well ; and I could
wish he would modestly examine himself, to see how much
he is unworthy so good a lady.

Leon. My lord, will you walk ? dinner is ready.

Claud. If he do not dote on her upon this, I will never trust
my expectation.

D. Pedro. Let there be the same net spread for her ; and that
must your daughter and her gentlewomen carry.   The sport
will be, when they hold one an opinion of another's dotage,
and no such matter : that's the scene that I would see, which
will be merely a dumb-show.   Let us send her to call him
in to dinner.   [*Exeunt Don Pedro, Claudio, and Leonato.*

Bene. [*Coming forward*] This can be no trick : the conference
was sadly borne.   They have the truth of this from Hero.
They seem to pity the lady : it seems her affections have
their full bent.   Love me ! why, it must be requited.   I hear
how I am censured : they say I will bear myself proudly, if I
perceive the love come from her ; they say too that she will
rather die than give any sign of affection.   I did never think to
marry : I must not seem proud : happy are they that hear their
detractions, and can put them to mending.   They say the lady
is fair,—'tis a truth, I can bear them witness ; and virtuous,
—'tis so, I cannot reprove it ; and wise, but for loving me,—by
my troth, it is no addition to her wit, nor no great argument of
her folly, for I will be horribly in love with her.   I may
chance have some odd quirks and remnants of wit broken
on me, because I have railed so long against marriage : but

doth not the appetite alter? a man loves the meat in his youth that he cannot endure in his age. Shall quips and sentences and these paper bullets of the brain awe a man from the career of his humour? No, the world must be peopled. When I said I would die a bachelor, I did not think I should live till I were married. Here comes Beatrice. By this day! she's a fair lady: I do spy some marks of love in her.

Enter Beatrice.

Beat. Against my will I am sent to bid you come in to dinner.

Bene. Fair Beatrice, I thank you for your pains.

Beat. I took no more pains for those thanks than you take pains to thank me: if it had been painful, I would not have

Bene. You take pleasure, then, in the message?   [come.

Beat. Yea, just so much as you may take upon a knife's point, and choke a daw withal. You have no stomach, signior: fare you well.   [*Exit.*

Bene. Ha! 'Against my will I am sent to bid you come in to dinner;' there's a double meaning in that. 'I took no more pains for those thanks than you took pains to thank me;' that's as much as to say, Any pains that I take for you is as easy as thanks. If I do not take pity of her, I am a villain; if I do not love her, I am a Jew. I will go get her picture.
                                                        [*Exit.*

ACT III—Scene I

Leonato's orchard.

Enter Hero, Margaret, and Ursula.

Hero. Good Margaret, run thee to the parlour;
   There shalt thou find my cousin Beatrice
   Proposing with the prince and Claudio:
   Whisper her ear, and tell her, I and Ursula
   Walk in the orchard, and our whole discourse
   Is all of her; say that thou overheard'st us;
   And bid her steal into the pleached bower,
   Where honeysuckles, ripen'd by the sun,
   Forbid the sun to enter; like favourites,
   Made proud by princes, that advance their pride
   Against that power that bred it: there will she hide her,
   To listen our propose. This is thy office;
   Bear thee well in it, and leave us alone.

Marg. I'll make her come, I warrant, you, presently.   [*Exit.*

Hero. Now, Ursula, when Beatrice doth come,
   As we do trace this alley up and down,
   Our talk must only be of Benedick.

When I do name him, let it be thy part
To praise him more than ever man did merit:
My talk to thee must be, how Benedick
Is sick in love with Beatrice.   Of this matter
Is little Cupid's crafty arrow made,
That only wounds by hearsay.

Enter Beatrice, behind.
        Now begin;
For look where Beatrice, like a lapwing, runs
Close by the ground, to hear our conference.

Urs. The pleasant'st angling is to see the fish
Cut with her golden oars the silver stream,
And greedily devour the treacherous bait:
So angle we for Beatrice; who even now
Is couched in the woodbine coverture.
Fear you not my part of the dialogue.

Hero. Then go we near her, that her ear lose nothing
Of the false sweet bait that we lay for it.

        [Approaching the bower.
No, truly, Ursula, she is too disdainful;
I know her spirits are as coy and wild
As haggerds of the rock.

Urs.   But are you sure
That Benedick loves Beatrice so entirely?

Hero. So says the prince and my new-trothed lord.

Urs. And did they bid you tell her of it, madam?

Hero. They did entreat me to acquaint her of it;
But I persuaded them, if they loved Benedick,
To wish him wrestle with affection,
And never to let Beatrice know of it.

Urs. Why did you so?   Doth not the gentleman
Deserve as full as fortunate a bed
As ever Beatrice shall couch upon?

Hero. O god of love!   I know he doth deserve
As much as may be yielded to a man:
But Nature never framed a woman's heart
Of prouder stuff than that of Beatrice;
Disdain and scorn ride sparkling in her eyes,
Misprising what they look on; and her wit
Values itself so highly, that to her
All matter else seems weak: she cannot love,
Nor take no shape nor project of affection,
She is so self-endeared.

Urs.   Sure, I think so;
And therefore certainly it were not good

    She knew his love, lest she make sport at it.
Hero. Why, you speak truth. I never yet saw man,
    How wise, how noble, young, how rarely featured,
    But she would spell him backward : if fair-faced,
    She would swear the gentleman should be her sister ;
    If black, why, Nature, drawing of an antique,
    Made a foul blot ; if tall, a lance ill-headed ;
    If low, an agate very vilely cut ;
    If speaking, why, a vane blown with all winds ;
    If silent, why, a block moved with none.
    So turns she every man the wrong side out ;
    And never gives to truth and virtue that
    Which simpleness and merit purchaseth.
Urs. Sure, sure, such carping is not commendable.
Hero. No, not to be so odd, and from all fashions,
    As Beatrice is, cannot be commendable :
    But who dare tell her so ? If I should speak,
    She would mock me into air ; O, she would laugh me
    Out of myself, press me to death with wit !
    Therefore let Benedick, like cover'd fire,
    Consume away in sighs, waste inwardly :
    It were a better death than die with mocks,
    Which is as bad as die with tickling.
Urs. Yet tell her of it : hear what she will say.
Hero. No ; rather I will go to Benedick,
    And counsel him to fight against his passion.
    And, truly, I 'll devise some honest slanders
    To stain my cousin with : one doth not know
    How much an ill word may empoison liking.
Urs. O, do not do your cousin such a wrong !
    She cannot be so much without true judgement,—
    Having so swift and excellent a wit
    As she is prized to have,—as to refuse
    So rare a gentleman as Signior Benedick.
Hero. He is the only man of Italy,
    Always excepted my dear Claudio.
Urs. I pray you, be not angry with me, madam,
    Speaking my fancy : Signior Benedick,
    For shape, for bearing, argument and valour,
    Goes foremost in report through Italy.
Hero. Indeed, he hath an excellent good name.
Urs. His excellence did earn it, ere he had it.
    When are you married, madam ?
Hero. Why, every day, to-morrow. Come, go in :
    I 'll show thee some attires ; and have thy counsel

Which is the best to furnish me to-morrow.

Urs. She's limed, I warrant you : we have caught her, madam.

Hero. If it prove so, then loving goes by haps :
Some Cupid kills with arrows, some with traps.

[*Exeunt Hero and Ursula.*

Beat. [*Coming forward*] What fire is in mine ears ?
    Can this·be true ?
    Stand I condemn'd for pride and scorn so much ?
Contempt, farewell ! and maiden pride, adieu !
    No glory lives behind the back of such.
And, Benedick, love on ; I will requite thee,
    Taming my wild heart to thy loving hand :
If thou dost love, my kindness shall incite thee
    To bind our loves up in a holy band ;
For others say thou dost deserve, and I
Believe it better than reportingly. [*Exit.*

SCENE II

A room in Leonato's house.

Enter Don Pedro, Claudio, Benedick, and Leonato.

D. Pedro. I do but stay till your marriage be consummate, and
then go I toward Arragon.

Claud. I'll bring you thither, my lord, if you'll vouchsafe me.

D. Pedro. Nay, that would be as great a soil in the new gloss
of your marriage, as to show a child his new coat and forbid
him to wear it. I will only be bold with Benedick for his
company ; for, from the crown of his head to the sole of his
foot, he is all mirth : he hath twice or thrice cut Cupid's
bow-string, and the little hangman dare not shoot at him ;
he hath a heart as sound as a bell, and his tongue is the
clapper, for what his heart thinks his tongue speaks.

Bene. Gallants, I am not as I have been.

Leon. So say I : methinks you are sadder.

Claud. I hope he be in love.

D. Pedro. Hang him, truant ! there's no true drop of blood in
him, to be truly touched with love ; if he be sad, he wants

Bene. I have the toothache. [*money.*

D. Pedro. Draw it.

Bene. Hang it !

Claud. You must hang it first, and draw it afterwards.

D. Pedro. What ! sigh for the toothache ?

Leon. Where is but a humour or a worm.

Bene. Well, every one can master a grief but he that has it.

Claud. Yet say I, he is in love.

D. Pedro. There is no appearance of fancy in him, unless it be a fancy that he hath to strange disguises; as, to be a Dutchman to-day, a Frenchman to-morrow; or in the shape of two countries at once, as, a German from the waist downward, all slops, and a Spaniard from the hip upward, no doublet. Unless he have a fancy to this foolery, as it appears he hath, he is no fool for fancy, as you would have it appear he is.

Claud. If he be not in love with some woman, there is no believing old signs: a' brushes his hat o' mornings; what should that bode?

D. Pedro. Hath any man seen him at the barber's?

Claud. No, but the barber's man hath been seen with him; and the old ornament of his cheek hath already stuffed tennis-balls.   [beard.

Leon. Indeed, he looks younger than he did, by the loss of a

D. Pedro. Nay, a' rubs himself with civet: can you smell him out by that?

Claud. That's as much as to say, the sweet youth's in love.

D. Pedro. The greatest note of it is his melancholy.

Claud. And when was he wont to wash his face?

D. Pedro. Yea, or to paint himself? for the which, I hear what they say of him.

Claud. Nay, but his jesting spirit; which is now crept into a lute-string, and now governed by stops.

D. Pedro. Indeed, that tells a heavy tale for him: conclude, conclude he is in love.

Claud. Nay, but I know who loves him.   [him not.

D. Pedro. That would I know too: I warrant, one that knows

Claud. Yes, and his ill conditions; and, in despite of all, dies for him.

D. Pedro. She shall be buried with her face upwards.

Bene. Yet is this no charm for the toothache. Old signior, walk aside with me: I have studied eight or nine wise words to speak to you, which these hobby-horses must not hear.

                              [*Exeunt Benedick and Leonato.*

D. Pedro. For my life, to break with him about Beatrice.

Claud. 'Tis even so. Hero and Margaret have by this played their parts with Beatrice; and then the two bears will not bite one another when they meet.

Enter Don John.

D. John. My lord and brother, God save you!

D. Pedro. Good den, brother.

D. John. If your leisure served, I would speak with you.

D. Pedro. In private?

D. John. If it please you: yet Count Claudio may hear; for what I would speak of concerns him.

D. Pedro. What's the matter?

D. John. [*To Claudio*] Means your lordship to be married to-

D. Pedro. You know he does. [morrow?

D. John. I know not that, when he knows what I know.

Claud. If there be any impediment, I pray you discover it.

D. John. You may think I love you not: let that appear hereafter, and aim better at me by that I now will manifest. For my brother, I think he holds you well, and in dearness of heart hath holp to effect your ensuing marriage,—surely suit ill spent and labour ill bestowed.

D. Pedro. Why, what's the matter?

D. John. I came hither to tell you; and, circumstances shortened, for she has been too long a talking of, the lady is

Claud. Who, Hero? [disloyal.

D. John. Even she; Leonato's Hero, your Hero, every man's

Claud. Disloyal? [Hero.

D. John. The word is too good to paint out her wickedness; I could say she were worse: think you of a worse title, and I will fit her to it. Wonder not till further warrant: go but with me to-night, you shall see her chamber-window entered, even the night before her wedding-day: if you love her then, to-morrow wed her; but it would better fit your honour to change your mind.

Claud. May this be so?

D. Pedro. I will not think it.

D. John. If you dare not trust that you see, confess not that you know: if you will follow me, I will show you enough; and when you have seen more, and heard more, proceed accordingly.

Claud. If I see any thing to-night why I should not marry her to-morrow, in the congregation, where I should wed, there will I shame her.

D. Pedro. And, as I wooed for thee to obtain her, I will join with thee to disgrace her.

D. John. I will disparage her no farther till you are my witnesses: bear it coldly but till midnight, and let the issue

D. Pedro. O day untowardly turned! [show itself.

Claud. O mischief strangely thwarting!

D. John. O plague right well prevented! so will you say when you have seen the sequel. [*Exeunt.*

SCENE III

A street.

Enter Dogberry and Verges with the Watch.

Dog. Are you good men and true?

Verg. Yea, or else it were pity but they should suffer salvation, body and soul.

Dog. Nay, that were a punishment too good for them, if they should have any allegiance in them, being chosen for the prince's watch.

Verg. Well, give them their charge, neighbour Dogberry.

Dog. First, who think you the most desartless man to be constable?

First Watch. Hugh Otecake, sir, or George Seacole; for they can write and read.

Dog. Come hither, neighbour Seacole.   God hath blessed you with a good name : to be a well-favoured man is the gift of fortune ; but to write and read comes by nature.

Sec. Watch. Both which, master constable,—

Dog. You have : I knew it would be your answer.   Well, for your favour, sir, why, give God thanks, and make no boast of it; and for your writing and reading, let that appear when there is no need of such vanity.   You are thought here to be the most senseless and fit man for the constable of the watch; therefore bear you the lantern.   This is your charge : you shall comprehend all vagrom men; you are to bid any man stand, in the prince's name.

Sec. Watch. How if a' will not stand?

Dog. Why, then, take no note of him, but let him go; and presently call the rest of the watch together, and thank God you are rid of a knave.

Verg. If he will not stand when he is bidden, he is none of the prince's subjects.

Dog. True, and they are to meddle with none but the prince's subjects.   You shall also make no noise in the streets; for the watch to babble and to talk is most tolerable and not to be endured.   [*to a watch.*

Watch. We will rather sleep than talk : we know what belongs

Dog. Why, you speak like an ancient and most quiet watchman; for I cannot see how sleeping should offend : only, have a care that your bills be not stolen.   Well, you are to call at all the ale-houses, and bid those that are drunk get them to bed.

Watch. How if they will not?

Dog. Why, then, let them alone till they are sober : if they

make you not then the better answer, you may say they are
not the men you took them for.

Watch. Well, sir.

Dog. If you meet a thief, you may suspect him, by virtue of
your office, to be no true man ; and, for such kind of men,
the less you meddle or make with them, why, the more is
for your honesty.   [on him ?

Watch. If we know him to be a thief, shall we not lay hands

Dog. Truly, by your office, you may; but I think they that
touch pitch will be defiled : the most peaceable way for you,
if you do take a thief, is to let him show himself what he is,
and steal out of your company.

Verg. You have been always called a merciful man, partner.

Dog. Truly, I would not hang a dog by my will, much more
a man who hath any honesty in him.

Verg. If you hear a child crying in the night, you must call to
the nurse and bid her still it.

Watch. How if the nurse be asleep and will not hear us ?

Dog. Why, then, depart in peace, and let the child wake her
with crying ; for the ewe that will not hear her lamb when it
baes will never answer a calf when he bleats.

Verg. 'Tis very true.

Dog. This is the end of the charge :—you, constable, are to
present the prince's own person : if you meet the prince in
the night, you may stay him.

Verg. Nay, by 'r lady, that I think a' cannot.

Dog. Five shillings to one on 't, with any man that knows the
statues, he may stay him : marry, not without the prince
be willing ; for, indeed, the watch ought to offend no man ;
and it is an offence to stay a man against his will.

Verg. By 'r lady, I think it be so.

Dog. Ha, ah, ha ! Well, masters, good night : an there be
any matter of weight chances, call up me : keep your fellows'
counsels and your own ; and good night.   Come, neighbour.

Watch. Well, masters, we hear our change : let us go sit here
upon the church-bench till two, and then all to bed.

Dog. One word more, honest neighbours.   I pray you, watch
about Signior Leonato's door ; for the wedding being there
to-morrow, there is a great coil to-night.   Adieu : be vigitant,
I beseech you.   [*Exeunt Dogberry and Verges.*

Enter Borachio and Conrade.

Bora. What, Conrade !

Watch. [*Aside*] Peace ! stir not.

Bora. Conrade, I say !

Con. Here, man; I am at thy elbow.　　　　　[a scab follow.

Bora. Mass, and my elbow itched; I thought there would

Con. I will owe thee an answer for that: and now forward with thy tale.

Bora. Stand thee close, then, under this pent-house, for it drizzles rain; and I will, like a true drunkard, utter all to thee.

Watch. [*Aside*] Some treason, masters: yet stand close.

Bora. Therefore know I have earned of Don John a thousand ducats.

Con. Is it possible that any villany should be so dear?

Bora. Thou shouldst rather ask, if it were possible any villany should be so rich; for when rich villains have need of poor ones, poor ones may make what price they will.

Con. I wonder at it.

Bora. That shows thou art unconfirmed. Thou knowest that the fashion of a doublet, or a hat, or a cloak, is nothing to a

Con. Yes, it is apparel.　　　　　　　　　　　　[man.

Bora. I mean, the fashion.

Con. Yes, the fashion is the fashion.

Bora. Tush! I may as well say the fool's the fool. But seest thou not what a deformed thief this fashion is?

Watch. [*Aside*] I know that Deformed; a' has been a vile thief this seven year; a' goes up and down like a gentleman: I remember his name.

Bora. Didst thou not hear somebody?

Con. No; 'twas the vane on the house.

Bora. Seest thou not, I say, what a deformed thief this fashion is? how giddily a' turns about all the hot bloods between fourteen and five-and-thirty? sometimes fashioning them like Pharaoh's soldiers in the reechy painting, sometime like god Bel's priests in the old church-window, sometime like the shaven Hercules in the smirched worm-eaten tapestry, where his codpiece seems as massy as his club?

Con. All this I see; and I see that the fashion wears out more apparel than the man. But art not thou thyself giddy with the fashion too, that thou has shifted out of thy tale into telling me of the fashion?

Bora. Not so, neither: but know that I have to-night wooed Margaret, the Lady Hero's gentlewoman, by the name of Hero: she leans me out at her mistress' chamber-window, bids me a thousand times good night,—I tell this tale vilely :—I should first tell thee how the prince, Claudio and my master, planted and placed and possessed by my master Don John, saw afar off in the orchard this amiable encounter.

Con. And thought they Margaret was Hero?

334

Bora. Two of them did, the prince and Claudio ; but the
devil my master knew she was Margaret ; and partly by his
oaths, which first possessed them, partly by the dark night,
which did deceive them, but chiefly by my villany, which did
confirm any slander that Don John had made, away went
Claudio enraged ; swore he would meet her, as he was
appointed, next morning at the temple, and there, before
the whole congregation, shame her with what he saw o'er
night, and send her home again without a husband.

First Watch. We charge you, in the prince's name, stand !

Sec. Watch. Call up the right master constable. We have here
recovered the most dangerous piece of lechery that ever was
known in the commonwealth.

First Watch. And one Deformed is one of them : I know
him ; a' wears a lock.

Con. Masters, masters,—

Sec. Watch. You'll be made bring Deformed forth, I warrant you.

Con. Masters,—

First Watch. Never speak : we charge you let us obey you to
go with us.

Bora. We are like to prove a goodly commodity, being taken
up of these men's bills.

Con. A commodity in question, I warrant you. Come, we'll
obey you.   [*Exeunt.*

SCENE IV

Hero's apartment.
Enter Hero, Margaret, and Ursula.

Hero. Good Ursula, wake my cousin Beatrice, and desire her

Urs. I will, lady.   [to rise.

Hero. And bid her come hither.

Urs. Well.   [*Exit.*

Marg. Troth, I think your other rabato were better.

Hero. No, pray thee, good Meg, I'll wear this.

Marg. By my troth 's not so good ; and I warrant your cousin
will say so.   [but this.

Hero. My cousin 's a fool, and thou art another : I'll wear none

Marg. I like the new tire within excellently, if the hair were a
thought browner ; and your gown 's a most rare fashion, i'
faith. I saw the Duchess of Milan's gown that they praise so.

Hero. O, that exceeds, they say.

Marg. By my troth 's but a night-gown in respect of yours,—
cloth o' gold, and cuts, and laced with silver, set with pearls,
down sleeves, side sleeves, and skirts, round underborne with

335

a bluish tinsel : but for a fine, quaint, graceful and excellent fashion, yours is worth ten on 't.

Hero. God give me joy to wear it ! for my heart is exceeding

Marg. 'Twill be heavier soon by the weight of a man. [heavy.

Hero. Fie upon thee ! art not ashamed ?

Marg. Of what, lady ? of speaking honourably ? Is not marriage honourable in a beggar ? Is not your lord honourable without marriage ? I think you would have me say, ' saving your reverence, a husband : ' an bad thinking do not wrest true speaking, I 'll offend nobody : is there any harm in ' the heavier for a husband ' ? None, I think, an it be the right husband and the right wife ; otherwise 'tis light, and not heavy : ask my Lady Beatrice else ; here she comes.

Enter Beatrice.

Hero. Good morrow, coz.

Beat. Good morrow, sweet Hero.

Hero. Why, how now ? do you speak in the sick tune ?

Beat. I am out of all other tune, methinks.

Marg. Clap 's into ' Light o' love ; ' that goes without a burden : do you sing it, and I 'll dance it.

Beat. Ye light o' love, with your heels ! then, if your husband have stables enough, you 'll see he shall lack no barns.

Marg. O illegitimate construction ! I scorn that with my heels.

Beat. 'Tis almost five o'clock, cousin ; 'tis time you were ready. By my troth, I am exceeding ill : heigh-ho !

Marg. For a hawk, a horse, or a husband ?

Beat. For the letter that begins them all, H

Marg. Well, an you be not turned Turk, there 's no more sailing

Beat. What means the fool, trow ?   [by the star.

Marg. Nothing I ; but God send every one their heart's desire !

Hero. These gloves the count sent me ; they are an excellent

Beat. I am stuffed, cousin ; I cannot smell.   [perfume.

Marg. A maid, and stuffed ! there 's goodly catching of cold.

Beat. O, God help me ! God help me ! how long have you professed apprehension ?   [rarely ?

Marg. Ever since you left it. Doth not my wit become me

Beat. It is not seen enough, you should wear it in your cap. By my troth, I am sick.

Marg. Get you some of this distilled Carduus Benedictus, and lay it to your heart : it is the only thing for a qualm.

Hero. There thou prickest her with a thistle.

Beat. Benedictus ! why Benedictus ? you have some moral in this Benedictus.

Marg. Moral ! no, by my troth, I have no moral meaning ; I meant, plain holy-thistle. You may think perchance that I

336

think you are in love: nay, by 'r lady, I am not such a fool
to think what I list; nor I list not to think what I can; nor,
indeed, I cannot think, if I would think my heart out of
thinking, that you are in love, or that you will be in love, or
that you can be in love.   Yet Benedick was such another,
and now is he become a man: he swore he would never
marry; and yet now, in despite of his heart, he eats his meat
without grudging: and how you may be converted, I know
not; but methinks you look with your eyes as other women

Beat. What pace is this that thy tongue keeps?   [do.

Marg. Not a false gallop.

Re-enter Ursula.

Urs. Madam, withdraw: the prince, the count, Signior Benedick, Don John, and all the gallants of the town, are come to
fetch you to church.

Hero. Help to dress me, good coz, good Meg, good Ursula.

[*Exeunt.*

SCENE V

Another room in Leonato's house.

Enter Leonato, with Dogberry and Verges.

Leon. What would you with me, honest neighbour?

Dog. Marry, sir, I would have some confidence with you that
decerns you nearly.

Leon. Brief, I pray you; for you see it is a busy time with me.

Dog. Marry, this it is, sir.

Verg. Yes, in truth it is, sir.

Leon. What is it, my good friends?

Dog. Goodman Verges, sir, speaks a little off the matter: an
old man, sir, and his wits are not so blunt as, God help, I
would desire they were; but, in faith, honest as the skin
between his brows.

Verg. Yes, I thank God I am as honest as any man living that
is an old man and no honester than I.

Dog. Comparisons are odorous: palabras, neighbour Verges.

Leon. Neighbours, you are tedious.

Dog. It pleases your worship to say so, but we are the poor
duke's officers; but truly, for mine own part, if I were as
tedious as a king, I could find in my heart to bestow it all of

Leon. All thy tediousness on me, ah?   [your worship.

Dog. Yea, an 't were a thousand pound more than 'tis; for I
hear as good exclamation on your worship as of any man in
the city; and though I be but a poor man, I am glad to

Verg. And so am I.   [hear it.

Leon. I would fain know what you have to say.

337

Verg. Marry, sir, our watch to-night, excepting your worship's presence, ha' ta'en a couple of as arrant knaves as any in Messina.

Dog. A good old man, sir; he will be talking: as they say, When the age is in, the wit is out: God help us! it is a world to see. Well said, i' faith, neighbour Verges: well, God's a good man; an two men ride of a horse, one must ride behind. An honest soul, i' faith, sir; by my troth he is, as ever broke bread; but God is to be worshipped; all men are not alike; alas, good neighbour!

Leon. Indeed, neighbour, he comes too short of you.

Dog. Gifts that God gives.

Leon. I must leave you.

Dog. One word, sir: our watch, sir, have indeed comprehended two aspicious persons, and we would have them this morning examined before your worship.

Leon. Take their examination yourself, and bring it me: I am now in great haste, as it may appear unto you.

Dog. It shall be suffigance.

Leon. Drink some wine ere you go: fare you well.

Enter a Messenger.

Mess. My lord, they stay for you to give your daughter to her
Leon. I 'll wait upon them: I am ready.　　　　　[husband.
　　　　　　　　　　　　　　　[*Exeunt Leonato and Messenger.*

Dog. Go, good partner, go, get you to Francis Seacole; bid him bring his pen and inkhorn to the gaol: we are now to examination these men.

Verg. And we must do it wisely.

Dog. We will spare for no wit, I warrant you; here 's that shall drive some of them to a noncome: only get the learned writer to set down our excommunication, and meet me at the gaol.　　　　　　　　　　　　　　　[*Exeunt.*

ACT IV—Scene I
A church.

Enter Don Pedro, Don John, Leonato, Friar Francis,
Claudio, Benedick, Hero, Beatrice, and attendants.

Leon. Come, Friar Francis, be brief; only to the plain form of marriage, and you shall recount their particular duties afterwards.

Friar. You come hither, my lord, to marry this lady.

Claud. No.

Leon. To be married to her: friar, you come to marry her.

Friar. Lady, you come hither to be married to this count.

Hero. I do.

Friar. If either of you know any inward impediment why you
   should not be conjoined, I charge you, on your souls, to

Claud. Know you any, Hero?   [utter it.

Hero. None, my lord.

Friar. Know you any, count?

Leon. I dare make his answer, none.

Claud. O, what men dare do! what men may do! what men
   daily do, not knowing what they do!

Bene. How now! interjections? Why, then, some be of
   laughing, as, ah, ha, he!

Claud. Stand thee by, friar. Father, by your leave:
   Will you with free and unconstrained soul
   Give me this maid, your daughter?

Leon. As freely, son, as God did give her me.

Claud. And what have I to give you back, whose worth
   May counterpoise this rich and precious gift?

D. Pedro. Nothing, unless you render her again.

Claud. Sweet prince, you learn me noble thankfulness.
   There, Leonato, take her back again:
   Give not this rotten orange to your friend;
   She's but the sign and semblance of her honour.
   Behold how like a maid she blushes here!
   O, what authority and show of truth
   Can cunning sin cover itself withal!
   Comes not that blood as modest evidence
   To witness simple virtue? Would you not swear,
   All you that see her, that she were a maid,
   By these exterior shows? But she is none:
   She knows the heat of a luxurious bed;
   Her blush is guiltiness, not modesty.

Leon. What do you mean, my lord?

Claud.   Not to be married,
   Not to knit my soul to an approved wanton.

Leon. Dear my lord, if you, in your own proof,
   Have vanquish'd the resistance of her youth,
   And made defeat of her virginity,—

Claud. I know what you would say: if I have known her,
   You will say she did embrace me as a husband,
   And so extenuate the 'forehand sin:
   No, Leonato,
   I never tempted her with word too large;
   But, as a brother to his sister, show'd
   Bashful sincerity and comely love.

Hero. And seem'd I ever otherwise to you?

339

Claud. Out on thee ! Seeming ! I will write against it :
  You seem to me as Dian in her orb,
  As chaste as is the bud ere it be blown ;
  But you are more intemperate in your blood
  Than Venus, or those pamper'd animals
  That rage in savage sensuality.

Hero. Is my lord well, that he doth speak so wide ?

Leon. Sweet prince, why speak not you ?

D. Pedro.   What should I speak ?
  I stand dishonour'd, that have gone about
  To link my dear friend to a common stale.

Leon. Are these things spoken, or do I but dream ?

D. John. Sir, they are spoken, and these things are true.

Bene. This looks not like a nuptial.

Hero.   True ! O God !

Claud. Leonato, stand I here ?
  Is this the prince ? is this the prince's brother ?
  Is this face Hero's ? are our eyes our own ?

Leon. All this is so : but what of this, my lord ?

Claud. Let me but move one question to your daughter ;
  And, by that fatherly and kindly power
  That you have in her, bid her answer truly.

Leon. I charge thee do so, as thou art my child.

Hero. O, God defend me ! how am I beset !
  What kind of catechising call you this ?

Claud. To make you answer truly to your name.

Hero. Is it not Hero ? Who can blot that name
  With any just reproach ?

Claud.   Marry, that can Hero ;
  Hero itself can blot out Hero's virtue.
  What man was he talk'd with you yesternight
  Out at your window betwixt twelve and one ?
  Now, if you are a maid, answer to this.

Hero. I talk'd with no man at that hour, my lord.

D. Pedro. Why, then are you no maiden. Leonato,
  I am sorry you must hear : upon mine honour,
  Myself, my brother, and this grieved count
  Did see her, hear her, at that hour last night
  Talk with a ruffian at her chamber-window ;
  Who hath indeed, most like a liberal villain,
  Confess'd the vile encounters they have had
  A thousand times in secret.

D. John. Fie, fie ! they are not to be named, my lord,
  Not to be spoke of ;
  There is not chastity enough in language,

Without offence to utter them.   Thus, pretty lady,
I am sorry for thy much misgovernment.

Claud. O Hero, what a Hero hadst thou been,
  If half thy outward graces had been placed
  About thy thoughts and counsels of thy heart !
  But fare thee well, most foul, most fair ! farewell,
  Thou pure impiety and impious purity !
  For thee I 'll lock up all the gates of love,
  And on my eyelids shall conjecture hang,
  To turn all beauty into thoughts of harm,
  And never shall it more be gracious.

Leon. Hath no man's dagger here a point for me ?

                                     [Hero swoons.

Beat. Why, how now, cousin ! wherefore sink you down ?

D. John. Come, let us go.   These things, come thus to light,
  Smother her spirits up.

             [Exeunt Don Pedro, Don John, and Claudio.

Bene. How doth the lady ?

Beat.   Dead, I think.   Help, uncle !
  Hero ! why, Hero ! Uncle ! Signior Benedick ! Friar !

Leon. O Fate ! take not away thy heavy hand.
  Death is the fairest cover for her shame
  That may be wish'd for.

Beat.   How now, cousin Hero !

Friar. Have comfort, lady.

Leon. Dost thou look up ?

Friar. Yea, wherefore should she not ?

Leon. Wherefore !   Why, doth not every earthly thing
  Cry shame upon her ?   Could she here deny
  The story that is printed in her blood ?
  Do not live, Hero ; do not ope thine eyes :
  For, did I think thou wouldst not quickly die,
  Thought I thy spirits were stronger than thy shames,
  Myself would, on the rearward of reproaches,
  Strike at thy life.   Grieved I, I had but one ?
  Chid I for that at frugal nature's frame ?
  O, one too much by thee !   Why had I one ?
  Why ever wast thou lovely in my eyes ?
  Why had I not with charitable hand
  Took up a beggar's issue at my gates,
  Who smirched thus and mired with infamy,
  I might have said, 'No part of it is mine ;
  This shame derives itself from unknown loins' ?
  But mine, and mine I loved, and mine I praised,
  And mine that I was proud on, mine so much

That I myself was to myself not mine,
Valuing of her,—why, she, O, she is fallen
Into a pit of ink, that the wide sea
Hath drops too few to wash her clean again,
And salt too little which may season give
To her foul-tainted flesh !

Bene.   Sir, sir, be patient.
For my part, I am so attired in wonder,
I know not what to say.

Beat. O, on my soul, my cousin is belied !

Bene. Lady, were you her bedfellow last night ?

Beat. No, truly, not ; although, until last night,
I have this twelvemonth been her bedfellow.

Leon. Confirm'd, confirm'd ! O, that is stronger made
Which was before barr'd up with ribs of iron !
Would the two princes lie, and Claudio lie,
Who loved her so, that, speaking of her foulness,
Wash'd it with tears ? Hence from her ! let her die.

Friar. Hear me a little ;
For I have only been silent so long,
And given way unto this course of fortune,
By noting of the lady : I have mark'd
A thousand blushing apparitions
To start into her face ; a thousand innocent shames
In angel whiteness beat away those blushes ;
And in her eye there hath appear'd a fire,
To burn the errors that these princes hold
Against her maiden truth. Call me a fool ;
Trust not my reading nor my observations,
Which with experimental seal doth warrant
The tenour of my book ; trust not my age,
My reverence, calling, nor divinity,
If this sweet lady lie not guiltless here
Under some biting error.

Leon.   Friar, it cannot be.
Thou seest that all the grace that she hath left
Is that she will not add to her damnation
A sin of perjury ; she not denies it :
Why seek'st thou, then, to cover with excuse
That which appears in proper nakedness ?

Friar. Lady, what man is he you are accused of ?

Hero. They know that do accuse me ; I know none :
If I know more of any man alive
Than that which maiden modesty doth warrant,
Let all my sins lack mercy ! O my father,

Prove you that any man with me conversed
At hours unmeet, or that I yesternight
Maintain'd the change of words with any creature,
Refuse me, hate me, torture me to death!
Friar. There is some strange misprision in the princes.
Beat. Two of them have the very bent of honour;
And if their wisdoms be misled in this,
The practice of it lives in John the bastard,
Whose spirits toil in frame of villanies.
Leon. I know not.   If they speak but truth of her,
These hands shall tear her; if they wrong her honour,
The proudest of them shall well hear of it.
Time hath not yet so dried this blood of mine,
Nor age so eat up my invention,
Nor fortune made such havoc of my means,
Nor my bad life reft me so much of friends,
But they shall find, awaked in such a kind,
Both strength of limb and policy of mind,
Ability in means and choice of friends,
To quit me of them thoroughly.
Friar.   Pause awhile,
And let my counsel sway you in this case.
Your daughter here the princes left for dead:
Let her awhile be secretly kept in,
And publish it that she is dead indeed;
Maintain a mourning ostentation,
And on your family's old monument
Hang mournful epitaphs, and do all rites
That appertain unto a burial.
Leon. What shall become of this? what will this do?
Friar. Marry, this, well carried, shall on her behalf
Change slander to remorse; that is some good:
But not for that dream I on this strange course,
But on this travail look for greater birth.
She dying, as it must be so maintain'd,
Upon the instant that she was accused,
Shall be lamented, pitied, and excused
Of every hearer: for it so falls out,
That what we have we prize not to the worth
Whiles we enjoy it; but being lack'd and lost,
Why, then we rack the value, then we find
The virtue that possession would not show us
Whiles it was ours.   So will it fare with Claudio:
When he shall hear she died upon his words,
The idea of her life shall sweetly creep

Into his study of imagination ;
And every lovely organ of her life
Shall come apparell'd in more precious habit,
More moving-delicate and full of life,
Into the eye and prospect of his soul,
Than when she lived indeed ; then shall he mourn,
If ever love had interest in his liver,
And wish he had not so accused her,
No, though he thought his accusation true.
Let this be so, and doubt not but success
Will fashion the event in better shape
Than I can lay it down in likelihood.
But if all aim but this be levell'd false,
The supposition of the lady's death
Will quench the wonder of her infamy :
And if it sort not well, you may conceal her,
As best befits her wounded reputation,
In some reclusive and religious life,
Out of all eyes, tongues, minds, and injuries.

Bene. Signior Leonato, let the friar advise you :
And though you know my inwardness and love
Is very much unto the prince and Claudio,
Yet, by mine honour, I will deal in this
As secretly and justly as your soul
Should with your body.

Leon.   Being that I flow in grief,
The smallest twine may lead me.

Friar. 'Tis well consented : presently away ;
For to strange sores strangely they strain the cure.
Come, lady, die to live : this wedding-day
Perhaps is but prolong'd : have patience and endure.
                    [*Exeunt all but Benedick and Beatrice.*

Bene. Lady Beatrice, have you wept all this while ?
Beat. Yea, and I will weep a while longer.
Bene. I will not desire that.
Beat. You have no reason ; I do it freely.
Bene. Surely I do believe your fair cousin is wronged.
Beat. Ah, how much might the man deserve of me that would
Bene. Is there any way to show such friendship ?   [right her !
Beat. A very even way, but no such friend.
Bene. May a man do it ?
Beat. It is a man's office, but not yours.   [that strange ?
Bene. I do love nothing in the world so well as you : is not
Beat. As strange as the thing I know not.   It were as possible
for me to say I loved nothing so well as you : but believe

344

me not ; and yet I lie not ; I confess nothing, nor I deny
nothing. I am sorry for my cousin.

Bene. By my sword, Beatrice, thou lovest me.

Beat. Do not swear, and eat it.

Bene. I will swear by it that you love me ; and I will make
him eat it that says I love not you.

Beat. Will you not eat your word ?

Bene. With no sauce that can be devised to it. I protest I

Beat. Why, then, God forgive me !   [love thee.

Bene. What offence, sweet Beatrice ?

Beat. You have stayed me in a happy hour : I was about to
protest I loved you.

Bene. And do it with all thy heart.

Beat. I love you with so much of my heart, that none is left to

Bene. Come, bid me do any thing for thee.   [protest.

Beat. Kill Claudio.

Bene. Ha ! not for the wide world.

Beat. You kill me to deny it. Farewell.

Bene. Tarry, sweet Beatrice.

Beat. I am gone, though I am here : there is no love in you :
nay, I pray you, let me go.

Bene. Beatrice,—

Beat. In faith, I will go.

Bene. We 'll be friends first.

Beat. You dare easier be friends with me than fight with mine

Bene. Is Claudio thine enemy ?   [enemy.

Beat. Is he not approved in the height a villain, that hath
slandered, scorned, dishonoured my kinswoman ? O that I
were a man ! What, bear her in hand until they come to
take hands ; and then, with public accusation, uncovered
slander, unmitigated rancour,—O God, that I were a man !
I would eat his heart in the market-place.

Bene. Hear me, Beatrice,—

Beat. Talk with a man out at a window ! A proper saying !

Bene. Nay, but, Beatrice,—

Beat. Sweet Hero ! She is wronged, she is slandered, she is

Bene. Beat—   [undone.

Beat. Princes and counties ! Surely, a princely testimony, a
goodly count, Count Comfect ; a sweet gallant, surely ! O
that I were a man for his sake ! or that I had any friend
would be a man for my sake ! But manhood is melted into
courtesies, valour into compliment, and men are only turned
into tongue, and trim ones too : he is now as valiant as
Hercules that only tells a lie, and swears it. I cannot be a
man with wishing, therefore I will die a woman with grieving.

Bene. Tarry, good Beatrice. By this hand, I love thee.

Beat. Use it for my love some other way than swearing by it.

Bene. Think you in your soul the Count Claudio hath wronged Hero ?

Beat. Yea, as sure as I have a thought or a soul.

Bene. Enough, I am engaged ; I will challenge him. I will kiss your hand, and so I leave you. By this hand, Claudio shall render me a dear account. As you hear of me, so think of me. Go, comfort your cousin : I must say she is dead : and so, farewell. [*Exeunt.*

Scene II

A prison.

Enter Dogberry, Verges, and Sexton, in gowns ; and the Watch, with Conrade and Borachio.

Dog. Is our whole dissembly appeared ?

Verg. O, a stool and a cushion for the sexton.

Sex. Which be the malefactors ?

Dog. Marry, that am I and my partner.

Verg. Nay, that's certain ; we have the exhibition to examine.

Sex. But which are the offenders that are to be examined ? let them come before master constable.

Dog. Yea, marry, let them come before me. What is your name, friend ?

Bora. Borachio.

Dog. Pray, write down, Borachio. Yours, sirrah ?

Con. I am a gentleman, sir, and my name is Conrade.

Dog. Write down, master gentleman Conrade. Masters, do you serve God ?

Con. } Yea, sir, we hope.
Bora. }

Dog. Write down, that they hope they serve God : and write God first ; for God defend but God should go before such villains ! Masters, it is proved already that you are little better than false knaves ; and it will go near to be thought so shortly. How answer you for yourselves ?

Con. Marry, sir, we say we are none.

Dog. A marvellous witty fellow, I assure you ; but I will go about with him. Come you hither, sirrah ; a word in your ear : sir, I say to you, it is thought you are false knaves.

Bora. Sir, I say to you we are none.

Dog. Well, stand aside. 'Fore God, they are both in a tale. Have you writ down, that they are none ?

Sex. Master Constable, you go not the way to examine : you must call forth the watch that are their accusers.

Dog. Yea, marry, that's the eftest way. Let the watch come forth. Masters, I charge you, in the prince's name, accuse these men.

First Watch. This man said, sir, that Don John, the prince's brother, was a villain.

Dog. Write down, Prince John a villain. Why, this is flat perjury, to call a prince's brother villain.

Bora. Master Constable,—

Dog. Pray thee, fellow, peace : I do not like thy look, I promise thee.

Sex. What heard you him say else?

Sec. Watch. Marry, that he had received a thousand ducats of Don John for accusing the Lady Hero wrongfully.

Dog. Flat burglary as ever was committed.

Verg. Yea, by mass, that it is.

Sex. What else, fellow?

First Watch. And that Count Claudio did mean, upon his words, to disgrace Hero before the whole assembly, and not marry her.

Dog. O villain! thou wilt be condemned into everlasting redemption for this.

Sex. What else?

Watch. This is all.

Sex. And this is more, masters, than you can deny. Prince John is this morning secretly stolen away ; Hero was in this manner accused, in this very manner refused, and upon the grief of this suddenly died. Master constable, let these men be bound, and brought to Leonato's : I will go before and show him their examination.   [*Exit.*

Dog. Come, let them be opinioned.

Verg. Let them be in the hands—

Con. Off, coxcomb!

Dog. God's my life, where's the sexton? let him write down, the prince's officer, coxcomb. Come, bind them. Thou naughty varlet!

Con. Away! you are an ass, you are an ass.

Dog. Dost thou not suspect my place? dost thou not suspect my years? O that he were here to write me down an ass! But, masters, remember that I am an ass ; though it be not written down, yet forget not that I am an ass. No, thou villain, thou art fully of piety, as shall be proved upon thee by good witness. I am a wise fellow ; and, which is more, an officer ; and, which is more, a householder ; and, which is more, as pretty a piece of flesh as any is in Messina ; and one that knows the law, go to ; and a rich fellow enough, go to ;

and a fellow that hath had losses ; and one that hath two
gowns, and every thing handsome about him.   Bring him
away.   O that I had been writ down as ass !   [*Exeunt.*

ACT V—SCENE I

Before Leonato's house.
Enter Leonato and Antonio.

Ant. If you go on thus, you will kill yourself ;
   And 'tis not wisdom thus to second grief
   Against yourself.
Leon.   I pray thee, cease thy counsel,
   Which falls into mine ears as profitless
   As water in a sieve : give not me counsel ;
   Nor let no comforter delight mine ear
   But such a one whose wrongs do suit with mine.
   Bring me a father that so loved his child,
   Whose joy of her is overwhelm'd like mine,
   And bid him speak of patience ;
   Measure his woe the length and breadth of mine,
   And let it answer every strain for strain,
   As thus for thus, and such a grief for such,
   In every lineament, branch, shape, and form :
   If such a one will smile, and stroke his beard,
   Bid sorrow wag, cry ' hem !' when he should groan,
   Patch grief with proverbs, make misfortune drunk
   With candle-wasters ; bring him yet to me,
   And I of him will gather patience.
   But there is no such man : for, brother, men
   Can counsel and speak comfort to that grief
   Which they themselves not feel ; but, tasting it,
   Their counsel turns to passion, which before
   Would give preceptial medicine to rage,
   Fetter strong madness in a silken thread,
   Charm ache with air, and agony with words :
   No, no ; 'tis all men's office to speak patience
   To those that wring under the load of sorrow,
   But no man's virtue nor sufficiency,
   To be so moral when he shall endure
   The like himself.   Therefore give me no counsel :
   My griefs cry louder than advertisement.
Ant. Therein do men from children nothing differ.
Leon. I pray thee, peace.   I will be flesh and blood ;
   For there was never yet philosopher
   That could endure the toothache patiently,

348

However they have writ the style of gods,
And made a push at chance and sufferance.
Ant. Yet bend not all the harm upon yourself;
Make those that do offend you suffer too.
Leon. There thou speak'st reason: nay, I will do so.
My soul doth tell me Hero is belied;
And that shall Claudio know; so shall the prince,
And all of them that thus dishonour her.
Ant. Here comes the prince and Claudio hastily.

Enter Don Pedro and Claudio.

D. Pedro. Good den, good den.
Claud.   Good day to both of you.
Leon. Hear you, my lords,—
D. Pedro.   We have some haste, Leonato.
Leon. Some haste, my lord! well, fare you well, my lord:
Are you so hasty now? well, all is one.
D. Pedro. Nay, do not quarrel with us, good old man.
Ant. If he could right himself with quarrelling,
Some of us would lie low.
Claud.   Who wrongs him:
Leon. Marry, thou dost wrong me, thou dissembler, thou:—
Nay, never lay thy hand upon thy sword;
I fear thee not.
Claud.   Marry, beshrew my hand,
If it should give your age such cause of fear:
In faith, my hand meant nothing to my sword.
Leon. Tush, tush, man; never fleer and jest at me:
I speak not like a dotard nor a fool,
As, under privilege of age, to brag
What I have done being young, or what would do,
Were I not old.   Know, Claudio, to thy head,
Thou hast so wrong'd mine innocent child and me,
That I am forced to lay my reverence by,
And, with grey hairs and bruise of many days,
Do challenge thee to trial of a man.
I say thou hast belied mine innocent child;
Thy slander hath gone through and through her heart,
And she lies buried with her ancestors;
O, in a tomb where never scandal slept,
Save this of hers, framed by thy villany!
Claud. My villany?
Leon.   Thine, Claudio; thine, I say.
D. Pedro. You say not right, old man.
Leon.   My lord, my lord,
I'll prove it on his body, if he dare,

349

Despite his nice fence and his active practice,
His May of youth and bloom of lustihood.

Claud. Away ! I will not have to do with you.

Leon. Canst thou so daff me ?   Thou hast kill'd my child :
If thou kill'st me, boy, thou shalt kill a man.

Ant. He shall kill two of us, and men indeed :
But that 's no matter ; let him kill one first ;
Win me and wear me ; let him answer me.
Come, follow me, boy ; come, sir boy, come, follow me :
Sir boy, I 'll whip you from your foining fence ;
Nay, as I am a gentleman, I will.

Leon. Brother,—

Ant. Content yourself.   God knows I loved my niece ;
And she is dead, slander'd to death by villains,
That dare as well answer a man indeed
As I dare take a serpent by the tongue :
Boys, apes, braggarts, Jacks, milksops !

Leon.   Brother Antony,—

Ant. Hold you content.   What, man ! I know them, yea,
And what they weigh, even to the utmost scruple,—
Scambling, out-facing, fashion-monging boys,
That lie, and cog, and flout, deprave, and slander,
Go antiquely, and show outward hideousness,
And speak off half a dozen dangerous words,
How they might hurt their enemies, if they durst ;
And this is all.

Leon. But, brother Antony,—

Ant.   Come, 'tis no matter :
Do not you meddle ; let me deal in this.

D. Pedro. Gentlemen both, we will not wake your patience.
My heart is sorry for your daughter's death :
But, on my honour, she was charged with nothing
But what was true, and very full of proof.

Leon. My lord, my lord,—

D. Pedro. I will not hear you.

Leon. No ?   Come, brother ; away ! I will be heard.

Ant. And shall, or some of us will smart for it.

                              [*Exeunt Leonato and Antonio.*

D. Pedro. See, see ; here come the man we went to seek.

Enter Benedick.

Claud. Now, signior, what news ?

Bene. Good day, my lord.

D. Pedro. Welcome, signior : you are almost come to part
almost a fray.

350

Claud. We had like to have had our two noses snapped off
with two old men without teeth.

D. Pedro. Leonato and his brother. What thinkest thou?
Had we fought, I doubt we should have been too young for
them.

Bene. In a false quarrel there is no true valour. I came to
seek you both.

Claud. We have been up and down to seek thee; for we are
high-proof melancholy, and would fain have it beaten away.
Wilt thou use thy wit?

Bene. It is in my scabbard: shall I draw it?

D. Pedro. Dost thou wear thy wit by thy side?

Claud. Never any did so, though very many have been beside
their wit. I will bid thee draw, as we do the minstrels;
draw, to pleasure us.

D. Pedro. As I am an honest man, he looks pale. Art thou
sick, or angry?

Claud. What, courage, man! What though care killed a cat,
thou hast mettle enough in thee to kill care.

Bene. Sir, I shall meet your wit in the career, an you charge it
against me. I pray you choose another subject.   [cross.

Claud. Nay, then, give him another staff: this last was broke

D. Pedro. By this light, he changes more and more: I think
he be angry indeed.

Claud. If he be, he knows how to turn his girdle.

Bene. Shall I speak a word in your ear?

Claud. God bless me from a challenge!

Bene. [*Aside to Claudio*] You are a villain; I jest not: I will
make it good how you dare, with what you dare, and when
you dare. Do me right, or I will protest your cowardice.
You have killed a sweet lady, and her death shall fall heavy
on you. Let me hear from you.

Claud. Well, I will meet you, so I may have good cheer.

D. Pedro. What, a feast, a feast?

Claud. I' faith, I thank him; he hath bid me to a calf's-head
and a capon; the which if I do not carve most curiously,
say my knife's naught. Shall I not find a woodcock too?

Bene. Sir, your wit ambles well; it goes easily.

D. Pedro. I'll tell thee how Beatrice praised thy wit the other
day. I said, thou hadst a fine wit: 'True,' said she, 'a fine
little one.' 'No,' said I, 'a great wit:' 'Right,' says she,
'a great gross one.' 'Nay,' said I, 'a good wit:' 'Just,'
said she, 'it hurts nobody.' 'Nay,' said I, 'the gentleman
is wise:' 'Certain,' said she, 'a wise gentleman.' 'Nay,'
said I, 'he hath the tongues:' 'That I believe,' said she,

'for he swore a thing to me on Monday night, which he
forswore on Tuesday morning; there's a double tongue;
there's two tongues.' Thus did she, an hour together, trans-
shape thy particular virtues: yet at last she concluded with
a sigh, thou wast the properest man in Italy.

Claud. For the which she wept heartily, and said she cared not.

D. Pedro. Yea, that she did; but yet, for all that, an if she did
not hate him deadly, she would love him dearly: the old
man's daughter told us all.

Claud. All, all; and, moreover, God saw him when he was hid
in the garden.

D. Pedro. But when shall we set the savage bull's horns on
the sensible Benedick's head?

Claud. Yea, and text underneath, 'Here dwells Benedick the
married man'?

Bene. Fare you well, boy: you know my mind. I will leave
you now to your gossip-like humour: you break jests as
braggarts do their blades, which, God be thanked, hurt not.
My lord, for your many courtesies I thank you: I must
discontinue your company: your brother the bastard is fled
from Messina: you have among you killed a sweet and
innocent lady. For my Lord Lackbeard there, he and I
shall meet: and till then peace be with him.   [*Exit.*

D. Pedro. He is in earnest.

Claud. In most profound earnest; and, I'll warrant you, for
the love of Beatrice.

D. Pedro. And hath challenged thee.

Claud. Most sincerely.

D. Pedro. What a pretty thing man is when he goes in his
doublet and hose, and leaves off his wit!

Claud. He is then a giant to an ape: but then is an ape a
doctor to such a man.

D. Pedro. But, soft you, let me be: pluck up, my heart, and
be sad.   Did he not say, my brother was fled?

*Enter Dogberry, Verges, and the Watch, with Conrade and
Borachio.*

Dog. Come, you, sir: if justice cannot tame you, she shall ne'er
weigh more reasons in her balance: nay, an you be a cursing
hypocrite once, you must be looked to.

D. Pedro. How now? two of my brother's men bound!

Claud. Hearken after their offence, my lord.   [Borachio one!

D. Pedro. Officers, what offence have these men done?

Dog. Marry, sir, they have committed false report; moreover,
they have spoken untruths; secondarily, they are slanders;
sixth and lastly, they have belied a lady; thirdly, they have

verified unjust things ; and, to conclude, they are lying
knaves.

D. Pedro. First, I ask thee what they have done ; thirdly, I ask
thee what's their offence ; sixth and lastly, why they are
committed ; and, to conclude, what you lay to their charge.

Claud. Rightly reasoned, and in his own division ; and, by my
troth, there's one meaning well suited.

D. Pedro. Who have you offended, masters, that you are thus
bound to your answer ? this learned constable is too cunning
to be understood : what's your offence ?

Bora. Sweet prince, let me go no farther to mine answer : do
you hear me, and let this count kill me. I have deceived
even your very eyes : what your wisdoms could not discover,
these shallow fools have brought to light ; who, in the night,
overheard me confessing to this man, how Don John your
brother incensed me to slander the Lady Hero ; how you
were brought into the orchard, and saw me court Margaret
in Hero's garments : how you disgraced her, when you should
marry her : my villany they have upon record ; which I had
rather seal with my death than repeat over to my shame.
The lady is dead upon mine and my master's false accusa
tion ; and, briefly, I desire nothing but the reward of a
villain.

D. Pedro. Runs not this speech like iron through your blood ?

Claud. I have drunk poison whiles he utter'd it.

D. Pedro. But did my brother set thee on to this ?

Bora. Yea, and paid me richly for the practice of it.

D. Pedro. He is composed and framed of treachery :
And fled he is upon this villany.

Claud. Sweet Hero ! now thy image doth appear
In the rare semblance that I loved it first.

Dog. Come, bring away the plaintiffs : by this time our sexton
hath reformed Signior Leonato of the matter : and, masters,
do not forget to specify, when time and place shall serve,
that I am an ass.   [too.

Verg. Here, here comes master Signior Leonato, and the sexton
      Re-enter Leonato and Antonio, with the Sexton.

Leon. Which is the villain ? let me see his eyes,
That, when I note another man like him,
I may avoid him : which of these is he ?

Bora. If you would know your wronger, look on me.

Leon. Art thou the slave that with thy breath hast kill'd
Mine innocent child ?

Bora.   Yea, even I alone.

Leon. No, not so, villain ; thou beliest thyself :

Here stand a pair of honourable men;
A third is fled, that had a hand in it.
I thank you, princes, for my daughter's death:
Record it with your high and worthy deeds:
'Twas bravely done, if you bethink you of it.

Claud. I know not how to pray your patience;
Yet I must speak.   Choose your revenge yourself
Impose me to what penance your invention
Can lay upon my sin : yet sinn'd I not
But in mistaking.

D. Pedro.   By my soul, nor I :
And yet, to satisfy this good old man,
I would bend under any heavy weight
That he 'll enjoin me to.

Leon. I cannot bid you bid my daughter live;
That were impossible: but, I pray you both,
Possess the people in Messina here
How innocent she died ; and if your love
Can labour aught in sad invention,
Hang her an epitaph upon her tomb,
And sing it to her bones, sing it to-night:
To-morrow morning come you to my house;
And since you could not be my son-in-law,
Be yet my nephew : my brother hath a daughter,
Almost the copy of my child that 's dead,
And she alone is heir to both of us :
Give her the right you should have given her cousin,
And so dies my revenge.

Claud.   O noble sir,
Your over-kindness doth wring tears from me !
I do embrace your offer; and dispose
For henceforth of poor Claudio.

Leon. To-morrow, then, I will expect your coming;
To-night I take my leave.   This naughty man
Shall face to face be brought to Margaret,
Who I believe was pack'd in all this wrong,
Hired to it by your brother.

Bora.   No, by my soul, she was not;
Nor knew not what she did when she spoke to me;
But always hath been just and virtuous
In any thing that I do know by her.

Dog. Moreover, sir, which indeed is not under white and black,
this plaintiff here, the offender, did call me ass : I beseech
you, let it be remembered in his punishment.   And also, the
watch heard them talk of one Deformed : they say he wears

354

a key in his ear, and a lock hanging by it; and borrows money in God's name, the which he hath used so long and never paid, that now men grow hard-hearted, and will lend nothing for God's sake : pray you, examine him upon that point.

Leon. I thank thee for thy care and honest pains.

Dog. Your worship speaks like a most thankful and reverend youth ; and I praise God for you.

Leon. There's for thy pains.

Dog. God save the foundation !

Leon. Go, I discharge thee of thy prisoner, and I thank thee.

Dog. I leave an arrant knave with your worship ; which I beseech your worship to correct yourself, for the example of others. God keep your worship ! I wish your worship well ; God restore you to health ! I humbly give you leave to depart ; and if a merry meeting may be wished, God prohibit it ! Come, neighbour.

[*Exeunt Dogberry and Verges.*

Leon. Until to-morrow morning, lords, farewell.

Ant. Farewell, my lords : we look for you to-morrow.

D. Pedro. We will not fail.

Claud.   To-night I'll mourn with Hero.

Leon. [*To the Watch*] Bring you these fellows on.
We'll talk with Margaret,
How her acquaintance grew with this lewd fellow.

[*Exeunt, severally.*

SCENE II

Leonato's garden.

Enter Benedick and Margaret, meeting.

Bene. Pray thee, sweet Mistress Margaret, deserve well at my hands by helping me to the speech of Beatrice.

Marg. Will you, then, write me a sonnet in praise of my beauty?

Bene. In so high a style, Margaret, that no man living shall come over it ; for, in most comely truth, thou deservest it.

Marg. To have no man come over me ! why, shall I always keep below stairs ?

Bene. Thy wit is as quick as the greyhound's mouth ; it catches.

Marg. And yours as blunt as the fencer's foils. which hit, but hurt not.

Bene. A most manly wit, Margaret ; it will not hurt a woman : and so, I pray thee, call Beatrice : I give thee the bucklers.

Marg. Give us the swords ; we have bucklers of our own.

Bene. If you use them, Margaret, you must put in the pikes with a vice ; and they are dangerous weapons for maids.

Marg. Well, I will call Beatrice to you, who I think hath legs.
Bene. And therefore will come.   [*Exit Margaret.*
    [*Sings*]   The god of love,
                        That sits above,
                    And knows me, and knows me,
                        How pitiful I deserve,—
I mean in singing ; but in loving, Leander the good swimmer,
Troilus the first employer of pandars, and a whole bookful of
these quondam carpetmongers, whose names yet run smoothly
in the even road of a blank verse, why, they were never so
truly turned over and over as my poor self in love.   Marry,
I cannot show it in rhyme ; I have tried : I can find out no
rhyme to 'lady' but 'baby,' an innocent rhyme ; for 'scorn,'
'horn,' a hard rhyme ; for 'school,' 'fool,' a babbling
rhyme ; very ominous endings : no, I was not born under a
rhyming planet, nor I cannot woo in festival terms.
                    Enter Beatrice.
Sweet Beatrice, wouldst thou come when I called thee?
Beat. Yea, signior, and depart when you bid me.
Bene. O, stay but till then !
Beat. 'Then' is spoken ; fare you well now : and yet, ere I go,
    let me go with that I came ; which is, with knowing what hath
    passed between you and Claudio.
Bene. Only foul words ; and thereupon I will kiss thee.
Beat. Foul words is but foul wind, and foul wind is but foul
    breath, and foul breath is noisome ; therefore I will depart
    unkissed.
Bene. Thou hast frighted the word out of his right sense, so
    forcible is thy wit.   But I must tell thee plainly, Claudio
    undergoes my challenge ; and either I must shortly hear
    from him, or I will subscribe him a coward.   And, I pray
    thee now, tell me for which of my bad parts didst thou first
    fall in love with me ?
Beat. For them all together ; which maintained so politic a
    state of evil, that they will not admit any good part to inter-
    mingle with them.   But for which of my good parts did you
    first suffer love for me ?
Bene. Suffer love,—a good epithet !   I do suffer love indeed,
    for I love thee against my will.
Beat. In spite of your heart, I think ; alas, poor heart !   If you
    spite it for my sake, I will spite it for yours ; for I will never
    love that which my friend hates.
Bene. Thou and I are too wise to woo peaceably.
Beat. It appears not in this confession : there's not one wise
    man among twenty that will praise himself.

Bene. An old, an old instance, Beatrice, that lived in the time of good neighbours. If a man do not erect in this age his own tomb ere he dies, he shall live no longer in monument than the bell rings and the widow weeps.

Beat. And how long is that, think you?

Bene. Question: why, an hour in clamour, and a quarter in rheum: therefore is it most expedient for the wise, if Don Worm, his conscience, find no impediment to the contrary, to be the trumpet of his own virtues, as I am to myself. So much for praising myself, who, I myself will bear witness, is praiseworthy: and now tell me, how doth your cousin?

Beat. Very ill.

Bene. And how do you?

Beat. Very ill too.

Bene. Serve God, love me, and mend. There will I leave you too, for here comes one in haste.

Enter Ursula.

Urs. Madam, you must come to your uncle. Yonder's old coil at home: it is proved my Lady Hero hath been falsely accused, the prince and Claudio mightily abused; and Don John is the author of all, who is fled and gone. Will you come presently?

Beat. Will you go hear this news, signior?

Bene. I will live in thy heart, die in thy lap, and be buried in thy eyes; and moreover I will go with thee to thy uncle's.

[Exeunt.

SCENE III
A church.
Enter Don Pedro, Claudio, and three or four with tapers.

Claud. Is this the monument of Leonato?

A Lord. It is, my lord.

Claud. [*Reading out of a scroll*]

> Done to death by slanderous tongues
> > Was the Hero that here lies:
> Death, in guerdon of her wrongs,
> > Gives her fame which never dies.
> So the life that died with shame
> Lives in death with glorious fame.

> Hang thou there upon the tomb
> Praising her when I am dumb.
Now, music, sound, and sing your solemn hymn.

SONG.

Pardon, goddess of the night,
Those that slew thy virgin knight;
For the which, with songs of woe,
Round about her tomb they go.
    Midnight, assist our moan;
    Help us to sigh and groan,
        Heavily, heavily:
    Graves, yawn, and yield your dead,
    Till death be uttered,
        Heavily, heavily.

Claud. Now, unto thy bones good night!
    Yearly will I do this rite.
D. Pedro. Good morrow, masters; put your torches out:
    The wolves have prey'd; and look, the gentle day,
  Before the wheels of Phœbus, round about
    Dapples the drowsy east with spots of grey.
  Thanks to you all, and leave us: fare you well.
Claud. Good morrow, masters: each his several way.
D. Pedro. Come, let us hence, and put on other weeds;
    And then to Leonato's we will go.
Claud. And Hymen now with luckier issue speed's
    Than this for whom we render'd up this woe.   [*Exeunt.*

SCENE IV

A room in Leonato's house.

Enter Leonato, Antonio, Benedick, Beatrice, Margaret,
Ursula, Friar Francis, and Hero.

Friar. Did I not tell you she was innocent?
Leon. So are the prince and Claudio, who accused her
  Upon the error that you heard debated:
  But Margaret was in some fault for this,
  Although against her will, as it appears
  In the true course of all the question.
Ant. Well, I am glad that all things sort so well.
Bene. And so am I, being else by faith enforced
  To call young Claudio to a reckoning for it.
Leon. Well, daughter, and you gentlewomen all,
  Withdraw into a chamber by yourselves,
  And when I send for you, come hither mask'd. [*Exeunt Ladies.*
  The prince and Claudio promised by this hour
  To visit me. You know your office, brother:
  You must be father to your brother's daughter,
  And give her to young Claudio.

Ant. Which I will do with confirm'd countenance.

Bene. Friar, I must entreat your pains, I think.

Friar. To do what, signior?

Bene. To bind me, or undo me; one of them.
Signior Leonato, truth it is, good signior,
Your niece regards me with an eye of favour.

Leon. That eye my daughter lent her: 'tis most true.

Bene. And I do with an eye of love requite her.

Leon. The sight whereof I think you had from me,
From Claudio, and the prince: but what's your will?

Bene. Your answer, sir, is enigmatical:
But, for my will, my will is, your good will
May stand with ours, this day to be conjoin'd
In the state of honourable marriage:
In which, good friar, I shall desire your help.

Leon. My heart is with your liking

Friar.   And my help.
Here comes the prince and Claudio.

    Enter Don Pedro and Claudio, and two or three others.

D. Pedro. Good morrow to this fair assembly.

Leon. Good morrow, prince; good morrow, Claudio:
We here attend you. Are you yet determined
To-day to marry with my brother's daughter?

Claud. I'll hold my mind, were she an Ethiope.

Leon. Call her forth, brother; here's the friar ready.

                          [Exit Antonio.

D. Pedro. Good morrow, Benedick. Why, what's the matter,
That you have such a February face,
So full of frost, of storm, and cloudiness?

Claud. I think he thinks upon the savage bull.
Tush, fear not, man; we'll tip thy horns with gold,
And all Europa shall rejoice at thee;
As once Europa did at lusty Jove,
When he would play the noble beast in love.

Bene. Bull Jove, sir, had an amiable low;
And some such strange bull leap'd your father's cow,
And got a calf in that same noble feat
Much like to you, for you have just his bleat.

Claud. For this I owe you: here comes other reckonings.

    Re-enter Antonio, with the Ladies masked.
Which is the lady I must seize upon?

Ant. This same is she, and I do give you her.

Claud. Why, then she's mine. Sweet, let me see your face.

Leon. No, that you shall not, till you take her hand
Before this friar, and swear to marry her.

Claud. Give me your hand : before this holy friar,
    I am your husband, if you like of me.
Hero. And when I lived, I was your other wife : [*Unmasking.*
    And when you loved, you were my other husband.
Claud. Another Hero !
Hero.   Nothing certainer :
    One Hero died defiled ; but I do live,
    And surely as I live, I am a maid.
D. Pedro. The former Hero ! Hero that is dead !
Leon. She died, my lord, but whiles her slander lived.
Friar. All this amazement can I qualify :
    When after that the holy rites are ended,
    I 'll tell you largely of fair Hero's death :
    Meantime let wonder seem familiar,
    And to the chapel let us presently.
Bene. Soft and fair, friar. Which is Beatrice ?
Beat. [*Unmasking*] I answer to that name. What is your will ?
Bene. Do not you love me ?
Beat.   Why, no ; no more than reason.
Bene. Why, then your uncle, and the prince, and Claudio
    Have been deceived ; they swore you did.
Beat. Do not you love me ?
Bene.   Troth, no ; no more than reason.
Beat. Why, then my cousin, Margaret, and Ursula
    Are much deceived ; for they did swear you did.
Bene. They swore that you were almost sick for me.
Beat. They swore that you were well-nigh dead for me.
Bene. 'Tis no such matter. Then you do not love me ?
Beat. No, truly, but in friendly recompence.
Leon. Come, cousin, I am sure you love the gentleman.
Claud. And I 'll be sworn upon 't that he loves her ;
    For here 's a paper, written in his hand,
    A halting sonnet of his own pure brain,
    Fashion'd to Beatrice.
Hero.   And here 's another,
    Writ in my cousin's hand, stolen from her pocket,
    Containing her affection unto Benedick.
Bene. A miracle ! here 's our own hands against our hearts.
    Come, I will have thee ; but, by this light, I take thee for pity.
Beat. I would not deny you ; but, by this good day, I yield
    upon great persuasion ; and partly to save your life, for I
    was told you were in a consumption.
Bene. Peace ! I will stop your mouth.   [*Kissing her.*
D. Pedro. How dost thou, Benedick, the married man ?
Bene. I 'll tell thee what, prince ; a college of wit-crackers

cannot flout me out of my humour.   Dost thou think I care
for a satire or an epigram?   No: if a man will be beaten with
brains, a' shall wear nothing handsome about him.   In brief,
since I do purpose to marry, I will think nothing to any
purpose that the world can say against it ; and therefore never
flout at me for what I have said against it ; for man is a giddy
thing, and this is my conclusion.   For thy part, Claudio, I
did think to have beaten thee ; but in that thou art like to
be my kinsman, live unbruised, and love my cousin.

Claud. I had well hoped thou wouldst have denied Beatrice,
that I might have cudgelled thee out of thy single life, to
make thee a double-dealer ; which, out of question, thou wilt
be, if my cousin do not look exceeding narrowly to thee.

Bene. Come, come, we are friends : let 's have a dance ere we
are married, that we may lighten our own hearts, and our

Leon. We 'll have dancing afterward.   [wives' heels.

Bene. First, of my word ; therefore play, music.   Prince, thou
art sad ; get thee a wife, get thee a wife: there is no staff
more reverend than one tipped with horn.

Enter a Messenger.

Mess. My lord, your brother John is ta'en in flight,
And brought with armed men back to Messina.

Bene. Think not on him till to-morrow : I 'll devise thee brave
punishments for him.   Strike up, pipers. [*Dance. Exeunt.*

TWELFTH NIGHT; OR, WHAT YOU WILL

DRAMATIS PERSONÆ

ORSINO, *Duke of Illyria.*
SEBASTIAN, *brother to Viola.*
ANTONIO, *a sea captain, friend to Sebastian.*
A Sea Captain, *friend to Viola.*
VALENTINE, } *gentlemen attending on the*
CURIO, } *Duke.*
SIR TOBY BELCH, *uncle to Olivia.*

SIR ANDREW AGUECHEEK.
MALVOLIO, *steward to Olivia.*
FABIAN, } *servants to Olivia.*
FESTE, *a clown,* }
OLIVIA.
VIOLA.
MARIA, *Olivia's woman.*

Lords, Priests, Sailors, Officers, Musicians, and other Attendants.
SCENE : *A city in Illyria, and the sea-coast near it.*

ACT I—SCENE I

An apartment in the Duke's palace.
Enter Duke, Curio, and other Lords ; Musicians attending.

Duke. If music be the food of love, play on ;
    Give me excess of it, that, surfeiting,
    The appetite may sicken, and so die.
    That strain again ! it had a dying fall :
    O, it came o'er my ear like the sweet sound,
    That breathes upon a bank of violets,
    Stealing and giving odour !   Enough ; no more .
    'Tis not so sweet now as it was before.
    O spirit of love, how quick and fresh art thou !
    That, notwithstanding thy capacity
    Receiveth as the sea, nought enters there.
    Of what validity and pitch soe'er,
    But falls into abatement and low price,
    Even in a minute ! so full of shapes is fancy,
    That it alone is high fantastical.

Cur. Will you go hunt, my lord ?
Duke.   What, Curio ?
Cur. The hart.
Duke. Why, so I do, the noblest that I have :
    O, when mine eyes did see Olivia first,
    Methought she purged the air of pestilence !
    That instant was I turn'd into a hart ;
    And my desires, like fell and cruel hounds,
    E'er since pursue me.

                Enter Valentine.
              How now ! what news from her ?

Val. So please my lord, I might not be admitted ;
    But from her handmaid do return this answer :
    The element itself, till seven years' heat,
    Shall not behold her face at ample view ;

But, like a cloistress, she will veiled walk
And water once a day her chamber round
With eye-offending brine: all this to season
A brother's dead love, which she would keep fresh
And lasting in her sad remembrance.

Duke. O, she that hath a heart of that fine frame
To pay this debt of love but to a brother,
How will she love, when the rich golden shaft
Hath kill'd the flock of all affections else
That live in her; when liver, brain and heart,
These sovereign thrones, are all supplied, and fill'd
Her sweet perfections with one self king!
Away before me to sweet beds of flowers:
Love-thoughts lie rich when canopied with bowers. [*Exeunt.*

SCENE II

The sea-coast.
Enter Viola, a Captain, and Sailors.

Vio. What country, friends, is this?
Cap. This is Illyria, lady.
Vio. And what should I do in Illyria?
My brother he is in Elysium.
Perchance he is not drown'd: what think you, sailors?
Cap. It is perchance that you yourself were saved.
Vio. O my poor brother! and so perchance may he be.
Cap. True, madam: and, to comfort you with chance,
Assure yourself, after our ship did split,
When you and those poor number saved with you
Hung on our driving boat, I saw your brother,
Most provident in peril, bind himself,
Courage and hope both teaching him the practice,
To a strong mast that lived upon the sea;
Where, like Arion on the dolphin's back,
I saw him hold acquaintance with the waves
So long as I could see.
Vio. For saying so, there's gold:
Mine own escape unfoldeth to my hope,
Whereto thy speech serves for authority,
The like of him. Know'st thou this country?
Cap. Ay, madam, well; for I was bred and born
Not three hours' travel from this very place.
Vio. Who governs here?
Cap. A noble Duke, in nature as in name.
Vio. What is his name?
Cap. Orsino.

363

Vio. Orsino! I have heard my father name him:
   He was a bachelor then.
Cap. And so is now, or was so very late;
   For but a month ago I went from hence,
   And then 'twas fresh in murmur,—as, you know,
   What great ones do the less will prattle of,—
   That he did seek the love of fair Olivia.
Vio. What 's she?
Cap. A virtuous maid, the daughter of a count
   That died some twelvemonth since; then leaving her
   In the protection of his son, her brother,
   Who shortly also died: for whose dear love,
   They say, she hath abjured the company
   And sight of men.
Vio.   O that I served that lady,
   And might not be delivered to the world,
   Till I had made mine own occasion mellow,
   What my estate is!
Cap.   That were hard to compass;
   Because she will admit no kind of suit,
   No, not the Duke's.
Vio. There is a fair behaviour in thee, captain;
   And though that nature with a beauteous wall
   Doth oft close in pollution, yet of thee
   I will believe thou hast a mind that suits
   With this thy fair and outward character.
   I prithee, and I 'll pay thee bounteously,
   Conceal me what I am, and be my aid
   For such disguise as haply shall become
   The form of my intent.   I 'll serve this Duke:
   Thou shalt present me as an eunuch to him:
   It may be worth thy pains; for I can sing,
   And speak to him in many sorts of music,
   That will allow me very worth his service.
   What else may hap to time I will commit;
   Only shape thou thy silence to my wit.
Cap. Be you his eunuch, and your mute I 'll be:
   When my tongue blabs, then let mine eyes not see.
Vio. I thank thee: lead me on.   [*Exeunt.*

Scene III

Olivia's house.
Enter Sir Toby Belch and Maria.

Sir To. What a plague means my niece, to take the death of
  her brother thus?   I am sure care 's an enemy to life.

Mar. By my troth, Sir Toby, you must come in earlier o' nights : your cousin, my lady, takes great exceptions to your ill hours.

Sir To. Why, let her except, before excepted.

Mar. Ay, but you must confine yourself within the modest limits of order.

Sir To. Confine ! I 'll confine myself no finer than I am : these clothes are good enough to drink in ; and so be these boots too : an they be not, let them hang themselves in their own straps.

Mar. That quaffing and drinking will undo you : I heard my lady talk of it yesterday ; and of a foolish knight that you brought in one night here to be her wooer.

Sir To. Who, Sir Andrew Aguecheek ?

Mar. Ay, he.

Sir To. He 's as tall a man as any 's in Illyria.

Mar. What 's that to the purpose?

Sir To. Why, he has three thousand ducats a year.

Mar. Ay, but he 'll have but a year in all these ducats : he 's a very fool and a prodigal.

Sir To. Fie, that you 'll say so ! he plays o' the viol-de-gamboys, and speaks three or four languages word for word without book, and hath all the good gifts of nature.

Mar. He hath indeed, almost natural : for besides that he 's a fool, he 's a great quarreller ; and but that he hath the gift of a coward to allay the gust he hath in quarrelling, 'tis thought among the prudent he would quickly have the gift of a grave.

Sir To. By this hand, they are scoundrels and subtractors that say so of him. Who are they ?

Mar. They that add, moreover, he 's drunk nightly in your company.

Sir To. With drinking healths to my niece : I 'll drink to her as long as there is a passage in my throat and drink in Illyria : he 's a coward and a coystrill that will not drink to my niece till his brains turn o' the toe like a parish-top. What, wench ! Castiliano vulgo ; for here comes Sir Andrew Agueface.

Enter Sir Andrew Aguecheek.

Sir And. Sir Toby Belch ! how now, Sir Toby Belch !

Sir To. Sweet Sir Andrew !

Sir And. Bless you, fair shrew.

Mar. And you too, sir.

Sir To. Accost, Sir Andrew, accost.

Sir And. What 's that ?

Sir To. My niece's chambermaid.

Sir And. Good Mistress Accost, I desire better acquaintance.

Mar. My name is Mary, sir.

Sir And. Good Mistress Mary Accost,—

Sir To. You mistake, knight: 'accost' is front her, board her, woo her, assail her.

Sir And. By my troth, I would not undertake her in this company. Is that the meaning of 'accost'?

Mar. Fare you well, gentlemen.

Sir To. An thou let part so, Sir Andrew, would thou mightst never draw sword again.

Sir And. An you part so, mistress, I would I might never draw sword again. Fair lady, do you think you have fools in

Mar. Sir, I have not you by the hand.   [hand?

Sir And. Marry, but you shall have; and here's my hand.

Mar. Now, sir, 'thought is free': I pray you, bring your hand to the buttery-bar and let it drink.

Sir And. Wherefore, sweet-heart? what's your metaphor?

Mar. It's dry, sir.

Sir And. Why, I think so: I am not such an ass but I can keep my hand dry. But what's your jest?

Mar. A dry jest, sir.

Sir And. Are you full of them?

Mar. Ay, sir, I have them at my fingers' ends: marry, now I let go your hand, I am barren.   [*Exit.*

Sir To. O knight, thou lackest a cup of canary: when did I see thee so put down?

Sir And. Never in your life, I think; unless you see canary put me down. Methinks sometimes I have no more wit than a Christian or an ordinary man has: but I am a great eater of beef, and I believe that does harm to my wit.

Sir To. No question.

Sir And. An I thought that, I'ld forswear it. I'll ride home to-morrow, Sir Toby.

Sir To. Pourquoi, my dear knight?

Sir And. What is 'pourquoi'? do or not do? I would I had bestowed that time in the tongues that I have in fencing, dancing and bear-baiting: O, had I but followed the arts!

Sir To. Then hadst thou had an excellent head of hair.

Sir And. Why, would that have mended my hair?

Sir To. Past question; for thou seest it will not curl by nature.

Sir And. But it becomes me well enough, does't not?

Sir To. Excellent; it hangs like flax on a distaff; and I hope to see a housewife take thee between her legs and spin it off.

Sir And. Faith, I'll home to-morrow, Sir Toby: your niece

366

will not be seen; or if she be, it's four to one she'll none
of me: the count himself here hard by woos her.

Sir To. She'll none o' the count: she'll not match above her
degree, neither in estate, years, nor wit; I have heard her
swear 't. Tut, there's life in 't, man.

Sir And. I'll stay a month longer. I am a fellow o' the
strangest mind i' the world; I delight in masques and revels
sometimes altogether.

Sir To. Art thou good at these kickshawses, knight?

Sir And. As any man in Illyria, whatsoever he be, under the
degree of my betters; and yet I will not compare with an
old man.

Sir To. What is thy excellence in a galliard, knight?

Sir And. Faith, I can cut a caper.

Sir To. And I can cut the mutton to 't.

Sir And. And I think I have the back-trick simply as strong
as any man in Illyria.

Sir To. Wherefore are these things hid? wherefore have these
gifts a curtain before 'em? are they like to take dust, like
Mistress Mall's picture? why dost thou not go to church in
a galliard and come home in a coranto? My very walk
should be a jig; I would not so much as make water but in
a sink-a-pace. What dost thou mean? Is it a world to
hide virtues in? I did think, by the excellent constitution
of thy leg, it was formed under the star of a galliard.

Sir And. Ay, 'tis strong, and it does indifferent well in a flame-
coloured stock. Shall we set about some revels?

Sir To. What shall we do else? were we not born under

Sir And. Taurus! That's sides and heart.   [Taurus?

Sir To. No, sir; it is legs and thighs. Let me see thee caper:
ha! higher: ha, ha! excellent!   [*Exeunt.*

Scene IV
The Duke's palace.
Enter Valentine, and Viola in man's attire.

Val. If the Duke continue these favours towards you, Cesario,
you are like to be much advanced: he hath known you but
three days, and already you are no stranger.

Vio. You either fear his humour or my negligence, that you
call in question the continuance of his love: is he inconstant,
sir, in his favours?

Val. No, believe me.

Vio. I thank you. Here comes the count.

Enter Duke, Curio, and Attendants.

Duke. Who saw Cesario, ho?

Vio. On your attendance, my lord; here.

Duke. Stand you a while aloof.   Cesario,
   Thou know'st no less but all; I have unclasp'd
   To thee the book even of my secret soul:
   Therefore, good youth, address thy gait unto her;
   Be not denied access, stand at her doors,
   And tell them, there thy fixed foot shall grow
   Till thou have audience.

Vio.   Sure, my noble lord,
   If she be so abandon'd to her sorrow
   As it is spoke, she never will admit me.

Duke. Be clamorous and leap all civil bounds
   Rather than make unprofited return.

Vio. Say I do speak with her, my lord, what then?

Duke. O, then unfold the passion of my love,
   Surprise her with discourse of my dear faith:
   It shall become thee well to act my woes;
   She will attend it better in thy youth
   Than in a nuncio's of more grave aspect.

Vio. I think not so, my lord.

Duke.   Dear lad, believe it;
   For they shall yet belie thy happy years,
   That say thou art a man: Diana's lip
   Is not more smooth and rubious; thy small pipe
   Is as the maiden's organ, shrill and sound;
   And all is semblative a woman's part.
   I know thy constellation is right apt
   For this affair.   Some four or five attend him;
   All, if you will; for I myself am best
   When least in company.   Prosper well in this,
   And thou shalt live as freely as thy lord,
   To call his fortunes thine.

Vio.   I'll do my best
   To woo your lady: [*Aside*] yet, a barful strife!
   Whoe'er I woo, myself would be his wife.   [*Exeunt.*

SCENE V

Olivia's house.
Enter Maria and Clown.

Mar. Nay, either tell me where thou hast been, or I will not
   open my lips so wide as a bristle may enter in way of thy
   excuse: my lady will hang thee for thy absence.

Clo. Let her hang me: he that is well hanged in this world
   needs to fear no colours.

Mar. Make that good.

Clo. He shall see none to fear.

Mar. A good lenten answer: I can tell thee where that saying was born, of 'I fear no colours.'

Clo. Where, good Mistress Mary?

Mar. In the wars; and that may you be bold to say in your foolery.

Clo. Well, God give them wisdom that have it; and those that are fools, let them use their talents.

Mar. Yet you will be hanged for being so long absent; or, to be turned away, is not that as good as a hanging to you?

Clo. Many a good hanging prevents a bad marriage; and, for turning away, let summer bear it out.

Mar. You are resolute, then?

Clo. Not so, neither; but I am resolved on two points.

Mar. That if one break, the other will hold; or, if both break, your gaskins fall.

Clo. Apt, in good faith; very apt. Well, go thy way; if Sir Toby would leave drinking, thou wert as witty a piece of Eve's flesh as any in Illyria.

Mar. Peace, you rogue, no more o' that. Here comes my lady: make your excuse wisely, you were best.   [*Exit.*

Clo. Wit, an't be thy will, put me into good fooling! Those wits, that think they have thee, do very oft prove fools; and I, that am sure I lack thee, may pass for a wise man: for what says Quinapalus? 'Better a witty fool than a foolish wit.'

Enter Lady Olivia with Malvolio.

God bless thee, lady!

Oli. Take the fool away.

Clo. Do you not hear, fellows? Take away the lady.

Oli. Go to, you're a dry fool; I'll no more of you: besides, you grow dishonest.

Clo. Two faults, madonna, that drink and good counsel will amend: for give the dry fool drink, then is the fool not dry: bid the dishonest man mend himself; if he mend, he is no longer dishonest; if he cannot, let the botcher mend him. Any thing that's mended is but patched: virtue that transgresses is but patched with sin; and sin that amends is but patched with virtue. If that this simple syllogism will serve, so; if it will not, what remedy? As there is no true cuckold but calamity, so beauty's a flower. The lady bade take away the fool; therefore, I say again, take her away.

Oli. Sir, I bade them take away you.

Clo. Misprision in the highest degree! Lady, cucullus non

facit monachum; that's as much to say as I wear not motley in my brain. Good madonna, give me leave to prove you a fool.

Oli. Can you do it?

Clo. Dexteriously, good madonna.

Oli. Make your proof.

Clo. I must catechize you for it, madonna: good my mouse of virtue, answer me.

Oli. Well, sir, for want of other idleness, I'll bide your proof.

Clo. Good madonna, why mournest thou?

Oli. Good fool, for my brother's death.

Clo. I think his soul is in hell, madonna.

Oli. I know his soul is in heaven, fool.

Clo. The more fool, madonna, to mourn for your brother's soul being in heaven. Take away the fool, gentlemen.

Oli. What think you of this fool, Malvolio? doth he not mend?

Mal. Yes, and shall do till the pangs of death shake him: infirmity, that decays the wise, doth ever make the better fool.

Clo. God send you, sir, a speedy infirmity, for the better increasing your folly! Sir Toby will be sworn that I am no fox; but he will not pass his word for two pence that you

Oli. How say you to that, Malvolio?   [are no fool.

Mal. I marvel your ladyship takes delight in such a barren rascal: I saw him put down the other day with an ordinary fool that has no more brain than a stone. Look you now, he's out of his guard already; unless you laugh and minister occasion to him, he is gagged. I protest, I take these wise men, that crow so at these set kind of fools, no better than the fools' zanies.

Oli. O, you are sick of self-love, Malvolio, and taste with a distempered appetite. To be generous, guiltless and of free disposition, is to take those things for bird-bolts that you deem cannon-bullets: there is no slander in an allowed fool, though he do nothing but rail; nor no railing in a known discreet man, though he do nothing but reprove.

Clo. Now Mercury endue thee with leasing, for thou speakest well of fools!

Re-enter Maria.

Mar. Madam, there is at the gate a young gentleman much desires to speak with you.

Oli. From the Count Orsino, is it?

Mar. I know not, madam: 'tis a fair young man, and well

Oli. Who of my people hold him in delay?   [attended.

Mar. Sir Toby, madam, your kinsman.

Oli. Fetch him off, I pray you ; he speaks nothing but madman :
fie on him ! [*Exit Maria.*]   Go you, Malvolio : if it be a
suit from the count, I am sick, or not at home ; what you
will, to dismiss it. [*Exit Malvolio.*]   Now you see, sir, how
your fooling grows old, and people dislike it.

Clo. Thou hast spoke for us, madonna, as if thy eldest son
should be a fool ; whose skull Jove cram with brains ! for,
—here he comes,—one of thy kin has a most weak pia mater

Enter Sir Toby.

Oli. By mine honour, half drunk.   What is he at the gate,

Sir To. A gentleman.   [cousin ?

Oli. A gentleman ! what gentleman ?

Sir To. 'Tis a gentleman here—a plague o' these pickle-herring !
How now, sot !

Clo. Good Sir Toby !

Oli. Cousin, cousin, how have you come so early by this lethargy ?

Sir To. Lechery ! I defy lechery.   There 's one at the gate.

Oli. Ay, marry, what is he ?

Sir To. Let him be the devil, an he will, I care not : give me
faith, say I.   Well, it 's all one.   [*Exit.*

Oli. What 's a drunken man like, fool ?

Clo. Like a drowned man, a fool and a mad man : one draught
above heat makes him a fool ; the second mads him ; and a
third drowns him.

Oli. Go thou and seek the crowner, and let him sit o' my coz ;
for he 's in the third degree of drink, he 's drowned : go look
after him.

Clo. He is but mad yet, madonna ; and the fool shall look to
the madman.   [*Exit.*

Re-enter Malvolio.

Mal. Madam, yond young fellow swears he will speak with you.
I told him you were sick ; he takes on him to understand so
much, and therefore comes to speak with you.   I told him
you were asleep ; he seems to have a foreknowledge of that
too, and therefore comes to speak with you.   What is to be
said to him, lady ? he 's fortified against any denial.

Oli. Tell him he shall not speak with me.

Mal. Has been told so ; and he says, he 'll stand at your door
like a sheriff's post, and be the supporter to a bench, but
he 'll speak with you.

Oli. What kind o' man is he ?

Mal. Why, of mankind.

Oli. What manner of man ?

Mal. Of very ill manner : he 'll speak with you, will you or no.

Oli. Of what personage and years is he?

Mal. Not yet old enough for a man, nor young enough for a boy; as a squash is before 'tis a peascod, or a codling when 'tis almost an apple: 'tis with him in standing water, between boy and man. He is very well-favoured and he speaks very shrewishly; one would think his mother's milk were scarce out of him.

Oli. Let him approach: call in my gentlewoman.

Mal. Gentlewoman, my lady calls.   [*Exit.*

Re-enter Maria.

Oli. Give me my veil: come, throw it o'er my face. We'll once more hear Orsino's embassy.

Enter Viola, and Attendants.

Vio. The honourable lady of the house, which is she?

Oli. Speak to me; I shall answer for her. Your will?

Vio. Most radiant, exquisite and unmatchable beauty,—I pray you, tell me if this be the lady of the house, for I never saw her: I would be loath to cast away my speech, for besides that it is excellently well penned, I have taken great pains to con it. Good beauties, let me sustain no scorn; I am very comptible, even to the least sinister usage.

Oli. Whence came you, sir?

Vio. I can say little more than I have studied, and that question's out of my part. Good gentle one, give me modest assurance if you be the lady of the house, that I may proceed in my

Oli. Are you a comedian?   [speech.

Vio. No, my profound heart: and yet, by the very fangs of malice I swear, I am not that I play. Are you the lady of

Oli. If I do not usurp myself, I am.   [the house?

Vio. Most certain, if you are she, you do usurp yourself; for what is yours to bestow is not yours to reserve. But this is from my commission: I will on with my speech in your praise, and then show you the heart of my message.

Oli. Come to what is important in 't: I forgive you the praise.

Vio. Alas, I took great pains to study it, and 'tis poetical.

Oli. It is the more like to be feigned. I pray you, keep it in. I heard you were saucy at my gates, and allowed your approach rather to wonder at you than to hear you. If you be not mad, be gone; if you have reason, be brief: 'tis not that time of moon with me to make one in so skipping a dialogue.

Mar. Will you hoist sail, sir? here lies your way.

Vio. No, good swabber; I am to hull here a little longer. Some mollification for your giant, sweet lady. Tell me your mind: I am a messenger.

Oli. Sure, you have some hideous matter to deliver, when the
courtesy of it is so fearful.   Speak your office.

Vio. It alone concerns your ear.   I bring no overture of war,
no taxation of homage: I hold the olive in my hand; my
words are as full of peace as matter.

Oli. Yet you began rudely.   What are you? what would you?

Vio. The rudeness that hath appeared in me have I learned
from my entertainment.   What I am, and what I would, are
as secret as maidenhead; to your ears, divinity, to any
other's, profanation.

Oli. Give us the place alone: we will hear this divinity.
[*Exeunt Maria and Attendants.*]   Now, sir, what is your text?

Vio. Most sweet lady,—

Oli. A comfortable doctrine, and much may be said of it.
Where lies your text?

Vio. In Orsino's bosom.

Oli. In his bosom!   In what chapter of his bosom?

Vio. To answer by the method, in the first of his heart.

Oli. O, I have read it: it is heresy.   Have you no more to say?

Vio. Good madam, let me see your face.

Oli. Have you any commission from your lord to negotiate
with my face?   You are now out of your text: but we will
draw the curtain and show you the picture.   Look you, sir,
such a one I was this present: is 't not well done?

[*Unveiling.*

Vio. Excellently done, if God did all.

Oli. 'Tis in grain, sir; 'twill endure wind and weather.

Vio. 'Tis beauty truly blent, whose red and white
Nature's own sweet and cunning hand laid on:
Lady, you are the cruell'st she alive,
If you will lead these graces to the grave
And leave the world no copy.

Oli. O, sir, I will not be so hard-hearted; I will give out divers
schedules of my beauty: it shall be inventoried, and every
particle and utensil labelled to my will: as, item, two lips,
indifferent red; item, two grey eyes, with lids to them; item,
one neck, one chin, and so forth.   Were you sent hither to
praise me?

Vio. I see you what you are, you are too proud;
But, if you were the devil, you are fair.
My lord and master loves you: O, such love
Could be but recompensed, though you were crown'd
The nonpareil of beauty!

Oli.   How does he love me?

Vio. With adorations, fertile tears,

With groans that thunder love, with sighs of fire.

Oli. Your lord does know my mind ; I cannot love him :
Yet I suppose him virtuous, know him noble,
Of great estate, of fresh and stainless youth ;
In voices well divulged, free, learn'd and valiant
And in dimension and the shape of nature
A gracious person : but yet I cannot love him ;
He might have took his answer long ago.

Vio. If I did love you in my master's flame,
With such a suffering, such a deadly life,
In your denial I would find no sense ;
I would not understand it.

Oli.   Why, what would you?

Vio. Make me a willow cabin at your gate,
And call upon my soul within the house ;
Write loyal cantons of contemned love
And sing them loud even in the dead of night ;
Halloo your name to the reverberate hills,
And make the babbling gossip of the air
Cry out 'Olivia !' O, you should not rest
Between the elements of air and earth,
But you should pity me !

Oli.   You might do much.
What is your parentage ?

Vio. Above my fortunes, yet my state is well :
I am a gentleman.

Oli.   Get you to your lord ;
I cannot love him : let him send no more ;
Unless, perchance, you come to me again,
To tell me how he takes it. Fare you well :
I thank you for your pains : spend this for me.

Vio. I am no fee'd post, lady ; keep your purse :
My master, not myself, lacks recompense.
Love make his heart of flint, that you shall love ;
And let your fervour, like my master's, be
Placed in contempt ! Farewell, fair cruelty.   [*Exit.*

Oli. 'What is your parentage ?'
'Above my fortunes, yet my state is well :
I am a gentleman.' I 'll be sworn thou art ;
Thy tongue, thy face, thy limbs, actions, and spirit,
Do give thee five-fold blazon : not too fast : soft, soft !
Unless the master were the man. How now !
Even so quickly may one catch the plague ?
Methinks I feel this youth's perfections
With an invisible and subtle stealth

To creep in at mine eyes.   Well, let it be.
What ho, Malvolio!
                        Re-enter Malvolio.
Mal.   Here, madam, at your service.
Oli. Run after that same peevish messenger,
    The county's man: he left this ring behind him,
    Would I or not: tell him I'll none of it.
    Desire him not to flatter with his lord,
    Nor hold him up with hopes; I am not for him:
    If that the youth will come this way to-morrow,
    I'll give him reasons for 't: hie thee, Malvolio.
Mal. Madam, I will.   [*Exit.*
Oli. I do I know not what, and fear to find
    Mine eye too great a flatterer for my mind.
    Fate, show thy force: ourselves we do not owe;
    What is decreed must be, and be this so.   [*Exit.*

ACT II—Scene I
The sea-coast.
Enter Antonio and Sebastian.

Ant. Will you stay no longer? nor will you not that I go with
    you?
Seb. By your patience, no.   My stars shine darkly over me:
    the malignancy of my fate might perhaps distemper yours;
    therefore I shall crave of you your leave that I may bear my
    evils alone: it were a bad recompense for your love, to lay
    any of them on you.
Ant. Let me yet know of you whither you are bound.
Seb. No, sooth, sir: my determinate voyage is mere extrava-
    gancy. But I perceive in you so excellent a touch of modesty,
    that you will not extort from me what I am willing to keep
    in; therefore it charges me in manners the rather to express
    myself. You must know of me then, Antonio, my name is
    Sebastian, which I called Roderigo. My father was that
    Sebastian of Messaline, whom I know you have heard of.
    He left behind him myself and a sister, both born in an
    hour: if the heavens had been pleased, would we had so
    ended! but you, sir, altered that; for some hour before you
    took me from the breach of the sea was my sister drowned.
Ant. Alas the day!
Seb. A lady, sir, though it was said she much resembled me,
    was yet of many accounted beautiful: but, though I could
    not with such estimable wonder overfar believe that, yet
    thus far I will boldly publish her; she bore a mind that

envy could not but call fair. She is drowned already, sir,
with salt water, though I seem to drown her remembrance
again with more.

Ant. Pardon me, sir, your bad entertainment.

Seb. O good Antonio, forgive me your trouble.   [servant.

Ant. If you will not murder me for my love, let me be your

Seb. If you will not undo what you have done, that is, kill him
whom you have recovered, desire it not. Fare ye well at
once : my bosom is full of kindness, and I am yet so near
the manners of my mother, that upon the least occasion
more mine eyes will tell tales of me. I am bound to the
Count Orsino's court : farewell.   [*Exit.*

Ant. The gentleness of all the gods go with thee !
  I have many enemies in Orsino's court,
  Else would I very shortly see thee there.
  But, come what may, I do adore thee so,
  That danger shall seem sport, and I will go.   *Exit.*

SCENE II

A street.

Enter Viola, Malvolio following.

Mal. Were not you even now with the Countess Olivia ?

Vio. Even now, sir ; on a moderate pace I have since arrived
but hither.

Mal. She returns this ring to you, sir : you might have saved
me my pains, to have taken it away yourself. She adds,
moreover, that you should put your lord into a desperate
assurance she will none of him : and one thing more, that
you be never so hardy to come again in his affairs, unless it
be to report your lord's taking of this. Receive it so.

Vio. She took the ring of me : I 'll none of it.

Mal. Come, sir, you peevishly threw it to her ; and her will is,
it should be so returned : if it be worth stooping for, there it
lies in your eye ; if not, be it his that finds it.   [*Exit.*

Vio. I left no ring with her : what means this lady ?
  Fortune forbid my outside have not charm'd her !
  She made good view of me ; indeed, so much,
  That methought her eyes had lost her tongue,
  For she did speak in starts distractedly.
  She loves me, sure ; the cunning of her passion
  Invites me in this churlish messenger.
  None of my lord's ring ! why, he sent her none.
  I am the man : if it be so, as 'tis,
  Poor lady, she were better love a dream.
  Disguise, I see, thou art a wickedness,

Wherein the pregnant enemy does much.
How easy is it for the proper-false
In women's waxen hearts to set their forms!
Alas, our frailty is the cause, not we!
For such as we are made of, such we be.
How will this fadge? my master loves her dearly;
And I, poor monster, fond as much on him;
And she, mistaken, seems to dote on me.
What will become of this?   As I am man,
My state is desperate for my master's love;
As I am woman—now alas the day!—
What thriftless sighs shall poor Olivia breathe!
O time! thou must untangle this, not I;
It is too hard a knot for me to untie!   [*Exit.*

SCENE III
Olivia's house.
Enter Sir Toby and Sir Andrew.

Sir To. Approach, Sir Andrew: not to be a-bed after midnight is to be up betimes; and 'diluculo surgere,' thou know'st,—

Sir And. Nay, by my troth, I know not: but I know, to be up late is to be up late.

Sir To. A false conclusion: I hate it as an unfilled can.   To be up after midnight and to go to bed then, is early: so that to go to bed after midnight is to go to bed betimes.   Does not our life consist of the four elements?

Sir And. Faith, so they say; but I think it rather consists of eating and drinking.

Sir To. Thou'rt a scholar; let us therefore eat and drink. Marian, I say! a stoup of wine!

Enter Clown.

Sir And. Here comes the fool, i' faith.

Clo. How now, my hearts! did you never see the picture of 'we three'?

Sir To. Welcome, ass.   Now let's have a catch.

Sir And. By my troth, the fool has an excellent breast.   I had rather than forty shillings I had such a leg, and so sweet a breath to sing, as the fool has.   In sooth, thou wast in very gracious fooling last night, when thou spokest of Pigrogromitus, of the Vapians passing the equinoctial of Queubus: 'twas very good, i' faith.   I sent thee sixpence for thy leman: hadst it?

Clo. I did impeticos thy gratillity; for Malvolio's nose is no

377

whipstock : my lady has a white hand, and the Myrmidons
are no bottle-ale houses.

Sir And. Excellent! why, this is the best fooling, when all is
  done. Now, a song.

Sir To. Come on ; there is sixpence for you : let 's have a song.

Sir And. There 's a testril of me too : if one knight give a—

Clo. Would you have a love-song, or a song of good life ?

Sir To. A love-song, a love-song.

Sir And. Ay, ay : I care not for good life.

Clo. [*Sings*]

> O mistress mine, where are you roaming ?
> O, stay and hear ; your true love 's coming,
> That can sing both high and low :
> Trip no further, pretty sweeting ;
> Journeys end in lovers meeting,
> Every wise man's son doth know.

Sir And. Excellent good, i' faith.

Sir To. Good, good.

Clo. [*Sings*]

> What is love ? 'tis not hereafter ;
> Present mirth hath present laughter ;
> What 's to come is still unsure :
> In delay there lies no plenty,
> Then come kiss me, sweet and twenty,
> Youth 's a stuff will not endure.

Sir And. A mellifluous voice, as I am true knight.

Sir To. A contagious breath.

Sir And. Very sweet and contagious, i' faith.

Sir To. To hear by the nose, it is dulcet in contagion. But
  shall we make the welkin dance indeed ? shall we rouse the
  night-owl in a catch that will draw three souls out of one
  weaver ? shall we do that ?

Sir And. An you love me, let 's do 't : I am dog at a catch.

Clo. By 'r lady, sir, and some dogs will catch well.

Sir And. Most certain. Let our catch be, 'Thou knave.'

Clo. 'Hold thy peace, thou knave,' knight ? I shall be constrained in 't to call thee knave, knight.

Sir And. 'Tis not the first time I have constrained one to call
  me knave. Begin, fool : it begins 'Hold thy peace.'

Clo. I shall never begin if I hold my peace.

Sir And. Good, i' faith. Come, begin.   [*Catch sung.*

Enter Maria.

Mar. What a caterwauling do you keep here ! If my lady
  have not called up her steward Malvolio and bid him turn
  you out of doors, never trust me.

Sir To. My lady's a Cataian, we are politicians, Malvolio's a
Peg-a-Ramsey, and 'Three merry men be we.' Am not I
consanguineous ? am I not of her blood ? Tillyvally.   Lady !
[*Sings*] 'There dwelt a man in Babylon, lady, lady !'

Clo. Beshrew me, the knight's in admirable fooling.

Sir And. Ay, he does well enough if he be disposed, and so
do I too : he does it with a better grace, but I do it more
natural.

Sir To. [*Sings*]   'O, the twelfth day of December,'—

Mar. For the love o' God, peace !

Enter Malvolio.

Mal. My masters, are you mad ? or what are you ? Have you
no wit, manners, nor honesty, but to gabble like tinkers at
this time of night ? Do ye make an alehouse of my lady's
house, that ye squeak out your coziers' catches without any
mitigation or remorse of voice ? Is there no respect of place,
persons, nor time in you ?

Sir To. We did keep time, sir, in our catches. Sneck up !

Mal. Sir Toby, I must be round with you. My lady bade me
tell you, that, though she harbours you as her kinsman, she's
nothing allied to your disorders. If you can separate yourself
and your misdemeanours, you are welcome to the house ; if
not, an it would please you to take leave of her, she is very
willing to bid you farewell.

Sir To. 'Farewell, dear heart, since I must needs be gone.'

Mar. Nay, good Sir Toby.

Clo. 'His eyes do show his days are almost done.'

Mal. Is 't even so ?

Sir To. 'But I will never die.'

Clo. Sir Toby, there you lie.

Mal. This is much credit to you.

Sir To. 'Shall I bid him go ?'

Clo. 'What an if you do ?'

Sir To. 'Shall I bid him go, and spare not ?'

Clo. 'O no, no, no, no, you dare not.'

Sir To. Out o' tune, sir : ye lie.   Art any more than a steward ?
Dost thou think, because thou art virtuous, there shall be no
more cakes and ale ?

Clo. Yes, by Saint Anne, and ginger shall be hot i' the
mouth too.

Sir To. Thou 'rt i' the right.   Go, sir, rub your chain with
crums.   A soup of wine, Marie !

Mal. Mistress Mary, if you prized my lady's favour at any thing
more than contempt, you would not give means for this
uncivil rule : she shall know of it, by this hand.   [*Exit.*

Mar. Go shake your ears.

Sir And. 'Twere as good a deed as to drink when a man's
a-hungry, to challenge him the field, and then to break
promise with him and make a fool of him.

Sir To. Do 't, knight : I 'll write thee a challenge ; or I 'll
deliver thy indignation to him by word of mouth.

Mar. Sweet Sir Toby, be patient for to-night : since the youth
of the count's was to-day with my lady, she is much out of
quiet. For Monsieur Malvolio, let me alone with him : if I
do not gull him into a nayword, and make him a common
recreation, do not think I have wit enough to lie straight in
my bed : I know I can do it.

Sir To. Possess us, possess us ; tell us something of him.

Mar. Marry, sir, sometimes he is a kind of puritan.

Sir And. O, if I thought that, I 'ld beat him like a dog !

Sir To. What, for being a puritan ? thy exquisite reason, dear
knight ?

Sir And. I have no exquisite reason for 't, but I have reason
good enough.

Mar. The devil a puritan that he is, or any thing constantly,
but a time-pleaser ; an affectioned ass, that cons state without
book and utters it by great swarths : the best persuaded of
himself, so crammed, as he thinks, with excellencies, that it
is his grounds of faith that all that look on him love him ;
and on that vice in him will my revenge find notable cause

Sir To. What wilt thou do?   [to work.

Mar. I will drop in his way some obscure epistles of love ;
wherein, by the colour of his beard, the shape of his leg, the
manner of his gait, the expressure of his eye, forehead, and
complexion, he shall find himself most feelingly personated.
I can write very like my lady your niece : on a forgotten
matter we can hardly make distinction of our hands.

Sir To. Excellent ! I smell a device.

Sir And. I have 't in my nose too.

Sir To. He shall think, by the letters that thou wilt drop, that
they come from my niece, and that she 's in love with him.

Mar. My purpose is, indeed, a horse of that colour.

Sir And. And your horse now would make him an ass.

Mar. Ass, I doubt not.

Sir And. O, 'twill be admirable !

Mar. Sport royal, I warrant you : I know my physic will work
with him. I will plant you two, and let the fool make a third,
where he shall find the letter : observe his construction of it.
For this night, to bed, and dream on the event. Farewell.
                                                                 [*Exit.*

Sir To. Good night, Penthesilea.

Sir And. Before me, she's a good wench.

Sir To. She's a beagle, true-bred, and one that adores me :
what o' that ?

Sir And. I was adored once too. [money.

Sir To. Let's to bed, knight. Thou hadst need send for more

Sir And. If I cannot recover your niece, I am a foul way out.

Sir To. Send for money, knight ; if thou hast her not i' the
end, call me cut.

Sir And. If I do not, never trust me, take it how you will.

Sir To. Come, come, I'll go burn some sack ; 'tis too late to
go to bed now : come, knight ; come, knight. [*Exeunt.*

Scene IV

The Duke's palace.
Enter Duke, Viola, Curio, and others.

Duke. Give me some music. Now, good morrow, friends,
Now, good Cesario, but that piece of song,
That old and antique song we heard last night :
Methought it did relieve my passion much,
More than light airs and recollected terms
Of these most brisk and giddy-paced times :
Come, but one verse, [it.

Cur. He is not here, so please your lordship, that should sing

Duke. Who was it ?

Cur. Feste, the jester, my lord ; a fool that the lady Olivia's
father took much delight in. He is about the house.

Duke. Seek him out, and play the tune the while.
[*Exit Curio. Music plays.*

Come hither, boy : if ever thou shalt love,
In the sweet pangs of it remember me ;
For such as I am all true lovers are,
Unstaid and skittish in all motions else,
Save in the constant image of the creature
That is beloved. How dost thou like this tune ?

Vio. It gives a very echo to the seat
Where love is throned.

Duke. Thou dost speak masterly :
My life upon 't, young though thou art, thine eye
Hath stay'd upon some favour that it loves :
Hath it not, boy ?

Vio. A little, by your favour.

Duke. What kind of woman is 't ?

Vio. Of your complexion.

Duke. She is not worth thee, then. What years, i' faith ?

Vio. About your years, my lord.

Duke. Too old, by heaven : let still the woman take
 An elder than herself ; so wears she to him,
 So sways she level in her husband's heart :
 For, boy, however we do praise ourselves,
 Our fancies are more giddy and unfirm,
 More longing, wavering, sooner lost and worn,
 Than women's are.

Vio.   I think it well, my lord.

Duke. Then let thy love be younger than thyself,
 Or thy affection cannot hold the bent ;
 For women are as roses, whose fair flower
 Being once display'd, doth fall that very hour.

Vio. And so they are : alas, that they are so ;
 To die, even when they to perfection grow !

Re-enter Curio and Clown.

Duke. O, fellow, come, the song we had last night.
 Mark it, Cesario, it is old and plain ;
 The spinsters and the knitters in the sun
 And the free maids that weave their thread with bones
 Do use to chant it : it is silly sooth,
 And dallies with the innocence of love,
 Like the old age.

Clo. Are you ready, sir ?

Duke. Ay ; prithee, sing.   [*Music.*

SONG.

Clo.   Come away, come away, death,
                 And in sad cypress let me be laid ;
               Fly away, fly away, breath ;
                 I am slain by a fair cruel maid.
               My shroud of white, stuck all with yew,
                      O, prepare it !
               My part of death, no one so true
                      Did share it.

               Not a flower, not a flower sweet,
                 On my black coffin let there be strown ;
               Not a friend, not a friend greet
                 My poor corpse, where my bones shall be thrown :
               A thousand thousand sighs to save,
                      Lay me, O, where
               Sad true lover never find my grave,
                      To weep there !

382

Duke. There's for thy pains.

Clo. No pains, sir; I take pleasure in singing, sir.

Duke. I'll pay thy pleasure then.

Clo. Truly, sir, and pleasure will be paid, one time or another.

Duke. Give me now leave to leave thee.

Clo. Now, the melancholy god protect thee; and the tailor
make thy doublet of changeable taffeta, for thy mind is a
very opal. I would have men of such constancy put to sea,
that their business might be every thing and their intent
every where; for that's it that always makes a good voyage
of nothing.   Farewell.   [*Exit.*

Duke. Let all the rest give place. [*Curio and Attendants retire.*
                              Once more, Cesario,
Get thee to yond same sovereign cruelty :
Tell her, my love, more noble than the world,
Prizes not quantity of dirty lands ;
The parts that fortune hath bestow'd upon her,
Tell her, I hold as giddily as fortune ;
But 'tis that miracle and queen of gems
That nature pranks her in attracts my soul.

Vio. But if she cannot love you, sir?

Duke. I cannot be so answer'd.

Vio.   Sooth, but you must.
Say that some lady, as perhaps there is,
Hath for your love as great a pang of heart
As you have for Olivia : you cannot love her ;
You tell her so ; must she not then be answer'd?

Duke. There is no woman's sides
Can bide the beating of so strong a passion
As love doth give my heart ; no woman's heart
So big, to hold so much ; they lack retention.
Alas, their love may be call'd appetite,—
No motion of the liver, but the palate,—
That suffer surfeit, cloyment and revolt ;
But mine is all as hungry as the sea,
And can digest as much : make no compare
Between that love a woman can bear me
And that I owe Olivia.

Vio.   Ay, but I know,—

Duke. What dost thou know?

Vio. Too well what love women to men may owe:
In faith, they are as true of heart as we.
My father had a daughter loved a man,
As it might be, perhaps, were I a woman,
I should your lordship.

Duke. And what's her history?

Vio. A blank, my lord.   She never told her love,
But let concealment, like a worm i' the bud,
Feed on her damask cheek : she pined in thought
And with a green and yellow melancholy
She sat like patience on a monument,
Smiling at grief.   Was not this love indeed?
We men may say more, swear more : but indeed
Our shows are more than will ; for still we prove
Much in our vows, but little in our love.

Duke. But died thy sister of her love, my boy?

Vio. I am all the daughters of my father's house,
And all the brothers too : and yet I know not.
Sir, shall I to this lady?

Duke. Ay that's the theme.
To her in haste ; give her this jewel : say,
My love can give no place, bide no denay.   [*Exeunt.*

SCENE V

Olivia's garden
Enter Sir Toby, Sir Andrew, and Fabian.

Sir To. Come thy ways, Signior Fabian.

Fab. Nay, I'll come: if I lose a scruple of this sport, let me
be boiled to death with melancholy.

Sir To. Wouldst thou not be glad to have the niggardly rascally
sheep-biter come by some notable shame?

Fab. I would exult, man: you know, he brought me out o'
favour with my lady about a bear-baiting here.

Sir To. To anger him we'll have the bear again ; and we will
fool him black and blue: shall we not, Sir Andrew?

Sir And. An we do not, it is pity of our lives.

Sir To. Here comes the little villain.

Enter Maria.

How now, my metal of India!

Mar. Get ye all three into the box-tree: Malvolio's coming
down this walk: he has been yonder i' the sun practising
behaviour to his own shadow this half hour: observe him,
for the love of mockery ; for I know this letter will make a
contemplative idiot of him.   Close, in the name of jesting!
Lie thou there [*throws down a letter*] ; for here comes the
trout that must be caught with tickling.   [*Exit.*

Enter Malvolio.

Mal. 'Tis but fortune ; all is fortune.   Maria once told me she
did affect me: and I have heard herself come thus near,
that, should she fancy, it should be one of my complexion.

384

Besides, she uses me with a more exalted respect than any one else that follows her.   What should I think on 't?

Sir To. Here 's an overweening rogue!

Fab. O, peace!   Contemplation makes a rare turkey-cock of him: how he jets under his advanced plumes!

Sir And. 'Slight, I could so beat the rogue!

Sir To. Peace, I say.

Mal. To be Count Malvolio!

Sir To. Ah, rogue!

Sir And. Pistol him, pistol him.

Sir To. Peace, peace!

Mal. There is example for 't; the lady of the Strachy married the yeoman of the wardrobe.

Sir And. Fie on him, Jezebel!   [blows him.

Fab. O, peace! now he 's deeply in: look how imagination

Mal. Having been three months married to her, sitting in my

Sir To. O, for a stone-bow, to hit him in the eye!   [state,—

Mal. Calling my officers about me, in my branched velvet gown; having come from a day-bed, where I have left Olivia

Sir To. Fire and brimstone!   [sleeping,—

Fab. O, peace, peace!

Mal. And then to have the humour of state; and after a demure travel of regard, telling them I know my place as I would they should do theirs, to ask for my kinsman Toby,—

Sir To. Bolts and shackles!

Fab. O, peace, peace, peace! now, now.

Mal. Seven of my people, with an obedient start, make out for him: I frown the while; and perchance wind up my watch, or play with my—some rich jewel. Toby approaches; courtesies there to me,—

Sir To. Shall this fellow live?   [peace.

Fab. Though our silence be drawn from us with cars, yet

Mal. I extend my hand to him thus, quenching my familiar smile with an austere regard of control,—

Sir To. And does not Toby take you a blow o' the lips then?

Mal. Saying, 'Cousin Toby, my fortunes having cast me on your niece give me this prerogative of speech,'—

Sir To. What, what?

Mal. 'You must amend your drunkenness.'

Sir To. Out, scab!

Fab. Nay, patience, or we break the sinews of our plot.

Mal. 'Besides, you waste the treasure of your time with a foolish knight,'—

Sir And. That 's me, I warrant you.

Mal. 'One Sir Andrew,'—

Sir And. I knew 'twas I ; for many do call me fool.

Mal. What employment have we here ?   [*Taking up the letter.*

Fab. Now is the woodcock near the gin.   [aloud to him.

Sir To. O, peace ! and the spirit of humours intimate reading

Mal. By my life, this is my lady's hand : these be her very
   C's, her U's, and her T's ; and thus makes she her great P's.
   It is, in contempt of question, her hand.

Sir And. Her C's, her U's, and her T's : why that ?

Mal. [*reads*] To the unknown beloved, this, and my good
   wishes :—her very phrases ! By your leave, wax. Soft ! and
   the impressure her Lucrece, with which she uses to seal: 'tis
   my lady. To whom should this be ?

Fab. This wins, him, liver and all.

Mal. [*reads*]   Jove knows I love :
                  But who ?
               Lips, do not move ;
               No man must know.

'No man must know.'   What follows ? the numbers altered !
'No man must know :' if this should be thee, Malvolio ?

Sir To. Marry, hang thee, brock !

Mal. [*reads*] I may command where I adore ;
               But silence, like a Lucrece knife,
               With bloodless stroke my heart doth gore :
               M, O, A, I, doth sway my life.

Fab. A fustian riddle !

Sir To. Excellent wench, say I.

Mal. ' M, O, A, I, doth sway my life.'   Nay, but first, let me
   see, let me see, let me see.

Fab. What dish o' poison has she dressed him !

Sir To. And with what wing the staniel checks at it !

Mal. ' I may command where I adore.'   Why, she may command me : I serve her ; she is my lady.   Why, this is evident
   to any formal capacity ; there is no obstruction in this : and
   the end,—what should that alphabetical position portend ?
   If I could make that resemble something in me,—Softly !
   M, O, A, I,—

Sir To. O, ay, make up that : he is now at a cold scent.

Fab. Sowter will cry upon 't for all this, though it be as rank as
   a fox.

Mal. M,—Malvolio ; M,—why, that begins my name.

Fab. Did not I say he would work it out ? the cur is excellent
   at faults.

Mal. M,—but then there is no consonancy in the sequel ; that
   suffers under probation : A should follow, but O does.

Fab. And O shall end, I hope.

Sir To. Ay, or I'll cudgel him, and make him cry O!

Mal. And then I comes behind.

Fab. Ay, an you had any eye behind you, you might see more detraction at your heels than fortunes before you.

Mal. M, O, A, I; this simulation is not as the former: and yet, to crush this a little, it would bow to me, for every one of these letters are in my name. Soft! here follows prose. [*Reads*] If this fall into thy hand, revolve. In my stars I am above thee; but be not afraid of greatness: some are born great, some achieve greatness, and some have greatness thrust upon 'em. Thy Fates open their hands; let thy blood and spirit embrace them; and, to inure thyself to what thou art like to be, cast thy humble slough and appear fresh. Be opposite with a kinsman, surly with servants; let thy tongue tang arguments of state; put thyself into the trick of singularity: she thus advises thee that sighs for thee. Remember who commended thy yellow stockings, and wished to see thee ever cross-gartered: I say, remember. Go to, thou art made, if thou desirest to be so; if not, let me see thee a steward still, the fellow of servants, and not worthy to touch Fortune's fingers. Farewell. She that would alter services with thee,　　　　　　THE FORTUNATE-UNHAPPY.

Daylight and champain discovers not more: this is open. I will be proud, I will read politic authors, I will baffle Sir Toby, I will wash off gross acquaintance, I will be point-devise, the very man. I do not now fool myself, to let imagination jade me; for every reason excites to this, that my lady loves me. She did commend my yellow stockings of late, she did praise my leg being cross-gartered; and in this she manifests herself to my love, and with a kind of injunction drives me to these habits of her liking. I thank my stars I am happy. I will be strange, stout, in yellow stockings, and cross-gartered, even with the swiftness of putting on. Jove and my stars be praised! Here is yet a postscript. [*Reads*] Thou canst not choose but know who I am. If thou entertainest my love, let it appear in thy smiling; thy smiles become thee well; therefore in my presence still smile, dear my sweet, I prithee.

Jove, I thank thee: I will smile; I will do everything that thou wilt have me.　　　　　　　　　　　　[*Exit.*

Fab. I will not give my part of this sport for a pension of thousands to be paid from the Sophy.

Sir To. I could marry this wench for this device,—

Sir And. So could I too.

Sir To. And ask no other dowry with her but such another jest.

Sir And. Nor I neither.

Fab. Here comes my noble gull-catcher.

Re-enter Marie.

Sir To. Wilt thou set thy foot o' my neck?

Sir And. Or o' mine either?

Sir To. Shall I play my freedom at tray-trip, and become thy
   bond-slave?

Sir And. I' faith, or I either?

Sir To. Why, thou hast put him in such a dream, that when
   the image of it leaves him he must run mad.

Mar. Nay, but say true; does it work upon him?

Sir To. Like aqua-vitæ with a midwife.

Mar. If you will then see the fruits of the sport, mark his first
   approach before my lady: he will come to her in yellow
   stockings, and 'tis a colour she abhors, and cross-gartered, a
   fashion she detests; and he will smile upon her, which will
   now be so unsuitable to her disposition, being addicted to a
   melancholy as she is, that it cannot but turn him into a
   notable contempt.   If you will see it, follow me.

Sir To. To the gates of Tartar, thou most excellent devil of
   wit!

Sir And. I'll make one too.   [*Exeunt.*

ACT III—Scene I

Olivia's garden.

Enter Viola, and Clown with a tabor.

Vio. Save thee, friend, and thy music: dost thou live by thy

Clo. No, sir, I live by the church.   [tabor?

Vio. Art thou a churchman?

Clo. No such matter, sir: I do live by the church; for I do
   live at my house, and my house doth stand by the church.

Vio. So thou mayst say, the king lies by a beggar, if a beggar
   dwell near him; or, the church stands by thy tabor, if thy
   tabor stand by the church.

Clo. You have said, sir.   To see this age!   A sentence is but
   a cheveril glove to a good wit: how quickly the wrong side
   may be turned outward!

Vio. Nay, that's certain; they that dally nicely with words may
   quickly make them wanton.

Clo. I would, therefore, my sister had had no name, sir.

Vio. Why, man?

Clo. Why, sir, her name's a word; and to dally with that word
   might make my sister wanton.   But indeed words are very
   rascals since bonds disgraced them.

Vio. Thy reason, man?

Clo. Troth, sir, I can yield you none without words; and words are grown so false, I am loath to prove reason with them.

Vio. I warrant thou art a merry fellow and carest for nothing.

Clo. Not so, sir, I do care for something; but in my conscience, sir, I do not care for you: if that be to care for nothing, sir, I would it would make you invisible.

Vio. Art not thou the Lady Olivia's fool?

Clo. No, indeed, sir; the Lady Olivia has no folly: she will keep no fool, sir, till she be married; and fools are as like husbands as pilchards are to herrings; the husband's the bigger: I am indeed not her fool, but her corrupter of words.

Vio. I saw thee late at the Count Orsino's.

Clo. Foolery, sir, does walk about the orb like the sun, it shines every where. I would be sorry, sir, but the fool should be as oft with your master as with my mistress: I think I saw your wisdom there.

Vio. Nay, an thou pass upon me, I'll no more with thee. Hold, there's expenses for thee. [beard!

Clo. Now Jove, in his next commodity of hair, send thee a

Vio. By my troth, I'll tell thee, I am almost sick for one; [*Aside*] though I would not have it grow on my chin. Is thy lady within?

Clo. Would not a pair of these have bred, sir?

Vio. Yes, being kept together and put to use.

Clo. I would play Lord Pandarus of Phrygia, sir, to bring a Cressida to this Troilus.

Vio. I understand you, sir; 'tis well begged.

Clo. The matter, I hope, is not great, sir, begging but a beggar: Cressida was a beggar. My lady is within, sir. I will construe to them whence you come; who you are and what you would are out of my welkin, I might say 'element,' but the word is over-worn. [*Exit.*

Vio. This fellow is wise enough to play the fool;
And to do that well craves a kind of wit:
He must observe their mood on whom he jests,
The quality of persons, and the time,
And, like the haggard, check at every feather
That comes before his eye. This is a practice
As full of labour as a wise man's art:
For folly that he wisely shows is fit;
But wise men, folly-fall'n, quite taint their wit.

Enter Sir Toby and Sir Andrew.

Sir To. Save you, gentleman.

Vio. And you, sir.

Sir And. Dieu vous garde, monsieur.

Vio. Et vous aussi ; votre serviteur.

Sir And. I hope, sir, you are ; and I am yours.

Sir To. Will you encounter the house ? my niece is desirous
you should enter, if your trade be to her.   [my voyage.

Vio. I am bound to your niece, sir ; I mean, she is the list of

Sir To. Taste your legs, sir ; put them to motion.

Vio. My legs do better understand me, sir, than I understand
what you mean by bidding me taste my legs.

Sir To. I mean, to go, sir, to enter.   [prevented.

Vio. I will answer you with gait and entrance.   But we are

                Enter Olivia and Maria.

Most excellent accomplished lady, the heavens rain odours
on you !

Sir And. That youth's a rare courtier : ' Rain odours ;' well.

Vio. My matter hath no voice, lady, but to your own most
pregnant and vouchsafed ear.

Sir And. 'Odours,' 'pregnant,' and 'vouchsafed :' I 'll get 'em
all three all ready.

Oli. Let the garden door be shut, and leave me to my hearing.
   [Exeunt Sir Toby, Sir Andrew, and Maria.]   Give me your

Vio. My duty, madam, and most humble service.   [hand, sir.

Oli. What is your name ?

Vio. Cesario is your servant's name, fair princess.

Oli. My servant, sir ! 'Twas never merry world
Since lowly feigning was call'd compliment :
You 're servant to the Count Orsino, youth.

Vio. And he is yours, and his must needs be yours :
Your servant's servant is your servant, madam.

Oli. For him, I think not on him : for his thoughts,
Would they were blanks, rather than fill'd with me !

Vio. Madam, I come to whet your gentle thoughts
On his behalf.

Oli.   O, by your leave, I pray you ;
I bade you never speak again of him :
But, would you undertake another suit,
I had rather hear you to solicit that
Than music from the spheres.

Vio.   Dear lady,—

Oli. Give me leave, beseech you.   I did send,
After the last enchantment you did here,
A ring in chase of you : so did I abuse
Myself, my servant and, I fear me, you :
Under your hard construction must I sit,

To force that on you, in a shameful cunning,
Which you knew none of yours : what might you think?
Have you not set mine honour at the stake
And baited it with all the unmuzzled thoughts
That tyrannous heart can think?   To one of your receiving
Enough is shown ; a cypress, not a bosom,
Hides my heart.   So, let me hear you speak.

Vio. I pity you.

Oli.   That's a degree to love.

Vio. No, not a grize ; for 'tis a vulgar proof,
That very oft we pity enemies.

Oli. Why, then, methinks 'tis time to smile again.
O world, how apt the poor are to be proud!
If one should be a prey, how much the better
To fall before the lion than the wolf!   [*Clock strikes.*
The clock upbraids me with the waste of time.
Be not afraid, good youth, I will not have you :
And yet, when wit and youth is come to harvest,
Your wife is like to reap a proper man ;
There lies your way, due west.

Vio.   Then westward-ho!
Grace and good disposition attend your ladyship!
You 'll nothing madam, to my lord by me?

Oli. Stay :
I prithee, tell me what thou think'st of me.

Vio. That you do think you are not what you are.

Oli. If I think so, I think the same of you.

Vio. Then think you right : I am not what I am.

Oli. I would you were as I would have you be!

Vio. Would it be better, madam, than I am?
I wish it might, for now I am your fool.

Oli. O, what a deal of scorn looks beautiful
In the contempt and anger of his lip!
A murderous guilt shows not itself more soon
Than love that would seem hid : love's night is noon.
Cesario, by the roses of the spring,
By maidhood, honour, truth and every thing,
I love thee so, that, maugre all thy pride,
Nor wit nor reason can my passion hide.
Do not extort thy reasons from this clause,
For that I woo, thou therefore hast no cause ;
But rather reason thus with reason fetter,
Love sought is good, but given unsought is better.

Vio. By innocence I swear, and by my youth,
I have one heart, one bosom and one truth,

391

And that no woman has; nor never none
Shall mistress be of it, save I alone.
And so adieu, good madam : never more
Will I my master's tears to you deplore.

Oli. Yet come again; for thou perhaps mayst move
That heart, which now abhors, to like his love.   [*Exeunt.*

SCENE II
Olivia's house.
Enter Sir Toby, Sir Andrew, and Fabian.

Sir And. No, faith, I'll not stay a jot longer.

Sir To. Thy reason, dear venom, give thy reason.

Fab. You must needs yield your reason, Sir Andrew.

Sir And. Marry, I saw your niece do more favours to the count's serving-man than ever she bestowed upon me; I saw 't i' the orchard.

Sir To. Did she see thee the while, old boy? tell me that.

Sir And. As plain as I see you now.

Fab. This was a great argument of love in her toward you.

Sir And. 'Slight, will you make an ass o' me?

Fab. I will prove it legitimate, sir, upon the oaths of judgement and reason.   [was a sailor.

Sir To. And they have been grand-jurymen since before Noah

Fab. She did show favour to the youth in your sight only to exasperate you, to awake your dormouse valour, to put fire in your heart, and brimstone in your liver. You should then have accosted her; and with some excellent jests, fire-new from the mint, you should have banged the youth into dumbness. This was looked for at your hand, and this was balked : the double gilt of this opportunity you let time wash off, and you are now sailed into the north of my lady's opinion; where you will hang like an icicle on a Dutchman's beard, unless you do redeem it by some laudable attempt either of valour or policy.

Sir And. An't be any way, it must be with valour; for policy I hate : I had as lief be a Brownist as a politician.

Sir To. Why, then, build me thy fortunes upon the basis of valour. Challenge me the count's youth to fight with him; hurt him in eleven places : my niece shall take note of it; and assure thyself, there is no love-broker in the world can more prevail in man's commendation with woman than report of valour.

Fab. There is no way but this, Sir Andrew.

Sir And. Will either of you bear me a challenge to him?

Sir To. Go, write it in a martial hand; be curst and brief; it is

no matter how witty, so it be eloquent and full of invention :
taunt him with the license of ink : if thou thou 'st him some
thrice, it shall not be amiss ; and as many lies as will lie in
thy sheet of paper, although the sheet were big enough for
the bed of Ware in England, set 'em down : go, about it.
Let there be gall enough in thy ink, though thou write with
a goose-pen, no matter : about it.

Sir And. Where shall I find you ?

Sir To. We 'll call thee at the cubiculo : go.

[*Exit Sir Andrew.*

Fab. This is a dear manakin to you, Sir Toby.

Sir To. I have been dear to him, lad, some two thousand
strong, or so.   [deliver 't ?

Fab. We shall have a rare letter from him : but you 'll not

Sir To. Never trust me, then ; and by all means stir on the
youth to an answer. I think oxen and wainropes cannot
hale them together. For Andrew, if he were opened, and
you find so much blood in his liver as will clog the foot of
a flea, I 'll eat the rest of the anatomy.

Fab. And his opposite, the youth, bears in his visage no great
presage of cruelty.

Enter Maria.

Sir To. Look, where the youngest wren of nine comes.

Mar. If you desire the spleen, and will laugh yourselves into
stitches, follow me. Yond gull Malvolio is turned heathen,
a very renegado ; for there is no Christian, that means to be
saved by believing rightly, can ever believe such impossible
passages of grossness. He 's in yellow stockings.

Sir To. And cross-gartered ?

Mar. Most villanously ; like a pedant that keeps a school i'
the church. I have dogged him, like his murderer. He
does obey every point of the letter that I dropped to betray
him : he does smile his face into more lines than is in the
new map with the augmentation of the Indies : you have
not seen such a thing as 'tis. I can hardly forbear hurling
things at him. I know my lady will strike him : if she do,
he 'll smile and tak 't for a great favour.

Sir To. Come, bring us, bring us where he is.   [*Exeunt.*

Scene III

A street.

Enter Sebastian and Antonio.

Seb. I would not by my will have troubled you ;
    But, since you make your pleasure of your pains,
    I will no further chide you.

Ant. I could not stay behind you : my desire,
    More sharp than filed steel, did spur me forth ;
    And not all love to see you, though so much
    As might have drawn one to a longer voyage,
    But jealousy what might befall your travel,
    Being skilless in these parts ; which to a stranger,
    Unguided and unfriended, often prove
    Rough and unhospitable : my willing love,
    The rather by these arguments of fear,
    Set forth in your pursuit.
Seb.   My kind Antonio,
    I can no other answer make but thanks,
    And thanks ; and ever . . . . . . oft good turns
    Are shuffled off with such uncurrent pay :
    But, were my worth as is my conscience firm,
    You should find better dealing.   What 's to do ?
    Shall we go see the reliques of this town ?
Ant. To-morrow, sir : best first go see your lodging.
Seb. I am not weary, and 'tis long to night :
    I pray you, let us satisfy our eyes
    With the memorials and the things of fame
    That do renown this city.
Ant.   Would you 'ld pardon me ;
    I do not without danger walk these streets :
    Once, in a sea-fight, 'gainst the count his galleys
    I did some service ; of such note indeed,
    That were I ta'en here it would scarce be answer'd.
Seb. Belike you slew great number of his people.
Ant. The offence is not of such a bloody nature ;
    Albeit the quality of the time and quarrel
    Might well have given us bloody argument.
    It might have since been answer'd in repaying
    What we took from them ; which, for traffic's sake,
    Most of our city did : only myself stood out ;
    For which, if I be lapsed in this place,
    I shall pay dear.
Seb.   Do not then walk too open.
Ant. It doth not fit me.   Hold, sir, here 's my purse.
    In the south suburbs, at the Elephant,
    Is best to lodge : I will bespeak our diet,
    Whiles you beguile the time and feed your knowledge
    With viewing of the town : there shall you have me.
Seb. Why I your purse ?
Ant. Haply your eye shall light upon some toy
    You have desire to purchase ; and your store,

I think, is not for idle markets, sir.

Seb. I 'll be your purse-bearer and leave you
    For an hour.

Ant.   To the Elephant.

Seb.   I do remember.   *[Exeunt.*

SCENE IV
Olivia's garden.
Enter Olivia and Maria.

Oli. I have sent after him : he says he 'll come ;
    How shall I feast him ? what bestow of him ?
    For youth is bought more oft than begg'd or borrow'd.
    I speak too loud.
    Where is Malvolio ? he is sad and civil,
    And suits well for a servant with my fortunes :
    Where is Malvolio ?

Mar. He 's coming, madam ; but in very strange manner.
    He is, sure, possessed, madam.

Oli. Why, what 's the matter ? does he rave ?

Mar. No, madam, he does nothing but smile : your ladyship
    were best to have some guard about you, if he come ; for,
    sure, the man is tainted in 's wits.

Oli. Go call him hither. *[Exit Maria.]* I am as mad as he,
    If sad and merry madness equal be.
        Re-enter Maria, with Malvolio.
    How now, Malvolio !

Mal. Sweet lady, ho, ho.

Oli. Smilest thou ?
    I sent for thee upon a sad occasion.

Mal. Sad, lady ? I could be sad : this does make some ob-
    struction in the blood, this cross-gartering ; but what of
    that ? if it please the eye of one, it is with me as the very true
    sonnet is, ' Please one, and please all.'

Oli. Why, how dost thou, man ? what is the matter with thee ?

Mal. Not black in my mind, though yellow in my legs. It did
    come to his hands, and commands shall be executed : I
    think we do know the sweet Roman hand.

Oli. Wilt thou go to bed, Malvolio ?

Mal. To bed ! ay, sweet-heart, and I 'll come to thee.

Oli. God comfort thee ! Why dost thou smile so and kiss thy
    hand so oft ?

Mar. How do you, Malvolio ?

Mal. At your request ! yes ; nightingales answer daws.

Mar. Why appear you with this ridiculous boldness before
    my lady ?

Mal. 'Be not afraid of greatness : ' 'twas well writ.

Oli. What meanest thou by that, Malvolio ?

Mal. 'Some are born great,'—

Oli. Ha !

Mal. 'Some achieve greatness,'—

Oli. What sayest thou ?

Mal. 'And some have greatness thrust upon them.'

Oli. Heaven restore thee !

Mal. 'Remember who commended thy yellow stockings,'—

Oli. Thy yellow stockings !

Mal. 'And wished to see thee cross-gartered.'

Oli. Cross-gartered !

Mal. 'Go to, thou art made, if thou desirest to be so ; '—

Oli. Am I made ?

Mal. 'If not, let me see thee a servant still.'

Oli. Why, this is very midsummer madness.

Enter Servant.

Ser. Madam, the young gentleman of the Count Orsino's is returned : I could hardly entreat him back : he attends your ladyship's pleasure.

Oli. I 'll come to him. [*Exit Servant.*] Good Maria, let this fellow be looked to. Where 's my cousin Toby ? Let some of my people have a special care of him : I would not have him miscarry for the half of my dowry.

[Exeunt Olivia and Maria.

Mal. O, ho ! do you come near me now ? no worse man than Sir Toby to look to me ! This concurs directly with the letter : she sends him on purpose, that I may appear stubborn to him ; for she incites me to that in the letter. 'Cast thy humble slough,' says she ; 'be opposite with a kinsman, surly with servants ; let thy tongue tang with arguments of state ; put thyself into the trick of singularity ; ' and consequently sets down the manner how ; as, a sad face, a reverend carriage, a slow tongue, in the habit of some sir of note, and so forth. I have limed her ; but it is Jove's doing, and Jove make me thankful ! And when she went away now, 'Let this fellow be looked to : ' fellow ! not Malvolio, nor after my degree, but fellow. Why, every thing adheres together, that no dram of a scruple, no scruple of a scruple, no obstacle, no incredulous or unsafe circumstance—What can be said ? Nothing that can be can come between me and the full prospect of my hopes. Well, Jove, not I, is the doer of this, and he is to be thanked.

Re-enter Maria, with Sir Toby and Fabian.

Sir To. Which way is he, in the name of sanctity ? If all the devils of hell be drawn in little, and Legion himself possessed him, yet I 'll speak to him.

Fab. Here he is, here he is.   How is 't with you, sir? how is 't with you, man?

Mal. Go off; I discard you : let me enjoy my private : go off.

Mar. Lo, how hollow the fiend speaks within him! did not I tell you? Sir Toby, my lady prays you to have a care of

Mal. Ah, ha! does she so?   [him.

Sir To. Go to, go to; peace, peace; we must deal gently with him; let me alone.   How do you, Malvolio? how is 't with you?   What, man! defy the devil: consider, he 's an enemy to mankind.

Mal. Do you know what you say?

Mar. La you, an you speak ill of the devil, how he takes it at heart!   Pray God, he be not bewitched!

Fab. Carry his water to the wise woman.

Mar. Marry, and it shall be done to-morrow morning, if I live. My lady would not lose him for more than I 'll say.

Mal. How now, mistress!

Mar. O Lord!

Sir To. Prithee, hold thy peace; this is not the way: do you not see you move him? let me alone with him.

Fab. No way but gentleness; gently, gently : the fiend is rough, and will not be roughly used.

Sir To. Why, how now, my bawcock! how dost thou, chuck?

Mal. Sir!

Sir To. Ay, Biddy, come with me.   What, man! 'tis not for gravity to play at cherry-pit with Satan: hang him, foul collier!

Mar. Get him to say his prayers, good Sir Toby, get him to

Mal. My prayers, minx!   [pray.

Mar. No, I warrant you, he will not hear of godliness.

Mal. Go, hang yourselves all! you are idle shallow things : I am not of your element : you shall know more hereafter.

[*Exit.*

Sir To. Is 't possible?

Fab. If this were played upon a stage now, I could condemn it as an improbable fiction.

Sir To. His very genius hath taken the infection of the device, man.

Mar. Nay, pursue him now, lest the device take air and taint.

Fab. Why, we shall make him mad indeed.

Mar. The house will be the quieter.

Sir To. Come, we 'll have him in a dark room and bound. My niece is already in the belief that he 's mad : we may carry

it thus, for our pleasure and his penance, till our very pastime, tired out of breath, prompt us to have mercy on him :
at which time we will bring the device to the bar and crown
thee for a finder of madmen.   But see, but see.

Enter Sir Andrew.

Fab. More matter for a May morning.

Sir And. Here's the challenge, read it : I warrant there's vinegar
and pepper in 't.

Fab. Is 't so saucy ?

Sir And. Ay, is 't, I warrant him : do but read.

Sir To. Give me.   [*Reads*] Youth, whatsoever thou art, thou
art but a scurvy fellow.

Fab. Good, and valiant.

Sir To. [*reads*] Wonder not, nor admire not in thy mind, why
I do call thee so, for I will show thee no reason for 't.

Fab. A good note ; that keeps you from the blow of the law.

Sir To. [*reads*] Thou comest to the lady Olivia, and in my
sight she uses thee kindly : but thou liest in thy throat ; that
is not the matter I challenge thee for.

Fab. Very brief, and to exceeding good sense—less.

Sir To. [*reads*] I will waylay thee going home ; where if it be
thy chance to kill me,—

Fab. Good.

Sir To. [*reads*] Thou killest me like a rogue and a villain.

Fab. Still you keep o' the windy side of the law : good.

Sir To. [*reads*] Fare thee well ; and God have mercy upon one
of our souls !   He may have mercy upon mine ; but my hope
is better, and so look to thyself.   Thy friend, as thou usest
him, and thy sworn enemy, ANDREW AGUECHEEK.   If this
letter move him not, his legs cannot : I 'll give 't him.

Mar. You may have very fit occasion for 't : he is now in some
commerce with my lady, and will by and by depart.

Sir To. Go, Sir Andrew ; scout me for him at the corner of the
orchard like a bum-baily : so soon as ever thou seest him,
draw ; and, as thou drawest, swear horrible ; for it comes to
pass oft that a terrible oath, with a swaggering accent sharply
twanged off, gives manhood more approbation than ever proof
itself would have earned him.   Away !

Sir And. Nay, let me alone for swearing.   [*Exit.*

Sir To. Now will not I deliver his letter : for the behaviour of
the young gentleman gives him out to be of good capacity
and breeding ; his employment between his lord and my niece
confirms no less : therefore this letter, being so excellently
ignorant, will breed no terror in the youth : he will find it
comes from a clodpole.   But, sir, I will deliver his challenge

by word of mouth ; set upon Aguecheek a notable report of valour ; and drive the gentleman, as I know his youth will aptly receive it, into a most hideous opinion of his rage, skill, fury and impetuosity. This will so fright them both, that they will kill one another by the look, like cockatrices.

Re-enter Olivia, with Viola.

Fab. Here he comes with your niece : give them way till he take leave, and presently after him.

Sir To. I will meditate the while upon some horrid message for a challenge.   [*Exeunt Sir Toby, Fabian, and Maria.*

Oli. I have said too much unto a heart of stone,
And laid mine honour too unchary out :
There's something in me that reproves my fault ;
But such a headstrong potent fault it is,
That it but mocks reproof.

Vio. With the same 'haviour that your passion bears
Goes on my master's grief.

Oli. Here, wear this jewel for me, 'tis my picture ;
Refuse it not ; it hath no tongue to vex you ;
And I beseech you come again to-morrow.
What shall you ask of me that I 'll deny,
That honour saved may upon asking give ?

Vio. Nothing but this ;—your true love for my master.

Oli. How with mine honour may I give him that
Which I have given to you ?

Vio.   I will acquit you.

Oli. Well, come again to-morrow : fare thee well :
A fiend like thee might bear my soul to hell.   [*Exit.*

Re-enter Sir Toby and Fabian.

Sir To. Gentleman, God save thee.

Vio. And you, sir.

Sir To. That defence thou hast, betake thee to 't : of what nature the wrongs are thou hast done him, I know not ; but thy intercepter, full of despite, bloody as the hunter, attends thee at the orchard-end : dismount thy tuck, be yare in thy preparation, for thy assailant is quick, skilful and deadly.

Vio. You mistake, sir ; I am sure no man hath any quarrel to me : my remembrance is very free and clear from any image of offence done to any man.

Sir To. You 'll find it otherwise, I assure you : therefore, if you hold your life at any price, betake you to your guard ; for your opposite hath in him what youth, strength, skill and wrath can furnish man withal.

Vio. I pray you, sir, what is he ?

Sir To. He is knight, dubbed with unhatched rapier and on

carpet consideration; but he is a devil in private brawl: souls
and bodies hath he divorced three; and his incensement at
this moment is so implacable, that satisfaction can be none
but by pangs of deaths and sepulchre. Hob, nob, is his
word; give 't or take 't.

Vio. I will return again into the house and desire some conduct
of the lady. I am no fighter. I have heard of some kind of
men that put quarrels purposely on others, to taste their
valour: belike this is a man of that quirk.

Sir To. Sir, no; his indignation derives itself out of a very
competent injury: therefore, get you on and give him his
desire. Back you shall not to the house, unless you undertake that with me which with as much safety you might
answer him: therefore, on, or strip your sword stark naked;
for meddle you must, that's certain, or forswear to wear iron
about you.

Vio. This is as uncivil as strange. I beseech you, do me this
courteous office, as to know of the knight what my offence to
him is: it is something of my negligence, nothing of my
purpose.

Sir To. I will do so. Signior Fabian, stay you by this gentleman
till my return.   [*Exit.*

Vio. Pray you, sir, do you know of this matter?

Fab. I know the knight is incensed against you, even to a mortal
arbitrement; but nothing of the circumstance more.

Vio. I beseech you, what manner of man is he?

Fab. Nothing of that wonderful promise, to read him by his
form, as you are like to find him in the proof of his valour.
He is, indeed, sir, the most skilful, bloody and fatal opposite
that you could possibly have found in any part of Illyria.
Will you walk towards him? I will make your peace with
him if I can.

Vio. I shall be much bound to you for 't: I am one that had
rather go with sir priest than sir knight: I care not who
knows so much of my mettle.   [*Exeunt.*

Re-enter Sir Toby, with Sir Andrew.

Sir To. Why, man, he 's a very devil; I have not seen such a
firago. I had a pass with him, rapier, scabbard and all, and
he gives me the stuck in with such a mortal motion, that it is
inevitable; and on the answer, he pays you as surely as your
feet hit the ground they step on. They say he has been
fencer to the Sophy.

Sir And. Pox on 't, I 'll not meddle with him.

Sir To. Ay, but he will not now be pacified: Fabian can scarce
hold him yonder.

Sir And. Plague on 't, an I thought he had been valiant and
  so cunning in fence, I 'ld have seen him damned ere I 'ld have
  challenged him.   Let him let the matter slip, and I 'll give
  him my horse, grey Capilet.
Sir To. I 'll make the motion: stand here, make a good show
  on 't: this shall end without the perdition of souls.   [*Aside*]
  Marry, I 'll ride your horse as well as I ride you.
                 Re-enter Fabian and Viola.
[*To Fab.*] I have his horse to take up the quarrel: I have
  persuaded him the youth 's a devil.
Fab. He is as horribly conceited of him; and pants and looks
  pale, as if a bear were at his heels.
Sir To. [*To Vio.*] There 's no remedy, sir; he will fight with
  you for 's oath sake: marry, he hath better bethought him of
  his quarrel, and he finds that now scarce to be worth talking
  of: therefore draw, for the supportance of his vow; he protests
  he will not hurt you.
Vio. [*aside*] Pray God defend me!   A little thing would make
  me tell them how much I lack of a man.
Fab. Give ground, if you see him furious.
Sir To. Come, Sir Andrew, there 's no remedy; the gentleman
  will, for his honour's sake, have one bout with you; he cannot
  by the duello avoid it: but he has promised me, as he is a
  gentleman and a soldier, he will not hurt you.   Come on; to 't.
Sir And. Pray God, he keep his oath!
Vio. I do assure you, 'tis against my will.   [*They draw.*
                      Enter Antonio.
Ant. Put up your sword.   If this young gentleman
  Have done offence, I take the fault on me:
  If you offend him, I for him defy you.
Sir To. You, sir! why, what are you?
Ant. One, sir, that for his love dares yet do more
  Than you have heard him brag to you he will.
Sir To. Nay, if you be an undertaker, I am for you. [*They draw.*
                      Enter Officers.
Fab. O good Sir Toby, hold! here come the officers.
Sir To. I 'll be with you anon.
Vio. Pray, sir, put your sword up, if you please.
Sir And. Marry, will I, sir; and, for that I promised you, I 'll
  be as good as my word: he will bear you easily and reins well.
First Off. This is the man; do thy office.
Sec. Off. Antonio, I arrest thee at the suit of Count Orsino.
Ant. You do mistake me, sir.
First Off. No, sir, no jot; I know your favour well,
  Though now you have no sea-cap on your head.

Take him away : he knows I know him well.

Ant. I must obey. [*To Vio.*] This comes with seeking you :
But there 's no remedy ; I shall answer it.
What will you do, now my necessity
Makes me to ask you for my purse ? It grieves me
Much more for what I cannot do for you
Than what befalls myself. You stand amazed ;
But be of comfort.

Sec. Off. Come, sir, away.

Ant. I must entreat of you some of that money.

Vio. What money, sir ?
For the fair kindness you have show'd me here,
And, part, being prompted by your present trouble,
Out of my lean and low ability
I 'll lend you something : my having is not much ;
I 'll make division of my present with you :
Hold, there 's half my coffer.

Ant.   Will you deny me now ?
Is 't possible that my deserts to you
Can lack persuasion ?   Do not tempt my misery,
Lest that it make me so unsound a man
As to upbraid you with those kindnesses
That I have done for you.

Vio.   I know of none ;
Nor know I you by voice or any feature :
I hate ingratitude more in a man
Than lying vainness, babbling drunkenness,
Or any taint of vice whose strong corruption
Inhabits our frail blood.

Ant.   O heavens themselves !

Sec. Off. Come, sir, I pray you, go.

Ant. Let me speak a little. This youth that you see here
I snatch'd one half out of the jaws of death ;
Relieved him with such sanctity of love ;
And to his image, which methought did promise
Most venerable worth, did I devotion.

First Off. What 's that to us ?   The time goes by : away !

Ant. But O how vile an idol proves this god !
Thou hast, Sebastian, done good feature shame.
In nature there 's no blemish but the mind ;
None can be call'd deform'd but the unkind :
Virtue is beauty ; but the beauteous evil
Are empty trunks, o'erflourish'd by the devil.   [sir.

First Off. The man grows mad : away with him ! Come, come,

Ant. Lead me on.   [*Exit with Officers.*

Vio. Methinks his words do from such passion fly,
  That he believes himself: so do not I.
  Prove true, imagination, O prove true,
  That I, dear brother, be now ta'en for you!
Sir To. Come hither, knight; come hither, Fabian: we'll
  whisper o'er a couplet or two of most sage saws.
Vio. He named Sebastian: I my brother know
  Yet living in my glass; even such and so
  In favour was my brother, and he went
  Still in this fashion, colour, ornament,
  For him I imitate: O, if it prove,
  Tempests are kind and salt waves fresh in love!   [*Exit.*
Sir To. A very dishonest paltry boy, and more a coward than a
  hare: his dishonesty appears in leaving his friend here in
  necessity and denying him; and for his cowardship, ask
Fab. A coward, a most devout coward, religious in it. [*Fabian.*
Sir And. 'Slid, I'll after him again and beat him.
Sir To. Do; cuff him soundly, but never draw thy sword.
Sir And. An I do not,—   [*Exit.*
Fab. Come, let's see the event.
Sir To. I dare lay any money 'twill be nothing yet.   [*Exeunt*

ACT IV—SCENE I
Before Olivia's house.
Enter Sebastian and Clown.

Clo. Will you make me believe that I am not sent for you?
Seb. Go to, go to, thou art a foolish fellow:
  Let me be clear of thee.
Clo. Well held out, i' faith! No, I do not know you; nor I
  am not sent to you by my lady, to bid you come speak with
  her; nor your name is not Master Cesario; nor this is not
  my nose neither. Nothing that is so is so.
Seb. I prithee, vent thy folly somewhere else:
  Thou know'st not me.
Clo. Vent my folly! he has heard that word of some great
  man and now applies it to a fool. Vent my folly! I am
  afraid this great lubber, the world, will prove a cockney. I
  prithee now, ungird thy strangeness and tell me what I shall
  vent to my lady: shall I vent to her that thou art coming?
Seb. I prithee, foolish Greek, depart from me:
  There's money for thee: if you tarry longer,
  I shall give worse payment.
Clo. By my troth, thou hast an open hand. These wise men

that give fools money get themselves a good report—after
fourteen years' purchase.

Enter Sir Andrew, Sir Toby, and Fabian.

Sir And. Now, sir, have I met you again ? there's for you.

Seb. Why, there's for thee, and there, and there.
   Are all the people mad ?

Sir To. Hold, sir, or I'll throw your dagger o'er the house.

Clo. This will I tell my lady straight : I would not be in some
   of your coats for two pence.   [*Exit.*

Sir To. Come on, sir ; hold.

Sir And. Nay, let him alone : I'll go another way to work with
   him ; I'll have an action of battery against him, if there be
   any law in Illyria : though I struck him first, yet it's no

Seb. Let go thy hand.   [matter for that.

Sir To. Come, sir, I will not let you go. Come, my young
   soldier, put up your iron : you are well fleshed ; come on.

Seb. I will be free from thee. What wouldst thou now ? If
   thou darest tempt me further, draw thy sword.

Sir To. What, what ? Nay, then I must have an ounce or two
   of this malapert blood from you.

Enter Olivia.

Oli. Hold, Toby ; on thy life, I charge thee, hold !

Sir To. Madam !

Oli. Will it be ever thus ?   Ungracious wretch,
   Fit for the mountains and the barbarous caves,
   Where manners ne'er were preach'd ! out of my sight !
   Be not offended, dear Cesario.
   Rudesby, be gone !

[*Exeunt Sir Toby, Sir Andrew, and Fabian*
                     I prithee, gentle friend,
   Let thy fair wisdom, not thy passion, sway
   In this uncivil and unjust extent
   Against thy peace.   Go with me to my house ;
   And hear thou there how many fruitless pranks
   This ruffian hath botch'd up, that thou thereby
   Mayst smile at this : thou shalt not choose but go :
   Do not deny.   Beshrew his soul for me,
   He started one poor heart of mine in thee.

Seb. What relish is in this ? how runs the stream ?
   Or I am mad, or else this is a dream :
   Let fancy still my sense in Lethe steep ;
   If it be thus to dream, still let me sleep !

Oli. Nay, come, I prithee : would thou 'ldst be ruled by me !

Seb. Madam, I will.

Oli.   O, say so, and so be !   [*Exeunt.*

SCENE II

Olivia's house.
Enter Maria and Clown.

Mar. Nay, I prithee, put on this gown and this beard ; make
him believe that thou art Sir Topas the curate : do it
quickly ; I'll call Sir Toby the whilst.   *[Exit.*

Clo. Well, I'll put it on, and I will dissemble myself in 't ; and
I would I were the first that ever dissembled in such a
gown. I am not tall enough to become the function well,
nor lean enough to be thought a good student ; but to be
said an honest man and a good housekeeper goes as fairly
as to say a careful man and a great scholar. The com-
petitors enter.

Enter Sir Toby and Maria.

Sir To. Jove bless thee, master Parson.

Clo. Bonos dies, Sir Toby : for, as the old hermit of Prague,
that never saw pen and ink, very wittily said to a niece of
King Gorboduc, 'That that is is ;' so I, being master
Parson, am master Parson ; for, what is 'that' but 'that,'
and 'is' but 'is'?

Sir To. To him, Sir Topas.

Clo. What, ho, I say ! peace in this prison !

Sir To. The knave counterfeits well ; a good knave.

Mal. [*within*] Who calls there ?

Clo. Sir Topas the curate, who comes to visit Malvolio the
lunatic.

Mal. Sir Topas, Sir Topas, good Sir Topas, go to my lady.

Clo. Out, hyperbolical fiend ! how vexest thou this man !
talkest thou nothing but of ladies ?

Sir To. Well said, master Parson.

Mal. Sir Topas, never was man thus wronged : good Sir Topas,
do not think I am mad : they have laid me here in hideous
darkness.

Clo. Fie, thou dishonest Satan ! I call thee by the most
modest terms ; for I am one of those gentle ones that will
use the devil himself with courtesy : sayest thou that house
is dark ?

Mal. As hell, Sir Topas.

Clo. Why, it hath bay windows transparent as barricadoes, and
the clearstories toward the south north are as lustrous as
ebony ; and yet complainest thou of obstruction ?

Mal. I am not mad, Sir Topas : I say to you, this house is
dark.

Clo. Madman, thou errest : I say, there is no darkness

but ignorance; in which thou art more puzzled than the Egyptians in their fog.

Mal. I say, this house is as dark as ignorance, though ignorance were as dark as hell; and I say, there was never man thus abused. I am no more mad than you are: make the trial of it in any constant question.

Clo. What is the opinion of Pythagoras concerning wild fowl?

Mal. That the soul of our grandam might haply inhabit a bird.

Clo. What thinkest thou of his opinion?

Mal. I think nobly of the soul, and no way approve his opinion.

Clo. Fare thee well. Remain thou still in darkness: thou shalt hold the opinion of Pythagoras ere I will allow of thy wits; and fear to kill a woodcock, lest thou dispossess the soul of thy grandam. Fare thee well.

Mal. Sir Topas, Sir Topas!

Sir To. My most exquisite Sir Topas!

Clo. Nay, I am for all waters.

Mar. Thou mightst have done this without thy beard and gown: he sees thee not.

Sir To. To him in thine own voice, and bring me word how thou findest him: I would we were well rid of this knavery. If he may be conveniently delivered, I would he were; for I am now so far in offence with my niece, that I cannot pursue with any safety this sport to the upshot. Come by and by to my chamber.   [*Exeunt Sir Toby and Maria.*

Clo. [*Singing*] Hey, Robin, jolly Robin,
            Tell me how thy lady does.

Mal. Fool,—

Clo. My lady is unkind, perdy.

Mal. Fool,—

Clo. Alas, why is she so?

Mal. Fool, I say,—

Clo. She loves another—Who calls, ha?

Mal. Good fool, as ever thou wilt deserve well at my hand, help me to a candle, and pen, ink and paper: as I am a gentleman, I will live to be thankful to thee for 't.

Clo. Master Malvolio!

Mal. Ay, good fool.

Clo. Alas, sir, how fell you besides your five wits?

Mal. Fool, there was never man so notoriously abused: I am as well in my wits, fool, as thou art.

Clo. But as well? then you are mad indeed, if you be no better in your wits than a fool.

Mal. They have here propertied me; keep me in darkness,

406

send ministers to me, asses, and do all they can to face me
out of my wits.

Clo. Advise you what you say; the minister is here. Malvolio,
Malvolio, thy wits the heavens restore! endeavour thyself to
sleep, and leave thy vain bibble babble.

Mal. Sir Topas,—

Clo. Maintain no words with him, good fellow. Who, I, sir?
not I, sir. God be wi' you, good Sir Topas. Marry, amen.
I will, sir, I will.

Mal. Fool, fool, fool, I say,—

Clo. Alas, sir, be patient. What say you, sir? I am shent for
speaking to you.

Mal. Good fool, help me to some light and some paper: I tell
thee, I am as well in my wits as any man in Illyria.

Clo. Well-a-day that you were, sir!

Mal. By this hand, I am. Good fool, some ink, paper and
light; and convey what I will set down to my lady: it shall
advantage thee more than ever the bearing of letter did.

Clo. I will help you to 't. But tell me true, are you not mad
indeed? or do you but counterfeit?

Mal. Believe me, I am not; I tell thee true.

Clo. Nay, I'll ne'er believe a madman till I see his brains.
I will fetch you light and paper and ink.

Mal. Fool, I'll requite it in the highest degree: I prithee,
be gone.

Clo. [*Singing*]   I am gone, sir,
                And anon, sir,
            I'll be with you again,
                In a trice,
                Like to the old vice,
            Your need to sustain;
                Who, with dagger of lath,
                In his rage and his wrath,
                Cries, ah, ha! to the devil:
                Like a mad lad,
                Pare thy nails, dad;
                Adieu, goodman devil.

SCENE III

Olivia's garden.
Enter Sebastian.

Seb. This is the air; that is the glorious sun;
This pearl she gave me, I do feel 't and see 't;
And though 'tis wonder that enwraps me thus,
Yet 'tis not madness. Where's Antonio, then?

I could not find him at the Elephant:
Yet there he was; and there I found this credit,
That he did range the town to seek me out.
His counsel now might do me golden service;
For though my soul disputes well with my sense,
That this may be some error, but no madness,
Yet doth this accident and flood of fortune
So far exceed all instance, all discourse,
That I am ready to distrust mine eyes
And wrangle with my reason, that persuades me
To any other trust but that I am mad,
Or else the lady's mad; yet, if 'twere so,
She could not sway her house, command her followers,
Take and give back affairs and their dispatch
With such a smooth, discreet, and stable bearing
As I perceive she does: there's something in't
That is deceivable.   But here the lady comes.

Enter Olivia and Priest.

Oli. Blame not this haste of mine.   If you mean well,
Now go with me and with this holy man
Into the chantry by: there, before him,
And underneath that consecrated roof,
Plight me the full assurance of your faith;
That my most jealous and too doubtful soul
May live at peace.   He shall conceal it
Whiles you are willing it shall come to note,
What time we will our celebration keep
According to my birth.   What do you say?
Seb. I'll follow this good man, and go with you;
And having sworn truth, ever will be true.
Oli. Then lead the way, good father; and heavens so shine,
That they may fairly note this act of mine!   [*Exeunt.*

ACT V—Scene I
Before Olivia's house.
Enter Clown and Fabian.

Fab. Now, as thou lovest me, let me see his letter.
Clo. Good Master Fabian, grant me another request.
Fab. Any thing.
Clo. Do not desire to see this letter.
Fab. This is, to give a dog, and in recompense desire my
dog again.

Enter Duke, Viola, Curio, and Lords.

Duke. Belong you to the Lady Olivia, friends?

Clo. Ay, sir; we are some of her trappings.

Duke. I know thee well: how dost thou, my good fellow?

Clo. Truly, sir, the better for my foes and the worse for my friends.

Duke. Just the contrary; the better for thy friends.

Clo. No, sir, the worse.

Duke. How can that be?

Clo. Marry, sir, they praise me and make an ass of me; now my foes tell me plainly I am an ass: so that by my foes, sir, I profit in the knowledge of myself; and by my friends I am abused: so that, conclusions to be as kisses, if your four negatives make your two affirmatives, why then, the worse for my friends, and the better for my foes.

Duke. Why, this is excellent.

Clo. By my troth, sir, no; though it please you to be one of my friends.

Duke. Thou shalt not be the worse for me: there's gold.

Clo. But that it would be double-dealing, sir, I would you could make it another.

Duke. O, you give me ill counsel.

Clo. Put your grace in your pocket, sir, for this once, and let your flesh and blood obey it.

Duke. Well, I will be so much a sinner, to be a double-dealer: there's another.

Clo. Primo, secundo, tertio, is a good play; and the old saying is, the third pays for all: the triplex, sir, is a good tripping measure; or the bells of Saint Bennet, sir, may put you in mind; one, two, three.

Duke. You can fool no more money out of me at this throw: if you will let your lady know I am here to speak with her, and bring her along with you, it may awake my bounty further.

Clo. Marry, sir, lullaby to your bounty till I come again. I go, sir; but I would not have you to think that my desire of having is the sin of covetousness: but, as you say, sir, let your bounty take a nap, I will awake it anon.   [*Exit.*

Vio. Here comes the man, sir, that did rescue me.

Enter Antonio and Officers.

Duke. That face of his I do remember well;
Yet, when I saw it last, it was besmear'd
As black as Vulcan in the smoke of war:
A bawbling vessel was he captain of,
For shallow draught and bulk unprizable;
With which such scathful grapple did he make
With the most noble bottom of our fleet,

That very envy and the tongue of loss
Cried fame and honour on him.   What 's the matter?
First Off. Orsino, this is that Antonio
That took the Phœnix and her fraught from Candy;
And this is he that did the Tiger board,
When your young nephew Titus lost his leg:
Here in the streets, desperate of shame and state,
In private brabble did we apprehend him.
Vio. He did me kindness, sir, drew on my side;
But in conclusion put strange speech upon me:
I know not what 'twas but distraction.
Duke. Notable pirate! thou salt-water thief!
What foolish boldness brought thee to their mercies,
Whom thou, in terms so bloody and so dear,
Hast made thine enemies?
Ant.   Orsino, noble sir,
Be pleased that I shake off these names you give me:
Antonio never yet was thief or pirate,
Though I confess, on base and ground enough,
Orsino's enemy.   A witchcraft drew me hither:
That most ingrateful boy there by your side,
From the rude sea's enraged and foamy mouth
Did I redeem; a wreck past hope he was:
His life I gave him and did thereto add
My love, without retention or restraint,
All his in dedication; for his sake
Did I expose myself, pure for his love,
Into the danger of this adverse town;
Drew to defend him when he was beset:
Where being apprehended, his false cunning,
Not meaning to partake with me in danger,
Taught him to face me out of his acquaintance,
And grew a twenty years removed thing
While one would wink; denied me mine own purse,
Which I had recommended to his use
Not half an hour before.
Vio.   How can this be?
Duke. When came he to this town?
Ant. To-day, my lord; and for three months before,
No interim, not a minute's vacancy,
Both day and night did we keep company.
                    Enter Olivia and Attendants.
Duke. Here comes the countess; now heaven walks on earth.
But for thee, fellow; fellow, thy words are madness:
Three months this youth hath tended upon me;

But more of that anon.   Take him aside.

Oli. What would my lord, but that he may not have,
　Wherein Olivia may seem serviceable?
　Cesario, you do not keep promise with me.

Vio. Madam!

Duke. Gracious Olivia,—

Oli. What do you say, Cesario?   Good my lord,—

Vio. My lord would speak; my duty hushes me.

Oli. If it be aught to the old tune, my lord,
　It is as fat and fulsome to mine ear
　As howling after music.

Duke.　　　　　　　　Still so cruel?

Oli. Still so constant, lord.

Duke. What, to perverseness? you uncivil lady,
　To whose ingrate and unauspicious altars
　My soul the faithfull'st offerings hath breathed out
　That e'er devotion tender'd!   What shall I do?

Oli. Even what it please my lord, that shall become him.

Duke. Why should I not, had I the heart to do it,
　Like to the Egyptian thief at point of death,
　Kill what I love?—a savage jealousy
　That sometime savours nobly.   But hear me this:
　Since you to non-regardance cast my faith,
　And that I partly know the instrument
　That screws me from my true place in your favour,
　Live you the marble-breasted tyrant still;
　But this your minion, whom I know you love,
　And whom, by heaven I swear, I tender dearly,
　Him will I tear out of that cruel eye,
　Where he sits crowned in his master's spite.
　Come, boy, with me; my thoughts are ripe in mischief:
　I'll sacrifice the lamb that I do love,
　To spite a raven's heart within a dove.

Vio. And I, most jocund, apt and willingly,
　To do you rest, a thousand deaths would die.

Oli. Where goes Cesario?

Vio.　　　　　　　　After him I love
　More than I love these eyes, more than my life,
　More, by all mores, than e'er I shall love wife.
　If I do feign, you witnesses above
　Punish my life for tainting of my love!

Oli. Ay me, detested! how am I beguiled!

Vio. Who does beguile you? who does do you wrong?

Oli. Hast thou forgot thyself? is it so long?
　Call forth the holy father.

Duke.   Come, away!
Oli. Whither, my lord? Cesario, husband, stay.
Duke. Husband!
Oli.   Ay, husband: can he that deny?
Duke. Her husband, sirrah!
Vio.   No, my lord, not I.
Oli. Alas, it is the baseness of thy fear
    That makes thee strangle thy propriety:
    Fear not, Cesario; take thy fortunes up;
    Be that thou know'st thou art, and then thou art
    As great as that thou fear'st.
                    Enter Priest.
                        O, welcome, father!
    Father, I charge thee, by thy reverence,
    Here to unfold, though lately we intended
    To keep in darkness what occasion now
    Reveals before 'tis ripe, what thou dost know
    Hath newly pass'd between this youth and me.
Priest. A contract of eternal bond of love,
    Confirm'd by mutual joinder of your hands,
    Attested by the holy close of lips,
    Strengthen'd by interchangement of your rings;
    And all the ceremony of this compact
    Seal'd in my function, by my testimony:
    Since when, my watch hath told me, toward my grave
    I have travell'd but two hours.
Duke. O thou dissembling cub! what wilt thou be
    When time hath sow'd a grizzle on thy case?
    Or will not else thy craft so quickly grow,
    That thine own trip shall be thine overthrow?
    Farewell, and take her; but direct thy feet
    Where thou and I henceforth may never meet.
Vio. My lord, I do protest—
Oli.   O, do not swear!
    Hold little faith, though thou hast too much fear.
                    Enter Sir Andrew.
Sir And. For the love of God, a surgeon! Send one presently
    to Sir Toby.
Oli. What's the matter?
Sir And. He has broke my head across and has given Sir Toby
    a bloody coxcomb too: for the love of God, your help! I had
    rather than forty pound I were at home.
Oli. Who has done this, Sir Andrew?
Sir And. The count's gentleman, one Cesario: we took him for
    a coward, but he's the very devil incarnate.

Duke. My gentleman, Cesario?

Sir And. 'Od's lifelings, here he is! You broke my head for
  nothing; and that that I did, I was set on to do 't by Sir
  Toby.

Vio. Why do you speak to me? I never hurt you:
  You drew your sword upon me without cause;
  But I bespake you fair, and hurt you not.

Sir And. If a bloody coxcomb be a hurt, you have hurt me: I
  think you set nothing by a bloody coxcomb.

Enter Sir Toby and Clown.

Here comes Sir Toby halting; you shall hear more: but if
  he had not been in drink, he would have tickled you other
  gates than he did.

Duke. How now, gentleman! how is 't with you?

Sir To. That 's all one: has hurt me, and there 's the end on 't.
  Sot, didst see Dick surgeon, sot?

Clo. O, he 's drunk, Sir Toby, an hour agone; his eyes were set
  at eight i' the morning.

Sir To. Then he 's a rogue, and a passy measures pavin: I hate
  a drunken rogue.

Oli. Away with him! Who hath made this havoc with them?

Sir And. I 'll help you, Sir Toby, because we 'll be dressed
  together.

Sir To. Will you help? an ass-head and a coxcomb and a
  knave, a thin-faced knave, a gull!

Oli. Get him to bed, and let his hurt be look'd to.

  [*Exeunt Clown, Fabian, Sir Toby, and Sir Andrew.*
Enter Sebastian.

Seb. I am sorry, madam, I have hurt your kinsman;
  But, had it been the brother of my blood,
  I must have done no less with wit and safety.
  You throw a strange regard upon me, and by that
  I do perceive it hath offended you:
  Pardon me, sweet one, even for the vows
  We made each other but so late ago.

Duke. One face, one voice, one habit, and two persons.
  A natural perspective, that is and is not!

Seb. Antonio, O my dear Antonio!
  How have the hours rack'd and tortured me,
  Since I have lost thee!

Ant. Sebastian are you?

Seb.   Fear'st thou that, Antonio?

Ant. How have you made division of yourself?
  An apple, cleft in two, is not more twin
  Than these two creatures. Which is Sebastian?

Oli. Most wonderful!

Seb. Do I stand there? I never had a brother;
  Nor can there be that deity in my nature,
  Of here and every where. I had a sister,
  Whom the blind waves and surges have devour'd.
  Of charity, what kin are you to me?
  What countryman? what name? what parentage?

Vio. Of Messaline: Sebastian was my father;
  Such a Sebastian was my brother too,
  So went he suited to his watery tomb:
  If spirits can assume both form and suit,
  You come to fright us.

Seb.   A spirit I am indeed;
  But am in that dimension grossly clad
  Which from the womb I did participate.
  Were you a woman, as the rest goes even,
  I should my tears let fall upon your cheek,
  And say 'Thrice-welcome, drowned Viola!'

Vio. My father had a mole upon his brow.

Seb. And so had mine.

Vio. And died that day when Viola from her birth
  Had number'd thirteen years.

Seb. O, that record is lively in my soul!
  He finished indeed his mortal act
  That day that made my sister thirteen years.

Vio. If nothing lets to make us happy both
  But this my masculine usurp'd attire,
  Do not embrace me till each circumstance
  Of place, time, fortune, do cohere and jump
  That I am Viola: which to confirm,
  I'll bring you to a captain in this town,
  Where lie my maiden weeds; by whose gentle help
  I was preserved to serve this noble count.
  All the occurrence of my fortune since
  Hath been between this lady and this lord.

Seb. [*To Olivia*] So comes it, lady, you have been mistook:
  But nature to her bias drew in that.
  You would have been contracted to a maid;
  Nor are you therein, by my life, deceived,
  You are betroth'd both to a maid and man.

Duke. Be not amazed; right noble is his blood.
  If this be so, as yet the glass seems true,
  I shall have share in this most happy wreck.
  [*To Viola*] Boy, thou hast said to me a thousand times
  Thou never shouldst love woman like to me.

414

Vio. And all those sayings will I over-swear;
   And all those swearings keep as true in soul
   As doth that orbed continent the fire
   That severs day from night.
Duke.   Give me thy hand;
   And let me see thee in thy woman's weeds.
Vio. The captain that did bring me first on shore
   Hath my maid's garments: he upon some action
   Is now in durance, at Malvolio's suit,
   A gentleman, and follower of my lady's.
Oli. He shall enlarge him: fetch Malvolio hither:
   And yet, alas, now I remember me,
   They say, poor gentleman, he's much distract.
            Re-enter Clown with a letter, and Fabian.
   A most extracting frenzy of mine own
   From my remembrance clearly banish'd his.
   How does he, sirrah?
Clo. Truly, madam, he holds Belzebub at the stave's end as
   well as a man in his case may do: has here writ a letter to
   you; I should have given 't you to-day morning, but as a
   madman's epistles are no gospels, so it skills not much when
   they are delivered.
Oli. Open 't and read it.
Clo. Look then to be well edified when the fool delivers the
   madman. [*Reads*] By the Lord, madam,—
Oli. How now! art thou mad?
Clo. No, madam, I do but read madness: an your ladyship
   will have it as it ought to be, you must allow Vox.
Oli. Prithee, read i' thy right wits.
Clo. So I do, madonna; but to read his right wits is to read
   thus: therefore perpend, my princess, and give ear.
Oli. Read it you, sirrah.   [*To Fabian.*
Fab. By the Lord, madam, you wrong me, and the world shall
   know it: though you have put me into darkness and given
   your drunken cousin rule over me, yet have I the benefit of
   my senses as well as your ladyship. I have your own letter
   that induced me to the semblance I put on; with the which
   I doubt not but to do myself much right, or you much shame.
   Think of me as you please. I leave my duty a little un-
   thought of, and speak out of my injury.
                          THE MADLY-USED MALVOLIO.

Oli. Did he write this?
Clo. Ay, madam.
Duke. This savours not much of distraction.

Oli. See him deliver'd, Fabian ; bring him hither. [*Exit Fabian.*
My lord, so please you, these things further thought on,
To think me as well a sister as a wife,
One day shall crown the alliance on 't, so please you,
Here at my house and at my proper cost.
Duke. Madam, I am most apt to embrace your offer.
[*To Viola*] Your master quits you ; and for your service done
So much against the mettle of your sex,   [him,
So far beneath your soft and tender breeding,
And since you call'd me master for so long,
Here is my hand : you shall from this time be
Your master's mistress.
Oli.   A sister ! you are she.
        Re-enter Fabian, with Malvolio.
Duke. Is this the madman ?
Oli.   Ay, my lord, this same.
How now, Malvolio !
Mal.   Madam, you have done me wrong,
Notorious wrong.
Oli.   Have I, Malvolio ? no.
Mal. Lady, you have.   Pray you, peruse that letter.
You must not now deny it is your hand :
Write from it, if you can, in hand or phrase ;
Or say 'tis not your seal, not your invention :
You can say none of this : well, grant it then
And tell me, in the modesty of honour,
Why you have given me such clear lights of favour,
Bade me come smiling and cross-garter'd to you,
To put on yellow stockings and to frown
Upon Sir Toby and the lighter people ;
And, acting this in an obedient hope,
Why have you suffer'd me to be imprison'd,
Kept in a dark house, visited by the priest,
And made the most notorious geck and gull
That e'er invention play'd on ? tell me why.
Oli. Alas, Malvolio, this is not my writing,
Though, I confess, much like the character :
But out of question 'tis Maria's hand.
And now I do bethink me, it was she
First told me thou wast mad ; then camest in smiling,
And in such forms which here were presupposed
Upon thee in the letter.   Prithee, be content :
This practice hath most shrewdly pass'd upon thee ;
But when we know the grounds and authors of it,
Thou shalt be both the plaintiff and the judge

Of thine own cause.

Fab.   Good madam, hear me speak,
And let no quarrel nor no brawl to come
Taint the condition of this present hour,
Which I have wonder'd at.   In hope it shall not,
Most freely I confess, myself and Toby
Set this device against Malvolio here,
Upon some stubborn and uncourteous parts
We had conceived against him : Maria writ
The letter at Sir Toby's great importance ;
In recompense whereof he hath married her.
How with a sportful malice it was follow'd
May rather pluck on laughter than revenge ;
If that the injuries be justly weigh'd
That have on both sides pass'd.

Oli. Alas, poor fool, how have they baffled thee !

Clo. Why, 'some are born great, some achieve greatness, and
some have greatness thrown upon them.'   I was one, sir, in
this interlude ; one Sir Topas, sir ; but that's all one.   'By
the Lord, fool, I am not mad.'   But do you remember?
'Madam, why laugh you at such a barren rascal? an you
smile not, he's gagged :' and thus the whirligig of time brings
in his revenges.

Mal. I'll be revenged on the whole pack of you.   [*Exit.*

Oli. He hath been most notoriously abused.

Duke. Pursue him, and entreat him to a peace :
He hath not told us of the captain yet :
When that is known, and golden time convents,
A solemn combination shall be made
Of our dear souls.   Meantime, sweet sister,
We will not part from hence.   Cesario, come ;
For so you shall be, while you are a man ;
But when in other habits you are seen,
Orsino's mistress and his fancy's queen.

                              [*Exeunt all, except Clown.*

Clo. [*Sings*]
          When that I was and a little tiny boy,
               With hey, ho, the wind and the rain,
          A foolish thing was but a toy,
               For the rain it raineth every day

          But when I came to man's estate,
               With hey, ho, &c.
          'Gainst knaves and thieves men shut their gate,
               For the rain, &c.

417

But when I came, alas! to wive,
    With hey, ho, &c.
By swaggering could I never thrive,
    For the rain, &c.

But when I came unto my beds,
    With hey, ho, &c.
With toss-pots still had drunken heads,
    For the rain, &c.

A great while ago the world begun,
    With hey, ho, &c.
But that's all one, our play is done,
    And we'll strive to please you every day.   *[Exit.*

THE WINTER'S TALE

DRAMATIS PERSONÆ

LEONTES, *king of Sicilia.*
MAMILLIUS, *young prince of Sicilia.*
CAMILLO,
ANTIGONUS,
CLEOMENES, } *Four Lords of Sicilia.*
DION,
POLIXENES, *king of Bohemia.*
FLORIZEL, *prince of Bohemia.*
ARCHIDAMUS, *a Lord of Bohemia.*
Old Shepherd, *reputed father of Perdita.*
Clown, *his son.*

AUTOLYCUS, *a rogue.*
A Mariner,
A Gaoler.

HERMIONE, *queen to Leontes.*
PERDITA, *daughter to Leontes and Hermione.*
PAULINA, *wife to Antigonus.*
EMILIA, *a lady attending on Hermione.*
MOPSA,
DORCAS, } *Shepherdesses.*

Other Lords and Gentlemen, Ladies, Officers, and Servants, Shepherds, and Shepherdesses.

Time, as Chorus.

SCENE: *Partly in Sicilia, and partly in Bohemia.*

ACT I—SCENE I

Antechamber in Leontes' palace.
Enter Camillo and Archidamus.

Arch. If you shall chance, Camillo, to visit Bohemia, on the like occasion whereon my services are now on foot, you shall see, as I have said, great difference betwixt our Bohemia and your Sicilia.

Cam. I think, this coming summer, the King of Sicilia means to pay Bohemia the visitation which he justly owes him.

Arch. Wherein our entertainment shall shame us we will be justified in our loves; for indeed—

Cam. Beseech you,—

Arch. Verily, I speak it in the freedom of my knowledge: we cannot with such magnificence—in so rare—I know not what to say. We will give you sleepy drinks, that your senses, unintelligent of our insufficience, may, though they cannot praise us, as little accuse us.

Cam. You pay a great deal too dear for what's given freely.

Arch. Believe me, I speak as my understanding instructs me, and as mine honesty puts it to utterance.

Cam. Sicilia cannot show himself over-kind to Bohemia. They were trained together in their childhoods; and there rooted betwixt them then such an affection, which cannot choose but branch now. Since their more mature dignities and royal necessities made separation of their society, their encounters, though not personal, have been royally attorneyed with interchange of gifts, letters, loving embassies; that they have seemed to be together, though absent; shook hands, as over a vast; and embraced, as it were, from the ends of opposed winds. The heavens continue their loves!

Arch. I think there is not in the world either malice or matter

to alter it. You have an unspeakable comfort of your young
prince Mamillius : it is a gentleman of the greatest promise
that ever came into my note.

Cam. I very well agree with you in the hopes of him : it is a
gallant child ; one that indeed physics the subject, makes
old hearts fresh : they that went on crutches ere he was born
desire yet their life to see him a man.

Arch. Would they else be content to die ?

Cam. Yes ; if there were no other excuse why they should
desire to live.

Arch. If the king had no son, they would desire to live on
crutches till he had one.   [*Exeunt.*

SCENE II

A room of state in the same.
Enter Leontes, Hermione, Mamillius, Polixenes, Camillo,
and Attendants.

Pol. Nine changes of the watery star hath been
The shepherd's note since we have left our throne
Without a burthen : time as long again
Would be fill'd up, my brother, with our thanks ;
And yet we should, for perpetuity,
Go hence in debt : and therefore, like a cipher,
Yet standing in rich place, I multiply
With one 'We thank you,' many thousands moe
That go before it.

Leon.   Stay your thanks a while ;
And pay them when you part.

Pol.   Sir, that 's to-morrow.
I am question'd by my fears, of what may chance
Or breed upon our absence ; that may blow
No sneaping winds at home, to make us say
'This is put forth too truly :' besides, I have stay'd
To tire your royalty.

Leon.   We are tougher, brother,
Than you can put us to 't.

Pol.   No longer stay.

Leon. One seven-night longer.

Pol.   Very sooth, to-morrow.

Leon. We 'll part the time between 's, then : and in that I 'll no
gainsaying.

Pol.   Press me not, beseech you, so.
There is no tongue that moves, none, none i' the world,
So soon as yours could win me : so it should now,
Were there necessity in your request, although

420

'Twere needful I denied it.   My affairs
Do even drag me homeward : which to hinder
Were in your love a whip to me ; my stay
To you a charge and trouble : to save both,
Farewell, our brother.

Leon.   Tongue-tied our queen ? speak you.

Her. I had thought, sir, to have held my peace until
You had drawn oaths from him not to stay.   You, sir,
Charge him too coldly.   Tell him, you are sure
All in Bohemia 's well ; this satisfaction
The by-gone day proclaim'd : say this to him,
He 's beat from his best ward.

Leon.   Well said, Hermione.

Her. To tell, he longs to see his son, were strong :
But let him say so then, and let him go ;
But let him swear so, and he shall not stay,
We 'll thwack him hence with distaffs.
Yet of your royal presence I 'll adventure
The borrow of a week.   When at Bohemia
You take my lord, I 'll give him my commission
To let him there a month behind the gest
Prefix'd for 's parting : yet, good deed, Leontes,
I love thee not a jar o' the clock behind
What lady she her lord.   You 'll stay?

Pol.   No, madam.

Her. Nay, but you will ?

Pol.   I may not, verily.

Her. Verily !
You put me off with limber vows ; but I,
Though you would seek to unsphere the stars with oaths,
Should yet say 'Sir, no going.'   Verily,
You shall not go : a lady's 'Verily' 's
As potent as a lord's.   Will you go yet ?
Force me to keep you as a prisoner,
Not like a guest ; so you shall pay your fees
When you depart, and save your thanks.   How say you ?
My prisoner? or my guest ? by your dread 'Verily,'
One of them you shall be.

Pol.   Your guest, then, madam :
To be your prisoner should import offending ;
Which is for me less easy to commit
Than you to punish.

Her.   Not your gaoler, then,
But your kind hostess.   Come, I 'll question you
Of my lord's tricks and yours when you were boys :

You were pretty lordings then?

Pol. 　　　　　　　　　　We were, fair queen,
　Two lads that thought there was no more behind,
　But such a day to-morrow as to-day,
　And to be boy eternal.

Her. 　　　　　　　　　　Was not my lord
　The verier wag o' the two?

Pol. We were as twinn'd lambs that did frisk i' the sun,
　And bleat the one at the other: what we changed
　Was innocence for innocence; we knew not
　The doctrine of ill-doing, nor dream'd
　That any did. Had we pursued that life,
　And our weak spirits ne'er been higher rear'd
　With stronger blood, we should have answer'd heaven
　Boldly 'not guilty;' the imposition clear'd
　Hereditary ours.

Her. 　　　　　　　　By this we gather
　You have tripp'd since.

Pol. 　　　　　　　　O my most sacred lady!
　Temptations have since then been born to's: for
　In those unfledged days was my wife a girl;
　Your precious self had then not cross'd the eyes
　Of my young play-fellow.

Her. 　　　　　　　　Grace to boot!
　Of this make no conclusion, lest you say
　Your queen and I are devils: yet go on;
　The offences we have made you do we'll answer,
　If you first sinn'd with us, and that with us
　You did continue fault, and that you slipp'd not
　With any but with us.

Leon. 　　　　　　　　Is he won yet?

Her. He'll stay, my lord.

Leon. 　　　　　　　　At my request he would not
　Hermione, my dearest, thou never spokest
　To better purpose.

Her. 　　　　　　　Never?

Leon. 　　　　　　　Never, but once.

Her. What! have I twice said well? when was't before?
　I prithee tell me; cram 's with praise, and make 's
　As fat as tame things: one good deed dying tongueless
　Slaughters a thousand waiting upon that.
　Our praises are our wages: you may ride 's
　With one soft kiss a thousand furlongs ere
　With spur we heat an acre. But to the goal:
　My last good deed was to entreat his stay:

What was my first? it has an elder sister,
Or I mistake you : O, would her name were Grace !
But once before I spoke to the purpose : when ?
Nay, let me have 't ; I long.

Leon.   Why, that was when
Three crabbed months had sour'd themselves to death,
Ere I could make thee open thy white hand,
And clap thyself my love : then didst thou utter
' I am yours for ever.'

Her.   'Tis Grace indeed.
Why, lo you now, I have spoke to the purpose twice :
The one for ever earn'd a royal husband ;
The other for some while a friend.

Leon.   [*Aside*] Too hot, too hot !
To mingle friendship far is mingling bloods.
I have tremor cordis on me : my heart dances ;
But not for joy ; not joy.   This entertainment
May a free face put on, derive a liberty
From heartiness, from bounty, fertile bosom,
And well become the agent ; 't may, I grant ;
But to be paddling palms and pinching fingers,
As now they are, and making practised smiles,
As in a looking-glass, and then to sigh, as 'twere
The mort o' the deer ; O, that is entertainment
My bosom likes not, nor my brows !   Mamillius,
Art thou my boy ?

Mam.   Ay, my good lord.

Leon.   I' fecks !
Why, that 's my bawcock.   What, hast smutch'd thy nose ?
They say it is a copy out of mine.   Come, captain,
We must be neat ; not neat, but cleanly, captain :
And yet the steer, the heifer and the calf
Are all call'd neat.—Still virginalling
Upon his palm !—How now, you wanton calf !
Art thou my calf ?

Mam.   Yes, if you will, my lord.

Leon. Thou want'st a rough pash and the shoots that I have
To be full like me : yet they say we are
Almost as like as eggs ; women say so,
That will say any thing : but were they false
As o'er-dyed blacks, as wind, as waters, false
As dice are to be wish'd by one that fixes
No bourn 'twixt his and mine, yet were it true
To say this boy were like me.   Come, sir page,
Look on me with your welkin eye : sweet villain !

Most dear'st! my collop! Can thy dam?—may't be?—
Affection! thy intention stabs the centre:
Thou dost make possible things not so held,
Communicatest with dreams;—how can this be?—
With what's unreal thou coactive art,
And fellow'st nothing: then 'tis very credent
Thou mayst co-join with something; and thou dost,
And that beyond commission, and I find it,
And that to the infection of my brains
And hardening of my brows.
Pol.   What means Sicilia?
Her. He something seems unsettled.
Pol.   How, my lord!
What cheer? how is't with you, best brother?
Her.   You look
As if you held a brow of much distraction:
Are you moved, my lord?
Leon.   No, in good earnest.
How sometimes nature will betray its folly,
Its tenderness, and make itself a pastime
To harder bosoms! Looking on the lines
Of my boy's face, methoughts I did recoil
Twenty-three years, and saw myself unbreech'd,
In my green velvet coat, my dagger muzzled
Lest it should bite its master, and so prove,
As ornaments oft do, too dangerous:
How like, methought, I then was to this kernel,
This squash, this gentleman   Mine honest friend,
Will you take eggs for money?
Mam. No, my lord, I'll fight.
Leon. You will! why, happy man be's dole! My brother,
Are you so fond of your young prince, as we
Do seem to be of ours?
Pol.   If at home, sir,
He's all my exercise, my mirth, my matter:
Now my sworn friend, and then mine enemy;
My parasite, my soldier, statesman, all:
He makes a July's day short as December;
And with his varying childness cures in me
Thoughts that would thick my blood.
Leon.   So stands this squire
Officed with me: we two will walk, my lord,
And leave you to your graver steps. Hermione,
How thou lovest us, show in our brother's welcome;
Let what is dear in Sicily be cheap:

Next to thyself and my young rover, he's
Apparent to my heart.
Her.   If you would seek us,
  We are yours i' the garden: shall's attend you there?
Leon. To your own bents dispose you: you'll be found,
  Be you beneath the sky. *[Aside]* I am angling now,
  Though you perceive me not how I give line.
  Go to, go to!
  How she holds up the neb, the bill to him!
  And arms her with the boldness of a wife
  To her allowing husband!
          [Exeunt Polixenes, Hermione, and Attendants.
               Gone already!
  Inch-thick, knee-deep, o'er head and ears a fork'd one!
  Go, play, boy, play: thy mother plays, and I
  Play too; but so disgraced a part, whose issue
  Will hiss me to my grave: contempt and clamour
  Will be my knell. Go, play, boy, play. There have been,
  Or I am much deceived, cuckolds ere now;
  And many a man there is, even at this present,
  Now, while I speak this, holds his wife by the arm,
  That little thinks she has been sluiced in's absence
  And his pond fish'd by his next neighbour, by
  Sir Smile, his neighbour: nay, there's comfort in't,
  Whiles other men have gates and those gates open'd,
  As mine, against their will. Should all despair
  That have revolted wives, the tenth of mankind
  Would hang themselves. Physic for 't there is none;
  It is a bawdy planet, that will strike
  Where 'tis predominant; and 'tis powerful, think it,
  From east, west, north and south: be it concluded,
  No barricado for a belly; know 't;
  It will let in and out the enemy
  With bag and baggage: many thousand on 's
  Have the disease, and feel 't not. How now, boy!
Mam. I am like you, they say.
Leon.   Why, that's some comfort.
  What, Camillo there?
Cam. Ay, my good lord.
Leon. Go play, Mamillius; thou'rt an honest man.
                   [Exit Mamillius.
  Camillo, this great sir will yet stay longer.
Cam. You had much ado to make his anchor hold:
  When you cast out, it still came home.
Leon.   Didst note it?

Cam. He would not stay at your petitions ; made
　　His business more material.
Leon.　　　　　　　　　　　Didst perceive it ?
　　[*Aside*] They 're here with me already ; whispering, rounding
　　' Sicilia is a so-forth :' 'tis far gone,
　　When I shall gust it last.—How came 't, Camillo,
　　That he did stay ?
Cam.　　　　　　　At the good queen's entreaty.
Leon. At the queen's be 't : ' good ' should be pertinent ;
　　But, so it is, it is not.　Was this taken
　　By any understanding pate but thine ?
　　For thy conceit is soaking, will draw in
　　More than the common blocks : not noted, is 't,
　　But of the finer natures ? by some severals
　　Of head-piece extraordinary ? lower messes
　　Perchance are to this business purblind ? say.
Cam. Business, my lord !　I think most understand
　　Bohemia stays here longer.
Leon.　　　　　　　　　Ha !
Cam.　　　　　　　　　　Stays here longer.
Leon. Ay, but why ?
Cam. To satisfy your highness, and the entreaties
　　Of our most gracious mistress.
Leon.　　　　　　　　　Satisfy !
　　The entreaties of your mistress ! satisfy !
　　Let that suffice.　I have trusted thee, Camillo,
　　With all the nearest things to my heart, as well
　　My chamber-councils ; wherein, priest-like, thou
　　Hast cleansed my bosom, I from thee departed
　　Thy penitent reform'd : but we have been
　　Deceived in thy integrity, deceived
　　In that which seems so.
Cam.　　　　　　　Be it forbid, my lord !
Leon. To bide upon 't, thou art not honest ; or,
　　If thou inclinest that way, thou art a coward,
　　Which hoxes honesty behind, restraining
　　From course required ; or else thou must be counted
　　A servant grafted in my serious trust
　　And therein negligent ; or else a fool
　　That seest a game play'd home, the rich stake drawn,
　　And takest it all for jest.
Cam.　　　　　　　My gracious lord,
　　I may be negligent, foolish and fearful ;
　　In every one of these no man is free,
　　But that his negligence, his folly, fear,

Among the infinite doings of the world,
Sometime puts forth.   In your affairs, my lord,
If ever I were wilful-negligent,
It was my folly ; if industriously
I play'd the fool. it was my negligence,
Not weighing well the end ; if ever fearful
To do a thing, where I the issue doubted,
Whereof the execution did cry out
Against the non-performance, 'twas a fear
Which oft infects the wisest : these, my lord,
Are such allow'd infirmities that honesty
Is never free of.   But, beseech your Grace,
Be plainer with me ; let me know my trespass
By its own visage : if I then deny it,
'Tis none of mine.

Leon.   Ha' not you seen, Camillo,—
But that's past doubt, you have, or your eye-glass
Is thicker than a cuckold's horn,—or heard,—
For to a vision so apparent rumour
Cannot be mute,—or thought,—for cogitation
Resides not in that man that does not think,—
My wife is slippery ?   If thou wilt confess,
Or else be impudently negative,
To have nor eyes nor ears nor thought, then say
My wife's a hobby-horse ; deserves a name
As rank as any flax-wench that puts to
Before her troth-plight : say 't and justify 't.

Cam. I would not be a stander-by to hear
My sovereign mistress clouded so, without
My present vengeance taken : 'shrew my heart,
You never spoke what did become you less
Than this ; which to reiterate were sin
As deep as that, though true.

Leon.   Is whispering nothing ?
Is leaning cheek to cheek ? is meeting noses ?
Kissing with inside lip ? stopping the career
Of laughter with a sigh ?—a note infallible
Of breaking honesty ;—horsing foot on foot ?
Skulking in corners ? wishing clocks more swift ?
Hours, minutes ? noon, midnight ? and all eyes
Blind with the pin and web but theirs, theirs only,
That would unseen be wicked ? is this nothing ?
Why, then the world and all that's in 't is nothing ;
The covering sky is nothing ; Bohemia nothing ;
My wife is nothing ; nor nothing have these nothings,

If this be nothing.
Cam.   Good my lord, be cured
Of this diseased opinion, and betimes;
For 'tis most dangerous.
Leon.   Say it be, 'tis true.
Cam. No, no, my lord.
Leon.   It is; you lie, you lie:
I say thou liest, Camillo, and I hate thee,
Pronounce thee a gross lout, a mindless slave,
Or else a hovering temporizer, that
Canst with thine eyes at once see good and evil,
Inclining to them both: were my wife's liver
Infected as her life, she would not live
The running of one glass.
Cam.   Who does infect her?
Leon. Why, he that wears her like her medal, hanging
About his neck, Bohemia: who, if I
Had servants true about me, that bare eyes
To see alike mine honour as their profits,
Their own particular thrifts, they would do that
Which should undo more doing: ay, and thou,
His cupbearer,—whom I from meaner form
Have bench'd and rear'd to worship, who mayst see
Plainly as heaven sees earth and earth sees heaven,
How I am gall'd,—mightst bespice a cup,
To give mine enemy a lasting wink;
Which draught to me were cordial.
Cam.   Sir, my lord,
I could do this, and that with no rash potion,
But with a lingering dram, that should not work
Maliciously like poison: but I cannot
Believe this crack to be in my dread mistress,
So sovereignly being honourable.
I have loved thee,—
Leon.   Make that thy question, and go rot!
Dost think I am so muddy, so unsettled,
To appoint myself in this vexation; sully
The purity and whiteness of my sheets,
Which to preserve is sleep, which being spotted
Is goads, thorns, nettles, tails of wasps;
Give scandal to the blood o' the prince my son,
Who I do think is mine and love as mine,
Without ripe moving to 't? Would I do this?
Could man so blench?
Cam.   I must believe you, sir:

I do; and will fetch off Bohemia for't;
Provided that, when he's removed, your highness
Will take again your queen as yours at first,
Even for your son's sake; and thereby for sealing
The injury of tongues in courts and kingdoms
Known and allied to yours.

Leon.   Thou dost advise me
Even so as I mine own course have set down:
I'll give no blemish to her honour, none.

Cam. My lord,
Go then; and with a countenance as clear
As friendship wears at feasts, keep with Bohemia
And with your queen.   I am his cupbearer:
If from me he have wholesome beverage,
Account me not your servant.

Leon.   This is all:
Do't, and thou hast the one half of my heart;
Do't not, thou splitt'st thine own.

Cam.   I'll do't, my lord.

Leon. I will seem friendly, as thou hast advised me.   [*Exit.*

Cam. O miserable lady!   But, for me,
What case stand I in?   I must be the poisoner
Of good Polixenes: and my ground to do't
Is the obedience to a master, one
Who, in rebellion with himself, will have
All that are his so too.   To do this deed,
Promotion follows.   If I could find example
Of thousands that had struck anointed kings
And flourish'd after, I'ld not do't; but since
Nor brass nor stone nor parchment bears not one,
Let villany itself forswear't.   I must
Forsake the court: to do't, or no, is certain
To me a break-neck.   Happy star reign now!
Here comes Bohemia.

Re-enter Polixenes.

Pol.   This is strange: methinks
My favour here begins to warp.   Not speak?
Good day, Camillo.

Cam.   Hail, most royal sir!

Pol. What is the news i' the court?

Cam.   None rare, my lord.

Pol. The king hath on him such a countenance
As he had lost some province, and a region
Loved as he loves himself: even now I met him
With customary compliment; when he,

　　Wafting his eyes to the contrary, and falling
　　A lip of much contempt, speeds from me and
　　So leaves me, to consider what is breeding
　　That changes thus his manners.
Cam. I dare not know, my lord.
Pol. How! dare not! do not.　Do you know, and dare not?
　　Be intelligent to me: 'tis thereabouts;
　　For, to yourself, what you do know, you must,
　　And cannot say, you dare not.　Good Camillo,
　　Your changed complexions are to me a mirror
　　Which shows me mine changed too; for I must be
　　A party in this alteration, finding
　　Myself thus alter'd with 't.
Cam.　　　　　　　　　There is a sickness
　　Which puts some of us in distemper; but
　　I cannot name the disease; and it is caught
　　Of you that yet are well.
Pol.　　　　　　　　　How! caught of me!
　　Make me not sighted like the basilisk:
　　I have look'd on thousands, who have sped the better
　　By my regard, but kill'd none so.　Camillo,—
　　As you are certainly a gentleman; thereto
　　Clerk-like experienced, which no less adorns
　　Our gentry than our parents' noble names,
　　In whose success we are gentle,—I beseech you,
　　If you know aught which does behove my knowledge
　　Thereof to be inform'd, imprison 't not
　　In ignorant concealment.
Cam.　　　　　　　　　I may not answer.
Pol. A sickness caught of me, and yet I well!
　　I must be answer'd.　Dost thou hear, Camillo?
　　I conjure thee, by all the parts of man
　　Which honour does acknowledge, whereof the least
　　Is not this suit of mine, that thou declare
　　What incidency thou dost guess of harm
　　Is creeping toward me; how far off, how near:
　　Which way to be prevented, if to be;
　　If not, how best to bear it.
Cam.　　　　　　　　　Sir, I will tell you;
　　Since I am charged in honour and by him
　　That I think honourable: therefore mark my counsel,
　　Which must be ev'n as swiftly follow'd as
　　I mean to utter it, or both yourself and me
　　Cry lost, and so good night!
Pol.　　　　　　　　　On, good Camillo.

Cam. I am appointed him to murder you.
Pol. By whom, Camillo?
Cam.   By the king.
Pol.   For what?
Cam. He thinks, nay, with all confidence he swears,
    As he had seen 't, or been an instrument
    To vice you to 't, that you have touch'd his queen
    Forbiddenly.
Pol.   O then, my best blood turn
    To an infected jelly, and my name
    Be yoked with his that did betray the Best!
    Turn then my freshest reputation to
    A savour that may strike the dullest nostril
    Where I arrive, and my approach be shunn'd,
    Nay, hated too, worse than the great'st infection
    That e'er was heard or read!
Cam.   Swear his thought over
    By each particular star in heaven and
    By all their influences, you may as well
    Forbid the sea for to obey the moon,
    As or by oath remove or counsel shake
    The fabric of his folly, whose foundation
    Is piled upon his faith, and will continue
    The standing of his body.
Pol.   How should this grow?
Cam. I know not: but I am sure 'tis safer to
    Avoid what's grown than question how 'tis born.
    If therefore you dare trust my honesty,
    That lies enclosed in this trunk which you
    Shall bear along impawn'd, away to-night!
    Your followers I will whisper to the business;
    And will by twos and threes at several posterns,
    Clear them o' the city. For myself, I'll put
    My fortunes to your service, which are here
    By this discovery lost. Be not uncertain;
    For, by the honour of my parents, I
    Have utter'd truth: which if you seek to prove,
    I dare not stand by; nor shall you be safer
    That one condemn'd by the king's own mouth, thereon
    His execution sworn.
Pol.   I do believe thee:
    I saw his heart in 's face. Give me thy hand:
    Be pilot to me and thy places shall
    Still neighbour mine. My ships are ready, and
    My people did expect my hence departure

Two days ago.   This jealousy
Is for a precious creature : as she 's rare,
Must it be great ; and, as his person 's mighty,
Must it be violent ; and as he does conceive
He is dishonour'd by a man which ever
Profess'd to him, why, his revenges must
In that be made more bitter.   Fear o'ershades me
Good expedition be my friend, and comfort
The gracious queen, part of his theme, but nothing
Of his ill-ta'en suspicion !   Come, Camillo ;
I will respect thee as a father if
Thou bear'st my life off hence : let us avoid.
Cam. It is in mine authority to command
The keys of all the posterns : please your highness
To take the urgent hour.   Come, sir, away.   [*Exeunt.*

ACT II—Scene I

A room in Leontes' palace.
Enter Hermione, Mamillius, and Ladies.

Her. Take the boy to you ; he so troubles me,
'Tis past enduring.
First Lady. Come, my gracious lord,
Shall I be your playfellow ?
Mam.   No, I 'll none of you.
First Lady. Why, my sweet lord ?
Mam. You 'll kiss me hard, and speak to me as if
I were a baby still.   I love you better.
Sec. Lady. And why so, my lord ?
Mam.   Not for because
Your brows are blacker ; yet black brows, they say,
Become some women best, so that there be not
Too much hair there, but in a semicircle,
Or a half-moon made with a pen.
Sec. Lady.   Who taught you this ?
Mam. I learn'd it out of women's faces.   Pray now
What colour are your eyebrows ?
First Lady.   Blue, my lord.
Mam. Nay, that 's a mock : I have seen a lady's nose
That has been blue, but not her eyebrows.
First Lady.   Hark ye ;
The queen your mother rounds apace : we shall
Present our services to a fine new prince
One of these days ; and then you 'ld wanton with us,
If we would have you.

Sec. Lady.   She is spread of late
 Into a goodly bulk : good time encounter her !
Her. What wisdom stirs amongst you ? Come, sir, now
 I am for you again : pray you, sit by us,
 And tell 's a tale.
Mam.   Merry or sad shall 't be ?
Her. As merry as you will.
Mam. A sad tale 's best for winter : I have one
 Of sprites and goblins.
Her.   Let 's have that, good sir.
 Come on, sit down : come on, and do your best
 To fright me with your sprites ; you 're powerful at it.
Mam. There was a man—
Her.   Nay, come, sit down ; then on.
Mam. Dwelt by a churchyard : I will tell it softly ;
 Yond crickets shall not hear it.
Her.   Come on, then,
 And give 't me in mine ear.
        Enter Leontes, with Antigonus, Lords, and others.
Leon. Was he met there ? his train ? Camillo with him ?
First Lord. Behind the tuft of pines I met them ; never
 Saw I men scour so on their way : I eyed them
 Even to their ships.
Leon.   How blest am I
 In my just censure, in my true opinion !
 Alack, for lesser knowledge ! how accursed
 In being so blest ! There may be in the cup
 A spider steep'd, and one may drink, depart,
 And yet partake no venom ; for his knowledge
 Is not infected : but if one present
 The abhorr'd ingredient to his eye, make known
 How he hath drunk, he cracks his gorge, his sides,
 With violent hefts. I have drunk, and seen the spider.
 Camillo was his help in this, his pandar :
 There is a plot against my life, my crown ;
 All 's true that is mistrusted : that false villain
 Whom I employ'd was pre-employ'd by him :
 He has discover'd my design, and I
 Remain a pinch'd thing ; yea, a very trick
 For them to play at will. How came the posterns
 So easily open ?
First Lord.   By his great authority ;
 Which often hath no less prevail'd than so
 On your command.
Leon.   I know 't too well.

433

Give me the boy : I am glad you did not nurse him .
Though he does bear some signs of me, yet you
Have too much blood in him.

Her.   What is this ? sport ?

Leon. Bear the boy hence ; he shall not come about her ;
Away with him ! and let her sport herself
With that she 's big with ; for 'tis Polixenes
Has made the swell thus.

Her.   But I 'ld say he had not,
And I 'll be sworn you would believe my saying,
Howe 'er you lean to the nayward.

Leon.   You, my lords,
Look on her, mark her well ; be but about
To say ' she is a goodly lady,' and
The justice of your hearts will thereto add
' 'Tis pity she 's not honest, honourable : '
Praise her but for this her without-door form,
Which on my faith deserves high speech, and straight
The shrug, the hum or ha, these pretty brands
That calumny doth use ; O, I am out,
That mercy does, for calumny will sear
Virtue itself : these shrugs, these hums and ha's,
When you have said ' she 's goodly,' come between
Ere you can say ' she 's honest : ' but be 't known,
From him that has most cause to grieve it should be,
She 's an adulteress.

Her.   Should a villain say so,
The most replenish'd villain in the world,
He were as much more villain : you, my lord,
Do but mistake.

Leon.   You have mistook, my lady,
Polixenes for Leontes : O thou thing !
Which I 'll not call a creature of thy place,
Lest barbarism, making me the precedent,
Should a like language use to all degrees,
And mannerly distinguishment leave out
Betwixt the prince and beggar : I have said
She 's an adulteress ; I have said with whom :
More, she 's a traitor and Camillo is
A federary with her ; and one that knows,
What she should shame to know herself
But with her most vile principal, that she 's
A bed-swerver, even as bad as those
That vulgars give bold'st titles ; ay, and privy
To this their late escape.

Her.   No, by my life,
    Privy to none of this.   How will this grieve you,
    When you shall come to clearer knowledge, that
    You thus have publish'd me!   Gentle my lord,
    You scarce can right me thoroughly then to say
    You did mistake.
Leon.   No; if I mistake
    In those foundations which I build upon,
    The centre is not big enough to bear
    A school-boy's top.   Away with her, to prison!
    He who shall speak for her is afar off guilty
    But that he speaks.
Her.   There's some ill planet reigns:
    I must be patient till the heavens look
    With an aspect more favourable.   Good my lords,
    I am not prone to weeping, as our sex
    Commonly are; the want of which vain dew
    Perchance shall dry your pities: but I have
    That honourable grief lodged here which burns
    Worse than tears drown: beseech you all, my lords,
    With thoughts so qualified as your charities
    Shall best instruct you, measure me; and so
    The king's will be perform'd!
Leon.   Shall I be heard?
Her. Who is 't that goes with me?   Beseech your highness,
    My women may be with me; for you see
    My plight requires it.   Do not weep, good fools;
    There is no cause: when you shall know your mistress
    Has deserved prison, then abound in tears
    As I come out: this action I now go on
    Is for my better grace.   Adieu, my lord:
    I never wish'd to see you sorry; now
    I trust I shall.   My women, come; you have leave.
Leon. Go, do our bidding; hence!
                    [*Exit Queen, guarded; with Ladies.*
First Lord. Beseech your highness, call the queen again.
Ant. Be certain what you do, sir, lest your justice
    Prove violence; in the which three great ones suffer,
    Yourself, your queen, your son.
First Lord.   For her, my lord,
    I dare my life lay down and will do 't, sir,
    Please you to accept it, that the queen is spotless
    I' the eyes of heaven and to you; I mean,
    In this which you accuse her.
Ant.   If it prove

435

    She's otherwise, I'll keep my stables where
    I lodge my wife; I'll go in couples with her;
    Than when I feel and see her no farther trust her;
    For every inch of woman in the world,
    Ay, every dram of woman's flesh is false,
    If she be.
Leon.   Hold your peaces.
First Lord.   Good my lord,
Ant. It is for you we speak, not for ourselves:
    You are abused, and by some putter-on
    That will be damn'd for't; would I knew the villain,
    I would land-damn him. Be she honour-flaw'd,
    I have three daughters; the eldest is eleven;
    The second and the third, nine, and some five;
    If this prove true, they'll pay for't: by mine honour,
    I'll geld 'em all; fourteen they shall not see,
    To bring false generations: they are co-heirs;
    And I had rather glib myself than they
    Should not produce fair issue.
Leon.   Cease; no more.
    You smell this business with a sense as cold
    As is a dead man's nose: but I do see't and feel't,
    As you feel doing thus; and see withal
    The instruments that feel.
Ant.   If it be so,
    We need no grave to bury honesty:
    There's not a grain of it the face to sweeten
    Of the whole dungy earth.
Leon.   What! lack I credit?
First Lord. I had rather you did lack than I, my lord,
    Upon this ground; and more it would content me
    To have her honour true than your suspicion,
    Be blamed for't how you might.
Leon.   Why, what need we
    Commune with you of this, but rather follow
    Our forceful instigation? Our prerogative
    Calls not your counsels, but our natural goodness
    Imparts this; which if you, or stupified
    Or seeming so in skill, cannot or will not
    Relish a truth like us, inform yourselves
    We need no more of your advice: the matter,
    The loss, the gain, the ordering on't, is all
    Properly ours.
Ant.   And I wish, my liege,
    You had only in your silent judgement tried it,

Without more overture.
Leon.   How could that be?
Either thou art most ignorant by age,
Or thou wert born a fool.   Camillo's flight,
Added to their familiarity,
Which was as gross as ever touch'd conjecture,
That lack'd sight only, nought for approbation
But only seeing, all other circumstances
Made up to the deed,—doth push on this proceeding:
Yet, for a greater confirmation,
For in an act of this importance 'twere
Most piteous to be wild, I have dispatch'd in post
To sacred Delphos, to Apollo's temple,
Cleomenes and Dion, whom you know
Of stuff'd sufficiency: now from the oracle
They will bring all; whose spiritual counsel had,
Shall stop or spur me.   Have I done well?
First Lord. Well done, my lord.
Leon. Though I am satisfied and need no more
Than what I know, yet shall the oracle
Give rest to the minds of others, such as he
Whose ignorant credulity will not
Come up to the truth.   So have we thought it good
From our free person she should be confined,
Lest that the treachery of the two fled hence
Be left her to perform.   Come, follow us;
We are to speak in public; for this business
Will raise us all.
Ant.   [*Aside*] To laughter, as I take it,
If the good truth were known.   [*Exeunt.*

Scene II
A prison.
Enter Paulina, a Gentleman, and Attendants.

Paul. The keeper of the prison, call to him;
Let him have knowledge who I am.   [*Exit Gent.*
                              Good lady,
No court in Europe is too good for thee;
What dost thou then in prison?
              Re-enter Gentleman, with the Gaoler.
                         Now, good sir,
You know me, do you not?
Gaol.   For a worthy lady
And one who much I honour.
Paul.   Pray you, then,

Conduct me to the queen.
Gaol.   I may not, madam:
To the contrary I have express commandment.
Paul. Here's ado,
To lock up honesty and honour from
The access of gentle visitors! Is't lawful, pray you,
To see her women? any of them? Emilia?
Gaol. So please you, madam,
To put apart these your attendants, I
Shall bring Emilia forth.
Paul.   I pray now, call her.
Withdraw yourselves.   [*Exeunt Gentleman and Attendants.*
Gaol.   And, madam,
I must be present at your conference.
Paul. Well, be't so, prithee.   [*Exit Gaoler.*
Here's such ado to make no stain a stain
As passes colouring.
                    Re-enter Gaoler, with Emilia.
                          Dear gentlewoman,
How fares our gracious lady?
Emil. As well as one so great and so forlorn
May hold together: on her frights and griefs,
Which never tender lady hath borne greater,
She is something before her time deliver'd.
Paul. A boy?
Emil.   A daughter; and a goodly babe,
Lusty and like to live: the queen receives
Much comfort in't; says 'My poor prisoner,
I am innocent as you.'
Paul.   I dare be sworn:
These dangerous unsafe lunes i' the king, beshrew them!
He must be told on't, and he shall: the office
Becomes a woman best; I'll take't upon me:
If I prove honey-mouth'd, let my tongue blister,
And never to my red-look'd anger be
The trumpet any more.   Pray you, Emilia,
Commend my best obedience to the queen:
If she dares trust me with her little babe,
I'll show't the king and undertake to be
Her advocate to the loud'st.   We do not know
How he may soften at the sight o' the child:
The silence often of pure innocence
Persuades when speaking fails.
Emil.   Most worthy madam,
Your honour and your goodness is so evident,

That your free undertaking cannot miss
A thriving issue: there is no lady living
So meet for this great errand.   Please your ladyship
To visit the next room, I 'll presently
Acquaint the queen of your most noble offer;
Who but to-day hammer'd of this design,
But durst not tempt a minister of honour,
Lest she should be denied.

Paul.   Tell her, Emilia,
I 'll use that tongue I have: if wit flow from 't
As boldness from my bosom, let 't not be doubted
I shall do good.

Emil.   Now be you blest for it!
I 'll to the queen: please you, come something nearer.

Gaol. Madam, if 't please the queen to send the babe,
I know not what I shall incur to pass it,
Having no warrant.

Paul.   You need not fear it, sir:
This child was prisoner to the womb, and is
By law and process of great nature thence
Freed and enfranchised; not a party to
The anger of the king, nor guilty of,
If any be, the trespass of the queen.

Gaol. I do believe it.

Paul. Do not you fear: upon mine honour, I
Will stand betwixt you and danger.   [*Exeunt.*

Scene III

A room in Leontes' palace.
Enter Leontes, Antigonus, Lords, and Servants.

Leon. Nor night nor day no rest: it is but weakness
To bear the matter thus; mere weakness.   If
The cause were not in being,—part o' the cause,
She the adulteress; for the harlot king
Is quite beyond mine arm, out of the blank
And level of my brain, plot-proof; but she
I can hook to me: say that she were gone,
Given to the fire, a moiety of my rest
Might come to me again.   Who 's there?

First Serv.   My lord?

Leon. How does the boy?

First Serv.   He took good rest to-night;
'Tis hoped his sickness is discharged.

Leon. To see his nobleness!
Conceiving the dishonour of his mother,

He straight declined, droop'd, took it deeply,
Fasten'd and fix'd the shame on 't in himself,
Threw off his spirit, his appetite, his sleep,
And downright languish'd. Leave me solely: go,
See how he fares. [*Exit Serv.*] Fie, fie! no thought of him:
The very thought of my revenges that way
Recoil upon me: in himself too mighty,
And in his parties, his alliance; let him be
Until a time may serve: for present vengeance,
Take it on her. Camillo and Polixenes
Laugh at me, make their pastime at my sorrow:
They should not laugh if I could reach them, nor
Shall she within my power.

Enter Paulina, with a child.

First Lord.   You must not enter.

Paul. Nay, rather, good my lords, be second to me:
Fear you his tyrannous passion more, alas,
Than the queen's life? a gracious innocent soul,
More free than he is jealous.

Ant.   That's enough.

Sec. Serv. Madam, he hath not slept to-night; commanded
None should come at him.

Paul.   Not so hot, good sir:
I come to bring him sleep. 'Tis such as you,
That creep like shadows by him, and do sigh
At each his needless heavings, such as you
Nourish the cause of his awaking: I
Do come with words as medicinal as true,
Honest as either, to purge him of that humour
That presses him from sleep.

Leon.   What noise there, ho?

Paul. No noise, my lord; but needful conference
About some gossips for your highness.

Leon.   How?
Away with that audacious lady! Antigonus,
I charged thee that she should not come about me:
I knew she would.

Ant.   I told her so, my lord,
On your displeasure's peril and on mine,
She should not visit you.

Leon.   What, canst not rule her?

Paul. From all dishonesty he can: in this,
Unless he take the course that you have done,
Commit me for committing honour, trust it,
He shall not rule me.

Ant.   La you now, you hear:
When she will take the rein I let her run;
But she 'll not stumble.
Paul.   Good my liege, I come;
And, I beseech you, hear me, who professes
Myself your loyal servant, your physician,
Your most obedient counsellor, yet that dares
Less appear so in comforting your evils,
Than such as most seem yours: I say, I come
From your good queen.
Leon.   Good queen!
Paul.   Good queen, my lord,
Good queen; I say good queen;
And would by combat make her good, so were I
A man, the worst about you.
Leon.   Force her hence.
Paul. Let him that makes but trifles of his eyes
First hand me: on mine own accord I 'll off;
But first I 'll do my errand. The good queen,
For she is good, hath brought you forth a daughter;
Here 'tis; commends it to your blessing.
                                   [*Laying down the child.*
Leon.   Out!
A mankind witch! Hence with her, out o' door:
A most intelligencing bawd!
Paul.   Not so:
I am as ignorant in that as you
In so entitling me, and no less honest
Than you are mad; which is enough, I 'll warrant,
As this world goes, to pass for honest.
Leon.   Traitors!
Will you not push her out? Give her the bastard.
Thou dotard! thou art woman-tired, unroosted
By thy dame Partlet here. Take up the bastard;
Take 't up, I say; give 't to thy crone.
Paul.   For ever
Unvenerable be thy hands, if thou
Takest up the princess by that forced baseness
Which he has put upon 't!
Leon.   He dreads his wife.
Paul. So I would you did; then 'twere past all doubt
You 'ld call your children yours.
Leon.   A nest of traitors!
Ant. I am none, by this good light.
Paul.   Nor I; nor any

441

But one that 's here, and that 's himself; for he
The sacred honour of himself, his queen's,
His hopeful son's, his babe's, betrays to slander,
Whose sting is sharper than the sword's; and will not,—
For, as the case now stands, it is a curse
He cannot be compell'd to 't,—once remove
The root of his opinion, which is rotten
As ever oak or stone was sound.

Leon.   A callat
Of boundless tongue, who late hath beat her husband
And now baits me!   This brat is none of mine;
It is the issue of Polixenes:
Hence with it, and together with the dam
Commit them to the fire!

Paul.   It is yours;
And, might we lay the old proverb to your charge,
So like you, 'tis the worse.   Behold, my lords,
Although the print be little, the whole matter
And copy of the father, eye, nose, lip;
The trick of 's frown; his forehead; nay, the valley,
The pretty dimples of his chin and cheek; his smiles;
The very mould and frame of hand, nail, finger:
And thou, good goddess Nature, which hast made it
So like to him that got it, if thou hast
The ordering of the mind too, 'mongst all colours
No yellow in 't, lest she suspect, as he does,
Her children not her husband's!

Leon.   A gross hag!
And, lozel, thou art worthy to be hang 'd,
That wilt not stay her tongue.

Ant.   Hang all the husbands
That cannot do that feat, you 'll leave yourself
Hardly one subject.

Leon.   Once more, take her hence.

Paul. A most unworthy and unnatural lord
Can do no more.

Leon.   I 'll ha' thee burnt.

Paul.   I care not:
It is an heretic that makes the fire,
Not she which burns in 't.   I 'll not call you tyrant;
But this most cruel usage of your queen—
Not able to produce more accusation
Than your own weak-hinged fancy—something savours
Of tyranny, and will ignoble make you,
Yea, scandalous to the world.

Leon.   On your allegiance,
    Out of the chamber with her ! Were I a tyrant,
    Where were her life? she durst not call me so,
    If she did know me one. Away with her !
Paul. I pray you, do not push me ; I 'll be gone.
    Look to your babe, my lord ; 'tis yours : Jove send her
    A better guiding spirit ! What needs these hands?
    You, that are thus so tender o'er his follies,
    Will never do him good, not one of you.
    So, so : farewell ; we are gone.   [*Exit.*
Leon. Thou, traitor, hast set on thy wife to this.
    My child? away with 't ! Even thou, that hast
    A heart so tender o'er it, take it hence
    And see it instantly consumed with fire ;
    Even thou and none but thou. Take it up straight :
    Within this hour bring me word 'tis done,
    And by good testimony, or I 'll seize thy life,
    With what thou else call'st thine. If thou refuse
    And wilt encounter with my wrath, say so ;
    The bastard brains with these my proper hands
    Shall I dash out. Go, take it to the fire ;
    For thou set'st on thy wife.
Ant.   I did not, sir :
    These lords, my noble fellows, if they please,
    Can clear me in 't.
Lords.   We can : my royal liege,
    He is not guilty of her coming hither.
Leon. You 're liars all.
First Lord. Beseech your highness, give us better credit :
    We have always truly served you ; and beseech you
    So to esteem of us : and on our knees we beg,
    As recompense of our dear services
    Past and to come, that you do change this purpose,
    Which being so horrible, so bloody, must
    Lead on to some foul issue : we all kneel.
Leon. I am a feather for each wind that blows :
    Shall I live on to see this bastard kneel
    And call me father? better burn it now
    Than curse it then. But be it ; let it live.
    It shall not neither. You, sir, come you hither ;
    You that have been so tenderly officious
    With Lady Margery, your midwife there,
    To save this bastard's life,—for 'tis a bastard,
    So sure as this beard 's grey,—what will you adventure
    To save this brat's life ?

Ant.   Any thing, my lord,
  That my ability may undergo,
  And nobleness impose: at least thus much:
  I'll pawn the little blood which I have left
  To save the innocent: any thing possible.
Leon. It shall be possible. Swear by this sword
  Thou wilt perform my bidding.
Ant   I will, my lord.
Leon. Mark and perform it: seest thou? for the fail
  Of any point in 't shall not only be
  Death to thyself but to thy lewd-tongued wife,
  Whom for this time we pardon. We enjoin thee,
  As thou art liege-man to us, that thou carry
  This female bastard hence, and that thou bear it
  To some remote and desert place, quite out
  Of our dominions; and that there thou leave it,
  Without more mercy, to its own protection
  And favour of the climate. As by strange fortune
  It came to us, I do in justice charge thee,
  On thy soul's peril and thy body's torture,
  That thou commend it strangely to some place
  Where chance may nurse or end it. Take it up.
Ant. I swear to do this, though a present death
  Had been more merciful. Come on, poor babe:
  Some powerful spirit instruct the kites and ravens
  To be thy nurses! Wolves and bears, they say,
  Casting their savageness aside have done
  Like offices of pity. Sir, be prosperous
  In more than this deed does require! And blessing
  Against this cruelty fight on thy side,
  Poor thing, condemn'd to loss!   [*Exit with the child.*
Leon.   No, I'll not rear
  Another's issue.
                    Enter a Servant.
Serv.   Please your highness, posts
  From those you sent to the oracle are come
  An hour since: Cleomenes and Dion,
  Being well arrived from Delphos, are both landed,
  Hasting to the court.
First Lord.   So please you, sir, their speed
  Hath been beyond account.
Leon.   Twenty three days
  They have been absent: 'tis good speed; foretells
  The great Apollo suddenly will have
  The truth of this appear. Prepare you, lords;

Summon a session, that we may arraign
Our most disloyal lady ; for, as she hath
Been publicly accused, so shall she have
A just and open trial.   While she lives
My heart will be a burthen to me.   Leave me,
And think upon my bidding.   [*Exeunt.*

ACT III—SCENE I
A seaport in Sicilia.
Enter Cleomenes and Dion.

Cleo. The climate 's delicate, the air most sweet,
  Fertile the isle, the temple much surpassing
  The common praise it bears.
Dion.   I shall report,
  For most it caught me, the celestial habits,
  Methinks I so should term them, and the reverence
  Of the grave wearers.   O, the sacrifice !
  How ceremonious, solemn and unearthly
  It was i' the offering !
Cleo.   But of all, the burst
  And the ear-deafening voice o' the oracle,
  Kin to Jove's thunder, so surprised my sense,
  That I was nothing.
Dion.   If the event o' the journey
  Prove as successful to the queen,—O be 't so !—
  As it hath been to us rare, pleasant, speedy,
  The time is worth the use on 't.
Cleo.   Great Apollo
  Turn all to the best !   These proclamations,
  So forcing faults upon Hermione,
  I little like.
Dion.   The violent carriage of it
  Will clear or end the business : when the oracle,
  Thus by Apollo's great divine seal'd up,
  Shall the contents discover, something rare
  Even then will rush to knowledge.   Go : fresh horses !
  And gracious be the issue.   [*Exeunt.*

SCENE II
A court of Justice.
Enter Leontes, Lords, and Officers.

Leon. This sessions, to our great grief we pronounce,
  Even pushes 'gainst our heart : the party tried
  The daughter of a king, our wife, and one

Of us too much beloved.   Let us be clear'd
Of being tyrannous, since we so openly
Proceed in justice, which shall have due course,
Even to the guilt or the purgation.
Produce the prisoner.

Off. It is his highness' pleasure that the queen
Appear in person here in court.   Silence!

Enter Hermione guarded ; Paulina and Ladies attending.

Leon. Read the indictment.

Off. [*reads*] Hermione, queen to the worthy Leontes, king of
Sicilia, thou art here accused and arraigned of high treason, in
committing adultery with Polixenes, king of Bohemia, and
conspiring with Camillo to take away the life of our sovereign
lord the king, thy royal husband : the pretence whereof being
by circumstances partly laid open, thou, Hermione, contrary
to the faith and allegiance of a true subject, didst counsel and
aid them, for their better safety, to fly away by night.

Her. Since what I am to say must be but that
Which contradicts my accusation, and
The testimony on my part no other
But what comes from myself, it shall scarce boot me
To say ' not guilty:' mine integrity,
Being counted falsehood, shall, as I express it,
Be so received.   But thus, if powers divine
Behold our human actions, as they do,
I doubt not then but innocence shall make
False accusation blush, and tyranny
Tremble at patience.   You, my lord, best know,
Who least will seem to do so, my past life
Hath been as continent, as chaste, as true,
As I am now unhappy ; which is more
Than history can pattern, though devised
And play'd to take spectators.   For behold me
A fellow of the royal bed, which owe
A moiety of the throne, a great king's daughter,
The mother to a hopeful prince, here standing
To prate and talk for life and honour 'fore
Who please to come and hear.   For life, I prize it
As I weigh grief, which I would spare : for honour,
'Tis a derivative from me to mine,
And only that I stand for.   I appeal
To your own conscience, sir, before Polixenes
Came to your court, how I was in your grace,
How merited to be so ; since he came,
With what encounter so uncurrent I

Have strain'd, to appear thus: if one jot beyond
The bound of honour, or in act or will
That way inclining, harden'd be the hearts
Of all that hear me, and my near'st of kin
Cry fie upon my grave!
Leon.   I ne'er heard yet
That any of these bolder vices wanted
Less impudence to gainsay what they did
Than to perform it first.
Her.   That's true enough;
Though 'tis a saying, sir, not due to me.
Leon. You will not own it.
Her.   More than mistress of
Which comes to me in name of fault, I must not
At all acknowledge.   For Polixenes,
With whom I am accused, I do confess
I loved him as in honour he required,
With such a kind of love as might become
A lady like me, with a love even such,
So and no other, as yourself commanded:
Which not to have done I think had been in me
Both disobedience and ingratitude
To you and toward your friend; whose love had spoke,
Even since it could speak, from an infant, freely
That it was yours.   Now, for conspiracy,
I know not how it tastes; though it be dish'd
For me to try how: all I know of it
Is that Camillo was an honest man;
And why he left your court, the gods themselves,
Wotting no more than I, are ignorant.
Leon. You knew of his departure, as you know
What you have underta'en to do in's absence.
Her. Sir,
You speak a language that I understand not:
My life stands in the level of your dreams,
Which I'll lay down.
Leon.   Your actions are my dreams;
You had a bastard by Polixenes,
And I but dream'd it.   As you were past all shame,—
Those of your fact are so,—so past all truth:
Which to deny concerns more than avails; for as
Thy brat hath been cast out, like to itself,
No father owning it,—which is, indeed,
More criminal in thee than it,—so thou
Shalt feel our justice, in whose easiest passage

Look for no less than death.

Her.   Sir, spare your threats :
The bug which you would fright me with I seek.
To me can life be no commodity :
The crown and comfort of my life, your favour,
I do give lost ; for I do feel it gone,
But know not how it went.   My second joy
And first-fruits of my body, from his presence
I am barr'd, like one infectious.   My third comfort,
Starr'd most unluckily, is from my breast,
The innocent milk in its most innocent mouth,
Haled out to murder : myself on every post
Proclaim'd a strumpet : with immodest hatred
The child-bed privilege denied, which 'longs
To women of all fashion ; lastly, hurried
Here to this place, i' the open air, before
I have got strength of limit.   Now, my liege,
Tell me what blessings I have here alive,
That I should fear to die ?   Therefore proceed.
But yet hear this ; mistake me not ; no life,
I prize it not a straw, but for mine honour,
Which I would free, if I shall be condemn'd
Upon surmises, all proofs sleeping else
But what your jealousies awake, I tell you
'Tis rigour and not law.   Your honours all,
I do refer me to the oracle :
Apollo be my judge !

First Lord.   This your request
Is altogether just : therefore bring forth,
And in Apollo's name, his oracle.   [*Exeunt certain Officers.*

Her. The Emperor of Russia was my father :
O that he were alive, and here beholding
His daughter's trial ! that he did but see
The flatness of my misery, yet with eyes
Of pity, not revenge !
            Re-enter Officers, with Cleomenes and Dion.

Off. You here shall swear upon this sword of justice,
That you, Cleomenes and Dion, have
Been both at Delphos, and from thence have brought
This seal'd-up oracle, by the hand deliver'd
Of great Apollo's priest, and that since then
You have not dared to break the holy seal
Nor read the secrets in 't.

Cleo. Dion.   All this we swear.

Leon. Break up the seals and read.

Off. [*reads*] Hermione is chaste; Polixenes blameless; Camillo
a true subject; Leontes a jealous tyrant; his innocent babe
truly begotten; and the king shall live without an heir, if
that which is lost be not found.

Lords. Now blessed be the great Apollo!

Her.   Praised!

Leon. Hast thou read truth?

Off.   Ay, my lord; even so
As it is here set down.

Leon. There is no truth at all i' the oracle:
The sessions shall proceed: this is mere falsehood.

Enter Servant.

Serv. My lord the king, the king!

Leon.   What is the business?

Serv. O sir, I shall be hated to report it!
The prince your son, with mere conceit and fear
Of the queen's speed, is gone.

Leon.   How! gone!

Serv.   Is dead.

Leon. Apollo's angry; and the heavens themselves
Do strike at my injustice. [*Hermione faints.*] How now
Paul. This news is mortal to the queen: look down   [there!
And see what death is doing.

Leon.   Take her hence:
Her heart is but o'ercharged; she will recover:
I have too much believed mine own suspicion:
Beseech you, tenderly apply to her
Some remedies for life.

                    [*Exeunt Paulina and Ladies with Hermione.*
                                Apollo, pardon
My great profaneness 'gainst thine oracle!
I'll reconcile me to Polixenes;
New woo my queen; recall the good Camillo,
Whom I proclaim a man of truth, of mercy;
For, being transported by my jealousies
To bloody thoughts and to revenge, I chose
Camillo for the minister to poison
My friend Polixenes: which had been done,
But that the good mind of Camillo tardied
My swift command, though I with death and with
Reward did threaten and encourage him,
Not doing it and being done: he, most humane
And fill'd with honour, to my kingly guest
Unclasp'd my practice, quit his fortunes here,
Which you knew great, and to the hazard

Of all incertainties himself commended,
No richer than his honour : how he glisters
Thorough my rust ! and how his piety
Does my deeds make the blacker !

Re-enter Paulina.

Paul.   Woe the while !
O, cut my lace, lest my heart, cracking it,
Break too !

First Lord.   What fit is this, good lady ?

Paul. What studied torments, tyrant, hast for me ?
What wheels ? racks ? fires ? what flaying ? boiling ?
In leads or oils ? what old or newer torture
Must I receive, whose every word deserves
To taste of thy most worst ?   Thy tyranny
Together working with thy jealousies,
Fancies too weak for boys, too green and idle
For girls of nine, O, think what they have done
And then run mad indeed, stark mad ! for all
Thy by-gone fooleries were but spices of it.
That thou betray'dst Polixenes, 'twas nothing ;
That did but show thee, of a fool, inconstant
And damnable ingrateful : nor was 't much,
Thou wouldst have poison'd good Camillo's honour,
To have him kill a king ; poor trespasses,
More monstrous standing by : whereof I reckon
The casting forth to crows thy baby-daughter
To be or none or little ; though a devil
Would have shed water out of fire ere done 't :
Nor is 't directly laid to thee, the death
Of the young prince, whose honourable thoughts,
Thoughts high for one so tender, cleft the heart
That could conceive a gross and foolish sire
Blemish'd his gracious dam : this is not, no,
Laid to thy answer : but the last,—O lords,
When I have said, cry ' woe !'—the queen, the queen,
The sweet'st, dear'st creature 's dead, and vengeance for 't
Not dropp'd down yet.

First Lord.   The higher powers forbid !

Paul. I say she 's dead, I 'll swear 't.   If word nor oath
Prevail not, go and see : if you can bring
Tincture or lustre in her lip, her eye,
Heat outwardly or breath within, I 'll serve you
As I would do the gods.   But, O thou tyrant !
Do not repent these things, for they are heavier
Than all thy woes can stir : therefore betake thee

To nothing but despair.   A thousand knees
Ten thousand years together, naked, fasting,
Upon a barren mountain, and still winter
In storm perpetual, could not move the gods
To look that way thou wert.

Leon.   Go on, go on :
Thou canst not speak too much ; I have deserved
All tongues to talk their bitterest.

First Lord.   Say no more :
Howe'er the business goes, you have made fault
I' the boldness of your speech.

Paul.   I am sorry for 't :
All faults I make, when I shall come to know them,
I do repent.   Alas ! I show'd too much
The rashness of a woman : he is touch'd
To the noble heart.   What 's gone and what 's past help
Should be past grief : do not receive affliction
At my petition ; I beseech you, rather
Let me be punish'd, that have minded you
Of what you should forget.   Now, good my liege,
Sir, royal sir, forgive a foolish woman :
The love I bore your queen, lo, fool again !
I 'll speak of her no more, nor of your children ;
I 'll not remember you of my own lord,
Who is lost too : take your patience to you,
And I 'll say nothing.

Leon.   Thou didst speak but well
When most the truth ; which I receive much better
Than to be pitied of thee.   Prithee, bring me
To the dead bodies of my queen and son :
One grave shall be for both ; upon them shall
The causes of their death appear, unto
Our shame perpetual.   Once a day I 'll visit
The chapel where they lie, and tears shed there
Shall be my recreation : so long as nature
Will bear up with this exercise, so long
I daily vow to use it.   Come and lead me
To these sorrows.   [*Exeunt.*

SCENE III

Bohemia.   A desert country near the sea.
Enter Antigonus with a Child, and a Mariner.

Ant. Thou art perfect, then, our ship hath touch'd upon
The deserts of Bohemia ?

Mar.   Ay, my lord ; and fear
We have landed in ill time : the skies look grimly

And threaten present blusters. In my conscience,
The heavens with that we have in hand are angry
And frown upon 's.

Ant. Their sacred wills be done ! Go, get aboard ;
Look to thy bark : I 'll not be long before
I call upon thee.

Mar. Make your best haste, and go not
Too far i' the land : 'tis like to be loud weather
Besides, this place is famous for the creatures
Of prey that keep upon 't.

Ant.   Go thou away :
I 'll follow instantly.

Mar.   I am glad at heart
To be so rid o' the business.   [*Exit.*

Ant.   Come, poor babe :
I have heard, but not believed, the spirits o' the dead
May walk again : if such thing be, thy mother
Appear'd to me last night, for ne'er was dream
So like a waking.   To me comes a creature,
Sometimes her head on one side, some another ;
I never saw a vessel of like sorrow,
So fill'd and so becoming : in pure white robes,
Like very sanctity, she did approach
My cabin where I lay ; thrice bow'd before me,
And, gasping to begin some speech, her eyes
Became two spouts : the fury spent, anon
Did this break from her : 'Good Antigonus,
Since fate, against thy better disposition,
Hath made thy person for the thrower-out
Of my poor babe, according to thine oath,
Places remote enough are in Bohemia,
There weep and leave it crying ; and, for the babe
Is counted lost for ever, Perdita,
I prithee, call 't.   For this ungentle business,
Put on thee by my lord, thou ne'er shalt see
Thy wife Paulina more.'   And so, with shrieks,
She melted into air.   Affrighted much,
I did in time collect myself, and thought
This was so, and no slumber.   Dreams are toys :
Yet for this once, yea, superstitiously,
I will be squared by this.   I do believe
Hermione hath suffer'd death ; and that
Apollo would, this being indeed the issue
Of King Polixenes, it should here be laid,
Either for life or death, upon the earth

Of its right father.   Blossom, speed thee well!
There lie, and there thy character: there these;
Which may, if fortune please, both breed thee, pretty,
And still rest thine.   The storm begins: poor wretch,
That for thy mother's fault art thus exposed
To loss and what may follow!   Weep I cannot,
But my heart bleeds; and most accursed am I
To be by oath enjoin'd to this.   Farewell!
The day frowns more and more: thou 'rt like to have
A lullaby too rough: I never saw
The heavens so dim by day.   A savage clamour!
Well may I get aboard!   This is the chase:
I am gone for ever.   [*Exit, pursued by a bear.*
                    Enter a Shepherd.
Shep. I would there were no age between ten and three-and-
    twenty, or that youth would sleep out the rest; for there is
    nothing in the between but getting wenches with child,
    wronging the ancientry, stealing, fighting—Hark you now!
    Would any but these boiled brains of nineteen and two-and-
    twenty hunt this weather?   They have scared away two of
    my best sheep, which I fear the wolf will sooner find than
    the master: if any where I have them, 'tis by the sea-side,
    browzing of ivy.   Good luck, an 't be thy will!   what have we
    here?   Mercy on 's, a barne; very pretty barne!   A boy or
    a child, I wonder?   A pretty one; a very pretty one: sure,
    some scape: though I am not bookish, yet I can read
    waiting-gentlewoman in the scape.   This has been some
    stair-work, some trunk-work, some behind-door-work: they
    were warmer that got this than the poor thing is here.   I 'll
    take it up for pity: yet I 'll tarry till my son come; he
    hallooed but even now.   Whoa, ho, hoa!
                    Enter Clown.
Clo. Hilloa, loa!
Shep. What, art so near?   If thou 'lt see a thing to talk on
    when thou art dead and rotten, come hither.   What ailest
    thou, man?
Clo. I have seen two such sights, by sea and by land! but I
    am not to say it is a sea, for it is now the sky: betwixt the
    firmament and it you cannot thrust a bodkin's point.
Shep. Why, boy, how is it?
Clo. I would you did but see how it chafes, how it rages, how
    it takes up the shore! but that 's not to the point.   O, the
    most piteous cry of the poor souls! sometimes to see 'em,
    and not to see 'em; now the ship boring the moon with her
    main-mast, and anon swallowed with yest and froth, as you 'ld

thrust a cork into a hogshead. And then for the land-service, to see how the bear tore out his shoulder-bone; how he cried to me for help and said his name was Antigonus, a nobleman. But to make an end of the ship, to see how the sea flap-dragoned it: but, first, how the poor souls roared, and the sea mocked them; and how the poor gentleman roared and the bear mocked him, both roaring louder than the sea or weather.

Shep. Name of mercy, when was this, boy?

Clo. Now, now: I have not winked since I saw these sights: the men are not yet cold under water, nor the bear half dined on the gentleman: he 's at it now.

Shep. Would I had been by, to have helped the old man!

Clo. I would you had been by the ship side, to have helped her: there your charity would have lacked footing.

Shep. Heavy matters! heavy matters! but look thee here, boy. Now bless thyself: thou mettest with things dying, I with things newborn. Here 's a sight for thee; look thee, a bearing-cloth for a squire's child! look thee here; take up, take up, boy; open 't. So, let 's see: it was told me I should be rich by the fairies. This is some changeling: open 't. What 's within, boy?

Clo. You 're a made old man: if the sins of your youth are forgiven you, you 're well to live. Gold! all gold!

Shep. This is fairy gold, boy, and 'twill prove so: up with 't, keep it close: home, home, the next way. We are lucky, boy; and to be so still requires nothing but secrecy. Let my sheep go: come, good boy; the next way home.

Clo. Go you the next way with your findings. I 'll go see if the bear be gone from the gentleman and how much he hath eaten: they are never curst but when they are hungry: if there be any of him left, I 'll bury it.

Shep. That 's a good deed. If thou mayest discern by that which is left of him what he is, fetch me to the sight of him.

Clo. Marry, will I; and you shall help to put him i' the ground.

Shep. 'Tis a lucky day, boy, and we 'll do good deeds on 't.

[*Exeunt.*

ACT IV—Scene I
Enter Time, the Chorus.

Time. I, that please some, try all, both joy and terror
  Of good and bad, that makes and unfolds error,
  Now take upon me, in the name of Time,
  To use my wings. Impute it not a crime

To me or my swift passage, that I slide
O'er sixteen years and leave the growth untried
Of that wide gap, since it is in my power
To o'erthrow law and in one self-born hour
To plant and o'erwhelm custom.   Let me pass
The same I am, ere ancient'st order was
Or what is now received : I witness to
The times that brought them in ; so shall I do
To the freshest things now reigning, and make stale
The glistering of this present, as my tale
Now seems to it.   Your patience this allowing,
I turn my glass and give my scene such growing
As you had slept between : Leontes leaving,
The effects of his fond jealousies so grieving
That he shuts up himself, imagine me,
Gentle spectators, that I now may be
In fair Bohemia ; and remember well,
I mentioned a son o' the king's, which Florizel
I now name to you ; and with speed so pace
To speak of Perdita, now grown in grace
Equal with wondering : what of her ensues
I list not prophesy ; but let Time's news
Be known when 'tis brought forth.   A shepherd's daughter,
And what to her adheres, which follows after,
Is the argument of Time.   Of this allow,
If ever you have spent time worse ere now ;
If never, yet that Time himself doth say
He wishes earnestly you never may.   [*Exit.*

SCENE II

Bohemia.   The palace of Polixenes.
Enter Polixenes and Camillo.

Pol. I pray thee, good Camillo, be no more importunate : 'tis
a sickness denying thee any thing ; a death to grant this.

Cam. It is fifteen years since I saw my country : though I
have for the most part been aired abroad, I desire to lay my
bones there.   Besides, the penitent king, my master, hath
sent for me ; to whose feeling sorrows I might be some allay,
or I o'erween to think so, which is another spur to my
departure.

Pol. As thou lovest me, Camillo, wipe not out the rest of thy
services by leaving me now : the need I have of thee, thine
own goodness hath made ; better not to have had thee than
thus to want thee : thou, having made me businesses, which
none without thee can sufficiently manage, must either stay to

455

execute them thyself, or take away with thee the very services thou hast done; which if I have not enough considered, as too much I cannot, to be more thankful to thee shall be my study; and my profit therein, the heaping friendships. Of that fatal country, Sicilia, prithee speak no more; whose very naming punishes me with the remembrance of that penitent, as thou callest him, and reconciled king, my brother; whose loss of his most precious queen and children are even now to be afresh lamented. Say to me, when sawest thou the Prince Florizel, my son? Kings are no less unhappy, their issue not being gracious, than they are in losing them when they have approved their virtues.

Cam. Sir, it is three days since I saw the prince. What his happier affairs may be, are to me unknown: but I have missingly noted, he is of late much retired from court and is less frequent to his princely exercises than formerly he hath appeared.

Pol. I have considered so much, Camillo, and with some care; so far, that I have eyes under my service which look upon his removedness; from whom I have this intelligence, that he is seldom from the house of a most homely shepherd; a man, they say, that from very nothing, and beyond the imagination of his neighbours, is grown into an unspeakable estate.

Cam. I have heard, sir, of such a man, who hath a daughter of most rare note: the report of her is extended more than can be thought to begin from such a cottage.

Pol. That's likewise part of my intelligence; but, I fear, the angle that plucks our son thither. Thou shalt accompany us to the place; where we will, not appearing what we are, have some question with the shepherd; from whose simplicity I think it not uneasy to get the cause of my son's resort thither. Prithee, be my present partner in this business, and lay aside the thoughts of Sicilia.

Cam. I willingly obey your command.

Pol. My best Camillo! We must disguise ourselves. [*Exeunt.*

Scene III

A road near the Shepherd's cottage.
Enter Autolycus, singing.

When daffodils begin to peer,
  With heigh! the doxy over the dale,
Why, then comes in the sweet o' the year;
  For the red blood reigns in the winter's pale.

The white sheet bleaching on the hedge,
  With heigh! the sweet birds, O, how they sing!
Doth set my pugging tooth on edge;
  For a quart of ale is a dish for a king.

The lark, that tirra-lyra chants,
  With heigh! with heigh! the thrush and the jay,
Are summer songs for me and my aunts,
  While we lie tumbling in the hay.

I have served Prince Florizel and in my time wore three-
pile; but now I am out of service:

But shall I go mourn for that, my dear?
  The pale moon shines by night:
And when I wander here and there,
  I then do most go right.

If tinkers may have leave to live,
  And bear the sow-skin budget,
Then my account I well may give,
  And in the stocks avouch it.

My traffic is sheets; when the kite builds, look to lesser
linen. My father named me Autolycus; who being, as I
am, littered under Mercury, was likewise a snapper-up of
unconsidered trifles. With die and drab I purchased this
caparison, and my revenue is the silly cheat. Gallows and
knock are too powerful on the highway: beating and hanging
are terrors to me: for the life to come, I sleep out the
thought of it. A prize! a prize!

Enter Clown.

Clo. Let me see: every 'leven wether tods; every tod yields
pound and odd shilling; fifteen hundred shorn, what comes
the wool to?
Aut. [*Aside*] If the springe hold, the cock's mine.
Clo. I cannot do 't without counters. Let me see; what am I
to buy for our sheep-shearing feast? Three pound of sugar;
five pound of currants; rice—what will this sister of mine do
with rice? But my father hath made her mistress of the
feast, and she lays it on. She hath made me four and
twenty nosegays for the shearers, three-man song-men all,
and very good ones; but they are most of them means and
bases; but one puritan amongst them, and he sings psalms
to hornpipes. I must have saffron to colour the warden
pies; mace; dates, none, that's out of my note; nutmegs,

seven ; a race or two of ginger, but that I may beg ; four pound of prunes, and as many of raisins o' the sun.

Aut. O that ever I was born !   [*Grovelling on the ground.*

Clo. I' the name of me—   [death, death !

Aut. O, help me, help me ! pluck but off these rags ; and then,

Clo. Alack, poor soul ! thou hast need of more rags to lay on thee, rather than have these off.

Aut. O sir, the loathsomeness of them offends me more than the stripes I have received, which are mighty ones and millions.   [great matter.

Clo. Alas, poor man ! a million of beating may come to a

Aut. I am robbed, sir, and beaten ; my money and apparel ta'en from me, and these detestable things put upon me.

Clo. What, by a horseman, or a footman ?

Aut. A footman, sweet sir, a footman.

Clo. Indeed, he should be a footman by the garments he has left with thee : if this be a horseman's coat, it hath seen very hot service. Lend me thy hand, I 'll help thee : come, lend me thy hand.   [*Helping him up.*

Aut. O, good sir, tenderly, O !

Clo. Alas, poor soul !

Aut. O, good sir, softly, good sir ! I fear, sir, my shoulder-blade is out.

Clo. How now ! canst stand ?

Aut. Softly, dear sir [*picks his pocket*] ; good sir, softly. You ha' done me a charitable office.

Clo. Dost lack any money ? I have a little money for thee.

Aut. No, good sweet sir ; no, I beseech you, sir : I have a kinsman not past three quarters of a mile hence, unto whom I was going ; I shall there have money, or any thing I want : offer me no money, I pray you ; that kills my heart.

Clo. What manner of fellow was he that robbed you ?

Aut. A fellow, sir, that I have known to go about with troll-my-dames : I knew him once a servant of the prince : I cannot tell, good sir, for which of his virtues it was, but he was certainly whipped out of the court.

Clo. His vices, you would say ; there 's no virtue whipped out of the court : they cherish it to make it stay there ; and yet it will no more but abide.

Aut. Vices I would say, sir. I know this man well : he hath been since an ape-bearer ; then a process-server, a bailiff ; then he compassed a motion of the Prodigal Son, and married a tinker's wife within a mile where my land and living lies ; and, having flown over many knavish professions, he settled only in rogue : some call him Autolycus.

Clo. Out upon him ! prig, for my life, prig : he haunts wakes,
fairs and bear-baitings.

Aut. Very true, sir ; he, sir, he ; that's the rogue that put me
into this apparel.

Clo. Not a more cowardly rogue in all Bohemia : if you had
but looked big and spit at him, he 'ld have run.

Aut. I must confess to you, sir, I am no fighter. I am false of
heart that way ; and that he knew, I warrant him.

Clo. How do you now?

Aut. Sweet sir, much better than I was ; I can stand and walk :
I will even take my leave of you, and pace softly towards my
kinsman's.

Clo. Shall I bring thee on the way?

Aut. No, good-faced sir ; no, sweet sir.   [*shearing.*

Clo. Then fare thee well : I must go buy spices for our sheep-

Aut. Prosper you, sweet sir ! [*Exit Clown.*] Your purse is
not hot enough to purchase your spice. I 'll be with you at
your sheep-shearing too : if I make not this cheat bring out
another and the shearers prove sheep, let me be unrolled
and my name put in the book of virtue !

SONG.

Jog on, jog on, the foot-path way,
　　And merrily hent the stile-a :
A merry heart goes all the day,
　　Your sad tires in a mile-a.   [*Exit.*

SCENE IV

The Shepherd's cottage.
Enter Florizel and Perdita.

Flo. These your unusual weeds to each part of you
Do give a life : no shepherdess, but Flora
Peering in April's front. This your sheep-shearing
Is as a meeting of the petty gods,
And you the queen on 't.

Per.   Sir, my gracious lord,
To chide at your extremes it not becomes me :
O, pardon, that I name them ! Your high self,
The gracious mark o' the land, you have obscured
With a swain's wearing, and me, poor lowly maid,
Most goddess-like prank'd up : but that our feasts
In every mess have folly and the feeders
Digest it with a custom, I should blush
To see you so attired, sworn, I think,
To show myself a glass.

Flo.   I bless the time

Which you say adds to nature, is an art
That nature makes. You see, sweet maid, we marry
A gentler scion to the wildest stock,
And make conceive a bark of baser kind
By bud of nobler race: this is an art
Which does mend nature, change it rather, but
The art itself is nature.
Per.   So it is.
Pol. Then make your garden rich in gillyvors,
And do not call them bastards.
Per.   I 'll not put
The dibble in earth to set one slip of them ;
No more than were I painted I would wish
This youth should say 'twere well, and only therefore
Desire to breed by me. Here 's flowers for you ;
Hot lavender, mints, savory, marjoram ;
The marigold, that goes to bed wi' the sun
And with him rises weeping : these are flowers
Of middle summer, and I think they are given
To men of middle age. You 're very welcome.
Cam. I should leave grazing, were I of your flock,
And only live by gazing.
Per.   Out, alas !
You 'ld be so lean, that blasts of January
Would blow you through and through. Now, my fair'st friend,
I would I had some flowers o' the spring that might
Become your time of day ; and yours, and yours,
That wear upon your virgin branches yet
Your maidenheads growing : O Proserpina,
For the flowers now, that frighted thou let'st fall
From Dis's waggon ! daffodils,
That come before the swallow dares, and take
The winds of March with beauty ; violets dim,
But sweeter than the lids of Juno's eyes
Or Cytherea's breath ; pale primroses,
That die unmarried, ere they can behold
Bright Phœbus in his strength, a malady
Most incident to maids ; bold oxlips and
The crown imperial ; lilies of all kinds,
The flower-de-luce being one ! O, these I lack,
To make you garlands of ; and my sweet friend,
To strew him o'er and o'er !
Flo.   What, like a corse ?
Per. No, like a bank for love to lie and play on ;
Not like a corse ; or if, not to be buried,

But quick and in mine arms.   Come, take your flowers:
Methinks I play as I have seen them do
In Whitsun pastorals : sure this robe of mine
Does change my disposition.

Flo.   What you do
Still betters what is done.   When you speak, sweet,
I 'ld have you do it ever : when you sing,
I 'ld have you buy and sell so, so give alms,
Pray so ; and, for the ordering your affairs,
To sing them too : when you do dance, I wish you
A wave o' the sea, that you might ever do
Nothing but that ; move still, still so,
And own no other function : each your doing,
So singular in each particular,
Crowns what you are doing in the present deeds,
That all your acts are queens.

Per.   O Doricles,
Your praises are too large : but that your youth,
And the true blood which peeps fairly through 't,
Do plainly give you out an unstain'd shepherd,
With wisdom I might fear, my Doricles,
You woo'd me the false way.

Flo.   I think you have
As little skill to fear as I have purpose
To put you to 't.   But come ; our dance, I pray :
Your hand, my Perdita : so turtles pair,
That never mean to part.

Per.   I 'll swear for 'em.

Pol. This is the prettiest low-born lass that ever
Ran on the green-sward : nothing she does or seems
But smacks of something greater than herself,
Too noble for this place.

Cam.   He tells her something
That makes her blood look out : good sooth, she is
The queen of curds and cream.

Clo.   Come on, strike up !

Dor. Mopsa must be your mistress : marry, garlic,
To mend her kissing with !

Mop.   Now, in good time !

Clo. Not a word, a word, we stand upon our manners.
Come, strike up !
          [*Music.   Here a dance of Shepherds and Shepherdesses.*

Pol. Pray, good shepherd, what fair swain is this
Which dances with your daughter ?

Shep. They call him Doricles ; and boasts himself

To have a worthy feeding: but I have it
Upon his own report and I believe it;
He looks like sooth.   He says he loves my daughter:
I think so too; for never gazed the moon
Upon the water, as he 'll stand and read
As 'twere my daughter's eyes: and, to be plain,
I think there is not half a kiss to choose
Who loves another best.

Pol.   She dances featly.

Shep. So she does any thing; though I report it,
That should be silent: if young Doricles
Do light upon her, she shall bring him that
Which he not dreams of.

Enter Servant.

Ser. O master, if you did but hear the pedlar at the door, you
would never dance again after a tabor and pipe; no, the
bagpipe could not move you: he sings several tunes faster
than you 'll tell money; he utters them as he had eaten
ballads and all men's ears grew to his tunes.

Clo. He could never come better; he shall come in.   I love a
ballad but even too well, if it be doleful matter merrily
set down, or a very pleasant thing indeed and sung
lamentably.

Serv. He hath songs for man or woman, of all sizes; no
milliner can so fit his customers with gloves: he has the
prettiest love-songs for maids; so without bawdry, which is
strange; with such delicate burthens of dildos and fadings,
'jump her and thump her;' and where some stretch-
mouthed rascal would, as it were, mean mischief and break
a foul gap into the matter, he makes the maid to answer
'Whoop, do me no harm, good man;' puts him off, slights
him, with 'Whoop, do me no harm, good man.'

Pol. This is a brave fellow.

Clo. Believe me, thou talkest of an admirable conceited fellow.
Has he any unbraided wares?

Serv. He hath ribbons of all the colours i' the rainbow; points
more than all the lawyers in Bohemia can learnedly handle,
though they come to him by the gross: inkles, caddisses,
cambrics, lawns: why, he sings 'em over as they were gods
or goddesses; you would think a smock were a she-angel,
he so chants to the sleeve-hand and the work about the
square on 't.

Clo. Prithee bring him in; and let him approach singing.

Per. Forewarn him that he use no scurrilous words in 's tunes.

[Exit Servant.

462

Clo. You have of these pedlars, that have more in them than you 'ld think, sister.

Per. Ay, good brother, or go about to think.

Enter Autolycus, singing.

Lawn as white as driven snow ;
Cypress black as e'er was crow ;
Gloves as sweet as damask roses;
Masks for faces and for noses ;
Bugle bracelet, necklace amber,
Perfume for a lady's chamber ;
Golden quoifs and stomachers,
For my lads to give their dears ;
Pins and poking-sticks of steel,
What maids lack from head to heel :
Come buy of me, come ; come buy, come buy ;
Buy, lads, or else your lasses cry
Come buy.

Clo. If I were not in love with Mopsa, thou shouldst take no money of me ; but being enthralled as I am, it will also be the bondage of certain ribbons and gloves.

Mop. I was promised them against the feast ; but they come not too late now.

Dor. He hath promised you more than that, or there be liars.

Mop. He hath paid you all he promised you : may be, he has paid you more, which will shame you to give him again.

Clo. Is there no manners left among maids ? will they wear their plackets where they should bear their faces ? Is there not milking-time, when you are going to bed, or kiln-hole, to whistle off these secrets, but you must be tittle-tattling before all our guests ? 'tis well they are whispering : clamour your tongues, and not a word more.

Mop. I have done. Come, you promised me a tawdry-lace and a pair of sweet gloves.

Clo. Have I not told thee how I was cozened by the way and lost all my money ?

Aut. And indeed, sir, there are cozeners abroad ; therefore it behoves men to be wary.

Clo. Fear not thou, man, thou shalt lose nothing here.

Aut. I hope so, sir ; for I have about me many parcels of charge.

Clo. What hast here ? ballads ?

Mop. Pray now, buy some : I love a ballad in print o' life, for then we are sure they are true.

Aut. Here 's one to a very doleful tune, how a usurer's wife was brought to bed of twenty money-bags at a burthen, and how she longed to eat adders' heads and toads carbonadoed.

Mop. Is it true, think you?

Aut. Very true, and but a month old.

Dor. Bless me from marrying a usurer!

Aut. Here's the midwife's name to 't, one Mistress Tale-porter, and five or six honest wives that were present. Why should I carry lies abroad?

Mop. Pray you now, buy it.

Clo. Come on, lay it by: and let's first see moe ballads; we'll buy the other things anon.

Aut. Here's another ballad of a fish, that appeared upon the coast, on Wednesday the fourscore of April, forty thousand fathom above water, and sung this ballad against the hard hearts of maids: it was thought she was a woman, and was turned into a cold fish for she would not exchange flesh with one that loved her: the ballad is very pitiful and as true.

Dor. Is it true too, think you?   [pack will hold.

Aut. Five justices' hands at it, and witnesses more than my

Clo. Lay it by too: another.

Aut. This is a merry ballad, but a very pretty one.

Mop. Let's have some merry ones.

Aut. Why, this is a passing merry one and goes to the tune of 'Two maids wooing a man:' there's scarce a maid westward but she sings it; 'tis in request, I can tell you.

Mop. We can both sing it: if thou'lt bear a part, thou shalt hear; 'tis in three parts.

Dor. We had the tune on 't a month ago.

Aut. I can bear my part; you must know 'tis my occupation: have at it with you.

Song.

  A. Get you hence, for I must go
   Where it fits not you to know.
     D. Whither? *M.* O, whither? *D.* Whither?
  M. It becomes thy oath full well,
   Thou to me thy secrets tell:
     D. Me too, let me go thither.

  M. Or thou goest to the grange or mill:
  D. If to either, thou dost ill.
     A. Neither. *D.* What, neither? *A.* Neither
  D. Thou hast sworn my love to be;
  M. Thou hast sworn it more to me:
    Then whither goest? say, whither?

Clo. We'll have this song out anon by ourselves: my father
  and the gentlemen are in sad talk, and we'll not trouble
  them.   Come, bring away thy pack after me.   Wenches, I'll
  buy for you both.   Pedlar, let's have the first choice.
  Follow me, girls.   [*Exit with Dorcas and Mopsa.*
Aut. And you shall pay well for 'em.   [*Follows singing.*

> Will you buy any tape,
>   Or lace for your cape,
> My dainty duck, my dear-a?
>   Any silk, any thread,
>   Any toys for your head,
> Of the new'st, and finest, finest wear-a?
>   Come to the pedlar;
>   Money's a medler,
> That doth utter all men's ware-a.   [*Exit.*

Re-enter Servant.

Serv. Master, there is three carters, three shepherds, three neat-
  herds, three swine-herds, that have made themselves all men
  of hair, they call themselves Saltiers, and they have a dance
  which the wenches say is a gallimaufry of gambols, because
  they are not in't; but they themselves are o' the mind, if it
  be not too rough for some that know little but bowling, it
  will please plentifully.
Shep. Away! we'll none on't: here has been too much homely
  foolery already.   I know, sir, we weary you.
Pol. You weary those that refresh us: pray, let's see these four
  threes of herdsmen.
Serv. One three of them, by their own report, sir, hath danced
  before the king; and not the worst of the three but jumps
  twelve foot and a half by the squier.
Shep. Leave your prating: since these good men are pleased,
  let them come in; but quickly now.
Serv. Why, they stay at door, sir.   [*Exit.*

Here a dance of twelve Satyrs.

Pol. O, father, you'll know more of that hereafter.
  [*To Cam.*] Is it not too far gone?   'Tis time to part them.
  He's simple and tells much.   How now, fair shepherd!
  Your heart is full of something that does take
  Your mind from feasting.   Sooth, when I was young
  And handed love as you do, I was wont
  To load my she with knacks: I would have ransack'd
  The pedlar's silken treasury and have pour'd it
  To her acceptance; you have let him go

And nothing marted with him. If your lass
Interpretation should abuse and call this
Your lack of love or bounty, you were straited
For a reply, at least if you make a care
Of happy holding her.

Flo.   Old sir, I know
She prizes not such trifles as these are :
The gifts she looks from me are pack'd and lock'd
Up in my heart ; which I have given already,
But not deliver'd.   O, hear me breathe my life
Before this ancient sir, who, it should seem,
Hath sometime loved !   I take thy hand, this hand,
As soft as dove's down and as white as it,
Or Ethiopian's tooth, or the fann'd snow that's bolted
By the northern blasts twice o'er.

Pol.   What follows this ?
How prettily the young swain seems to wash
The hand was fair before !   I have put you out :
But to your protestation ; let me hear
What you profess.

Flo.   Do, and be witness to 't.

Pol. And this my neighbour too ?

Flo.   And he, and more
Than he, and men, the earth, the heavens, and all :
That, were I crown'd the most imperial monarch,
Thereof most worthy, were I the fairest youth
That ever made eye swerve, had force and knowledge
More than was ever man's, I would not prize them
Without her love ; for her employ them all ;
Commend them and condemn them to her service
Or to their own perdition.

Pol.   Fairly offer'd.

Cam. That shows a sound affection.

Shep.   But, my daughter,
Say you the like to him ?

Per.   I cannot speak
So well, nothing so well ; no, nor mean better :
By the pattern of mine our thoughts I cut out
The purity of his.

Shep.   Take hands, a bargain !
And, friends unknown, you shall bear witness to 't :
I give my daughter to him, and will make
Her portion equal his.

Flo.   O, that must be
I' the virtue of your daughter : one being dead,

466

I shall have more than you can dream of yet ;
Enough then for your wonder.   But, come on,
Contract us 'fore these witnesses.
Shep.   Come, your hand ;
And, daughter, yours.
Pol.   Soft, swain, awhile, beseech you ;
Have you a father ?
Flo.   I have : but what of him ?
Pol. Knows he of this ?
Flo.   He neither does nor shall.
Pol. Methinks a father
Is at the nuptial of his son a guest
That best becomes the table.   Pray you once more,
Is not your father grown incapable
Of reasonable affairs ? is he not stupid
With age and altering rheums ? can he speak ? hear ?
Know man from man ? dispute his own estate ?
Lies he not bed-rid ? and again does nothing
But what he did being childish ?
Flo.   No, good sir ;
He hath his health and ampler strength indeed
Than most have of his age.
Pol.   By my white beard,
You offer him, if this be so, a wrong
Something unfilial : reason my son
Should choose himself a wife, but as good reason
The father, all whose joy is nothing else
But fair posterity, should hold some counsel
In such a business.
Flo.   I yield all this ;
But for some other reasons, my grave sir,
Which 'tis not fit you know, I not acquaint
My father of this business.
Pol.   Let him know 't.
Flo. He shall not.
Pol.   Prithee, let him.
Flo.   No, he must not.
Shep. Let him, my son : he shall not need to grieve
At knowing of thy choice.
Flo.   Come, come, he must not.
Mark our contract.
Pol.   Mark your divorce, young sir,
                              [*Discovering himself.*
Whom son I dare not call ; thou art too base
To be acknowledged : thou a sceptre's heir,

That thus affects a sheep-hook! Thou old traitor,
I am sorry that my hanging thee I can
But shorten thy life one week. And thou, fresh piece
Of excellent witchcraft, who of force must know
The royal fool thou copest with,—

Shep.   O, my heart!

Pol. I 'll have thy beauty scratch'd with briers, and made
More homely than thy state. For thee, fond boy,
If I may ever know thou dost but sigh
That thou no more shalt see this knack, as never
I mean thou shalt, we 'll bar thee from succession;
Not hold thee of our blood, no, not our kin,
Far than Deucalion off: mark thou my words:
Follow us to the court. Thou churl, for this time,
Though full of our displeasure, yet we free thee
From the dead blow of it. And you, enchantment,—
Worthy enough a herdsman; yea, him too,
That makes himself, but for our honour therein,
Unworthy thee,—if ever henceforth thou
These rural latches to his entrance open,
Or hoop his body more with thy embraces,
I will devise a death as cruel for thee
As thou art tender to 't.   [*Exit.*

Per.   Even here undone!
I was not much afeard; for once or twice
I was about to speak and tell him plainly,
The selfsame sun that shines upon his court
Hides not his visage from our cottage, but
Looks on alike. Will 't please you, sir, be gone?
I told you what would come of this: beseech you,
Of your own state take care: this dream of mine,—
Being now awake, I 'll queen it no inch farther,
But milk my ewes and weep.

Cam.   Why, how now, father:
Speak ere thou diest.

Shep.   I cannot speak, nor think,
Nor dare to know that which I know. O sir!
You have undone a man of fourscore three,
That thought to fill his grave in quiet; yea,
To die upon the bed my father died,
To lie close by his honest bones: but now
Some hangman must put on my shroud and lay me
Where no priest shovels in dust. O cursed wretch,
That knew'st this was the prince, and wouldst adventure
To mingle faith with him! Undone! undone!

468

If I might die within this hour, I have lived
To die when I desire.   [*Exit*

Flo.   Why look you so upon me?
I am but sorry, not afeard; delay'd,
But nothing alter'd: what I was, I am;
More straining on for plucking back, not following
My leash unwillingly.

Cam.   Gracious my lord,
You know your father's temper: at this time
He will allow no speech, which I do guess
You do not purpose to him; and as hardly
Will he endure your sight as yet, I fear:
Then, till the fury of his highness settle,
Come not before him.

Flo.   I not purpose it.
I think, Camillo?

Cam.   Even he, my lord.

Per. How often have I told you 'twould be thus!
How often said, my dignity would last
But till 'twere known!

Flo.   It cannot fail but by
The violation of my faith; and then
Let nature crush the sides o' the earth together
And mar the seeds within! Lift up thy looks:
From my succession wipe me, father, I
Am heir to my affection.

Cam.   Be advised.

Flo. I am, and by my fancy: if my reason
Will thereto be obedient, I have reason;
If not, my senses, better pleased with madness,
Do bid it welcome.

Cam.   This is desperate, sir.

Flo. So call it: but it does fulfil my vow;
I needs must think it honesty. Camillo,
Not for Bohemia, nor the pomp that may
Be thereat glean'd; for all the sun sees, or
The close earth wombs, or the profound seas hide
In unknown fathoms, will I break my oath
To this my fair beloved: therefore, I pray you,
As you have ever been my father's honour'd friend,
When he shall miss me,—as, in faith, I mean not
To see him any more,—cast your good counsels
Upon his passion: let myself and fortune
Tug for the time to come. This you may know
And so deliver, I am put to sea

469

With her whom here I cannot hold on shore ;
And most opportune to our need I have
A vessel rides fast by, but not prepared
For this design.   What course I mean to hold
Shall nothing benefit your knowledge, nor
Concern me the reporting.

Cam.   O my lord !
I would your spirit were easier for advice,
Or stronger for your need.

Flo.   Hark, Perdita. [*Drawing her aside.*
I 'll hear you by and by.

Cam.   He 's irremoveable,
Resolved for flight.   Now were I happy, if
His going I could frame to serve my turn,
Save him from danger, do him love and honour,
Purchase the sight again of dear Sicilia
And that unhappy king, my master, whom
I so much thirst to see.

Flo.   Now, good Camillo ;
I am so fraught with curious business that
I leave out ceremony.

Cam.   Sir, I think
You have heard of my poor services, i' the love
That I have borne your father ?

Flo.   Very nobly
Have you deserved : it is my father's music
To speak your deeds, not little of his care
To have them recompensed as thought on.

Cam.   Well, my lord,
If you may please to think I love the king,
And through him what is nearest to him, which is
Your gracious self, embrace but my direction,
If your more ponderous and settled project
May suffer alteration, on mine honour
I 'll point you where you shall have such receiving
As shall become your highness ; where you may
Enjoy your mistress, from the whom, I see,
There 's no disjunction to be made, but by,
As heavens forefend ! your ruin ; marry her,
And, with my best endeavours in your absence,
Your discontenting father strive to qualify
And bring him up to liking.

Flo.   How, Camillo,
May this, almost a miracle, be done ?
That I may call thee something more than man

And after that trust to thee.

Cam.   Have you thought on
A place whereto you'll go?

Flo.   Not any yet:
But as the unthought-on accident is guilty
To what we wildly do, so we profess
Ourselves to be the slaves of chance, and flies
Of every wind that blows.

Cam.   Then list to me:
This follows, if you will not change your purpose
But undergo this flight, make for Sicilia,
And there present yourself and your fair princess,
For so I see she must be, 'fore Leontes:
She shall be habited as it becomes
The partner of your bed.   Methinks I see
Leontes opening his free arms and weeping
His welcomes forth; asks thee the son forgiveness,
As 'twere i' the father's person; kisses the hands
Of your fresh princess; o'er and o'er divides him
'Twixt his unkindness and his kindness; the one
He chides to hell and bids the other grow
Faster than thought or time.

Flo.   Worthy Camillo,
What colour for my visitation shall I
Hold up before him?

Cam.   Sent by the king your father
To greet him and to give him comforts.   Sir,
The manner of your bearing towards him, with
What you as from your father shall deliver,
Things known betwixt us three, I'll write you down:
The which shall point you forth at every sitting
What you must say; that he shall not perceive
But that you have your father's bosom there
And speak his very heart.

Flo.   I am bound to you:
There is some sap in this.

Cam.   A course more promising
Than a wild dedication of yourselves
To unpath'd waters, undream'd shores, most certain
To miseries enough: no hope to help you,
But as you shake off one to take another:
Nothing so certain as your anchors, who
Do their best office, if they can but stay you
Where you'll be loath to be: besides you know
Prosperity's the very bond of love,

Whose fresh complexion and whose heart together
Affliction alters.

Per.   One of these is true:
I think affliction may subdue the cheek,
But not take in the mind.

Cam.   Yea, say you so?
There shall not at your father's house these seven years
Be born another such.

Flo.   My good Camillo,
She is as forward of her breeding as
She is i' the rear o' her birth.

Cam.   I cannot say 'tis pity
She lacks instructions, for she seems a mistress
To most that teach.

Per.   Your pardon, sir; for this
I 'll blush you thanks.

Flo.   My prettiest Perdita!
But O, the thorns we stand upon! Camillo,
Preserver of my father, now of me,
The medicine of our house, how shall we do?
We are not furnish'd like Bohemia's son,
Nor shall appear in Sicilia.

Cam.   My lord,
Fear none of this: I think you know my fortunes
Do all lie there: it shall be so my care
To have you royally appointed as if
The scene you play were mine. For instance, sir,
That you may know you shall not want, one word.

[*They talk aside.*

Re-enter Autolycus.

Aut. Ha, ha! what a fool Honesty is! and Trust, his sworn
brother, a very simple gentleman! I have sold all my
trumpery; not a counterfeit stone, not a ribbon, glass,
pomander, brooch, table-book, ballad, knife, tape, glove,
shoe-tie, bracelet, horn-ring, to keep my pack from fasting:
they throng who should buy first, as if my trinkets had been
hallowed and brought a benediction to the buyer: by which
means I saw whose purse was best in picture; and what I
saw, to my good use I remembered. My clown, who wants
but something to be a reasonable man, grew so in love with
the wenches' song, that he would not stir his pettitoes till he
had both tune and words; which so drew the rest of the
herd to me, that all their other senses stuck in ears: you
might have pinched a placket, it was senseless; 'twas nothing
to geld a codpiece of a purse; I would have filed keys off

that hung in chains: no hearing, no feeling, but my sir's
song, and admiring the nothing of it. So that in this time
of lethargy I picked and cut most of their festival purses;
and had not the old man come in with a whoo-bub against
his daughter and the king's son and scared my choughs
from the chaff, I had not left a purse alive in the whole
army.   [*Camillo, Florizel, and Perdita come forward.*

Cam. Nay, but my letters, by this means being there
So soon as you arrive, shall clear that doubt.

Flo. And those that you'll procure from King Leontes—

Cam. Shall satisfy your father.

Per.   Happy be you!
All that you speak shows fair.

Cam.   Who have we here?
                [*Seeing Autolycus.*
We'll make an instrument of this; omit
Nothing may give us aid.

Aut. If they have overheard me now, why, hanging.

Cam. How now, good fellow! why shakest thou so? Fear
not, man; here's no harm intended to thee.

Aut. I am a poor fellow, sir.

Cam. Why, be so still; here's nobody will steal that from
thee: yet for the outside of thy poverty we must make an
exchange; therefore discase thee instantly,—thou must
think there's a necessity in 't,—and change garments with
this gentleman: though the pennyworth on his side be the
worst, yet hold thee, there's some boot.

Aut. I am a poor fellow, sir. [*Aside*] I know ye well enough.

Cam. Nay, prithee, dispatch: the gentleman is half flayed
    already.

Aut. Are you in earnest, sir? [*Aside*] I smell the trick on 't.

Flo. Dispatch, I prithee.

Aut. Indeed, I have had earnest; but I cannot with conscience

Cam. Unbuckle, unbuckle.   [take it.
                [*Florizel and Autolycus exchange garments.*
Fortunate mistress,—let my prophecy
Come home to ye!—you must retire yourself
Into some covert: take your sweetheart's hat
And pluck it o'er your brows, muffle your face,
Dismantle you, and, as you can, disliken
The truth of your own seeming; that you may—
For I do fear eyes over—to shipboard
Get undescried.

Per.   I see the play so lies
That I must bear a part.

Cam.   No remedy.
Have you done there?
Flo.   Should I now meet my father,
He would not call me son.
Cam.   Nay, you shall have no hat.
                                        [*Giving it to Perdita.*
Come, lady, come.   Farewell, my friend.
Aut.   Adieu, sir.
Flo. O Perdita, what have we twain forgot?
Pray you, a word.
Cam. [*Aside*] What I do next, shall be to tell the king
Of this escape and whither they are bound;
Wherein my hope is I shall so prevail
To force him after: in whose company
I shall review Sicilia, for whose sight
I have a woman's longing.
Flo.   Fortune speed us!
Thus we set on, Camillo, to the sea-side.
Cam. The swifter speed the better.
                        [*Exeunt Florizel, Perdita, and Camillo.*
Aut. I understand the business, I hear it: to have an open
ear, a quick eye, and a nimble hand, is necessary for a
cut-purse; a good nose is requisite also, to smell out work
for the other senses.   I see this is the time that the unjust
man doth thrive.   What an exchange had this been without
boot!   What a boot is here with this exchange!   Sure the
gods do this year connive at us, and we may do any thing
extempore.   The prince himself is about a piece of iniquity,
stealing away from his father with his clog at his heels: if I
thought it were a piece of honesty to acquaint the king
withal, I would not do't: I hold it the more knavery to
conceal it; and therein am I constant to my profession.

                Re-enter Clown and Shepherd.
Aside, aside; here is more matter for a hot brain: every
lane's end, every shop, church, session, hanging, yields a
careful man work.
Clo. See, see; what a man you are now!   There is no other
way but to tell the king she's a changeling and none of your
flesh and blood.
Shep. Nay, but hear me.
Clo. Nay, but hear me.
Shep. Go to, then.
Clo. She being none of your flesh and blood, your flesh and
blood has not offended the king; and so your flesh and
blood is not to be punished by him.   Show those things

you found about her, those secret things, all but what she has with her: this being done, let the law go whistle: I warrant you.

Shep. I will tell the king all, every word, yea, and his son's pranks too; who, I may say, is no honest man, neither to his father nor to me, to go about to make me the king's brother-in-law.

Clo. Indeed, brother-in-law was the farthest off you could have been to him and then your blood had been the dearer by I know how much an ounce.

Aut. [*Aside*] Very wisely, puppies!

Shep. Well, let us to the king: there is that in this fardel will make him scratch his beard.

Aut. [*Aside*] I know not what impediment this complaint may be to the flight of my master.

Clo. Pray heartily he be at palace.

Aut. [*Aside*] Though I am not naturally honest, I am so sometimes by chance: let me pocket up my pedlar's excrement. [*Takes off his false beard.*] How now, rustics! whither are you bound?

Shep. To the palace, an it like your worship.

Aut. Your affairs there, what, with whom, the condition of that fardel, the place of your dwelling, your names, your ages, of what having, breeding, and any thing that is fitting to be known, discover.

Clo. We are but plain fellows, sir.

Aut. A lie; you are rough and hairy. Let me have no lying: it becomes none but tradesmen, and they often give us soldiers the lie: but we pay them for it with stamped coin, not stabbing steel; therefore they do not give us the lie.

Clo. Your worship had like to have given us one, if you had not taken yourself with the manner.

Shep. Are you a courtier, an 't like you, sir?

Aut. Whether it like me or no, I am a courtier. Seest thou not the air of the court in these enfoldings? hath not my gait in it the measure of the court? receives not thy nose court-odour from me? reflect I not on thy baseness court-contempt? Thinkest thou, for that I insinuate, or toaze from thee thy business, I am therefore no courtier? I am courtier cap-a-pe; and one that will either push on or pluck back thy business there: whereupon I command thee to open thy

Shep. My business, sir, is to the king.   [affair.

Aut. What advocate hast thou to him?

Shep. I know not, an 't like you.   [none.

Clo. Advocate 's the court-word for a pheasant: say you have

Shep. None, sir ; I have no pheasant, cock nor hen.

Aut. How blessed are we that are not simple men !
Yet nature might have made me as these are,
Therefore I will not disdain.

Clo. This cannot be but a great courtier.

Shep. His garments are rich, but he wears them not handsomely.

Clo. He seems to be the more noble in being fantastical : a
great man, I 'll warrant ; I know by the picking on 's teeth.

Aut. The fardel there ? what 's i' the fardel ?   Wherefore that
box ?

Shep. Sir, there lies such secrets in this fardel and box, which
none must know but the king ; and which he shall know
within this hour, if I may come to the speech of him.

Aut. Age, thou hast lost thy labour.

Shep. Why, sir ?

Aut. The king is not at the palace ; he is gone aboard a
new ship to purge melancholy and air himself : for, if
thou beest capable of things serious, thou must know the
king is full of grief.

Shep. So 'tis said, sir ; about his son, that should have married
a shepherd's daughter.

Aut. If that shepherd be not in hand-fast, let him fly : the
curses he shall have, the tortures he shall feel, will break
the back of man, the heart of monster.

Clo. Think you so, sir ?

Aut. Not he alone shall suffer what wit can make heavy
and vengeance bitter ; but those that are germane to him,
though removed fifty times, shall all come under the hangman : which though it be great pity, yet it is necessary.
An old sheep-whistling rogue, a ram-tender, to offer to
have his daughter come into grace ! Some say he shall
be stoned ; but that death is too soft for him, say I :
draw our throne into a sheep-cote ! all deaths are too few,
the sharpest too easy.   [sir ?

Clo. Has the old man e'er a son, sir, do you hear, an 't like you,

Aut. He has a son, who shall be flayed alive ; then, 'nointed
over with honey, set on the head of a wasp's nest ; then
stand till he be three quarters and a dram dead ; then
recovered again with aqua-vitæ or some other hot infusion ;
then, raw as he is, and in the hottest day prognostication
proclaims, shall he be set against a brick-wall, the sun
looking with a southward eye upon him, where he is to
behold him with flies blown to death.   But what talk we
of these traitorly rascals, whose miseries are to be smiled

476

at, their offences being so capital? Tell me, for you seem
to be honest plain men, what you have to the king:
being something gently considered, I 'll bring you where
he is aboard, tender your persons to his presence, whisper
him in your behalfs; and if it be in man besides the king
to effect your suits, here is man shall do it.

Clo. He seems to be of great authority: close with him,
give him gold; and though authority be a stubborn bear,
yet he is oft led by the nose with gold: show the inside
of your purse to the outside of his hand, and no more
ado. Remember 'stoned,' and 'flayed alive.'

Shep. An 't please you, sir, to undertake the business for us,
here is that gold I have: I 'll make it as much more and
leave this young man in pawn till I bring it you.

Aut. After I have done what I promised?

Shep. Ay, sir.

Aut. Well, give me the moiety. Are you a party in this
business?

Clo. In some sort, sir: but though my case be a pitiful one,
I hope I shall not be flayed out of it.

Aut. O, that 's the case of the shepherd's son: hang him,
he 'll be made an example.

Clo. Comfort, good comfort! We must to the king and show
our strange sights: he must know 'tis none of your daughter nor my sister; we are gone else. Sir, I will give you as
much as this old man does when the business is performed,
and remain, as he says, your pawn till it be brought you.

Aut. I will trust you. Walk before toward the sea-side; go on
the right hand: I will but look upon the hedge and follow
you.

Clo. We are blest in this man, as I may say, even blest.

Shep. Let 's before as he bids us: he was provided to do us
good. [*Exeunt Shepherd and Clown.*

Aut. If I had a mind to be honest, I see Fortune would not
suffer me: she drops booties in my mouth. I am courted
now with a double occasion, gold and a means to do the
prince my master good; which who knows how that may
turn back to my advancement? I will bring these two
moles, these blind ones, aboard him: if he think it fit to
shore them again and that the complaint they have to the
king concerns him nothing, let him call me rogue for being
so far officious; for I am proof against that title and what
shame else belongs to 't. To him will I present them:
there may be matter in it. [*Exit*

ACT V.—Scene I

A room in Leontes' palace.
Enter Leontes, Cleomenes, Dion, Paulina, and Servants.

Cleo. Sir, you have done enough, and have perform'd
　　A saint-like sorrow: no fault could you make,
　　Which you have not redeem'd; indeed, paid down
　　More penitence than done trespass: at the last,
　　Do as the heavens have done, forget your evil;
　　With them forgive yourself.

Leon.　　　　　　　　　Whilst I remember
　　Her and her virtues, I cannot forget
　　My blemishes in them, and so still think of
　　The wrong I did myself: which was so much,
　　That heirless it hath made my kingdom; and
　　Destroy'd the sweet'st companion that e'er man
　　Bred his hopes out of.

Paul.　　　　　　　　True, too true, my lord:
　　If, one by one, you wedded all the world,
　　Or from the all that are took something good,
　　To make a perfect woman, she you kill'd
　　Would be unparallel'd.

Leon.　　　　　　　I think so.　Kill'd!
　　She I kill'd!　I did so: but thou strikest me
　　Sorely, to say I did; it is as bitter
　　Upon thy tongue as in my thought: now, good now,
　　Say so but seldom.

Cleo.　　　　　　Not at all, good lady:
　　You might have spoken a thousand things that would
　　Have done the time more benefit and graced
　　Your kindness better.

Paul.　　　　　　You are one of those
　　Would have him wed again.

Dion.　　　　　　　　If you would not so,
　　You pity not the state, nor the remembrance
　　Of his most sovereign name; consider little
　　What dangers, by his highness' fail of issue,
　　May drop upon his kingdom and devour
　　Incertain lookers-on.　What were more holy
　　Than to rejoice the former queen is well?
　　What holier than, for royalty's repair,
　　For present comfort and for future good,
　　To bless the bed of majesty again
　　With a sweet fellow to 't?

Paul.   There is none worthy,
Respecting her that's gone.   Besides, the gods
Will have fulfill'd their secret purposes;
For has not the divine Apollo said,
Is't not the tenor of his oracle,
That King Leontes shall not have an heir
Till his lost child be found? which that it shall,
Is all as monstrous to our human reason
As my Antigonus to break his grave
And come again to me; who, on my life,
Did perish with the infant.   'Tis your counsel
My lord should to the heavens be contrary,
Oppose against their wills.   [*To Leontes.*] Care not for issue;
The crown will find an heir: great Alexander
Left his to the worthiest; so his successor
Was like to be the best.
Leon.   Good Paulina,
Who hast the memory of Hermione,
I know, in honour, O, that ever I
Had squared me to thy counsel!—then, even now,
I might have look'd upon my queen's full eyes;
Have taken treasure from her lips,—
Paul.   And left them
More rich for what they yielded.
Leon.   Thou speak'st truth.
No more such wives; therefore, no wife: one worse,
And better used, would make her sainted spirit
Again possess her corpse, and on this stage,
Where we offenders now, appear soul-vex'd,
And begin, 'Why to me?'
Paul.   Had she such power,
She had just cause.
Leon.   She had; and would incense me
To murder her I married.
Paul.   I should so.
Were I the ghost that walk'd, I'ld bid you mark
Her eye, and tell me for what dull part in't
You chose her; then I'ld shriek, that even your ears
Should rift to hear me; and the words that follow'd
Should be 'Remember mine.'
Leon.   Stars, stars,
And all eyes else dead coals!   Fear thou no wife;
I'll have no wife, Paulina.
Paul.   Will you swear
Never to marry but by my free leave?

Leon. Never, Paulina; so be blest my spirit !
Paul. Then, good my lords, bear witness to his oath.
Cleo. You tempt him over-much.
Paul.   Unless another
  As like Hermione as is her picture,
  Affront his eye.
Cleo.   Good madam,—
Paul.   I have done.
  Yet, if my lord will marry,—if you will, sir,
  No remedy, but you will,—give me the office
  To choose you a queen : she shall not be so young
  As was your former ; but she shall be such
  As, walk'd your first queen's ghost, it should take joy
  To see her in your arms.
Leon.   My true Paulina,
  We shall not marry till thou bid'st us.
Paul.   That
  Shall be when your first queen's again in breath ;
  Never till then.

Enter a Gentleman.

Gent. One that gives out himself Prince Florizel,
  Son of Polixenes, with his princess, she
  The fairest I have yet beheld, desires access
  To your high presence.
Leon.   What with him ? he comes not
  Like to his father's greatness : his approach,
  So out of circumstance and sudden, tells us
  'Tis not a visitation framed, but forced
  By need and accident.   What train ?
Gent.   But few,
  And those but mean.
Leon.   His princess, say you, with him ?
Gent. Ay, the most peerless piece of earth, I think,
  That e'er the sun shone bright on.
Paul.   O Hermione,
  As every present time doth boast itself
  Above a better gone, so must thy grave
  Give way to what's seen now !   Sir, you yourself
  Have said and writ so, but your writing now
  Is colder than that theme, 'She had not been,
  Nor was not to be equall'd ;'—thus your verse
  Flow'd with her beauty once ; 'tis shrewdly ebb'd,
  To say you have seen a better.
Gent.   Pardon, madam :
  The one I have almost forgot,—your pardon,—

480

The other, when she has obtain'd your eye,
Will have your tongue too.   This is a creature,
Would she begin a sect, might quench the zeal
Of all professors else ; make proselytes
Of who she but bid follow.

Paul.   How ! not women ?

Gent. Women will love her, that she is a woman
More worth than any man ; men, that she is
The rarest of all women.

Leon.   Go, Cleomenes ;
Yourself, assisted with your honour'd friends,
Bring them to our embracement.

                    [*Exeunt Cleomenes and others.*
                              Still, 'tis strange
He thus should steal upon us.

Paul.   Had our prince,
Jewel of children, seen this hour, he had pair'd
Well with this lord : there was not full a month
Between their births.

Leon. Prithee, no more ; cease ; thou know'st
He dies to me again when talk'd of : sure,
When I shall see this gentleman, thy speeches
Will bring me to consider that which may
Unfurnish me of reason.   They are come.

     Re-enter Cleomenes and others, with Florizel and Perdita.
Your mother was most true to wedlock, prince ;
For she did print your royal father off,
Conceiving you : were I but twenty one,
Your father's image is so hit in you,
His very air, that I should call you brother,
As I did him, and speak of something wildly
By us perform'd before.   Most dearly welcome !
And your fair princess,—goddess !—O, alas !
I lost a couple, that 'twixt heaven and earth
Might thus have stood begetting wonder, as
You, gracious couple, do : and then I lost,
All mine own folly, the society,
Amity too, of your brave father, whom,
Though bearing misery, I desire my life
Once more to look on him.

Flo.   By his command
Have I here touch'd Sicilia, and from him
Give you all greetings, that a king, at friend,
Can send his brother : and, but infirmity,
Which waits upon worn times, hath something seized

His wish'd ability, he had himself
The lands and waters 'twixt your throne and his
Measured to look upon you; whom he loves,
He bade me say so, more than all the sceptres
And those that bear them living.

Leon.   O my brother,
Good gentleman! the wrongs I have done thee stir
Afresh within me; and these thy offices,
So rarely kind, are as interpreters
Of my behind-hand slackness!   Welcome hither,
As is the spring to the earth.   And hath he too
Exposed this paragon to the fearful usage,
At least ungentle, of the dreadful Neptune,
To greet a man not worth her pains, much less
The adventure of her person?

Flo.   Good my lord,
She came from Libya.

Leon.   Where the warlike Smalus,
That noble honour'd lord, is fear'd and loved?

Flo. Most royal sir, from thence; from him, whose daughter
His tears proclaim'd his, parting with her: thence,
A prosperous south-wind friendly, we have cross'd,
To execute the charge my father gave me,
For visiting your highness: my best train
I have from your Sicilian shores dismiss'd;
Who for Bohemia bend, to signify
Not only my success in Libya, sir,
But my arrival, and my wife's, in safety
Here where we are.

Leon.   The blessed gods
Purge all infection from our air whilst you
Do climate here!   You have a holy father,
A graceful gentleman; against whose person,
So sacred as it is, I have done sin:
For which the heavens, taking angry note,
Have left me issueless; and your father's blest,
As he from heaven merits it, with you
Worthy his goodness.   What might I have been,
Might I a son and daughter now have look'd on,
Such goodly things as you!

Enter a Lord.

Lord.   Most noble sir,
That which I shall report will bear no credit,
Were not the proof so nigh.   Please you; great sir,
Bohemia greets you from himself by me;

Desires you to attach his son, who has—
His dignity and duty both cast off—
Fled from his father, from his hopes, and with
A shepherd's daughter.
Leon.   Where's Bohemia ? speak.
Lord. Here in your city ; I now came from him :
I speak amazedly ; and it becomes
My marvel and my message. To your court
Whiles he was hastening, in the chase, it seems,
Of this fair couple, meets he on the way
The father of this seeming lady and
Her brother, having both their country quitted
With this young prince.
Flo.   Camillo has betray'd me ;
Whose honour and whose honesty till now
Endured all weathers.
Lord.   Lay 't so to his charge :
He 's with the king your father.
Leon.   Who ? Camillo ?
Lord. Camillo, sir ; I spake with him ; who now
Has these poor men in question. Never saw I
Wretches so quake : they kneel, they kiss the earth ;
Forswear themselves as often as they speak :
Bohemia stops his ears, and threatens them
With divers deaths in death.
Per.   O my poor father !
The heaven sets spies upon us, will not have
Our contract celebrated.
Leon.   You are married ?
Flo. We are not, sir, nor are we like to be ;
The stars, I see, will kiss the valleys first :
The odds for high and low 's alike.
Leon.   My lord,
Is this the daughter of a king ?
Flo.   She is,
When once she is my wife.
Leon. That ' once,' I see by your good father's speed,
Will come on very slowly. I am sorry,
Most sorry, you have broken from his liking
When you were tied in duty, and as sorry
Your choice is not so rich in worth as beauty,
That you might well enjoy her.
Flo.   Dear, look up :
Though Fortune, visible an enemy,
Should chase us with my father, power no jot

Hath she to change our loves.   Beseech you, sir,
Remember since you owed no more to time
Than I do now : with thought of such affections,
Step forth mine advocate ; at your request
My father will grant precious things as trifles.

Leon. Would he do so, I 'ld beg your precious mistress,
Which he counts but a trifle.

Paul.   Sir, my liege,
Your eye hath too much youth in 't : not a month
'Fore your queen died, she was more worth such gazes
Than what you look on now.

Leon.   I thought of her,
Even in these looks I made.   [*To Florizel*] But your petition
Is yet unanswer'd.   I will to your father :
Your honour not o'erthrown by your desires,
I am friend to them and you : upon which errand
I now go toward him ; therefore follow me
And mark what way I make : come, good my lord. [*Exeunt.*

SCENE II
Before Leontes' palace.
Enter Autolycus and a Gentleman.

Aut. Beseech you, sir, were you present at this relation ?

First Gent. I was by at the opening of the fardel, heard the old
shepherd deliver the manner how he found it : whereupon,
after a little amazedness, we were all commanded out of the
chamber ; only this methought I heard the shepherd say, he
found the child.

Aut. I would most gladly know the issue of it.

First Gent. I make a broken delivery of the business ; but the
changes I perceived in the king and Camillo were very notes
of admiration : they seemed almost, with staring on one
another, to tear the cases of their eyes ; there was speech in
their dumbness, language in their very gesture ; they looked
as they had heard of a world ransomed, or one destroyed : a
notable passion of wonder appeared in them ; but the wisest
beholder, that knew no more but seeing, could not say if the
importance were joy or sorrow ; but in the extremity of the
one, it must needs be.

Enter another Gentleman.

Here comes a gentleman that haply knows more.   The news,
Rogero ?

Sec. Gent. Nothing but bonfires : the oracle is fulfilled ; the king's
daughter is found : such a deal of wonder is broken out within
this hour, that ballad-makers cannot be able to express it.

Enter a Third Gentleman.

Here comes the Lady Paulina's steward: he can deliver you more.   How goes it now, sir? this news which is called true is so like an old tale, that the verity of it is in strong suspicion: has the king found his heir?

Third Gent. Most true, if ever truth were pregnant by circumstance: that which you hear you'll swear you see, there is such unity in the proofs.   The mantle of Queen Hermione's, her jewel about the neck of it, the letters of Antigonus found with it, which they know to be his character, the majesty of the creature in resemblance of the mother, the affection of nobleness which nature shows above her breeding, and many other evidences proclaim her with all certainty to be the king's daughter.   Did you see the meeting of the two kings?

Sec. Gent. No.

Third Gent. Then have you lost a sight, which was to be seen, cannot be spoken of.   There might you have beheld one joy crown another, so and in such manner, that it seemed sorrow wept to take leave of them, for their joy waded in tears. There was casting up of eyes, holding up of hands, with countenance of such distraction, that they were to be known by garment, not by favour.   Our king, being ready to leap out of himself for joy of his found daughter, as if that joy were now become a loss, cries 'O, thy mother, thy mother!' then asks Bohemia forgiveness; then embraces his son-in-law; then again worries he his daughter with clipping her; now he thanks the old shepherd, which stands by like a weather-bitten conduit of many kings' reigns.   I never heard of such another encounter, which lames report to follow it and undoes description to do it.

Sec. Gent. What, pray you, became of Antigonus, that carried hence the child?

Third Gent. Like an old tale still, which will have matter to rehearse, though credit be asleep and not an ear open.   He was torn to pieces with a bear: this avouches the shepherd's son; who has not only his innocence, which seems much, to justify him, but a handkerchief and rings of his that Paulina knows.

First Gent. What became of his bark and his followers?

Third Gent. Wrecked the same instant of their master's death and in the view of the shepherd: so that all the instruments which aided to expose the child were even then lost when it was found.   But O, the noble combat that 'twixt joy and sorrow was fought in Paulina!   She had one eye declined for the loss of her husband, another elevated that the oracle was

fulfilled : she lifted the princess from the earth, and so locks
her in embracing, as if she would pin her to her heart that
she might no more be in danger of losing.

First Gent. The dignity of this act was worth the audience of
kings and princes ; for by such was it acted.

Third Gent. One of the prettiest touches of all and that which
angled for mine eyes, caught the water though not the fish,
was when, at the relation of the queen's death, with the
manner how she came to 't bravely confessed and lamented
by the king, how attentiveness wounded his daughter; till,
from one sign of dolour to another, she did, with an ' Alas,' I
would fain say, bleed tears, for I am sure my heart wept blood.
Who was most marble there changed colour ; some swooned,
all sorrowed : if all the world could have seen 't, the woe had
been universal.

First Gent. Are they returned to the court ?

Third Gent. No : the princess hearing of her mother's statue,
which is in the keeping of Paulina,—a piece many years in
doing and now newly performed by that rare Italian master,
Julio Romano, who, had he himself eternity and could put
breath into his work, would beguile Nature of her custom, so
perfectly he is her ape: he so near to Hermione hath done
Hermione, that they say one would speak to her and stand in
hope of answer :—thither with all greediness of affection are
they gone, and there they intend to sup.

Sec. Gent. I thought she had some great matter there in hand ;
for she hath privately twice or thrice a day, ever since the
death of Hermione, visited that removed house. Shall we
thither and with our company piece the rejoicing ?

First Gent. Who would be thence that has the benefit of access ?
every wink of an eye, some new grace will be born : our
absence makes us unthrifty to our knowledge. Let 's along.

                                        [*Exeunt Gentlemen.*

Aut. Now, had I not the dash of my former life in me, would
preferment drop on my head. I brought the old man and
his son aboard the prince; told him I heard them talk of a
fardel and I know not what : but he at that time, overfond of
the shepherd's daughter, so he then took her to be, who
began to be much sea-sick, and himself little better, extremity
of weather continuing, this mystery remained undiscovered.
But 'tis all one to me ; for had I been the finder out of this
secret, it would not have relished among my other discredits.

                    Enter Shepherd and Clown.

Here comes those I have done good to against my will, and
already appearing in the blossoms of their fortune.

Shep. Come, boy; I am past moe children, but thy sons and daughters will be all gentlemen born.

Clo. You are well met, sir. You denied to fight with me this other day, because I was no gentleman born. See you these clothes? say you see them not and think me still no gentleman born: you were best say these robes are not gentleman born: give me the lie, do, and try whether I am not now a gentleman born.

Aut. I know you are now, sir, a gentleman born.

Clo. Ay, and have been so any time these four hours.

Shep. And so have I, boy.

Clo. So you have: but I was a gentleman born before my father; for the king's son took me by the hand, and called me brother; and then the two kings called my father brother; and then the prince my brother and the princess my sister called my father father; and so we wept, and there was the first gentleman-like tears that ever we shed.

Shep. We may live, son, to shed many more.

Clo. Ay; or else 'twere hard luck, being in so preposterous estate as we are.

Aut. I humbly beseech you, sir, to pardon me all the faults I have committed to your worship, and to give me your good report to the prince my master.   [gentlemen.

Shep. Prithee, son, do; for we must be gentle, now we are

Clo. Thou wilt amend thy life?

Aut. Ay, an it like your good worship.

Clo. Give me thy hand: I will swear to the prince thou art as honest a true fellow as any is in Bohemia.

Shep. You may say it, but not swear it.

Clo. Not swear it, now I am a gentleman? Let boors and franklins say it, I'll swear it.

Shep. How if it be false, son?

Clo. If it be ne'er so false, a true gentleman may swear it in the behalf of his friend: and I'll swear to the prince thou art a tall fellow of thy hands and that thou wilt not be drunk; but I know thou art no tall fellow of thy hands and that thou wilt be drunk: but I'll swear it, and I would thou wouldst be a tall fellow of thy hands.

Aut. I will prove so, sir, to my power.

Clo. Ay, by any means prove a tall fellow: if I do not wonder how thou darest venture to be drunk, not being a tall fellow, trust me not. Hark! the kings and the princes, our kindred, are going to see the queen's picture. Come, follow us: we'll be thy good masters.   [*Exeunt.*

SCENE III

A chapel in Paulina's house.

Enter Leontes, Polixenes, Florizel, Perdita, Camillo, Paulina, Lords, and Attendants.

Leon. O grave and good Paulina, the great comfort
  That I have had of thee !
Paul.   What, sovereign sir,
  I did not well, I meant well. All my services
  You have paid home : but that you have vouchsafed
  With your crown'd brother and these your contracted
  Heirs of your kingdoms, my poor house to visit,
  It is a surplus of your grace, which never
  My life may last to answer.
Leon.   O Paulina,
  We honour you with trouble : but we came
  To see the statue of our queen : your gallery
  Have we pass'd through, not without much content
  In many singularities ; but we saw not
  That which my daughter came to look upon,
  The statue of her mother.
Paul.   As she lived peerless,
  So her dead likeness, I do well believe,
  Excels whatever yet you look'd upon
  Or hand of man hath done ; therefore I keep it
  Lonely, apart. But here it is : prepare
  To see the life as lively mock'd as ever
  Still sleep mock'd death : behold, and say 'tis well.
                [Paulina draws a curtain, and discovers
                    Hermione standing like a statue.
  I like your silence, it the more shows off
  Your wonder : but yet speak ; first, you, my liege.
  Comes it not something near ?
Leon.   Her natural posture !
  Chide me, dear stone, that I may say indeed
  Thou art Hermione ; or rather, thou art she
  In thy not chiding, for she was as tender
  As infancy and grace. But yet, Paulina,
  Hermione was not so much wrinkled, nothing
  So aged as this seems.
Pol.   O, not by much.
Paul. So much the more our carver's excellence ;
  Which lets go by some sixteen years and makes her
  As she lived now.
Leon.   As now she might have done,

So much to my good comfort, as it is
Now piercing to my soul.   O, thus she stood,
Even with such life of majesty, warm life,
As now it coldly stands, when first I woo'd her !
I am ashamed : does not the stone rebuke me
For being more stone than it ?   O royal piece,
There 's magic in thy majesty, which has
My evils conjured to remembrance, and
From thy admiring daughter took the spirits,
Standing like stone with thee.

Per.   And give me leave,
And do not say 'tis superstition, that
I kneel and then implore her blessing.   Lady,
Dear queen, that ended when I but began,
Give me that hand of yours to kiss.

Paul.   O, patience !
The statue is but newly fix'd, the colour 's
Not dry.

Cam. My lord, your sorrow was too sore laid on,
Which sixteen winters cannot blow away,
So many summers dry : scarce any joy
Did ever so long live ; no sorrow
But kill'd itself much sooner.

Pol.   Dear my brother,
Let him that was the cause of this have power
To take off so much grief from you as he
Will piece up in himself.

Paul.   Indeed, my lord,
If I had thought the sight of my poor image
Would thus have wrought you, for the stone is mine,
I 'ld not have show'd it.

Leon.   Do not draw the curtain.

Paul. No longer shall you gaze on 't, lest your fancy
May think anon it moves.

Leon.   Let be, let be.
Would I were dead, but that, methinks, already—
What was he that did make it ?   See, my lord,
Would you not deem it breathed ? and that those veins
Did verily bear blood ?

Pol.   Masterly done :
The very life seems warm upon her lip.

Leon. The fixure of her eye has motion in 't,
As we are mock'd with art.

Paul.   I 'll draw the curtain :
My lord 's almost so far transported that

He 'll think anon it lives.

Leon.   O sweet Paulina,
Make me to think so twenty years together !
No settled senses of the world can match
The pleasure of that madness.   Let 't alone.

Paul. I am sorry, sir, I have thus far stirr'd you : but
I could afflict you farther.

Leon.   Do, Paulina ;
For this affliction has a taste as sweet
As any cordial comfort.   Still, methinks,
There is an air comes from her : what fine chisel
Could ever yet cut breath ?   Let no man mock me,
For I will kiss her.

Paul.   Good my lord, forbear :
The ruddiness upon her lip is wet ;
You 'll mar it if you kiss it, stain your own
With oily painting.   Shall I draw the curtain ?

Leon. No, not these twenty years.

Per.   So long could I
Stand by, a looker on.

Paul.   Either forbear,
Quit presently the chapel, or resolve you
For more amazement.   If you can behold it,
I 'll make the statue move indeed, descend
And take you by the hand : but then you 'll think,
Which I protest against, I am assisted
By wicked powers.

Leon.   What you can make her do,
I am content to look on : what to speak,
I am content to hear ; for 'tis as easy
To make her speak as move.

Paul.   It is required
You do awake your faith.   Then all stand still ;
On : those that think it is unlawful business
I am about, let them depart.

Leon.   Proceed :
No foot shall stir.

Paul.   Music, awake her ; strike !   [*Music.*
'Tis time ; descend ; be stone no more ; approach ;
Strike all that look upon with marvel.   Come,
I 'll fill your grave up : stir, nay, come away,
Bequeath to death your numbness, for from him
Dear life redeems you.   You perceive she stirs :

                                        [*Hermione comes down.*

Start not ; her actions shall be holy as

490

You hear my spell is lawful: do not shun her
Until you see her die again; for then
You kill her double.   Nay, present your hand :
When she was young you woo'd her; now in age
Is she become the suitor?
Leon.   O, she 's warm !
If this be magic, let it be an art
Lawful as eating.
Pol.   She embraces him.
Cam. She hangs about his neck:
If she pertain to life let her speak too.
Pol. Ay, and make 't manifest where she has lived,
Or how stolen from the dead.
Paul.   That she is living,
Were it but told you, should be hooted at
Like an old tale : but it appears she lives,
Though yet she speak not.   Mark a little while.
Please you to interpose, fair madam : kneel
And pray your mother's blessing.   Turn, good lady ;
Our Perdita is found.
Her.   You gods, look down,
And from your sacred vials pour your graces
Upon my daughter's head !   Tell me, mine own,
Where hast thou been preserved? where lived? how found
Thy father's court? for thou shalt hear that I,
Knowing by Paulina that the oracle
Gave hope thou wast in being, have preserved
Myself to see the issue.
Paul.   There 's time enough for that
Lest they desire upon this push to trouble
Your joys with like relation.   Go together,
You precious winners all ; your exultation
Partake to every one.   I, an old turtle,
Will wing me to some wither'd bough and there
My mate, that 's never to be found again,
Lament till I am lost.
Leon.   O, peace, Paulina !
Thou shouldst a husband take by my consent,
As I by thine a wife : this is a match,
And made between 's by vows.   Thou hast found mine ;
But how, is to be question'd ; for I saw her,
As I thought, dead ; and have in vain said many
A prayer upon her grave.   I 'll not seek far,—
For him, I partly know his mind,—to find thee
An honourable husband.   Come, Camillo,

And take her by the hand, whose worth and honesty
Is richly noted and here justified
By us, a pair of kings.   Let's from this place.
What! look upon my brother : both your pardons,
That e'er I put between your holy looks
My ill suspicion.   This your son-in-law,
And son unto the king, whom heavens directing,
Is troth-plight to your daughter.   Good Paulina,
Lead us from hence, where we may leisurely
Each one demand, and answer to his part
Perform'd in this wide gap of time, since first
We were dissever'd : hastily lead away.   *[Exeunt.*

A MIDSUMMER-NIGHT'S DREAM

DRAMATIS PERSONÆ

THESEUS, *Duke of Athens.*
EGEUS, *father to Hermia.*
LYSANDER, } *in love with Hermia.*
DEMETRIUS, }
PHILOSTRATE, *master of the revels to Theseus.*
QUINCE, *a carpenter.*
SNUG, *a joiner.*
BOTTOM, *a weaver.*
FLUTE, *a bellows-mender.*
SNOUT, *a tinker.*
STARVELING, *a tailor.*

HIPPOLYTA, *queen of the Amazons, betrothed to Theseus.* [*Lysander.*
HERMIA, *daughter to Egeus, in love with*
HELENA, *in love with Demetrius.*

OBERON, *king of the fairies.*
TITANIA, *queen of the fairies.*
PUCK, *or Robin Goodfellow.*
PEASEBLOSSOM, }
COBWEB, }
MOTH, } *fairies.*
MUSTARDSEED, }

Other fairies attending their King and Queen. Attendants on Theseus and Hippolyta.
SCENE : *Athens, and a wood near it.*

ACT I—SCENE I
Athens. The palace of Theseus.
Enter Theseus, Hippolyta, Philostrate, and Attendants.

The. Now, fair Hippolyta, our nuptial hour
    Draws on apace ; four happy days bring in
    Another moon : but, O, methinks, how slow
    This old moon wanes ! she lingers my desires,
    Like to a step-dame, or a dowager,
    Long withering out a young man's revenue.
Hip. Four days will quickly steep themselves in night ;
    Four nights will quickly dream away the time ;
    And then the moon, like to a silver bow
    New-bent in heaven, shall behold the night
    Of our solemnities.
The.   Go, Philostrate,
    Stir up the Athenian youth to merriments ;
    Awake the pert and nimble spirit of mirth :
    Turn melancholy forth to funerals ;
    The pale companion is not for our pomp. [*Exit Philostrate.*
    Hippolyta, I woo'd thee with my sword,
    And won thy love, doing thee injuries ;
    But I will wed thee in another key,
    With pomp, with triumph and with revelling.
    Enter Egeus, Hermia, Lysander, and Demetrius.
Ege. Happy be Theseus, our renowned duke !
The. Thanks, good Egeus : what 's the news with thee ?
Ege. Full of vexation come I, with complaint
    Against my child, my daughter Hermia.
    Stand forth, Demetrius. My noble lord,
    This man hath my consent to marry her.
    Stand forth, Lysander : and, my gracious duke,
    This man hath bewitch'd the bosom of my child :

Thou, thou, Lysander, thou hast given her rhymes,
And interchanged love-tokens with my child :
Thou hast by moonlight at her window sung,
With feigning voice, verses of feigning love ;
And stolen the impression of her fantasy
With bracelets of thy hair, rings, gawds, conceits,
Knacks, trifles, nosegays, sweetmeats, messengers
Of strong prevailment in unharden'd youth :
With cunning hast thou filch'd my daughter's heart ;
Turn'd her obedience, which is due to me,
To stubborn harshness : and, my gracious duke,
Be it so she will not here before your Grace
Consent to marry with Demetrius,
I beg the ancient privilege of Athens,
As she is mine, I may dispose of her :
Which shall be either to this gentleman
Or to her death, according to our law
Immediately provided in that case.

The. What say you, Hermia ? be advised, fair maid :
To you your father should be as a god ;
One that composed your beauties ; yea, and one
To whom you are but as a form in wax
By him imprinted and within his power
To leave the figure or disfigure it.
Demetrius is a worthy gentleman.

Her. So is Lysander.

The.   In himself he is ;
But in this kind, wanting your father's voice,
The other must be held the worthier.

Her. I would my father look'd but with my eyes.

The. Rather your eyes must with his judgement look.

Her. I do entreat your Grace to pardon me.
I know not by what power I am made bold,
Nor how it may concern my modesty,
In such a presence here to plead my thoughts ;
But I beseech your Grace that I may know
The worst that may befall me in this case,
If I refuse to wed Demetrius.

The. Either to die the death, or to abjure
For ever the society of men.
Therefore, fair Hermia, question your desires ;
Know of your youth, examine well your blood,
Whether, if you yield not to your father's choice,
You can endure the livery of a nun ;
For aye to be in shady cloister mew'd,

To live a barren sister all your life,
Chanting faint hymns to the cold fruitless moon.
Thrice-blessed they that master so their blood,
To undergo such maiden pilgrimage ;
But earthlier happy is the rose distill'd,
Than that which, withering on the virgin thorn,
Grows, lives, and dies in single blessedness.

Her. So will I grow, so live, so die, my lord,
Ere I will yield my virgin patent up
Unto his lordship, whose unwished yoke
My soul consents not to give sovereignty.

The. Take time to pause ; and, by the next new moon,—
The sealing-day betwixt my love and me
For everlasting bond of fellowship,—
Upon that day either prepare to die
For disobedience to your father's will,
Or else to wed Demetrius, as he would ,
Or on Diana's altar to protest
For aye austerity and single life.

Dem. Relent, sweet Hermia : and, Lysander, yield
Thy crazed title to my certain right.

Lys. You have her father's love, Demetrius ;
Let me have Hermia's : do you marry him.

Ege. Scornful Lysander ! true, he hath my love,
And what is mine my love shall render him.
And she is mine, and all my right of her
I do estate unto Demetrius.

Lys. I am, my lord, as well derived as he,
As well possess'd ; my love is more than his ;
My fortunes every way as fairly rank'd,
If not with vantage, as Demetrius' ;
And, which is more than all these boasts can be,
I am beloved of beauteous Hermia :
Why should not I then prosecute my right?
Demetrius, I 'll avouch it to his head,
Made love to Nedar's daughter, Helena,
And won her soul ; and she, sweet lady, dotes,
Devoutly dotes, dotes in idolatry,
Upon this spotted and inconstant man.

The. I must confess that I have heard so much,
And with Demetrius thought to have spoke thereof ;
But, being over-full of self-affairs,
My mind did lose it. But, Demetrius, come ;
And come, Egeus ; you shall go with me,
I have some private schooling for you both.

For you, fair Hermia, look you arm yourself
To fit your fancies to your father's will ;
Or else the law of Athens yields you up,—
Which by no means we may extenuate,—
To death, or to a vow of single life.
Come, my Hippolyta : what cheer, my love ?
Demetrius and Egeus, go along :
I must employ you in some business
Against our nuptial, and confer with you
Of something nearly that concerns yourselves.

Ege. With duty and desire we follow you.

                    [Exeunt all but Lysander and Hermia.

Lys. How now, my love ! why is your cheek so pale ?
How chance the roses there do fade so fast ?

Her. Belike the want of rain, which I could well
Beteem them from the tempest of my eyes.

Lys. Ay me ! for aught that I could ever read,
Could ever hear by tale or history,
The course of true love never did run smooth ;
But, either it was different in blood,—

Her. O cross ! too high to be enthrall'd to low.

Lys. Or else misgraffed in respect of years,—

Her. O spite ! too old to be engaged to young.

Lys. Or else it stood upon the choice of friends,—

Her. O hell ! to choose love by another's eyes.

Lys. Or, if there were a sympathy in choice,
War, death, or sickness did lay siege to it,
Making it momentary as a sound,
Swift as a shadow, short as any dream ;
Brief as the lightning in the collied night,
That, in a spleen, unfolds both heaven and earth,
And ere a man hath power do say ' Behold ! '
The jaws of darkness do devour it up :
So quick bright things come to confusion.

Her. If then true lovers have been ever cross'd,
It stands as an edict in destiny :
Then let us teach our trial patience,
Because it is a customary cross,
As due to love as thoughts and dreams and sighs,
Wishes and tears, poor fancy's followers.

Lys. A good persuasion : therefore, hear me, Hermia.
I have a widow aunt, a dowager
Of great revenue, and she hath no child :
From Athens is her house remote seven leagues ;
And she respects me as her only son.

There, gentle Hermia, may I marry thee ;
And to that place the sharp Athenian law
Cannot pursue us.   If thou lovest me, then,
Steal forth thy father's house to-morrow night ;
And in the wood, a league without the town,
Where I did meet thee once with Helena,
To do observance to a morn of May,
There will I stay for thee.

Her.   My good Lysander !
I swear to thee, by Cupid's strongest bow,
By his best arrow with the golden head,
By the simplicity of Venus' doves,
By that which knitteth souls and prospers loves,
And by that fire which burn'd the Carthage queen,
When the false Troyan under sail was seen,
By all the vows that ever men have broke,
In number more than ever women spoke,
In that same place thou hast appointed me,
To-morrow truly will I meet with thee.

Lys. Keep promise, love.   Look, here comes Helena.

Enter Helena.

Her. God speed fair Helena ! whither away ?

Hel. Call you me fair ? that fair again unsay.
Demetrius loves your fair : O happy fair !
Your eyes are lode-stars ; and your tongue's sweet air
More tuneable than lark to shepherd's ear,
When wheat is green, when hawthorn buds appear.
Sickness is catching : O, were favour so,
Yours would I catch, fair Hermia, ere I go ;
My ear should catch your voice, my eye your eye,
My tongue should catch your tongue's sweet melody.
Were the world mine, Demetrius being bated,
The rest I 'ld give to be to you translated.
O, teach me how you look ; and with what art
You sway the motion of Demetrius' heart !

Her. I frown upon him, yet he loves me still.

Hel. O that your frowns would teach my smiles such skill !

Her. I give him curses, yet he gives me love.

Hel. O that my prayers could such affection move !

Her. The more I hate, the more he follows me.

Hel. The more I love, the more he hateth me.

Her. His folly, Helena, is no fault of mine.

Hel. None, but your beauty : would that fault were mine !

Her. Take comfort : he no more shall see my face ;
Lysander and myself will fly this place.

Before the time I did Lysander see,
Seem'd Athens as a paradise to me :
O, then, what graces in my love do dwell,
That he hath turn'd a heaven unto a hell !
Lys. Helen, to you our minds we will unfold :
To-morrow night, when Phœbe doth behold
Her silver visage in the watery glass,
Decking with liquid pearl the bladed grass,
A time that lovers' flights doth still conceal,
Through Athens' gates have we devised to steal.
Her. And in the wood, where often you and I
Upon faint primrose-beds were wont to lie,
Emptying our bosoms of their counsel sweet,
There my Lysander and myself shall meet ;
And thence from Athens turn away our eyes,
To seek new friends and stranger companies.
Farewell, sweet playfellow : pray thou for us ;
And good luck grant thee thy Demetrius !
Keep word, Lysander : we must starve our sight
From lovers' food till morrow deep midnight.
Lys. I will, my Hermia.   [*Exit Herm.*
                Helena, adieu :
As you on him, Demetrius dote on you !   [*Exit.*
Hel. How happy some o'er other some can be !
Through Athens I am thought as fair as she.
But what of that ? Demetrius thinks not so ;
He will not know what all but he do know :
And as he errs, doting on Hermia's eyes,
So I, admiring of his qualities :
Things base and vile, holding no quantity,
Love can transpose to form and dignity :
Love looks not with the eyes, but with the mind ;
And therefore is wing'd Cupid painted blind :
Nor hath Love's mind of any judgement taste ;
Wings, and no eyes, figure unheedy haste :
And therefore is Love said to be a child,
Because in choice he is so oft beguiled.
As waggish boys in game themselves forswear,
So the boy Love is perjured everywhere :
For ere Demetrius look'd on Hermia's eyne,
He hail'd down oaths that he was only mine ;
And when this hail some heat from Hermia felt,
So he dissolved, and showers of oaths did melt.
I will go tell him of fair Hermia's flight :
Then to the wood will he to-morrow night

Pursue her ; and for this intelligence
If I have thanks, it is a dear expense :
But herein mean I to enrich my pain,
To have his sight thither and back again.   ⌊*Exit.*

Scene II

The same.   Quince's house.

Enter Quince, Snug, Bottom, Flute, Snout, and Starveling.

Quin. Is all our company here ?

Bot. You were best to call them generally, man by man, according to the scrip.

Quin. Here is the scroll of every man's name, which is thought fit, through all Athens, to play in our interlude before the duke and the duchess, on his wedding-day at night.

Bot. First, good Peter Quince, say what the play treats on ; then read the names of the actors ; and so grow to a point.

Quin. Marry, our play is, The most lamentable comedy, and most cruel death of Pyramus and Thisby.

Bot. A very good piece of work, I assure you, and a merry. Now, good Peter Quince, call forth your actors by the scroll. Masters, spread yourselves.

Quin. Answer as I call you.   Nick Bottom, the weaver.

Bot. Ready.   Name what part I am for, and proceed.

Quin. You, Nick Bottom, are set down for Pyramus.

Bot. What is Pyramus ? a lover, or a tyrant ?

Quin. A lover, that kills himself most gallant for love.

Bot. That will ask some tears in the true performing of it : if I do it, let the audience look to their eyes ; I will move storms, I will condole in some measure.   To the rest : yet my chief humour is for a tyrant : I could play Ercles rarely, or a part to tear a cat in, to make all split.

> The raging rocks
> And shivering shocks
> Shall break the locks
>   Of prison-gates ;
> And Phibbus' car
> Shall shine from far,
> And make and mar
>   The foolish Fates.

This was lofty ! Now name the rest of the players.   This is Ercles' vein, a tyrant's vein ; a lover is more condoling.

Quin. Francis Flute, the bellows-mender.

Flu. Here, Peter Quince.

Quin. Flute, you must take Thisby on you.

Flu. What is Thisby? a wandering knight?

Quin. It is the lady that Pyramus must love.　　　　　[coming.

Flu. Nay, faith, let not me play a woman; I have a beard

Quin. That's all one: you shall play it in a mask, and you may speak as small as you will.

Bot. An I may hide my face, let me play Thisby too, I'll speak in a monstrous little voice, 'Thisne, Thisne;' 'Ah Pyramus, my lover dear! thy Thisby dear, and lady dear!'

Quin. No, no; you must play Pyramus: and, Flute, you Thisby.

Bot. Well, proceed.

Quin. Robin Starveling, the tailor.

Star. Here, Peter Quince.

Quin. Robin Starveling, you must play Thisby's mother. Tom Snout, the tinker.

Snout. Here, Peter Quince.

Quin. You, Pyramus' father: myself, Thisby's father: Snug, the joiner; you, the lion's part: and, I hope, here is a play fitted.

Snug. Have you the lion's part written? pray you, if it be, give it me, for I am slow of study.

Quin. You may do it extempore, for it is nothing but roaring.

Bot. Let me play the lion too: I will roar, that I will do any man's heart good to hear me; I will roar, that I will make the duke say, 'Let him roar again, let him roar again.'

Quin. An you should do it too terribly, you would fright the duchess and the ladies, that they would shriek; and that were enough to hang us all.

All. That would hang us, every mother's son.

Bot. I grant you, friends, if you should fright the ladies out of their wits, they would have no more discretion but to hang us: but I will aggravate my voice so, that I will roar you as gently as any sucking dove; I will roar you an 'twere any nightingale.

Quin. You can play no part but Pyramus; for Pyramus is a sweet-faced man; a proper man, as one shall see in a summer's day; a most lovely, gentleman-like man: therefore you must needs play Pyramus.

Bot. Well, I will undertake it. What beard were I best to play it in?

Quin. Why, what you will.

Bot. I will discharge it in either your straw colour beard, your orange-tawny beard, your purple-in-grain beard, or your French crown colour beard, your perfect yellow.

Quin. Some of your French crowns have no hair at all, and

then you will play barefaced. But, masters, here are your
parts : and I am to entreat you, request you, and desire you,
to con them by to-morrow night ; and meet me in the palace
wood, a mile without the town, by moonlight ; there will we
rehearse, for if we meet in the city, we shall be dogged with
company, and our devices known. In the mean time I will
draw a bill of properties, such as our play wants. I pray
you, fail me not.

Bot. We will meet ; and there we may rehearse most ob-
scenely and courageously. Take pains ; be perfect : adieu.

Quin. At the duke's oak we meet.

Bot. Enough ; hold or cut bow-strings   [*Exeunt.*

ACT II—Scene I

A wood near Athens.

Enter, from opposite sides, a Fairy, and Puck.

Puck. How now, spirit ! whither wander you ?

Fai.   Over hill, over dale,
                    Thorough bush, thorough brier,
                Over park, over pale,
                    Thorough flood, thorough fire,
                I do wander every where,
                Swifter than the moon's sphere ;
                And I serve the fairy queen,
                To dew her orbs upon the green.
                The cowlips tall her pensioners be :
                In their gold coats spots you see ;
                Those be rubies, fairy favours,
                In those freckles live their savours :
            I must go seek some dewdrops here,
            And hang a pearl in every cowslip's ear.
            Farewell, thou lob of spirits ; I 'll be gone :
            Our queen and all her elves come here anon.

Puck. The king doth keep his revels here to-night :
            Take heed the queen come not within his sight ;
            For Oberon is passing fell and wrath,
            Because that she as her attendant hath
            A lovely boy, stolen from an Indian king ;
            She never had so sweet a changeling :
            And jealous Oberon would have the child
            Knight of his train, to trace the forests wild ;
            But she perforce withholds the loved boy,
            Crowns him with flowers, and makes him all her joy :

And now they never meet in grove or green,
By fountain clear, or spangled starlight sheen,
But they do square, that all their elves for fear
Creep into acorn cups and hide them there.

Fai. Either I mistake your shape and making quite,
Or else you are that shrewd and knavish sprite
Call'd Robin Goodfellow: are not you he
That frights the maidens of the villagery;
Skim milk, and sometimes labour in the quern,
And bootless make the breathless housewife churn;
And sometime make the drink to bear no barm;
Mislead night-wanderers, laughing at their harm?
Those that Hobgoblin call you, and sweet Puck,
You do their work, and they shall have good luck:
Are not you he?

Puck.   Thou speak'st aright;
I am that merry wanderer of the night.
I jest to Oberon, and make him smile,
When I a fat and bean-fed horse beguile,
Neighing in likeness of a filly foal:
And sometime lurk I in a gossip's bowl,
In very likeness of a roasted crab;
And when she drinks, against her lips I bob
And on her withered dewlap pour the ale.
The wisest aunt, telling the saddest tale,
Sometime for three-foot stool mistaketh me;
Then slip I from her bum, down topples she,
And 'tailor' cries, and falls into a cough;
And then the whole quire hold their hips and laugh;
And waxen in their mirth, and neeze, and swear
A merrier hour was never wasted there.
But, room, fairy! here comes Oberon.

Fai. And here my mistress.   Would that he were gone!

*Enter, from one side, Oberon, with his train; from the
      other, Titania, with hers.*

Obe. Ill met by moonlight, proud Titania.

Tita. What, jealous Oberon!   Fairies, skip hence:
I have forsworn his bed and company.

Obe. Tarry, rash wanton: am not I thy lord?

Tita. Then I must be thy lady: but I know
When thou hast stolen away from fairy land,
And in the shape of Corin sat all day,
Playing on pipes of corn, and versing love
To amorous Phillida.   Why art thou here,
Come from the farthest steppe of India?

But that, forsooth, the bouncing Amazon,
Your buskin'd mistress and your warrior love,
To Theseus must be wedded, and you come
To give their bed joy and prosperity.

Obe. How canst thou thus for shame, Titania,
Glance at my credit with Hippolyta,
Knowing I know thy love to Theseus?
Didst thou not lead him through the glimmering night
From Perigenia, whom he ravished?
And make him with fair Ægle break his faith,
With Ariadne and Antiopa?

Tita. These are the forgeries of jealousy:
And never, since the middle summer's spring,
Met we on hill, in dale, forest, or mead,
By paved fountain or by rushy brook,
Or in the beached margent of the sea,
To dance our ringlets to the whistling wind,
But with thy brawls thou hast disturb'd our sport.
Therefore the winds, piping to us in vain,
As in revenge, have suck'd up from the sea
Contagious fogs; which, falling in the land,
Have every pelting river made so proud,
That they have overborne their continents:
The ox hath therefore stretch'd his yoke in vain,
The ploughman lost his sweat; and the green corn
Hath rotted ere his youth attain'd a beard:
The fold stands empty in the drowned field,
And crows are fatted with the murrion flock,
The nine men's morris is fill'd up with mud;
And the quaint mazes in the wanton green,
For lack of tread, are undistinguishable:
The human mortals want their winter here;
No night is now with hymn or carol blest:
Therefore the moon, the governess of floods,
Pale in her anger, washes all the air,
That rheumatic diseases do abound:
And thorough this distemperature we see
The seasons alter: hoary-headed frosts
Fall in the fresh lap of the crimson rose;
And on old Hiems' thin and icy crown
An odorous chaplet of sweet summer buds
Is, as in mockery, set: the spring, the summer,
The childing autumn, angry winter, change
Their wonted liveries; and the mazed world,
By their increase, now knows not which is which:

And this same progeny of evils comes
From our debate, from our dissension;
We are their parents and original.

Obe. Do you amend it, then; it lies in you:
Why should Titania cross her Oberon?
I do but beg a little changeling boy,
To be my henchman.

Tita.   Set your heart at rest.
The fairy land buys not the child of me.
His mother was a votaress of my order:
And, in the spiced Indian air, by night,
Full often hath she gossip'd by my side;
And sat with me on Neptune's yellow sands,
Marking the embarked traders on the flood;
When we have laugh'd to see the sails conceive
And grow big-bellied with the wanton wind;
Which she, with pretty and with swimming gait
Following,—her womb then rich with my young squire,—
Would imitate, and sail upon the land,
To fetch me trifles, and return again,
As from a voyage, rich with merchandise.
But she, being mortal, of that boy did die;
And for her sake do I rear up her boy;
And for her sake I will not part with him.

Obe. How long within this wood intend you stay?

Tita. Perchance till after Theseus' wedding-day.
If you will patiently dance in our round,
And see our moonlight revels, go with us;
If not, shun me, and I will spare your haunts.

Obe. Give me that boy, and I will go with thee.

Tita. Not for thy fairy kingdom. Fairies, away!
We shall chide downright, if I longer stay.
                                        [*Exit Titania and her Train.*

Obe. Well, go thy way: thou shalt not from this grove
Till I torment thee for this injury.
My gentle Puck, come hither. Thou rememberest
Since once I sat upon a promontory,
And heard a mermaid, on a dolphin's back,
Uttering such dulcet and harmonious breath,
That the rude sea grew civil at her song,
And certain stars shot madly from their spheres,
To hear the sea-maid's music.

Puck.   I remember.

Obe. That very time I saw, but thou couldst not,
Flying between the cold moon and the earth,

Cupid all arm'd : a certain aim he took
At a fair vestal throned by the west,
And loosed his love-shaft smartly from his bow,
As it should pierce a hundred thousand hearts :
But I might see young Cupid's fiery shaft
Quench'd in the chaste beams of the watery moon,
And the imperial votaress passed on,
In maiden meditation, fancy-free.
Yet mark'd I where the bolt of Cupid fell :
It fell upon a little western flower,
Before milk-white, now purple with love's wound,
And maidens call it love-in-idleness.
Fetch me that flower ; the herb I shew'd thee once
The juice of it on sleeping eye-lids laid
Will make or man or woman madly dote
Upon the next live creature that it sees.
Fetch me this herb ; and be thou here again
Ere the leviathan can swim a league.

Puck. I 'll put a girdle round about the earth
In forty minutes.   [*Exit.*

Obe.   Having once this juice,
I 'll watch Titania when she is asleep,
And drop the liquor of it in her eyes.
The next thing then she waking looks upon,
Be it on lion, bear, or wolf, or bull,
On meddling monkey, or on busy ape,
She shall pursue it with the soul of love :
And ere I take this charm from off her sight,
As I can take it with another herb,
I 'll make her render up her page to me.
But who comes here ? I am invisible ;
And I will overhear their conference.

Enter Demetrius, Helena following him.

Dem. I love thee not, therefore pursue me not.
Where is Lysander and fair Hermia ?
The one I 'll slay, the other slayeth me.
Thou told'st me they were stolen unto this wood ;
And here am I, and wode within this wood,
Because I cannot meet my Hermia.
Hence, get thee gone, and follow me no more.

Hel. You draw me, you hard-hearted adamant ;
But yet you draw not iron, for my heart
Is true as steel : leave you your power to draw,
And I shall have no power to follow you.

Dem. Do I entice you ? do I speak you fair ?

Or, rather, do I not in plainest truth
Tell you, I do not nor I cannot love you?

Hel. And even for that do I love you the more.
　I am your spaniel; and, Demetrius,
　The more you beat me, I will fawn on you:
　Use me but as your spaniel, spurn me, strike me,
　Neglect me, lose me; only give me leave,
　Unworthy as I am, to follow you.
　What worser place can I beg in your love,—
　And yet a place of high respect with me,—
　Than to be used as you use your dog?

Dem. Tempt not too much the hatred of my spirit;
　For I am sick when I do look on thee.

Hel. And I am sick when I look not on you.

Dem. You do impeach your modesty too much,
　To leave the city, and commit yourself
　Into the hands of one that loves you not;
　To trust the opportunity of night
　And the ill counsel of a desert place
　With the rich worth of your virginity.

Hel. Your virtue is my privilege: for that
　It is not night when I do see your face,
　Therefore I think I am not in the night;
　Nor doth this wood lack worlds of company,
　For you in my respect are all the world:
　Then how can it be said I am alone,
　When all the world is here to look on me?

Dem. I'll run from thee and hide me in the brakes,
　And leave thee to the mercy of wild beasts.

Hel. The wildest hath not such a heart as you.
　Run when you will, the story shall be changed:
　Apollo flies, and Daphne holds the chase;
　The dove pursues the griffin; the mild hind
　Makes speed to catch the tiger; bootless speed,
　When cowardice pursues, and valour flies.

Dem. I will not stay thy questions; let me go:
　Or, if thou follow me, do not believe
　But I shall do thee mischief in the wood.

Hel. Ay, in the temple, in the town, the field,
　You do me mischief. Fie, Demetrius!
　Your wrongs do set a scandal on my sex:
　We cannot fight for love, as men may do;
　We should be woo'd, and were not made to woo. [*Exit Dem.*
　I'll follow thee, and make a heaven of hell,
　To die upon the hand I love so well. [*Exit.*

506

Obe. Fare thee well, nymph : ere he do leave this grove,
  Thou shalt fly him, and he shall seek thy love.
                    Re-enter Puck.
  Hast thou the flower there ?   Welcome, wanderer.
Puck. Ay, there it is.
Obe.   I pray thee, give it me.
  I know a bank where the wild thyme blows,
  Where oxlips and the nodding violet grows ;
  Quite over-canopied with luscious woodbine,
  With sweet musk-roses, and with eglantine :
  There sleeps Titania sometime of the night,
  Lull'd in these flowers with dances and delight ;
  And there the snake throws her enamell'd skin,
  Weed wide enough to wrap a fairy in :
  And with the juice of this I 'll streak her eyes,
  And make her full of hateful fantasies.
  Take thou some of it, and seek through this grove :
  A sweet Athenian lady is in love
  With a disdainful youth : anoint his eyes ;
  But do it when the next thing he espies
  May be the lady : thou shalt know the man
  By the Athenian garments he hath on.
  Effect it with some care that he may prove
  More fond on her than she upon her love :
  And look thou meet me ere the first cock crow.
Puck. Fear not, my lord, your servant shall do so.   [*Exeunt.*

SCENE II

Another part of the wood.
Enter Titania, with her train.

Tita. Come, now a roundel and a fairy song ;
  Then, for the third part of a minute, hence ;
  Some to kill cankers in the musk-rose buds ;
  Some war with rere-mice for their leathern wings,
  To make my small elves coats ; and some keep back
  The clamorous owl, that nightly hoots and wonders
  At our quaint spirits.   Sing me now asleep ;
  Then to your offices, and let me rest.

SONG.

Fir. Fairy. You spotted snakes with double tongue,
          Thorny hedgehogs, be not seen ;
        Newts and blind-worms, do no wrong,
          Come not near our fairy queen.

507

CHORUS.

Philomel, with melody
Sing in our sweet lullaby ;
Lulla, lulla, lullaby, lulla, lulla, lullaby :
Never harm,
Nor spell, nor charm,
Come our lovely lady nigh ;
So, good night, with lullaby.

Fir. Fairy. Weaving spiders, come not here ;
Hence, you long-legg'd spinners, hence !
Beetles black, approach not near ;
Worm nor snail, do no offence.

CHORUS.

Philomel, with melody, &c.

Sec. Fairy.   Hence, away ! now all is well :
One aloof stand sentinel.
[Exeunt Fairies. Titania sleeps.

Enter Oberon, and squeezes the flower on Titania's eyelids.

Obe.   What thou seest when thou dost wake,
Do it for thy true-love take ;
Love and languish for his sake :
Be it ounce, or cat, or bear,
Pard, or boar with bristled hair,
In thy eye that shall appear
When thou wakest, it is thy dear :
Wake when some vile thing is near.   *[Exit.*
Enter Lysander and Hermia.

Lys. Fair love, you faint with wandering in the wood ;
And to speak troth, I have forgot our way :
We 'll rest us, Hermia, if you think it good,
And tarry for the comfort of the day.
Her. Be it so, Lysander : find you out a bed ;
For I upon this bank will rest my head.
Lys. One turf shall serve as pillow for us both ;
One heart, one bed, two bosoms, and one troth.
Her. Nay, good Lysander ; for my sake, my dear,
Lie further off yet, do not lie so near.
Lys. O, take the sense, sweet, of my innocence !
Love takes the meaning in love's conference.
I mean, that my heart unto yours is knit.
So that but one heart we can make of it :

Two bosoms interchained with an oath ;
So then two bosoms and a single troth.
Then by your side no bed-room me deny ;
For lying so, Hermia, I do not lie.

Her. Lysander riddles very prettily :
Now much beshrew my manners and my pride,
If Hermia meant to say Lysander lied.
But, gentle friend, for love and courtesy
Lie further off ; in human modesty,
Such separation as may well be said
Becomes a virtuous bachelor and a maid,
So far be distant ; and, good night, sweet friend :
Thy love ne'er alter till thy sweet life end !

Lys. Amen, amen, to that fair prayer, say I ;
And then end life when I end loyalty !
Here is my bed : sleep give thee all his rest !

Her. With half that wish the wisher's eyes be press'd ! [*They sleep.*

Enter Puck.

Puck.   Through the forest have I gone,
But Athenian found I none,
On whose eyes I might approve
This flower's force in stirring love.
Night and silence.—Who is here ?
Weeds of Athens he doth wear :
This is he, my master said,
Despised the Athenian maid ;
And here the maiden, sleeping sound,
On the dank and dirty ground.
Pretty soul ! she durst not lie
Near this lack-love, this kill-courtesy.
Churl, upon thy eyes I throw
All the power this charm doth owe.
When thou wakest, let love forbid
Sleep his seat on thy eyelid !
So awake when I am gone ;
For I must now to Oberon.   [*Exit.*

Enter Demetrius and Helena, running.

Hel. Stay, though thou kill me, sweet Demetrius.
Dem. I charge thee, hence, and do not haunt me thus :
Hel. O, wilt thou darkling leave me ? do not so.
Dem. Stay, on thy peril : I alone will go.   [*Exit.*
Hel. O, I am out of breath in this fond chase !
The more my prayer, the lesser is my grace.
Happy is Hermia, wheresoe'er she lies ;
For she hath blessed and attractive eyes.

How came her eyes so bright? Not with salt tears:
If so, my eyes are oftener wash'd than hers.
No, no, I am as ugly as a bear;
For beasts that meet me run away for fear:
Therefore no marvel though Demetrius
Do, as a monster, fly my presence thus.
What wicked and dissembling glass of mine
Made me compare with Hermia's sphery eyne?
But who is here? Lysander! on the ground!
Dead? or asleep? I see no blood, no wound.
Lysander, if you live, good sir, awake.

Lys. [*Awaking*] And run through fire I will for thy sweet sake.
Transparent Helena! Nature shews art,
That through thy bosom makes me see thy heart.
Where is Demetrius? O, how fit a word
Is that vile name to perish on my sword!

Hel. Do not say so, Lysander; say not so.
What though he love your Hermia? Lord, what though?
Yet Hermia still loves you: then be content.

Lys. Content with Hermia! No; I do repent
The tedious minutes I with her have spent.
Not Hermia but Helena I love:
Who will not chance a raven for a dove?
The will of man is by his reason sway'd
And reason says you are the worthier maid.
Things growing are not ripe until their season:
So I, being young, till now ripe not to reason;
And touching now the point of human skill,
Reason becomes the marshal to my will,
And leads me to your eyes; where I o'erlook
Love's stories, written in love's richest book.

Hel. Wherefore was I to this keen mockery born?
When at your hands did I deserve this scorn?
Is 't not enough, is 't not enough, young man,
That I did never, no, nor never can,
Deserve a sweet look from Demetrius' eye,
But you must flout my insufficiency?
Good troth, you do me wrong, good sooth, you do,
In such disdainful manner me to woo.
But fare you well: perforce I must confess
I thought you lord of more true gentleness.
O, that a lady, of one man refused,
Should of another therefore be abused!   [*Exit.*

Lys. She sees not Hermia. Hermia, sleep thou there:
And never mayst thou come Lysander near!

For as a surfeit of the sweetest things
The deepest loathing to the stomach brings,
Or as the heresies that men do leave
Are hated most of those they did deceive,
So thou, my surfeit and my heresy,
Of all be hated, but the most of me!
And, all my powers, address your love and might
To honour Helen and to be her knight!   [*Exit.*

Her. [*Awaking*] Help me, Lysander, help me! do thy best
To pluck this crawling serpent from my breast!
Ay me, for pity! what a dream was here!
Lysander, look how I do quake with fear:
Methought a serpent eat my heart away,
And you sat smiling at his cruel prey.
Lysander! what, removed? Lysander! lord!
What, out of hearing? gone? no sound, no word?
Alack, where are you? speak, an if you hear;
Speak, of all loves! I swoon almost with fear.
No? then I well perceive you are not nigh:
Either death or you I'll find immediately.   [*Exit.*

ACT III—SCENE I

The wood.   Titania lying asleep.

Enter Quince, Snug, Bottom, Flute, Snout, and Starveling.

Bot. Are we all met?
Quin. Pat, pat; and here's a marvellous convenient place for
our rehearsal. This green plot shall be our stage, this
hawthorn-brake our tiring-house; and we will do it in action
as we will do it before the duke.
Bot. Peter Quince,—
Quin. What sayest thou, Bully Bottom?
Bot. There are things in this comedy of Pyramus and Thisby
that will never please. First, Pyramus must draw a sword to
kill himself; which the ladies cannot abide. How answer
Snout. By'r lakin, a parlous fear.   [you that?
Star. I believe we must leave the killing out, when all is done.
Bot. Not a whit: I have a device to make all well. Write me
a prologue; and let the prologue seem to say, we will do
no harm with our swords, and that Pyramus is not killed
indeed; and, for the more better assurance, tell them that I
Pyramus am not Pyramus, but Bottom the weaver: this will
put them out of fear.
Quin. Well, we will have such a prologue; and it shall be
written in eight and six.

Bot. No, make it two more ; let it be written in eight and eight.

Snout. Will not the ladies be afeard of the lion ?

Star. I fear it, I promise you.

Bot. Masters, you ought to consider with yourselves : to bring in,—God shield us !—a lion among ladies, is a most dreadful thing ; for there is not a more fearful wild-fowl than your lion living : and we ought to took to 't.

Snout. Therefore another prologue must tell he is not a lion.

Bot. Nay, you must name his name, and half his face must be seen through the lion's neck ; and he himself must speak through, saying thus, or to the same defect,—' Ladies,'—or, 'Fair ladies,—I would wish you,'—or, ' I would request you,' —or, ' I would entreat you,—not to fear, not to tremble : my life for yours. If you think I come hither as a lion, it were pity of my life : no, I am no such thing ; I am a man as other men are : ' and there indeed let him name his name, and tell them plainly, he is Snug the joiner.

Quin. Well, it shall be so. But there is two hard things ; that is, to bring the moonlight into a chamber ; for, you know, Pyramus and Thisby meet by moonlight.

Snout. Doth the moon shine that night we play our play ?

Bot. A calendar, a calendar ! look in the almanac ; find out moonshine, find out moonshine.

Quin. Yes, it doth shine that night.

Bot. Why, then may you leave a casement of the great chamber window, where we play, open, and the moon may shine in at the casement.

Quin. Ay ; or else one must come in with a bush of thorns and a lantern, and say he comes to disfigure, or to present, the person of moonshine. Then, there is another thing : we must have a wall in the great chamber ; for Pyramus and Thisby, says the story, did talk through the chink of a wall.

Snout. You can never bring in a wall. What say you, Bottom ?

Bot. Some man or other must present wall : and let him have some plaster, or some loam, or some rough-cast about him, to signify wall ; and let him hold his fingers thus, and through that cranny shall Pyramus and Thisby whisper.

Quin. If that may be, then all is well. Come, sit down, every mother's son, and rehearse your parts. Pyramus, you begin : when you have spoken your speech, enter into that brake : and so every one according to his cue.

Enter Puck behind.

Puck. What hempen home-spuns have we swaggering here,
     So near the cradle of the fairy queen ?

What, a play toward! I 'll be an auditor;
An actor too perhaps, if I see cause.

Quin. Speak, Pyramus. Thisby, stand forth.

Bot. Thisby, the flowers of odious savours sweet,—

Quin. Odours, odours.

Bot. ——odours savours sweet:
 So hath thy breath, my dearest Thisby dear.
 But hark, a voice! stay thou but here awhile,
 And by and by I will to thee appear. [*Exit.*

Puck. A stranger Pyramus than e'er play'd here. [*Exit.*

Flu. Must I speak now?

Quin. Ay, marry, must you; for you must understand he goes
but to see a noise that he heard, and is to come again.

Flu. Most radiant Pyramus, most lily-white of hue,
 Of colour like the red rose on triumphant brier,
 Most brisky juvenal, and eke most lovely Jew,
 As true as truest horse, that yet would never tire,
 I 'll meet thee, Pyramus, at Ninny's tomb.

Quin. 'Ninus' tomb,' man: why, you must not speak that yet;
that you answer to Pyramus: you speak all your part at once,
cues and all. Pyramus enter: your cue is past; it is, 'never
tire.'

Flu. O,—As true as truest horse, that yet would never tire.

 Re-enter Puck, and Bottom with an ass's head.

Bot. If I were fair, Thisby, I were only thine.

Quin. O monstrous! O strange! we are haunted.
 Pray, masters! fly, masters! Help!
 [*Exeunt Quince, Snug, Flute, Snout, and Starveling.*

Puck. I 'll follow you, I 'll lead you about a round,
 Through bog, through bush, through brake, through brier:
 Sometime a horse I 'll be, sometime a hound,
 A hog, a headless bear, sometime a fire;
 And neigh, and bark, and grunt, and roar, and burn,
 Like horse, hound, hog, bear, fire, at every turn. [*Exit.*

Bot. Why do they run away? this is a knavery of them to
make me afeard.

 Re-enter Snout.

Snout. O Bottom, thou art changed! what do I see on thee?

Bot. What do you see? you see an ass-head of your own, do
you? [*Exit Snout.*

 Re-enter Quince.

Quin. Bless thee, Bottom! bless thee! thou art translated.
 [*Exit.*

Bot. I see their knavery: this is to make an ass of me; to
fright me, if they could. But I will not stir from this place,

do what they can: I will walk up and down here, and I will
sing, that they shall hear I am not afraid.　　　　　*[Sings.*

The ousel cock so black of hue,
　　With orange-tawny bill,
The throstle with his note so true,
　　The wren with little quill;

Tita. [*Awaking*] What angel wakes me from my flowery bed?
Bot. [*Sings*]

The finch, the sparrow, and the lark,
　　The plain-song cuckoo gray,
Whose note full many a man doth mark,
　　And dares not answer nay;—

for, indeed, who would set his wit to so foolish a bird? who
would give a bird the lie, though he cry ' cuckoo ' never so?
Tita. I pray thee, gentle mortal, sing again:
　Mine ear is much enamour'd of thy note;
　So is mine eye enthralled to thy shape;
　And thy fair virtue's force perforce doth move me
　On the first view to say, to swear, I love thee.
Bot. Methinks, mistress, you should have little reason for that:
　and yet, to say the truth, reason and love keep little company
　together now-a-days; the more the pity, that some honest
　neighbours will not make them friends. Nay, I can gleek
　upon occasion.
Tita. Thou art as wise as thou art beautiful.
Bot. Not so, neither: but if I had wit enough to get out of
　this wood, I have enough to serve mine own turn.
Tita. Out of this wood do not desire to go:
　Thou shalt remain here, whether thou wilt or no.
　I am a spirit of no common rate:
　The summer still doth tend upon my state;
　And I do love thee: therefore, go with me;
　I'll give thee fairies to attend on thee;
　And they shall fetch thee jewels from the deep,
　And sing, while thou on pressed flowers dost sleep:
　And I will purge thy mortal grossness so,
　That thou shalt like an airy spirit go.
　Peaseblossom! Cobweb! Moth! and Mustardseed!
　　Enter Peaseblossom, Cobweb, Moth, and Mustardseed.
First Fai. Ready.
Sec. Fai.　　　　And I.
Third Fai.　　　　　And I.

514

Fourth Fai.   And I.
All.   Where shall we go?
Tita. Be kind and courteous to this gentleman;
      Hop in his walks, and gambol in his eyes;
      Feed him with apricocks and dewberries,
      With purple grapes, green figs, and mulberries;
      The honey-bags steal from the humble-bees,
      And for night-tapers crop their waxen thighs,
      And light them at the fiery glow-worm's eyes,
      To have my love to bed and to arise;
      And pluck the wings from painted butterflies,
      To fan the moonbeams from his sleeping eyes:
      Nod to him, elves, and do him courtesies.
First Fai. Hail, mortal!
Sec. Fai. Hail!
Third Fai. Hail!
Fourth Fai. Hail!
Bot. I cry your worships mercy heartily: I beseech your
Cob. Cobweb.   [worship's name.
Bot. I shall desire you of more acquaintance, good Master
      Cobweb: if I cut my finger, I shall make bold with you.
      Your name, honest gentleman?
Peas. Peaseblossom.
Bot. I pray you, commend me to Mistress Squash, your
      mother, and to Master Peascod, your father. Good Master
      Peaseblossom, I shall desire you of more acquaintance too.
      Your name, I beseech you, sir?
Mus. Mustardseed.
Bot. Good Master Mustardseed, I know your patience well:
      that same cowardly, giant-like ox-beef hath devoured many
      a gentleman of your house: I promise you your kindred
      hath made my eyes water ere now. I desire your more
      acquaintance, good Master Mustardseed.
Tita. Come, wait upon him; lead him to my bower.
          The moon methinks looks with a watery eye;
          And when she weeps, weeps every little flower,
            Lamenting some enforced chastity.
          Tie up my love's tongue, bring him silently.   [*Exeunt.*

SCENE II

Another part of the wood.
Enter Oberon.

Obe. I wonder if Titania be awaked;
      Then, what it was that next came in her eye,
      Which she must dote on in extremity.

515

Enter Puck.

Here comes my messenger.

　　　　　　　　　　How now, mad spirit!
What night-rule now about this haunted grove?
Puck. My mistress with a monster is in love.
Near to her close and consecrated bower,
While she was in her dull and sleeping hour,
A crew of patches, rude mechanicals,
That work for bread upon Athenian stalls,
Were met together to rehearse a play,
Intended for great Theseus' nuptial-day.
The shallowest thick-skin of that barren sort,
Who Pyramus presented, in their sport
Forsook his scene, and enter'd in a brake:
When I did him at this advantage take,
An ass's nole I fixed on his head:
Anon his Thisbe must be answered,
And forth my mimic comes.　When they him spy,
As wild geese that the creeping fowler eye,
Or russet-pated choughs, many in sort,
Rising and cawing at the gun's report,
Sever themselves and madly sweep the sky,
So, at his sight, away his fellows fly;
And, at our stamp, here o'er and o'er one falls;
He murder cries, and help from Athens call.
Their sense thus weak, lost with their fears thus strong,
Made senseless things begin to do them wrong;
For briers and thorns at their apparel snatch;
Some sleeves, some hats, from yielders all things catch.
I led them on in this distracted fear,
And left sweet Pyramus translated there:
When in that moment, so it came to pass,
Titania waked, and straightway loved an ass.
Obe. This falls out better than I could devise.
But hast thou yet latch'd the Athenian's eyes
With a love-juice, as I did bid thee do?
Puck. I took him sleeping,—that is finish'd too,—
And the Athenian woman by his side;
That, when he waked, of force she must be eyed.

Enter Hermia and Demetrius.

Obe. Stand close: this is the same Athenian.
Puck. This is the woman, but not this the man.
Dem. O, why rebuke you him that loves you so?
Lay breath so bitter on your bitter foe.

Her. Now I but chide; but I should use thee worse,
    For thou, I fear, hast given me cause to curse.
    If thou hast slain Lysander in his sleep,
    Being o'er shoes in blood, plunge in the deep,
    And kill me too.
    The sun was not so true unto the day
    As he to me: would he have stolen away
    From sleeping Hermia? I'll believe as soon
    This whole earth may be bored, and that the moon
    May through the centre creep, and so displease
    Her brother's noontide with the Antipodes.
    It cannot be but thou hast murder'd him;
    So should a murderer look, so dead, so grim.

Dem. So should the murder'd look; and so should I,
    Pierced through the heart with your stern cruelty:
    Yet you, the murderer, look as bright, as clear,
    As yonder Venus in her glimmering sphere.

Her. What's this to my Lysander? where is he?
    Ah, good Demetrius, wilt thou give him me?

Dem. I had rather give his carcass to my hounds.

Her. Out, dog! out, cur! thou drivest me past the bounds
    Of maiden's patience. Hast thou slain him, then?
    Henceforth be never number'd among men!
    O, once tell true, tell true, even for my sake!
    Durst thou have look'd upon him being awake,
    And hast thou kill'd him sleeping? O brave touch!
    Could not a worm, an adder, do so much?
    An adder did it; for with doubler tongue
    Than thine, thou serpent, never adder stung.

Dem. You spend your passion on a misprised mood:
    I am not guilty of Lysander's blood;
    Nor is he dead, for aught that I can tell.

Her. I pray thee, tell me then that he is well.

Dem. An if I could, what should I get therefore

Her. A privilege, never to see me more.
    And from thy hated presence part I so:
    See me no more, whether he be dead or no.   [*Exit.*

Dem. There is no following her in this fierce vein:
    Here therefore for a while I will remain.
    So sorrow's heaviness doth heavier grow
    For debt that bankrupt sleep doth sorrow owe;
    Which now in some slight measure it will pay,
    If for his tender here I make some stay. [*Lies down and sleeps.*

Obe. What hast thou done? thou hast mistaken quite,
    And laid the love-juice on some true-love's sight:

Of thy misprision must perforce ensue
Some true love turn'd, and not a false turn'd true.

Puck. Then fate o'er-rules, that, one man holding troth,
A million fail, confounding oath on oath.

Obe. About the wood go swifter than the wind,
And Helena of Athens look thou find:
All fancy-sick she is and pale of cheer,
With sighs of love, that costs the fresh blood dear:
By some illusion see thou bring her here:
I'll charm his eyes against she do appear.

Puck. I go, I go; look how I go,
Swifter than arrow from the Tartar's bow.   [*Exit.*

Obe.   Flower of this purple dye,
Hit with Cupid's archery,
Sink in apple of his eye.
When his love he doth espy,
Let her shine as gloriously
As the Venus of the sky.
When thou wakest, if she be by,
Beg of her for remedy.

Re-enter Puck.

Puck.   Captain of our fairy band,
Helena is here at hand;
And the youth, mistook by me,
Pleading for a lover's fee.
Shall we their fond pageant see?
Lord, what fools these mortals be!

Obe.   Stand aside: the noise they make
Will cause Demetrius to awake.

Puck.   Then will two at once woo one;
That must needs be sport alone;
And those things do best please me
That befal preposterously.

Enter Lysander and Helena.

Lys. Why should you think that I should woo in scorn?
Scorn and derision never come in tears:
Look, when I vow, I weep; and vows so born,
In their nativity all truth appears.
How can these things in me seem scorn to you,
Bearing the badge of faith, to prove them true?

Hel. You do advance your cunning more and more.
When truth kills truth, O devilish-holy fray!
These vows are Hermia's: will you give her o'er?
Weigh oath with oath, and you will nothing weigh:

Your vows to her and me, put in two scales,
Will even weigh; and both as light as tales.

Lys. I had no judgement when to her I swore.

Hel. Nor none, in my mind, now you give her o'er.

Lys. Demetrius loves her, and he loves not you.

Dem. [*Awaking*] O Helen, goddess, nymph, perfect, divine!
To what, my love, shall I compare thine eyne?
Crystal is muddy. O, how ripe in show
Thy lips, those kissing cherries, tempting grow!
That pure congealed white, high Taurus' snow,
Fann'd with the eastern wind, turns to a crow
When thou hold'st up thy hand: O, let me kiss
This princess of pure white, this seal of bliss!

Hel. O spite; O hell! I see you all are bent
To set against me for your merriment:
If you were civil and knew courtesy,
You would not do me thus much injury.
Can you not hate me, as I know you do,
But you must join in souls to mock me too?
If you were men, as men you are in show,
You would not use a gentle lady so;
To vow, and swear, and superpraise my parts,
When I am sure you hate me with your hearts.
You both are rivals, and love Hermia;
And now both rivals, to mock Helena:
A trim exploit, a manly enterprise,
To conjure tears up in a poor maid's eyes
With your derision! none of noble sort
Would so offend a virgin, and extort
A poor soul's patience, all to make you sport.

Lys. You are unkind, Demetrius; be not so;
For you love Hermia; this you know I know:
And here, with all good will, with all my heart,
In Hermia's love I yield you up my part;
And yours of Helena to me bequeath,
Whom I do love, and will do till my death.

Hel. Never did mockers waste more idle breath.

Dem. Lysander, keep thy Hermia; I will none:
If e'er I loved her, all that love is gone.
My heart to her but as guest-wise sojourn'd,
And now to Helen is it home return'd,
There to remain.

Lys.   Helen, it is not so.

Dem. Disparage not the faith thou dost not know,
Lest, to thy peril, thou aby it dear.

Look, where thy love comes; yonder is thy dear.

Re-enter Hermia.

Her. Dark night, that from the eye his function takes,
The ear more quick of apprehension makes;
Wherein it doth impair the seeing sense,
It pays the hearing double recompence.
Thou art not by mine eye, Lysander, found;
Mine ear, I thank it, brought me to thy sound.
But why unkindly didst thou leave me so?
Lys. Why should he stay, whom love doth press to go?
Her. What love could press Lysander from my side?
Lys. Lysander's love, that would not let him bide,
Fair Helena, who more engilds the night
Than all yon fiery oes and eyes of light.
Why seek'st thou me? could not this make thee know,
The hate I bare thee made me leave thee so?
Her. You speak not as you think: it cannot be.
Hel. Lo, she is one of this confederacy!
Now I perceive they have conjoin'd all three
To fashion this false sport, in spite of me.
Injurious Hermia! most ungrateful maid!
Have you conspired, have you with these contrived
To bait me with this foul derision?
Is all the counsel that we two have shared,
The sisters' vows, the hours that we have spent,
When we have chid the hasty-footed time
For parting us,—O, is all forgot?
All school-days' friendship, childhood innocence?
We, Hermia, like two artificial gods,
Have with our needles created both one flower,
Both on one sampler, sitting on one cushion,
Both warbling of one song, both in one key;
As if our hands, our sides, voices, and minds,
Had been incorporate. So we grew together,
Like to a double cherry, seeming parted,
But yet an union in partition;
Two lovely berries moulded on one stem;
So, with two seeming bodies, but one heart;
Two of the first, like coats in heraldry,
Due but to one, and crowned with one crest.
And will you rent our ancient love asunder,
To join with men in scorning your poor friend?
It is not friendly, 'tis not maidenly:
Our sex, as well as I, may chide you for it,

Though I alone do feel the injury.
Her. I am amazed at your passionate words.
  I scorn you not: it seems that you scorn me.
Hel. Have you not set Lysander, as in scorn,
  To follow me and praise my eyes and face?
  And made your other love, Demetrius,
  Who even but now did spurn me with his foot,
  To call me goddess, nymph, divine and rare,
  Precious, celestial? Wherefore speaks he this
  To her he hates? and wherefore doth Lysander
  Deny our love, so rich within his soul,
  And tender me, forsooth, affection,
  But by your setting on, by your consent?
  What though I be not so in grace as you,
  So hung upon with love, so fortunate,
  But miserable most, to love unloved?
  This you should pity rather than depise.
Her. I understand not what you mean by this.
Hel. Ay, do, persever, counterfeit sad looks,
  Make mouths upon me when I turn my back;
  Wink each at other; hold the sweet jest up:
  This sport, well carried, shall be chronicled.
  If you have any pity, grace, or manners,
  You would not make me such an argument.
  But fare ye well: 'tis partly my own fault;
  Which death or absence soon shall remedy.
Lys. Stay, gentle Helena; hear my excuse:
  My love, my life, my soul, fair Helena!
Hel. O excellent!
Her.   Sweet, do not scorn her so.
Dem. If she cannot entreat, I can compel.
Lys. Thou canst compel no more than she entreat:
  Thy threats have no more strength than her weak prayers.
  Helen, I love thee; by my life, I do:
  I swear by that which I will lose for thee,
  To prove him false that says I love thee not.
Dem. I say I love thee more than he can do.
Lys. If thou say so, withdraw, and prove it too.
Dem. Quick, come!
Her.   Lysander, whereto tends all this?
Lys. Away, you Ethiope!
Dem.   No, no; he 'll . . .
  Seem to break loose; take on as you would follow,
  But yet come not: you are a tame man, go!
Lys. Hang off, thou cat, thou burr! vile thing, let loose,

　　Or I will shake thee from me like a serpent!

Her. Why are you grown so rude? what change is this?
　　Sweet love,—

Lys. 　　　　　Thy love! out, tawny Tartar, out!
　　Out, loathed medicine! hated potion, hence!

Her Do you not jest?

Hel. 　　　　　Yes, sooth; and so do you.

Lys. Demetrius, I will keep my word with thee.

Dem. I would I had your bond, for I perceive
　　A weak bond holds you: I'll not trust your word.

Lys. What, should I hurt her, strike her, kill her dead?
　　Although I hate her, I'll not harm her so.

Her. What, can you do me greater harm than hate?
　　Hate me! wherefore? O me! what news, my love!
　　Am not I Hermia? are not you Lysander?
　　I am as fair now as I was erewhile.
　　Since night you loved me; yet since night you left me:
　　Why, then you left me,—O, the gods forbid!—
　　In earnest, shall I say?

Lys. 　　　　　Ay, by my life;
　　And never did desire to see thee more.
　　Therefore be out of hope, of question, of doubt;
　　Be certain, nothing truer; 'tis no jest
　　That I do hate thee, and love Helena.

Her. O me! you juggler! you canker-blossom!
　　You thief of love! what, have you come by night
　　And stolen my love's heart from him?

Hel. 　　　　　Fine, i' faith!
　　Have you no modesty, no maiden shame,
　　No touch of bashfulness? What, will you tear
　　Impatient answers from my gentle tongue?
　　Fie, fie! you counterfeit, you puppet, you!

Her. Puppet? why so? ay, that way goes the game.
　　Now I perceive that she hath made compare
　　Between our statures; she hath urged her height;
　　And with her personage, her tall personage,
　　Her height, forsooth, she hath prevail'd with him.
　　And are you grown so high in his esteem,
　　Because I am so dwarfish and so low?
　　How low am I, thou painted maypole? speak;
　　How low am I? I am not yet so low
　　But that my nails can reach unto thine eyes.

Hel. I pray you, though you mock me, gentlemen,
　　Let her not hurt me: I was never curst;
　　I have no gift at all in shrewishness;

I am a right maid for my cowardice :
Let her not strike me.   You perhaps may think,
Because she is something lower than myself,
That I can match her.

Her.   Lower ! hark, again.

Hel. Good Hermia, do not be so bitter with me.
I evermore did love you, Hermia,
Did ever keep your counsels, never wrong'd you ;
Save that, in love unto Demetrius,
I told him of your stealth unto this wood.
He follow'd you ; for love I follow'd him ;
But he hath chid me hence, and threaten'd me
To strike me, spurn me, nay, to kill me too :
And now, so you will let me quiet go,
To Athens will I bear my folly back,
And follow you no further : let me go :
You see how simple and how fond I am.

Her. Why, get you gone : who is 't that hinders you ?

Hel. A foolish heart, that I leave here behind.

Her. What, with Lysander ?

Hel.   With Demetrius.

Lys. Be not afraid ; she shall not harm thee, Helena.

Dem. No, sir, she shall not, though you take her part.

Hel. O, when she 's angry, she is keen and shrewd !
She was a vixen when she went to school ;
And though she be but little, she is fierce.

Her. Little again ! nothing but low and little !
Why will you suffer her to flout me thus ?
Let me come to her.

Lys.   Get you gone, you dwarf ;
You minimus, of hindering knot-grass made ;
You bead, you acorn.

Dem.   You are too officious
In her behalf that scorns your services.
Let her alone : speak not of Helena ;
Take not her part ; for, if thou dost intend
Never so little show of love to her,
Thou shalt aby it.

Lys.   Now she holds me not ;
Now follow, if thou darest, to try whose right,
Of thine or mine, is most in Helena.

Dem. Follow ! nay, I 'll go with thee, cheek by jole.

[*Exeunt Lysander and Demetrius.*

Her. You, mistress, all this coil is 'long of you :
Nay, go not back.

Hel.   I will not trust you, I,
　Nor longer stay in your curst company.
　Your hands than mine are quicker for a fray.
　My legs are longer though, to run away.   [*Exit.*
Her. I am amazed, and know not what to say.   [*Exit.*
Obe. This is thy negligence: still thou mistakest,
　Or else committ'st thy knaveries wilfully.
Puck. Believe me, king of shadows, I mistook.
　Did not you tell me I should know the man
　By the Athenian garments he had on?
　And so far blameless proves my enterprise,
　That I have 'nointed an Athenian's eyes;
　And so far am I glad it so did sort,
　As this their jangling I esteem a sport.
Obe. Thou see'st these lovers seek a place to fight:
　Hie therefore, Robin, overcast the night;
　The starry welkin cover thou anon
　With drooping fog, as black as Acheron;
　And lead these testy rivals so astray,
　As one come not within another's way.
　Like to Lysander sometime frame thy tongue,
　Then stir Demetrius up with bitter wrong;
　And sometime rail thou like Demetrius;
　And from each other look thou lead them thus,
　Till o'er their brows death-counterfeiting sleep
　With leaden legs and batty wings doth creep:
　Then crush this herb into Lysander's eye;
　Whose liquor hath this virtuous property,
　To take from thence all error with his might,
　And make his eyeballs roll with wonted sight.
　When they next wake, all this derision
　Shall seem a dream and fruitless vision;
　And back to Athens shall the lovers wend,
　With league whose date till death shall never end,
　Whiles I in this affair do thee employ,
　I'll to my queen and beg her Indian boy;
　And then I will her charmed eye release
　From monster's view, and all things shall be peace.
Puck. My fairy lord, this must be done with haste,
　For night's swift dragons cut the clouds full fast,
　And yonder shines Aurora's harbinger;
　At whose approach, ghosts, wandering here and there,
　Troop home to churchyards: damned spirits all,
　That in crossways and floods have burial,
　Already to their wormy beds are gone;

For fear lest day should look their shames upon,
They wilfully themselves exile from light,
And must for aye consort with black-brow'd night.

Obe. But we are spirits of another sort :
  I with the morning's love have oft made sport ;
  And, like a forester, the groves may tread,
  Even till the eastern gate, all fiery-red,
  Opening on Neptune with fair blessed beams,
  Turns into yellow gold his salt green streams.
  But, notwithstanding, haste : make no delay :
  We may effect this business yet ere day.   *[Exit.*

Puck.   Up and down, up and down,
        I will lead them up and down :
        I am fear'd in field and town :
        Goblin, lead them up and down.
  Here comes one.

Re-enter Lysander.

Lys. Where art thou, proud Demetrius ? speak thou now.
Puck. Here, villain ; drawn and ready.   Where art thou ?
Lys. I will be with thee straight.
Puck.   Follow me, then,
  To plainer ground.
          [Exit Lysander, as following the voice.

Re-enter Demetrius.

Dem.   Lysander ! speak again :
  Thou runaway, thou coward, art thou fled ?
  Speak !   In some bush ?   Where dost thou hide thy head ?
Puck. Thou coward, art thou bragging to the stars,
  Telling the bushes that thou look'st for wars,
  And wilt not come ?   Come, recreant ; come, thou child ;
  I 'll whip thee with a rod : he is defiled
  That draws a sword on thee.
Dem.   Yea, art thou there ?
Puck. Follow my voice : we 'll try no manhood here.   *[Exeunt*

Re-enter Lysander.

Lys. He goes before me and still dares me on :
  When I come where he calls, then he is gone.
  The villain is much lighter-heel'd than I :
  I follow'd fast, but faster he did fly ;
  That fallen am I in dark uneven way,
  And here will rest me. *[Lies down.]* Come, thou gentle day
  For if but once thou show me thy grey light,
  I 'll find Demetrius, and revenge this spite.   *[Sleeps.*

Re-enter Puck and Demetrius.

Puck. Ho, ho, ho! Coward, why comest thou not?

Dem. Abide me, if thou darest; for well I wot
　　Thou runn'st before me, shifting every place,
　　And darest not stand, nor look me in the face.
　　Where art thou now?

Puck. 　　　　　　　Come hither: I am here.

Dem. Nay, then, thou mock'st me. Thou shalt buy this dear,
　　If ever I thy face by daylight see:
　　Now, go thy way. Faintness constraineth me
　　To measure out my length on this cold bed.
　　By day's approach look to be visited. 　　[*Lies down and sleeps.*

Re-enter Helena.

Hel. O weary night, O long and tedious night,
　　　Abate thy hours! Shine comforts from the east,
　　That I may back to Athens by daylight,
　　　From these that my poor company detest:
　　And sleep, that sometimes shuts up sorrow's eye,
　　Steal me awhile from mine own company.

　　　　　　　　　　　　　[*Lies down and sleeps.*

Puck. 　　　　　Yet but three? Come one more;
　　　　　　　Two of both kinds makes up four.
　　　　　　　Here she comes, curst and sad:
　　　　　　　Cupid is a knavish lad,
　　　　　　　Thus to make poor females mad.

Re-enter Hermia.

Her. Never so weary, never so in woe;
　　　Bedabbled with the dew, and torn with briers;
　　I can no further crawl, no further go;
　　　My legs can keep no pace with my desires.
　　Here will I rest me till the break of day.
　　Heavens shield Lysander, if they mean a fray!

　　　　　　　　　　　　　[*Lies down and sleeps.*

Puck. 　　　　　　　On the ground
　　　　　　　　　Sleep sound:
　　　　　　　　　I 'll apply
　　　　　　　　　To your eye,
　　　　　　　Gentle lover, remedy.

　　　　　　[*Squeezing the juice on Lysander's eye.*
　　　　　　　　　When thou wakest,
　　　　　　　　　Thou takest
　　　　　　　　　True delight
　　　　　　　　　In the sight

Of thy former lady's eye :
And the country proverb known,
That every man should take his own,
In your waking shall be shown :
          Jack shall have Jill ;
          Nought shall go ill ;
The man shall have his mare again, and all shall be
well.   [*Exit.*

ACT IV—Scene I
The same.

Lysander, Demetrius, Helena, and Hermia, lying asleep.

*Enter Titania and Bottom; Peaseblossom, Cobweb, Moth.
Mustardseed, and other Fairies attending; Oberon behind unseen.*

Tita. Come, sit thee down upon this flowery bed,
      While I thy amiable cheeks do coy,
   And stick musk-roses in thy sleek smooth head,
      And kiss thy fair large ears, my gentle joy.

Bot. Where 's Peaseblossom ?

Peas. Ready.

Bot. Scratch my head, Peaseblossom. Where 's Mounsieur

Cob. Ready.   [Cobweb ?

Bot. Mounsieur Cobweb, good mounsieur, get you your
weapons in your hand, and kill me a red-hipped humble-bee
on the top of a thistle ; and, good mounsieur, bring me
the honey bag. Do not fret yourself too much in the
action, mounsieur ; and, good mounsieur, have a care the
honey-bag break not ; I would be loth to have you overflown
with a honey-bag, signior. Where 's Mounsieur Mustardseed ?

Mus. Ready.

Bot. Give me your neaf, Mounsieur Mustardseed. Pray you,
leave your courtesy, good mounsieur.

Mus. What 's your will ?

Bot. Nothing, good mounsieur, but to help Cavalery Cobweb
to scratch. I must to the barber's, mounsieur ; for methinks
I am marvellous hairy about the face ; and I am such a
tender ass, if my hair do but tickle me, I must scratch.

Tita. What, wilt thou hear some music, my sweet love ?

Bot. I have a reasonable good ear in music. Let 's have the
tongs and the bones.

Tita. Or say, sweet love, what thou desirest to eat.

Bot. Truly, a peck of provender : I could munch your good
dry oats. Methinks I have a great desire to a bottle of hay :
good hay, sweet hay, hath no fellow.

Tita. I have a venturous fairy that shall seek
  The squirrel's hoard, and fetch thee new nuts.
Bot. I had rather have a handful or two of dried peas. But,
  I pray you, let none of your people stir me: I have an
  exposition of sleep come upon me.
Tita. Sleep thou, and I will wind thee in my arms.
  Fairies, be gone, and be all thy ways away. [*Exeunt Fairies.*
  So doth the woodbine the sweet honeysuckle
  Gently entwist; the female ivy so
  Enrings the barky fingers of the elm.
  O, how I love thee! how I dote on thee!   [*They sleep.*
                    Enter Puck.
Obe. [*Advancing*] Welcome, good Robin. See'st thou this
  Her dotage now I do begin to pity: [sweet sight?
  For, meeting her of late behind the wood,
  Seeking sweet favours for this hateful fool,
  I did upbraid her, and fall out with her;
  For she his hairy temples then had rounded
  With coronet of fresh and fragrant flowers;
  And that same dew, which sometime on the buds
  Was wont to swell, like round and orient pearls,
  Stood now within the pretty flowerets' eyes,
  Like tears, that did their own disgrace bewail.
  When I had at my pleasure taunted her,
  And she in mild terms begg'd my patience,
  I then did ask of her her changeling child;
  Which straight she gave me, and her fairy sent
  To bear him to my bower in fairy land.
  And now I have the boy, I will undo
  This hateful imperfection of her eyes:
  And, gentle Puck, take this transformed scalp
  From off the head of this Athenian swain;
  That, he awaking when the other do,
  May all to Athens back again repair,
  And think no more of this night's accidents,
  But as the fierce vexation of a dream.
  But first I will release the fairy queen.
            Be as thou wast wont to be;
            See as thou was wont to see:
            Dian's bud o'er Cupid's flower
            Hath such force and blessed power.
  Now, my Titania; wake you, my sweet queen.
Tita. My Oberon! what visions have I seen!
  Methought I was enamour'd of an ass.
Obe. There lies your love.

Tita.   How came these things to pass?
O, how mine eyes do loathe his visage now!
Obe. Silence awhile.   Robin, take off this head.
Titania, music call; and strike more dead
Than common sleep of all these five the sense.
Tita. Music, ho! music, such as charmeth sleep! [*Music, still.*
Puck. Now, when thou wakest, with thine own fool's eyes peep.
Obe. Sound, music!   Come, my queen, take hands with me,
And rock the ground whereon these sleepers be.
Now thou and I are new in amity,
And will to-morrow midnight solemnly
Dance in Duke Theseus' house triumphantly,
And bless it to all fair prosperity:
There shall the pairs of faithful lovers be
Wedded, with Theseus, all in jollity.
Puck.   Fairy king, attend, and mark:
                    I do hear the morning lark.
Obe.   Then, my queen, in silence sad,
                    Trip we after night's shade:
                    We the globe can compass soon,
                    Swifter than the wandering moon.
Tita.   Come, my lord; and in our flight,
                    Tell me how it came this night,
                    That I sleeping here was found
                    With these mortals on the ground.   [*Exeunt.*
                                                [*Horns winded within.*
         Enter Theseus, Hippolyta, Egeus, and train.

The. Go, one of you, find out the forester;
For now our observation is perform'd;
And since we have the vaward of the day,
My love shall hear the music of my hounds.
Uncouple in the western valley; let them go:
Dispatch, I say, and find the forester.   [*Exit an Attendant.*
We will, fair queen, up to the mountain's top,
And mark the musical confusion
Of hounds and echo in conjunction.
Hip. I was with Hercules and Cadmus once,
When in a wood of Crete they bay'd the bear
With hounds of Sparta: never did I hear
Such gallant chiding; for, besides the groves,
The skies, the fountains, every region near
Seem'd all one mutual cry: I never heard
So musical a discord, such sweet thunder.
The. My hounds are bred out of the Spartan kind,
So flew'd, so sanded; and their heads are hung

With ears that sweep away the morning dew;
Crook-knee'd, and dew-lapp'd like Thessalian bulls;
Slow in pursuit, but match'd in mouth like bells,
Each under each. A cry more tuneable
Was never holla'd to, nor cheer'd with horn,
In Crete, in Sparta, nor in Thessaly:
Judge when you hear. But, soft! what nymphs are these?
Ege. My lord, this is my daughter here asleep;
And this, Lysander; this Demetrius is;
This Helena, old Nedar's Helena:
I wonder of their being here together.
The. No doubt they rose up early to observe
The rite of May; and, hearing our intent,
Came here in grace of our solemnity.
But speak, Egeus; is not this the day
That Hermia should give answer of her choice?
Ege. It is, my lord.
The. Go, bid the huntsmen wake them with their horns.

              [Horns and shout within. Lys., Dem.,
                Hel., and Her., wake and start up.

Good morrow, friends. Saint Valentine is past:
Begin these wood-birds but to couple now?
Lys. Pardon, my lord.
The.   I pray you all, stand up.
I know you two are rival enemies:
How comes this gentle concord in the world,
That hatred is so far from jealousy,
To sleep by hate, and fear no enmity?
Lys. My lord, I shall reply amazedly,
Half sleep, half waking: but as yet, I swear,
I cannot truly say how I came here;
But, as I think,—for truly would I speak,
And now I do bethink me, so it is,—
I came with Hermia hither: our intent
Was to be gone from Athens, where we might,
Without the peril of the Athenian law.
Ege. Enough, enough, my lord; you have enough:
I beg the law, the law, upon his head.
They would have stolen away; they would, Demetrius,
Thereby to have defeated you and me,
You of your wife and me of my consent,
Of my consent that she should be your wife.
Dem. My lord, fair Helen told me of their stealth,
Of this their purpose hither to this wood;
And I in fury hither follow'd them,

Fair Helena in fancy following me.
But, my good lord, I wot not by what power,—
But by some power it is,—my love to Hermia,
Melted as the snow, seems to me now
As the remembrance of an idle gaud,
Which in my childhood I did dote upon ;
And all the faith, the virtue of my heart,
The object and the pleasure of mine eye,
Is only Helena. To her, my lord,
Was I betroth'd ere I saw Hermia :
But, like in sickness, did I loathe this food ;
But, as in health, come to my natural taste,
Now I do wish it, love it, long for it,
And will for evermore be true to it.

The. Fair lovers, you are fortunately met :
Of this discourse we more will hear anon.
Egeus, I will overbear your will ;
For in the temple, by and by, with us
These couples shall eternally be knit :
And, for the morning now is something worn,
Our purposed hunting shall be set aside.
Away with us to Athens ! three and three,
We'll hold a feast in great solemnity.
Come, Hippolyta.   [*Exeunt The., Hip., Ege., and train.*

Dem. These things seem small and undistinguishable,
Like far-off mountains turned into clouds.

Her. Methinks I see these things with parted eye,
When every thing seems double.

Hel.   So methinks :
And I have found Demetrius like a jewel,
Mine own, and not mine own.

Dem.   Are you sure
That we are awake ? It seems to me
That yet we sleep, we dream.   Do not you think
The Duke was here, and bid us follow him ?

Her. Yea ; and my father.

Hel.   And Hippolyta.

Lys. And he did bid us follow to the temple.

Dem. Why, then, we are awake : let 's follow him ;
And by the way let us recount our dreams.   [*Exeunt.*

Bot. [*Awaking*] When my cue comes, call me, and I will
answer : my next is, 'Most fair Pyramus.' Heigh-ho ! Peter
Quince ! Flute, the bellows-mender ! Snout, the tinker !
Starveling ! God 's my life, stolen hence, and left me asleep !
I have had a most rare vision.   I have had a dream, past the

wit of man to say what dream it was : man is but an ass, if
he go about to expound this dream. Methought I was—
there is no man can tell what. Methought I was,—and
methought I had,—but man is but a patched fool, if he will
offer to say what methought I had. The eye of man hath
not heard, the ear of man hath not seen, man's hand is not
able to taste, his tongue to conceive, nor his heart to report,
what my dream was. I will get Peter Quince to write a
ballad of this dream : it shall be called Bottom's Dream,
because it hath no bottom ; and I will sing it in the latter
end of a play, before the Duke : peradventure, to make it the
more gracious, I shall sing it at her death.   [*Exit.*

SCENE II
Athens.   Quince's house.
Enter Quince, Flute, Snout, and Starveling.

Quin. Have you sent to Bottom's house ? is he come home yet ?
Star. He cannot be heard of.   Out of doubt he is transported.
Flu. If he come not, then the play is marred : it goes not
     forward, doth it ?
Quin. It is not possible : you have not a man in all Athens
     able to discharge Pyramus but he.   [Athens
Flu. No, he hath simply the best wit of any handicraft man in
Quin. Yea, and the best person too ; and he is a very paramour
     for a sweet voice.
Flu. You must say 'paragon': a paramour is, God bless us,
     a thing of naught.
Enter Snug.
Snug. Masters, the Duke is coming from the temple, and there
     is two or three lords and ladies more married : if our sport
     had gone forward, we had all been made men.
Flu. O sweet bully Bottom !   Thus hath he lost sixpence a day
     during his life ; he could not have scaped sixpence a day :
     an the Duke had not given him sixpence a day for playing
     Pyramus, I'll be hanged ; he would have deserved it :
     sixpence a day in Pyramus, or nothing.
Enter Bottom.
Bot. Where are these lads ? where are these hearts ?   [hour !
Quin. Bottom ! O most courageous day ! O most happy
Bot. Masters, I am to discourse wonders : but ask me not
     what ; for if I tell you, I am no true Athenian.   I will tell
     you every thing, right as it fell out.
Quin. Let us hear, sweet Bottom.
Bot. Not a word of me. All that I will tell you is, that the
     Duke hath dined.   Get your apparel together, good strings

to your beards, new ribbons to your pumps; meet presently at the palace; every man look o'er his part; for the short and the long is, our play is preferred. In any case, let Thisby have clean linen; and let not him that plays the lion pare his nails, for they shall hang out for the lion's claws. And, most dear actors, eat no onions nor garlic, for we are to utter sweet breath; and I do not doubt but to hear them say, it is a sweet comedy. No more words: away! go, away!

                                    [Exeunt.

ACT V—SCENE I

Athens. The palace of Theseus.

Enter Theseus, Hippolyta, Philostrate, Lords, and Attendants

Hip. 'Tis strange, my Theseus, that these lovers speak of.
The. More strange than true: I never may believe
   These antique fables, nor these fairy toys.
   Lovers and madmen have such seething brains,
   Such shaping fantasies, that apprehend
   More than cool reason ever comprehends.
   The lunatic, the lover and the poet
   Are of imagination all compact:
   One sees more devils than vast hell can hold,
   That is, the madman: the lover, all as frantic,
   See Helen's beauty in a brow of Egypt:
   The poet's eye in a fine frenzy rolling,
   Doth glance from heaven to earth, from earth to heaven;
   And as imagination bodies forth
   The forms of things unknown, the poet's pen
   Turns them to shapes, and gives to airy nothing
   A local habitation and a name.
   Such tricks hath strong imagination,
   That, if it would but apprehend some joy,
   It comprehends some bringer of that joy;
   Or in the night, imagining some fear,
   How easy is a bush supposed a bear!
Hip. But all the story of the night told over,
   And all their minds transfigured so together,
   More witnesseth than fancy's images,
   And grows to something of great constancy;
   But, howsoever, strange and admirable.
The. Here come the lovers, full of joy and mirth.

    Enter Lysander, Demetrius, Hermia, and Helena.

   Joy, gentle friends! joy and fresh days of love
   Accompany your hearts!

Lys.   More than to us
Wait in your royal walks, your board, your bed !
The. Come now ; what masques, what dances shall we have,
To wear away this long age of three hours
Between our after-supper and bed-time ?
Where is our usual manager of mirth ?
What revels are in hand ?   Is there no play,
To ease the anguish of a torturing hour ?
Call Philostrate.
Phil.   Here, mighty Theseus.
The. Say, what abridgement have you for this evening ?
What masque ? what music ?   How shall we beguile
The lazy time, if not with some delight?
Phil. There is a brief how many sports are ripe :
Make choice of which your highness will see first.
                                        [*Giving a paper.*
The. [*reads*] The battle with the Centaurs, to be sung.
By an Athenian eunuch to the harp.
We 'll none of that : that have I told my love,
In glory of my kinsman Hercules.
[*Reads*] The riot of the tipsy Bacchanals,
Tearing the Thracian singer in their rage.
That is an old device ; and it was play'd
When I from Thebes came last a conqueror.
[*Reads*] The thrice three Muses mourning for the death
Of Learning, late deceased in beggary.
That is some satire, keen and critical,
Not sorting with a nuptial ceremony.
[*Reads*] A tedious brief scene of young Pyramus
And his love Thisbe ; very tragical mirth.
Merry and tragical ! tedious and brief !
That is, hot ice and wondrous strange snow.
How shall we find the concord of this discord ?
Phil. A play there is, my lord, some ten words long,
Which, is as brief as I have known a play ;
But by ten words, my lord, it is too long,
Which makes it tedious ; for in all the play
There is not one word apt, one player fitted :
And tragical, my noble lord, it is ;
For Pyramus therein doth kill himself.
Which, when I saw rehearsed, I must confess,
Made mine eyes water ; but more merry tears
The passion of loud laughter never shed.
The. What are they that do play it ?
Phil. Hard-handed men, that work in Athens here.

Which never labour'd in their minds till now;
And now have toil'd their unbreathed memories
With this same play, against your nuptial.

The. And we will hear it.

Phil.   No, my noble lord;
It is not for you: I have heard it over,
And it is nothing, nothing in the world;
Unless you can find sport in their intents,
Extremely stretch'd and conn'd with cruel pain,
To do you service.

The.   I will hear that play;
For never any thing can be amiss,
When simpleness and duty tender it.
Go, bring them in: and take your places, ladies.

                                        [*Exit Philostrate.*

Hip. I love not to see wretchedness o'ercharged,
And duty in his service perishing.

The. Why, gentle sweet, you shall see no such thing.

Hip. He says they can do nothing in this kind.

The. The kinder we, to give them thanks for nothing.
Our sport shall be to take what they mistake:
And what poor duty cannot do, noble respect
Takes it in might, not merit.
Where I have come, great clerks have purposed
To greet me with premeditated welcomes;
Where I have seen them shiver and look pale,
Make periods in the midst of sentences,
Throttle their practised accent in their fears,
And, in conclusion, dumbly have broke off,
Not paying me a welcome. Trust me, sweet,
Out of this silence yet I picked a welcome;
And in the modesty of fearful duty
I read as much as from the rattling tongue
Of saucy and audacious eloquence.
Love, therefore, and tongue-tied simplicity
In least speak most, to my capacity.

Re-enter Philostrate.

Phil. So please your Grace, the Prologue is address'd.

The. Let him approach.   [*Flourish of trumpets.*

Enter Quince for the Prologue.

Pro. If we offend, it is with our good will.
    That you should think, we come not to offend,
  But with good will. To show our simple skill,
    That is the true beginning of our end.

Consider, then, we come but in despite.
  We do not come, as minding to content you,
Our true intent is.   All for your delight,
  We are not here.   That you should here repent you,
The actors are at hand; and, by their show,
You shall know all, that you are like to know.

Th. This fellow doth not stand upon points.

Lys. He hath rid his prologue like a rough colt; he knows not
  the stop. A good moral, my lord: it is not enough to speak,
  but to speak true.

Hip. Indeed he hath played on his prologue like a child on a
  recorder; a sound, but not in government.

The. His speech was like a tangled chain; nothing impaired.
  but all disordered.   Who is next?

  Enter Pyramus and Thisbe, Wall, Moonshine, and Lion.

Pro. Gentles, perchance you wonder at this show;
  But wonder on, till truth make all things plain.
This man is Pyramus, if you would know;
  This beauteous lady Thisby is certain.
This man, with lime and rough-cast, doth present
  Wall, that vile Wall which did these lovers sunder;
And through Wall's chink, poor souls, they are content
  To whisper.   At the which let no man wonder.
This man, with lanthorn, dog, and bush of thorn,
  Presenteth Moonshine; for, if you will know,
By moonshine did these lovers think no scorn
  To meet at Ninus' tomb, there, there to woo.
This grisly beast, which Lion hight by name,
The trusty Thisby, coming first by night,
Did scare away, or rather did affright;
And, as she fled, her mantle she did fall,
  Which Lion vile with bloody mouth did stain.
Anon comes Pyramus, sweet youth and tall,
  And finds his trusty Thisby's mantle slain:
Whereat, with blade, with bloody blameful blade,
  He bravely broach'd his boiling bloody breast;
And Thisby, tarrying in mulberry shade,
  His dagger drew, and died.   For all the rest,
Let Lion, Moonshine, Wall, and lovers twain
  At large discourse, while here they do remain.
  [*Exeunt Prologue, Pyramus, Thisbe, Lion, and Moonshine.*

The. I wonder if the lion be to speak.

Dem. No wonder, my lord: one lion may, when many asses do.

Wall. In this same interlude it doth befall
  That I, one Snout by name, present a wall;

And such a wall, as I would have you think,
That had in it a crannied hole or chink,
Through which the lovers, Pyramus and Thisby,
Did whisper often very secretly.
This loam, this rough-cast, and this stone, doth show
That I am that same wall; the truth is so:
And this the cranny is, right and sinister,
Through which the fearful lovers are to whisper.

The. Would you desire lime and hair to speak better?

Dem. It is the wittiest partition that ever I heard discourse, my
lord.

The. Pyramus draws near the wall: silence!

Re-enter Pyramus.

Pyr. O grim-look'd night! O night with hue so black!
O night, which ever art when day is not!
O night, O night! alack, alack, alack,
I fear my Thisby's promise is forgot!
And thou, O wall, O sweet, O lovely wall,
That stands't between her father's ground and mine!
Thou wall, O wall, O sweet and lovely wall,
Show me thy chink, to blink through with mine eyne!
                                   [*Wall holds up his fingers.*
Thanks, courteous wall: Jove shield thee well for this!
But what see I? No Thisby do I see.
O wicked wall, through whom I see no bliss!
Cursed be thy stones for thus deceiving me!

The. The wall, methinks, being sensible, should curse again.

Pyr. No, in truth, sir, he should not. 'Deceiving me' is
Thisby's cue: she is to enter now, and I am to spy her
through the wall. You shall see, it will fall pat as I told you.
Yonder she comes.

Re-enter Thisbe.

This. O wall, full often hast thou heard my moans,
For parting my fair Pyramus and me.
My cherry lips have often kissed thy stones,
Thy stones with lime and hair knit up in thee.

Pyr. I see a voice: now will I to the chink,
To spy an I can hear my Thisby's face.
Thisby!

This. My love thou art, my love I think.

Pyr. Think what thou wilt, I am thy lover's grace;
And, like Limander, am I trusty still,

This. And I like Helen, till the Fates me kill.

Pyr. Not Shafalus to Procrus was so true.

This. As Shafalus to Procrus, I to you.

Pyr. O, kiss me through the hole of this vile wall!

This. I kiss the wall's hole, not your lips at all.

Pyr. Wilt thou at Ninny's tomb meet me straightway?

This. 'Tide life, 'tide death, I come without delay.

　　　　　　　　　　　[*Exeunt Pyramus and Thisbe.*

Wall. Thus have I, wall, my part discharged so;

　　And, being done, thus wall away doth go.　　　[*Exit.*

The. Now is the mural down between the two neighbours.

Dem. No remedy, my lord, when walls are so wilful to hear without warning.

Hip. This is the silliest stuff that ever I heard.

The. The best in this kind are but shadows; and the worst are no worse, if imagination amend them.

Hip. It must be your imagination then, and not theirs.

The. If we imagine no worse of them than they of themselves, they may pass for excellent men.　Here come two noble beasts in, a man and a lion.

Re-enter Lion and Moonshine.

Lion. You, ladies, you, whose gentle hearts do fear

　　The smallest monstrous mouse that creeps on floor,

　May now perchance both quake and tremble here,

　　When lion rough in wildest rage doth roar.

　Then know that I, one Snug the joiner, am

　A lion-fell, nor else no lion's dam;

　For, if I should as lion come in strife

　Into this place, 'twere pity on my life.

The. A very gentle beast, and of a good conscience.

Dem. The very best at a beast, my lord, that e'er I saw.

Lys. This lion is a very fox for his valour.

The. True; and a goose for his discretion.

Dem. Not so, my lord; for his valour cannot carry his discretion; and the fox carries the goose.

The. His discretion, I am sure, cannot carry his valour; for the goose carries not the fox.　It is well: leave it to his discretion, and let us listen to the moon.

Moon. This lanthorn doth the horned moon present;—

Dem. He should have worn the horns on his head.

The. He is no crescent, and his horns are invisible within the circumference.

Moon. This lanthorn doth the horned moon present;

　Myself the man i' the moon do seem to be.

The. This is the greatest error of all the rest: the man should be put into the lantern.　How is it else the man i' the moon?

Dem. He dares not come there for the candle; for you see, it is already in snuff.

A Midsummer-Night's Dream [Act V, Sc. i

Hip. I am aweary of this moon: would he would change!

The. It appears, by his small light of discretion, that he is in the wane; but yet, in courtesy, in all reason, we must stay

Lys. Proceed, Moon. [the time.

Moon. All that I have to say, is, to tell you that the lanthorn is the moon; I, the man i' the moon; this thorn-bush, my thorn-bush; and this dog, my dog.

Dem. Why, all these should be in the lantern; for all these are in the moon. But, silence! here comes Thisbe.

Re-enter Thisbe.

This. This is old Ninny's tomb. Where is my love?

Lion. [*Roaring*] Oh—— [*Thisbe runs off.*

Dem. Well roared, Lion.

The. Well run, Thisbe.

Hip. Well shone, Moon. Truly, the moon shines with a good grace. [*The Lion shakes Thisbe's mantle, and exit.*

The. Well moused, Lion.

Dem. And then came Pyramus.

Lys. And so the lion vanished.

Re-enter Pyramus.

Pyr. Sweet Moon, I thank thee for thy sunny beams,
    I thank thee, Moon, for shining now so bright;
For, by thy gracious, golden, glittering gleams,
    I trust to take of truest Thisby sight.
        But stay, O spite!
        But mark, poor knight,
    What dreadful dole is here!
        Eyes, do you see?
        How can it be?
O dainty duck! O dear!
        Thy mantle good,
        What, stain'd with blood!
Approach, ye Furies fell!
        O Fates, come, come,
        Cut thread and thrum;
    Quail, crush, conclude, and quell!

The. This passion, and the death of a dear friend, would go near to make a man look sad.

Hip. Beshrew my heart, but I pity the man.

Pyr. O wherefore, Nature, didst thou lions frame?
    Since lion vile hath here deflower'd my dear:
Which is—no, no—which was the fairest dame
    That lived, that loved, that liked, that look'd with cheer.
        Come, tears, confound;
        Out, sword, and wound

539

            The pap of Pyramus;
                Ay, that left pap,
                Where heart doth hop :   [*Stabs himself.*
            Thus die I, thus, thus, thus.
                Now am I dead,
                Now am I fled ;
            My soul is in the sky :
                Tongue, lose thy light ;
                Moon, take thy flight :   [*Exit Moonshine.*
            Now die, die, die, die, die.   [*Dies.*

Dem. No die, but an ace, for him ; for he is but one.

Lys. Less than an ace, man ; for he is dead ; he is nothing.

The. With the help of a surgeon he might yet recover, and prove an ass.

Hip. How chance Moonshine is gone before Thisbe comes back and finds her lover ?

The. She will find him by starlight. Here she comes ; and her passion ends the play.

Re-enter Thisbe.

Hip. Methinks she should not use a long one for such a Pyramus : I hope she will be brief.

Dem. A mote will turn the balance, which Pyramus, which Thisbe, is the better ; he for a man, God warrant us ; she for a woman, God bless us.

Lys. She hath spied him already with those sweet eyes.

Dem. And thus she means, videlicet :—

This.   Asleep, my love ?
                What, dead, my dove ?
            O Pyramus, arise !
                Speak, speak.   Quite dumb ?
                Dead, dead ?   A tomb
            Must cover thy sweet eyes.
                These lily lips,
                This cherry nose,
            These yellow cowslip cheeks,
                Are gone, are gone :
                Lovers, make moan :
            His eyes were green as leeks.
                O Sisters Three,
                Come, come to me,
            With hands as pale as milk :
                Lay them in gore,
                Since you have shore
            With shears his thread of silk.

> Tongue, not a word :
> Come, trusty sword ;
> Come, blade, my breast imbrue :   [*Stabs herself.*
> And, farewell, friends :
> Thus Thisbe ends :
> Adieu, adieu, adieu.   [*Dies.*

The. Moonshine and Lion are left to bury the dead.

Dem. Ay, and Wall too.

Bot. [*Starting up*] No, I assure you ; the wall is down that parted their fathers. Will it please you to see the epilogue, or to hear a Bergomask dance between two of our company ?

The. No epilogue, I pray you ; for your play needs no excuse. Never excuse ; for when the players are all dead, there need none to be blamed. Marry, if he that writ it had played Pyramus and hanged himself in Thisbe's garter, it would have been a fine tragedy : and so it is, truly ; and very notably discharged. But, come, your Bergomask : let your epilogue alone.   [*A dance.*

> The iron tongue of midnight hath told twelve :
> Lovers, to bed ; 'tis almost fairy time.
> I fear we shall out-sleep the coming morn,
> As much as we this night have overwatch'd.
> This palpable-gross play hath well beguiled
> The heavy gait of night. Sweet friends, to bed.
> A fortnight hold we this solemnity,
> In nightly revels and new jollity.   [*Exeunt.*

Enter Puck.

Puck.
> Now the hungry lion roars,
>   And the wolf behowls the moon ;
> Whilst the heavy ploughman snores,
>   All with weary task foredone.
> Now the wasted brands do glow,
>   Whilst the screech-owl, screeching loud,
> Puts the wretch that lies in woe
>   In remembrance of a shroud.
> Now it is the time of night,
>   That the graves, all gaping wide,
> Every one lets forth his sprite,
>   In the church-way paths to glide :
> And we fairies, that do run
>   By the triple Hecate's team,
> From the presence of the sun,
>   Following darkness like a dream,
> Now are frolic : not a mouse
> Shall disturb this hallow'd house :

541

I am sent with broom before,
To sweep the dust behind the door.

Enter Oberon and Titania with their train.

Obe.   Through the house give glimmering light,
      By the dead and drowsy fire:
    Every elf and fairy sprite
      Hop as light as bird from brier;
    And this ditty, after me,
    Sing, and dance it trippingly.

Tita.   First, rehearse your song by rote,
    To each word a warbling note:
    Hand in hand, with fairy grace,
    Will we sing, and bless this place.   [*Song and dance.*

Obe.   Now, until the break of day,
    Through this house each fairy stray.
    To the best bride-bed will we,
    Which by us shall blessed be;
    And the issue there create
    Ever shall be fortunate.
    So shall all the couples three
    Ever true in loving be;
    And the blots of Nature's hand
    Shall not in their issue stand;
    Never mole, hare lip, nor scar,
    Nor mark prodigious, such as are
    Despised in nativity,
    Shall upon their children be.
    With this field-dew consecrate,
    Every fairy take his gait;
    And each several chamber bless,
    Through this palace, with sweet peace,
    Ever shall in safety rest,
    And the owner of it blest.
    Trip away; make no stay;
    Meet me all by break of day,
            [*Exeunt Oberon, Titania, and train.*

Puck.   If we shadows have offended,
    Think but this, and all is mended,
    That you have but slumber'd here,
    While these visions did appear.
    And this weak and idle theme,
    No more yielding but a dream,
    Gentles, do not reprehend:
    If you pardon, we will mend.

And, as I am an honest Puck,
If we have unearned luck
Now to scape the serpent's tongue,
We will make amends ere long ;
Else the Puck a liar call :
So, good night unto you all.
Give me your hands, if we be friends,
And Robin shall restore amends.   [*Exit.*

GLOSSARY

J. = Johnson.   D. = Dyce.   S. = Schmidt.   H.E.D. = A new English Dictionary on
Historical Principles (Murray, Bradley).

ABATED, subdued, depressed.
ABHOR, " protest against.'
ABLE, answer for.
ABODE, forebode.
ABRIDGMENT, (?) a means of shortening
or whiling away ; or, epitome, abstract
(H.E.D.).
ABSOLUTE, perfect ; decided.
ABUSE, deception ; v. deceive.
ACCITE, cite, summon.
ACKNOWN, confessedly acquainted with.
ADDITION, title.
ADDRESS, prepare.
ADMITTANCE, fashion (D.) ; sanction ;
admissibility (H.E.D.).
ADVANCE, raise to honour.
ADVERTISEMENT, admonition (D.) ; public
notice or announcement (H.E.D.).
ADVERTISING, attentive.
ADVISED, act with deliberation ; informed.
AFFECTION, affectation.
AFFEER'D, confirmed.
AFFRONT, encounter.
AFFY, betroth.
AGAZ'D, amazed, aghast.
AGLET, tag.
AGLET-BABY, " image or head cut on a
tag."
AGNIZE, acknowledge.
AIM, conjecture.
ALDER-LIEFEST, most beloved, dearest.
ALLOW, approve.
AMES-ACE, both aces, the lowest throw.
ANCHOR, anchorite.
ANCIENT, ensign.
ANGEL, coin.
ANTHROPOPHAGINIAN, cannibal.
ANTRE, cave.
APE, " lead apes in hell," punishment pre-
dicted for old maids.
APPELLANT, challenger.
APPLE-JOHN, a variety of apple.
APPREHENSION, anticipation ; perception by
the senses ; sarcasm (D.).
ARCH, chief.
ARGAL, corruption of *ergo*.
ARGUMENT, subject.
ARM-GAUNT, (?) with gaunt limbs (H.E.D.).
AROINT, away ! avaunt !
ARROSE, water.
ARTICULATE, set forth in articles, particu-
larize (H.E.D.).
ASCAUNT, across.
ASINEGO, ASINICO, donkey, fool.
ASSAY, assault.
ASSURED, betrothed.
ATTACH, arrest.
AWFUL, filled with awe.

BACCARE, " Go back."
BAFFLE, a punishment inflicted on recreant
knights, who were hung up by their heels
and beaten.

BALDRICK, belt.
" BALK LOGIC," chop logic ; balked (?)
heaped up (H.E.D.).
BALLOW, cudgel.
BAN-DOG, dog tied or chained up.
BANQUET, dessert.
BARBED, in horse armour.
BASE, prisoner's base, a game.
BASES, " a kind of embroidered mantle,
which hung down from the middle, worn
by knights on horseback."
BASILISK, cocatrice, a creature fabled to
kill by its look ; piece of ordnance.
BASTARD, a sweet wine.
BAT, cudgel.
BATE, strife, dispute ; v. flutter with the
wings.
BATLET, small bat for beating clothes.
BATTEN, fatten.
BAVIN, faggot of brushwood.
BEADSMAN, one hired to pray for another.
BEAR A BRAIN, have remembrance.
BEAR-HERD, BEAR-WARD, bear keeper.
BEAR-IN-HAND, hold in expectation, in
false hopes.
BEARING-CLOTH, mantle in which a child
was carried to the font.
BEAVER, movable vizor of helmet.
BECK, bow.
BENT, " utmost degree of any passion or
mental quality " (J.).
BERGOMASK, a dance imitated from that of
the peasants of Bergamasco.
BESONIAN, needy, base fellow.
BESORT, suite, escort.
BETEEM, allow, suffer.
BIAS, " swelled as the bowl on the biassed
side " (J.).
BIGGEN, cap, resembling that worn by the
Beguines.
BILBO, sword, from *Bilboa*, famous for its
steel work.
BILBOES, iron bar and fetters for confining
refractory sailors.
BILL, kind of pike, halbert.
BIRD-BOLT blunt-pointed arrow used for
killing birds.
BISSON, blind.
BLACK MONDAY, a reference to the Monday
after Easter-day 1360, when many men
of King Edward III's host, then before
Paris, died of cold as they sat on their
horses.
BLANK, white in centre of target.
BLOCK, fashion of hat.
BLOOD, " in blood," in good condition.
BLOOD-BOLTERED, matted with blood.
BOB, taunt ; v. to cheat.
BODGE, " old form of botch " (H.E.D.).
BODKIN, small dagger.
BOGGLE, swerve, shy.
BOLINS, bowlines, ropes for governing the
sails of a ship.

545

Glossary

BOLLEN, swollen.
BOLTED, sifted.
BOLTER, sieve.
BOLTING-HATCH, receptacle into which meal is sifted.
BOMBARD, large leather drinking vessel.
BOMBAST, cotton, or other material, used for stuffing.
BONA-ROBA, "good, wholesome, plum-cheeked wench;" Courtesan.
BOOT, profit, something over and above; booty.
BOOTS, "give the boots," allusion to an instrument of torture, or "make a laughing-stock of."
BORE, calibre of a gun, capacity of the barrel.
BOSKY, woody.
BOTTLE, truss (of hay).
BOTTOM, low-lying land.
BRABBLE, quarrel.
BRACE, (?) coat of armour (H.E.D.), state of defence.
BRACH, scent-hound; bitch.
BRAID, (?) deceitful (H.E.D.); v. upbraid.
BRAKES ("brakes of vice"), thickets; "engines of torture" (D.).
BRAVE, defy; adorn, make fine.
BRAVERY, finery; bravado.
BRAWL, lively dance.
BRAWN, arm.
BREAK UP, carve; used metaphorically for opening a letter.
BREED-BATE, a hatcher of quarrels.
BREESE, BRIZE, gadfly.
BROCK, badger.
BROGUES, shoes.
BRUIT, report.
BUCK, lye in which linen is washed; linen so washed.
BUCKLE, join in fight.
BUCKLERS, "give the bucklers," yield the victory.
BUG, bugbear.
BULLY, term of familiar affection.
BULLY-ROOK, "jolly comrade, boon companion" (H.E.D.).
BUNG, sharper, cut-purse.
BURGONET, particular kind of helmet.
BUTT-SHAFT, a kind of arrow, used for shooting at butts.
BUTTERY, room where provisions are laid up.
BUZZARD, hawk; various insects that fly by night; large moths, cockchafers (H.E.D.).
BY AND BY, immediately.

CADDIS, worsted tape, riband.
CADE, barrel.
CALIVER, light musket, harquebus.
CANARY, a wine; a lively dance.
CANKER, dog-rose; canker-worm.
CANSTICK, candlestick.
CANTLE, piece, portion.
CANVASS, toss.
CAPTIOUS, "capable of receiving" (D.).
CARACK, large trading vessel; galleon.
CARBONADO, meat sliced for broiling.
CARDED, adulterated.

CAREER, space within the lists; race-course; "short turning of a nimble horse," frisk, gambol (H.E.D., "he passes some . . . careires").
CARKANET, necklace.
CARL, CARLOT, churl, boor.
CASTLE, close helmet.
CATAIAN, Chinese (Cataia, Cathay, old name for China).
CATER-COUSIN, cousin of "quatre," fourth degree.
CATES, table delicacies.
CATLING, lute, violin-string.
CAUTEL, craftiness, caution.
CENSURE, opinion, judgment.
CEREMENTS, waxed cloths for enwrapping embalmed bodies.
CESS, measure, "out of all cess."
CHACES, "a chace at tennis is that spot where a ball falls, beyond which the adversary must strike his ball to gain a point or chace" (Douce).
CHAMBER, piece of ordnance; "Camera Regis," old name of London.
CHAMBERLAIN, one in charge of chambers.
CHANNEL, kennel.
CHAPE, metal mounting of scabbard, "particularly that which covers the point," possibly the scabbard itself (H.E.D.).
CHARACT, distinctive mark, character.
CHARACTER, handwriting.
CHARNECO, wine, probably Portuguese.
CHAUDRON, entrails.
CHEATER, escheator.
CHECK, turn from pursuing one prey to follow another (falconry).
CHERRY-PIT, game in which cherry-stones were thrown into a small hole.
CHEVERIL, leather made of kid-skin.
CHEWET, chough, jackdaw.
CHILDING, fruitful.
CHOPINE, a high clog worn by Venetian ladies, etc.
CINQUE-PACE, a dance, the steps of which were regulated by the number five.
CITTERN, musical instrument, similar to guitar.
CLACK-DISH, or CLAP-DISH, carried about by beggars, who clacked the cover to attract attention.
CLAW, flatter.
CLEPE, call.
CLIFF, clef, key in music.
CLING, shrivel.
CLINQUANT, glittering.
CLIP, embrace.
CLOUD IN'S FACE, signifying that the horse has a dark-coloured spot between the eyes.
CLOUT, "the mark shot at" (H.E.D.), nail or pin in centre of white of target (D.).
CLOUTED, hobnailed "clouted brogues."
CLOY, claw.
COAST, approach; assail, accost.
COASTING, "coasting welcome," an amorous approach (Nares); some eds., "accosting welcome."
COBLOAF, small round-shaped loaf.
COCKATRICE. See Basilisk.
COCKLED, within a shell.
COCKREL, a young cock.

Glossary

COFFIN, raised crust of a pie.

COG, cheat.

COIL, turmoil, confusion.

COLLOP, slice of meat, portion of flesh.

COLOURS, false appearances; " fear no—"
fear no enemy.

COLT, fool.

COMMODITY, advantage, profit.

COMPARATIVE, " quick at comparisons "
(S.); one ready to make comparisons;
or, compeer, rival (H.E.D.).

COMPASSED, bow (window).

COMPETITOR, confederate.

COMPOSURE, combination.

COMPROMISED, having mutually promised.

COMPTIBLE, sensitive.

CONCEIT, conception, fancy; trifle.

CONCENT, accord, harmony.

CONEY-CATCH, swindle.

CONFECT, a sweetmeat.

CONTEMPTIBLE, contemptuous.

CONTINENT, that which envelops, contains;
the thing contained.

CONTRIVE, spend, while away.

CONVENT, cite; suit.

CONVINCE, overpower.

COPATAIN HAT, high-crowned hat.

CORANTO, quick dance.

CORINTHIAN, debauchee.

CORKY, withered.

COSTARD, head.

COTE, overtake, pass by.

COT-QUEAN, a meddler in women's affairs.

COUNTER, debtor's prison.

COUNTERFEIT, likeness; false coin.

COUNTERPOINT, counterpane.

COURSER'S HAIR, old idea that a horse's
hair came to life in water.

COURT-CUPBOARD, a movable cupboard,
sideboard.

COVSTRIL, low fellow, knave.

COZIER, cobbler.

CRAB, wild apple.

CRACK, lively, forward boy.

CRANTS, garland.

CREDIT, accepted report.

CRESCIVE, increasing, growing.

CRESSET, a beacon light, suspended in an
iron vessel or basket.

CRISP, curled.

CROSS, coin stamped with a cross.

CROSS-ROW, alphabet.

CROW-KEEPER, scarecrow.

CRUSADO, Portuguese coin.

CRY, pack.

CUCKOO-BUD, buttercup, cowslip, marsh
marigold; " orchis, or cuckoo-pint in
bud " (H.E.D.).

CUCKOO-FLOWER, name given to various
flowers in bloom when cuckoo is heard :
lady's smock, ragged robin, etc. (H.E.D.).

CUISSES, armour for the thighs.

CULLION, low fellow, lout.

CUNNING, skill, knowledge; skilful.

CURB, cringe, crouch.

CURIOUS, CURIOSITY, scrupulous; precision.

CURST, ill-tempered, shrewish, vicious.

CURTAIL, CURTAL-DOG, originally a dog
with its tail cut to show that his master
was unqualified for hunting; later, a
dog not meant, or not good, for sport.

CURTLE-AXE, cutlass.

CUT, a docked horse; term of contempt.

CUT AND LONG TAIL, dogs of every kind.

CUTS, lots.

CUTTLE, knife.

CYPRUS, CYPRESS, material similar to
crape.

DAFF, doff.

DANSKERS, Danes.

DARE, terrify.

DARNEL, said to be injurious to the eyes if
taken in food or drink.

DARRAIGN, set in order of battle.

DAY-WOMAN, dairy-woman.

DEAR, loving; important; " heartfelt " (S.);
used to express the extreme of any
emotion, pleasurable or otherwise, aroused
by the object to which it is applied.

DEARTH, dearness, value.

DEBATE, fighting.

DEBITOR AND CREDITOR, an account book.

DECEIVABLE, deceptive.

DECK (of cards), pack.

DECKED, " deck'd the sea," sprinkled (D.);
covered (S.).

DEFEAT, DEFEATURE, disfigure; disfigure-
ment.

DEFEND, forbid.

DEFIANCE, " declaration of aversion or
contempt " (H.E.D., " take my defiance ").

DEFUSE, DEFUSED, confuse; disordered,
" irregular, uncouth " (J.).

DEFY, renounce, disdain.

DELATION, denunciation, information.

DEMERIT, desert, in good or bad sense
(S.).

DENAY, denial; v. deny.

DENIER, piece of money of lowest value.

DEPART, departure; v. part.

DEPRAVE, DEPRAVATION, detract; detraction.

DEROGATE, disparage; a. debased, degen-
erate.

DESCANT, variations.

DESIGN, designate.

DESPERATE, hopeless; reckless (S.)

DESPITE, hatred, malice.

DETERMINATE, bring to an end; a. fixed,
final.

DICH, corruption of " do it."

DISABLE, disparage.

DISAPPOINTED, not properly equipped,
unprepared.

DISASTER, " obnoxious planet."

DISCANDY, melt.

DISCLOSE, hatch.

DISCOURSE, reasoning power.

DISEASE, discomfort; trouble.

DISEDGE, blunt the edge of appetite.

DISLIMN, obliterate.

DISME, tenth.

DISNATURED, unnatural.

DISPARK, convert into common land.

DISPITEOUS, without pity.

DISPOSE, disposition.

DISTAIN, stain, dishonour.

DISTEMPERED, out of humour; deranged.

DISTEMPERATURE, disorder of mind or
body.

DISTRACT, divide.
DISTRACTION, detachment.
DIVIDANT, divided, different.
DIVISION, florid passage in music.
DOFF, do off, put off.
DOGGED, cruel.
DOLPHIN, dauphin.
DOUT, put out.
DOWLAS, coarse linen.
DOWLE, fibre of down.
DOWN-GYVED, hanging round the ankles.
DRAFF, refuse.
DRAW, track.
DROLLERY, puppet show.
DRUG, drudge.
DRUM, " John Drum's entertainment,"
   proverbial expression for ill-treatment.
DRUMBLE, dawdle.
DUDGEON, handle of a dagger.
DUMP, melancholy tune.
DUN, "dun's the mouse"; proverb;
   "frequently a mere quibble on the word
   ' done.'"
DUN IS IN THE MIRE, old game; a log
   of wood being dragged out of the sup-
   posed mire by the company.
DUP, do up, open.
DURANCE, "robe, suits, of durance," dur-
   able (quibble with other meaning of word).

EAGER, sharp, keen; sour.
EANING, when young are brought forth.
EANLING, new-born lamb.
EAR, till.
ECHE, eke out.
ECSTACY, madness.
EFT, (?) ready, convenient (H.E.D.).
EGMA, enigma.
EISEL (eysell), vinegar.
ELF, mat; elf-locks=hair matted by the
   elves.
EMBALLING, carrying the ball at a corona-
   tion (D.), "investing with the ball as an
   emblem of royalty."
EMBARQUEMENT, embargo.
EMBOSS, drive a hunted animal to ex-
   tremity (H.E.D.).
EMBOSSED, swollen; foaming at the
   mouth.
EMBRASURE, embrace.
EMULATE, emulous, envious.
ENGROSS, fatten; bring together from all
   quarters.
ENGROSSMENT, accumulation.
ENSEAM, grease.
ENTERTAIN, take into, or retain in,
   service.
ENTERTAINMENT, service.
ENTREAT, treat; entertain, "beguile"
   (H.E.D.).
ENTREATMENT, entertainment, "con-
   versation, interview" (H.E.D.).
ENVY, ENVIOUS, spite; spiteful, malicious.
EPHESIAN, jovial companion.
ESCOTED, paid for.
ESPIAL, spy.
ESTRIDGE, ostrich.
EXCREMENT, hair, beard, nails.
EXEQUIES, funeral ceremonies.
EXPEDIENT, EXPEDIENCE, expeditious, ex-
   pedition.

EXSUFFLICATE, (?) puffed up, inflated
   (H.E.D.).
EXTENT, seizure.
EYAS, EYAS-MUSKET, young hawk.
EYE, slight shade of colour.
EYLIAD, œillade, ogle.

FACINOROUS, wicked, infamous.
FACTIONARY, partisan.
FACTIOUS," characterized by party spirit "
   (H.E.D.); active, urgent (J.).
FADGE, fit in, suit.
FAITOR, vagabond.
FANCY, love.
FANGLED, "characterized by crotchets
   and fopperies" (H.E.D.); "given to
   tinsel finery" (S.).
FANTASTICAL, a thing of phantasy, im-
   agination.
FARCE, stuff.
FARDEL, burden.
FAR-FET, far-fetched.
FASHIONS, disease of horses.
FAVOUR, countenance, appearance.
FAVOURS, features.
FAY, faith.
FEAR, frighten.
FEAT, trim, neat, elegant, dexterous.
FEATURE, person in general, form.
FEDARY (fedarary), confederate.
FEE-FARM, grant of lands for all time.
FELL, skin, hide; a. savage.
FELLOWLY, sympathetic.
FERE, companion, mate.
FERN-SEED, thought to have power of ren-
   dering persons invisible.
FESTINATE, speedy.
FETCH trick, artifice.
FETTLE, make ready.
FIGHTS, cloths put up to screen men in
   action during a sea-fight.
FILE, list; v. defile.
FILL-HORSE, shaft horse.
FILLS, shafts.
FINELESS, endless.
FIRE-DRAKE, fiery dragon, meteor, fire-
   work (D.).
FIRK, thrash.
FIT, division in a song.
FITCHEW, pole-cat.
FIVES, disease in horses.
FLAP-DRAGON, small combustible body
   floated alight in liquor; to be drunk
   down, or caught up by the mouth and
   swallowed.
FLAP-JACK, pancake.
FLAW, sudden gust of wind; "flake of
   snow" (H.E.D.).
FLESH, initiate; give the first taste of
   blood; feed angry or lustful passion.
FLESHMENT, pride of successful attempt.
FLEWED, with hanging chaps.
FLIBBERTIGIBBET, name of a demon.
FLIGHT, light arrow.
FLOTE, sea.
FLOUTING-STOCK, laughing-stock.
FOB, cheat.
FOIN, a thrust in fencing.
FOISON, abundance.
FOND, foolish; "fond and winnowed"=
   trite, trivial (S.).

548

Glossary

FOOT-CLOTH, horse trappings.
FORCED, stuffed.
FORDO, undo.
FOREFEND, forbid.
FOREHAND, previous.
FORGETIVE, inventive.
FORMAL, having right use of senses; in a usual form, customary.
FOX, sword; perhaps on account of the figure of a wolf engraved on some blades being mistaken for a fox (H.E.D.).
FRAMPOLD, peevish, vexatious.
FRANK, pig-sty.
FRAUGHT, FRAUTAGE, freight.
FRAYED, frightened.
FRET, stop used for regulating the fingering of stringed instrument.
FRET, chequer.
FRIPPERY, old clothes-shop.
FRONTIER, outwork.
FRUSH, dash violently to pieces.
FULLAM, a kind of false dice.

GABERDINE, loose coarse outer garment.
GAD, spur; "upon the gad"=on the spur of the moment.
GAIN-GIVING, misgiving.
GALLIARD, sprightly dance.
GALLIAS, galley of large size.
GALLOW, frighten.
GALLOWGLASSES, heavy-armed foot soldiers of Ireland.
GAPE, bawl.
GARBOIL, uproar, commotion.
GASKINS, wide breeches.
GEAR, matter, business in general.
GECK, dupe, fool.
GENEROUS, GENEROSITY, of high birth; nobility.
GENTLE, raise to the rank of gentleman.
GENTRY, complaisance.
GERMAN (germane), akin.
GEST, resting stage, and time allotted for pause at same.
GESTS, deeds.
GIB, old tom-cat.
GIG, top.
GIGLET (giglot), wanton.
GILLYVORS (gilliflowers), of the same genus (*Dianthus*) as the carnation.
GIMMAL, composed of links or rings.
GIMMOR (gimmer), contrivance of machinery; (?) a hinge (H.E.D.).
GING, gang.
GIRD, sarcasm.
GIRDLE, "turn his girdle," turn buckle behind to prepare for wrestling.
GLEEK, jeer.
GLOZE, flatter; interpret.
GLUT, swallow.
GOD 'ILD, God yield.
GONGARIAN, Hungarian.
GOOD DEN, good even.
GORBELLIED, corpulent.
GOSSIP, sponsor.
GOUT, drop.
GOVERNMENT, self-control, well-mannered behaviour.
GRATULATE, gratifying (S.), worthy of gratulation (D.).
GREAVES, 'eg armour.

GRIPE, griffin.
GRISE, degree, step.
GROUNDLINGS, spectators in a theatre who had pit seats, or *ground-stands*.
GUARD, trim.
GUARDS, facings, trimmings.
GUIDON, standard, and standard-bearer.
GULES, heraldic term for red.
GULF, anything which engulfs or swallows.
GULL, dupe; cheat, imposition; unfledged nestling.
GUNSTONES, balls of stone.
GUST, taste.

HAGGARD, untrained hawk.
HALCYON, kingfisher; it was supposed that the body of this bird, if hung up, would always turn its breast to the wind.
HALF-FACED, with face in profile; "half-faced groats."
HALF-KIRTLE, a *kirtle* consisted of jacket and petticoat.
HALL, "a hall"; an exclamation used to make space in a crowd.
HAND, "at any hand," at all events; "of his hands," of valour, skill (H.E.D.).
HANDFAST, marriage contract; confinement.
HANGER, part of sword-belt in which the weapon was suspended.
HAPPILY, haply.
HARLOCK, unidentified (H.E.D.).
HATCHED, engraved.
HAVOC, to cry "havoc" was a signal for general slaughter.
HAY, dance, "of the nature of a reel" (H.E.D.).
HEBENON, ebony.
HEFT, heaving; "tender-hefted"=agitated by tender emotion.
HENCHMAN, page.
HENT, seized.
HERB OF GRACE, rue.
HEST, command.
HIDE FOX AND ALL AFTER, hide and seek.
HIGHT, named.
HILDING, low, menial wretch.
HOBBIDIDANCE, name of a demon.
HOBBY-HORSE, personage in the Morris-dance who had the figure of a horse fastened round his waist.
HOB-NOB, have or have not.
HOLDING, burden of a song.
HOODMAN-BLIND, blind man's buff.
HOPDANCE, name of a demon.
HORN, "thy horn is dry;" the Bedlam beggars had a horn slung round their necks which they wound as they came to a house for alms.
HOSE, stockings, breeches, or both in one.
HOX, cut the hamstrings.
HUGGER-MUGGER, "in huggermugger," in secrecy.
HUMOUR, mood, disposition, caprice. The fashionable abuse of this word is satirized by Shakespeare in his character of Nym, and elsewhere.
HUMOUROUS, capricious; moody, out of humour (H.E.D.).
HURLY, hurly-burly.
HURRICANO, water-spout.

Glossary

HURTLE, clash together.
HUSBAND, husbandman; *v.* cultivate, manage economically.
HUSBANDRY, cultivation; thrift, household economy.
HUSWIFE, HOUSEWIFE, hussy.

IDLE, frivolous, useless, foolish.
ILL-FAVOURED, of an ill-countenance.
IMMANITY, savagery.
IMMOMENT, not momentous.
IMP, graft, insert new feathers.
IMPAIR, unequal.
IMPARTIAL, not taking part with either side; used also for *partial*.
IMPARTMENT, something imparted, communication.
IMPEACHMENT, hindrance.
IMPERSEVERANT (imperceiverant), undiscerning (H.E.D.); giddy-headed, thoughtless (S.).
IMPONE, lay down as a wager.
IMPORTANCE, importunity, import.
IMPORTANT, importunate.
INCENSE, instigate; perhaps *insense* = inform, school.
INCH, island.
INCH-MEAL, piece-meal.
INCONTINENT, immediately.
INCONY, pretty, delicate.
INCORPSED, incorporated.
INDENT, bargain, make agreement.
INDEX, prologue; anything which gives brief account of, or is preparatory to, what is coming in story, play, or pageant (in the latter case possibly a painted emblem).
INDIFFERENCY, impartiality; moderate size.
INDIFFERENT, impartial; ordinary, "indifferent children," "indifferent knit."
INDIGEST, without form; chaos (S.), formless mass.
INDIRECTION, opposed to direct and honest practice or means.
INDURANCE, confinement (D.); endurance (S.).
INFORMAL. *See* Formal.
INGENIOUS, ingenuous; "ingenious studies" = befitting a well-born person; "liberal" (H.E.D.); "ingenious feeling," "sense" = conscious, heartfelt (S.).
INHOOPED—cocks, while fighting, were confined within hoops.
INKLE, tape.
INNOCENT, idiot.
INSANE ROOT, hemlock, or henbane.
INSISTURE, persistency, constancy (S.); fixedness, stability (D.).
INSTANCE, motive; proof, example.
INTEND, pretend.
INTENDMENT, intention.
INTENIBLE, unable to hold.
INTRINSE, INTRINSICATE, intricate.
INTRENCHANT, which cannot be cut, not divisible.
INVESTMENTS, dress.
INWARD, intimate acquaintance; *a.* intimate.
IRREGULOUS, irregular, disorderly.
ITERANCE, iteration.

JACK, used in contempt, "Jack priest," etc.; "play the Jack" = play the knave, do a mean trick (H.E.D.); "Jack o' the clock" = figure that strikes the bell on the outside of clocks; Jack-a-Lent = puppet thrown at during Lent; Minute-Jack = "fellows who watch the minutes to offer their adulation;" marking every minute, changing with every minute (S.).
Jack = bowl at which the players aim in game of bowls; a quarter or half-pint measure.
JAR, tick.
JAUNCE, ride hard.
JESSES, straps round the legs of a hawk to which the leash was attached.
JET, strut.
JOINT-RING, ring made of closely-fitted, separable halves.
JOURNAL, daily.
JUMP, exactly, just; *v.* agree; take the risk of.
JUTTY, projection, *v.* project.

KAM, crooked.
KECKSY, kex; dry stem of hemlock, and other plants.
KEECH, "tallow-keech," fat rolled up in a lump.
KEEL, cool.
KEISAR, cæsar, emperor.
KERNE, Irish foot-soldier.
KIBE, a sore on the heel from chap or chilblain.
KID-FOX, young fox (? H.E.D.).
KIND, nature, natural disposition; *a.* kindly, natural.
KINDLESS, unnatural.
KIRTLE. *See* Half-kirtle.
KISSING-COMFITS, perfumed, to sweeten the breath.
KNOT, flower-bed; company, band.
KNOT-GRASS, supposed to hinder growth.
KNOTTY-PATED, block-headed (H.E.D.).

LABRAS, lips (Span.).
LACED MUTTON, courtesan.
LADY-SMOCK, cuckoo flower (local: convolvulus, H.E.D.).
LAKIN, ladykin.
LAMMAS, August 1st.
LAMPASS, disease of horses.
LAND-RAKER, foot-pad.
LARUM, alarm; alarum.
LATCH, catch; "latched the Athenian's eyes" = anointed (S. and D.).
LATED, belated.
LATTEN, a mixed metal.
LAUND, lawn; glade (S.).
LAVOLT, LAVOLTA, a dance, consisting in part of high bounds.
LEASING, lying.
LEATHER-COAT, kind of apple.
LEER, complexion.
LEESE, lose.
LEET, "manor court, private jurisdiction for petty offences.
LEVEL, aim; guess.
LEWD, vile.
LIBBARD, leopard.

Glossary

LIBERAL, licentious, frank.
LIGHTLY, usually.
LIMB-MEAL, limb by limb.
LIMBECK, alembic.
LIMBO, borders of hell; hell.
LINE, draw, paint.
LINE-GROVE, linden, lime.
LIST, boundary; *v.* listen; please.
LISTS, enclosed space where tournaments were held, or the surrounding barricades.
LITHER, soft, pliable.
LIVELIHOOD, liveliness, vigour.
LIVERY, "delivery, or grant of possession."
LOACH, small fish.
LOCKRAM, cheap sort of linen.
LODE-STAR, pole-star.
LODGE, lay flat.
LOFFE, laugh.
LOGGATS, small logs: the game consisted of throwing loggats at a stake fixed in the ground.
LONG STAFF SIXPENNY STRIKERS, "fellows that infest the road with long staffs and knock men down for sixpence" (J.).
LONGLY, longingly.
LOOFED, luffed, brought close to the wind.
LOON, LOWN, a stupid rascal.
LOUTED, flouted, mocked.
LOVE-IN-IDLENESS, pansy.
LUCE, pike.
LUNES, fits of frenzy.
LURCH, lurk, rob.
LUXURIOUS, unchaste.
LYM, sporting-dog.

MACULATE, spotted, stained.
MAGOT-PIE, magpie.
MAINED, maimed.
MAKELESS, mateless.
MALKIN, diminutive of Mary.
MALT-HORSE, heavy dray horse; used as a term of reproach.
MALT-WORM, lover of ale.
MAMMERING, hesitating, muttering.
MAMMET, puppet.
MAMMOCK, rend in pieces.
MANAGE, management, administration; training (horse); career, course.
MANDRAGORA, MANDRAKE, supposed when torn from the ground to utter groans; a powerful narcotic.
MANKIND, masculine, mannish.
MANNER, "taken with the," caught in the act.
MANNINGTREE OX, fairs were held at this place.
MAN-QUELLER, murderer.
MARCH-PANE, sweet biscuits, made of sugar, flour, and almonds.
MARE, RIDE THE WILD, play see-saw.
MARGENT, margin.
MARTLEMAS, Martinmas, November 11th.
MARY-BUDS, marigold.
MATE, confound, stupefy.
MAUGRE, in spite of.
MAZARD, MAZZARD, head.
MEACOCK, tame coward.
MEAL'D, mingled; sprinkled, tainted (S.).
MEAN, tenor, "means and basses."
MEASURE, slow dignified dance.
MEASLES, leprosy.

MEINY, attendants composing the household; retinue.
MELL, meddle.
MEMORY, memorial.
MERE, simple, only; absolute.
MERELY, simply, absolutely, entirely.
MESS, party of four, "lower messes" = those who sat below the salt.
METAL, used frequently for mettle.
METE-YARD, yard measure.
METHEGLIN, a mixture of various ingredients, of which the main was honey.
MEW, keep shut up.
MICHER, truant.
MICHING MALLECHO, concealed mischief (mich = skulk; mallecho, probably from Spanish malhecho = evil action).
MICKLE, much.
MILCH, "draw tears."
MILL SIXPENCES, coined by a mill or machine.
MIND, call to mind.
MINIM, at one time the shortest note in music.
MIRABLE, admirable.
MISER, a miserable wretch.
MISERY, avarice (D.); S. gives ordinary signification.
MISPRISE, underrate; mistake.
MISPRISION, undervaluing; mistake.
MISSIVE, messenger.
MISTHINK, judge wrongly, think wrongly of.
MO, more.
MOBLE, cover up the head.
MODERN, common, trivial, worthless.
MODESTY, moderation (D.).
MOLDWARP, mole.
MOME, blockhead.
MOMENTANY, lasting for a moment.
MOON-CALF, a deformed creature, monster.
MOP, grimace.
MORAL, meaning.
MORALIZE, interpret, expound.
MORISCO, morris-dancer.
MORRIS-PIKE, moorish pike.
MORT O' THE DEER, certain set of notes blown by the huntsmen at the death of the deer.
MORTAL, fatal, deadly.
MORTIFIED, lifeless, inert, insensible; "the mortified man" = ascetic (D.).
MOSE IN THE CHINE, disease of horses.
MOTION, puppet-show, puppet.
MOTIVE, moving agent; cause.
MOTLEY, parti-coloured dress worn by fools.
MOUSE, to tear in pieces, devour (as a cat a mouse) (D.), "mousing the flesh of men."
MOW, grimace.
MOY, piece of money.
MUM-BUDGET, a cant word implying silence.
MURE, wall.
MUSCADEL, a rich wine.
MUSE, wonder.
MUSS, scramble after things that are thrown down.
MUTINES, mutineers.

MYSTERY, art, trade.

NAPKIN, handkerchief.

NAUGHT, naughty, bad; "be naught awhile," a malediction equivalent to our "be hanged."

NAUGHTY, good for nothing, worthless.

NAYWARD, inclining to a negative, to a denial.

NAYWORD, watchword; by-word.

NEAT, horned cattle.

NEB, bill of a bird.

NEEDLY, necessarily.

NEEZE, sneeze.

NEIF, fist or hand.

NETHER-STOCKS, stockings.

NICE, dainty, precise; over-punctilious; foolish, trifling.

NICELY, NICENESS, punctiliously, subtilely (S.); scrupulousness, coyness (S.).

NICK, notch in a tally; "out of all nick" = out of all reckoning"; cut in notches, fools being "shaved and nicked in a particular manner."

NIGHT-RULE, night revel.

NINE-MEN'S-MORRIS, a game in which nine holes were made in the ground, some of the players having pegs, the others stones.

NOBLE, gold coin worth 6s. 8d.

NOISE, company.

NONCE, purpose.

NOOK-SHOTTEN, "shooting out into capes, etc."

NOTT-PATED, having the hair cut close; or equivalent to knotty-pated (q. v.).

NOURISH, nourice, nurse.

NOVUM, a game at dice.

NOWL, head.

NUTHOOK, metaphorically used for a bailiff.

OB, abbreviation of obolus, halfpenny.

OBLIGATION, bond.

OBSEQUIOUS, pertaining to funeral rites; careful of performing all funeral rites.

OBSEQUIOUSLY, as one at a funeral.

OBSERVANCE, observation.

OBSERVANTS, obsequious attendants.

ODDLY, unevenly.

O'ERCOUNT, out-number, perhaps "over-reach."

O'ERLOOKED, bewitched.

O'ER-PARTED, having a part assigned to him beyond his powers.

O'ER-RAUGHT, over-reached, overtaken.

OLD, wold; a. frequent, abundant, "old swearing," "old abusing of God's patience."

ONCE, at some time or other; once for all.

ONEYERS, "great oneyers," of uncertain meaning; S. suggests, "persons who converse with great ones."

OPINION, credit, reputation; conceit.

OPPOSITE, antagonist; a. antagonistic, hostile.

ORB, orbit; fairy-ring.

ORDINANCE, rank; ordnance; fate, or "divine dispensation" (S.).

ORDINANT, ORDINATE, ordaining.

ORDINARY, public dinner where each pays his share.

ORGULOUS, proud.

ORT, scrap.

OSTENT, OSTENTATION, show, appearance.

OTHERGATES, otherways.

OUPH, fairy, sprite.

OUSEL, blackbird.

OVER-PEER, overhang, look down on; rise above (S.).

OVERSCUTCHED, possibly corruption of "overswitched;" whipped at the cart's tail; "worn in the service" (Malone).

OUCH, OWCH, brooch, or other precious ornament.

OWE, own.

OYES (Fr. oyez), hear ye! the word with which the crier begins his proclamation.

PACK, enter into clandestine agreement with, intrigue; arrange or shuffle cards in a cheating way.

PACKING, underhand connivance.

PACTION, pact, compact.

PADDOCK, toad, frog.

PAINTED CLOTH, cloth, or canvas, painted with subjects and devices or mottoes, with which rooms were hung.

PALABRAS, Spanish for words "paucas pallabris" (pocas palabras), few words.

PALE, enclose.

PALL, fail, wane.

PALLIAMENT, robe.

PALTER, shuffle, equivocate.

PANTLER, servant in care of the pantry.

PARAGON, excel, compare; set forth as a model.

PARCEL, part; v. "enumerate by items"(S.).

PARCELED, "particular" (S.).

PARISH-TOP, a top kept in villages to keep the peasants in exercise and out of mischief when work was slack.

PARITOR, officer of the Bishop's Court, who delivers summonses.

PARLOUS, perilous.

PARTAKE, communicate.

PARTAKER, confederate.

PARTED, gifted with parts, endowed.

PARTISAN, pike, halberd.

PARTLET, ruff.

PASH, head (H.E.D.); v. strike violently.

PASS, care for, regard.

PASSADO, a forward thrust in fencing.

PASSAGE, passing to and fro of people, ("no passage"?); event, circumstance.

PASSIONATE, give expression in words to passion.

PASSIONATE, sorrowful.

PASSY-MEASURE, a slow dance.

PASTRY, pastry-room.

PATCH, fool.

PATCHERY, knavery; "botchery intended to hide faults" (S.).

PATHETICAL, pathetic (H.E.D.), "pleasing or displeasing in a high degree" (S.).

PATINE, plate on which the bread is laid at the Eucharist; or the cover of chalice.

PAVIN, a grave Spanish dance.

PAX, a plate of various material passed round to the people at mass to be kissed.

Glossary

PEAK, (?) droop in health and spirits, waste away (H.E.D.) ; mope, sneak.

PEAKING, skulking, mean-spirited (H.E.D.).

PEAT, pet.

PEDASCULE, pedant, preceptor.

PEEVISH, foolish, idle, trifling.

PEISE, weigh down, oppress.

PELT, rage.

PELTING, paltry.

PERDURABLE, lasting.

PEREGRINATE, foreign in ways and manners.

PERFECT, certain.

PERIAPT, amulet.

PERIOD, end.

PERPEND, consider, think over.

PERSPECTIVE, a picture or figure constructed so as to produce some fantastic effect " (H.E.D.).

PERTLY, alertly.

PETAR, PETARD, engine used to blow up gates, etc.

PHEEZE, beat; "any kind of teazing and annoying " (S.).

PHILIP, a familiar appellation for a sparrow.

PICKT-HATCH, noted resort for bad characters.

PIGHT, pitched.

PILCHER, scabbard.

PILL, pillage.

PIN-AND-WEB, disease of the eye.

PINK, small, half-shut, "pink eyne."

PITCH, the height to which a falcon soars.

PLACKET, (?) petticoat, or opening in it, stomacher.

PLAIN-SONG, simple notes without variation, opposed to "prick song."

PLANCHED, planked.

PLANTAGE, plants generally.

PLASH, pool.

PLATE, piece of silver money.

PLATFORM, plan.

PLAUSIVE, pleasing, plausible.

PLEACH, intertwine.

PLEASANCE, pleasure, delight.

POINT, tagged lace.

POINT-DEVISE, nice to excess.

POISE, weight, importance.

POKING-STICK, stick, or iron, for setting the plaits of ruffs.

POLACK, Pole; much controversy as to the meaning of the "sledded Polacks."

POLLED, stripped, shorn, plundered.

POMANDER, ball filled with perfumes.

POMEWATER, kind of apple.

POOR-JOHN, hake.

POPINJAY, parrot.

PORPENTINE, porcupine.

PORT, state ; gate ; bearing.

PORTABLE, bearable.

PORTAGE, port ; port-hole.

PORTANCE, carriage, deportment.

POTABLE, drinkable.

POTCH (POACH), thrust.

POTENT, potentate.

POTTLE, two quarts.

POULTER, poulterer.

POUNCET-BOX, perforated perfume-box.

PRACTICE, treachery, deceit, artifice.

PRACTISANTS, confederates in treachery.

PRACTISE, to use artifice, plot.

PRECEDENT, rough draft.

PRECEPT, warrant.

PREGNANT, ready, apt, quick of perception ; artful, designing ; full of meaning, conviction, intelligence, information.

PREMISED, sent beforehand.

PRE NOMINATE, foretell ; name beforehand.

PRESCRIPT, direction, written order ; a. prescribed, written ; prescriptive, immemorial (? S.).

PRESENTLY, immediately.

PRESS, commission for forcing men into military service ; v. impress, force into service.

PRESSURE, impression.

PREST, ready.

PRETENCE, intention, design.

PRETEND, intend.

PREVENT, anticipate.

PRICK-SONG, music written down, noted down with pricks or dots.

PRICKET, buck of the second year.

PRIME, eager.

PRIMERO, game at cards.

PRINCOX, pert, forward youth.

PRINT, "in print," with exactness.

PRIZE, privilege.

PRODIGIOUS, portentous, unnatural, horrible.

PRODITOR, traitor.

PROLIXIOUS, prolix, causing delay.

PRONE, prompt, ready.

PROPER, belonging to a particular person, own ; private ; handsome.

PROPOSE, conversation ; v. converse.

PUGGING, thievish (S.); "pegging, pegtooth = canine tooth" (Walter, quoted by S.).

PUKE (stocking), either colour or material, in either case "dark-coloured."

PUN, pound.

PUNTO, thrust, hit in fencing; "punto reverso" = back-handed stroke.

PURCHASE, cant term used by thieves for their plunder.

PURPLES, purple orchis.

PUT ON, instigate.

PUTTOCK, kite.

PUZZEL, drab.

QUAIL, overpower ; faint

QUAINT, neat, elegant, ingenious; "my quaint Ariel" = ingenious, clever (D.); fine, neat, pretty (S.).

QUALITY, profession.

QUARREL, ("that quarrel fortune"); a square dart ; or, quarreller (S.).

QUAT, spot on the skin.

QUATCH, square, flat.

QUEAN, slut.

QUEASY, fastidious, delicate ; disgusted.

QUELL, kill.

QUERN, hand-mill.

QUEST, inquest.

QUESTANT, candidate, competitor.

QUESTION, conversation.

QUESTIONABLE, "provoking question"; "capable of being conversed with."

QUICK, living.

Glossary

QUIDDITS, quiddities, legal subtleties.
QUILLETS, sly turn in argument, chicanery.
QUINTAIN, a figure set up for riders to tilt at.
QUIT, requite.
QUITTANCE, acquittance; requital.
QUIVER, nimble.
QUOIF, cap.
QUOTE, note, mark.

R, "for the dog," because of the sound being like a dog's snarl.
RABATO, ruff, band; originally a turned-back collar.
RABBIT-SUCKER, sucking rabbit.
RACE, flavour; natural disposition (S.); breed.
RACE "OF GINGER," root.
RACK, floating vapourous clouds; v. move like clouds.
RAMPALLIAN, a term of low abuse.
RANK, row; "rank to market" = some interpret "pace."
RAPTURE, fit.
RASCAL, lean deer, unfit to hunt.
RASH, strike (applied particularly to the stroke of a boar).
RAT, "Irish rat," it was believed in Ireland that rats could be rhymed to death.
RAUGHT, reached.
RAVIN, devour.
RAWNESS, hasty, unprepared manner.
RAYED, defiled, dirtied (S.).
RAZE, race, root; package (? S.).
RAZED, slashed.
READ, REDE, counsel.
REAR (rere) MOUSE, bat.
REBATE, render obtuse, blunt.
REBECK, stringed instrument.
RECEIVING, "ready apprehension."
RECHEAT, notes sounded on the horn to call the dogs off.
RECORDER, a kind of flute, or flageolet.
RED LATTICE, pertaining to the ale-house, formerly distinguished by its coloured lattice.
REDUCE, bring back.
REECHY, smoky, greasy, filthy.
REFELLED, refuted.
REGIMENT, government, sovereign sway.
REMONSTRANCE, manifestation.
REMORSE, pity, compassion.
REMOTION, "act of keeping aloof, non-appearance" (S.).
REMOVED, secluded, remote.
RENEGE, deny.
REPLICATION, reply.
REPORT, "so likely to report," = "so near to speech" (J.).
REPROOF, disproof.
REPROVE, disprove.
REPUGN, resist.
REPURED, purified.
REPUTING, "valuing at a high rate" (S.).
RESOLUTION, assurance, conviction.
RESOLVE, dissolve; convince, satisfy; "make up one's mind fully" (D.).
RESOLVED, convinced.
RESPECT, regard.
RESPECTIVE, worthy of regard; considerate; respectful, formal.

REST, "set up one's rest," to be fully determined; a metaphor borrowed from gaming.
REVERB, reverberate.
RHEUMATIC, choleric.
RIGOL, circle.
RIVAL, associate.
RIVALITY, equality, association.
RIVE, split; used to express the bursting sound of artillery.
ROAD, roadstead.
ROISTING, bullying, defying.
ROMAGE, tumultuous movement.
RONYON, mangy animal.
ROOKED, squatted.
ROPERY, roguery.
ROTE, repeat from memory.
ROTHER, horned cattle (some editions, "brother").
ROUND, plain spoken; v. whisper.
ROUSE, carouse.
RUB, an expression borrowed from game of bowls.
RUDDOCK, redbreast.
RUDESBY, a rude, underbred person.
RUFFLE, to be turbulent and boisterous.
RUSH, rush-ring; used for rural marriages, or mock marriages.
RUSH, openly, eagerly evade (S.); "rush'd aside the law."

SACK, a dry Spanish wine.
SACKBUT, kind of trumpet, trombone.
SACKERSON, a famous bear at Paris-garden; name probably that of his master.
SAD, serious.
SADLY, seriously.
SAG, hang down, flag.
SAGITTARY, the Centaur who fought in the armies of the Trojans; building in Venice bearing sign of.
SALLET, helmet, headpiece; salad.
SALT, licentious.
SALTIERS, blunder for satyrs.
SALUTE, touch, affect (S.).
SAND-BLIND, having imperfect sight.
SANDED, sandy.
SAVAGERY, wildness of growth.
SAW, saying.
SAY, a kind of silk, or satin; taste, relish; assay.
SCALD, low, shabby, "scabby."
SCALE, weigh.
SCAMBLE, scramble.
SCAMEL, uncertain meaning; perhaps sea-mell, i. e. sea-mew.
SCANTLING, a given portion.
SCAPE, escape; misdemeanour.
SCAR, broken precipice.
SCARFED, hung with flags.
SCATHE, injury.
SCONCE, round fortification; head.
SCOTCH, score, make shallow cuts.
SCRIMER, fencer.
SCRIP, slip of writing, list; a small bag "scrip and scrippage."
SCROYLE, low wretch.
SCULL, shoal.
SCUT, tail.
SEAM, grease, lard.

Glossary

SEASON, temper; "seasons him his enemy," "my blessing season this in thee," confirm (D.); mature (S.).

SECT, sex; section, cutting.

SECURE, SECURELY, SECURITY, rashly confident, etc.

SEEL, close the eyes; the eyes of hawks were seeled by passing a fine thread or small feather through the eyelids.

SEEN, skilled; "well seen in music."

SEIZED, possessed (legal term).

SELDOM-WHEN, rarely.

SELF, same, self-same; "that self hand."

SEMBLABLE, likeness.

SEMBLATIVE, resembling; appearing, seeming (S.).

SENNET, set of notes, or flourish, on the trumpet.

SENSELESS, without feeling, perception.

SENSIBLE, having feeling, sensation, perception.

SERE, catch in a gunlock; "tickle of the sere," a gun which explodes on the least touch on the sere. (See Wright, quoted by S.)

SERPIGO, eruption.

SESSA, "probably a cry exciting to swift running" (S.).

SEVERAL, private, "inclosed pasture, as opposed to common land."

SEWER, the attendant who set on and removed dishes.

SHALE, shell.

SHARD, hard wing-case, "shard-borne," "sharded"; fragment of broken pottery.

SHARKED, "collected in a banditti-like manner."

SHEER, clear, transparent; nothing but, mere.

SHENT, scolded, reproached, disgraced.

SHIP-TIRE, head-dress in some way resembling a ship.

SHIVE, a small slice.

SHOTTEN, "having cast its spawn" (D.).

SHOUGH, shaggy dog.

SHOVE-GROAT, SHOVEL-BOARD, game in which coins were pushed to reach a certain mark.

SHRIEVE, sheriff.

SHRIFT, confession.

SHROWD, shelter.

SIB, akin.

SIEGE, seat; rank.

SIGHTLESS, invisible; unsightly.

SILLY, simple, rustic, harmless.

SIMPLICITY, foolishness.

SIMULAR, counterfeited.

SINK-A-PACE. See Cinque-pace.

SIR-REVERENCE, save-reverence.

SITH, SITHENCE, since.

SIZES, portions, allowances.

SKAINS-MATES, sword-mates (S.); skain = "scapegrace" (Staunton); "swaggering-companions" (Nares).

SKILL, matter, "it skills not."

SKIRR, scour.

SLAB, moist and glutinous.

SLEAVE, soft floss silk used for weaving.

SLEEVELESS, useless, fruitless.

SLEIDED, raw, untwisted, "sleided silk."

SLIP, counterfeit coin; noose in which greyhounds were held, before they were let loose to start for the game.

SLIVER, slip, portion broken off.

SLOP, SLOPS, loose trousers, or breeches.

SLUBBER, to do things in a slovenly way; to obscure "by smearing over."

SMATCH, taste, smack.

SMOOTH, flatter.

SNEAK-CUP, one who sneaks from his glass.

SNEAP, snubbing, rebuke; check, nip.

SNEEK-UP, "go and be hanged."

SNUFF, anger; "take in snuff" = take offence.

SOILED, high fed.

SOLIDARE, small coin.

SONTIES, supposed corruption of saints, or sanctity.

SOOTH, truth; sweetness.

SOOTH, SOOTHER, flatter, smooth over; flatterer.

SOP O' THE MOONSHINE, "old dish of eggs in moonshine: i. e. broken and boiled in salad-oil till the yolks become hard, and eaten with slices of onion" (Douce).

SORE, buck of the fourth year.

SOREL, buck of the third year.

SORT, company; v. choose; suit, fit; contrive (S.).

SOUSED, pickled.

SOWL, pull by the ears.

SOWTER, cobbler, name of a hound.

SPAN-COUNTER, a player throws a coin, or counter, to try and hit another, or come within a span of it; sometimes played with marbles.

SPAVIN, disease of horses.

SPECULATION, power of vision, "speculators, observers" (S.).

SPECULATIVE, visual (D.); "speculative . . . instruments."

SPERR, make fast.

SPILL, destroy (D.).

SPILTH, spilling.

SPIRIT OF SENSE, "utmost refinement of sensation"; "sense or sensibility itself" (S.).

SPLEEN, caprice, humour; impetuous haste; "hate; any uncontrollable impulse, fit; fire, eagerness" (S.).

SPLEENY, ill-tempered, peevish (D.); eager, headstrong (S.).

SPLINTER, put into splints.

SPRAG, sprack, alert.

SPRIGHTED, haunted.

SPRINGHALT, a kind of lameness in horses.

SQUARE, quarrel.

SQUASH, unripe peas pod.

SQUINY, squint.

SQUIRE, square, or measure.

STAIN, disgrace; "stain to all nymphs" = that sullies by contrast (D.); v. taint, dim, disfigure.

STALE, decoy; stalking-horse.

STALKING-HORSE, a real or artificial horse, behind which the shooter hid himself from the game.

STANIEL, an inferior kind of hawk.

STARRED, fated by the stars.

START-UP, up-start.

STATE, chair of state.

555

Glossary

STATION, mode of standing; state of rest, as opposed to motion.

STATUTE-CAPS, woollen caps, worn, as decreed by statute, by all but the nobility, after a certain age, on Sundays and holidays.

STELLED, "quenched the stelled fires," starry; fixed (S.).

STERNAGE, steerage.

STICKLER, umpire.

STIGMATIC, one who has been stigmatised, branded; stigmatised with deformity.

STIGMATICAL, marked with a stigma of deformity.

STINT, stop.

STITHY, smithy.

STOCCADO, a thrust in fencing.

STOCK. See Stoccado.

STOMACH, arrogance, anger; stubborn courage; inclination; v. resent (D.).

STOUT, bold; unbending, obstinate (D.); overbearing (S.).

STRAIGHT-PIGHT, straight-pitched, straight-built, upright (D.).

STRAIN, lineage; disposition.

STRAIT, close-fitted.

STRAITED, puzzled.

STRANGE, foreign; shy.

STRANGELY, wonderfully; distantly, like a stranger.

STRANGENESS, coyness, shyness.

STRAPPADO, a torture which broke and dislocated the arms and joints.

STRATAGEM, calamity, dire event.

STRICTURE, strictness.

STRIKE, blast by secret influence, "then no planets strike."

STROND, strand.

STROSSERS, trossers, trousers.

SUBSCRIBE, yield, submit.

SUBTILTIES, "when a dish appeared unlike what it really was, they called it a subtilty" (Steevens).

SUCCESS, succession; result, consequence.

SUGGEST, prompt, tempt.

SUMPTER, horse or mule to carry baggage.

SUPER-SERVICEABLE, over-officious.

SUPPLIANCE, supply, gratification, pastime (S.); "suppliance of a minute."

SUR-REINED, over-worked.

SWEETING, a kind of apple.

SWINGE-BUCKLER, a roisterer.

SWINGED, whipped.

TABLE, palm of the hand; tablet.

TABLE-BOOK, memorandum-book.

TABOR, a small drum.

TAKE, blast, bewitch.

TAKE IN, conquer.

TAKE UP, borrow; obtain on credit.

TALL, valiant.

TALLOW-KEECH. See Keech.

TANLING, one tanned by the sun.

TARRE, set on.

TARTAR, Tartarus.

TASK, tax.

TASSEL-GENTLE, tiercel, male goshawk.

TAXATION, sarcasm, censure, vituperation.

TEEN, grief, misfortune.

TENDER-HEFTED. See Heft.

TENT, probe a wound. Tent being a roll of lint, used as a probe.

TERMAGANT, a Saracen god.

TERMLESS, "beyond the power of words" (D.).

TESTER, a coin worth sixpence.

TETCHY, touchy.

THARBOROUGH, corruption of Thirdborough; constable, or constable's assistant.

THRASONICAL, boastful.

THREAD AND THRUM, "the thread is the substance of the warp, the thrum the small tuft beyond, where it is tied."

THREE-MAN BEETLE, implement for pile-driving.

THROSTLE, thrush.

THRUM. See Thread.

THRUMMED, made of thrums, or of very coarse cloth.

THUNDER-STONE, thunder-bolt.

TICK-TACK, sort of backgammon (D.).

TICKLE, ticklish, precarious(ly).

TIKE, common sort of dog.

TILTH, tilled land; tillage.

TIMELESS, untimely.

TIRE, head-dress; v. pull, tear, seize eagerly, as birds of prey their food.

TOD, twenty-eight pounds of wool.

TOGE, gown.

TOKEN'D, shewing plague tokens, spots.

TOM O' BEDLAM, the Bedlam beggars were men who had recovered sufficiently to be let out of Bedlam, and were licensed to go begging; many impostors were about who had never seen the inside of a madhouse.

TOPLESS, not to be topped, surpassed.

TORTIVE, tortuous.

TOUCH, test by the touchstone.

TOUSE, drag, tear, pluck.

TOYS, "there's toys abroad" = "rumours, idle reports," "tricks, devices," "follies in the world" (S.).

TOZE. See Touse.

TRADE, traffic; in the "gap and trade" = "practised method, general course" (J.).

TRAIN, artifice, stratagem.

TRAMMEL, confine, tie up.

TRANECT, probably from Italian traghetto = ferry (S.).

TRASH, "trash for overtopping," lop, crop (S.); Nares decided that it was some kind of strap, or implement to hold back a hound; according to Madden (quoted by S.) "when the hound was running, the long strap, dragged along the ground, handicapped the overtopping hound."

TRAY-DRIP, a game played with cards and dice; success in it depended upon throwing a trois (treys).

TREACHER, traitor.

TRENCH, cut, carve.

TRIBULATION, probably name of a puritanical society; or applied to the whole sect of Puritans (S.).

TRICKING, dress, ornament.

TRICKSY, clever, adroit (D.); full of tricks and devices (S.).

TRIGON, astrological term, signifying the meeting of the three upper planets, which were then called the "fiery Trigon."

Glossary

TROJAN, cant term for thief; "a familiar name for any equal or inferior" (Nares).

TROLL-MY-DAMES, TROLL-MADAM, TROU-MADAM, a game known in England as pigeon-holes, small balls being bowled into these from the farther end of the board.

TROPICALLY, figuratively.

TRUNDLE-TAIL, dog with a curly tail.

TUCKET, flourish, certain set of notes on the trumpet.

TUN-DISH, funnel.

TURK, "turn Turk," undergo a complete change (S. adds "for the worse").

TURLYGOOD, TURLYGOD, apparently a name for a "bedlam-beggar."

TWIGGEN, covered with wicker-work.

TYPE, symbol.

UNANELED, not having received extreme unction.

UNAVOIDED, unavoidable.

UNBARBED, unbarbered, unshorn.

UNBATED, not blunted, as foils are.

UNBOLTED, unsifted.

UNBRAIDED, not counterfeit, or, blunder for embroidered (? S.).

UNCAPE, probably "uncouple" (S.); it has been interpreted as "unearth"; "turn fox out of bag."

UNCLEW, UNCLUE, unwind.

UNCOINED, "not counterfeit"; real, unrefined, unadorned; having received no previous impression; "without the current stamp, i. e. insinuating words, etc." (S.).

UNCONFIRMED, without experience.

UNCOUTH, unknown, strange.

UNDERBEAR, undergo, bear.

UNDERSKINKER, undertapster.

UNEARED, untilled.

UNEATH, hardly, scarcely.

UNEXPERIENT, inexperienced.

UNEXPRESSIVE, inexpressible.

UNHAPPY, UNHAPPILY, waggish(ly); mischievous(ly), evilly (S.).

UNHAPPINESS, mischief, "dreamed of unhappiness," = wanton or mischievous tricks (S.).

UNHOUSELED, without receiving the sacrament.

UNIMPROVED, unreproved, unimpeached (D.); not yet used to advantage, turned to account (S.).

UNION, pearl of fine quality.

UNKIND, unnatural.

UNMANNED, untamed (term in falcony).

UNOWED, unowned.

UNPLAUSIVE, unapplauding.

UNPREGNANT. See Pregnant.

UNPROPER, not the property of one alone.

UNQUALITIED, deprived of faculties.

UNQUESTIONABLE, opposed to conversation.

UNRECURING, incurable.

UNRESPECTIVE, without respect, inconsiderate; "unrespective sieve," unvalued (D.), used at random (S.).

UNSISTING, unresting (? S.).

UNSQUARED, unfitted to the purpose.

UNTENTED, not to be probed, incurable (S.).

UNVALUED, invaluable.

UPSPRING, upstart; or, a wild German dance "Hüpfauf."

URCHIN, hedgehog.

USANCE, interest on money.

UTIS (Fr. huit), eighth day, or space of eight days, after a feast = the octave; festivities during same.

UTTERANCE (Fr. outrance), extremity.

VADE, fade.

VAIL, lower, "angels vailing-clouds" = "letting these clouds which obscured their brightness sink from before them" (J.), clouds letting down, bearing down, angels (? S.).

VALIDITY, value.

VANTAGE, advantage; "to the vantage" = in addition, to boot; "of vantage" = same sense (S.).

VANTBRACE, VAMBRACE, armour for the arm.

VARLET, servant to a knight.

VARY, variation.

VAST (Waste), "the darkness of midnight in which the prospect is not bounded in by distinct objects" (S.).

VASTIDITY, immensity.

VASTY, vast.

VAUNT, van, beginning.

VAWARD, vanward.

VENEW, VENEY, VENUE, thrust, attack, bout in fencing.

VENGEANCE, harm.

VENTAGE, hole or stop in a flute.

VERBAL, verbose, or plain-spoken.

VICE, a personage in the old moralities, sometimes dressed as a buffoon; armed at times with a wooden dagger, "Vice's dagger."

VIE, wager, contend in rivalry.

VIEWLESS, invisible.

VILLIAGO (VILLIACO), villain.

VINEWEDST, most mouldy.

VIOL-DE-GAMBOYS, a viol held between the legs, bass-viol, violoncello.

VIRGINALLING, playing with the fingers as on a virginal.

VULGAR, common, general, "the vulgar air;" of common report, "most sure and vulgar."

VULGARLY, publicly.

WAFT, beckon; turn, "wafting his eyes."

WAFTAGE, passage by water.

WAKE, to keep night revel.

WANION, WANNION, "with a wanion," apparently equivalent to "with a vengeance."

WAPPENED, worn.

WARD, posture of defence.

WARDEN, hard pear used for baking, "warden-pie."

WARDER, kind of truncheon.

WASSAIL, festivity, drinking-bout.

WATCH, "I'll watch him tame;" hawks were kept awake to tame them.

WATER-WORK, water-colour painting.

WAX, grow, increase.

WEAL, welfare; commonwealth.

Glossary

WEALS-MAN, commonwealth man, statesman.
WEAR, fashion.
WEEDS, dress.
WEEN, suppose, imagine.
WEET, know.
WEIRD, concerned with fate, "subservient to destiny" (S.); "weird sisters"= Fates.
WELKIN, sky.
WELKIN-EVE, blue, "heavenly" (S.).
WELL-FOUND, tried, approved (S.).
WELL-SEEN, accomplished.
WHEEL "how the wheel becomes it," burden of a ballad (this is queried by S.).
WHELK, wheal, protuberance.
WHELKED, with protuberances, or "twisted, convolved."
WHIFFLER, a person who cleared the way for a procession; originally a fifer.
WHILE, until.
WHIPSTOCK, handle of whip.
WHITING-TIME, bleaching-time.
WHITSTER, WHITESTER, bleacher.
WHITTLE, small clasp-knife.
WHOOBUB, hubbub.
WIDE "speak so wide," far from the mark.
WILDERNESS, wildness.
WIMPLED, veiled, hoodwinked.
WINTER-GROUND, protect from winter weather.
WIS, think, suppose (i-wis = certainly, indeed).

WISH, recommend, "desire, invite, bid" (S.).
WISTLY, earnestly, eagerly.
WIT, know.
WITHOUT, beyond.
WONDERED, able to perform wonders.
WOOD, mad.
WOODCOCK, a proverbially foolish bird.
WOOLWARD, dressed in wool only.
WORLD, "go to the world," = marry; "woman of the world," = married.
WORM, serpent.
WORT, cabbages, and similar plants; sweet infusion of malt before it ferments.
WOT, know.
WREAK, revenge.
WREST, tuning key.
WRITHLED, wrinkled.
WROTH, ruth, misfortune.
WRY, go astray.

YARE, quick, ready, active.
YCLEPED, named.
YEARN, grieve.
YELLOWS, jaundice in horses.
YELLOWNESS, jealousy.
YESTY, frothy.

ZANY, fool, buffoon.
ZED, "unnecessary letter," since "its place may be supplied by S."
ZENITH, highest point of fortune.

END OF VOL I.